War and Democracy

War and Democracy

PETER T. MANICAS

Basil Blackwell

Copyright © Peter T. Manicas 1989

First published 1989

Basil Blackwell, Inc.
3 Cambridge Center,
Cambridge, Massachusetts 02142, USA

Basil Blackwell Ltd
108 Cowley Road, Oxford, OX4 1JF, UK

Library of Congress Cataloging in Publication Data

Manicas, Peter T.
  War and democracy.

  Bibliography: p.
  Includes index.
  1. Democracy. 2. War. I. Title.
JC423.M34 1989   355.02   88–7914
ISBN 0–631–15836–7

British Library Cataloguing in Publication Data

A CIP catalogue record for this book is available from the British Library.

Typeset in 10 on 12 pt Ehrhardt
by Setrite Typesetters Ltd
Printed in Great Britain by Billing and Sons Ltd, Worcester

Contents

Acknowledgments

The author and publishers are grateful for permission to use portions of the following previously published essays:

'The Foreclosure of Democracy in America,' *History of Political Thought* (1988)

'The Legitimation of the Modern State,' in Ronald Cohen and Judith D. Toland (ed.) *State Formation and Political Legitimacy* (New Brunswick, New Jersey and Oxford: Transaction Books, 1988)

'Marx or Dewey?' in M. Murphey (ed.) *Values and Value Theory in Twentieth Century America* (Philadelphia: Temple University Press, 1988)

'War, Stasis, and Greek Political Theory,' *Comparative Studies in Society and History*, 24 (Oct. 1982), pp. 673–88

'John Dewey: Anarchism and the Political State,' *Transactions of the Charles S. Peirce Society*, 18 (Spring 1982), pp. 133–58

'Montesquieu and the Eighteenth Century Vision of the State,' *History of Political Thought*, 2 (June 1981), pp. 313–47

Introduction

Few words are more familiar and less useful than "war" and "democracy."
Fernand Braudel wrote, with no exaggeration, that "we are as ignorant of
war as the physicist is of the true nature of matter. We talk about it because
we have to; it has never ceased to trouble the lives of men." In the era of
nuclear war and of cold war, talk of war as "troubling" our lives seems
lame. As for democracy, the condition is different. Up to the end of the
eighteenth century, nobody − or almost nobody − approved of it; whereas
today everybody does − after all, the United States, the Union of Soviet
Socialist Republics, the People's Republic of China, El Salvador, and
Nicaragua are all "democracies." There is reason to wonder, then, what
happened to make this possible.

This book is a historical study of war and democracy. Its main aim is to
contribute to an understanding of our present situation. By looking at war
and democracy together, I hope to develop an important, frequently overlooked perspective, one that will make both of them more comprehensible.
For example, there is the obvious, and not unimportant fact that there was
a time when no one who had to fight in a war was excluded from the
decision to go to war. Citizens ruled, and only citizens fought and died.
Today, people who have had no say in the matter have to face the enemy.
Worse, entire populations who have not had the slightest say in the decision
to go to war may be subject to enormous suffering and sacrifice. How did
this come to be? More important, what can we do in response to this? It
may well be that the problem of "democracy," construed as an ideal,
cannot be solved until there is a solution to the problem of war, and
conversely, that the human blight of war will not be eliminable until
mankind takes some significant steps in the direction of greater democracy.

The study is somewhat idiosyncratic, in that it combines history, the
history of ideas, and political philosophy; but is neither a history of war or
the idea of war nor a history of democracy or the idea of democracy. The

argument proceeds selectively, with an eye to identifying critical junctures in the development of the relations of war and democracy.

It begins with the epoch of the ancient Greek *polis*, locus of the first reflections in the West on war and democracy. This is the topic of Part I. There is then a long in-between period, with rumblings of new forms in the Germanic Middle Ages, a period terminated, as far as the "tradition" is concerned, by Renaissance interest in "republicanism" and by the transition to the early modern state, the subject of Part II. Next comes the invention in North America of both modern democracy and modern war − also in the new United States. Part III is concerned with this critical period.

But the end of the eighteenth century also saw the French Revolution and the quite remarkable French Wars of Liberation. The conceptual materials developed in the American War of Independence and the re-invention of a citizen-army by Americans were put to explosive use in France, for the reasons sketched in Part IV. While Kant was writing of "perpetual peace," Clausewitz saw, prophetically, that "absolute war" could now be conceived and, under appropriate conditions, realized. These four parts, then, covering the period from Solon to Napoleon, are an attempt to show in some detail how war and democracy were related in ancient times, and how different are modern war, modern democracy and their relations, as well as how these differences came to be.

The second chapter of Part IV looks at the implications of modern war and modern democracy against the revolutionary idea of Social Democracy, also born during the French Revolution. There is a sense, in which there came to be but two parties in the world after the French Revolution: those who sought to complete the French Revolution and those who believed, not without reason, that the Americans, in 1787, went as far as one could go. The struggle between these two parties is still very much with us. In this chapter the discussion focuses on the much overlooked views of Marx and Engels on war and democracy. They wrote against the background not only of Hegel, but also of Clausewitz; their views and the misunderstandings to which they gave rise became critical in the World War I period, the topic of Part V.

World War I, the so-called Great War, has in many, many ways defined the twentieth century. But in my view, not only is the significance of World War I too little appreciated, but there have been some disastrous mis-understandings of the period generally, misunderstandings which can be exposed and explained only by retracing the critical stages in the period that preceded it.

Some common themes and methodological features propel the argument. First, the book opposes the idea that meanings can be grasped apart from context. On the present view, all ideas, including those of war, democracy, republic, a sovereign people, social democracy, Marxism, workers' and soldiers' councils, Bolshevism, and so forth are given concrete, particularized meaning. Because ideas are seen as practical attempts to address existing problems and circumstances, they are treated in close connection with the events and conditions which gave rise to them. To the extent that what follows involves a foray into the history of ideas, there will be more historical detail than might otherwise be expected. Indeed, this was an enormous problem in writing the book, not so much because it entailed reading many histories, but because it required making judgments about these histories. Since the book is not intended as history or political philosophy, as generally understood, it may be that the history is too philosophical and the philosophy too historical to suit either historians or philosophers. Yet in my view, these disciplines are not natural kinds; rather, the way they are practiced reflects particular circumstances in the history of Western civilization. Moreover, the separation of history, philosophy, and the social sciences from one another, a division reproduced in academic institutions the world over, has been nothing less than a disaster, in that it has had detrimental effects on all three branches of inquiry an idea developed in my *A History and Philosophy of the Social Sciences.*[1]

In this study, accordingly, I take the position of a nonspecialist writing for nonspecialists, even if I entertain hopes that the study will also be of use to specialists and general readers. There is a sense in which I have tried to do what many philosophers in the nineteenth century tried to do — namely, provide a general understanding of Western civilization. Indeed, in my view, we remain victims of such nineteenth-century efforts. Today philosophers tend to define more manageable tasks for themselves. But not only is there a need to rethink the history of the Western world periodically; there is also a certain urgency, if I am correct, to reject some of the conventional understandings of that history. I have tried to control my history by appeal to critical primary materials, as well as a wide variety of secondary sources. By using history to re-understand theory and theory to re-understand history, I have arrived at interpretations of both which are unconventional. I can only hope that they are not also implausible.

Second, and here agreeing with R. R. Palmer, I hope to undercut the historiographical argument as to whether events — for example, the American War of Independence — arose from ideas or from circumstances. In the view of history I assume, there is a critical place for both ideas and agents, because people with ideas make history, and do so not just as they please or with materials of their own choosing. Marx was surely correct in this, although the materials are not solely "instruments of production," but include the particular problems people face and the legacy of human ideas which constitute, inform, justify, and sometimes mystify their practices and activities. But this is precisely why it is essential to have a concrete historical understanding of that legacy. For, though the *words* may be the same, the *worlds* of the ancient *polis* and the eighteenth century were remarkably different. There is a sense, then, in which this study is an attempt at demystification, by going beyond words to realities, the latter including the inherited, but profoundly transformed, *mentalités* which are so profoundly constitutive of these very different social worlds.

Third, we need to see that not only are social forms human creations – particular incarnations at a given time and place of previous human ideas and practices – but that history is radically contingent, the outcome of both accident and will. If there are imperatives so called, stemming from social forces which, like the seasons, seem unbending to our will, there are always choices, and sometimes opportunities. Thus, when Thucydides writes that the growth of Athenian power "compelled" (*anankasai*) the Spartans to go to war, he does not mean that they had no choice. To be sure, the situation which had been created, the unintended consequences of a host of "rational" decisions made by "rational" people, left them with nothing but unpleasant alternatives, equally disastrous alternatives, perhaps. Still, there were choices; and informed by their beliefs, some true, some false, they opted for war. More generally, history is the unintended result of countless decisions made by countless people in circumstances which they did not choose and would often not have chosen had they had the choice.

This is not however, to say, as C. Wright Mills has so wisely noted, that we all have an *equal* share in the making of history. Indeed, this is the very problem of democracy, and it is crucial that the reader keep it firmly in mind. When Thucydides wrote that the Athenians decided to go to war against Sicily, almost all Athenian males were participants, or were at least eligible to participate, in the decision. Hence they were all responsible for the disaster which befell Athens. By contrast, when historians write of Prussia's decision in 1792 to join Austria in a war against France, they are referring to a decision made by the Hohenzollern monarch Frederick William II.

But this is no fatalism. There is a sense in which what happened had to happen; but that can only mean that, given those concrete circumstances and those particular decisions, the outcome was what it was. The Athenians might have chosen otherwise; they did not. *We* know what happened; *they*, in advance, could not have known. Most of them believed that the encounter would be swift and to their advantage, just as previous encounters with the Corinthians, the Mytileneans, and even the Persians had been.

The radical openness of history suggests the place for counterfactuals, even if historians sometimes pretend a certain distance from them. If the Spartans had not chosen war, then Athenian power would have grown and, in due course, would have upset the stability of Spartan hegemony in the Peloponnesus. If the Athenians had not invaded Sicily, they could have sustained themselves indefinitely against the Peloponnesian League. In either case, the course of Western civilization would have been different. We can see why keeping a certain distance is desirable. How can one possibly say what *might* have happened? As historians, we should restrict ourselves to what did happen. Yet there are problems in this.

First, if one wants to explain what happened, then one must look for causes. And if one seeks causes, then one must construct counterfactual hypotheses. One way to make sense of Spartan policy — Thucydides' way — is to "show" that the Spartans were "compelled" in just the sense that, had they not gone to war against Athens, growing Athenian power would have threatened the continued viability of Sparta. If this is true, and if we can see how the Spartans came to believe this, we approach an understanding of the war.

While it is not my main purpose in this book to give the causes of the wars discussed, the Persian and Peloponnesian wars, the American War of Independence, the wars of revolutionary France, the Great War, and the cold war, the view of history here assumed (and illustrated) leads me to conclude that to give an explanation of a war is to give a causal explanation, and that in principle this is no different from giving an explanation of a fire or any other phenomenon. As long as there are things which are combustible and there is oxygen, the causal conditions for a fire are present. Thus when an arsonist lights a match or a circuit breaker fails to open, for example, we can have a fire. But whether we actually have a fire depends on other causes, whether somebody intervenes at the right moment, whether sufficient heat is generated by the short circuit, and so forth. Similarly as regards war. Analogous to the combustible things and oxygen are the social structures which are the medium of action, the materials which enable and constrain the actors. These may present the actors with choices which either directly or indirectly produce a war. It is plain, then, that actors *are* the causes of wars, even when their situations are such that in Thucydides' sense they were compelled.

This suggests that we should beware of abstractions in ascribing responsibility. In considering whether responsibility should be assigned to the Spartans or the Athenians, Thucydides knew that in both cities, all male citizens were direct parties to the pertinent decisions. In discussing the situations of the Germans or the Russians in more recent history, we have to remember that neither Germany nor the Germans decided to go to war against the Russians; it was the Kaiser, Bethmann-Hollweg, and General Moltke.

This also implies that in so far as it suggests a dualism, the language of "underlying" and "proximate" causes misleads. For the underlying causes of a war can only be materials of action employed by actors in circumstances which they did not create. They are not causes of war unless actors choose to use them as such. Many societies have faced domestic conflict or scarcity or, more generally, have been structured by economies which made conquest one possible solution to their problems. But in most of them, the key actors have not sought to solve these problems in this way. Similarly, many societies have had ambitious rulers who, nevertheless, did not seek to enhance their power through war. Domestic conflict or shrinking profits are conditions which may lead to war, but, equally, may not. Moreover, sometimes domestic consensus and abundance can have this outcome. Likewise, ambition can be played out in all sorts of ways, depending on the historical circumstances, the contingent opportunities, and so on. Thus again, the importance of concrete history.

Finally, while historians are reluctant to assess critical decisions in history, it is well nigh impossible to avoid this. "The Spartans were threatened by Athenian hegemony." "The Athenian policy regarding Sicily was a gigantic blunder." "The United States needed the Constitution drafted at Philadelphia." But then we must not only construct counterfactuals as hypotheses, but must go further and assess them for their truth. This will never be easy, and sometimes it will be quite impossible.

There are a number of counterfactuals of particular relevance to this study. One relates to the question of the American Confederation. It is widely held that, given the situation as it existed, the Constitution of the United States was as inevitable as anything could be. Yet, I will argue that the circumstances, the array of forces, and the conceptual materials available at the time allowed for a number of genuine alternatives, including one, actually articulated in Philadelphia, that would have left open the possibility of the flowering of institutions which would have been far more democratic than those that were realized. Any such judgment needs to be discussed concretely, of course. Still other counterfactual questions arise in the context of my discussion of the French Revolution and of the revolutions in Russia and Germany following World War I.

There is little doubt that my effort to articulate and judge such alternative possibilities will displease many. Nor do I expect that my arguments will convince everyone. All I can hope is that there is no evidence which would contradict the views expressed here, and that there might be further evidence that could be mustered in support of my interpretations. Much of the force of successive interpretations will depend on the force of arguments of previous chapters in the development of the argument.

Nevertheless, it would be well to keep in mind that historical judgments about what was possible and what was right or wrong about the decisions made are found in *all* historical writing, even when the evidence on which they rest is less substantial than it is in the cases I discuss. Further, when historians demur from considering what might have been, it may be that they have succumbed to fatalism, the view that history could not have gone

any other way than the one it did. Sometimes they do this in an unconsciously Hegelian way, by arguing that this or that decision *had* to be made
because it was *right* and that those who championed alternatives were
wrong − and happily, for this reason, failed to persuade.

But if we are not to be fatalists, whether in an optimistic, celebratory
mode, or, conversely, in a pessimistic, apocalyptic mode we must admit
that there were unrealized possibilities in history, that opportunities have
been missed, mistakes made, and that different decisions would have had
different outcomes, perhaps for the better, perhaps for the worse. Indeed, I
believe with Barrington Moore, that the "intellectual liberation from the
inevitable may be one of the most important next steps we have to take."[2]
This study is an attempt to contribute to taking this step.

Fourth, this book is an exploration in political theory made concrete. It is
guided by the conviction that the question of a good − well-ordered, just,
and so on − constitution cannot be discussed intelligently apart from
considerations of the international environment, in particular apart from
considerations of war. Such a view is explicit in Plato, though for the most
part it goes unnoticed, and is manifest in Machiavelli and those influenced
by him. We also find it in Montesquieu, Kant, Hegel, Marx and Engels,
and perhaps a few others. Regrettably, the majority of modern theorists
(including Hobbes, Locke, and almost all twentieth-century authors) write
as if one could speak of justice, freedom, and democracy without regard for
the empirical and normative relations of "states." An important aspect of
my effort, then, is to make a case for this older view.

Finally, I wish to stress two further points. This effort to comprehend
the past, to at least identify the critical junctures in the development of war
and democracy, is not simply for its own sake, although that would be
sufficient justification. My concern is also with the present. For not only
does the present rest on incorporation and transformation of the past, a
legacy put to use, but the very constitution of a "present" necessarily
involves "present" interpretations of the past, recent and remote. Current
ideas about democracy are critical in the constitution of present political
practices; and these depend, in some measure at least, on current understandings of past practices and problems. But our present ideas of democracy
are very much influenced by eighteenth-century ideas, and these, in turn,
were profoundly shaped by early modern perceptions of ancient democracy.
Indeed, the central terms of the discourse of politics were established by
literate elites in ancient Greece and were passed on by successions of
literate elites. Until the very recent past, the anonymous *demos* has lacked
an effective political voice. This is especially critical as regards the problem
of democracy. Indeed since nearly all the major writers in the Western
tradition have been antidemocratic − excepting, notably, those who are
today least likely to be either taken seriously or called democrats − the

understanding of democracy which they have passed on is necessarily biased. Hence, alternative understandings to what, in the course of time, have come to be conventional understandings may offer possibilities for alternative present practices. The attempt to understand the past can thus have genuine practical import.

But perhaps the deep philosophical message of the book is the fact, already noted, that individuals always and everywhere have choices, but that these are made in circumstances not of their own choosing. And this is just as true in the ordinary lives of ordinary people as it is in the lives of key historical figures. A person is free insofar as he or she has the capacity to make choices, including choices of things which may be desirable, wanted or wished for. Largely by virtue of historical circumstances, some societies have done better than others in distributing this freedom. In so far as historical contingency is a key factor, the distribution of freedom has been part of the lottery of life. Thus we return to the question of democracy. The more democratic a society, the greater are the possibilities for collectively controlling the conditions of the common lives of its members, and the less is the distribution of freedom left to the contingencies of one's place in the inherited structures which define the character of an undemocratic societies.

Part I

War and Democracy in Ancient Greece

Introduction

As everyone knows, democracy was born in ancient Greece. Like most of what has happened in history, it was the product as much of accident as intention. Crucial in this instance was war and *stasis* – conflict, strife, and revolution. Both war and *stasis* were important elements in Greek thinking; but it may seem odd to modern readers that for intellectuals in ancient Greece, *stasis* was the greater evil. Plato summarized the situation aptly when he said that while the best condition was neither war nor *stasis*, "*stasis* is the most dangerous kind of war." In designing a constitution, it is *stasis*, first and foremost, that the lawgiver must guard against (Laws, 628a).[1]

There is no one English word which suitably translates *stasis*. Sometimes its meaning seems best rendered "civil disorder" or "civil strife," sometimes "sedition" or "revolution." While *stasis* connotes the opposite of domestic tranquility, none of these terms is exactly right, and each of them may sometimes be appropriate. A *stasis* could simmer and be contained for a long time; moreover, it might or might not be violent. It might result in a change of regime, the result of struggles between the powerful who by means of *coups* replace one oligarchy by another. Or it could be something far more serious, the form of revolution characteristic of the late fifth century and important to writers of the fourth century and every century since, one resulting in a change in constitution, from an aristocracy, oligarchy, or tyranny to a democracy, or the other way round.

The concern with *stasis* in Greek political thinking is important. But it was important to the Greeks precisely because it was the Greeks who quite literally invented *politics*, construed here as a struggle for a share of the ruling power, for a voice in the decisions which affect the community. This struggle eventually came to include all free males in the political community. Indeed, the Greeks unsettled what had once been a settled question, namely, the question of who can be excluded from sharing in decisions of major social importance. As Aristotle was later to put it, if a citizen (*polites*) was defined by nothing so much as having a right "to participate in judging and ruling" (*metachein kriseos kai arches*) (*Politics*, III. 1), then the critical question, in both theory and practice, was who was to be a citizen.

Particular features of the world of the Greek *polis* gave rise to this idea of politics, an idea alien to other ancient societies and, despite the manifest but superficial similarities, alien also to our own. The most critical feature in this was the idea of the *polis* itself, a provincial, autonomous, self-sufficient ensemble of citizens. Critical too, however, was the special character of Greek war, not only what it was like, its limits, and the extraordinary complexity of inter-*polis* and "international" relations, but also the critical relation between "citizen" and "soldier," between who ruled and who fought. Politics produced *stasis*, which in turn produced democracy; but war was the variable which finally destroyed both democracy and the world of the *polis*. The philosophers who reflected on this left an enormous legacy; but, as I will suggest, this legacy was not merely instruction, it was also in many ways an enormous burden.

1

The Invention of Politics

The invention of the *polis* was surely the most decisive factor in the Greek invention of politics, but it is also the factor which we stand least chance of ever explaining.[1] It seems to have emerged in Greek prehistory, in the eighth century. It spread quickly, however, and by end of the fifth century there may well have been 1,000 or more such enclaves, stretching from all around the Black Sea, through the Hellespont, down across Ionia, throughout the Cyclades and Crete, on mainland Greece (*Magna Graeca*, the Latin for Greek "Hellene"), across to Sicily, and as far west as Massalia, present-day Marseilles. All were near the sea; yet geography is not a sufficient explanation of their appearance.

We can characterize a *polis* as a territory of modest size — Athens was as large as any, about the size of Rhode Island, but most were much smaller — in which there was an urban center (the word *polis* originally meant "citadel"), surrounded by a region of countryside and villages. But — and this is critical — the *polis* was politically united and autonomous *(autonomia)*: it gave itself its own laws. Ideally, as the philosophers later insisted, it was also autarchic — self-sufficient and complete in itself.

The older form of association, the *ethnos*, could be a territory of many thousands of square miles, with its population thinly scattered, of which the Court formed the center, even though it was not the center of the "community." An *ethnos* might have shared customs and a shared religion; and in some extended sense it might even have constituted an "ethnic" unit. It was ruled by a king, often in conjunction with an assembly of aristocrats. Looked at from a distance, a small *ethnos* might be difficult to distinguish from a large *polis*; but the typical *ethnos* had the advantage of larger size, and it survived much past the time of the appearance — and demise — of the *polis*. One thinks here especially of Macedonia and Epirus.

Four developments coincided more or less with the emergence, and gestation of the *polis*. First, there seems to have been a shift from an exclusively pastoral economy, loosely associated with "tribalism," to arable farming, probably as a result of a phenomenal increase in population during the period. For our purposes it is important to note that it established a critical link between citizenship in the *polis* and ownership of the land.

Second, and tied to this, if surprisingly, it was during this period that chattel slavery came to the fore in the Greek world. Third, there was the development of hoplite warfare; and finally, and almost surely related in some way to the foregoing, there was the disappearance of hereditary monarchies.

It would be wonderful to be able to show that these four developments reduce to a single fundamental factor: demography, geography, a change in the mode of production, a technical innovation in warfare, or a new ideology. But such an effort would, I think, be misguided. For what happens in the world, natural and social, is the result of a plurality of causes; and in general, efforts to explain it will inevitably be guided by particular interests and, just as inevitably, suffer from incompleteness. No one would try to explain a hotel fire by pointing to the presence of oxygen, regardless of the fact that, there can be no combustion without it. It is the arsonist or the failed fire-detector in which we are interested. No one would be deluded into supposing that the maturing of a particular acorn into a handsome oak-tree could be explained without appeal to background facts concerning the genetic materials of acorn cells, the local climate, and local geography, or, lest we forget, to contingent facts regarding human intervention (or nonintervention.) We say, "The acorn will become an oak, other things being equal." But of course, in the concrete, they never are equal. In the case of aged stately oaks, they were sufficiently "equal" in that they got the rain they needed as seedlings, were saved from the bulldozers of developers, and so forth.

Indeed, the critical causal agent in human history is the human agent, struggling for a livelihood and the satisfaction of material and spiritual needs. This is not to subscribe to a "great man" theory of history, since even so-called unimportant people play necessary causal roles. After all, it is the countless everyday activities of countless individuals which unintentionally reproduce and transform, usually imperceptibly, the ensemble of practices which constitute the changing social order. Of course, some of these acts − for example, the decision to go to war − set in motion events which may have rather more dramatic consequences than were intended; how these decisions are structured and who makes them are critically important facts. Because history is best understood as the outcome of conjunctural "accidents," of opportunities taken or missed, we need to remember the overwhelming presence of agency. But if agents are decisive, they always act with the materials at hand: the existing geography, technologies, social relations, and beliefs.

In the present case, arable farming and beliefs regarding the possession of land, chattel slavery, the household, freedom, religion, rule, war, especially hoplite warfare, and the disappearance of hereditary monarchies were surely elements in the causal nexus which produced the *polis*. It is the combined outcome of all these things, along with others certainly, which generated the world of the *polis*. But our effort to reach an understanding is doubly burdened. For we are still in the era of Greek prehistory, before the age of written documents, which means that we must rely on archeology, inference, and the writings of later authors. Aristotle is here an important source.

The Genesis of Politics in Ancient Greece

In his effort "to study things in the process of development from the beginning," Aristotle began with an account of the "household" *(oikos)*, the "partnership" which includes "the female and the slave," "the persons whom Charondos speaks of as 'meal-tubfellows.'" When several households come together, we have a village *(kome)*, "formed of those whom people speak of as 'fellow-nurslings,' sons and sons' sons." According to Aristotle, "it is owing to this that our cities were at first under royal sway and that foreign races are so still ... for every household is under the royal rule of its eldest member" *(Politics, I. 1)*. For the Greeks, these masters *(despotes)* of households, the "fathers," *(patres)* who ruled, were seen as having natural authority. Indeed, this was self-evident to Aristotle — as it has been for many after him. It is easy to suppose that some of these men became chiefs of the "tribes" *(gene)*, and thus, by the side of their king *(basileus)*, formed an aristocracy, literally, the rule of the *aristoi*, the "best" families.

We know that over the course of history, the ideas underpinning such a system have convinced millions. Not only is the male parent, the *despotes*, considered to be the natural head of the household, but when some of these heads of families come together to constitute a so-called natural ruling group, one may be made king. The ancients never reconsidered the idea of the *despotes*, but, remarkably, these Greeks did abandon the idea of a hereditary king. Because the question of who was to be a citizen could now be asked, a conceptual floodgate was opened. The changes were probably barely noticed, at least for a long time. After all, it was not until 300 years later, after the Greeks had stumbled and fought their way to democracy, that Aristotle wrote. Nor can we be sure why in so many cities, kingly authority was rejected. As Aristotle says, "Some renounced this power voluntarily, from others it was taken by force, and nothing was left to these kings but the care of the sacrifices" *(Politics, III. 9)*. In Sparta, it is Lycurgus who, in the myth, is given credit for ending the *stasis* which balanced power in a "mixed constitution" of dual kings, a senate *(gerousia)*, and "citizens." In Athenian lore, it is Theseus.

It may be best to consider separately the early histories of the "constitutions" of Athens and Sparta, the two key cities in all accounts.

Archaic Athens

For the earliest period, we can perhaps do no better than follow Aristotle, who offers a subtle, if confusing, account of the different forms of monarchy (*Politics*, III. 9). It seems clear, however, that, as he understands it, in the monarchies of "heroic times" there were no institutions whose function it was to constrain a king in his decision making. He was "despotic" (*despotikai*) even though, as in an *oikos*, he ruled over "willing subjects." Aristotle suggests that a critical change occurred sometime before the time of Drakon (ca. 620?), in whose reign "archons or supreme magistrates were elected in accordance partly with aristocratic, partly with oligarchic qualifications, originally for life, afterwards for ten years" (*Athenian Constitution*, 3). He tells us that these included the king and the polemarch − literally the archon of war, created "to supply the generalship in which some of the kings were wanting." In addition to the king and the polemarch, there seem to have been six other archons, the *themistothetai*, literally "givers of the *themis*," or law, whose function was "to commit the ordinances to writing." Taken together, the body of archons constituted, as the name indicates, "rulers" of the city. We know nothing of how these rulers were elected. Nor can we be sure that Aristotle is correct in suggesting that non-nobles had a vote or that they may have been eligible for at least some of these offices. The point is critical. Aristotle rightly sees that there are enormous differences between an oligarchy and an aristocracy, for the former would include only a wealthy few, the latter only a hereditary caste. If aristocratic control had already been broken, conditions for continuous *statis* might already have been realized.

There was, evidently, an aristocratic body, the Council of the Areopagus. Aristotle writes that it had "the duty of watching over observance of the laws." Again, it is not at all clear what this means: whether, for example, it was a body which gave advice to those who actually ruled and whose consent was required for action, or whether it controlled the "magistrates" or something else. Regardless, Aristotle, always the political sociologist, makes it clear that in this constitution "power was . . . wielded by the class of persons capable of providing their own equipment in war" (ibid., 4). It may be, accordingly, that power was in the hands not only of aristocrats but of wealthy "commoners" as well. The point is important and requires an excursion on the development of hoplite warfare in ancient Greece.

Hoplite Warfare

There was a critical relation − as well as continuous tension − between the ruling and military functions in Greek cities; and at the bottom of this was the problem of war. Though, again, the evidence is extremely thin, it is possible to guess, with Thucydides, that during the period of the gestation of the *polis*, the word "war" typically referred to a raid, limited in terms of both its objectives and the number of persons and sorts of organizations involved. Conducted on a private basis, these so-called wars were, as Thucydides remarks, pillaging forays conducted "under the lead of their powerful men, whose motive was their private gain and support of their weaker followers" (I. 15). Fighting, it seems, was conducted by individual champions, some Achilles who could afford a horse-drawn chariot, a shield, a breastplate, a helmet, a pair of javelins, and a sword. The "heroes" of ancient Greece, the warriors so beautifully and extravagantly captured in the epic poetry of Homer, belong to this time and condition in all probability.[2]

A genuinely juridical concept of war becomes appropriate with the emergence of the *polis*. War, so understood, implies a confrontation between distinct political entities and involves some sort of organized commitment on the part of their members. Piracy and brigandage continued, but, as Thucydides suggests, with less frequency. Moreover, frontier skirmishes became better organized and more reasonably identified as wars.

By 650 BC, at least, we know that all the items of hoplite equipment were available, and that hoplite phalanx warfare had been invented.[3] Some detail on the technical points is important. First, the hoplite gets his name from the particular type of shield he used, the *hoplon*, made of wood but rimmed or faced with bronze and with two interior handles. One of these handles, a detachable armband, the *propax*, allowed the bearer to insert his left arm up to the elbow and grip a leather thong (the *antilabe*) at the rim of the shield. This meant that the shield could be larger and heavier than the earlier varieties of shield. The hoplite would also wear a breastplate made of bronze, a bronze helmet with a felt or leather cap sewn in for comfort, and bronze shin-guards (*knemides*). His weapons included a spear, perhaps one and a half times his own height, and a sword. A line of hoplites in very close formation was called a "phalanx". In such an array the offensive might of the spears was maximized, and the vulnerable right side – apart from the last row on the right – was protected. In combat, what was required was "above all disciplined cohesion and unyielding physical and moral strength." Fighting consisted mainly of "a concerted shoving (*othismos*) akin to the tight scrummaging of modern rugby football," [4] and usually the first shock of confrontation decided the issue. As Adcock neatly summarized the situation, Greek battles were "mass duels."[5]

Everyone agrees, it seems, that the full hoplite "panoply" was expensive, and that many landowners – probably most – could not afford one. It seems clear too that a hereditary aristocracy might well be too small to effectively engage in phalanx warfare, in which sheer numbers would be decisive. But a number of other questions, still hotly contested, are also pertinent to this development. In the first place, why was hoplite warfare introduced into Greece, and why did it remain the dominant form of warfare throughout the entire classical period? After all, there were alternatives: cavalry or missiles could have been used to a greater extent; so could more lightly armed infantry, *peltastes* (or skirmishers), who were more mobile. Indeed, hoplite warfare, prima facie, is, not suited to the predominantly mountainous terrain of Greece. As Cartledge points out, "If a hoplite is to keep in step and maintain his position in the phalanx, he needs a plain that is at once level and not conducive to ambush."[6] One would have thought that the terrain of Greece would have made it ideal for radically different tactics, those of the *peltastes*, which would have opened up the possibilities of both surprise and guerrilla fighting. Nor, it seems, were alternatives not considered. Indeed, Herodotus has Mardonius the Persian remark that "Greeks wage wars in a most senseless way, through sheer wrongheadedness and folly. When they have declared war against one another, they search out the smoothest and fairest plain . . . and there assemble and fight" (VII. 9). If there is an answer to this puzzle, it seems to lie in social and political factors; indeed, it seems to be connected to the belief that ruling and citizenship were linked.

Second, and not unrelated, did the change in tactics, by introduction of the phalanx, promote the changes in the hoplite panoply, especially the double-handle arrangement, or did these changes precede the new tactic? An answer would go some way to explaining whether aristocratic rule was broken as a consequence of the hoplite reform, or whether it was the cause of that reform, a point that has been contested. However, the question is badly put; for it suggests a reductionist, monocausal choice of alternatives. The practices which, taken together, constitute the ensemble which came to be the *polis* had been undergoing gradual change at this time. The shift to arable farming, the increasing population, the use of slave labor, and so on had each had its effects; but these were probably transactional, interrelated, and uneven. Most critical, perhaps, was the development in the countryside of a body of substantial farmers who were not part of the aristocracy. Against this background, we can assent, if we like, to the view that the crucial modifications of the shield were introduced to improve aristocratic dominance, both political and military. But, given the existence of these farmers and their need for defense of property, and given that at some point the integrity of the *polis* was acknowledged by all, it can also be envisaged that the *aristoi* might invite those farmers who could afford the hoplite panoply to aid in defending the *polis*. The phalanx might or might not have preceded this enlargement of the hoplite force. Either way, numbers were clearly important, especially after the commitment to the hoplite shield and its employment in a phalanx.

I should stress here that the hoplite reform was essentially defensive, a point that will be developed later, and that even after the massive confrontation of the Persians and the Greeks, even after the long, complex series of engagements which we call the Peloponnesian War, the Greeks continued to think of war in terms of their heroic past. As Cartledge writes:

> In fact, hoplite warfare continued for centuries as it had begun – a gentlemanly, amateur affair confined to a campaigning "season" in spring and early summer before the harvest, a "walking tour ending in combat" and demanding a minimum of training and theoretical analysis .... As Marx neatly phrased it, "antiquity unanimously esteemed agriculture as the proper occupation of the free man, the soldier's school."[7]

But of course there were unintended consequences, not least the potential for *stasis* which was unleased everywhere except Sparta, the most stable *polis* in the Greek world. Indeed, as fourth-century theory never fails to remind us. Sparta was free of *stasis* for most of its 700-year history.

Sparta

Sparta was exceptional, in that it was one of only a few of the early cities to conquer and subject its neighbors. It seems – although we are guessing here – that as early as the tenth century perhaps, before she became a *polis*, Sparta had subjected the Lakonians to the institution called "helotage." "Helots" were not chattel slaves in that, unlike the slaves of Athens, say, they were members of "native" peoples who had been subjected through conquest of their native territory; nor were they "commodities" to be bought or sold. Further, they were self-perpetuating – that is, they lived as family units. They were thus like serfs. Around 735, Sparta had conquered the neighboring city of Messenia, in the so-called First Messenian War. But it was the Second Messenian War, a war of independence fought around the middle of the seventh century, that seems to have been decisive. What emerged, following the famous reforms of Lycurgus, was a structure very nearly unique in the Greek world, or indeed, anywhere else.[8]

The most crucial factor was the noncoincidence of the *polis*, Sparta, and the territory, Lakedaimonia, in which a single class of Spartans (*Spartiates*), the *homoioi* ("peers" or "equals"), ruled over a very large subject population. Sparta became, in effect, a police state, continuously at war with an internal enemy. To avoid the "unholy" (*euages*) killing of a helot, which would have amounted to murder, the Ephors made an annual, formal declaration of war upon the helots. The ratio of *Spartiates* to their subjects may have been ten to one; and the subject population were not only Greeks, but were comprised of homogeneous communities who never lost their "tribal" identities. If ancient writers persistently applauded the absence of *stasis* in Sparta, they did not fail to notice that helot revolts were a permanent feature of Spartan history. The point is worth emphasizing; for people who struggled against those with power were said to engage in *stasis* only if they had some claim to membership in the city. Poor Athenian farmers did; helots did not. There have been similarities throughout history, of course, whether the nonmembers have been black slaves, Jews, Armenians, or Palestinians.

Another important feature of the Spartan *polis* was that the Spartan *homoioi* were allowed both full economic security and complete freedom from economic activity, these being provided by helots and *perioikoi*, communities of subjects who maintained some local autonomy but were entirely subordinate to the Spartans as regards the waging of war and the making of foreign policy. They were not slaves, like the helots; on the other hand, they were not "foreign allies" either, as, for example, were the citizens of Corinth.[9] This extraordinary arrangement allowed a Spartan to be not only a full-time citizen, the ideal of every notable theorist of antiquity, but also a full-time soldier, and in particular a hoplite. Although we cannot be sure, it seems that at no point in Spartan history did the number of *Spartiates* ever exceed 9,000, and that by 371, their number had shrunk to perhaps 1,500.[10] Indeed, two years later, when a large force of hostile hoplites penetrated the Peloponnese, the helots staged a successful rebellion, and Sparta was reduced to a second-rate power.

A further, important feature is that the *Spartiates* were equal in that all were subject to a highly disciplined process of education known as the *agoge*. Young Spartan males were obliged to enter competitions and at twenty or twenty-one were elected to a common mess, where they continued to live simply, train, and develop martial skills. As Plato recognized so well in appropriating these ideas, this was not only the most direct way to socialize the "guardians" (*phylakai*) of the *polis*; it served to maximize just those virtues of solidarity, selflessness, and courage so essential to their role.

But there were two ways in which Spartans were not equals. Some were richer than others – a problem of increasing significance, as Aristotle noted (*Politics* II. 6) – and the decision-making structure was based on a mix of hereditary right, election, and appointment. The second is directly pertinent here; for Sparta was not a monarchy, in that she had two kings – an utterly unique, unexplained situation in the world of the *polis*. Moreover, as Aristotle emphasized, a Spartan king was a "lifelong general" (*strategia dia biou*). This was no small matter. Given that in the Greek *polis* there was a strong relation between the ruling and the military functions, two hereditary generals would have considerable political power. The relations between a hereditary general and his men and an elected general and his men, the situation in Athens, would be very different. The Spartan arrangement of dual kings-cum-commanders certainly created problems, even if, as ancient sources suggest, it also contributed to the absence of "tyranny" in Sparta.

The two kings were automatically members of the *Gerousia* (the elders, in Latin the *senatus*), which numbered thirty, including the kings. Many much later writers — among them Isocrates, Plutarch, and Polybius — say that the *Gerousia* was the governing body; but this seems to be part of the mythology of Sparta's so-called mixed constitution. There is nothing in the historical record which suggests that this was the case. As the exclusive judiciary in the Spartan *polis*, it undoubtedly had great power, however. There were also five Ephors, who, Aristotle says, were elected "in a childish manner" from "the entire people" (*ek tou demon pantos*). In the Spartan case, the reference to "the entire people" is always clear. It refers to the Equals, who presumably comprised an assembly when convened. The "childish mode of election" was by shouting, there being no ballots, never mind secret ballots. Aristotle gives the Ephors "absolute control over the most important affairs" and complains that this is a poor arrangement because "quite poor men often happen to get into office." Not only are they easily "corrupted with money," but they also tend to pander to "the people" (*Politics*, II. 6). The Ephors presided over all meetings, virtually conducted foreign policy, and could compel even the kings to face trial by the *Gerousia*. This is an instance of the kind of checks and balances so greatly favored by later writers. Evidence suggests that the Assembly, the famous "democratic element" in the Spartan constitution, could ratify or reject proposals brought before it. However, its members lacked the right to make speeches and to criticize and propose amendments (*isegoria*), and not all decisions required the consent of the Assembly. As we shall see, these are two of the many differences between the constitution of Sparta and that of Athens.

Nonetheless, it was a stable constitution, and the *Spartiates* managed to suppress for a long time the many efforts of the Messenian helots to revolt. Sparta avoided "tyranny" (in the Greek sense) altogether, a fact which drew continuous praise from the philosophers; but, of course, it also avoided democracy. To be sure, in the Spartan *polis*, the *least* democratic of the cities, decisions about war and peace required the consent of those who fought, a fact which should give us pause; but the decision-making process never came close to what it was in Athens. Even if we restrict ourselves to Spartans and ignore altogether the non-Spartans who were subordinate to them, there was little democracy. Power was almost fully lodged in the hands of a very few. Not only were there constitutional constraints on participation, such as the fact, noted above, that Spartans had no right to speak in the Assembly, but, to quote Finley, "Can we imagine that the obedient, disciplined Spartan soldier dropped his normal habits on those occasions when he was assembled not as a soldier but as a citizen, while he listened to debates among those from whom he otherwise was taught to take orders without questioning or hesitation?"[11] Just as Achilles and Agamemnon "harangued each other before the assembled people," so too did King Archidamus and the Ephor, Sthenelaidas, at the critical moment when the fateful vote was taken to go to war with Athens (Thucydides, I. 78, 86).

The Beginnings of Democracy in Athens

The early history of Athens followed a trajectory which was more typical of the history of Greek cities.[12] Once the monarchy had declined and after the exclusive grip of the aristocracy had been broken, Athens, like other cities, seems to have experienced a continued polarization of rich and poor, a fact which plainly impressed both Plato and Aristotle. Large numbers were reduced to debt-bondage. Some of these were the *hektemoroi*, who were liable to be taken into slavery if they defaulted on the obligatory payments of at least one-sixth of their produce. In ca. 594, the archon Solon was appointed to address this problem which threatened to undo the community. Extraordinarily, he abolished the debts, redeemed the Athenians who had been sold into slavery, and introduced laws prohibiting such practices in the future. For these actions, later writers have called him the first "champion of the people" (*prostates tou demou*).

It is not clear what sort of support Solon had for these remarkable moves, although it is evident enough that they had enduring consequences. At the same time, perhaps doing no more than codifying the *de facto* situation, he redefined eligibility for the highest magistracies, including the Council of the Areopagus, which was now to be based on agricultural wealth, not aristocratic descent. Other rights were similarly allocated on the basis of landed wealth. Aristotle identifies four Solonian "classes." At the top were the *pentakosiomedimnoi*, literally those who produced annually, in grain, wine, or oil, 500 medimni (perhaps 6,000 imperial gallons). Below these were the *hippeis*, (or cavalry, the 300-medimni class), then the *zeugitai*, (who produced 200 medimni), and finally the class of *thetes*.

There are some difficulties as regards *thetes*. In ordinary Greek, *thetes*, "laborers", were understood to be those who had *no* property and were thus *forced* to sell their labor-power. But it is extremely doubtful that Solon made citizens of men defined as *thetes* in this sense. From Homer to Aristotle – indeed to Jefferson! – landless, hence dependent, laborers were regarded as utterly unfit for participation in the political process. As Finley remarks, "a *thes*, not a slave, was the lowest creature on earth that Achilles could think of."[13] Aristotle was more explicit regarding the reasoning behind this persistent attitude: "No man can practice virtue who is living the life of manual toil or as a hired laborer" (*zonta bion bananoun n thetikon*). It was for this reason that, "in ancient times, and among some nations, before the development of extreme democracy, the working classes did not participate in ruling" (*Politics III. 3*). Aristotle does say that with Solon's reforms, *thetes* were "only admitted to participate in the assembly (*ekklesia*) and the law courts (*dikasterion*)" (*Athenian Constitution*, 7), yet this does suggest "citizenship" in some sense. But it is by no means clear what sense, for surely Solon had not created an "extreme democracy" (*demos tou eschatou*)!

It might be well to pause here to develop, if briefly, the idea, analyzed by Aristotle, that citizenship, like democracy, could admit of degrees and types. Nowadays we tend to think in black-and-white terms; either one is a citizen or one is not. But we must remember that the idea of a citizen was only being invented in the sixth century BC.

There were at least three criteria (or sets of rights) which could be invoked. There was the question of whether a man — and only men were eligible, regardless of the particular criteria — had, in our terms, "civil rights." Was he protected by law, and more radically, was this a condition of *isonomia* — that "what is regarded as valid and binding is so regarded by and for all classes of society"?[14] People could have rights without having equal rights. *Isonomia* meant equal rights. Second, were there restrictions on direct participation, in juries, legislation, and administration? And third, what was the mechanism for being granted decision-making power — for example, was it by lot, appointment, or election? I should stress here that answers to these questions still leave open the question of the actual powers assigned to various institutions — for example, the archonship, the Council of the Areopagus, the Assembly, and so forth. The possible combinations are many: for example, there could have been a fair degree of equality of "civil rights" and participation in "popular" courts, but highly restricted access to the institutions which made law and had the power to declare war. Aristotle was content to call such an arrangement "democratic," but it is minimally democratic by later standards.

At the minimum, then, *thetes* may have been given some measure of what we call "civil rights" — for example, the right to appeal decisions by magistrates. Aristotle says that there were three "democratic" parts to Solon's reform. The first and most important was "stopping loans on the person." Second was the right of "he who wishes" (*ho boulomenos*) to prosecute someone who has done a wrong. Thus, the "private" system of personal "revenge," in which only the person (or relative of that person) wronged could prosecute was rejected. With Solon's reform, anyone who knew of wrongdoing could bring charges. Third, there was "the thing which they say has most strengthened the people (*plethos*), appeal to the lawcourt (*dikasterion*)." This seems to imply that "the people" were given *some* protection against the powerful, a considerable step forward, but not in any sense full-fledged citizen's rights. Indeed, not only is there confusion over the term Eliaia, which seems etymologically to mean "assembly", but there is question as well — and this is critical of the powers of the Assembly and the rights of its members. As Ostwald points out, before the time of Cleisthenes, we know nothing of the powers of the Assembly. Further, we should at least notice that Solon's frequent references to "the people" — as when he says, "I protected with a strong shield" both "the people" (*demos*) and "those with power and wealth" (*dynamin kai chremasin*) — leave much room for different interpretations, since not only are there different mechanisms for protecting a group against oppression, but there is no specification of who "the people" are and what rights they have. We know that slaves and "foreign residents" (metics) were not included among "the people." But were "the people" non-aristocratic landowners? Or were they all poor Athenians, including *thetes,* who in Solon's day, might have constituted only a small, inconsequential number? Solon, it is worth mentioning, was attacked from the left as well as the right. As Aristotle writes, "the people (*demos*) had expected that the land would be equally divided, the nobles that the old system would be restored" (*Athenian Constitution*, 11).

Tyranny

Still, the road to democracy continued to be rocky, and included the Athenian experience of "tyranny" (*tyrannes*). The word is foreign, perhaps coming from Lydia and may initially have been just another word for kingship. But it soon came to designate a "special kind of monarchy, one that is usurped by force and not inherited." Snodgrass, here quoted, would seem to be on firm ground in saying that "through tyranny . . . most Greek states had their first taste of radical policies and, conversely, there were few leading progressive states which had not passed through a phase of tyranny."[15] If one views "progress" as increased participation in decisions affecting one's life, then "tyranny" was progressive in the sense that it broke the grip of the traditional power-holders and opened the way for an extended citizenship. Indeed, it seems clear that the poorer mass of people fared well under tyrants, and that at least some of the Greek tyrants were quite popular. Faced with Solon's problem, Cypselos of Corinth, for example, took the very radical step of redistributing the land, one of the consequences of which was the growth of a class of small landowners who came to make up the notable citizen-army of Corinth. [16]

No doubt the first emergence of tyrannies, in various places at various times from ca. 675 on, was deeply connected with both the problem of insufficient land for the poor and the hoplite reform noted earlier (again, leading to misplaced argument as to whether the tyrants created the reform or the other way round.) But these early tyrannies need to be distinguished from the later, much less frequent tyrannies of the late fifth and the fourth centuries.

At least three questions need to be addressed at this point. First, can tyrannies be "progressive"? We have already noted that, viewed from the standpoint of early Greek history, as a first step in breaking the hold of hereditary kings, the answer is yes. Second, does the successful usurper, whatever the subsequent regime, usually find popular support? Aristotle was probably correct in answering this question in the affirmative; for on his view, "kings came into existence for the purpose of helping the better classes (*epieikeis*) against the people (*demos*) ... while a tyrant is set up from among the people and the multitude to oppose the notables (*gnorimoi*), in order that the people may suffer no injustice from them." On this ground he concludes that "almost the greatest number of tyrants have arisen ... from being demagogues, having won the people's confidence in slandering the nobles" (*Politics* V. 8). The third question, not to be confused with the second, is whether democracies are especially vulnerable to tyranny, the view clearly promulgated by Plato. But it is by no means self-evident that democracies give rise to tyrants. We know that democracy came late to Athens and was accelerated by her successes; but it was not demagogues in democracies who caused trouble in the fourth century, but Persian gold, oligarchic reaction, and, finally, Macedonian power. Indeed, perhaps despite himself, Aristotle gives a different picture from Plato.

Aristotle rightly appeals to the "facts of history" and acknowledges that tyranny is not always to be laid at the feet of democratic demagogues. He writes, "Some tyrannies were set up when the cities had already grown great, but others which came before them arose from kings departing from the ancestral customs." The latter, of course, were the early tyrannies. He then says that the tyrannies which arose "after the cities had already grown great" did so in various ways: some "from the men elected to fill the supreme magistrates ... and others from oligarchies." There is no reason to assume that either of these ways involved democratic constitutions. He give examples of kings who became tyrants, presumably violating their rightful trust by so doing, of other tyrants who "arose from offices of honor"; and then gives four examples of demagogues, Panaetius at Leontini, Cypselos at Corinth, Peisistratus at Athens, and Dionysius at Syracuse of which *only* Dionysius emerged from a democracy to become tyrant.

To some extent at least, it is an aristocratic prejudice, promoted by Plato, Aristotle, and many others, to suppose that the tyrants were all evil demagogues, with no legitimacy, who imposed on the Greek world the worst of all political conditions. Fourth-century writers persistently assimilate the tyrannies of the archaic period to the later tyrannies. Indeed, Plato's prime example of a tyrant, that most wretched of all men, the demagogue who rose to power in a democracy by virtue of its mediocrity and corruption and then went on to destroy it, is Dionysius, who in 405, destroyed the Syracusan democracy, which, in a profound irony, was the very democracy which had crushed democratic Athens in the famous Sicilian campaign of 411. Plato's influence here has been great. Nobody wants a tyranny, but if demagogues have their way in democracies, then democracies are critically flawed. In his famous hierarchy of cities, only tyrannies are worse than democracies, which are bad because of what they are and because they give way, inevitably, to tyrannies. Plato's version of Greek history was the version which influenced the American Founding Fathers, a fact of some importance in the Constitution of the American Republic.

Finally, one must not confuse the condition of the ancient *polis* with that of a modern republic. In the modern world, republican governments, beginning with France's First Republic, have often yielded to authoritarian regimes; but none of these governments were democracies in the ancient Greek sense. In modern republics, "representatives" of the people have power, but not the people themselves; hence the switch to authoritarian power does not require taking power from the people.

Solon's reforms did not prevent Athens from becoming a tyranny, but this was en route to its becoming a democracy. After gaining fame in a war against Megara, Peisistratus (ca. 560) seems to have been voted a bodyguard by the oligarchic assembly; but he used this force to seize power, almost certainly with a considerable number of hoplites behind him. Peisistratus was careful not to alter the core of Solon's reforms – excepting, of course, the election of the chief magistrate. As in other cities, tyranny further undermined the aristocratic control of the *polis* and contributed to the politicizing of the city.

The Reforms of Cleisthenes

Peisistratus is not thought of as a champion of the people (*prostates tou demou*); but Cleisthenes is. No doubt the complex familial relations of the Alcmaeonidae, the *genos* headed by Cleisthenes, and the competing Cimonids, Isagoras and his kin and associates, were critical in Athens's next step toward democracy. But I turn directly to the ironical, but critical, decision made by Sparta in ca. 511/10 to "liberate" Athens from tyranny. Sparta succeeded, and Athens returned, albeit only temporarily, to "aristocratic politics as usual." In suggesting an irony in Sparta's intervention, I mean not to suggest that Sparta usually defended tyranny – it was committed to aristocracy – but the unintended consequence of its action. For, after a short period of stability, ca. 508/7, Cleisthenes managed, remarkably, to introduce reforms which effectively "gave authority to the common people" (*Athenian Constitution*, 20).

Cleisthenes achieved at least two monumental reforms. First, there was the reorganization of the electoral rolls of the *polis*, which increased the number of "tribes" from four to ten. This was coupled with a complicated arrangement of subdivisions of *trittyes* and *demes*, the *deme*, of which there were 139 in Attica, being the smallest voting unit. As a consequence, the older system of aristocratic control of the *phratries* (the religious association of "families", which was the unit of a tribe) was undermined; and at the same time, a greater measure of local autonomy was promoted. Residence in a locality, rather than kinship, became the criterion of citizenship. Ten generals (*strategoi*), one from each tribe, were elected, and the Council of Five Hundred now included fifty members from each tribe. Similarly, in the villages outside the central city, Archarnae, Marathon, Eleusis, and so on, the *deme* assembly and its leader, the *demarch*, provided a new locus of pride and political control for the *polis*. The second major reform was that the Assembly now became the fundamental legislative body of the *polis*. The idea of equal rights (*isonomia*) thus took a giant step forward.

That these were radical measures is well attested by the fact that within three years oligarchs in Athens were happy to again invite Spartan hoplites, and that the Spartan, Cleomenes, was now fully prepared to install Isagoras as tyrant of Athens. In this, he established a principle which in various forms still seems to exist: that a regime of the few is far more threatened by a democracy than it is by a tyranny.

Better prepared, Cleomenes arranged for Corinth, an ally in the Peloponnesian League, and Boeotia and Chalchis to join in the invasion. Athens could then be attacked from the west, the east, and the north. But things did not go as planned. The Corinthians, assembled at Eleusis with the Spartans, "thinking that they were perpetrating a wrong, changed their minds, and drew off the main army" (Herodotus, V. 66). The Two Spartan kings Cleomenes and Demaratus, quarreled and finally decided to follow suit. This subsequently led to a new law in Sparta, forbidding the two monarchs from going out together with an army. This reluctance and indecision, which was characteristically Spartan, gave Athens considerable room for maneuver. On a single day the Athenians defeated the Boeotians and then crossed into Euboea and defeated the Chalcidians. In a famous text, Herodotus compared the military prowess of Athens then and before the democracy: "While undergoing oppression," he wrote, "they let themselves be beaten, since then they worked for a master." "It is plain enough, not from this instance only, but from many everywhere, that freedom is an excellent thing.... [As] soon as they got their freedom, each man was as eager to do the best he could for himself. So fared it now with the Athenians" (V. 78). The idea is powerful, surely. No longer servants, but masters of their community, the Athenians were not going to let themselves be beaten. With this text in mind perhaps, Snodgrass concludes that "the individual Greek had begun by expressing himself in poetry, in thought and in art; now the individual Athenian was claiming, as of right, the responsibility of political participation in a democracy, and backing that claim with extraordinary success."[17] Born in fire, the democracy of Athens would prove to be, as Pericles was later to say, an example to the world. Today we still celebrate freedom and democracy. But whether, 2,000 years later, we have any sort of clear sense of the meanings of these two extraordinary notions is far from self-evident. Yet our account has not yet reached that "extreme democracy" which Pericles praised and Aristotle condemned. Moreover, before we look at the further development of democracy in Athens, in the remarkable fifth century, we need to broaden our outlook and look at war in the ancient world and in particular the war of the Greeks against the Persians.

Greek Warfare

It is often said that "war was an ever present reality in Greek life."[18] This may well be true; but we should not infer from this that it was a reality in the same way that war has been an ever present reality for, say, a European born in 1898, a Vietnamese born in 1930 or, indeed, for a more fortunate American born in this century. Nor should we conclude that the Greeks were always at war, a statement that is true of the Roman polity, but not of the world of the Greek *polis*.

We are up against the problem of historical selection; since the great wars were great "events," it is hardly surprising that the two greatest histories of the period, by Herodotus and Thucydides, were accounts of wars. Similarly, because these great events "made history," it is unsurprising that later writers should have given them so such attention. Nevertheless, if we are talking about war in ancient Greece, we are talking about several hundreds of years and the inter-*polis* relations of hundreds of cities. Many of these cities are of little general interest, tiny dry Seriphos, Ios in the Cyclades, Locri and Caulonia in Italy, the string of cities along the coast of the Black Sea, Ialysos on Rhodes, and Naupactus on the mainland of Greece, to name but a few. Many more are of marginal interest only, being utterly uninvolved in inter-*polis* hostilities and remaining undisturbed for long periods of time. For example, Miletus and large, important Corinth seem to have experienced continuous peace for more than a hundred years. Still more of these cities, though involved in various wars from time to time, were never in the situation of Athens during its war with the Peloponnesians. It is inevitable that we should concentrate on Athens and Sparta. Not only do we have very little detail about the hundreds of other cities, the main writers being either Athenian or resident in Athens when they wrote, but the populations of Athens and Sparta were, from our point of view, the decisive actors in Greek history. But we fall into a trap if we speak of them as if they were the only actors. Indeed, this is a good place to remind ourselves that democracy came not just to Athens in the fifth century, but to hundreds of other cities as well.

Moreover, we are talking about a relatively uncomplicated social structure. For the Greeks, the idea of total war or of a war economy would have made no sense. As we have seen, the technology of war was primitive, and Greek cities, with the notable exception of Sparta, did not have significant citizen military levies and did not have either long or strong military traditions. Most of the people continued to be engaged in peaceful tasks, even at the height of the most significant wars of the period; thus, at the famous battle of Marathon (in 490), there were no more than 10,000 and 15,000 fighting men on each side.

As suggested, wars were generally not fought on a continuous basis. With a few exceptions, mainly in the late Peloponnesian War period, there was a campaigning "season," and wars, not just battles, might begin and end on a single day. There were few sieges – and again these were late – and the idea of war "without decision" – a war without decisive battles to settle the issues which prompted the war – makes no sense until we come to the series of "wars" which we, though not Thucydides, call "the Peloponnesian War." Typically, a war was announced, the forces gathered for the clash or a series of clashes, and the war ended with one side victorious, the other vanquished. Both the beginning and the end were signaled by highly ritualized declarations and symbolic acts, with a symbolic victory sometimes being the only prize. What we call "cold war" was, albeit possible, unusual. Not only was it clear to all when a war was on; but, once the fighting formally ended, there was – with exceptions, of course – little of the lingering enmity between former adversaries which we take for granted. At the cessation of hostilities, the *polis* simply returned to completely peaceful conditions.

This helps to explain the amazing readiness of Greek cities to ally themselves for a specific purpose with other cities, perhaps with a city with which they had quite recently been at war. To cite but one famous example, as the result of a war with Corinth about a disputed territory, Megara, long aligned with Sparta through the Peloponnesian League, deserted ca. 460 to ally herself with Athens, a recent adversary, and then returned again to the Spartan fold in 446 (Thucydides, I. 103).

Finally, the enormous emphasis on ritual and symbol which attended ancient war does not necessarily imply that ritual was important because war was ever-present. Indeed, the reverse may have been true: namely, that it was because war was a clear departure from life as usual that it was so ceremoniously decked out. Similar considerations might well apply to the treatment of war themes in fifth-century drama, as in the *Oresteia, Antigone,* Euripides' *Trojan Women*, produced in 415 after some fifteen years of hostilities with the Peloponnesians, or his relentlessly anti-Spartan *Andromache* which teaches that "If Death were in full view when votes are cast, Greece would never be destroying itself by war madness."

Yet Greek war was different from war in later periods, not only because the same people who voted for war fought, but because the aims and objects were different. In the ancient world, here including not merely the Greek *polis*, one might go to war for the sake of booty — slaves or gold — or to ensure the supply of necessaries; alternatively, one might go to war with the idea of establishing a tribute-paying empire, like that of Alexander or Rome. But given the nature of ancient economies, a war — or indeed, any other state activity — motivated by competition for markets or trading advantage or by other forms of mercantile or capitalistic imperialism simply was not possible. To be sure, "commercial rivalry" and other such explanations of ancient wars are found in many books; but these must be dismissed as anachronisms. Of course, establishing a tribute-paying empire, as did Persia and Rome, required means of coercively extracting tribute, and this, if the empire were either extensive or far away or both, required resources well beyond those at the disposal of a typical Greek *polis*, especially if cities formed defensive leagues precisely to keep this from happening. At least up until the intervention of Persia, the Greek world may well have realized the dream of "balance of power" theorists.

Critical in this regard was the fact that the *polis* was "territorially inelastic." It could not be expanded beyond certain rather restricted limits without fundamentally altering its nature. The idea that the "true nature" of a *polis* strictly determined its size is carefully defended by Plato and Aristotle who asserts:

> A polis consisting of too few people will not be self-sufficing (*autarkes*), an essential quality of a *polis*, and one consisting of too many, though self-sufficing as regards necessaries, is an *ethnos*, but not a *polis*. It will not be easy for it to be "constitutional" (*politeian*) — for who will command its over-swollen multitude in war? Or who will serve as its herald, unless he have the lungs of a Stentor. (*Politics* VII. 4) [19]

The jealously guarded *polis* structure put definite limits on wars of expansion, including those aimed at "empire." This was not unrelated to the point noted earlier, that the original equivalence of the military and ruling functions was preserved with the hoplite reform. We can now say, therefore, that there was a close relation between citizen-armies, the problem of *stasis*, and the scope of the military activities of a *polis*. In general, any "overextension of military activities beyond "agricultural poker" — protecting one's crops or menacing or destroying the enemy's — severely tested the integrity of the *polis*.

Sparta's early success in conquering its neighbors forced it into an extraordinary situation and, as everyone agrees, thenceforth dictated that its foreign policy be extremely conservative. It simply could not send off many *Spartiates* for too long without risking a successful slave revolt.

With these considerations in mind, we should note that it is too easy to argue that "in view of the scale and conditions of ancient warfare it was difficult for a state to follow up its victory with territorial extension and military occupation on a large scale," and that "few states could either afford or provide the manpower, whether of citizens or mercenaries, to maintain their [newly conquered] territory." This is true of course; but it assumes precisely what needs to be explained, which is why the Greeks clung so tenaciously to this form of organization, given that it restricted the available manpower. It is plain enough that they valued it. Indeed, not only did they see the *polis* as the only "civilized" form — note the Latin root of this translation of the Greek word *polis* — but, when challenged by alien "empires," they firmly maintained their commitment to the idea of an "autonomous" *polis*. Persia was an empire. Philip and then Alexander ruled an *ethnos*. Roman desire for aggrandizement required the abandonment of the *polis* form of organization altogether, as Machiavelli may have been the first to understand. There was, however, one solution to empire that was consistent with the *polis* form. It was, as we shall see, Athenian thalassocracy, rule of the sea. But before we examine this and its relation to "extreme democracy," we must consider the factor that upset the balance of power in the Greek Mediterranean, the war of the Persians against the Greeks.

2

War, *Stasis*, and Empire

The Persian Wars

"If the history of Assyria touches only a remote fringe of the Hellenic world, it is otherwise with the story of those who destroyed the Assyrian empire. The Medes and Persians, folks of Aryan speech like the Greeks, were marked out by destiny to be the adversaries of the Greeks throughout the chief two centuries of Grecian history." So writes Bury in his classic *History of Greece*. Plainly, this is not the place to describe or even sketch the complicated histories of Assyria, the Medes and Persians, and all the other "nations" which comprised what came to be known as the Persian Empire.[1] But we should note two further pertinent facts. First, if the Medes and Persians were like Greeks in being "folks of Aryan speech," they were unlike Greeks in not being *polis*-dwellers. Second, being organized in *ethnos*, they did not restrict their armies to "citizens." Indeed, the greater part of their armies consisted of either peoples who came under their domination, or mercenaries, here including Greeks.[2]

It was Croesus, son of the Assyrian king Alyattes, who conquered, ca. 550, all the Greek cities of the Ionian coast except Miletus. Miletus had established a treaty with Alyattes which his son had respected. When the Persian monarch Cyrus sought to crush Croesus, however, he invited Ionian Greeks to join him. They stubbornly refused to "medize" and were conquered by Cyrus, thus exchanging subjection to the Lydian lord of Sardis for subjection to Cyrus, a very distant monarch. Cyrus's Persian Empire was vast, and he could not have ruled it in anything like the sense in which a modern government rules its citizens. Nonetheless, he counted as his all territories which his armies, headed by satraps, had conquered; and his empire now included Ionian Greeks separated from Athens, Sparta, and the cities of *Magna Graeca* by the Aegean Sea.

According to Herodotus's account, "the troubles" which brought on the confrontation between the Persians and the Greeks began with a *stasis* in the Ionian island *polis* of Naxos ca. 494. Certain of the "fat men" (*andres ton pacheon*) had been banished from Naxos by the people (*demos*) and had fled to Miletus. Aristagoras, regent of Miletus, decided that if he were to help these oligarchs "recover their country," he might be able to make himself "lord of Naxos." Accordingly, he traveled to Sardis to convince "his friend" Artaphernes, the Persian satrap of Sardis (and future king), that "Naxos is an island of no great size, but fair and fertile, and containing much treasure and vast numbers of slaves." Aristagoras argued that if Artaphernes were to reinstate the exiles, he would not only be richly rewarded, but this would give him power not only over Naxos but over "the other islands which depend on it." With success at Naxos, Euboea (on the Greek mainland) would also become an easy prey (VI. 31).

Things did not go as planned. When the Persians arrived at Naxos to begin their quest for domination, the Naxians were prepared. After a siege of four months, the Persians withdrew, having failed to accomplish their mission. Aristagoras, unable to keep his promise but still ambitious, then decided to lead a revolt against the Persians! By relinquishing his own claims to rule and by establishing *isonomia* − "equality of government" − in Miletus, he induced the Milesians to follow him. He then succeeded in his campaign to promote rebellion in *all* of Ionia. Thus what began as a plot on the part of Aristagoras to reinstate the "fat men" of Naxos with Persian help, became a full-scale Ionian Greek rebellion *for* democracy and *against* Persian power.

Aristagoras appreciated, clearly, that King Darius would soon be down on them all, and that if the Ionian cities were to preserve the autonomy they had reclaimed, their inhabitants would need help. So he traveled to Sparta. Every Greek knew that the warriors of Sparta were among the best in the world. With their help, the Ionians would be invincible. But Aristagoras had no appreciation of Sparta's situation at home or of the fact that the Spartans would be reluctant to be away from home for long. Herodotus reports that the negotiations were proceeding nicely when Aristagoras blundered and told the Spartans the truth: that their force would need to travel to Asia for three months (V. 50). The Spartans balked. Not ready to give up, Aristagoras proceeded to Athens in the hope that the Athenians would help.

He was not wrong. Some years previously, Hippias, banished tyrant of Athens, had journeyed to Sardis to persuade Artaphernes to restore him to power. Artaphernes had cooperated by threatening the Athenians, but had done nothing to enforce his threat. It was thus that the Athenians were, as Herodotus says, "already in bad odor with the Persians." In reporting the outcome of Aristagoras's mission, Herodotus cannot resist editorializing: "Truly it would seem that it is easier to deceive many than one; for Aristagoras, though he failed to impose on Cleomenes, the Lakedaemonian,

succeeded with the Athenians, who were 30,000." "Won by his per-
suasions," he continues, "they voted that twenty ships should be sent to the
aid of the Ionians." But of course Athens was a democracy and already
large. Unlike Sparta, it had no helots to control and could easily spare men
and ships for limited ventures. Herodotus concluded ominously: "These
ships were the beginning of the mischief both to the Greeks and to the
barbarians" (V. 97).

The campaign was an enormous success. The Milesians and Chalcideans,
now assisted by Athens and Eretria, seem to have had little difficulty in
marching straight to Sardis, "no man opposing them; the whole city fell
into their hands, except only the citadel, which Artaphernes defended in
person, having with him no contemptible force" (V. 100). Though some
histories suggest that it was an accident, Herodotus makes it clear that the
burning of the city was deliberate. On returning from inland Sardis, the
Greeks met a force at Ephesus (the important coastal city), where they
surely had the worst of it. The Athenians then returned to Athens. When
Darius heard the news, he is reported to have asked who the Athenians
were and to have pledged, " 'O Zeus, grant me revenge on the Athenians' "
(V. 105). But he had first to reconquer Ionia.

The Ionians, combined, were by no means impotent. But it was no easy
task to get and then keep them together. Moreover, enormously complicating matters were Darius's successful efforts to promote *stasis* by pledging
support to the ousted oligarchs. Ionia was experiencing a struggle both for
democracy and for independence from Persian domination, and it is important to emphasize that Hippias and Aristagoras were not the only
Greeks who were ready to sell out their cities, that class loyalties could and
often did supersede *polis* loyalties − a point at the center of the analysis
and lament of the fourth-century democrat Demosthenes.

In this instance, a combined force which had assembled at Lade finally
disintegrated when the hoplites refused obedience to the leader, Dionysius
of Phocea. The cities which remained to fight were easily defeated,
and Ionia again became subject, albeit this time with differences. First,
Artaphernes forced the cities to sign a pledge that all inter-*polis* quarrels
would be settled by legal means. Second, and perhaps more startling,
under the young Mardonius, Greek despotisms were replaced by Greek
democracies. For perhaps the first time in Greek history, but surely not the
last, Greek cities, having lost their autonomy, found that for different
actors, there were different, if difficult, choices to be made. Moreover,
these choices depended critically on the nature and interests of powers
which could not be resisted. We can only guess at why Mardonius acted as
he did. It may be, however, that even if Mardonius's motives were good, he
judged that his capacity to dominate Ionia would not be threatened
through ousting "tyrannies" and implementing democracies.

Nor, egged on by Hippias, who now resided in the court at Susa, did King Darius forget his promise. Proceeding along the northern coastline of the Aegean and requiring tokens of submission from free Greek cities, the Persian force of perhaps 600 ships attacked and burned Naxos, forcing the inhabitants to flee to the hills, and then proceeded to Eretria, subjecting the inhabitants and burning the city. The force then crossed the strait to the Bay of Marathon, in 490.

Everyone knows of the famous run of Philippides, sent to Sparta by the Athenian Assembly to ask for help; and everyone knows of the victory of the Athenians. But we should emphasize that the Spartans, refusing to violate their law against marching out when the moon was not full, arrived well after the battle was over, and that Militiades the Athenian deserves credit not only for his courage but also for discerning, as Adcock puts it, "that a moment had come when, for whatever reasons, he could take the Persians at a disadvantage, when he could launch a decisive attack in which the weight and thrust of his hoplites came into their own."[3] Here was the first real confrontation between two very different kinds of armies, the hoplites of Greece and the mixed force of archers, cavalry, and light infantry of the Persian force.

The Athenian Assembly had to decide that day whether to go to Marathon to meet the Persians or to give them battle within sight of the Acropolis. Militiades persuaded them to send the force of 9,000 to Marathon, where they encamped in an invulnerable position with their backs to the hills. Help for the Athenians came when 1,000 Plataeans arrived. Days passed, and the Persians, numbering perhaps 15,000, could wait no longer. On that September day, then, the Greeks found a place and a tactic which brought them an overwhelming victory.

This was the first great battle between the Persians and the Greeks. There were only four others. The second and third, the land battle at Thermopylae and the sea battle at Salamis, were fought within weeks of each other, in September 480. The defense of Thermopylae, a critical element in the overall strategy, involved the combined Peloponnesian armies of Sparta (numbering 300), Tegea and Mantinea (500 each), Orchomenus (120), Corinth (400), Philius (200), and Mycenae (80), along with 700 Thespians and 400 Thebans. The Greek fleet which won at Salamis consisted of some 324 triremes and 9 penteconters, of which 200 were Athenian. The fourth and fifth battles, which were final and decisive, were at Plataea and Mycale, in August 479. At Plataea there were 1,500 Tegeans, 300 Potideans, 600 Arcadians of Orchomenus, 800 Epidaurians, 1,000 Troezenians, 200 Lepreats, 400 Mycenaeans and Tirynthians, 1,000 Phliasians, 300 Hermionians, 600 Eretrians and Styreans, 400 Chalcideans, 500 Ambraciots, 800 Leucadians and Anactorians, 200 Paleans, 600 Plataeans, 500 Aeginetans, 3,000 Sicyonians, 3,000 Megarians, 5,000

Corinthians, some 5,000 Spartans, along with 35,000 helots "who were lightly armed — seven to each Spartan" (IX. 28) and the largest force of all, 8,000 Athenians under Aristides.

I have not taken the short cut and lumped them all together as "the Greeks," because it is critical to have some concrete appreciation of the fact that while they were all Greeks and had much in common, they were first of all Plataeans, Leucadians, and so on. Referring to them as "the Greeks" makes us think that we have here a "nation" in some modern sense, and hence that the expression "the Greeks" had some political content — indeed that here was an incipient state which, tragically, "failed" to be realized. Bound up as we are with the idea of the nation-state, this bears emphasis. Not only did the Greeks believe in the *polis* form, but the alternative was not a "state" as we think of it, but either a huge *ethnos* or an empire. The Greeks wanted neither. Further, it is useful to have some concrete appreciation of the relative numbers involved (all taken from Herodotus). The men of the cities fought in phalanxes, under their own generals, side by side. It is hardly surprising, given the numbers, though, that the overall commander of the alliance would be either a Spartan or an Athenian.

Up until now we have not discussed Greek sea power, and this may be as good a place as any to remedy this omission. In the heroic period, ships were only transports. But, as Adcock points out, "post-Heroic ships become capable of fighting against each other," and "when that happens, the art of naval warfare begins."[4] Sometime in the sixth century, the penteconter, with 25 oarsmen on each side, became standard. It was a dual-purpose vessel, used for trade as well as war. The standard mode of attack was to propel the ram into the hull of the enemy ship. In the second half of the sixth century, the trireme, a vessel which could be used *only* for war, was developed. The trireme required as many as 170 oarsmen and in addition carried perhaps 30 "marines" or hoplites, but it was no longer than a penteconter. How this was possible was for decades disputed, as was the arrangement of oarsmen, whether in a single tier or in three tiers. Today, we feel confident that there were three.[5] The trireme was fast and highly maneuverable, and it took considerable skill to master this huge fighting scull. The crews of Athens were famous for their prowess. Prior to the fifth century, we have no hard data on the distribution of triremes among the numerous cities; we know only that Syracuse, Corcyra, Athens, Corinth, Samos, and a few others were already cognizant of their potential.

When the fifth century began, Athens was a naval power in so far as there was such a thing. Hence it could feel some confidence after sending its twenty ships, carrying a substantial hoplite force, to assist the Ionians. But it was Themistocles who seems to have grasped that naval power could be more than an adjunct to hoplite forces, and as archon, in 494, he convinced the Assembly that it should abandon the badly exposed harbor at Phaleron as its naval base and fortify the harbor at Piraeus, several miles away. Although a threatening Persia on the horizon and, nearer to home, the hostility of neighboring Aegina provided a motive, the idea of developing Athenian naval power was nonetheless an extraordinary one, with extraordinary consequences.

Work on the new facility was under way when the Persian sea and land force arrived at Marathon. This surely helped Themistocles to convince the Athenian Assembly that the silver newly discovered at Laurion should not be distributed to the citizens as had been proposed, but should be put towards the building of new ships. Two years later, in 481, Athens had the 200 triremes which were to be so critical at Salamis. Indeed, these ships were the basis for what would later become the Athenian Empire.

Democracy and Empire

The Greek view of the relation between the political and the military functions was critical in the development of the *polis*. Moreover, in democratic Athens, the development of a navy was to propel both democracy and an extraordinary solution to empire.

The new triremes needed crews, and this meant an enormous increase in the fighting force, perhaps by as many as 34,000 men. Clearly there were not that many citizens who were not already hoplites. Perhaps that number approximated the total number of free males in Athens, most of whom would be poor, of course. Nevertheless, in a democracy, this did not have to be a bar. Indeed, over the years, less prosperous men had increasingly been added to the franchise, and there was no reason now not to bring in even the poorest of men. As Aristotle remarks, "hoplites are for the well-to-do rather that the poor and thus for oligarchies, light infantry and naval forces are entirely democratic" (*Politics*, VI. 4). Although, as with regard to all numbers in ancient history, we have far from adequate information, Jones estimates that at the time of the Persian wars there may have been 30,000 adult male citizens in Athens, of whom perhaps 10,000 were hoplites.[6] If so, then it would not be unreasonable to infer that the remaining 20,000 could make up the crews of the triremes or were archers or peltastes, and that these were poor men, poor landowners and *thetes*. These numbers increased considerably over the next fifty years – indeed, Thucydides and later writers make more than occasional reference to "the maritime mob" (*nautikos ochlos*), the poorer sorts who came to have a voice in the Assembly of Athens.

It was in the decades following the victory at Plataea that further novelties were introduced: pay for those manning the ships, per diem pay for office-holders and jurors, restriction of tenure to one or two years depending on the office, multiplication of offices and selection by lot for all except the *strategoi*, and emasculation of the power of the Council of the Areopagus. Aristotle seems to have had just this democracy – "extreme democracy" – in mind when, in writing about "a fourth kind of democracy, latest in the history of the *polis*," he says:

> Because there are poleis which have far outgrown their original size, their revenues have increased and while all citizens have a share in governing, because of the preponderance of the multitude (*tou plethous*), all really take part since even the poor who receive pay are able to take part. Indeed, the multitude in this kind of polis has a very great deal of leisure for they are not hampered by the care of their private affairs. (*Politics* IV. 6)

Thus poor farmers and *thetes*, now paid for military duty and civic responsibility received small, but perhaps significant, supplements to their income. If Aristotle is correct, such men were free to participate in a way that they never had been before. But this was expensive. It is not possible to distinguish cause and consequence here, but it seems clear that accession of Athens to *hegemon* of what we call the Delian League and thence to Empire was a critical aspect of the development of "extreme democracy."

Athens stumbled into empire.[7] The alliance of cities – sometimes called "the Hellenic League," although it had no official name – which fought the Persians in effect collapsed when Sparta refused to respond to an Ionian call for help. As before, Athens did respond, sending a force off to the Hellespont to destroy the bridges which Xerxes had built. Subsequent misconduct by Pausanias, the Spartan king, led to Athenian leadership. In 478–7, then, some 158 cities, including *none* from the Peloponnesian League of which Sparta was *hegemon*, swore an oath "to have the same friends and the same enemies." *Mydroi* (symbolic iron weights) were sunk into the sea, thereby establishing the alliance (*symmachia*) as permanent, with Athens as *hegemon*. The purpose of the alliance, which we call "the Delian League," is about as clear as such matters can be: it was designed to liberate any city still subject to Persia, to take revenge on Persia by engaging in pillaging and outright banditry, and to keep Greek cities free from Persian domination.[8]

Hegemon answers well enough to "leader," but, of course, few concepts are looser than that. We begin to get some handle on it in the present context by noticing that there have been two interpretations of the nature of the league.[9] First, some have held that the cities swore to have the same friends and the same enemies as the *hegemon*. In return, a city gained the protection of the *hegemon* but wholly lost control of its foreign policies. This was the way it was with the Peloponnesian League with Sparta as *hegemon*. As we will see, a critical feature of Spartan foreign policy was maintenance of the league, which included from the beginning of the fifth century most of the cities of the Peloponnese – Corinth, Mycenae, Tiryns, Sikyon, and others – apart from Argos and the Achaea and outside the Peloponnese, Megara and Aigina, at least.

But this seems not to have been the arrangement in the case of the Delian League, in which it appears that the oaths were fully reciprocal. On the other hand, it seems unlikely that Athens would have subjected its foreign policy to a synod decision in which she had only one vote. Accordingly, it is likely that the alliance was between two parties, Athens and all the others combined. The cities did not swear to follow Athens whithersoever she might lead, as was the case with Sparta and the Peloponnesian League; the others did have a voice in policy, but, because Athens's vote counted for as much as all the others combined, she was clearly in command.

The Delian League had real powers, including the power to assess each of its members. The cities were assessed a commitment of ships and crews or, as in the more usual case, money to pay for the maintenance of crews and ships. The original assessment was made by Aristides, described as "the just," and it seems that, initially at least, the cities cheerfully met their obligations. The treasury of the allies was originally at Delos, but in 454–3, it was moved to Athens. This step suggests that the transformation of Athens from *hegemon* to *arche* was by then complete.

Initially, the league decided policy, including what was to be done with delinquent or rebellious states. But the allies gradually tired of their responsibility, and Athens accepted more of it. The first test was in 470 when Naxos rebelled and was then "subjugated" (*edoulothe*) by an Athenian force (I. 98). Thucydides does not explain what this means, but there seems little doubt that Athens acted with the approval of the synod. As time wore on, Athens grew more powerful, and more arrogant. Thucydides writes:

> For all this the allies themselves were responsible; for most of them, on account of their aversion to military service, in order to avoid being away from home got themselves rated in sums of money instead of ships ... and consequently the fleet of the Athenians was increased by the funds which they contributed, while they themselves, whenever they revolted, entered on the war without preparation and without experience. (I. 99)

Interpretation of this text is not straightforward, however. On the one hand, the immediate threat from Persia had passed; but Persia itself had not disappeared. On the other hand, as Finley remarks, the crews of the cities would be serving "an alien, imperial state"; yet it may well have been less expensive for a city to pay "tribute" (*phoron*, originally meaning a contribution, and thus voluntary (I. 96) than to contribute a naval force. However this may be, by the time of the war with the Peloponnesians, Pericles was perfectly willing to admit that "by this time the empire you hold is a tyranny." Indeed, "it may seem wrong to have assumed [the empire]," but "certainly it is dangerous to let go" (II. 63). Pericles was probably correct on both counts, even if as regards the former we ought to try to be critical about what this means, and even if as regards the latter we can only speculate, since Athens did not "let go" of her empire.

There is little point in pretending that Athens had no empire, that it was "merely" the *hegemon*, for example, even if it is critical to acknowledge that it was very unlike the empire of Persia or later of Rome. Because of the Greek commitment to maintaining an identity between the ruling and the military functions, there was no compulsory military service; nor was there any thought, as later in Rome, of making subjugated peoples "citizens" who would then serve in Roman armies. Athens did pay its naval service, but these were native citizens, and it was not until the Sicilian expedition that any "foreigners" (paid, noncitizens) were involved. The fact that anybody was paid, however, lies behind the scorn that fourth-century conservatives associated with the term "mercenary" (*misthophoros*).

Nor did Athens tithe or tax the land of the cities in its empire, although she did confiscate properties, which were then awarded to Athenian citizens, usually poorer ones. Finley estimates that this "most naked kind of imperial exploitation" directly benefited perhaps 8−10 percent of the Athenian citizen body, but of course these citizens then left Athens to farm their properties. Nor can there be any doubt that the cities of the empire were no longer autonomous (*autonomia*) in the sense that they could have an independent foreign policy; for that had been abrogated by the terms of the initial alliance. Moreover, they were not entirely free to alter their constitutions. Athens sustained democracies and undermined oligarchies − just as Sparta did the reverse (see, for example, Thucydides, I. 19 and 144). Still, it seems that a city in the Athenian Empire was able to choose and control its magistrates, try its own citizens, and more generally maintain its own laws.

The cities were surely coerced into paying the tribute. On the other hand, given the basis for this, as well as the foregoing considerations regarding "autonomy," the degree to which this constitutes exploitation in unclear. Finally, as is obvious, when we speak of Abdera or Lampsacus or any of the cities, we are really speaking of associations of individuals. But then, if, as seems the case, the tribute collected within each city was paid by the rich households, not the poorer ones, while it might well have been a source of legitimate indignation, it was unlikely to have been a burden. The cities were certainly part of Athens's "empire"; but did this amount to a form of slavery, as ancient — and many modern — commentators say? Or is the label in part, at least, the product of fierce Greek pride in "freedom" (*eleutheria*) and in part, perhaps, aristocratic — anti-Athenian — prejudice? As Ste Croix writes: "The prospect of enjoying a very considerable degree of political freedom in a democracy upheld by Athens would involve a far smaller degree of *douleia* (slavery) than the total, or almost total, subjection to their own propertied class which would necessarily occur in an oligarchy, dependent upon Sparta or Persia or even completely free from outside control."[10] But, of course, at this point in Greek history, the choice to be completely free from outside control was not available. The poorer people in the cities need not have loved Athens, and, given Greek commitment to full autonomy, it is unlikely that they did. A story told by Thucydides suggests the response of the lower classes. The Mytilenaeans, expecting food from the Peloponnese, "equipped the people (*demos*) as hoplites, instead of their former light arms, intending to attack the Athenians." But when they got the equipment, the people refused to obey, ordered the powerful men (*dynatoi*) to bring out whatever food there was, and then threatened to make terms themselves with the Athenians. The oligarchs, realizing that "they would be in peril if excluded from the capitulation, joined the people in making an agreement with Paches [the Athenian *strategoi*] and his army" (III. 27).

But this story has another aspect in that it suggests both that Athens was more than capable of injustice and that, as Cleon put it, "a democracy is incompetent to rule others" (III. 37). Paches, we are told, had difficulty convincing the oligarches of Mytilene that he would do them no injury (III. 28); and after he left, they renewed their efforts to bring in Spartan intervention. When Paches returned, he decided to make these men his prisoners and take them back with him to Athens. Upon his return, the Assembly "held a debate, and under the impulse of anger finally determined to put to death, not only the Mytilenaeans who were there in Athens, but also all who were of adult age, and to enslave their women and children" (III. 36). Paches was dispatched to carry out the massacre. But the next day, "a feeling of repentance came over them [the Assembly] and they began to reflect that their plan was cruel and monstrous." The Assembly was therefore reconvened, and another vote was taken. It was during this debate that Cleon noted that a democracy was unfit for empire. He argued that because the daily life of Athenians was "unaffected by fear and intrigue," Athenians had the same attitude towards their allies. But this he saw as a fatal weakness, since it did not win gratitude. Indeed, though the Athenians might be reluctant to admit it, the citizens of other cities saw the empire as a tyranny. Cleon did not persuade them, however, and the order was rescinded. Fortunately for the Mytilenaeans, word reached Paches just before the massacre commenced. The Melians, by constrast, were not to be so fortunate.[11]

The War between Athens and her Allies and Sparta and her Allies

Athens never did "let go" of her empire. Thirty years of intermittent warfare with Sparta and her Peloponnesian allies ended in Athens being forced to give it up. Moreover, the argument over the causes of the series of battles which we call the Peloponnesian War continues to rage.[12] Yet if we refuse to ignore the obvious in favor of an endless search for "deeper" causes, there is considerable agreement that Sparta began it for the good reason that she judged, rightly or wrongly, that the alternative was worse. Athens had already become too powerful, and continued stability in the Peloponnesus was thus threatened. After Themistocles, whose anti-Spartan policy was well known, was ostracized, in about 472, and as long as Cimon was influential in Athens, Sparta might count on acknowledgment of a system of "dual hegemony." Indeed, Cimon was the key voice in bringing the 4,000-men hoplite force to Ithome in 462. Sparta had requested this force to suppress revolting helots. It is therefore interesting to see why Sparta subsequently decided to send the Athenians home: "For the Lacedaemonians, when they failed to take the place by storm, fearing the audacity and the capriciousness of the Athenians, whom they regarded, besides, as men of another race, thought that, if they remained, they might be persuaded by the rebels to change sides" (Thucydides, I. 192)!

It was not necessarily that Sparta believed that Athens would invade her; it may have been more that, even if she did not, given the power and character of Athens, the character of the Peloponnesian League, and the requirements for maintaining the uniquely structured Spartan *polis*, the Spartans believed that they had to go to war. Not only was it essential that the whole peninsula be sealed off from the outside world, but democratic revolution in her sister cities would have imperiled her ability to keep the Peloponnese under control, and thus her ability to maintain control over helot Messenia. Indeed, the possibility of democratic revolutions was also a motivation for the oligarchs who ruled the cities in the Peloponnesian League to maintain the alliance with Sparta.[13]

Sparta felt "compelled," but not without reason. There was a deeper cause. It was the *situation* faced by the actors, the set of relations and beliefs which were the outcome of the radically different histories of Athens and Sparta. In a speech by a Corinthian addressed to the Spartans, Thucydides offers a summary of this contrast between the Athenians and the Spartans:

> [The Athenians] are given to innovation and quick to form plans and
> to put their decisions into execution, whereas you are disposed merely
> to keep what you have, to devise nothing new, and, when you do take
> action, not to carry to completion even what is indispensable. Again,

they are bold beyond their strength, venturesome beyond their better judgment, and sanguine in the face of dangers; while your way is to do less than your strength warrants . . . Nay more, they are prompt in their decision while you are dilatory; they stir abroad, while you are perfect stay-at-homes; for they expect by absence from the home to gain something, while you are afraid that, if you go out after something, you may imperil even what you have. (I. 70)

The struggle between the Athenians and the Lacedaemonians was a struggle between the old and the new, between two radically different conceptions of the *polis*, as manifest in the innovative, venturesome, democratic Athens and old-fashioned, conservative, aristocratic Sparta. This contrast, never absent from the background of fourth-century political writing, reflects a struggle rooted in an exacerbated, ultimately fatal *stasis* in the cities of the Greek world. It was a situation which neither side could escape. It was a war which nobody wanted; and given the trajectory of the respective and interlocking histories of Athens and Sparta, it was a clash which *seemed* as "inevitable" as could be.

But, of course, "seemed" is the operative word here. Thucydides was no fatalist. He appreciated that both sides had genuine choices and that there was nothing inevitable about Sparta's decision to go to war. He sketched the genesis of the situation, which neither side had created or controlled, and then, given this situation, gave reasons why the Spartans chose as they did. The war was not inevitable; but, given that it had happened, Thucydides set out to explain it.

This is not the place to give even a sketch of what turned out to be a thirty-year struggle, a consequence not anticipated by anyone, and certainly not by Sparta and her allies. Presumably Sparta predicted that this clash would be like previous ones with Athens and other cities, that it would be quick, if bloody, and that the "problem" which prompted the decision to go to war would be resolved in short order, one way or the other.

But Athens, still the innovator, adopted Pericles' policy of containment: secure the city, avoid direct hoplite confrontation, and maintain the sea lanes, thereby guaranteeing vital grain imports and continuing tribute. It was, as Ste Croix agrues, mainly a defensive strategy with some offensive elements; Athens "could never hope to *win* the war in the only way Greek wars could be won, by invading Sparta's heart-land."[14] This policy was abandoned, of course, and there is supreme irony in the fact that it was a democratic *polis* in far-off Sicily which delivered the fatal blow to democratic Athens, in 411. Thucydides writes:

Great had been their miscalculation, and far greater still their regret at having made the expedition. For of all the cities with which they had gone to war, these alone were at that time similar in character to their own, democratic in constitution like themselves, and strong in ships, cavalry and size. And so, finding themselves unable either to bring about a change in their constitution, and thus introduce among them that element of discord by which they might have brought them over to the Athenian side, or to subdue them ... and now that they had suffered defeat even with their fleet, a thing they could never have anticipated, they were in far greater perplexity still. (VII. 55)

When news of the Sicilian disaster reached the cities in the Athenian alliance, the rebellion against Athens began in earnest: Chios, Miletus, Teos, Lebedus, Methymnia, Mytilene, and the rest. When the news reached Athens, *stasis* was unleashed there, this time involving the loudest voice in the Sicilian adventure, that of Alcibiades, now banished.

Aligned with "the best people" (*oi beltistoi*), Alcibiades was negotiating with the Persian Tissaphernes to return to Athens, arguing that "the King would be a friend of them and would furnish money if Alcibiades were restored and they were not ruled by a democracy" (VIII. 47). A debate followed in the Assembly, in which various members urged the Assembly to recall Alcibiades, and to "adopt a different form of democracy, both to have the King as their ally and to prevail over the Peloponnesians" (VIII. 52). But the Assembly as a whole remained unconvinced. In the end, however, believing that "there was no other salvation, through fear and at the same time because they expected to make a change later, [they] yielded" (VIII. 54). The result was the sham government of the Five Thousand, sham because four hundred oligarchs ruled in the name of the Five Thousand, who, in fact, were never concretely identified. The idea was to assent to the principle of an extended oligarchy, but for "the best men" to retain power.

Presumably there were still at least 5,000 hoplites, "competent to serve the polis with both property and person" (VIII. 40, 92). But some of these, discerning the treachery of "the best men," took matters into their own hands. Demolishing the fortification at Piraeus, they exhorted the crowd thus: "Whoever wants the Five Thousand to rule in place of the Four Hundred, let him set to work." Thucydides suggests, however, that they were even more radical: "For in spite of everything they were still concealing their purpose under the name of the 'Five Thousand' so as not say outright, 'Whoever wants the *people* to rule'; for they were afraid that the Five Thousand did in reality exist and that one man in speaking to another might without knowing it get into trouble" (VIII. 92). Indeed, Thucydides had earlier discerned that the disintegration of the democracy was being propelled by misinformation, an "inability to find out the facts," and suspicion, "as though everyone had a hand in what was going on" (VIII. 46).

Just at that moment news arrived that the Peloponnesians were hovering in the neighborhood, and "neither the disaster in Sicily, ... nor any other event ever yet so frightened them." Fortunately for the Athenians, they were saved by Lacedaemonian alacrity. A meeting of the Assembly was hastily called, twenty ships were manned and dispatched, and the Spartans receded. Knowing that the men of the main fleet, still in Samos, had already firmly rejected the Four Hundred, the Assembly voted to give "the management of affairs" to the Five Thousand and to abandon pay for office-holders. Thucydides, like Aristotle after him, here reveals his preference: during the period which followed, "the Athenians appear to have enjoyed the best constitution they ever had, at least in my time; for there was a moderate blending of the few and the many" (VIII. 97). It is another question, of course, whether one should call this "constitution" a democracy at all, given that in Aristotle's own terms, it was rule by the wealthier few — albeit 5,000 hoplites!

Stasis had not run its course in the Greek world, still less in Athens, needless to say. Following acceptance of the terms of peace and dismemberment of the Empire, in 404, another revolution took place, this time instigated by the Oligarchic Thirty, led by Critias, companion of Socrates, a cousin of Plato named Charmides, Plato's uncle, Theramenes, and Dracontides, among others. This constitution, according to Plato's Seventh Letter, "made the former constitution seem like a paradise." It is usually taken for granted that "the former constitution" referred to here is Periclean democracy. But this is hardly likely. The "former constitution" is rather the constitution of the Five Thousand, the rule by the wealthier hoplites of Athens.

The "best men," the Oligarchic Thirty, clearly had the support of some of the hoplites. But they were were quickly put to the test by exiled democrats in league with Thebans, who took over the Attic fortress of Phyle. The Thirty were deposed and were replaced by a Council of Ten, who immediately appealed to Sparta. The Spartans dispatched a force, which was met by the Athenians. By this time, however, all parties were ready for a reconciliation. The Athenians agreed to become part of the Spartan alliance, and "lawgivers" were appointed to revise the Athenian constitution.

Initially the franchise was restricted to the first three Solonian classes, namely, those who could serve as hoplites; but pressure from Thrasyboulos and the democrats subsequently forced a restoration of the old democracy, with unlimited franchise. Athens had experienced democracy for too long to go back. "The people" were not going to give up so easily. Thrasyboulos is reported by Xenophon to have said that it was a victory of the "have-nots" over the "haves."

Athens remained a democracy for some sixty more years, until Macedonia decisively overwhelmed the Greek cities. Indeed, once the Greek cities lost their autonomy to Philip, the era of the *polis* was over, strictly speaking. But Demosthenes was correct in judging that it would be war and *stasis* which would ultimately doom the *polis*. In his remarkable *Third Philipic*, delivered in May 341, just three years before the decisive battle of Chaeronea, he said:

> I am told that in former times the Lacedaemonians and all the other Greeks would invade and ravage the enemy's land with hoplites and citizen armies for four or five months only during the campaigning season, and then return home. They were so old-fashioned in outlook, or rather so civic-spirited, that they would not purchase any service [mercenaries] from anyone, but war was waged according to rules and openly. But now you see that the greatest damage has been done by traitors [that is, those who conspire against the democracies], and not as a result of pitched battles. You hear of Philip marching where he pleases followed not by a phalanx of hoplites, but by light-armed troops (*peltastes*), cavalry, archers and mercenaries — this is the kind of army he has around him. When, further, he falls upon a people torn by *stasis* and no one marches out to defend the land, so suspicious are they of one another, he brings up his engines and lays siege to the city. I pass over the fact that he draws no distinction between summer and winter, and that he has no season set apart for suspending operations. (*Third Philipic*, 47–50)

The idea of freedom and democracy, discovered by the Greeks only some 200 years before this was written, already seemed like a dream from the past to Demosthenes, as was the "old-fashioned idea" of war, fought during "the campaigning season," "according to rules and openly." The era of the *polis* was over, and with it went democracy, undone by oligarchic reaction, Persian gold, fear, hubris and war. Of course, people continued to live in what were nominally *polis* units; but once they had lost their capacity to make their own laws and once the poor in the democratic cities had lost the ability to protect themselves, they were no longer "city-states."

The Legacy

Greek democracy was something extraordinary, a startling achievement, especially so perhaps, given that so many peoples, then and for centuries afterward, continued to live under forms of rule in which aristocratic domination was taken for granted and in which even any consciousness of politicial freedom, understood as the Greeks understood it, had vanished.

Further, much of the legacy of this experience has been distorted, beginning with the powerful pictures painted by the great philosophers of the fourth century. In this final section of the chapter, therefore, we will reconsider the character of Greek democracy, discuss the question of whether it depended upon slavery and empire, and finally, return to the views of "the philosophers."

Four aspects of this democracy should be stressed. First, while everyone realizes that citizens were members of the Assembly, the policy-making and war-making body of the city, the democratic principle of equality in Athens was realized perhaps most fundamentally in the extraordinary fact that all offices, excepting *strategoi*, were filled by lot and that tenure was restricted to one year. This seems not to have come about all at once. The election of archons was a critical departure from ancient practices, of course. A modern democrat would not want more. But this practice was replaced, perhaps by 487, with the selection of archons by lot, albeit from a preselected group. Then, by 457 perhaps, the lottery drew from the *entire* citizen body. At this point even membership of the Council of Five Hundred, the primary "executive" body of the *polis*, was determined by lot. As Finley sees it, "in any decade, something between a fourth and a third of the total citizenry over thirty would have been Council members, serving daily (in principle) throughout the year and for a tenth of that year on full duty as so-called *prytaneis*. Given the range of importance of Council business, Lotze is therefore justified in calling the Council 'a school for democracy'."[15]

A host of other offices were also filled in this way, about 700 according to Aristotle. There were market controllers (*agoranomoi*), guardians of grain (*sitophylakes*), special supervisors for wholesale grain trading (*epimeletai tou emporiou*), controllers of measures (*metronomoi*), controllers of the town (*astynomoi*), auditors (*logistai*), various sorts of officers of the courts, and many many others (*Athenian Constitution*, 51). We can say that this was indeed a "government" of amateurs; but if we do, we must remember that these "officials" were "magistrates" in the sense that they "executed" the laws and decisions of "the people." They did not make them. Like decisions to go to war or to make peace, the laws were also made by "amateurs," of course, so that, as Rousseau was to argue much later, the Athenians had no government at all in the modern sense of the word.

One is tempted to say that this extraordinary level of direct participation in all the affairs of the city was possible only insofar as the polity was small and the level of "development" low, for no modern society could be managed by amateurs. The argument from size is surely persuasive. In a large, complexly connected society, it may be that there is an increasing demand for specialized knowledge in management and so forth, and that a permanent bureaucracy is essential. Still, one wonders how much validity there is to the view, so widely held, that none of the administrative tasks of a modern bureaucracy can be managed by nonspecialists. We know that incapacity, as well as capacity, can be learned; we know too that, when challenged, people sometimes discover powers they did not know they had. We know too that modern arrangements were called into being as much by accident as intention. Accordingly, the fact that they exist as they do does not guarantee that they are required to satisfy some need.

A second feature of Greek democracy, a precondition for *any* democracy, was the existence of a "public," to use John Dewey's apt term. If any place ever had a public, it was Athens. Not only was it the case that by virtue of the extraordinary level of direct experience in matters of state, at least half the "multitude" had been "schooled in democracy," but Athens was a face-to-face community. Information was *totally* unmediated. There were no media – *a fortiori*, no *mass* media – and no Defense Department, Budget Office, or National Security Council. People congregated and talked. As Finley notes, people were members of households, neighborhoods, squadrons, upper-class dining clubs, and private associations (*hetaireia*). And in these formal and informal settings, they talked, shared views, tested them, and so learned. The business of the city was everybody's business in a way that is almost incomprehensible today.

Third, because of *isegoria*, the right to speak and debate in the Assembly, and because it was the Assembly which decided which decisions needed to be made and then made them, the public had an instrument by which it could be involved in making public policy. As Finley say, "on controversial matters, the debates were 'real': there were no formal party line-ups, no whips, or machinery to predetermine the final vote irrespective of speech-making. It was in those debates that leadership was tested."[16] This is not to say that the citizen could not be fooled or manipulated, or that the right decisions were always made, however one construes "right." The decision to invade Sicily was a poor one, no doubt. But the problem was not, as is so frequently stated by fourth-century critics and so readily believed by people thereafter, that "demagogues" had manipulated "the mob," but especially, that "maritime mob," whose direct interests would have been promoted by success in Sicily. W. S. Ferguson offers a characteristic modern view when he writes that, "misled by Alcibiades and Cleophon, they [The Athenians] were convicted by disaster of being unsound judges of foreign policy."[17] Ferguson's widely shared judgment might have been influenced by the "demagogues" themselves. According to Alcibiades, "democracy was manifest folly." Nor did Isocrates see any value in it: "Monarchies are not just better at ordinary everyday affairs, but encompass superiority in war. Tyrannies are better than republics at gathering forces, deploying them to deceive and get there first, using persuasion and force" (III. 15).

The decision to invade Sicily was misguided; but, as Thucydides remarks, "there was a passion for the expedition which seized everyone alike" (VI. 24). Whether it was arrogance, pride, desperation, impatience, or, more likely, all these together, which fueled this passion, we will never know. Nor was the problem ignorance of the citizens, who were chastised by Thucydides for not knowing the size of the the island or the number of its inhabitants (VI. 31). This was technical knowledge given to the citizens; but it seems not to have had any effect in deterring their decision. According to Thucydides, when Nicias saw that Alcibiades' position was coming to be the position of the Assembly, he hoped that the members might change their minds if they fully understood the enormity of the venture and the magnitude of the force required. In the end, Nicias's counsel failed to persuade them; but at least, as Thucydides admits, the expedition was fully prepared. Indeed, it might well have succeeded. The men who voted were experienced in both government and war. If they were wrong, it was not because they were stupid or ignorant or because they had been lied to or manipulated. Athenian democracy was by no means perfect, and it certainly made its share of mistakes, just as, to be sure, it committed its share of injustices. Still, one may reasonably wonder what justification there is for indicting nearly 200 years of democracy for its obvious mistakes (or injustices), even if, as in the instance of Sicily, the mistake was fatal. Worse, it is manifestly preposterous to assume that "experts" or other elites were not at least as capable of making gigantic errors and of committing even worse injustices. Indeed, those who paid for the mistakes that were made at least had the chance to make them.

Finally, recent scholarship has convincingly demonstrated that the view, so frequently put forward by modern and contemporary defenders of the liberal state, that there were no "constitutional" restraints in the democracy of Athens cannot be sustained. As the foregoing sketch of Solon's reforms hinted, there was a long tradition according to which citizens had "rights," which must be protected. The basis for guaranteeing these rights was guardianship of the laws (*nomophylakein*) and a mandate of vigilance, not only against the "tyranny" of one or a few, but against that of the many as well. One example is the odd *graphe paranonomon*, a procedure which allowed any citizen to prosecute another simply for having made an "illegal proposal" in the Assembly – even if, as Finley notes, "the sovereign Assembly had approved it."[18]

It is true, of course, that this was not a secular culture. Nor was there any bifurcation, as in modern liberal societies, of "society" and "the state." Accordingly, "individualism" was not a distinguishing trait. As Arendt has remarked, for the Greek, "a life spent in the privacy of 'one's own' (*idion*), outside the world of the common, is 'idiotic' by definition."[19] But this presupposes not only that there was "a clear and sharp distinction between what is his own and what is communal (*koinon*)," but that maintenance of that distinction was a matter for the law. This was well summarized by Pericles in an oft-quoted text from his rightly famous Funeral Oration. Just after telling us that all men are equal as regards law and that poverty is no bar to public life, Thucydides reports:

> And not only in our public life are we free (*eleutheros*), but also as regards our freedom from suspicion of one another in the pursuits of everyday life; for we do not feel resentment at our neighbor if he does what he likes, nor yet do we put on sour looks which, though harmless, are painful to behold. But while we thus avoid giving offense in our private intercourse, in our public life we are restrained from lawlessness chiefly through reverent fear, for we listen to those in authority and conform to the laws (*ton te aiei en arche onton akroasei kai ton nomon*) and especially to those laws which are ordained for the succor of the oppressed and those which though unwritten, bring upon the transgressor a disgrace which all men recognize. (II. 36)

From the modern point of view, tyranny involves violation of rights, crucial among which are rights of property. It is important to emphasize, however, that, even if Solon did relieve the debt, at no time did the Athenian democracy attack the institutions of private property, despite the fears of Plato and Aristotle and the illusions – and hopes – characteristic of modern writers. One might insist here that it could have done so. But indeed, there is nothing in the American Constitution to prevent a Congress of the United States from doing the same thing. Athens lacked a constitution in the modern sense, but it did not lack what we think of as fundamental law, written, but especially unwritten. Indeed, because laws were intended to have permanent validity, new laws were inscribed on stone or wood and then put in places where they could be seen by all who wanted to see them. Similarly, democratic Athens lacked a "supreme court" – although in the sixth century the Council of Areopagus perhaps played such a role. But it did not lack courts or procedures to insure that people lived by the laws and that "rights" were protected. Indeed, not only were there numerous courts, the *Eliaia* of the *thesmothetai*, the *Odeion*, the the *Stoa Poikile*, and so on, but, as MacDowell remarks, "in proportion to their population, the Athenians must have spent more man-hours in judging than any other people in history. Not for nothing did the juror become a symbol of Athens in comic cross-talk. In *Clouds*, Aristophanes writes: 'Look, this is Athens.' 'What? I don't believe it; I can't see any jurors sitting.' "[20]

Isonomia, so often identified with democracy, involved not merely that those who make the law live under the law, but that each rightfully have a share in making that law under which they all live.[21] The idea still seems powerful, however little it is realized in practice.

Empire and Slavery

It has often been held that Athens needed its empire to be a democracy. I have already noted that the full development of its democracy, "extreme democracy," attended empire. Moreover, it can hardly be doubted that empire brought wealth to Athens, not only via the tribute, but indirectly through tourism, through income generated by properties owned by Athenians abroad, and through the increased flow of goods into the Piraeus. Jones has suggested that increasing Athenian prosperity probably explains, in part at least, the increasing numbers of men who achieved hoplite status, which perhaps doubled in the years following the Persian War; and such prosperity was almost certainly the source of the reliable income paid to the *thetes* who manned the triremes. Further, as Aristotle hinted, pay for political services was a further supplement for poor Athenians. Still, Jones asserts that it is "demonstrably false" that poor Athenians could live on state pay for political services.[22] What seems most crucial, however, is the fact that Athens was a democracy before it became an empire, and that it was an "extreme democracy" even after it lost its empire. Thus one may legitimately conclude, with Jones, that empire was not necessary to its democracy, however much it may have simplified matters and however much it may have contributed to its full flowering.[23]

Athens, of course, was a slave society. And it may well be that the democracy it realized, limited as it was to free males — women were in any reasonable sense *also* "slaves" — would not have been possible without slavery. But there is no way to test this, since Athens was always a slave society. Still, there are excellent theoretical grounds for inferring that the requisite surpluses depended on slave labor, especially the wealth which made some Athenians "rich," thereby freeing them to render the public services (*leitourgia*) which were so vital to Athens. Not only were athletic and dramatic festivals supported by "private" funds, but the institution of the triarchy allowed a wealthy Athenian to support and command a trireme for one year.[24] On the other hand, how much surplus can be said to have been essential to the democracy is not easily decided. But the question is wrongly posed in any case. Ancient democracy and slavery were contingently part of the same fabric of causes which generated the world of the *polis*. It is easy enough to imagine conditions such that there were no slaves and democracy was achieved — for example, if, as Plato noted so remarkably, the *polis* had rejected "luxury" (*Republic*, II. 372). But this was almost certainly not a genuine option, as Plato well knew. And it is not the way it happened.

More interesting is the question of whether, in the absence of slavery, even the *idea* of freedom which became so central to Athenian political practice would have emerged in the way that it did, and whether, in the absence of a very substantial slave population, it would have been *politically* possible to enlarge the franchise to the same extent. All this is guesswork, obviously. Still, it may be useful to say a bit more.

It may be supposed that slaves outnumbered free men in the dominant category of surplus production namely, agricultural production, and that, accordingly, democracy was possible. But Jones estimates that in Athens in the fourth century there were some 20,000 slaves, male and female, versus 62,000 free adults. Perhaps all the slaves were owned by one-third to one-quarter of the free persons. Moreover, on Jones's estimates, perhaps 60 percent of the citizen population earned its living by working on very small holdings or as craftsmen or shopkeepers.[25]

Nor should we assume that, were some anthropologist from Mars, say, to descend into the *polis* world, he would easily be able to distinguish between slaves and free men. For not only did most free men have to work for a livelihood (except in Sparta), but free and slave were not marked out by their appearance or style (as the "Old Oligarch" so bitterly complained); and they worked side by side in almost all occupations, from agriculture to what surely amounts to "high art."

Rather, we should notice that, during the classical period, chattel slavery emerged from a more general category of dependent (or involuntary) labor, in which the "dependency" was rooted more vaguely. As Finley suggests, this category included all who worked for another and were "bound to do so by some precondition, birth into a class of dependents or debt or capture or any other situation which, by law of custom, automatically removed some measure of . . . freedom of choice and action, usually for a long term or for life."[26] Further, "the more advanced the city-state, the more it will be found to have had true slavery instead of the "hybrid" types of helotage."[27] That is, the articulation of "freedom" went hand in hand with the articulation of slavery.

Indeed, "freedom" (*eleutheria*) for the Greek was not some kind of noninterference; it had the connotation of ruling oneself (*autonomia*). One might say that this became the ideology of freedom in the Greek world, that a man was thought to be free only insofar as he was master of his household, and that, as far as possible, he ought to be "independent" (*autarcheia*) — that is, not dependent on another. But, remarkably, the Greek saw also that it would then be necessary for him to have a share in making those decisions which affected him and his household. Slaves, men in debt-bondage, wage-workers (*thetes*), and all the peasants in Asia and Egypt were "slaves" by Greek reckoning.

Few Greeks ever approached this ideal of freedom, clearly, and it was just this thirst for freedom which both propelled *stasis* and perhaps allowed for a clear stopping place in the fight for rights, A freeman was not a slave, whatever the limitations on his freedom. Hence it was entirely reasonable that he should expect to participate in society. On the other hand, as long as there were slaves (and women), the struggle unleashed by the breaking of hereditary power could be stopped well short of including the whole population, an advantage rightly discerned by some of the American Founding Fathers.

Plato and Aristotle

This is a natural place to consider some further views of the philosophers relevant to the assessment of democracy. As is well known, Aristotle believed that "the best *polis*" will not admit to citizenship either working people (*banausoi*) or slaves, for two independent but related reasons. His more general argument is that "a person living a life of manual toil (*bion banauson*) or as a hired laborer (*thetes*) cannot practice the pursuits in which goodness (*arete*) is exercised" (III. 3), for "leisure (*scholia*) is needed both for the development of virtue (*arete*) and for active participation in politics" (VII. 8).

This supports the ideology of freedom in the Greek world, even if, *contra* Aristotle, increasing numbers of free males may have seen themselves as *sufficiently* independent to be both virtuous and active politically. These men certainly lacked the leisure which Aristotle so prized; but independence was a relative matter, and they could easily point to others who were less independent and hence less fit. Moreover, as Jones argues, for the average Greek, the crucial issue was not work — including hauling the oars of a trireme — but class, whether one was another man's servant: "He would work as an independent craftsman or at a pinch as a casual laborer, but he would not take even a black-coated job as a regular employee."[28] Slaves, women, and wage-laborers had a different place in society for precisely this reason.

But Aristotle had a more specific argument regarding slavery, an argument which he also applied albeit with some adjustment, to women and wage-workers. They were incapable, he insisted, of ruling themselves; *a fortiori* they were incapable of sharing in the ruling of others (*Politics* I. 2). They were dependent and needed direction, either because of "nature" or by virtue of their condition of propertylessness. With this, the majority of free Greek males would probably have agreed. When Aristotle wrote that "the condition of a free man is that he does not live at another's beck and call" (*Rhetoric*, I. 9), he was saying what every Greek believed.[29]

It is, of course, striking that Aristotle's argument in defense of slavery is a non-argument. Indeed, could there be a good argument for it? But it is probably erroneous to maintain that there were no objections to the conventional wisdom on such matters, as Aristotle's own discussion shows. While no fifth-century text which condemns slavery as such is extant, some Sophists, at least, seem to have seen straight through Aristotelian arguments regarding the "naturalness" of slavery. And Plato himself had already exposed the foolishness of the assumption that women were not, "by nature" fit to rule (*Republic*, V. 451–7). Yet it is true and important that, as far as we know, no Greek ever suggested that slavery be eliminated, and there was no "faction" or movement which ever made an effort to abolish either slavery or patriarchy.

Aristotle's famous classification of constitutions, following Plato, has been put to all kinds of ideological purposes; so we would do well to get straight just what he did say. In at least two places he outlines three forms of *polis*: constitutions of one, a few, and many. Each category is subdivided into "true," because it aimed to realize the common interest, and "deviant," because it failed to do this. The true forms are labeled by him "kingship" (*basileia*), "aristocracy" (*aristocratein*), and *politeia*. The corresponding "deviant" (*parekbaseis*) forms are "tyranny," "oligarchy," and "democracy," rule in the interests of the tyrant, the rich, and the poor, respectively (*Politics*, III. 5). Of the true forms, Aristotle clearly preferred monarchy (it was "most divine") and aristocracy to *politeia*. Moreover, since tyranny was surely the worst form, it would seem – and has often been held – that democracy must be the best of the bad forms. Yet Aristotle is perfectly clear on this; for him, this is a confusion, for "we say that the deviations are wholly wrong" (IV. 2). Moreover, there is no reason to assume that, for him, the true forms could not exist.

He also rejected the definition of democracy as "the constitution in which the multitude (*plethos*) rule." He says: "If the whole number were thirteen hundred, and a thousand of these were rich and did not give the three hundred poor a share in ruling although they were free and like themselves in all other respects, no one would say that this people was governed democratically" (IV. 3). As he notes elsewhere, the problem results from confusing a matter of fact with a matter of principle. It is merely a contingent fact that the few are rich and the poor are many (III. 5).

His concept of *politeia*, the "generic" term for the generic constitution, is filled with problems. At one point he says that a *politeia* "does not often occur" and later that, though it is not really a "deviation," it should be counted as one of the deviant forms. He then says that it is "a fusion of democracy and oligarchy" (IV. 6), yet notes that "aristocracy and *politeia* are not widely apart from one another" (IV. 7). Aristotle allowed that a constitution could introduce democracy in more than one way, depending upon who makes the law (and war), how courts are constituted, and the mode of selecting "magistrates." "Extreme democracy" is extreme because it is *thoroughly* democratic. "A good mixture" would make critical restrictions. But the central problem, as he rightly saw, was who made law and war – who, in our terms, was sovereign.

This perplexing ensemble of ideas falls into place, however, when we recognize that his fundamental concern was that the propertied should rule. It was in this way that a broadly based, property-owning "democracy" from which the poor were excluded would be like an "aristocracy." "Where some own a very great deal of property and others none there comes about either an extreme democracy, or an unmixed oligarchy, or a tyranny may result from both of the two extremes" (IV. 9). It is nonsense to say that Aristotle saw a strong "middle class" as vital to "democracy." It is also nonsense to call the arrangement which Aristotle favored a "constitutional democracy," which would imply that the many ruled, albeit under law, or that it was a "republic," "democratic" but not subject to the manifest vices of that awful form "extreme democracy." Indeed, the short-lived regime of the Five Thousand came as close as any society in history to Aristotle's ideal of a *politeia*, exactly because, as he so clearly argued, in the ideal *politeia* the citizens are independent because they own sufficient land − the means of production in the ancient world − and they are warriors, who, as they grow older, become the rulers. As he summarizes the matter, "the land ought to belong to those who possess arms and have a share in government" (VII. 9 and III. 7). "Tillers of the soil, craftsmen and the laboring classes are necessary for a polis but have no share (*meris*) in it." Those that do are "the hoplites who engage in war and those who deliberate" (*meri de tis poleos to te hoplitikon kai boulevtikon*) (VIII. 8).

Tradition has generally acknowledged that Plato was no friend of Athenian democracy, even though, as in the case of Aristotle, there has been an incredible reluctance to admit that he was against any sort of democracy. Much of the force of Plato's writing depends on the assumption that in Athens a *mob* ruled, that it murdered Socrates, that corruption was fueled by imperialism, and that he, Plato, had the incredible burden of fighting off the terrible relativist philosophies of the late fifth-century Sophists.[30]

But few writers, if any, have noticed that Plato's political views were essentially related to his views on war. Indeed, it is extraordinary to find that commentators have usually said that Greek thinkers paid little attention to war as a theoretical problem, and that instead, they turned their eyes to constitutional questions, and expecially the question of *stasis*. It is true that they say little about war and much about *stasis*; it is also true that what they say about war is sometimes banal, as, for example, when Aristotle tells us that "there is great harm" in engaging in conquest "with a view to ruling over one's neighbors." And his paternalism is remarkable when, following the phrases just quoted, he remarks that men should not study war "with a view to the enslavement of those who do not deserve to be enslaved." For, "first of all," he continues, "they should provide against their own enslavement, and in the second place, obtain empire for the good of the governed, and not for the sake of exercising a general despotism" (VII. 13). Aristotle, unlike Plato, had no problems with imperialism – "for the good of the governed."

But Plato, like Aristotle, never relinquished the Greek idea that the military and ruling functions should be coincident; moreover, both were clear that, insofar as this was so, war was a problem whose solution posed critical questions for the resolution of *stasis*. Indeed, Plato's remarkable *Republic* (a very misleading mistranslation of *Politeia*) is a *radical* solution to the problem of a *polis* which must fight wars and at the same time avoid *stasis*.

It will be remembered that in his search for justice (*dikaios*), Socrates offers to construct an ideal state, but that he appears to be content with what Glaucon calls "a community of pigs." Socrates' community of pigs is a subsistence society, producing only enough to reproduce itself. But, insists Socrates, it is "healthy and at peace," its citizens "naturally coming to old age, and leaving their children to live after them in the same manner." The picture painted is nostalgic and idyllic: they "make merry with their children," drink wine, and feast on loaves of bread. They may lack couches and dishes and sweets, but they "sing the praises of the gods" and "live pleasantly together." Indeed, "a prudent fear of poverty and war will keep them from begetting children beyond their means" (*Republic*, II. 372.

It should not go unnoticed here that Plato seems to hold, remarkably, not only that such a society would control its population so as to stay within its means, but that it *could not* be at war, since, first, it would not be motivated to conquer and second, a conqueror from outside would have no motivation to conquer it! This little society contains only producers, who produce only what is needed to reproduce themselves. There is nothing to exploit and no possibility of exploiting it. Hence there is no need for "guardians" or "rulers."

But Glaucon wants "luxuries." In this he merely represents what seems inevitable, perhaps. Now everything changes. A vast number of new people are introduced, most of whom are not themselves producers. But they too will have to be fed and clothed. The country will now be too small, and the people will have "to cut off a slice of [their] neighbor's territory; and if they too are not content with necessaries, but give themselves up to getting unlimited wealth, they will want a slice of ours too" (II. 273). War is now inevitable. Not only is there an imperative to exploit the surpluses of neighbors, but the "luxurious state" itself becomes vulnerable to surplus exploitation by conquerors.

One might pause here and ask whether this theory on the causes of war, brilliant though it is, is adequate. There is something intuitively convincing about the idea that insatiable desire in a world of scarcity makes war as inevitable as death itself. On the other hand, if we are willing to concede that there may be non-economic causes of war — for example, honor, · ideology, security — and, conversely, that economically motivated aggression may be constrained for all sorts of reasons, then we can see that the theory is inadequate.

Still, it is probable that the war between Athens and Sparta is Plato's inspiration here. If, then, we assign *imperial* Athens the "ultimate" responsibility for the war, Plato's abstract theoretical schema does give us an insight into the deeper causes of the Peloponnesian War. Democratic Athens is the luxurious imperial state, and its extravagance did threaten conservative and prudent Sparta. What Plato suggests is true; yet to explain this war, as any other, requires a concrete understanding of the particular events and relations which constituted the specific situation which brought about the confrontation. We need an account both of the pertinent structures and of how, given these, one thing led to another, an account of how hopes and beliefs, some true and some false, finally led to the Spartan decision to make war on Athens. What Plato suggests needs to be joined to the kind of account which the historian Thucydides gives us.

Plato knows, of course, that the luxurious state is with us, and that it will remain with us; moreover, his notion that "guardians," a military force, are necessary is not contestable. Given this, the familiar lines of the *Republic* fall into place. Once the principle of specialization through the division of labor has been established it follows that the necessary military function must be filled by specialists, who, as Aristotle will later agree, will be the source of the ruling group. Indeed, it may well be that Plato found a "principle" which would guarantee the result he was looking for.[31]

Moreover, like Thucydides before him and Aristotle after him, Plato certainly exploits the very profound differences between Sparta and Athens. In the *Republic*, the *polis* that comes closest to the perfectly just *polis* is orderly, conservative, and frugal — a Spartan "timocracy." As already noted, Athens is the very paradigm of the imperialist luxury state; its democracy is the *reductio ad absurdum* of the attempt to enlarge the military and maintain its coincidence with the ruling group. Instead of solving the problem of "guardians," Athens destroyed the city. In Plato's view, "democracy" is not merely Athens's form of constitution; it became the key feature of its entire being. No one has a place or knows his place. "Chockfull of liberty and freedom of speech," a "diversity of characters, like the different colours in a patterned dress," Athens is surely "an anarchic form of society, with plenty of variety, which treats all men as equal, whether they are equal or not (*Republic*, VIII. 558). But if that is not bad enough, because it has permitted unbridled *stasis*, it must succumb to the worst of all forms, tyranny.

Plato returned to these themes in his *Laws*, written perhaps in the years just prior to his death in 347. He began that dialogue by posing a fundamental question of politics, a question which is raised and answered in exactly the opposite way in Machiavelli's monumental *Discourses* (see Part II below). Plato asks whether the lawgiver should design his constitution with an eye to peace or war. Which alternative should have priority in the construction of institutions, and which should be the primary object of policy? His answer begins with a critical distinction between external war and internal war, or *stasis*. Clinias, the Cretan protagonist of the dialogue, admires the venerable constitution of his city and the similar constitution of Sparta, which is also a constitution of long duration (and also, significantly, a *polis* with the institution of helotage). But Clinias must surely be wrong, argues the Athenian, if he regards *external* wars as "the first and foremost object of the law-giver's regard" (*Laws*, I. 628). The constitutions of Crete and Sparta are good, but not for the reasons which Clinias supposes. Despite the common misunderstanding of Spartan militarism, Sparta, unlike Athens, is not an imperializing city. It *avoids* war and makes war only to preserve itself. Its citizens, as Thucydides said, try only to maintain what they have. Spartan and Cretan excellence reside in the stability and conservatism of the two cities. Indeed, not only should a constitution aim at virtue and the happiness of its citizens, but it must not be forgotten that "*stasis* is the most dangerous kind of war."

Plato disliked "politics," especially the idea of politics which characterized the "extreme democracy" of Athens. Yet, while his portrait of democracy (*Republic*, VIII. 10−1), could be endorsed − *without* his brilliant irony − by J. S. Mill and Marx, it has terrified most.[32] Plato saw rightly that the goal of advocates of democracy was to realize as much freedom and equality as possible, and he succeeded, it seems, in convincing those who read him and contemplated Athens that too much of either was more than anyone could stand. Yet Finley catches what is perhaps the even more important truth when he writes that, "to put it bluntly, if Plato was right about Athens, then we are desperately wrong in our most influential political notions today." Finley assumes that *we* believe that "people are capable of popular self-government" and that "politics are a legitimate and necessary activity in which all members of society ought to take some share and some responsibility."[33] But even if we *believe* these things, it is mostly ideology to believe that these ideas are realized in practice. Indeed, it will take 2,000 years and a whole series of additional distortions and mystifications before Americans come up with an entirely novel solution to the problem of "democracy," "domestic tranquility," "citizen-armies," and war.

Part II

Early Modern War and State Formation

Introduction

Between the time of Machiavelli (1469–1527) and that of Napoleon I (1769–1821), Western Europe underwent a remarkable transformation. The social relations which we call "capitalism" emerged from what we call "feudal society"; there was a "revolution" in the nature and aims of warfare; the "modern state" emerged from the Renaissance kingdom; and at the end of this, came what we call "modern democracy."

In this part of the book, we will focus on the transformation in early modern warfare and the foundations of the early modern state up until the Seven Years' War (1756–63). What is given is only a sketch, intended to highlight critical, but usually ignored, features. Central here is the thought of Machiavelli and Montesquieu, the theorists with the most profound and influential voices in these concomitant developments. All this is preparatory to Parts III and IV, which deal respectively with the American War of Independence and the wars of the French Revolution. These, the first modern wars, unleash the idea of self-government. But we must begin here, in the fifteenth century.

As the fifteenth century began, "the Mediterranean belonged to its towns, the city-states scattered around its shores." There were some "territorial states, homogeneous in character and comparatively large," such as the kingdom of Naples, and there were also what must be called "empires." First, there was the Ottoman Empire, centered in the key cities of Constantinople, captured by Ottoman Turks in 1453, and Salonica and the possessions united under Ferdinand and Isabella in 1469 with the union of Castille and

Aragon. Of course, Spain, along with Portugal, soon came to be among the first modern maritime empires. Then there was France, with the annexation and absorption of Burgundy (1477) and Brittany, an empire in fact if not word. Further to the north was the Confederation of Swiss Cities, and still further away the Belorussian, Ruthenian, and Lithuanian "kingdom" of Poland, along with the agglomeration of free cities, duchies, and fiefdoms identified as the two Prussias. There was the multinational Habsburg Empire, the seventeen "provinces" of the Netherlands, and the kingdoms of Denmark and Sweden. Then there was England, which was more than a kingdom but not yet quite an empire or a modern state.

Indeed in 1500, Europe was comprised of some 500 more or less independent political units answering to a variety of descriptions: principate, *città*, empires, real and not so real, *républiques*, kingdoms, baronies, and duchies, grand and not so grand. While it takes us ahead of our story, we can say that it was through conquest, rebellion, secession, treaties, assassinations, intermarriages, purchases, "the extinction of palatine independencies, the consolidation of expired fiefs, and the falling of feudal inheritances," that, some 200 years later, the states system of modern Europe finally emerged. "The history of modern Europe," Oakeshott remarks, "is the history of Poland only a little more so."[1]

Countless pages narrate the histories encapsulated in the foregoing paragraph, and no doubt the trajectory of change was the "accidental" outcome of infinitely many decisions and circumstances. Still, one does not "belittle the role played by individuals and circumstances" by acknowledging that, of critical importance in the development of the large entity which came to be called "the modern state," were both war and those underlying structural changes which in the long course of events came to be what we call "capitalism." Briefly stated, the spread of commodity production, so intimately linked with Mediterranean trade, made the lord a landlord and sometimes a warlord and generated immense new opportunities, as well as immense new problems. Among the new opportunities were new possibilities for aggrandizement. Among the new problems was a transformation in the nature and aims of war. As summarized by Perry Anderson:

> The late feudal aristocracy was obliged to abandon old traditions and acquire many new skills. It had to shed military exercise of private violence, social patterns of vassal loyalty, economic habits of hereditary insouciance, political rights of representative autonomy, and cultural attributes of unlettered

ignorance. It had to learn the new avocations of a disciplined officer, a literate functionary, a polished courtier, and a more or less prudent estate owner.[2]

This process, "a great silent structural" change, extended at least across the period identified in the beginning sentences of this part, but one of its most obvious features is well put by Braudel: "The city-state was already losing ground," and "it was becoming clear that only the rival of the city-state, the territorial state, rich in land and manpower, would in future be able to meet the expense of modern warfare." Braudel is quite clear about what this means: "It could maintain paid armies and afford costly artillery; it was soon to indulge in the added extravagance of full-scale naval wars." It was, as he writes, no accident that Italian thinkers, pressed by these forces, "were to meditate above all upon politics and the destiny of the state."[3]

3

Machiavelli and the Imperative of Modern Politics

Machiavelli was the great prophet of the modern state, fit, as no other entity ever had been, to carry on war. Although the popular imagination sees him as a political immoralist, this is to do him an injustice. For, if Machiavelli is a political immoralist, then who among public persons in the modern world is not?

Machiavelli began his remarkable *Discourses on the First Ten Books of Titus Livius* with the complaint that, for all the admiration his generation had heaped on antiquity, antiquity was in fact ignored when it came to really important matters. The text is worth quoting in full: "And yet to found a republic, maintain states, to govern a kingdom, organize an army, conduct a war, dispense justice, and extend empires, you will find neither prince, nor republic, nor captain, nor citizen, who has recourse to the examples of antiquity!"[1] There were plenty of lessons to be learned by "recourse to the examples of antiquity," good ones and bad ones, and despite his occasional failure to adapt the old to the new, as in his account of the pertinence of the new technologies of war, Machiavelli seems to appreciate fully that times have changed, and changed drastically, and that, accordingly, one must be careful in applying to the present circumstances the examples of antiquity.

Chapter 1 of *Discourses* sets the problem, the securing of the "liberty" and the "security" of the body politic. It is a theme which runs throughout his work. For failure to secure its "liberty," its capacity to provide itself with laws, and its security, its capacity to resist being conquered, makes all else impossible. Indeed, the problem of acquiring offensive and defensive strength against other states which seek aggrandizement *defines* modern politics.

A second premise also makes an early appearance in this chapter: "A people cannot make themselves secure except by being powerful." It follows, then, that to be free and secure, a polity must be powerful. But this merely states the problem; it does not solve it. It was here, then, that "recourse to the examples of antiquity" would be informative. How did the states which endured secure their liberty and security? How did they become powerful and stay that way?

The philosophers of the fourth century had defined the legacy of ancient Greece. The worst constitution, as Plato had said, was that of Athens. Solon established "popular government," but it quickly gave way to the tyranny of Peisistratus. After forty years, Peisistratus was expelled; but the restored "popular government" did not last for more than a hundred years, a paltry performance compared to that of Sparta. Lycurgus "deserves the highest praise," for "in giving to the king, the nobles, and the people each their portion of authority and duties, he created a government (*uno stato*) which maintained itself for over eight hundred years in the most perfect tranquility" (I. 2).

But the legacy of Rome is even more important. Rome, even if she "did not attain the first degree of happiness," was far and away the most useful example. Machiavelli agreed that what the Greeks called *stasis* spelled the death knell of the body politic, and that first and foremost it had to be guarded against. For Machiavelli, as for Plato, the problem of how to prevent "civil strife" could not be settled unless one had answered a prior question, a question which, indeed, ultimately reflected an enormous difference between ancients and moderns.

There was, Machiavelli argued, a choice between two sorts of republics: one that "desires to extend its empire, as Rome," the other, as with Sparta or Venice, that "confines itself merely to its own preservation" (I. 69), a republic of expansion and a republic of conservation. In order to expand, Rome had "to employ the people in the armies" and "open the door to strangers." Venice refused to do the former, Sparta the latter. Both alternatives create "dissensions and troubles," especially as regards "the differences that will arise between the Senate and the people." Still, "to have removed the cause of trouble from Rome would have been to deprive her of her power of expansion" (ibid.).

Sparta and Venice are attractive. "Expansion is the poison of such republics; but if a republic is located "in some strong place" and is "sufficiently powerful, so that no one could hope to overcome her readily, and yet on the other hand not so powerful as to make her formidable to her neighbors ... she might long enjoy her independence." Plato had said as much in his *Laws*. But, after tempting his readers with what at first seem like genuine options, Machiavelli eliminates one:

All human beings are kept in perpetual movement .... [S]tates naturally either rise or decline, and necessity compels them to many acts which reason will not influence them; so that having organized a republic competent to maintain herself without expanding, still, if forced by necessity to extend her territory ... we shall see her foundations give way and herself quickly brought to ruin .... On the other hand, if Heaven favors her so as never to be involved in war, the continued tranquility will enervate her, or provoke internal dissensions which ... will be apt to prove her ruin. (I. 6)

Now the modern, Machiavelli rejects the Platonic solution. Echoing Thucydides' "necessity compels," Machiavelli judges that Spartan stability is no longer possible. Continued peace, were it possible, would provoke "internal dissensions." But in any case, continued peace is not possible, especially in a republic: "It impossible for a republic to remain long in the quiet enjoyment of her freedom within her limited confines; for even if she does not molest others, others will molest her, and from being thus molested will spring desire and necessity of conquests" (III. 19). There is, for Machiavelli then, no "perfect equilibrium," no "middle course." "I believe it therefore necessary," he concludes, "to take the constitution of Rome as a model" (I. 6). Rome endured, and Rome was expansionist. In this, Machiavelli had discerned, prophetically, the imperative of modern politics: that the only republic possible in the modern world is a republic of expansion. If a state is to preserve its liberty and security, it is necessary that it be "powerful"; but if it is to compete in a world seeking aggrandizement, it cannot adopt a policy of preservation. In a world of many incipient Romes, each seeking offensive and defensive power, each competing with the other for the ability to dominate those lacking the means, one must try to achieve "great empire." "*Crescit interea Roma, Albae ruinis.* Those who desire to become a great empire must endeavor by all possible means to make her populous, for without an abundance of inhabitants, it is impossible ever to make a city powerful" (II. 3). But this generates the fundamental dilemma:

If therefore you wish to make a people numerous and warlike, so as to create a great empire, you will have to constitute it in such a manner as will cause you more difficulty in managing it; and if you keep it either small or unarmed, and you acquire other dominions, you will not be able to hold them, or you will become so feeble that you will fall prey to whoever attacks you. (I. 6)

All else in Machiavelli flows from this fundamental perception. Although Machiavelli is remembered for a politics which shrinks at nothing as long as it is aimed at ensuring security and liberty, he is also, rightly, thought of as a defender of "republican" institutions. It will pay us first, then, to be clear about what "republican" meant to him.

The Republic of Rome and Renaissance Republics

Plato's *Politeia* is always translated "Republic," English for the Latin *respublica*, "the public thing." "Republic," however, is often the translation of the Latin *civitas* or the Greek *polis*. To complicate matters further, *respublica* is often translated "commonwealth." This confusion results, in part, from an inability to break with the Greek categories of "constitutions," defined in terms of the *polis*. Thus, for the Greeks, "kingdoms" and "empires" were not *polis* forms at all, even though a *polis* might have a king (or, as in Sparta, two kings). A kingdom was an *ethnos* form. As we shall see, it was not until Montesquieu's *Spirit of the Laws* of 1748 that any writer broke with the Greek three- or six-fold classification of forms of the *polis*. The confusion also stems in part, from conflating the *idea* of the *polis* with *forms* of the *polis*, especially that peculiar form which Aristotle called *politeia*. Roman practice is critical here, and Machiavelli knew his Roman history well enough.

As far as we can tell, the early history of Rome was similar to that of the Greek "cities." It was ruled by a king-priest (*rex*) and a hereditary aristocracy (*optimates, patricii*).[2] As with the Greeks, the fundamental social and economic unit was the *familia* (Greek *oikos*) with its *paterfamilias* (*patripotestas*). These constituted tribes (*tribus, gens*) and military and religious groups (*curiae*). The self-supporting farmer, the *assiduus*, was the heart of the polity. Below him were *proletarii*, people without property, whose service to the city consisted in raising offspring (*proles*); and of course, there were slaves. Kingly rule was broken, perhaps with Numa, but certainly after Lucius Tarquinius (ca. 500 BC).

During the early "republic," the king was replaced by two consuls, elected by the *comitia curiata*, which consisted of thirty curiae, ten from each of the three archaic tribes. As with the Greek *strategoi* who served exactly the same military functions, consuls were elected annually. Initially, consularship was restricted to patricians, who comprised a senate which was self-perpetuating. As Crawford notes in summary: "It was a form of government to which modern notions of being in or out of power are almost wholly inappropriate."[3]

The first attack on this system came from wealthy and ambitious *plebeians*, free, nonpatrician *assidui* who combined with the poorer plebs to extort concessions. By 366 BC, the consularship was open to them too. The assembly of the *plebes*, the *Concilium Plebis*, with its officials, the tribunes, evolved earlier; and it seems that the first efforts of the tribunes were aimed at securing protection of the weak against injustice. In 451–50, for example, they won codification and publication of the laws. By 287, the patricians had made a further concession; and the resolutions of the assembly of *plebes*, the *plebiscita*, acquired a binding effect on the state.

Concomitantly, the right of the tribunes to nullify oppressive acts committed by magistrates against individuals led to the right, finally, to veto even legislative acts of the Senate. If the tribunes "represented" the plebs, it must be emphasized that tribunes were hardly poor. Indeed, they were extremely rich, not merely by Roman standards, but by anybody's standards.

But this development and its effect are unintelligible apart from another development for which there is *no* precedent in the Greek world. It was the conquest by Rome of much of Italy. By the beginning of the fifth century, Rome was annexing by conquest and agreement parts of Latium. In the fourth century it extended its hegemony over the Sabines, the Etruscan city of Veii, and the Volci and Aequi. Rostovtzeff summarizes the situation thus: "As the Roman territory expanded, the number of free non-patrician landowners increased; for free plebeians who took part in successful campaigns received grants out of the conquered land; and many clients of the ruling families were perhaps rewarded in the same way for military service." The threat from the Gauls (ca. 400 BC) subsequently made radical reforms in Rome's military organization necessary. It also meant that "a national army must be created to take the place of the purely patrician force which had been sufficient for the kings and the infant republic."[4] It was thus that Rome broke with the Greek idea that a coincidence of the ruling and military functions was essential if a "city" was to be both free and secure.

The consequences were enormous. Rome articulated an utterly novel concept of "citizen" as one who had rights under Roman law, but who need not, as Aristotle had said, "participate in judging and ruling." The original definition of "patrician-citizen" as warrior came to include first, those *assidui* who could, as in the Greek world, provide their own equipment and eventually, even those who could not. By the third century BC, continued expansion had forced differentiation of a number of statuses, from those who could participate in ruling to those who had rights in the Roman republic to those who, as "allies," lacked such rights although they contributed men to the armies of Rome. In between there were those *cives sine suffragio*, citizens without a vote, who were potential citizens.

By the time of Polybius's *Histories* (ca. 150 BC), the Roman republic was *huge* by Greek standards. By then, too, it could be identified as a "republic" by virtue of its "mixed constitution," its senate, assemblies, and consuls. Rome already had many "citizens," even though it was not until 212 AD that Caracalla decreed that almost all free inhabitants of Rome's gigantic empire were citizens.[5]

Yet this was no *politeia* as Aristotle understood that word. In the first place, Rome, by then, was no *polis*. Hence it could not satisfy Aristotelian constraints on the political order. For Aristotle, Athens was "an overswollen multitude." What then of a "republic" which included the whole of Italy? It would take more than the voice of a Stentor to be heard from the tip of

Sicily to the hills of Verona! As is plain, "the history of Republican government [in Rome] is to a large extent the history of competition within a group of men formally peers, always within the framework of the over-riding decisions of this group."[6] Cicero came close to seeing what had happened when he wrote that "the people, though free, performed few functions themselves" (*De Re Publica*, II. 32). In his *De Legibus*, he was even more frank, writing that "Our law grants the appearance of freedom, retains the authority of the aristocrats and eliminates the causes of strife" (III. 17). But in a Greek *politeia* – for example, the short-lived regime of the Five Thousand – there was more than "the appearance of freedom." But there was also *stasis*. As Cicero and Machiavelli saw, it was precisely the "appear-ance of freedom," promoted by the Roman laws of citizenship in an aggrandizing empire, which had eliminated the causes of "strife."

Rome was a republic which desired to expand its empire. Once it had dominated Italy, it did not stop there. Indeed, it may well be that in its entire history, there was not a single day on which "Romans" were not at war. Soon, of course, it came to identify as its "provinces" all of Gaul, the entire European side of the Mediterranean to Syria and Cyrene, and Carthage and "Africa nova" on the African side of the Mediterranean.

This history was well known to Machiavelli – which is not to say that he altogether approved of what had happened and how it had come about. It is clear that he did not approve of the destruction of the "Republic" and the ascendancy, following "the civil war" (27 BC) of an emperor (when Octavius took the title "Augustus" and "*princeps*"). It is clear enough that, for him, there were "two causes of her [Rome's] decadence; the one was the dis-sensions consequent upon the agrarian laws, and the other the prolongation of her military commands" (III. 24). There is nothing new in Machiavelli's assignment of the first cause. It represents an antidemocratic bias as old as that of Solon's aristocratic opponents. Machiavelli believed that Rome was "well ordered" until the time of the Gracchi. For him, the agrarian proposals of Tiberius Gracchus, who was tribune in 133 BC and was lynched by a group of senators the following year, sowed the seeds of the *stasis* which, ultimately was fatal to the republic.

Roman expansion into Italy meant booty, land, and the obligation of Latin communities to provide legionnaires. After 197 BC, Rome imposed tribute in the form of cash and indemnities. To get a sense of the scale of the wealth accumulated in this way, we might note that whereas Athens spent the equivalent of 12 million Roman denarii on the Parthenon, the statue of Athena, and the entrance to the Acropolis, Rome, in the mid-second century BC, spent 45 million on its aqueduct and was literally transformed by the construction of new public buildings. Further, conquering generals had almost unlimited opportunities for private aggrandizement. Cornelius Scipio Africanus, Cicero's hero in *De Re Publica*, received 18 million denarii from Antiochus, presumably for the unkeep of his army (at a time when a legionnaire received 108 denarii per annum!). The process, once in motion, had an inner logic to propel it — and ultimately to undermine it. New victories brought new slaves, new tribute to invest in land — there were no other possibilities — and thus the continuing expropriation of *assidui*, who comprised new legions. As slave-worked properties of immense size, *latifundia*, became commonplace, the poor were increasingly displaced. Tiberius Gracchus is said by Plutarch to have insisted that "the savage beasts in Italy, have their particular dens, they have their places of repose and refuge; but the men who bear arms, and expose their lives for the safety of their country, enjoy in the meantime nothing in it but the air and light; and having no houses or settlements of their own, are constrained to wander from place to place with their children" (*Lives* vol. 10. IX).

The problem was not inconsequential. By the middle of the first century BC, almost half Rome's population of some 750,000 lived exclusively off the free grain dole, the famous "bread and circuses." Gracchus offered land reform as a solution. The core of his proposal was "the reenactment of an earlier prohibition on the holding by an individual of more than 500 *iugera* [approximately 312.5 acres] of public land" and the appointment of a commission to distribute land to landless peasants.

Machiavelli approved of the tribunate, one of the responses to the earlier "troubles of Rome." The tribunes were established, he said, "as the most assured guardians of Roman liberty" (I. 4). It was only when the tribunes mobilized the poor that "opposition" between Senate and "people" became disastrous. Nor did Machiavelli disapprove of Roman expansionism, the success of which was due, he insisted, less to the "favors of Fortune" than to Rome's own merits (II. 1). Indeed, this was precisely what made Rome such a valuable example. Like Sparta, it endured. With its conservative foreign policy, Sparta lasted 700 years. But in the conditions of the sixteenth century would Sparta endure? Indeed, could Venice?

To Renaissance "republicans," Venice was the contemporary paradigm of a conservative republic. "Self-centered" and, as Burckhardt put it, perhaps with Sparta in mind, "the city of apparent stagnation and of political silence."[7] Venice had managed to resist entangling alliances and to maintain her security with a large army of mercenaries. She was also the paradigm of "domestic tranquility." Machiavelli's near contemporary Sanuto put it well: "This holy republic is governed with such order that it is a marvellous thing. She has neither popular sedition nor discord among her patricians, but all unite in promoting her greatness; and therefore, as wise men say, she will last forever."[8]

Sanuto's words are well chosen. The constitution of Venice, a genuine *città*, approximated the ideal of Thucydides and Aristotle, Athens under the rule of the Five Thousand, who in effect constituted an oligarchy composed of the relatively numerous *optimates* of Venice, perhaps some 4–5 percent of the whole population. Every "noble" over twenty-five had a place in the Great Council, the seat of "sovereignty" in Venice. There was also a senate of Three Hundred, which exercised supervisory authority over all agencies of the state, waged war, and concluded peace, and a Council of Ten, which dealt with "urgent and extraordinary problems," especially those requiring secrecy and speed of execution. The doge, referred to as a "prince," represented sovereignty but did not in fact exercise it.

But, as Machiavelli saw, Venice had been shaken by events in the last part of the fifteenth century and would be further shaken by events in the early sixteenth century. Her prosperity as a link between East and West, her well-cultivated isolation, and in consequence, her capacity to maintain a Spartan-like foreign policy were all challenged. Bouwsma summarizes these events thus:

> Economic setbacks on several fronts, mounting Turkish pressure in the Levant, the domination of Italy by ultramontane powers too formidable to be either ignored or manipulated, and the hostility of a militant pope prepared to ally with the invaders and to humiliate the Republic with spiritual weapons, combined to bring about a general crisis which substantially altered the circumtances of Venetian existence.[9]

Machiavelli was correct: there was no longer any real choice. Only Rome could serve as a model for the "founder" of any polity which would have any hope of maintaining its liberty and security.

Before turning to Machiavelli's military insights and their relation to his analysis of the imperative of modern politics, it would be well to insert in the context so far developed the texts for which Machiavelli is best known, those of his striking *"The Prince"* (1513).

The Prince

Machiavelli began his *Discourses* by lamenting the failure of moderns to use the lessons of antiquity regarding all the really critical matters of politics, when what was at issue was "to found a republic, maintain states, to govern a kingdom, organize an army, conduct a war, dispense justice, [or] extend empires." He believed, too, that antiquity demonstrated that these activities sometimes required "extraordinary means," especially if the task was "to found a new republic, or to reform entirely the old institutions of an existing one" (*Discourses*, I. 9). Although it is often overlooked, Machiavelli is clear that his account in *The Prince* is directed not at governors of republics, but at new monarchs faced with the task of building a strong, unified state. Accordingly, he dedicated *Il Principe* to Lorenzo the Magnificent, in the hope that the latter might become the "liberator" of Italy. But Machiavelli concluded *The Prince* with words that could be said of *any* modern liberator:

> I cannot express the love with which he would be received in all those provinces which have suffered under these foreign invasions. . . . What doors would be closed to him? What people could refuse him obedience? What envy would oppose him? What Italian would withhold him allegiance? This barbarous domination stinks in the nostrils of everyone.[10]

The message of *The Prince* is technical, not moral. It concerns how territories are to be aggregated if a new, powerful state is to be created and the sorts of things a prince must do if he is to maintain power in such a situation. Machiavelli writes as an advisor, a technician, and an expert, not as a moralist. Some selections may here be appropriate:

> Whoever becomes the ruler of a free city and does not destroy it can be expected to be destroyed by it. (V)

> In taking a state the conqueror must arrange to commit all his cruelties at once. (VIII)

> A wise prince will seek means by which his subjects will always and in every possible condition of things have need of his government. (IX)

> A prince must not mind incurring the charge of cruelty for the purpose of keeping his subjects united and faithful. (XVII)

> A prince should make himself feared in such a way that if he does not gain love, he at any rate avoids hatred . . . . [Such absence of hatred] will always be attained by one who abstains from interfering with the property of his citizens and subjects or with their women . . . for men forget more easily the death of their father than the loss of their patrimony. (XVII)

> It is not . . . necessary for a prince to have [the qualities of mercy, faith, humanity, sincerity and religion], but it is very necessary to seem to have them . . . . A prince must take great care that nothing goes out of his mouth which is not full of the above named five qualities. (XVIII)

> Princes should let the carrying out of unpopular duties devolve on others, and bestow favors themselves. (XIX)

A prudent prince [should choose] for his counsel wise men and [give] these alone full liberty to speak the truth to him, but only of those things that he asks and nothing else. (XXIII)

On the other hand, and not to be reduced to the foregoing, there is an incipient "moral doctrine," if not in *The Prince*, at least in the *Discourses*. It is often referred to as "reason of state" (*ragione di stato, raison d'état*), although Machiavelli himself did not use the expression.[11] Its essence is captured by his remark that, "when the act accuses him, the result should excuse him" (*accusandolo il fatto, lo effetto lo scusi*) (*Discourses*, I. 9).

As in *The Prince*, the context is clear. He says, "a wise mind will never censure any one for having employed any extraordinary means for the purpose of establishing a kingdom or constituting a republic" (ibid.). Machiavelli has been accused of being an immoralist on the grounds that, in his view, *any* end is justified by any means. But this is to misrepresent him. What he seems to have held − and quite plausibly − is that the continued existence of the body politic (*vivere civile*), its capacity to maintain itself as an independent entity, is the statesman's overriding responsibility, and hence that this is a *unique* moral obligation, the *one* end which justifies any means. This doctrine, as is quite clear, has been enormously influential in the modern world. Indeed, as I will subsequently suggest, it is taken for granted by *all* leaders of *all* modern states. On this view, although, for example, assassination is wrong, it is "excused" when the preservation of the state is at issue. Similarly, lying to countrymen is wrong but is excused for similar reasons. So too with any "extraordinary means" which statesmen may find necessary in carrying out their tasks as statesmen.

It would appear today that very few people believe that, when it comes to war and to dealings with other states and their leaders, Christian morality is a proper morality for statesmen. "Diplomacy," like war, requires different standards. That we resist the full implications of this and go on believing that a statesman ought to conform to the common morality in his dealings with his own countrymen, stems in part, at least, from our belief − ideologically sustained − that since we are "the state," statesmen ought to act within *our* law and not lie or do worse *to us* in the name of *our* security and *our* liberty. But once we subscribe to the idea, which would be anathema to the Greeks, of a radical separation between the government and those governed and thus between the *roles* of a private person and a public person, then morals and politics can each have their own, inherent rationale. The point is critical.

For the Greek, the citizen *was* the "government", for it was the citizens who ruled. A citizen was at once a private and a public person. But today this is no longer the case. Public persons constitute a government which presumably exists to serve the governed, persons in their private lives. It may do this well or badly; but it cannot do it well if its decisions and policies are persistently opposed, and if it cannot act for the body as whole. Machiavelli saw this clearly: "Government is the management of citizens so that they are neither able nor inclined to oppose you" (*Discourses*, II. 23).

The Greek was unhypocritical as regards the "justness" of the exercise of Athenian power over the Melians. It was an act explained by "necessity," though not justified by it. Moreover, no Greek would have accepted the idea that its magistrates could violated the laws of the city, even in the name of liberty. This was tyranny. Nor, finally, and for the same reasons, did the Greek ever go as far as Machiavelli in the advocacy of force and deception against fellow citizens. As Neal Wood rightly remarks, not only does a military caste of mind inform Machiavelli's political insights, but, critically, "the classic distinction between friend and foe is blurred."[12] The idea is hardly unfamiliar. Are protesters in the streets friends or foes? Indeed, are obstructionists in elective bodies, – for example, the "willful men" who opposed American entry into World War I – friends or foes?

Thus a public person can be condemned for cowardice or stupidity, for doing what was not necessary in carrying out his public responsibilities. But a public person is not to be condemned for breaches of the common morality if such acts were necessary to maintain the safety and security of the body politic. Nor should we here confuse immorality with illegality. Recent American presidents have been challenged as lacking the authority to instruct the Central Intelligence Agency to carry out acts which would otherwise be widely seen as immoral. But a challenge to the authority of the president is not about the morality or immorality of such acts themselves. It was surely the view of these presidents that what they did was both moral and legal, that it had to be done to maintain the national security, and, on their view at least, that the American constitution gave them authority to engage in such practices.

Seen from the point of view of morality, we need also to be clear that the claim is *not* that such acts are to be judged by the same standards as those of private persons, but that they should be looked at from some larger vantage point of justice or some other, more inclusive or ultimate good. The doctrine I am attributing to Machiavelli is no utilitarian moral philosophy, for it does not require that there be some ultimate good. Nor does it mean that if some measures justified as exceptional are carried out, they will never be needed again. For Machiavelli, there is neither hypocrisy nor anguish nor a millenarian vision. Rather, in his view, the rulers of *any* well-ordered, powerful state will and should *quite normally* employ measures which, from the standpoint of the common morality, are immoral.

There are *two* moralities, not one. There is one for the private person, another for the public person. There need be no visionary future – the "utilitarianism" of a Lenin – or exceptional circumstances or ultimate justification in terms of justice or happiness. Viewed from the perspective of the public man, the continued existence of the state is *sufficient* reason for whatever is done. It defines the task of the public man and justifies his behavior. Toward the end of his *Discourses*, Machiavelli concludes:

> Where the safety of the country depends upon the resolution to be taken, no considerations of justice or injustice, humanity or cruelty, nor of glory or shame, should be allowed to prevail. But putting all other considerations aside the only question should be, What course will save the life and liberty of the country. (III. 41)

In a world of aggrandizing "states," Machiavelli pursued the full implications of the primary imperative of modern politics: "A people cannot make themselves secure except by being powerful." The only question then is a *technical* question: namely, "What course will save the life and liberty of the country?" Isaiah Berlin observes:

> One may disagree with this. One may argue that the greatness, glory and wealth of a state are hollow ideals, or detestable . . . . If so, one is simply contradicting Machiavelli's thesis. He is convinced that states that have lost their appetite for power are doomed to decadence and likely to be destroyed by their more vigorous and better armed neighbors.[13]

But another contemporary scholar of politics, more sympathetic to Machiavelli, has put it differently:

> Politics needs all these dubious practices; it cannot be managed without violence, betrayal, secrecy, propaganda . . . . Politics is a hard thing, said the Romans, and they meant that it is a dangerous enterprise not suited for the sentimentalist and romantic. For the well-being of the political community is the necessary condition for all other human endeavors.[14]

Virtù

Machiavelli had little patience with medieval values regarding the conduct of war. It may be that membership in *Respublica Christiana* had mitigated, to some extent at least, the very total kind of activity that had characterized ancient wars. But, as Machiavelli saw it, *virtù*, a literally untranslatable concept, had disappeared from the world with the advent of *Respublica Christiana*. As a result of placing "the supreme happiness in humility, lowliness, and a contempt for worldly objects," men had become "feeble," an "easy prey to evil-minded men" (*Discourses*, II. 2). *Virtù* was a military quality, as Wood writes, involving the exhibition of "masculine," aggressive conduct "in a dangerous and uncertain situation of tension, stress, and conflict" and a capacity "to achieve great deeds."[15] Yet even if it was a military quality, Machiavelli agreed with the Greeks in associating it with a political quality; for the political man too had to be a man of *virtù*. The men of *virtù* in ancient days were military men; but this was hardly a bar to their being statesmen. However, in this view, Machiavelli went directly against prevailing opinion; for current opinion held that military and civilian life were antithetical, and that one must choose one or the other.

The "New" Art of War

It is an oversimplification, yet a useful one, to say that while in the medieval world, like the Greek world, those who ruled fought, by the time of Machiavelli, things had exactly reversed themselves. For in Machiavelli's day, those who ruled did *not* fight; instead, they hired mercenaries to do their fighting for them. How this came about is complicated; but the shift to a money economy was surely critical. As Felix Gilbert writes:

> When rapid expansion of the money economy shook the agricultural basis of medieval society, the effect of this development on military institutions was immediate. In the military field, those who were protagonists of the new economic developments — the cities and the wealthy overlords — could make use of new opportunities: namely to accept money payments instead of services, or to secure services by money rewards and salaries.[16]

Overlords and regimes in cities, freeing themselves from dependence on vassals and "citizens," were laying the foundations for permanent professional armies.

As the "chivalrous" role became discredited, writers like Castiglione, in his very influential and much copied *The Courtier* (1528), could joke about the medieval "men who fight." He tells of a "fierce," "blustering" man who, upon being asked to dance by a lady, "refused not only that, but to listen to the music," saying that "such silly trifles were not his business." What, then, she asked, was his business? "To fight," he replied; whereupon the lady said, "Now that you are in no war, and out of fighting trim, I should think that it were a good thing to have yourself well oiled, and to stow yourself and your battle harness in a closet until needed, lest you grow more rusty than you are."

New weapons and new forms of war contributed to this shift. The "man-at-arms," the heavily mailed cavalryman driving at full trot, equipped with a lance, a sword, and "his lobster-cracking tool," a mace, had been a formidable fighting man, able to strike terror in the heart of anyone. By the middle of the fifteenth century, however, when he reached his peak efficiency perhaps, he was no longer a sufficient instrument of war. The English longbow, formations of pikemen, brought to a refined art by the Swiss, and thence, the new firearms, initially "as much symbols as weapons," created a condition in which was again came to look much as it did in ancient times. As Gilbert writes, "in the battles of Morat and Nancy (1476), the knights of Charles the Bold, unable to break up the squares of Swiss foot soldiers and to penetrate into the forest of their pikes, were thoroughly defeated. This event was a European sensation. Infantry had won its place in the military organization of the period."[17] When infantry replaced the knight in shining armor, the problem of manpower again arose, just as it had in the ancient world of the *polis*. And again, as Machiavelli was quick to see, there was the question of a citizen-army.

The Art of War

Machiavelli's influential, but today little read, *The Art of War*, like his *Discourses*, looks to Rome. Its critical "innovation," not brought to its full realization until the armies of Napoleon, is the conscripted citizen-army. Machiavelli subscribed to the idea that "no man can be called a good man who in order to support himself, takes up a profession that obliges him at all times to be rapacious, fraudulent, and cruel, as of course must be all of those – no matter what their rank – who make a trade of war."[18] But to Machiavelli, the critical point is not that killing is a mortal sin; but rather, that no man who takes up soldiering *in order to support himself* can be called "good." Machiavelli's prejudice was Aristotelian. For Machiavelli, mercenaries were either useless, or dangerous, because they were reluctant to fight, because they were a potential threat to the body politic.

Machiavelli had become convinced that the foundation of a republic is "justice and arms," and that no state could succeed unless "the troops are natives of the same country and have lived together for some time." Rome was again the example. "As long as Rome continued to be well governed (which was until the time of the Gracchi) there was never any soldier who made war his only occupation" (*Art of War*, 18).

For Machiavelli there were, however, two straightforward problems which a revitalized "citizen's militia" had to overcome. First, ordinary, hard-working men will be "raw and inexperienced"; and second, it is unlikely that they will volunteer to serve. Machiavelli seems to have assumed, too quickly as it turns out, that just as Rome had managed to train and discipline its infantry legions, so their success could be replicated in a Renaissance city-state with men who were not "professionals." Here he had the chance to try his hand. The famous *Ordinanza* of 1505, drafted by Machiavelli, provided for the formation of a militia of 10,000, consisting of farmers, blacksmiths, and other men of the countryside — the city with its richer sorts would furnish cavalry — who would be drilled on festival days. Although it was hardly a *sufficient* test of his ideas, a test came in 1512, when his militiamen capitulated to professional Spanish troops, Florence fell, and the Medici were restored. Machiavelli paid a heavy price. Falsely accused of treason, he was imprisoned, then released and allowed to live in retirement. It is in this period, indeed, that Machiavelli had the leisure to produce all the works for which he is best remembered.

The second problem, that militiamen are unlikely to volunteer and will serve only if compelled by force, raises some large-scale issues highly pertinent to this book. The Greek citizen-armies, as we have seen, were comprised of citizens in the strictest sense. They fought *and* ruled. In consequence, there was no problem in securing the obedience of the army, in getting men not merely to fight, but to fight in the interest of the republic and its laws. For they had made the laws, and would defend them. But for Rome, what we must call the problem of legitimacy did arise. How could one constitute a large army of men who would be courageous, and not constitute a threat to the ruling order of society, even though they were excluded from power? That is, "if the militia consists of soldiers of *virtù*, the commander may very well use it to seize government power." As Machiavelli acknowledged, Rome was often cited for the very reason that the Romans "lost their liberties by maintaining a citizen's militia". Moreover, what of Venice and France as examples of successful polities who use only foreign troops? Venetian subjects cannot "stage a *coup*," and the king of France "has disarmed all his subjects in order to rule them more easily" (*Art of War*, 218–19).

Machiavelli was extraordinarily sensitive to this problem, but he almost certainly idealized Rome in this regard, principally in holding that — at least until the time of Gracchi — the Roman army had that civic spirit which he called "virtù." Common soldiers, he writes, "entered voluntarily into the service," but "they were no less glad to return to their families when they were no longer wanted."[19] Moreover, he wrote in a number of places that the difficulties began with the commanders, that "men who are well disciplined will always be cautious of violating the laws when they have arms . . . as when they have not; and so they will continue, if they are not corrupted by their commanders" (*Art of War*, 40). This shifts the problem, of course, making it far more tractable. One might assure that commanders are not kept in "constant pay," that they do not "receive any stipend or pension in peacetime," and that they "do not acquire too great an authority over their men."

All this may be true – as far as it goes – but Machiavelli seems utterly to discount the fact that conquest paid, not merely for the Roman state as a whole, but also in the form of pay, booty, and a promise of a secure future for many of its citizens individually.[20] Rome's armies were hardly "defensive" forces, called up to protect a "homeland" under periodic threat. On the contrary, from very early on they were armies of conquest. Moreover, Roman wars of conquest – unlike the wars of the early modern period – undoubtedly paid for themselves.

Machiavelli did emphasize Roman discipline, which he hoped to emulate. But again, while it was severe, it was, as Nicolet says, a skillful blend of punishment and reward. A man unwilling to answer the *dilectus* (the regular summons) could have his property sold by auction, or he might himself be sold into slavery. Having taken the oath for service, punishments for disobedience or cowardice were severe and included the possibility of "decimation." On the other hand, not only were there rewards for success, but gifts were made for individual acts of heroism and leadership. Although it is not easy to get an entirely satisfactory answer to the puzzle of Roman success on this score, one must look, it seems, at how choices for free males were structured by prevailing circumstances. The logic that created both *latifundia* and Rome's "social" problem goes some way to explaining the willingness of ordinary men to serve with such apparent enthusiasm in Rome's armies.

Machiavelli also suggested that love of one's country might be a sufficient motivation, and that men who were subjects, though not citizens, could be motivated to both make war and maintain the laws. In this, of course, he was more prophetic than descriptive, since it was clear to him that love of country could not function in an extended republic, at least not initially. "If a prince or state is able to raise an army of 15,000 to 20,000 strong, young men in his own dominions," then, he wrote, "nothing in the world can be more easily effected than the reduction of military discipline to the standard of the ancients." But if he cannot find men in his own country, then "nothing can be more difficult." All the great generals had "subjects of such a disposition that they could discipline and train them as they pleased." Indeed, without this, however great any of them might have been, they would never have been able to perform "anything memorable in a foreign country whose inhabitants were corrupt and averse to all good order and necessary obedience." Machiavelli is not so much begging the question as stating the problem. If one has "good" men who love their country, then they can be molded. If one is working with "foreigners" who are "corrupt," then nothing can be done to make them into a virtuous army. Men from the countryside of Florence spoke a vernacular Italian and were at least potentially virtuous; but, as he realized, one could not assume that they would love the Florentine republic, especially since they were not citizens and could not expect to become citizens. Still less did Machiavelli expect that, in the absence of a charismatic leader like Lorenzo the Magnificent, there was any chance that they would fight and die for an entity called "Italy."

We must be clear here. The problem was not a matter of securing the "legitimacy" of the government. Most people, as Machiavelli wrote, "only care to live in security, are easily satisfied by institutions and laws that confirm at the same time the general security of the people and the power of the prince" (*Discourses* I. 16). The problem, rather, was how to get "subjects" to risk their security in war. More generally, it is absolutely critical that we remember what is often forgotten: namely, that in Machiavelli's day, as Hale writes, "no government had such power or persuasiveness as to compel any large number of non-helpless men to do what they did not want to do."[21] Power and persuasiveness: both were critical. We take both for granted; but this is probably because the capacities of modern governments to persuade and compel are the outcome of several centuries of almost imperceptible change. Critical steps were taken in England in the seventeenth century, but perhaps the solution to the legitimation problem was not discovered until late in the eighteenth century, with the citizen-armies of the United States and the First Republic of France. In the interim, massive sums generated by the new opportunities were used to fund massive mercenary armies which engaged in wars whose organization and outcomes were the most decisive element in the building of the new states of Western Europe.

But if the problem of how to raise effective citizen-armies seemed all but insoluble to Machiavelli, the alternatives were hardly more desirable. Machiavelli could turn the argument around. For, as many Italian cities had already discovered, there was nothing to prevent "contract soldiers," *condottieri*, from using their hardened professionals to seize power. Indeed, if Machiavelli could not entirely solve the problems he had exposed, no one else could either. To put the matter simply: only in a republic could one preserve "liberty"; and, for a republic to be secure, it must be powerful and expansionist. But if so, it must have a large army of men of *virtù* headed by men of *virtù*, men who would maintain the laws as they maintained the state. As Montesquieu was to insist, kingdoms and despotisms could be warlike and expansionist; republics, if they were to survive, could not. As it turned out, Machiavelli's vision was capable of realization, but not immediately.

4

Monarchies, Despotisms, and Peaceful Republics

The "Revolution" in War

"Although it is generally so considered, money is not the sinews of war" (*Discourses*, II. 10). Machiavelli may have been correct in saying that "gold alone will not procure good soldiers, but good soldiers will always procure gold," especially if, given the fears he had so rightly discerned, a "good soldier" is not merely a bold adventurer. Nevertheless, if one fact stands out regarding war in the early modern period, it is that the costs of war escalated remarkably. The revolution in war was less technological than financial. Not only did the size of armies, made up almost exclusively of mercenaries, grow by leaps and bounds, but both artillery and naval war budgets increased by heretofore unimaginable proportions.

A few numbers serve to indicate what was happening. Spanish military expenditures (in millions of ducats per annum) increased as follows:

Before 1556	2
1560s	4.5
1570s	8
1590s	13

When Philip II took over from his father, Charles V, he had at his command about 150,000 men; by the end of his reign, he had 200,000, and by the 1630s, the Crown was able to assemble 300,000 men. Neither American silver nor the tripling of Castile's taxes was sufficient to support this many, and four times, in 1557, 1560, 1575, and 1596, Philip repudiated his debts. Nor did he ever pay his soldiers on time. After 1630, Louis XIV, with a better organized tax system and a much larger population to tax, managed to outdo Spain by far; in the 1630s France had 150,000 in paid service, but by the 1700s this had risen to 400,000. The war budget of 1683 was 38 million livres. In 1706 it was 145 million, including money for fortifications, artillery, and provisions. British military efforts, especially during the period of the wars with Louis XIV, also took on an unprecedented scale. Before 1688, annual revenue was at some £2 million, jumping to £72 million between 1689 and 1702 and £99 million between 1702 and 1711. Forty percent went to the army, which never exceeded 75,000 men, and 35 percent to its formidable navy. Meanwhile, the Dutch numbered 50,000 troops in the 1630s. 100,000 in the 1700s; the Swedes had 45,000 in the earlier period, 100,000 in the later period; and the Russians had 35,000 in the former, 170,000 in the latter.[1]

Many factors contributed to these developments, of course, but everyone agrees that the remarkable Chinese invention of gunpowder was an important element. Yet this was not because infantry armed with arquebuses, calivers, or muskets could fell a man-at-arms or drive pikemen to retreat. The early firearms were inaccurate and unreliable, and had long loading times. Machiavelli, accordingly, was not misguided in assigning these only a minor role in his idealized army. The initial push was for artillery which would be able to break down castle walls. This brought on an arms race, a second bronze age in Europe (1453–1553), and rapid technological improvements in cannon manufacture. Yet, inevitably, new offensive weapons called for new defenses: the *trace italienne*, bastion and outworks with masonry facing to a ditch, themselves defended by artillery. These were enormously expensive to build. Moreover, they gave new purpose and significance to the siege, and thus to increasingly large numbers of infantry.[2]

At the same time, the development of cannon radically altered naval warfare and led to increasingly costly investments. In the thirteenth century, all-weather vessels carrying men with crossbows began to replace the light, maneuverable ships in use since ancient times, ships which fought by ramming and boarding. By building even stouter ships and equipping them with cannon, one had in effect a floating gun platform. Heavy guns had to be carried near the waterline, and a ship built for Henry VIII in 1514 was the first to cut gunports in the hull. When Queen Elizabeth's ships were improved some seventy years later as McNeill writes, "the adaption of oceangoing vessels to the artillery revolution of the fifteenth century was effectively achieved." The Mediterranean states, here including Spain, which were accustomed to waging war against the Turks, lagged behind in adopting the new designs. The defeat of the Armada in 1588 by nimbler English ships, aided, as in the case Xerxes' great invasion fleet, by bad weather, was decisive. McNeill summarizes matters: "In effect, the roar of Dutch and English naval guns closed off the last avenue of escape from the economic and ecological impasse confronting Mediterranean populations."[3] Moreover, the early successes of Spain and Portugal as maritime empires were increasingly threatened by the highly rationalized imperial policy of the British and, to a lesser extent, the Dutch.

Sea power still had a quasi-private character, and most of the ships which fought the Armada were merchantmen. Turning to land forces, however, we find that mercenaries dominated. "National" wars were fought, as Sanuto remarked, by "Noah's arc" armies. According to Hale, "a sour Welsh professional" once observed that Henry VIII's French invasion army of 1544–5 contained "depraved brutish foreign soldiers from all nations under the sun . . . Scots, Spaniards, Gascons, Portingals, Italians, Albanians, Greeks, Turks, Tartars, Germans, Burgundians, Flemings."[4] Sovereigns knew that mercenaries could be extremely effective against rebellious "common people" intent on overthrowing the status quo. Indeed, it is not too much to say that money constituted the "sinews of war" precisely because mercenary forces were the sinews of sovereignty.

Although we cannot go into it here, perhaps the most remarkable example was the use of mercenaries (*Landsknechte*) by the members of the Swabian League in the German Peasants' War of 1525. According to one expert, the war is misnamed in that the rebels included "the poor common man in town and countryside," not just the peasant, but also the miner or journeyman or servant who lived in a territorial or imperial city. Such a man was politically powerless, of course. More to the point, we must not suppose that this was something like Shay's Rebellion in Massachusetts, since huge armies fought on both sides. The rebel army of Baltringen numbered perhaps 10,000, for example, and it was but one of many armies. Although ill-trained, these men were armed not only with swords and poled weapons but with firearms as well. They sorely lacked cavalry and experienced artillerymen and were very short of wall-breaking siege guns. No doubt their cause was improved by the presence, as officers and in the ranks, of disaffected former mercenaries. The military deficiencies of the revolutionaries do not wholly explain, it seems, the failure of the revolutions which spread throughout South Germany and which came to involve hundreds of thousands. Critical as well was "the rebel's failure to establish permanent communications and political solidarity across the historic territorial and regional divisions."[5]

The new developments in armaments, the cost of navies, and the increase in the size of armies put an enormous strain on the budgets of sovereigns, as the examples cited earlier indicate. Sovereigns faced with new imperatives to generate funds to sustain war accelerated their efforts to find such funds. If we compare military expenses with total "normal" expenses: namely, court expenses, administrative costs, and the defense costs of fortifications and garrisons, we can see that, as Hale argues, "in general it can be hazarded that the direct costs of war were seldom less than half the peacetime revenues." And sometimes, as with the papacy in 1529–31 and Holland in 1599, they even exceeded revenue. One or two further examples will suffice. Louis XI (reigned 1461–83) spent half his revenue on his small permanent establishment of some 9,000 and on contracts with Swiss mercenaries. In 1615 the war expenses of France accounted for 10 million livres out of a total revenue of 24.4 million. Sovereigns and the regimes of republics became desperate. Florence increased direct taxation, imposed loans on the wealthy, offered shares in government stock, commuted death and mutilation sentences in return for fines, allowed for a fee the rights of full citizenship, and confiscated silver from churches. Henry VIII expropriated hundreds of acres of monastic lands, which paid for about 32 percent of his French wars, and became indebted to foreign bankers, including the Fuggers, to the tune of £3 million. Between 1519 and 1556, when normal tax revenues amounted to some 55.5 million ducats, the Spanish Crown happily — or not so happily — borrowed 39 million. But, as Hale says, "recourse to expedients of this sort reflects not the theoretical inadequacy of the traditional tax structure but the difficulty of making it work." What we call the "modern state" is in large measure the outcome of having learned how to make it work.[6] But the "revolution" in war required one further development.

Maurice of Nassau, Prince of Orange (1567–1625), like Machiavelli, knew his Roman history well, and perhaps it is not an exaggeration to say that he not only solved some of the problems which the Florentine had addressed, but that, by appealing to the same historical sources, he found a way to lay firm foundations for the solution of others. He began by rejecting the idea that a mercenary force had to be undisciplined by its very nature. He discovered — or rediscovered — that drill was an effective method of instilling discipline, and that small tactical units under a strict chain of command which demanded unquestioned obedience could turn an otherwise motley crew of potentially dangerous adventurers into "an articulated organism with a central nervous system."[7]

We are accustomed to think of the manual-of-arms and close-order drill as ceremonial frills, aimed at keeping otherwise idle soldiers occupied. But Maurice's "Taylorist" innovations, which broke down soldierly acts into regular sequences which could be repeated until they became automatic made his armies incredibly effective, in part because, as McNeill writes, his methods tapped "a primitive reservoir of sociality directly." In the *polis* world, "affective community" came easily. Maurice may not have appreciated it fully, but what we call *esprit de corps* could be built, and once built, it gave armies that *virtù* which Machiavelli saw lacking in mercenaries. McNeill both summarizes the situation and suggests a deep explanation:

Prideful esprit de corps became a palpable reality for hundreds of thousands of human beings who had little else to be proud of. Human flotsam and jetsam found an honorable refuge from a world in which buying and selling had become so pervasive as to handicap severely those who lacked the necessaɪy pecuniary self-restraint, cunning, and foresight. An artificial community bureaucratically structured and controlled, came into existence, based on deep-seated, stable, and very powerful human sentiments. What an instrument in the hands of statesmen, diplomats, and Kings![8]

Just as for the Roman *assiduus*, taken from his land, the idea of a career as a legionnaire seemed desirable as compared with the alternatives, so too for men of the early modern period. And just as Roman discipline had been conducive to the growth of *virtù* among the troops, so Maurice's adaptation of Roman practice to fit the firearms of his day achieved more than he hoped.

The idea of an army with no personal stake in victory facing death in opposing rows in response to commands initiated by invisible, anonymous superiors is, as McNeill says, itself "as remarkable in its way as the birth of modern science or any of the breakthroughs of that age." But a further unintended consequence, remarkable in other ways, was the discovery, encouraged by the innovations of Maurice, that sharp cleavages in society might be entirely consistent with large armies made up mainly of the poorest of a nation's men. As we have seen, Machiavelli felt caught on the horns of a dilemma: for to arm "the people" would threaten civil order; but to hire mercenaries would do the same thing. The kings of Europe, however, proved that mercenaries could be sinews of their sovereignty – if only they could afford them. But Gustavus Adolphus (who was seventeen when he ascended to the Swedish throne in 1611), gave some evidence – soon to be tested by Charles I in England – that Machiavelli's dream of a conscripted militia might be realized. In 1625, he introduced a system which gave him "a substantial long-service national army, up to forty thousand men, perhaps the first such in Europe." Rothenberg, here quoted, cautions us against making too much of this.[9] The system was for home defense, and mercenaries were still prominent.

Two Contrasting Experiences

We should here look at the English experience with militias. Like the Italians, the English had long experimented with militia. Henry VII (reigned 1485–1509) had employed shire militias for home defense; but, favored by geography, these had scarcely been tested. Still, Machiavelli might not have been surprised at Ludlow's reflection on the English civil wars, that "the great quarrel between the king and us was the militia." In the last months of 1641, radicals achieved control of the Common Council of the City of London and the following January established a Committee of Public

Safety, the first appearance of such a body. Its explicit role was to control the city militia. The Royalists responded, and by August, as Stone writes, "the local authorities in every town and county were forced to make a choice, for they were faced with two incompatible demands: for the implementation of a Militia Ordinance from Parliament to raise troops 'to defend the King' — meaning to attack him, and for the implementation of a Commission of Array from the King to raise troops to defend him, meaning to attack Parliament."[10] Charles I, of course, did not survive that challenge, thereby establishing in the eyes of many the crucial connection between "standing armies" — or rather their absence — and absolutist monarchy. A king without a standing army could not be King; a republic, therefore, cannot suffer one.

One can hardly exaggerate the significance of this problem for seventeenth- and eighteenth-century thinking. In 1688 the "civil war" was finally settled, and William and Mary became King and Queen by an act of Parliament. In 1689 Parliament insisted on effective control of the army, a new departure of considerable importance. It then felt free to institute annual appropriations and to legislate a yearly mutiny act designed to keep the army under control. Along with this, it defined a code of military justice. Ideology did not quite catch up with reality, however, and the anti-army ideology which the struggles of the seventeenth century had produced would continue to have its effects, not merely on Englishmen but on people in the colonies as well. As one writer put it:

After the great standing army debate of the late 1690's and the outpouring of radical tracts, generations of Englishmen and Americans were unable to distinguish the varieties of militarism and military interference in politics, or the differences in military institutions. Henceforth, Rome's legions, the Turkish janissaries, and Cromwell's New Model Army would all qualify as "standing armies," a powerful, emotional phrase so easily understood and so universally accepted that it needed no further definition.[11]

But, sharply contrasted to the English experience was the Prussian experience. Both were firmly in the mind of Montesquieu when he set out his remarkable analysis of the European scene — indeed, the world scene — of his time.

Swedish troops had occupied Brandenburg during the Thirty Years' War, and in 1619 "Prussia" was still but a "clutch of distinct territories." Although he was but one of the Seven Electors who chose the Holy Roman Emperor, the Great Elector, Frederick William (reigned 1640—88), made a decision which effectively altered the course of central European history.

With peace restored, he decided that the Brandenburg territories should be restored to Prussia. He asked for funds to supplement his mere 1,300 mercenaries. Before he was through, he had 30,000 men permanently in arms and control of all of East Prussia, Eastern Pomerania, Cleves, and Ravensburg. As Palmer writes, "to support this army he virtually founded a new polity and a new economy."[12] That is, not only did Prussia virtually owe its existence to its army, but "military science, politics and economics merged inseparably into a great science of statecraft." Plainly, this is not the place to detail this quite amazing development; but its general outlines seem clear enough, and, of course, the consequences were critical.

Frederick wanted a general excise tax similar to the tax which the Dutch levied. But, not wanting to shift any of the tax burden from the peasants to themselves, Brandenburg's nobles refused to grant it. Frederick conceded that noble lands would be free from taxation. He further assented that the onus of deciding whether a peasant was free or servile fell on the peasant. The consequence was predictable. While west of the Elba, serfdom was being transformed, in Prussia it was effectively consolidated. The consequences of this were felt perhaps well into twentieth-century German history. In 1655 Frederick requested more money and was refused. Accordingly, he decided that the men of his army could collect the tax themselves. In 1680, then, he imposed an excise tax on the towns and created a bureaucracy to supervise its administration. As a result, local mayors and councils gradually disappeared. Thus, "with the new revenue, the bureaucracy, the standing army, the eclipse of the Estates and the extinction of local self-government, the Elector found himself absolute!"[13] Machiavelli would not have been surprised, for here was the *reductio ad absurdum* of the dilemma between security and liberty. Frederick had not built an army for Brandenburg but with his army had built an empire. From Montesquieu's vantage point in France, it looked much like "an oriental despotism."

Montesquieu and the Eighteenth-Century Vision of the State

Getting a handle on Montesquieu's brilliant *Spirit of the Laws* will, I believe, go some way to seeing how the changes in war and "the state" had altered the problem of democracy. Like us, Montesquieu found the situation bewildering. But wiser than many, even today, he saw clearly that the traditional three- or six-part classification of *gouvernements* on the basis of whether rule was by one (monarchy), a few (aristocracy), or many (democracy) was no longer applicable. A new classification was demanded, and a new understanding to go with it. This led him to offer as an alternative, republics, monarchies, and despotisms.

It is clear the Montesquieu was interested not simply in forms of government in the narrow sense in which we use the term, but in forms of society as politically organized. His concern was not merely laws in a statutory sense and "governments" as we understand them. The "spirit of the laws" was meant to convey the idea that all the many forms and types of societies are complex, interconnected wholes, the products of complex causal factors that determine their "nature" or "character." He was also the first modern political theorist to try to be thoroughly global in a second sense. "The laws of all peoples" referred not merely to laws in Europe and Asia, but to those in Africa, the Pacific, and the New World. He was almost completely ignorant of these last peoples, which in typical fashion he brought together under the heading of "barbarians" and "savages," what we might more aptly call "pre-state" peoples. Subscribing to the Greek prejudice that people who did not live in cities were uncivilized, he wrote that "savages" are "dispersed clans, which for some particular reason cannot find a body." "Barbarians," by contrast, are "commonly small nations, capable of being united."[14]

Montesquieu's new classification of "states" was extraordinarily insightful, even though, as he realized, it made China and especially England anomalous polities. Moreover, because he was not omniscient but was a great theorist writing during a period of crucial transition in the West, writers in America and France, responding to events at the end of his century will appeal to his views, even as these events and their responses made his central classification anachronistic.

Republics

What, in Montesquieu's view, was a republic? His characterization of republics makes it clear enough that he was thinking of the ancient "cities." Further, he seems to have believed that conditions still existed in which small self-sufficient "republics" could be sustained.

The most obvious feature of republics, which he repeats often, is that they last only in small territories (VIII. 16; XXIII. 17). Conversely, it is "natural that small states be governed as republics" (VIII. 20). Second, "virtue," which is the "spring" of republican government, requires both equality and frugality — a problem in the modern era, in which, as he sees clearly, luxury, ambition, and inequality are the rule. Third, there are two fundamental types of republics: either "the body or only part of the body is possessed of supreme power" (II. 1). If the former, the republic is a democracy; if the latter, an aristocracy. Montesquieu followed Aristotle exactly in holding that in republics the fundamental question was who should be a citizen, given that, crucially, "the citizen participated in judicial functions and ruling" (*Politics*, III. 1). The citizens *were* "the government."

It was precisely for this reason that "virtue" was the "principle" of republican government.

As a direct consequence of the foregoing, republics were characterized by "peace and moderation" and had as their direct object "liberty." *Republics could not be aggressors*; their foreign policy must be conservative, aimed at "preservation," to use Machiavelli's term. Montesquieu followed Machiavelli — up to a point at least — in holding that Rome, which seemed to be a critical exception, proved that imperial behaviour was inconsistent with republican institutions (*Spirit* XI. 2). Republics were subject to a fundamental dilemma: "If a republic be small, it is destroyed by a foreign force; if it be large, it is ruined by internal imperfection" (IX. 1).

In an age of greatness, was there any hope for the *small* republic? Montesquieu knew very well that his era was one of aggrandizement; that the world was comprised almost exclusively of "monarchies" and "despotisms," which, in their imperial behavior, were absorbing not only "cities," but also small principates; and that in the Americas and Asia, pre-state peoples not already subject to successful "despotisms" were quickly being absorbed. He understood perfectly well, furthermore, that monarchies and despotisms were in no way limited by any of the preconditions of the ancient republics. They could expand, perhaps indefinitely. Their "natures," territorially and structurally, their "principles," and their "spirits" were, therefore, entirely consistent with the modern age. Perhaps, then, the only serious alternatives were monarchies, such as France, or "despotisms," such as Prussia.

Monarchy and Despotism

Everyone recognizes that for Montesquieu, despotism is not simply monarchy "misliked," for despotisms and monarchies are shown to differ structurally. Yet it is usually overlooked that, in general, when he speaks about a despotism, he identifies it as an empire. In the eighteenth century Turkey, Persia, Russia, India, and China were always referred to as empires, a fact reflected still in our maps. To be sure, since the modern state had not yet quite emerged, the distinction between a kingdom and an empire was not clear. This was reflected in many ways, for example, in the ease with which Montesquieu, like his contemporaries, could interchange the vocabulary of "tax" with that of "tribute," in the ambiguity of the word "province," a legacy of the confusion, still with us, regarding whether Rome constituted an "empire" or whether it was merely an entity that happened to be ruled by an "emperor." Moreover, looked at from a modern point of view, eighteenth-century France, like China, was in reality a mixture of empire and kingdom. Neither France nor China were "nations" in the modern sense; for in both "the state," to use Dewey's language, was "hardly more than a shadow thrown upon the family and neighborhood by remote personages."[15] The "Prince" — whether he called himself a king or an emperor — ruled, but he did not regulate.

For Montesquieu, the key difference between a monarchy and a despotism was clear enough: it was the presence or absence of an "intermediate, subordinate, and dependent power" (II. 4). In both monarchies and despotisms, the prince is the source of all power; but only in monarchies are there "intermediate channels through which the power flows," channels which are "established" and "acknowledged," fixed, immovable, and of long standing. Moreover, "the most natural, intermediate and subordinate power is that of the nobility . . . . No monarch, no nobility; no nobility, no monarch; there can be but a despot" (ibid.).

Juridically, there must be "a depository of the laws," a *parlement*, persons "who promulgate the new laws, and revive the obsolete" (ibid.). For Montesquieu, France was surely the paradigm of a monarchy. But if this is the "nature" of a monarchy, its "principle" — what makes it work, function and live — is the concept of honor, surely. Thus, "the laws should support the nobility, in respect to whom honor may be" (V. 9). In sum, then, monarchy, with its nobility, clergy, and *parlements*, has feudal ancestors, the pyramidal, layered structure in which, with Bodin, sovereignty rested with the king, but power — understood as the effective means of realizing ends — was diffused and dispersed in the state at large. Western feudalism had given a perfectly natural solution to the problem of power in Montesquieu's view. In monarchies, there was a relative balance and relation between the prince and his lieutenants — the centralized state machinery, if you will — and the "intermediate" powers — the landed nobility who had an independent power-base.

With despotisms, by contrast, there were no intermediate powers, no effective nobility with an independent power-base, and hence no "depository of law." The absence of Western feudalism in Asia and the withering of the "estates" east of the Elba, then, were decisive. In the "Orient," "despotisms" were inevitable. As Perry Anderson points out, the canonical passage associating the "Orient" with "despotism" is in Aristotle, who asserts that, "Barbarians are more servile by nature than Greeks, and Asians are more servile than Europeans; hence they endure despotic power without protest" (*Politics*, III. 9). Here again the legacy of the philosophers can be seen to have had an impact. The Ottoman Empire was Montesquieu's paradigm of an oriental despotism, but Russia also very plainly fitted the bill.[16]

The military basis of despotisms is also clear: "Since strength does not lie in the state, but in the army that founded it, in order to defend the state the army must be preserved" (V. 14). The people are "timid, ignorant, and fainthearted," and fear and "the hope of the conveniences of life" motivate a despotism.

No doubt Montesquieu thought of empires as enormous by European standards. Yet he was puzzled by China. Observations by missionaries suggested that it did not fit his new classification: it seemed to combine as its principles fear, honor, *and* virtue. In China "industry and economy" are, he says, "as requisite as in any republic" (VII. 6); its rulers have displayed "virtue, attention, and vigilance" and have practiced "a method equally proper for moderating despotic power, and for preserving conquest." This is the device of insuring that "every military corps in the provinces" and "every court of adjudicature" is comprised half of Chinese and half of Tartars. This keeps both "within bounds" and has other "good effects," in particular, that "they both preserve the civil and military power, and the one is not destroyed by the other" (IX. 15).[17] But England was even more of an anomaly.

The English Constitution: A Republic Disguised as a Monarchy?

"The English," Montesquieu wrote, "to favor their liberty, have abolished all the intermediate powers of which their monarchy was composed" (II. 4). Yet, England was surely no despotism. It was "a republic disguised as a monarchy" (V. 19), whatever that might mean.

In his peculiar – and much misunderstood – discussion in Book XI, Montesquieu gave a detailed account of "the constitution of England." He wrote that monarchies do not have "liberty" as their object (XI. 6). But, if so, how could it be that England should have all the appearances of a monarchy yet be the "one nation . . . in the world that had for the direct end of its constitution political liberty" (XI. 5)? We have the answer to this puzzle once we see that this was a period of remarkable transition. Montesquieu seems to have seen, if dimly, that England had evolved from a feudal kingdom to become what, in our terms, is a modern state, a polity with a national government, centralized and effective, yet hardly despotic. The point is critical.

England was not a typical monarchy, because the "intermediate powers" – the feudal nobility – no longer represented fiefdoms. But it was not a despotism either, because it had discovered an utterly unique solution not only to the problem of power, but also to the problem of the legitimation of power. These two are distinct, even if they are often confused. Perhaps the best way to see what is at stake here is to consider England at the time when Montesquieu was writing. As Plumb has shown, it is a serious mistake, still repeated in textbooks in the United States, to hold that the ultimate Whig domination of English politics from 1675 to 1725 was the culmination of a "revolution" which destroyed "absolutism" and instituted "constitutional democracy." These ideas are ostensibly to be found in John Locke's *Two Treatises of Government* (1690). But the England which Montesquieu praised was no constitutional democracy. On the contrary, once Whiggery had separated itself from radicalism, succeeded in taming the enlarged electorate, and all but obliterated the Tory Party, it was able to fuse the interests of the aristocracy, high finance, and the executive power of the Crown.

By 1727 there was a reliable and effective Court Party, which included the richest and most widely connected aristocrats, the king's "household," and a parliament which was effectively in the hands not simply of men of property, but "particularly those of high social standing, either aristocrats or linked with the aristocracy, whose tap-root was in land but whose side-roots reached out to commerce, industry and finance."[18] The elected members of the House of Commons were not "common people" obviously; nor were they required to live in the boroughs from which they were elected. As Pole notes, an act of 1710 stipulated a landed qualification for knights and burgesses of the shire.[19] Although there had formally been a residence qualification since 1413, it had fallen into disuse in Elizabeth's reign. Pole comments, "If the rule of residence . . . had been insisted on, it would have been almost impossible for an upper class leadership to find seats in the House of Commons as a matter of legitimate reward for the attainment of a certain social or economic eminence."[20] Finally, from 1430 on, the suffrage franchise had been limited to holders of freehold property bringing in an income of 40s. a year clear of all charges.

Parliament had gained a new authority and had replaced the centralized governing structure of "King-in-council" with the far more powerful one of "King-in-parliament." The difference was fundamental, and Montesquieu knew it.[21] He also knew that the idea of a "mixed constitution" derived from Greek thought; but he insisted, rightly, that "the Greeks had no notion of the proper distribution of the three powers in the government of one person; they could see it only in that of many; and this kind of constitution they distinguished by the name of Polity" (XI. 11). His view of the "three powers" has led some people to suppose that he was confused, when instead, we should say that his views were merely different from both earlier and later views.[22] The three powers are "the legislative"; "the executive in respect to things dependent on the law of nations," for example, the declaring of war and foreign policy; and "the executive in regard to matters that depend on the civil law" (XI. 6). The two "executive" powers had been distinguished by Locke, who called the first the "federative" power, the special executive right of a king. The second executive power was judicial but was "executive" in that it referred to the king's justice.

"The ancients," in brief, "had not a clear idea of monarchy." Montesquieu attributed this to two causes: "The ancients had no notion of a government founded on a body of nobles, and even less of a legislative body composed of representatives of the nation" (XI. 8). On both counts, Montesquieu was correct. The English, then, had stumbled into an entirely new form of polity. Its main features can be summarized thus. First, "the executive power" was as it should be, "in the hands of the Monarch." Second, "the executive power ... ought to have a share in the legislature by the power of rejecting" — that is, a veto power. Third, "the legislative body being composed of two parts, they check one another by the mutual privilege of rejecting," and "they are both restrained by the executive power, as the executive is by the legislative." Montesquieu's analysis of the "legislature" and its relation to "the government" showed that it had *no* ancient parallels. It was a "Gothic" discovery, "found in the woods" (XI. 6)!

The "government" was the king and his bureaucracy. The idea of a government which actually governed was, at this time, itself a novel idea, vaguely distinct from the relation between "ruler" and "ruled." The difference, still not clear to modern readers, depended critically on Montesquieu's idea that "the government" was "founded on a body of nobles." That is, the "rightfulness" — authority, legitimacy" — of the "government" derived, as Locke had said, from "the Community"; but concretely, this meant that it got its authority from Parliament — the House of Lords and those lords who sat in the House of Commons.[23]

Moreover, the House of Commons, as "a legislative body composed of representatives of the nation," had no parallel in ancient practice. These remarkable innovations — and Montesquieu was correct in seeing them as such — made it possible to correct the "great faults" of ancient republics.[24] The "one great fault" of those republics was that "the people had a right to active resolutions, ... a thing of which they are absolutely incapable." Montesquieu was emphatic: "They ought to have no share in the government but for the choosing of representatives, which is within their reach." There was a second "great fault": the representatives should not be allowed executive power, for they may then be "corrupted by the people." A hereditary monarch and chamber of nobles can check "the licentiousness of the people" (XI. 6). Montesquieu's perception of Greek history, like that of Machiavelli, was profoundly influenced by the critics of fourth-century Athens.

Viewed from the perspective of today, the English arrangement may appear closest to Rome under the Republic; yet it was different in important ways, as Montesquieu rightly discerned. First, nothing in Rome could be compared to the British House of Commons, an elective legislative body "composed of representatives of the nation." Second, the "government" of Rome, if one wants to use that term, very nearly *was* the body of nobles, together with its "magistrates," of course. England had a modern civil bureaucracy directed by a king, but even more important, Roman rule was not legitimated by Whig principles. Indeed, for the ancients, the very idea that "government" needed legitimating would have made little sense. Finally, the absence of a monarchy in Rome was, for Montesquieu, critical. If "the executive power should be committed to a certain number of persons selected from the legislative body [the arrangement of the Consuls in Rome], there would be an end of liberty" (XI. 6). "Liberty" required that the monarch be both independent and have the power of veto. Indeed Montesquieu, following tradition, attributes Rome's loss of "liberty" to the fact that the power of veto "was entirely lodged in the people," through the mechanism of the tribunate (ibid.)

The New Politics

But if no one would have called the England of Montesquieu's *Spirit* "constitutional democracy," it might well have been called an example of "representative government."[24] For the first time anywhere, a sizeable electorate had come into being. Plumb gives as a conservative estimate for William III's reign, 200,000 voters, perhaps one in thirty of the entire population. But again, it is critical to see what this does *not* mean.

Whig doctrine, from at least the time of Locke, had insisted on the indispensability of constitutionally fixed meetings of Parliament and on the "supremacy" of the legislature. But nothing in the *Two Treatises* presupposed that *individuals* were to be represented by Parliament. Indeed, nothing in Locke or in standard Whig theory required that "representatives" be periodically elected![25] In the standard Whig view, boroughs and communes might be represented. So too, as Burke was soon to say, "the great and legitimate interests of the nation."[26] Yet, as Pole points out, until at least the nineteenth century, "English history had never known a period in which the common people, considered as a mass, or with more dignity, as an estate, had been formally represented as a matter of right." There was a great deal of difference between representing communes and representing commoners. Finally, from the Septennial Act of 1716, it was widely held that

> parliament ... was not created in order to express the will of the variety of shires and corporations; it did not exist to find the desires of the different constituences and translate them into legislative action .... Parliament existed because the nation needed government; the duty of the House of Commons was to take its share in the burden of providing good government, regardless of popularity and local opposition.[27]

The "nation" was represented; groups and "interests" shared by those who could not vote were "virtually represented." If this was "representative government," it was because the governors had a new role. They now functioned to "represent" the "nation." It was not "representative" because "the people" voted; nor, surely, because it was their will which was "represented." As Montesquieu saw, the parliament of England had been transformed from a feudal gathering of nobles into a national assembly.

Since it was *nothing like* Athens, there was no reason to fear that it would end up with a demagogic tyrant. "Patronage," the locus of "corruption," was an increasing problem, however, and "the people" were no doubt a source of new political concern. As Plumb writes:

> The new political nation proved very meddlesome, very contrary, very fickle in its moods; above all it helped to give substance to parties and to give them added power .... The battle to control this new electorate is a vital issue of this period .... It called into being new methods of propaganda and electioneering; it was subjected to vicious attacks by the Crown and to subtler forms of corruption and manipulation by the aristocracy and gentry.[28]

It would be hard to exaggerate the importance of these developments; but one must be clear about what they were. Here was a small, if significant, body of "citizens," all propertied, who voted; but, unlike the situation in Athens, they had no *direct* voice in *any* policy. To be sure, the men elected to the House of Commons were "accountable" to this electorate; and to be sure, "new methods of propaganda and electioneering" quickly became an essential part of this. These methods became ever more important, furthermore, especially in the first decade of the new United States. Since then, as we know only too well, "the new methods of propaganda and electioneering" have taken on a gigantic significance, one that is particularly critical to the problem of war and democracy.

Virtue: The Spring of Republican Government

Montesquieu could now also find new meaning to "republican virtue." With one foot solidly planted in the ancient world, he could write:

> When virtue is banished, ambition invades the hearts of those who are capable of receiving it, and avarice possesses the whole community. Desires then change their objects; what they were fond of before, becomes now indifferent; they were free with laws, and now they want to be free without them; every citizen is a slave who has escaped from his master's house; what was maxim is now called rigor; to rule they give the name of constraint; and of fear to attention. Frugality, then, and the thirst for gain, passes for avarice. (III. 3)

The similarity of this passage to lines in Book VIII of Plato's *Republic* cannot be accidental. Plato there portrayed the fall from the ideal state, from virtue as wisdom to timarchy, guided by the principle of the ambitious man's love of honor — the principle of monarchies in Montesquieu's view — to oligarchy to democracy. In "oligarchy," or more strictly "plutocracy," the principle which rules the *polis* is "love of money." In "democracy," it is avarice, lawlessness, and that base nature which reason and "spirit" once kept repressed but which now becomes "liberated," ultimately, of course, to enslave us. But Montesquieu, feeling the vibrations of Plato's influential diatribe against Athens, is no Greek.

First, he comes close to Machiavelli in saying that virtue "is a feeling, and not a consequence of knowledge, a feeling that may inspire the lowliest as well as the highest person in the state" (V. 2). It has nothing to do with wisdom or excellence. It is a kind of love which stirs men to preserve the *institutions* of their country. Hence it is not even "patriotism" as that is normally understood.

Second, according to this modern view, it is not true that virtue requires leisure, as Plato and Aristotle insisted. There is a difference, Montesquieu says, between "two sorts of republics, the one military like Sparta; the other commercial, like Athens. In one, the citizens were obliged to be idle; in the other endeavors were used to inspire them with the love of industry and labor" (V. 6). This is a complete inversion. For Plato and Aristotle, Sparta exemplified the virtuous *polis*. Athens, precisely because it acceded to the "maritime mob" (*nautikos ochlos*), rang the death knell of the just *polis*.

Finally, in a monarchy "it is extremely difficult for the people to be virtuous." "Sad and melancholy experience" proves this:

Ambition with idleness, baseness with pride, the thirst of riches without labor, aversion to truth, flattery, treason, perfidy, violation of engagements, contempt of civil duties, fear of the prince's virtue, hope from his weakness, but above all, perpetual ridicule of virtue, are ... the characteristics by which the courtiers of all ages and countries have been constantly distinguished. (III. 5)

Plainly, it is not ambition which is the problem, but ambition with idleness; it is not pride as such, but baseness with pride; it not thirst for riches *per se*, but such thirst without the requisite industriousness and labor. These are the vices of a leisured, nonproductive aristocracy, who constitute the backbone of a monarchy, the very "courtiers" praised by Castiglione! Evidently, one must include here their unwillingness to stoop to soldiering, even in defense of their "country." All other vices, lying, flattery, treason, breaking engagements, and so forth, are either vices in a commercial society — for how can one conduct business with men who "violate engagements"? — or vices associated with failure of military virtues.

Montesquieu said that the "spring" of monarchy was honor, not virtue. He found "virtue" only in republics. But could it be that England, that republic disguised as a monarchy, was also virtuous? After all, it had the happy fortune of liberating commerce, and Montesquieu knew this. As Plumb observed, England's aristocracy, unlike France's, had "tap-roots" in land, but "side-roots" in commerce, industry and finance. Its nobility were not "courtiers," even if they were rich, ambitious, and proud.

Commerce and the Powerful State

We can pursue this by a further comparison of how "commerce" functions in "republics" versus how it functions in "monarchies." In monarchies, according to Montesquieu, trade is "founded on luxury" and presupposes inequalities. "It is carried on to procure everything that can contribute to the pride, the pleasure, and the capricious whim of the nature" (XX. 4). Indeed, in monarchies, "there is an absolute necessity for luxury. Were the rich not to spend their money freely, the poor would starve" (VII. 4). The exact opposite is true in a republic. There, commerce is "founded on economy" and presupposes (relative) equality. Even "vast riches" held by private persons did not have "bad effect" if "the spirit of commerce was not destroyed." Some inkling of the meaning of this is contained in Montesquieu's observation that the "spirit of commerce" is attended by frugality, moderation, labor, prudence, and order.

Evidently he is juxtaposing two very different kinds of social order. In monarchies the rich are but an idle aristocracy, and the poor are *kept* in their place, essentially as peasants, bound to the land and deriving gratuities from the ostentatious spending and charity of the rich. In the other kind of society, a "trading republic," the majority of the population are engaged in productive commerce; hence "the spirit of commerce" is very much alive.

Was there a social mechanism which might account for this difference? And if so, might it be that it has some other beneficial effects, regarding the problems of inequality and war, for example? Montesquieu did not address these questions. But his associate and correspondent in England, David Hume, did.

Indeed, Hume's analysis, in his 1752 essay "Of Commerce," is absolutely brilliant.[29] If it did not provide all the insight needed to settle the problems which Montesquieu had exposed, it did settle them for a string of modern thinkers, not least Alexander Hamilton. It would be no exaggeration to say that a critical divide at this crucial juncture in European and American history was between those who internalized Hume's thesis and those who did not.

Hume saw that the crux of the matter was not simply "commerce"; for it was trade which stimulated "manufactures." It was this that propelled "the spirit of commerce." Moreover, where laborers "enjoyed the fruits of their labour" and were not reduced to bare subsistence, inequalities were no disaster, and a fully stable social order was possible, without massive repression.

Hume divided the "bulk" of the population into "husbandmen" and "manufacturers" and noted that "time and experience" so improve agricultural productivity that agricultural needs require less and less labor time. This creates "superfluous hands." Two alternatives result. These extra hands may apply themselves "to the finer arts, which are commonly denominated the arts of luxury," or they may be claimed by the sovereign and "employed in fleets and armies."

The latter alternative seems attractive and has "history and experience" to recommend it. Sparta is the perfect example. It was extremely powerful; it did not engage in commerce; and it cultivated austerity and *amour propriae*. But as if heeding Machiavelli, Hume asks whether "sovereigns may return to the maxims of ancient policy" and answers, with Machiavelli, that "it appears to me to be almost impossible." Hume gives his reasons. First, the ancient republics were free states, but they were small. Since everyone was "continually in arms," "public spirit" could be fostered. Second, every citizen was a self-maintained soldier who took the field in his turn. Relative equality of fortune made this possible. The wise legislator, however, has to adopt principles which are "natural" to the particular society, and it is clearly impossible that any modern state could duplicate the two conditions named. Thus Sparta cannot be emulated. Lack of trade and manufactures may sometimes has good effects "among a free and very martial people"; but "it is certain that, in the common course of human affairs, it will have a quite contrary tendency." Without manufactures and trade, "sloth and barbarity" are likely.

Moreover, an agricultural society cannot sustain a large army. People in agricultural societies have "no temptation ... to increase their skill and industry; since they cannot exchange superfluity for any commodities which may serve either to their pleasure or vanity." So there is no "superfluity" to pay for an army. One cannot increase productivity and develop skill and industry "on a sudden." Hence the modern state which requires a large military must encourage trade and manufacture. Not only is the eighteenth century not the ancient world of free, small republics, but "to consider the matter abstractly, manufactures increase the power of the state only as they store up so much labour, and that of a kind to which the public may lay claim."

The "only" is critical. The task is to identify a mechanism which will insure that "superfluity" benefits the nation. Hume discerned that through manufacture, the "stock of labor" − what we would call the product of labor — which in times of peace is used for the "ease and satisfaction" of individuals, in time of war can be "turned to the public advantage." If, he argued, one could "infuse into each breast" a "passion for public good" and "so martial a genius" that individuals would endure hardships for "the sake of the public," this would sustain what Montesquieu called "the spirit of commerce." As it is, however, this is to ask too much. But if "the labourer is furnished with manufactures and commodities," he will toil to acquire these. Thus "men become acquainted with the pleasures of luxury and the profits of commerce; and their delicacy and their industry, once awakened, carry them on to further improvements in every branch of domestic as well as foreign trade." Having discerned the mechanism of an acquisitive society, Hume discerned a further outcome. If everyone enjoys "the fruits of his labour" and has "full possession of all the necessaries and many of the conveniences," it adds to the happiness of the poor, without diminishing from the happiness of the rich. Finally, and of no small consequence, because "the greater is the stock of labour of all kinds, the greater quantity may be taken from the heap without any sensible alteration in it." There will be enough to sustain a large military, since the greater "heap" will make "extraordinary taxes and impositions to be paid with more cheerfulness." Indeed, Hume was able to conclude his breathtaking performance by noting that "in this circumstance consists the great advantage of England above any nation present in the world, or that appears in the records of any story."

England was doubly unique. Not only had she found a unique solution to the problem of power, but she had stumbled upon a unique solution to the problem of virtuous republics. Though formally a monarchy, she had none of its vices. Instead, the "spirit of commerce" was much alive, and so too were all the virtues of a commercial republic. But there is yet a third feature which Montesquieu seems to have perceived, again, if but dimly.

Aggrandizement

"The spirit of monarchy is war and enlargement of dominion; peace and moderation are the spirit of a republic" (IX. 2). By engaging in aggression, a republic "exposes its own liberty"; but even if successful, its government "is ever odious to the conquered states." Yet Montesquieu saw that there were differences as regards the problems of war and of conquest between his era and ancient times. In his *Considerations on the Causes of the Greatness of the Romans and their Decline* (1734), a book comparable to Machiavelli's *Discourses*, he agreed that Rome was a virtuous republic, but that she had clearly overstepped her limits. He wrote: "When the domination of Rome was limited to Italy, the republic could easily maintain itself. A soldier was equally a citizen .... Since the number of troops was not excessive, care was taken to admit into the militia only people who had enough property to have an interest in preserving the city."[30]

Earlier, he had noted that "constant experience has shown that a prince who has a million subjects cannot maintain more than ten thousand troops without ruining himself." Only great nations, therefore, have armies (*Considerations*, III). But crucially, "it was not the same in ancient republics." The difference is the result of changes in the nature of armies, especially in the enormously increased expenses of the huge numbers of modern armies, and in the training, organizing, and fielding of an army. In his *Reflections on Universal Monarchy* (1727), he had already judged, with the majority and against Machiavelli, that in the new order of things, *"ce sont les richesses qui font la puissance"* ("it is wealth which creates power"). In *Considerations*, he writes that in the new order a much larger population is needed to sustain an army, since, on his calculation, the proportion had shifted from one soldier to eight persons to one soldier to a hundred persons. Moreover, conquest has become more complicated. "The invention of postal service makes news spread like lightning." Since "every prince has ministers in all courts and can have traitors in all cabinets," plans cannot be kept in secret. Third, "great enterprises cannot be accomplished without money, and merchants have been in control of money since the invention of letters of exchange" (*Considerations*, XXI). Montesquieu has in mind here the enormous debts sustained by Europe's monarchs in their wars of conquest. All this suggests that small republics are doomed.

In *The Spirit*, he had allowed for the possibility of a "confederate republic," "a kind of constitution that has all the internal advantages of the republican, together with the external force of a monarchical government" (IX. 1). This is more than just a logical possibility, since Holland, Germany, and the Swiss cantons are named as examples, even if they differ in their degree of "perfections." Like solitary republics, republican confederations are ill designed for conquest. Still, they are not only "capable of withstanding an external force," but "may be able to support [their] greatness without any internal corruption." In particular, "should a popular insurrection happen in one of the confederated republics, the others are able to quell it" (ibid.). *Stasis* again.

Nevertheless, one of the remarkable features of Montesquieu's work and of contemporary theory in general is the marginality of the idea of confederated republics. Montesquieu has surprisingly little to say about them, despite the fact that, as indicated, they seem to satisfy a number of his primary desiderata. One may speculate here that he may have subscribed fully to the prescription of Machiavelli that, in the modern era, republics must be expansionist and thus model themselves on Rome, not Holland. Or perhaps he discerned in the new circumstances new possibilities as well.

In the first place, the new conditions might encourage peace, not war, in which case Machiavelli's dilemma of having to choose between preservation and expansion was dissolved. Montesquieu did in fact suggest this when he wrote: "Peace is the natural effect of trade. Two nations who traffic with each other become reciprocally dependent" (*Spirit*, XX. 2). Indeed, "We begin to be cured of Machiavellianism, and recover from it each day. More moderation has become necessary in the councils of princes .... Happy is it for men that they are in a situation in which, though their passions prompt them to be wicked, it is, nevertheless, to their interests to be humane and virtuous" (XXI. 20). This seems not to be a naive expression of "natural harmony" but a consequence of observations made in his *Considerations*. It takes a great deal of money to make war, and it is merchants, not sovereigns who have it. As Montesquieu saw rightly, at that time at least, the interests of merchants were not necessarily served by war. If we add the new problems which new means of communication had brought, the ease of treachery, and so forth, it may be that "moderation" is required.

However, it is by no means clear that Montesquieu believed that war was a thing of the past, nor indeed that he would have entirely disapproved of wars of conquest. Although he said that "commerce broke through the Barbarism of Europe" (*Spirit*, XXI. 20), he also said that as "riches consist in either lands or in movable effects," "the avarice of nations makes them quarrel for the movables of the whole universe" (XX. 23). Montesquieu does not say that a monarchy ought not to embark on conquest. He says, rather, that "it ought not ... to aim at conquests beyond the natural limits of its government" (X. 9). Exceeding that limit transforms it into a despotism, and despotisms, as noted, have no limits as regard their expansiveness.

But might there be, in the new circumstances, still a *third* alternative, perhaps close to the one which Athens very nearly brought off? Might this alternative be the one which England had succeeded in bringing about? Montesquieu quotes this very famous text from Xenophon:

"Athens", says Xenophon, "rules the sea; but as the country of Attica is joined to the continent, it is ravaged by enemies while the Athenians are engaged in distant expeditions .... But if the Athenians inhabited an island, and beside this, enjoyed the empire of the sea, they would, so long as they were possessed of these advantages, be able to annoy others, and at the same time to be out of danger of being annoyed." One would imagine that Xenophon was speaking of England. (*Spirit*, XXI. 7)

England was indeed an island, tested only rarely and with difficulty by invasion. It was thus that her militia and her very small army sufficed. But she was also a maritime empire with a large and powerful navy, "annoying others," but hard to annoy. More than this, from at least the time of Elizabeth, the English state had not compromised its commercial interests for purely political motives. It was, for its time, the most supremely "rational" of all the great powers. It had actively fostered and supported the far-flung interests of commerce — for example, through military intrusion into Spanish and Portuguese shipping — through a program of overseas colonization — for example, in the New World. Its colonization program differed from the programs of other great powers precisely in its organizational rationality and in the quasi-public chartering and protection of joint-stock companies with enormous privileges and powers from the Levant to India.[31]

Plainly, this is a most complicated story. But it is hard to believe that Montesquieu was blind to the preeminence that England was achieving day by day, or that he failed to see its deep causes. England had found a way of expanding which did not corrupt its "internal perfection." It had become wealthy and powerful without Spartan militarization and without the compromises which had cost Rome its liberty. It was achieving empire without risking either civil war or despotism. Indeed, by good fortune and circumstance, its transformed Gothic government, its geographical unity and isolation, its industry and commerce, England had solved Machiavelli's dilemma.

But was it a republic? Or was it a monarchy? After Montesquieu, apart from Rousseau, the models of ancient republics lost their force. It was England that became the paradigm, even if later "founders," "revolutionaries," and theoreticians of the modern state discovered that history never repeats itself.

The Americans, having fought a successful war of independence, sought another model of "republican government" and arrived, after a period of experimentation with confederation, at a solution as novel as the English state which they tried so hard to emulate. The revolt of the nobility in France issued in a violent social revolution in which both king and aristocracy were forced to give way to a series of "republican" efforts at constituting a modern state. But sketching some of this is the task of Part III.

Part III

Modern War and Modern Democracy

Introduction

What has been called "the Age of Democratic Revolution" began with a war in which thirteen British colonies secured their independence. It climaxed just a few years later with a social revolution in France, followed by fires across Europe and the wars of the French Revolution. War was a critical fact in all this. But there was also a revolution *in* war, a revolution that was critical to the emergence — or reemergence — of the idea of democracy. I say "the idea of democracy," because there is a great deal at stake in the label "Age of Democratic Revolution."[1] In this part of the book, I try to show that events in America were critical in redefining the idea of democracy.

Everyone knows, of course, that modern democracy, "representative democracy," is not the same as classical, "direct" democracy; and everyone also knows that the United States Constitution was a remarkable achievement, a radical, innovative document. In particular, it created an entirely new kind of "democratic" politics, a "democratic" politics for "an extended republic."[2] And this is precisely what made America the model for the world. But taken for granted in this is the idea of the modern state, and worse, that the American solution to the problem of government in the era of the modern state was not merely *a* solution but the best possible solution, one that was democratic without involving the tyrannies of ancient democracies. On this view, not only did French radicalism undermine the second effort at constituting a republic in the modern world, but the American Constitution was a natural, logical outgrowth of the development of older arrangements in America and of a successful war for independence.

Yet, since the modern state is not merely a large *polis*, the American "extended republic" under the Constitution was not the only possibility or necessarily the *best* possibility. In America conditions existed which allowed some very unique opportunities for realizing democratic forms; and if we want to be historical here, we should acknowledge not only a choice of alternative means to the solution of the problem posed, but that there were differrences among those who debated the different possibilities as to visions and goals. Among these differences were different visions of what we call "democracy." Moreover, the choice facing those who assembled in Philadelphia was not merely between the Articles of Confederation as they stood and the Constitution as it was subsequently defined.

It has been a prominent feature of a sizeable portion of American historiography – ill acknowledged in American textbooks and on commemorative occasions – that the Constitution was motivated by antidemocratic sentiment;[3] but the usual argument is incomplete and perhaps even misstated. In the present view, it needs to be seen in conjunction with the problem of war and of foreign policy, the problem articulated by Plato and Machiavelli, that of the relation of a "constitution" to the choice between a policy of preservation and a policy of expansion. The ideas of Machiavelli and Montesquieu were critical here.

But the American Founders were innovators. If, as a proto-modern state, England was a "republic disguised as a monarchy," that would make the United States a modern republic, the first of the truly modern states. This involved transformations of the older theories in subtle – and radical –ways, ways which turned out to be highly significant in terms of the world's understanding of democracy. While there is no way to assess sweeping counterfactual judgments in history, and hence no way to know what might have been the consequences had the Constitution failed, it might well have turned out that the consequence for democracy would have been enormous, not because the United States – a fraudulent name as it turned out – would have failed, but because it might have succeeded with institutions which were far more democratic. It may well be that the "democracy" which Americans got was far better than the democracy they thought they had and which they might have had. The American Founders were extraordinarily successful, not only in the sense that they managed to create an enduring form of modern polity suited to a world of aggrandizement, but also in that their ideological victory was so complete that it remains almost impossible in the era of the modern state to take seriously even the possibility of forms of polity which are *more* democratic.

5

The American War of Independence

Athens and America

The Seven Years' War (1756−63) was worldwide, beginning strictly with
hostilities between England and France in India in 1751 and in North
America in 1754. When it was over, the East India Company was able to
extend its hegemony over some two million square miles, from Afghanistan
to China, and France had yielded most of Canada to Great Britain and the
Upper Missouri to Spain. In North America, Britain had some fifteen
regiments totaling about 6,000 troops, sprinkled from St Augustine to
Quebec.[1] This was modern empire, the paradigm of empire for Hume and,
later, for Alexander Hamilton. All this was expensive; and the British
national debt stood at £122,603,336 in 1763. The colonists were lightly
taxed; yet it could hardly be denied that they had benefited from the war
fought by the redcoats. But it was when Grenville secured passage of the
Sugar Act in 1764 and the Stamp Act in 1765 so as to raise £200,000 to
help maintain the British army in the colonies that the troubles began.

Although there is still argument about who bears responsibility for what,
one or two points which sometimes go unnoticed bear emphasis.[2] First, the
colonists were nondependent citizens who were by no means unaccustomed
to soldiering. An extensive militia system was in existence in the colonies,
and able-bodied citizens were expected to attend regular − if sporadic and
inadequate − training sessions and to serve in defense of the colony if and
when they were needed. Unlike their opponents in the War of Independence, British redcoats and German mercenaries, the "patriots" were not
professionals, but ordinary productive citizens: farmers, mechanics, merchants, and lawyers. For the most part, they were defending their own
property. The point is critical, not just because it affected the attitudes of
soldiers to the war, but because it bears fundamentally on the character of
the "revolution" itself. To anticipate somewhat, because slavery had pre-

vented the growth of a large, propertyless class of indigent freemen, because, therefore, this was not a conflict between haves and have-nots, the war of liberation was not like twentieth-century wars of national liberation, or even, in this respect, like the French Revolution which followed on its heels. The point is well summarized by Edmund Morgan:

> Had the southern plantations not shifted from free to slave labor, had the planters continued to import masses of indentured servants and continued to pour them into their own and other colonies a few years later as indigent freedmen, then the picture of social mobility in the colonial period and of class conflict in the Revolution might have been quite different. The Minutesmen of 1775 might have been truly a rabble in arms, ready to turn from fighting the British to fighting their well-to-do neighbors. . . . But in the century between 1676 and 1776 the growth of slavery had curbed the growth of a free, depressed lower class and correspondingly magnified the social and economic opportunities of whites. It is perhaps the greatest irony of a Revolution fought in the name of freedom, a Revolution that indeed advanced the cause of freedom throughout the world, that the men who carried it out were able to unite against British oppression because they had so completely and successfully oppressed the largest segment of their own laboring population.[3]

The comparison to Athens is stunning!

If for the European, "the Life of the Soldier is the property of King," as General Burgoyne had put the matter, Americans now rediscovered the ancient principle that soldiers had to be citizens whose lives — and property — were their own. Indeed, because they fought so as to be able to return to their farms as free men, they increasingly thought of the government as theirs — and this in the strictest of senses.[4]

It is hard to overestimate the importance of this, both during the war, during the so-called crisis period, and later, with the return of Jacobin-inspired radicalism in the 1790s. Moreover, "the militia system reinforced the provincialism that was a salient characteristic of the colonial period. The county court, the town meeting, the church congregation, and the military unity consisted of local people under local leadership, meeting local needs."[5] If we are to grasp the nature of the explosion of democratic sentiment in America, American hostility to "standing armies," the problems of the Confederation, and the quasi-war with France in 1798–9, we will need to keep these facts firmly in mind.

Citizens versus Professionals

This is not to say that the war was won by militia units fighting British regulars and German professionals. One of the first acts of the Second Continental Congress was the creation of the "Continental Army." The democratic, provincialist character of the typical patriot, whether he served in a militia unit or as a volunteer or conscript in the Continental Army, caused enormous difficulties for General George Washington and his officers. Campaigns were planned with the terms of enlistment in mind. But the main problem, to quote Joseph Reed, Washington's secretary, echoing Machiavelli, was this: "To attempt to introduce discipline and subordination into a new army must always be a work of great difficulty, but where the principles of democracy so universally prevail, where so great an equality and so thorough a leveling spirit predominates, either no discipline can be established, or he who attempts it must become odious and detestable."[6]

The decamping of militia units and the expiration of enlistments was an ongoing problem. For example, within a week of the Battle of Long Island in August 1776, "the 8,000 Connecticut irregulars had dwindled to 2,000."[7]. At Trenton in December 1776, Pennsylvania militia left for home, and Washington offered a bounty of $10 to keep Continentals for another six weeks.[8] That Gates gave generous terms to Burgoyne after Saratoga was in part because "his militia dominated army might not remain through a protracted siege" otherwise.[9]

Everyone wanted the Continental Army to be a volunteer army, and as long as the duration of service was short, not more than a year, volunteers almost sufficed, at least to begin with. But as the war continued, seemingly interminably, Washington concluded in 1778 that "the country has been already pretty well drained of that class of Men whose tempers, attachments and circumstances disposed them to enter permanently [that is, for the duration] or for a length of time, into the army." Nor did "exorbitant bounties" and other inducements help. These had little effect, he complained, other than "to increase the rapacity and raise the demands of those to whom they were held out."[10] Accordingly, Congress assented to the need for short-term conscription, under the direction of the states. A specified number of soldiers was demanded, and it was the state's responsibility to fill its quota. Perhaps inevitably, this led not only to the drafting of men who were among the poorest in the states, including indentured servants, but to the inclusion of British deserters. Finally, in the northern states, as in ancient Greece, slaves came to be included in the lists. There appear to be no reliable figures for the numbers in any of these groups, which is unfortunate. As in ancient Greece, one may reasonably infer, however, that the inclusion of the poorest men contributed to the radicalization of the revolution, and that if slaves fought ably and some earned manumission, it was still easy enough to exclude them from sharing whatever political victories were at stake. Indeed, the Constitution was later to redefine the way in which even freemen would "share" in politics.

In any case, as noted, the main battles, both those lost and those won, were fought by "Continentals." The critical battle at Yorktown was "performed by the book," straight from the principles of Vauban. Militia units certainly played a vital role, keeping control of the countryside, preventing foraging by an enemy in the field, and harassing and intimidating loyalists.[11]

Not insignificantly, the numbers of loyalists were continually overestimated by the British War Office. Initially, the British believed that the agitators were an insignificant minority. As late as 1775, William Howe, who later came to change his mind, was led to concl·: .e: "I may safely assert that the insurgents are very few, in comparison with the whole of the people." Loyalists reinforced the myth by providing false information to unwitting decision-makers in London. In 1777, Howe was arguing that the loyalists would be useful, but that he was still short-handed and that the supplement he needed could not come from loyalists. But "the chimera of loyalism continued to make Germaine − 3,000 miles away [and the cabinet officer in charge] − starry-eyed to the point that he expressed confidence that the campaign [Philadelphia, 1777] would terminate the war."[12] When Howe moved on Philadelphia, he saw that he was no liberator. The people "excepting a few individuals are strongly against us," he complained to Germaine. Indeed, "the mirage of loyalism was coming home to roost."[13]

Involving the People

The American War of Independence also heralded the end of "the Age of Limited War." As Higginbotham writes, "In eighteenth century Europe war was generally the peculiar preoccupation of the monarchy. Seldom did the aims and objectives of the struggle arouse broad popular interest and support. Indeed, to put arms in the hands of the population was to court danger."[14] Accordingly, European armies of the period had been small and had been carefully trained and disciplined. Moreover, because strategy and tactics were designed for such armies, the general population might be scarcely aware of the hostilities. This changed in America. Not only did guerrilla warfare and atrocities against persons and property take on new, significant dimensions, but it became critical, if the conflict was to be justified and paid for, that the general citizenry be involved. This became a major task of the revolutionary committees and then of the Congress created to carry on the war. There can be little doubt that this fact contributed enormously to the politicization of countless ordinary Americans.

Third, and plainly related, in the American Revolution ideology became a critical factor of warfare. This was not a dynastic war, a war to increase the size of a king's treasury; nor was it a war for aggrandizement through conquest of new colonies and territories. It was a war fought for "principles" and was to have universal significance. According to an anonymous soldier, it was a "most just and holy war, in defense of our country, our wives, children, parents and sisters, and to secure to ourselves and our posterity the inestimable blessings of *Liberty*."[15]

The war also involved ideological novelties regarding the nature of the enemy, encouraged perhaps by the presence of Indians, whose customs and ceremonies seemed barbaric to "civilized" Europeans. An event on the first day of the violence seems to have set the tone. As reported by Higginbotham, it seems that a young man, perhaps on his way to join the aroused citizenry, crossed the North Bridge at Lexington, where several wounded British regulars were waiting for aid. We do not know, but it may be that one of them called out or attempted to get up. The boy, no doubt frightened, drove an axe into the skull of the man and left him dying. The spectacle of the soldier with his head and face covered with blood was no doubt horrible enough. But in the British telling or retelling of it, the victim was said to have been scalped and to have had his ears cut off! Did not everyone know that Americans, like the Indians with whom they had intercourse, were savages?

The opportunity to exploit both racism and ignorance did not go unnoticed, even if, as is usually forgotten, the Indian nations which participated mostly fought on the side of the British. The ideology of barbarism was put to good use by Benjamin Franklin in France, for example. In order to stir up French support for the American cause and to show the depths to which the British had stooped with their use of "savages," he had an American newspaper print a wholly concocted account of a captured British document which described "eight packs of Scalps, cured, dried, hooped and painted." The packs were labeled 62 farmers "surprised in the Night"; 88 women, "hair long ... to shew that they were Mothers;" "29 little Infant's Scalps of various sizes."[16]

There was a final novelty and irony, critical as regards the final outcome of the war and its significance. For Britain faced a task that had few, if any, parallels in the past, a task that would not be taken on again with similar commitment until the twentieth century: namely, the suppression of "rebels" in a war of liberation in a land that was geographically distant. Britain had little idea of what she had got herself into. Little did she expect that some two and half million colonists would be a match for the might of the British Empire, especially if, as her leaders believed, most of the colonists were unsympathetic to the claims being made by just a few "trouble-makers." But again, this is not to say that the colonists did not get significant French help in the struggle.

After the Seven Years' War, Britain had emerged as the great power of the world. France, surely the European territory with the largest population under one king, was financially depleted. By 1787, the debt was absorbing over half her receipts, and the deficit was worsening every day. But the Americans had succeeded, and the French Revolution which followed owed its occurrence in no small measure to French perception of how remarkable the American success had been, to the revolutionary ideas which Americans had been articulating during this critical period, and, ironically, to the economic crisis in France which had been greatly exacerbated by the loan of some two billion livres to the American cause.

A War Nobody Planned

Historians know, of course, that wars have often begun without someone making a decision to go to war. In this case, the King's Cabinet was convinced that a show of strength would be sufficient to end the nonsense. But it was clear to General Gage, commander of the British regulars in Boston, that the "embattled farmers" were ready to fight, even as they insisted that they were not fighting for their independence. It turned out to be an enormous miscalculation to suppose, as Sir Jeffrey Amherst boasted, that with 5,000 men he could subdue all the colonies, or, as Lord Sandwich predicted, that the Americans would run at "the very sound of cannon . . . as fast as their feet could carry them."[17] In Gage's estimation, it might take a year to subdue New England alone, and only then if he were given substantial reinforcements for his 3,500 men. Just as the Cabinet and Parliament continually overestimated the loyalist support that would be forthcoming, so they continually overestimated the capacites of their well-trained professionals in the hands of their highly regarded generals.

This war was something new, the first of what we now take to be a *characteristic* colonial response to European empire. Hence misjudgment on the part of the British was not unreasonable. After Gage was disgraced, so too were a string of distinguished British ranking officers, including General John Burgoyne and Sir William Howe and his brother, the admiral. The Howes both tendered their resignations, knowing that, as Higginbotham writes, "their assignment was hopeless, except perhaps by so vast an expenditure of manpower as to stagger the imagination of Whitehall."[18]

The beginning of the actual fighting at Lexington on 19 April 1775, was hardly a battle. The Lexington militiamen numbered about seventy, a little less than half the adult male population. There were eight father-and-son combinations and one Negro, Prince Estabrook. Major John Pitcairn led six British light-infantry companies. Pitcairn cantered toward the Americans and ordered them to thrown down their arms. But as his men approached the two straggling lines of militiamen, the British threw off their hard-won discipline and broke into a run, cheering wildly. Someone fired. Pitcairn tried to end the firing, but his regulars were "so wild they could hear no orders." The fighting lasted about twenty minutes. Eight Americans died and ten were wounded. One British regular was wounded. Even as fighting escalated that day along the sixteen-mile distance to Concord, the total British dead numbered seventy-three, while the total number of Americans killed or wounded was ninety-three. Yet, as we now know, a war which was to last eight years had begun. Moreover, almost up to the critical battle at Yorktown, this war was carried on by a Congress which was, in the strictest sense, a revolutionary committee — of some thirty-five members, more or less — with no authority from anyone.

The Continental Congress

It is sometimes said that the insurgent colonists found themselves "in a state of nature." But one must appreciate what is meant here. It refers to the fact that the existing sources of authority were being broken down; it does *not* imply that the people lacked either notions of law and order or habits by which to structure their daily lives. Nor does it mean, accordingly, that the institutions of government had utterly disappeared. Yet, as Palmer emphasizes:

> Governors, unable to control their assemblies, undertook to disband them, only to see most of the members continue to meet as unauthorized congresses or associations; or conventions of counties unknown to law, chose delegates to such congresses for provinces as a whole; or local people forcibly prevented the sitting of law courts.....
> Violence spread, militias formed, and the Continental Congress called into existence a Continental army.[19]

All this was extralegal, and in this sense "revolutionary." It was also decidedly "democratic." But before we address this issue, we should look further at the fact that the war was managed by a revolutionary committee, the Second Continental Congress, for it is highly significant.

The First Continental Congress, which convened in September 1774, had developed out of provincial conventions and committees of correspondence, which, in turn, were vehicles of communication between the many local pockets of "resistance." The idea was not to form a new "government," but to find a way to enlarge and solidify popular support for resistance and to institutionalize a common front for ongoing negotiations with the British Government. After considering pertinent actions of the British Parliament and drawing up a Declaration of Rights, the last order of business of the First Congress was to call for another Congress to meet in May 1775, "unless the redress of grievances, which we have desired, be obtained before that time."

The legitimacy of the Second Congress did not go unchallenged, either by the British and their loyalist supporters or by the colonial legislatures. Yet concerns in this regard did not undermine the perception that unity was essential. As John Dickinson put it, "The great point, *at present*, is to keep up the appearance of an unbroken Harmony in public measures ... for fear of encouraging Great Britain to hostilities, which, otherwise, she would avoid."[20] In order to preserve the peace, then, this Congress set about preparing for war. It recommended to the several colonies the manufacture and collection of munitions and created a Continental Army, with George Washington as its commander. Six days later, on 22 June it approved its first emission of bills of credit. This citizen-army, unlike the citizens of some ancient *polis*, had to be trained, fed, clothed, and paid. And somebody had to pay the bills.

Perhaps no single item lingers so thoroughly in the popular mind as the idea that the United Colonies – and then, under the Articles, the United States – was unable to tax or to manage the enormous fiscal problems of the war and the period which followed. The product of Gilded Age historiography, of the almost universal tendency to hold that, under the circumstances, the Constitution was inevitable, and of sheer propaganda, this perception is wildly distorted.

The men of the Congress knew that the total quantity of gold and silver in circulation was inadequate; there were no banks, corporations, or insurance companies. They knew also that paper money "had usually been a sound and successful method for obtaining a medium of exchange," and that "in the colonial wars many merchants and creditors as well as debtors (not infrequently substantial property-owners themselves) approved the use of commerical paper."[21] Further, they knew that the American economy was strong, and that it could easily support the effort they conceived. There was thus nothing foolish or irresponsible in the tactic adopted by the Congress. Even more critically, the problem was not that Congress could not tax, but that the states themselves were simply unable to collect the taxes which had been called for by the Congress and which they had been willing to impose on their citizens. Rakove summarizes the crucial facts thus:

> In fact, most of the states did attempt to levy taxes and fulfill other elements of the congressional program, with the exception of price regulations, which were too controversial and too difficult to enforce to be effectively set in motion. Nor did the states challenge the

propriety or rationale of the November [1777] recommendations. Where they did fall short was, first, in the size of the levies they nominally adopted; but second — what was probably more important — in their simple inability to collect taxes or once collected, to remit the currency to the treasury when their own pressing demands required its immediate return to circulation.[22]

Indeed, "it seems unlikely that any different result would have occurred had Congress rather than the states been vested with the power of taxation."[23]

The Congress was, to be sure, an anomalous institution, and there was little clarity regarding what it was. It was born of action, not theory. If, as Rakove rightly argues, there was no time for theory — at least until the immediate problems of the war were past — it is also true, as he says, that what was at stake "was not the creation of an enduring nation state but the continued legitimation of a resistance movement whose responsibilities were rapidly growing more extensive and complex."[24] Indeed, all the evidence suggests that as long as there was a war and the conduct of that war was the responsibility of the Congress, the exact status of Congress could be left open. But concrete problems did force theoretical issues to the fore. What, for example, were the responsibilities of the men of the Congress? Was the Congress, as Thomas Burke had said, "a deliberating Executive assembly," or as John Adams was to argue, "not a legislative but a diplomatic assembly"? Or was it, as Jefferson insisted, "both legislative and executive"? Further, even if in general it was acknowledged that states were bound by the legitimate recommendations and policies of the Congress, what would make a policy illegitimate? Could Maryland, for example, vote a cash bounty to enlistees, rather than a grant of land, as Congress had requested?

Much of the confusion regarding the "nature" of the Congress is perhaps more apparent than real, and much of what is real stems directly from the fact, usually unnoticed, that eighteenth-century "governments" were only just becoming governments as we understand them. In Europe, what we call the civil bureaucracy was the king's household in function, though in form a civil service. The Congress utterly lacked a bureaucracy, and, as in the world of the ancient *polis*, its members were "amateurs" who both deliberated and, in managing a war, carried out a host of difficult, time-consuming administrative duties. John Adams, just after independence, wanted many of the members of the Congress to be replaced by men skilled "in either Military or Commercial Branches of Knowledge." There were, he insisted, hundreds "better qualified" for these roles than he was.

Second, and adding to the confusion, was the fact that since 1688 the English Parliament had been a deliberating legislative assembly which shared power with the king. As Locke had put matters, there was, in the king, both "Federative" and "Executive Power." The executive power comprehended "the Execution of the Municipal Laws of the Society," and the federative power "contains the Power of War and Peace, Leagues and Alliances." The idea was substantially repeated by Montesquieu, who held that there were three "powers": "the legislative, the executive in regard to things dependent on the law of nations," and "the executive in regard to matters that depend upon civil law."

From Bodin on, a principal mark of sovereignty was the right to impose laws on subjects and to make war and peace. And everyone, even an eighteenth-century Whig, would have said that the king was sovereign. In these terms, then, was the Congress claiming some sort of sovereignty? It already had half a king's responsibilities and indeed had them without the authority which any eighteenth-century monarch could have commanded. More because the Congress was sensitive to the problem of its own legitimacy than because it was concerned about the division of powers, it sought to draft a constitution and have it ratified.

The Articles of Confederation

Two drafts for a constitution for the confederation preceded John Dickinson's draft of 1776, a draft which was much debated and very much amended before it was offered for ratification. The date 10 March 1778 was fixed for proceeding with ratification. But ratification required unanimity, and it was not until March 1781, when Maryland finally signed, that this was secured.

In the course of the debates, Dickinson's essentially nationalist ideas were eliminated from the document. As Rakove writes, "the effective powers of government were to be divided into two spheres of authority, with respective functions of Congress and the states clearly and exclusively distinguished."[25] This suggests that the majority, at least, had some clear ideas about their institution, even if subsequent developments obscured this.

An early debate between Thomas Burke and James Wilson, who was to be an influential voice in the 1787 Philadelphia Convention, posed the fundamental issue clearly. It was whether Congress's policies were to be directed toward states per se or toward agencies and individuals *within* states. As summarized by his opponent, Burke, Wilson argued that "every object of Continental Concern was the subject of Continental Councils, that all Provisions made by the Continental Councils must be carried into execution by Continental authority."[26]

This is not as clear as one would like. But Wilson, at least, seems to have believed that the Congress has the authority to direct local agencies and perhaps also individuals to do what it legislates. He based his conclusion on two facts: first, that at this time, 1777, there were no formal limits on the powers of the Congress; and second, that Congress had from time to time worked directly — supervening state authority — with local militias and committees. The implications of his notion were thus strongly "nationalist." Burke saw this, and he resisted it:

> It would be giving Congress a Power to prostrate all the laws and Constitutions of the states because they might create a Power within each that must act entirely Independent of them, and might act directly contrary to them .... [T]he states alone had Power to act coercively against their Citizens, and therefore were the only Power competent to carry into execution any Provisions whether Continental or Municipal.[27]

In calling for quotas for the Continental Army, for example, the Congress could not conscript individuals. Only the states could. The Congress had the authority to determine the quotas, perhaps even to force them on states. Did this make the states sovereign? The wording of Burke's amendment answered this question. It asserted that each state retained "its sovereignty, freedom, and independence, and every power, jurisdiction and right, which is not by this confederation expressly delegated."

Ancient theory utterly lacked any concept of "sovereignty." It was an invention of the modern period, probably that of Bodin, in a work published in 1576.[28] Ancient confederations were leagues of independent entitites joined together for some common purpose or purposes. Traditionally, this was usually a matter of foreign policy, relating to questions of mutual defense and war. States in confederation were thus not sovereign if that meant having the right to make war and peace. In a classic defensive league, it was precisely this right which was yielded to a "congress" of "ambassadors" which "represented" the states of the confederation. When the "Congress" — the word is itself critical — decided to make war, the units were bound. On all other matters, they made decisions unilaterally. When Burke entered Congress, he "arrived with an acutely defined sense of his responsibilities. No other delegate was more determined to act strictly as an ambassador from a sovereign state."[29] On his first day, he informed the Governor of his state (North Carolina) that it was his intention, one that he faithfully carried through, "to trouble you with a letter every post."

In effect, Burke divorced the federative from the executive power, locating the former in the Congress. Some members saw that the Congress was an "Executive body resembling [the] King." But perhaps they failed to appreciate sufficiently that the Congress was a representative body which, to carry out its "federative" function, had also to legislate, even though, as

Burke clearly insisted, it was to legistate over *states.* Thus it may have seemed to many that Burke's amendment was unnecessary. While "executive" and "deliberative" functions rested in the federative power, there was no inconsistency in this since, not only were the objects of federative power strictly limited, but, as Burke had contended, against Wilson, "the States alone had Power to act coercively against their Citizens."

The issue of sovereignty was here a red herring, strictly speaking. Sovereignty had been defined by Bodin as "the right to impose laws on subjects generally without their consent." But in this sense, even the king of England was not sovereign, because by this time, he lacked such a right. This is precisely why things became so confused. As the modern state was emerging, "sovereignty" took on a number of different meanings. It is essential that we be clear about these.

The Several Senses of "Sovereignty"

If by "sovereign" one refers to supreme coercive power, the capacity to use force or the threat of force, whether or not this power is legitimated, then in England, the king was sovereign. Prior to 1688 he might claim that right on the basis of custom or, as with James I and Sir Robert Filmer, via "divine right." But after 1688, one might hold that the ground of his legitimacy rested in some sense on consent. Alternatively, if by "sovereign,' one refers to the supreme legal authority, the entity which makes law and has the (constitutional) right to make war, then in Britain, sovereignty, as Montesquieu saw, was shared. King and Parliament made both law and war.

When we turn to the American Confederation (indeed, to any classic federation), if the question is the location of the supreme coercive power, then, prior to the American Constitution, the governments of the states were sovereign, just as Burke had insisted; for only they could use coercion against individuals. They alone were "competent" to execute orders by the Congress. Moreover, prior to ratification, the Congress, strictly speaking, had *no* legitimacy. To be sure, lacking coercive power altogether, it had *de facto* legitimacy insofar as its "authority" was acknowledged by the pertinent states in Congress. Indeed, the Congress had the possibility of acquiring coercive power over the states without itself becoming the *supreme* coercive power — without, that is, becoming the central government of a state. Thus, it could have had the power to coerce the states into complying with its directives — for example, in fulfilling its quotas — without having the power to supersede or contravene state law or coerce individuals. Coercive power, like authority, *can* be divided.

In the Confederation, then, sovereignty in the sense of legal authority was divided. Under the Articles, the Congress had (constitutional) authority over matters regarding war and foreign policy, and the states were sovereign – that is, had supreme legal authority – as regards all other matters. Not only was Burke's view perfectly coherent, but the Congress acknowledged that, in drawing up constitutions, the states had acted to define the powers of their governments and that any "power" (means of coercion) *or* "authority" the Congress was to have would have to depend on and be grounded in the authority of the several states.

Indeed, as Rakove says, it is a striking fact "that nothing in the general reception of the Articles suggests that Americans were deeply interested in discussing the nature of the union they were forming."[30] But this does not reflect apathy, confusion, or an atmosphere of crisis. Neither the Congress nor the populace "thought of confederation as an exercise in creating a conventional structure of government," precisely because, on the one hand, *within each state*, they had already done this, and because, on the other, the confederation *was, and was conceived as* merely "a league of sovereign states." Moreover, this was no "fiction." It was exactly what it was and what people thought it to be. The Congress had enormous legislative, diplomatic, and administrative reponsibilities in managing the fighting of the war against Britain. But these responsibilities, rendered complex by the greatly altered nature of war, did not – contrary to so much current opinion – make it in fact, though not in "theory," a *national* government. There was no such government. There was, to repeat, a congress of representatives, "ambassadors" from the several states, exercising federative power, the power to organize men and materials from thirteen states in order to fight a war against a common enemy.[31]

Wartime Problems of the Confederation

Washington and his Continental Army may well have suffered from the inadequacies of the Congress, and no doubt there were changes that could have been made which might have helped. There was, first, the question, new to republican institutions in the modern world, of how to have a commander-in-chief of military forces and yet keep the military subordinate to civilian authority. How does one draw the line between policy and strategy and institutionalize this? In ancient republics the "government" *was* the army. The *strategos* was elected by the citizen-army in Athens, and there could be no separation of the "civil" and the "military." In a kingdom, the army was the king's army – even if, after Cromwell and the resolution of 1688, the idea of king-in-Parliament put checks on the "sovereignty" of the king and thus on the military.

There was no "American army" before Congress created the Continental Army, elected its generals and ranking officers, formulated its rules of conduct, and made decisions about its size, what it needed, and how men and materials were to be allocated. Moreover, the Congress made itself responsible for overall strategy. Higginbotham points out that it never considered, for example, a full-scale guerrilla war which might result "in the razing of towns and cities, the pillaging of fields and farms." It might well have made military sense to do more of this kind of thing. Indeed, Washington may have contemplated becoming a guerrilla when, after the famous Christmas Eve crossing of the Delaware, his skeleton army was threatened by lapsing enlistments. More generally, while many of his problems could have been solved had he had dictatorial powers − Richard Henry Lee was arguing at the time for Congress "to vest some form of dictatorial powers in Washington" − a balance between his authority and congressional control was somehow kept.

Many − perhaps most − of Washington's officers had little faith in the Congress. A leading critic, General Philip Schuyler, echoed the ancient prejudice of Isocrates: "A degree of inertia pervades all popular bodies, they are unequal to that celerity so requisite to effectual prosecution of Military operations." He continued, "Perhaps Congress labours in a greater degree under this misfortune than any popular body that ever existed at the head of an Empire."[32] Not only is his choice of words significant, but he was probably correct in this judgment. Indeed, as is clear enough, it bears deeply on Montesquieu's perception that republics, even in confederation, are not especially fitted for war.

Second, there was the persistent problem of the power of the Congress. Could Congress, for example, not order Washington to use his army to compel "any State [which] is deficient in furnishing its Quota of Men, Money, Provisions or other Supplies ... to furnish its deficiency." This conclusion from a New York resolution of 1780 was not, prima facie at least, in violation of either the letter or the spirit of the Articles. As Governor Clinton, later a strong opponent of a national government, noted, "No objection has, that we know of, been made by any State to any of these Measures." Such power "necessarily existed in Congress," he continued, "and we cannot suppose that they should want the Power of compelling the several States to their Duty and thereby enabling the Confederacy to expel the common enemy."[33] As Jefferson was later to argue, to will the ends is necessarily to will the means to those ends; and, as Madison, Duane, and Varnum were then rightly insisting, Congress did have exclusive responsibility for the conduct of war and for foreign policy. Yet Congress was understandably reluctant to use coercion against delinquent states. It is impossible to know what might have happened had it taken this step. One outcome, perhaps the likeliest, is that the states would have acceded and that the entire debate over the "inadequacies" of the Articles would have been changed drastically.

A major flaw in the Articles, no doubt, was that amendments required unanimity of the parties. Recognizing the validity of Clinton's arguments, the Congress tried to secure the necessary authority, both to use compulsion and, under the redoubtable leadership of "the Financier" Robert Morris, to put its finances on a more secure footing. It would be well here to attempt to clarify certain matters which are too often obscured or relegated to the realm of the arcane.

At least three issues need to be distinguished. First and easiest is Morris's Bank of North America, the first commercial bank in North America. Its functions were to hold government funds, to make loans to the government, and to discount its notes. Congress accepted the idea, but "Gentlemen of monied interest," wary of the outcome, did not invest in it. Accordingly, Morris's hopes that eventually the bank's notes would provide a medium of exchange for the thirteen states were not realized. With the small capital of $254,000 (in borrowed French specie) and another $160,000 in private subscriptions, it did, undeniably, serve a useful purpose. Nor was the existence of the bank in any way inconsistent with existing political arrangements.

Second, there is the matter of the public debt, a source of difficulty until at least the so-called assumption thereof in the first months of the new United States. There are two issues here. First, there was the question of whether the debt was the responsibility of the states or the Congress. Most people seem to have assumed that the debts were the states', and that the states had the responsibility of liquidating them. But Morris saw otherwise. He saw, in the first place, that the public debt was potential capital for development and that when hostilities ended, if the debt was a Congressional responsibility, this would provide a role for the continuing existence of a "central government." Second, there was the question of how the debt should be liquidated. Morris saw that the states would be strongly motivated to do it with agrarian paper money rather than specie. Rhode Island in 1786 provided the classic example. As Ferguson points out, that year the legislature established a land bank, issued paper money on loan, and made it legal tender on all debts. A year later, the money had fallen to an exchange rate of 4 to 1 specie. The assembly then compelled its acceptance at par. But by November 1788 it had fallen to 10 to 1. While this gets ahead of our story, there can be hardly any doubt that this alarmed the propertied classes, even if, as Ferguson comments, many of the creditors had surely bought securities at a considerable discount, and that "perhaps there was no great injustice giving these people paper money worth half of a tenth of its face value for securities they had bought at the same rate."[34] Morris insisted, however, both that, since the debts were incurred by the Congress, they were its responsibility, and that they had to be liquidated in a more financially responsible way. He succeeded in centralizing receipts and disbursements and in 1782 began the "liquidation" of accounts with individuals by giving them a formal money value and entering this on Congress's books. But the issue of the debt remained in the air.

Third, there is the matter of the taxing powers of the Congress. Morris, along with most of the Congress and the elite leadership, accepted the idea that the Congress could achieve solvency only if it had some taxing power. The clearest (and safest) tax was an impost, a tax on imported goods. It is clear enough that Morris saw this as only a first step, and that other forms of taxation would inevitably follow. Indeed, the power to tax was the linchpin of his entire program. However, it is absolutely critical to notice here that it was by no means clear to his contemporaries whether this program violated the letter of the Articles, even if, in a sense, it violated its spirit. Moreover, in retrospect, it is easy enough to see that an amendment to the Articles would have guaranteed the letter and at the same time have preserved the spirit.

Congress hoped that the states would see the impost as not demanding an amendment to the Articles. But perhaps predictably, this was exactly what the states did demand, thus dooming the idea. One problem was the mode of collection: whether the states were to pass laws granting the impost to Congress, or whether they were to grant a power to Congress to levy a tax. Assuming that Congress had the power to compel compliance from recalcitrant states, even the outcomes would have been indiscernible; yet there was a subtle difference in theory. The first alternative is the most obviously confederal mode, most fully in the "spirit" of the Articles; states would have been obliged to generate impost funds and transfer them to the Congress. In the second, the states would have granted the Congress power to generate the impost and collect it. We should note here that under either arrangement, the debt could have been *either* Congress's responsibility or the states', depending on the decision of the parties. As with the impost, the latter would have been more fully in the spirit of the Articles, but there would have been no threat to the integrity of the states in the former. Morris could not accept the former solution, with good reason: in the absence of any coercive power, the impost would be no better than the requisitions which had already failed to meet with compliance. The tale of the impost is hoary indeed and includes the efforts by Morris and "the nationalists" to use an innocent effort on the part of Newburgh officers – the "Newburgh Conspiracy" – to threaten the Congress and the states, arguing that under the *implied* powers of the Articles, the states were obliged to *any* federal plan for liquidating the debt.

Morris did not get his way. Still, because historians know what did happen, the significance of his ideas is always overstated. It is surely true that, had they been implemented, there would have been a stronger "central government." But it is an error to argue that implementation of any of them, the bank, the assumption of responsibility of the debt by the Congress, or the impost would have constituted steps in the loss of "sovereignty" of the states, or that, had they been put into effect, the United States would have been anything like what it was after the Constitution was realized.

In the first place, once in alliance for the purposes of war and defense, the states had *already* alienated their right to an independent foreign policy and in this sense were no longer sovereign. Any number of particular powers consequent to this or in addition to this, including power over trade and commerce, could be granted to the Congress as long as they were consistent with the continuing existence of the states as independent states. While we will return to this in discussing the New Jersey Plan in chapter 6, we should note here that if there was to be a federal army or any sort of bureaucracy to carry out tasks delegated to the Congress by the states, this had to be paid for. But unless the Congress and/or its army overstepped the boundaries drawn by the members of the Confederation, all the funding arrangements realistically considered were fully consistent with the continuing existence of the states in confederation.

But, as already noted, the states in confederation thought of the Congress as only a temporary exigency. The states were at war. When the war ended, would there still be a need for a standing army and thus for institutions to fund and manage it? Alexander Hamilton was one of the first to see clearly what was at stake. Writing in 1780, he argued that were each state to retain "an uncontrollable sovereignty ... over its *internal police*" (my emphasis), the nation would be "feeble and precarious." Hamilton had understood his Machiavelli, and he had rejected the possibility of Montesquieu's notion of "peaceful republics" joined in a "league of friendship." If the United States was to be secure, it must be powerful. If it was to be powerful, it must not be vulnerable to the failings of ancient republics. In the modern world of aggrandizement, this meant having defensive *and* offensive strength. It meant the elimination of states' militias for a "national" standing army and a powerful navy. But Hamilton and his allies were to have a struggle on their hands before they won their case.

Preparing for Peace

Both sides knew that the capitulation of Cornwallis at Yorktown, on 19 October 1781 marked the effective end of the war. By April 1783, even before the war was formally brought to a close, Congress appointed a committee to study future military needs. It included Madison, Samuel Osgood, James Wilson, and Oliver Ellsworth. At the request of Hamilton, chairman of the committee, General Washington, in consultation with his officers, prepared his "Sentiments on a Peace Establishment." Washington called for a small standing army of 2,631 "Continental troops," and, assuming that the war debt would be paid, urged that, should a foreign danger arise, a navy be built and equipped. Too poor to maintain a large standing army, but heeding the lessons of Xenophon, Montesquieu, and common sense, the geography of the United States made a navy more logical. Though he had often berated the militia, he now spoke of them as "the great Bulwark of our Liberties and independence." We now know that in saying this, he had in mind to organize the militia very differently from the way it was when he had to deal with it. Indeed, there was *no* reason why a militia system could not have been made much more efficient. As he saw, such a system would be no threat to the safety of the polity and yet, along with a small standing army, would serve the military needs of the states in con-federation. Hamilton's final report, characteristically, went beyond Washington's proposals; but, as in the case of Congressional reluctance to use compulsion against the states, the "republican" fear of "standing armies" led Congress to emasculate Washington's altogether sensible pro-gram. Again, the conseqences of this decision were to be of considerable importance.

Most of the frontier was beyond the jurisdiction of the several states; hostilities with the Indians had not ceased; and the West could be opened for future settlement. Could this be managed under the existing arrange-ments? And what of the foreign policy of the United States? Could a federation of "peaceful republics," lacking both a "standing army" and a navy, subsist in a world of aggrandizing monarchies?[35] But we need to return to the earlier period to relate these questions to the problem of democracy.

Unique Conditions and Unique Opportunities

The break with the English monarchy gave each of the thirteen colonies unique opportunities to establish constitutions for themselves. These were continuous with past practices and deeply reflected inherited British con-stitutional practice. But, as Bernard Bailyn has emphasized, prior to the war, the American experience had led the colonies to move in the direction opposite to Britain. As argued in the last chapter, from its early beginnings, the Parliament of England had been transformed from a feudal gathering of nobles into a national assembly. By contrast, the Americans, "starting with seventeenth century assumptions, out of necessity . . . drifted backward, as it were, toward the medieval forms of attorneyship in representation. . . . The colonial towns and counties . . . were largely autonomous, and they stood to lose more than they were likely to gain from a loose acquiescence in the action of central government."[36]

As J. R. Pole, Jack P. Greene, and others have amply demonstrated,[37] in America, it was also the case that the representative houses in the colonies had thoroughly taken over legislative power, upsetting fundamentally the teachings of Montesquieu and the inferences drawn from the British constitution. The factors accounting for this were many. In part, it was the commitment to localism; in part, it resulted from the drive for power of an increasingly large group of planters, merchants, and professionals; and in part, it was the result of the fact that the American colonies were colonies, so that while the king was "represented" by his appointees, the lower houses "represented" the people of the colonies. After 1763, of course, this was crucial.

In the ideological struggle with the English Parliament over taxation, the Americans made another discovery: namely, they realized that all the people should be "represented," and that if a person was to represent others he — and they were all males — must be elected. Americans did not believe that every free male should have suffrage rights, and there were some like John Adams who saw — and did not like — the implications of the new ideas. As regards the principle of voting as a vehicle of consent, Adams wrote in 1776:

> But to what extent shall we carry this principle? Shall we say that every individual of the community, old and young, male and female, as well as rich and poor, must consent, expressly to every act of legislation? No, you will say, this is impossible. How, then, does the right arise in the majority to govern the minority, against their will? Whence arises the right of the men to govern the women, without their consent?[38]

The older ideas about representation, articulated in Whig theory, sufficed for that "republic disguised as a monarchy"; but they did not suffice for the colonists in the struggle over taxation. Initially, it was not a contention of the Americans that they did not *elect* representatives. They argued, rather, that because they were a people distinct, their interests differed. As Americans, they could not be "virtually represented" by non-Americans. This was consistent with Whig theory; but when this argument did not evoke what might have been the expected response, that after all, the colonists were Englishmen, the Americans, reinforced by Paine's incendiary *Common Sense*, shifted ground. Because, clearly, Americans elected no one to England's Parliament, this became the appeal of last resort.[39] Moreover, because they saw that the implications could be radical, it was an appeal made reluctantly.

These three factors, then, localism, the aggrandizement of government by the representative body, and the shift in the meaning of representation, were all signs of a shift towards democracy. Yet no one would have said that the new constitutions drawn up by the several states were democratic. Further, just as there were differences in the class character of the states, so there were differences in the thirteen constitutions. Still, following Montesquieu, since there was no king, all were conceived as "republics."

There would be a "governor" — the term is significant — who would be the executive head of state; there was a "representative legislature," one body in Pennsylvania and Vermont, two in the others, an "upper house," a "senate," and a "lower house." Although America lacked a hereditary aristocracy, it was clear to most eighteenth-century men that "political liberty" depended on a "balanced" constitution. In this the model was the British consitution as analyzed by Montesquieu; but if England was a republic "disguised as a monarchy," in America, republicanism would not be disguised.[40]

The war provoked new "nationalist" feelings in Americans, but, as noted, it also stimulated their belief that the government was theirs. This was no war waged by a prince to extend his dominions, to settle a dynastic struggle, or to secure either "empire" or commercial advantages. It was a war fought by men and women for their own freedom. And, as already noted, the concept of representation as in "no taxation without represent-ation" quickly came to mean that one who was taxed had a right to vote for those "representatives" who decided on matters of taxation. But the new spirit of self-government did not end there.

It is worthwhile here to distinguish two additional features of the radicalization which began in the 1770s. First, as Palmer (quoted above) and Wood argue, well before the war ended, many Americans had come to believe that representatives were indeed ambassadors, elected and controlled by quasi-independent local constituencies. This recovered an older sense of "representation." Second, there was the "revolutionary," or "extralegal," replacement of constitutional forms by conventions and associations. This occurred, for example, when a representative did not act in accordance with the wishes of his constituency, and Americans were willing to complement or replace a constituted form with a committee.[41]

Whether these developments can be said to have constituted a "crisis" of "law and order" depends, of course, as much on one's attitudes as on the degree and kind of extralegal activity and the amount of "disorder" being experienced. As I will argue in the chapter that follows, it is not usually emphasized that after hostilities ceased, most people were anxious to get on with their lives. Indeed, the fear expressed by Washington's oft-quoted remark "We are fast verging on anarchy and confusion" came *later*, following the episode with Shay in 1787. To this I return. At the moment we need to be clear on the problem of representatives as "ambassadors."

Two Concepts of Representation

During this period, Americans articulated two distinct and incompatible meanings of the word "represent." In one sense, a representative could be defined, as in Hobbes and Locke, in terms of his authority. It was a mark of the emerging conception of government that those who "legislate" be "authorized" by those "governed" by these laws. In this sense, a representative need not be elected, thought he might be. A representative in this sense might be "solicited," but not commanded. He might be "petitioned," and this could apply even to the king. By contrast, a representative could be conceived of merely as an agent, "a servant of the people," elected and controlled by those he represents in the sense that he is "instructed" by them. While the legal language of "agency" might refer to either, or to both ambiguously, the idea of a "servant," like that of "instruction," was clear. While it might be held that on both views "the people" retained their *authority*, only on the latter did they retain their *power*.[42] Sovereignty was in *this* sense, as Rousseau put it, "inalienable."

Americans, little influenced by Rousseau, if at all, had nevertheless a concrete sense of this latter idea, since, as noted, it was a version of the medieval idea of "attorneyship." Both conceptions rested on "compact" doctrine, a source of considerable confusion, then as now. But the issue was joined in a forceful, clear way in the Maryland debates of the winter of 1786–7. While Maryland was in no way the most "democratical" of the new states, the problem which precipitated the debate was typically "democratic," having, indeed, the precedent of Solon. It was an attack on the institutions of private property in the form of debtor relief and paper-money bills.

In their November 1785 session the House of Delegates had acted in favor of "an emission of credit," but the Senate had refused to ratify it. Did the people then have a right to instruct their representatives in the upper house? The defenders of instruction held, rightly, that during the time Maryland had been a colony, it was not denied, even by the Crown, that members of the lower house, the House of Delegates, were bound by their instructions from the people. Moreover, as Samuel Chase argued, no one then claimed the right to instruct the upper house, since that body was not elected by Marylanders. Appointed by the Crown, the upper house properly represented the Crown. For Chase, the power to elect implied the power to bind those elected. If so, the members of the upper house were now also "servants" of the people of Maryland. On this view, as an opponent pointed out, "Planters, Farmers, Parsons, Overseers, Lawyers, Constables, Petifoggers, Physicians, Mechanicks, Shopkeepers, Merchants, Apprentices, Watchmen, Barbers, Beaux, Drayman, Porters, Labourers, Coblers and Cooks, all are to order the honourable, the legislature of Maryland what they *must* do upon the most *intricate* questions in government."[43]

The idea was radical enough, which was precisely the trouble. But defenders of the idea showed their confusion, a confusion still with us, when they argued that this radical notion was required by standard "compact" arguments. The other side could easily show that this was not the case. Alexander Contee Hanson ("Aristides") insisted, rightly, that "the doctrine of the binding force of instructions has been adopted upon a mistaken idea, that it is connected with the principles of the English and American Revolution" (p. 89). The "mistake" was easily diagnosed. As an anonymous "Constituent" insisted, Locke, for example, had held that no government was "rightful" that did not rest on a compact with the governed. Locke had further argued that when the legislature "abuses its trust ... there is a supreme power in the people to *remove* or *alter* the legislature" (p. 102). This was indeed the basis of the "right of revolution," as "revolution" was then understood; but, as Hanson also insisted, "the right of the people to bind their representatives, chosen under this compact, is quite a different thing" (p. 89).

Hanson did not deny that representatives ought to listen to their constituents, that they might advise him, or, as Hume had said, "much less, that he ought to despise the sentiments of *those* he represents" (p. 123). But to suppose that a representative was "absolutely bound to follow instructions, as an ambassador or a general is bound by his orders," is "wicked, slavish and absurd." Such a practice, he concluded, was inconsistent with "free government" as that had been understood by Locke, Sidney, Hume, Montesquieu, and others; indeed, if followed, it would soon put Maryland into "a state of anarchy and confusion" (p. 127). It was not Hanson who had introduced a "newfangled" and "pernicious" doctrine; it was Chase, William Paca, and the defenders of instruction. To be sure, Hanson, like most Americans, had moved leftward from Locke's doctrine, since he accepted the idea, not found in Locke but by now familiar to Americans, that elections were the most appropriate machinery for "choosing" a government. Suffrage did not imply instruction, however. (p. 89). This was not to be found in the Maryland constitution any more than it was to be found in Whig theory.

Of course, the defenders of instruction did not want a "free government" as Locke, Sidney, and Montesquieu had defined it. They were republicans surely, albeit not republicans in the mold of James Harrington, John Trenchard, and Thomas Gordon. That what they wanted smacked of democracy created all sorts of problems; nevertheless, this is the best description of what it was that they wanted. Two years before the Maryland debate, Benjamin Rush had rightly diagnosed the issue:

The people of America have mistaken the meaning of the word "sovereignty" ... It is often said that "the sovereign and all other power is seated in the people." The idea is unhappily expressed. It should be − "all power is derived *from* the people." They possess it only on the days of their elections. After this it is the property of their rulers.[44]

If representatives were to be "deputies," "agents," or "servants of the people," then, as "magistrates," the ancient democratic republic was the model. On the other hand, as they had also been taught, no form of polity was more "turbulent." Democratic republics tended to tyranny: they attacked the institutions of private property by waiving debts, floating paper money, imposing taxes, and perhaps worse. Moreover, they had to be small and comprised of citizens who were "virtuous."

To be sure, even among the democratically inclined, these perceptions left ample room for argument on a host of questions. For example, what are the goals of the association, the cultivation of human excellence or the effective promotion of individual "interests" — an argument between "ancients" and "moderns"? Who should be admitted to the franchise, and what were to be the qualifying conditions for office? Should the laboring classes be admitted to the franchise, for example, and should they be eligible for office? One could be a "democrat" and deny women, slaves, and the propertyless suffrage rights, or one could be a *radical* democrat and argue that such exclusions were without ground.

One could debate questions about mechanisms of recall and referendum and questions regarding the tolerable limits of instruction for representatives. Finally, there were questions about the size and relations of units. Was any state, except perhaps Rhode Island, which was probably the most threateningly democratic of all, small enough to be a republic? What was the proper legislative relation between villages and towns, and between these and the assembly of the state government? All these were genuine questions. Yet, we must emphasize that the answers to them would almost certainly have had entirely different consequences had a true confederation of states been allowed to prevail.

The conditions which led the colonies to war gave rise also to a democratic ground swell, which in turn forced a debate on the forms of government that had not been heard before. All sorts of Americans, rooted in very different class relations[45] and divided on all sorts of issues, came to the conclusion that rule ought not to be in the hands of an elite leadership governing a passive citizenry. The existing arrangements and patterns, the confederation of sovereign states, legislative supremacy, localism, and the recovery of an older sense of "representation," now joined to suffrage rights, did not give way without a struggle. In the next chapter, we will look more closely at the conditions which prompted the Philadelphia Convention which drafted the Constitution, the arguments of that convention, and the circumstances which led to ratification. At this juncture, we need to join foreign policy to the problem of democracy and locate these concretely in the decade of the 1780s.

6

The Invention of Modern Democracy

The difference between Montesquieu's *The Spirit of the Laws* (1748) and Tocqueville's *Democracy in America* (1830) is a difference in worlds. It was the events of 1776, 1787, and 1789 that gave rise to this difference, a difference obscured by failure to see what was at stake during this crucial transitionary period.

By the end of the century Americans had achieved a large, powerful state, a state which would no longer be an embarrassment in the expansionist, aggrandizing modern world. No doubt Jefferson spoke for many Americans when he wrote to Madison in 1809 that "no constitution was ever before as well calculated as ours for extensive empire and self-government." On grounds set out by Montesquieu, a confederacy was capable of indefinite expansion, but in the manner of the Lycian confederacy, not that of Rome. Rome was an empire, and once it had expanded beyond Italy, it was in no sense a republic of self-governing citizens. Americans were to have both "empire" and "self-government" — as long as one did not look too critically at what "self-government" meant. But Jefferson was absolutely correct in asserting that the Constitution had "rendered useless almost everything written before on the structure of government." The American Constitution and its ideological defense made America the first fully modern state. In it people were not ruled, though they were governed. In it, "the people" were "sovereign," and political equality made all "citizens" equal. For it, foreign policy would be primary and would be in the name of "the nation."

This chapter examines the events and arguments which led to this situation. The critical idea is the idea of the sovereign people; but the institutionalization of this, as defined by the Constitution, is also fundamental. Yet if this much is widely recognized, it is not so widely acknowledged that there was nothing inevitable about the Philadelphia Convention, either that it should have been called or as regards the "solution" to the "crisis" to which it responded. We need here to consider critically the alternative New Jersey Plan. We begin with a sketch of the crisis, then turn to an account of the debate at Philadelphia, and then to the central arguments of the *Federalist Papers*, written to persuade New Yorkers that the Constitution drafted in Philadelphia by the fifty-five who came to be called "the American Founding Fathers" should be adopted. The arguments of the *Papers* succeeded, not so much because they convinced those who had the chance to vote for or against ratification, but because they have convinced so many who came later. In chapter 7, in an effort to reveal the very different understandings of what the United States was, the thought of Adams and Jefferson will be considered; and chapter 8 will sketch the consequences of this.

The "Crisis" Period

The idea that the period between the end of hostilities with Britain and the ratification of the Constitution was a "crisis period" has a long historical lineage – a critical fact in explaining the power of the standard view. Indeed, it is not easy to get a clear picture or to assess the significance of the picture one might draw "objectively." There was a division of opinion on the situation in the new states among articulate contemporaries, but some of this was surely hyperbole, and some was based on things not as they were, but as they were gloomily forecast to become. For most people, there was nothing like what the French experienced for years after the Bastille was stormed or indeed, what Americans experienced after the stock market crashed in 1929. For most people, things were returning to normal, even if there were a host of problems to be faced, problems which any people coming out of a long war have to face. These included the burying of loved ones, the inevitable dislocations, the problem of inflation, and for merchants the reestablishing of the former ties of commerce. Undoubtedly the poorest Americans were badly affected by inflation and until the economy recovered, there would be increasing hardship as the decade proceeded. Still, if we can call this period America's first "depression," it seems that no widespread deprivation was being experienced by Americans in the 1780s.[1]

There certainly had been turmoil; but this too was settling down. The populace had been highly politicized by the resistance movement and the war. The countless committees and associations provided opportunities for self-government and for the articulation of all sorts of grievances. However, not only was this no rabble, but, when hostilities ended, most people were happy to get on with their lives. Some were not; but despite the illegal activities of Shaysites in Massachusetts, it could not be said that there was a revolution in the streets.[2]

There was disagreement among the men in government about how to solve these and other problems – the problems of foreign relations, for example. We may judge that these were not of much concern to ordinary people. But before 1786, as Rakove writes, there was widespread agreement among elites as to what was the central problem to be faced: namely the lack of coercive power of the Congress. This was a major weakness because it seemed that the financial problems created by the war, along with the problems of interstate and foreign trade, could not be solved short of giving Congress coercive power to tax and to regulate commerce. Yet it is a striking fact that, as Rakove rightly remarks, "These were admittedly substantial powers. But the purposes for which they were solicited did not presuppose a radical alteration in the nature of the Confederation."[3] Moreover, and crucially, before 1786 "there had been little if any discussion of the idea of actively using the confederation to correct the internal political vices of the states."[4] Both points are important and are sometimes overlooked.

The state constitutions were not perfect, regardless of how one defines perfection. They might have been changed in this way or that. Still, there was little concern to change them. But the question of whether this was because these "vices" demanded a solution *outside* reformation of the state constitutions seems to turn on the question of whether Americans had become lawless democrats en route to "tyranny," that incredibly influential picture of the trajectory of societies so brilliantly painted by Plato.

The pertinent event in this regard is Shay's remarkable "rebellion," an event which took on fantastically exaggerated dimensions because it occurred four months *after* the defunct Annapolis Convention (see below) and some three months *before* the Philadelphia Convention in May 1787. By virtue of its place in this sequence, it was, although a minor, contingent event, one which had stunning effects.

The war was the background of Shay's "rebellion," of course. As inflation continued there was increasing concern among small farmers faced with the prospect of foreclosure proceedings. In Massachusetts, trouble was guaranteed by financial policies which were, as Ferguson writes, "as surely class legislation as any paper money bill."[5] Most of the states had sunk their wartime currency at full depreciation, with rates as high as 1,000 to 1 of specie. Massachusetts appraised her notes at the value when issued. For example, a note issued in 1778 when depreciation was 4 to 1 was in 1781 valued at 25 cents, whereas its actual value was nearer to 2.5 cents! This extraordinary policy of Massachusetts conferred enormous gains on holders of these notes and doubled the state's debt. Taxes were legislated to liquidate this, and very soon most people were drained of notes, and many were faced with foreclosure. In 1786 there was some estimated $931,000 in delinquent taxes. The trouble began in 1782 and increased steadily. In the fall of 1786 farmers began obstructing the proceedings of country courts in Massachusetts in an attempt to delay executions for debts and taxes until a new legislature could be elected. They hoped that they might be granted relief, as had happened in other states. The conservative governor, James Bowdoin, issued a proclamation forbidding their assemblies as unlawful. It was not surprising that this act would provoke the Springfield Committee, which had thrust into leadership a former sergeant in a Massachusetts line regiment, Daniel Shays. Not only were the farmers using methods employed by Samuel Adams just fifteen years earlier, but these were men who had fought a war to defend their property against unjust appropriations. To the governor, however, they exemplified the historic drift of "democracy."

When the group, now numbering some 1,100, moved on the federal arsenal (on 25 January 1787) in the hope of securing arms – their ultimate aims are unclear – Major General Shepherd, who was in command of a local militia, fired a volley from his cannon. The insurgents broke. Another militia unit arriving on the scene pursued the rebels through the snowy woods to Petersham, where they took prisoners. Shay himself managed to get to Vermont.

What is remarkable about the whole episode is the ease with which the matter was handled, both militarily and politically. There were no deaths. Fourteen captured leaders of the rebellion were sentenced to death but were subsequently either pardoned or given short prison terms. In the April elections, Bowdoin and a host of representatives were replaced. The newly elected legislature, sympathetic to the problem, granted many of the demands. As Morris writes, "clothing, household goods, and tools of trade were exempted by law from the debt process; personal property as well as real estate was now acceptable in payment for debts. Imprisoned debtors might now secure their freedom by taking a pauper's oath. A new fee was passed reducing court charges. No direct tax whatsoever was enacted in 1787, and the year following saw a lightened tax burden." As a consequence of the new laws and the recovering economy, "law and order" were thence not threatened.[6] This is the whole story.

Shay's Rebellion had an enormous impact – at least on contemporary and later defenders of the Constitution, including here, not insignificantly, the overwhelming majority of historians.[7] The weakness of the Confederation, which many had discerned, was now joined to another weakness: namely, the state governments were incapable of maintaining "domestic tranquility" – the American expression for the absence of what the Greeks called *stasis*. With the notable but important exception of Jefferson, Shay's Rebellion became *the* evidence for this, even if, manifestly, the Massachusetts state militia had proved itself capable of suppressing lawlessness. To be sure, the state's constitution was vulnerable to the influence of "mobs" – Greek *ochlos* – even if the difference between a "mob" and "a people" may, like beauty, be often in the eyes of the beholder. Shay's group was seen as the paradigm of a mob. Still, it did not constitute the *whole* of the people, and Massachusetts, still less New York or Virginia, had not been reduced to ochlocracy. Indeed, a quite different lesson should have been learned from this event.

As Pole writes, "no administration could entirely have averted the post-war economic crisis; but the form it took in Massachusetts was in large measure a product of the policies of the General Court, a point firmly grasped by the more articulate and better informed spokesmen of the protest movements."[8] Indeed, the question, usually overlooked, is "why a government consisting solely of duly elected representatives should have pursued a policy capable of alienating a large section of the people . . . and why, under a representative government, the opposition should have been able to find no means of attaining redress, both constitutional and effective."[9] Jefferson, writing from Paris, suggested an answer. It was in response to news of Shay's Rebellion that he asserted:

I hold it, that a little rebellion, now and then, is a good thing, and as necessary in the political world as storms in the physical. Unsuccessful rebellions, indeed, generally establish the encroachments on the rights of the people, which have produced them. An observation of this truth should render honest republican governors so mild in their punishment of rebellions, as not to discourage them too much. It is a medicine necessary for the sound health of government. (Letter to Madison, 1787)

Stasis was the heart of politics; it was not to be feared by a serious defender of democracy. The problem in Massachusetts was not too much democracy, but too little.

The Confederation, Land, and Trade

In August 1784 Madison wrote to Jefferson "Notwithstanding the languor of our direct trade in Europe, this Country has indirectly tasted some of the fruits of Independence. The price of our last crop of Tobacco has been in James River from 36/ to 42/6 per Ct. and has brought more specie into the Country than it ever before contained at one time."[10] Nevertheless, the British readiness to adopt unilateral trade policies was, understandably, a source of considerable consternation to many. Most serious was Britain's closure of the West Indies to American ships and the exclusion of American salt meat and fish from its ports – even if, at the same time, American ships entered England's ports on the same terms as British ships.

Moreover, the 1783 treaty between England and Spain acknowledged the Spanish conquest, during the war, of the Floridas. There was, as Varg writes, "an impending struggle," the "prize" being "nothing less than the Mississippi Valley." Further, the British refusal to evacuate forts in the Northwest was another source of anxiety. More generally, there was the whole question of the frontier, the evident direction for American expansion. These were realities that would not go away, and it was far from clear that the Articles, as constituted, would enable Congress to resolve them. Still, the last of these problems, the problem of the American empire was handled with surprising ease.

In 1780 Virginia set up a land office in its "Kentucky District" to sell land claims north of the Ohio. It was flooded with prospective speculators and settlers.[11] Congress moved to gain control. Virginia ceded her claims to the Congress in March 1784, an example subsequently followed by Massachusetts and Connecticut. With these cessions, the United States (in confederation) became an imperial power. The Territorial Ordinance of 1784, drafted by Jefferson, detailed the management of this empire and laid down the essential principles for the addition of new states some three years *before* the Constitution was adopted.

While the problem of the frontier was certainly an obstacle to the final ratification of the Articles, the states did not lapse into the prophesied "state of war." As Peter Onuf has argued, "the American states could never live up to the dire predictions of their bloody demise because, however willing, they were unable to act like true states."[12] Congress had "a superintending jurisdiction" which made possible the peaceful resolution of territorial problems. That this in fact occurred defied all previous experience. The states united were, as Onuf argues, "a community of states," different, both collectively and individually, from previous associations. In particular, the American states accepted the limitations of their sovereignty both in regard to matters of war and peace and in regard to the settlement of disputes over territory. The importance of this should not be underestimated, for it powerfully suggests the irrelevance of Madison's historical argument, offered in Philadelphia in 1787, that the examples of confederacies "prove the greater tendency in such systems to anarchy rather than to tyranny." Indeed, it suggests that he was quite wrong in asserting that "our own experience had fully illustrated this tendency."[13]

Madison played a singularly important role in what was to be. In the 1785 winter session, Madison had attempted to persuade the Virginia Assembly to grant Congress the power to regulate trade. Instead, it called for an interstate conference to consider the question of a uniform commercial policy. Seeing this as better than nothing, Madison supported the idea. The conference which had the enthusiastic support of Hamilton, was scheduled for September 1786 at Annapolis. In April of that year New

York rejected the impost which Congress was strenuously recommending to the states, and Madison concluded that, "if anything can be done, it seems as likely to result from the proposed Convention, and more likely to result [from] the present crisis, than from any other mode or time." But he was not optimistic. There was little hope that the Articles could be amended piecemeal, given the requirement of unanimity, and even less that the task could be accomplished by a convention.[14]

The Annapolis Convention was attended by delegates from only five states. In a gamble, the twelve men who came decided to recommend to the Congress a second convention, "to devise such further provisions as shall appear to them necessary to render the constitution of the Federal government adequate to the exigencies of the Union." After some five months the recommendation was endorsed by the Congress. Madison convinced Washington that he should participate, and the presence of Benjamin Franklin, James Wilson, Robert and Gouverneur Morris, John Dickinson, George Mason, and Elbridge Gerry, among others, ensured that the outcome would be taken seriously. Still, it may seem somewhat incredible that we know very little about how this particular group happened to come together. As Rakove notes, "Such evidence as there is suggests that the separate state decisions were neither the result of an intensive coordinated effort by committed 'nationalists' nor a source of significant partisan divisions within legislatures."[15] As he says, those who accepted the invitation to participate must have shared a belief that something had to be done. But in all probability, neither the legislatures nor the Philadelphia participants realized that they were embarking on a historic task. We can suppose that they hoped to do better than had been done at Annapolis and find some agreement on some critical amendments to the existing Articles. The group was no doubt heavily weighted in favor of those whom we think of as "nationalists," for many "antifederalists" refused to participate. As Morris comments, "Patrick Henry perhaps summed up their attitude when he declined, saying that he 'smelt a rat'."[16]

Thomas Jefferson and John Adams could not be present: Jefferson was in France and Adams in England, both serving as envoys for the United States in confederation. It is hard to guess the consequences of their absence.

Consolidation versus Confederation

Having convened in Philadelphia and electing Washington to the chair, the group decided to hold its meetings in absolute secrecy. Then, on the third day, the participants agreed to abandon their explicit mandate and to consider, *de nova*, plans for a "national government." That they opted for secrecy was not in itself remarkable. What *was* remarkable is that, sitting smack in the middle of America's largest city for four months, they were *able* to keep their negotiations secret. As Rakove writes, "It was a curious counterpoint to the tumult of state politics in the 1780's and indeed to a whole generation of political ferment, suggesting that the turbulence of the preceding years had crested somewhere below the national level, held within the limits of local conflicts over debts and taxes, roads and banks, and the rights of religious dissenters and loyalist refugees." He would also seem to be correct in suggesting that the subsequent ratification was primarily neither a function of the response to crisis nor the product of elite manipulation of mass opinion. "Deference on the part of those who were predisposed to favor a stronger federal government, indifference or simply ignorance among those who might later see the Constitution as a reaction against local autonomy; this is perhaps the most that can be said about the state of public opinion during the summer of 1787."[17]

The fundamental theme of the Convention was set when, in response to a doubt raised by General Pinckney, Gouverneur Morris "explained the distinction between a *federal* and *national, supreme,* Gov[ernment]."[18] Pinckney had doubted whether the act of Congress which recommended the Convention "could authorize a discussion of a System founded on different principles from the federal Constitution" (p. 35). Morris's "explanation" implied that this was not a problem, since a federal system was "a mere compact resting on the good faith of the parties; the latter [a national system] having a compleat [sic] and compulsive operation." Morris contended "that in all Communities there must be one supreme power, and one only." As we now know, it was exactly the task of Madison, Hamilton, and James Wilson to show that if it was "compulsion" that was needed, then there *had* to be a "national" government, and that this would *not* involve a different "set of principles." On the view they would go on to promote, if in any political society there had to be but one supreme power, a sovereign, then in the new republic, this power would rest in the people themselves. The equivocality of "sovereignty" would now come home to roost.

But, as in older debates in 1777 over the nature of the Congress, there were members present who were not misled by Morris's unhelpful "explanation." We can see this by considering, if briefly, the two plans which were considered: the Virginia Plan, brilliantly defended by Madison, and the New Jersey Plan, which offered a strengthened "confederation" as that had been classically understood. It was, as William Patterson rightly said, "purely federal," in contradistinction to the Virginia Plan. John Lansing Jr., who, along with his colleague from New York, Robert Yates, was later to leave the Convention in protest, pointed out that the Virginia Plan was "totally novel." There was, he said, "no parallel . . . to be found" (p. 122).

George Mason, Lansing, and Edmund Randolph, on opposite sides of the debate in Philadelphia, correctly grasped the difference between the two plans, even if Hamilton and Madison subsequently succeeded in convincing Americans that "in principle" there was no difference.

Colonel Mason rightly contended that, as "under the existing Confederacy, Cong[ress] represent[s] the *States*, not the *people* of the States; [its] acts operate on the *States*, not on the individuals" (p. 75). Alexander Martin supported this view, saying that "the General Gov[ernment] was meant merely to preserve the State Govern[ments], not to govern individuals." Randolph, acknowledging the point but denying its desirability, insisted that "we must resort to a National *Legislation over individuals*, for which Cong[resses] are unfit" (p. 128). The difference was perfectly clear, even if, as Madison and later writers would argue, there was in the Virginia Plan a "dual jurisdiction." At the Virginia ratification convention, Patrick Henry was to put the difference simply: "The question turns, sir, on that poor little thing – the expression, We the *people*, instead of the *states* of America."[19]

Lansing saw the two plans "as involving principles directly in contrast; that of Mr. Patterson says he sustains the sovereignty of the respective States, that of Mr. Randolph distroys [sic] it; the latter requires a negative on the laws of the particular states; the former only certain general powers for the general good" (p. 121). The "negative" was indeed the clearest test of this difference. Could laws made within states regarding the citizens of states be superseded or overturned by the national government? If so, then surely Congress had sovereign power; if not, then, at least as regards legislation over the citizens of states, state sovereignty was upheld.

The first proposition of the New Jersey Plan resolved that the Articles "be so revised, corrected, or enlarged, as to render the federal Constitution adequate to the exigencies of Government & the preservation of the Union" (p. 118). The second proposition resolved that Congress be authorized "to pass acts for raising revenue, by levying a duty or duties on all goods or merchandizes of foreign growth or manufacture," "to make rules and regulations for the collection thereof," and "to pass Acts for the regulation of trade and commerce as well as with foreign nations as with each other" (p. 119). The first two powers in no way affected the governance of citizens, even though the Congress would have needed a civil bureaucracy to carry out these tasks. To handle the infraction of trade regulations by individuals in states, the resolution envisaged that infractions and punishments would be determined by the state's judiciary, with an appeal process to a common federal judiciary.

The third proposition gave the Congress the authority to demand, when necessary, money requisitions from states (proportional to their free populations) *and* authorized it "to direct the collection thereof in the noncomplying States" (ibid.). This involved giving the Congress coercive powers against the states. But the resolution put limits on this: the specific exercise of these powers required the consent of some proportion of the existing states, the percent to be decided by the Convention. Unanimity would not work; but perhaps a simple majority of the states, two-thirds say, could authorize coercive compliance with regard to delinquent states.

On Tuesday 19 June, after a long speech by Madison, the New Jersey Plan was rejected by a vote of seven to three, with only New York, New Jersey, and Delaware voting in favor of it. The Maryland delegation was divided. It is impossible to say what motivated the individual decisions, but it is clear that in the subsequent debate, the defenders of the alternative, the Virginia Plan, were able to take enormous advantage of ambiguities in the key terms, ambiguities which they themselves had either introduced or propagated in Philadelphia.

As I have already noted, Morris began doing this on the first day. But perhaps the most important move was that of Hamilton. In his first comments at the Convention, the day before the vote on the New Jersey Plan, Hamilton argued that "different Confederacies have different powers, and exercise them in different ways. In some the powers are exercised over collective bodies; in others over individuals, as in the German diet – & among ourselves in the cases of piracy. Great latitude therefore must be given to the signification of the term."[20] No doubt "confederation," like "sovereignty" and "representation" (see chapter 5), was used equivocally, something that could be exploited to great advantage. The issues, however, were not semantic but real. Were there genuine distinctions to be drawn, whatever the terms used? As regards "confederation," Hamilton argued that the distinction between the older arrangement and the new one, regarding legislating over states versus individuals, was "arbitrary," that "there is no absolute rule on the subject," and that "so long as the separate organizations of the members be not abolished ... it would still be, in fact and theory, an association of states, or a confederacy." Hence Hamilton's ninth *Federalist Paper* concluded, falsely, that the proposed Constitution "fully corresponds, in every rational import of the terms, with the idea of a federal government."[21]

The move was brilliant. On the one hand, it was plain that legislation regarding war and peace by a national congress, even in a classic defensive league, had direct effects on individuals in the several states. Indeed, in arguing against the proposed Constitution at the New York ratifying convention, antinationalist Melancthon Smith had admitted that "the general government ought to operate on individuals to a certain degree."[22] But so, what was the quarrel about? On the other hand, the Constitution did not abolish "the separate organizations of the members," down to the most local of organizations. Nevertheless, it was more than intuition and confusion which prompted the anti-Federalists to stick to their guns. They discerned that if the national government were to be authorized to legislate over individuals, then effective control by local units would be lost and that, inevitably, the powers of the latter would be "residual." Indeed, it was pure nonsense to argue, as Hamilton did (*Federalist Paper* no. 84), that in the United States Constitution, "in strictness, the people surrender nothing," or, as James Wilson had argued, "[sovereignty] *resides* in the PEOPLE, as the fountain of government."[23]

But this was to be the next remarkable move, prompted by the fact, as Gordon Wood has argued, that it was clear that the problem of sovereignty "was the most powerful obstacle to the acceptance of the new Constitution the opponents could have erected." The Federalists groped to find a way to respond. The considerations at Philadelphia regarding "coequal sovereignties" and "dual jurisdiction" floundered on the rock of "divided sovereignty." How could there be one supreme legislature in each state *and* a federal government which could make laws which *superseded* those of the individual states. The Constitution created an "Imperia in Imperio," said Samuel Adams. This was "justly deemed a solecism in Politiks." John Adams agreed. However, as Wood concludes, "relocating sovereignty in the people by making them 'the fountain of all power' seemed to make sense of the entire system."[24] This became possible in an extraordinary way.

General Pinckney had not been alone in doubting the legitimacy of the proceedings in Philadelphia. Patterson, for example, had argued that "we have no power to go beyond the federal scheme, and if we had, the people are not ripe for any other. We must follow the people" (Madison, *Notes of Debates*, p. 95). When the Convention had all but finished its work, the question of the ratification process was broached. The existing law, the Articles, required that all amendments have the unanimous consent of all the states. But under these constraints, this proposal – perhaps no proposal – could have passed. The majority of those voting took Madison's suggestion that a special convention be set up for the purpose of ratification, and that nine states would be sufficient for adoption of the Constitution. In defense of the revolutionary act of bypassing the state legislatures, Madison offered what seemed to be an obvious revolutionary justification: "The people were in fact, the fountain of all power, and by resorting to them, all difficulties were got over. They could alter constitutions as they pleased. It was a principle in the Bill of Rights, that first principles might be resorted to" (ibid., p. 564).

The outcome was marvelous. Understood this way, the very ratification process became not merely the legitimation process of a new government, but the act of "a WHOLE PEOPLE exercising its first and greatest power – performing an act of SOVEREIGNTY, ORIGINAL, and UNLIMITED."[25] We can note in passing that no more than 160,000 voted in elections for delegates to ratifying conventions, and that no more than 100,000 favored the Constitution. This represents perhaps 5 percent of the total free population. Had the Constitution failed, we can only wonder what might have happened to the now familiar modern doctrine of the "sovereignty of the people"? To be sure, it became a fundamental feature of the French Revolution, and in 1789 the French might still have appropriated the notion as a way of making sense of their own national assembly. Nevertheless, it should be emphasized that the idea was an *American* invention, aimed precisely at making sense of an extensive "republic" in which the "citizens" did not themselves rule.

The question of whether the states were any longer sovereign did not go away easily. It was at the bottom of the Kentucky and Virginia resolutions of 1798 and of the later American Civil War. But the question of whether the people would rule themselves soon took on an entirely new meaning.

The ideological confusion, coupled with the utter novelty of some of the key concepts, is sufficient reason for holding that the defeat of the New Jersey Plan at Philadelphia was crucial. Once the debate became couched in terms of an ineffective "federation" versus a federation with the "improvements" of the document drawn up at Philadelphia, the Federalist forces had all the polemical advantages. Not only could they argue that the new Constitution included all the desirable features of the state constitutions, but they could also appropriate the language of "federation," "representation," and "democracy" itself. Indeed Hamilton, usually and rightly thought of as *less* of a democrat than either Madison or Jefferson, was perhaps the first person to use the term "representative democracy" to refer to the new system.[26] Yet, as Wood points out, we need not accuse the Federalists of deliberate manipulation of the language of popular democracy; for, even if they knowingly engaged in obfuscation, they were not wrong in insisting that their vision of representative government was the most radical experiment in the modern world. Moreover, it was radical precisely in its institutionalization of new meanings of "federation" and "representation," a fact which still bedevils even informed discussion.[27] The idea that sovereignty resides in, originates with, or derives from "the people," along with the electoral mechanisms which institutionalized this, were innovations, as the leading men of France who initiated the French Revolution perceived accurately.[28] But it was just this that explains how the older idea of democracy, democracy as direct participation, was undermined, a fact not fully appreciated by democratic radicals in America or by the sans-culottes of 1792, who never had a chance to realize their ancient vision of democracy. To see this, we should emphasize the contrast here.

From a classic democrat's point of view, expressed in the modern period by Rousseau, the people could be sovereign only insofar as they had power. To have power, they must have control over decisions which affected them, which meant, as everyone knew, that the units must be relatively small, and if the latter were integrated into larger units, that the "representatives" must truly represent, be circumscribed by "instructions." The idea of local control, realized in America through legally constituted bodies and, during the war, through "committees and conventions," must be combined with a strong sense of representation, "attorneyship," an idea also available. The United States, with its thirteen states in confederation for purposes of foreign policy and the satisfaction of other common needs, had a national character *without* fundamentally compromising strong democracy. Indeed, in view of the unique *social* conditions of America, the United States may well have been the historically most opportune place for a modern experiment in participatory democracy.[29]

Of course, there is no way of knowing how things would have proceeded if, say, the New Jersey Plan had been adopted. Nor am I claiming that at this time a form of "proletarian" democracy (as desired by the most radical elements in France) would have resulted. Paradoxically, the experiment might have succeeded precisely because the franchise was restricted. In the United States, as in Athens, slavery might well have worked in favor of constituting an incomplete democracy! Of course, if victory in the struggle against slavery and for an enlarged franchise had taken place *within* the constitutional forms as they existed, it is impossible to judge the outcome — whether blacks, women, and the poor would have achieved some real democratic muscle, or whether apartheid would have resulted. On the other hand, the American Civil War hardly represented a peaceful adjustment to the terrible legacy of slavery.

However all this may be, during the 1770s and 1780s in America, the idea of participation was no philosopher's dream. It was evolving in practice among ordinary Americans using the materials at hand. Indeed, this was just what elite intuition found so disturbing. A radically decentralized, layered arrangement of building blocks, in which constitutive units yield increasingly specific powers to "representative" bodies as the territory and scope are enlarged, had been fully articulated in America, initially in the nostalgic terms of "Anglo-Saxon government." As early as 1776, a Pennsylvania radical writing as "Demophilus" had argued that "the peculiar excellence" of Anglo-Saxon government "consisted in its incorporating small parcels of the people into little communities by themselves." The writer continued:

> In their small republics they often met in council upon their common concerns . . . . From this view of the gradual progression of the Saxon government from the smallest combinations of meer [sic] neighborhoods to the most extensive Commonwealth of the United Colonies they ever possessed, they conceived the power of all civil government as derived only from the voluntary delegations of the whole People.[30]

That this was the view held by Jefferson seems indisputable. In a famous letter of 12 July 1816 to Samuel Kercheval, Jefferson wrote:

> We should ... marshall our government into, 1, the general federal republic, for all concerns foreign and federal; 2, that of the State, for what relates to our own citizens exclusively; 3, the county republics, for the duties and concerns of the county; and 4, the ward republics, for the small, yet numerous and interesting concerns of the neighborhood.[31]

We need to return to the democratic philosophy of Jefferson, compare it with the utterly novel Federalist philosophy, and then examine the unintended consequences of Jefferson's "Revolution of 1800." But before doing this, we must consider a text which is often, rightly, taken to be *the* fundamental theoretical text of the philosophy of the American political system.

The Federalist Papers

The Federalist Papers, written by Hamilton, Madison, and Jay, brilliantly summarized all the arguments that the Federalist forces could muster.[32] What is most striking about them, aside from the evident hyperbole of many of the claims made, is their persistent attempt to refute the teachings of Montesquieu. In this effort, the authors codified novel answers to problems of war and republican government, problems which had first been raised by Machiavelli. In this regard, the *Papers* are an enduring triumph.

Hamilton set the tone in the first with his opening sentence: "After an unequivocal experience of the inefficacy of the subsisting Federal Government, you are called up to deliberate on a new Constitution for the United States of America." The subject "speaks of its own importance," "nothing less than the existence of the UNION, the safety and welfare of the parts of which it is composed, the fact of an empire, in many respects, the most interesting in the world." Versus those "who hope to aggrandize themselves by the confusions of their country," history teaches us that "behind the specious mask of zeal for the rights of the people" is a "dangerous ambition." It has been a "much more certain road to despotism" than "the forbidding appearance of zeal for the firmness and efficiency of government" (p. 3).

Hamilton developed these classically rooted themes in the sixth paper by appealing to some outrageous history. "The celebrated Pericles, in compliance with the resentments of a prostitute, ... attacked, vanquished, and destroyed, the city of Samnians." "The same man, stimulated by private pique" or "to avoid a prosecution" or "from a combination of all these causes, was the primitive author of that famous and fatal war, distinguished in the Grecian annals by the name of the Pelopponesian [sic] war; which, after various vicissitudes, intermissions and renewals, terminated in the ruin of the Athenian commonwealth" (p. 29). Further historical examples are adduced, ending, significantly, with Shay's Rebellion: "If Shay had not been a desperate debtor it is much to be doubted whether Massachusetts would have been plunged into a civil war" (p. 31).

The "prostitute" is Aspasia, wife of Pericles. Athens attacked Samos because, ironically, an oligarchy in control had revolted from the Peloponnesian League. Athens restored democracy. It was followed by an oligarchic counter-revolution which called for Phoenician help. As regards the Peloponnesian War, if only its cause was so easily comprehended! The hyperbole of Hamilton's initial claim that "unequivocal experience" demonstrates the "inefficacy of the subsisting Federal government" seems restrained compared to his claim that Shay plunged Massachusetts into a civil war.

Of course, given that the essays which constitute the *Papers* were not "scholarly" pieces written for an academic journal, but rather polemical essays written to persuade a public, we should expect some hyperbole and some distortion, and perhaps even some outright lies. Nonetheless, countless people have believed these claims as if they were the whole truth and nothing but the truth. Indeed, competent historians writing primers in American citizenship have been pleased to pass them on as "history."

"Domestic faction" and "insurrection," Greek *stasis*, constitute the theme of Hamilton's ninth paper and Madison's far more famous tenth. Both appeal to the new "science of politics" and to "wholly new discoveries" — "the regular distribution of power into distinct departments . . . the representation of the people in the legislature by deputies of their own choosing" (p. 50). These are "means, and powerful means by which the excellence of republican government may be retained and its imperfections lessened or improved." But seeing that anti-Federalists will *also* stand by these Montesquievian principles, Hamilton poses a dilemma.

Montesquieu had argued that a confederacy of states could "suppress faction" and offer a way to "increase their external force and security." But "when Montesquieu recommends a small extent for republics, the standards he has in view were of dimensions far short of the limits of almost every one of these States." If we follow him, then, "we shall be driven to the alternative, either of taking refuge at once in the arms of monarchy, or of splitting ourselves into an infinity of little jealous, clashing, tumultous commonwealths," like those in the Greek world, presumably "the wretched nurseries of unceasing discord and the miserable objects of universal pity or contempt" (pp. 52–3). The ninth and fourteenth paper, he tells us, show the way around this.

In the tenth paper, Madison followed Hume in turning Montesquieu on his head. It will be remembered that for Montesquieu republics must be small and their citizens virtuous. Hume seems to have seen the implications of Montesquieu's analysis of "republican liberty" in Book XI. If England was a republic "disguised as a monarchy," why not replicate British institutions without the monarch as executive? Agreeing with Machiavelli, Hume observed: "Though it is more difficult to form a republican government in an extensive territory than in a city, there is facility when once it is formed, of preserving it steady and uniform, without tumult and faction." The trick was, as Hume saw, representative machinery, including an indirectly elective executive.[33]

Madison picked this up and added to it some lessons from his understanding of the tradition. Arguing that "the most common and durable source of factions, has been the various and unequal distribution of property," Madison held that since a cure aimed at eliminating faction would be worse than the disease, an attempt must be made to control its effects. In one of the earliest uses of the term, Madison insisted that in a "pure Democracy" this would be impossible, since "a common passion or interest will, in almost every case, be felt by a majority of the whole." His remarkable conclusion was that an extensive territory coupled with a system of representative government could contain faction. First, "by passing [the public views] through the medium of a chosen body of citizens," the effect is "to enlarge and refine [them]." Second, in a large republic, it is more difficult for "men of factitious tempers, of local prejudices, or of sinister designs" to "first obtain the suffrages, and then betray the interests of the people" (p. 62). This is so because the proportion of representatives relative to the size of the electorate is far smaller. Accordingly, it is "more difficult for unworthy candidates to practice with success the vicious arts, by which elections are often carried." It is more likely that elections will "centre on men who possess the most attractive merit, and the most diffusive and established characters" (p. 63).

Of course, it could be that the opposite is the case, that in a large territory, "unworthy candidates" can more easily practice the "vicious arts." But if we put this problem aside for the present, it is clear enough that the whole point of this argument is to incapacitate popular majorities, to prevent majority rule.[34]

If a faction is defined as "a number of citizens . . . united and actuated by some common impulse of passion, or interest, adverse to the rights of others, or to the permanent and aggregate interests of the community," then necessarily "pure democracy" cannot prevent the bad effects of "faction." But this is an argument against democracy only if one assumes that popular majorities will act "adversely to the rights of others, or to the permanent and aggregate interests of the community." Madison clearly assumes this, but one would have to search far to find convincing evidence to support it. Greek history provides none; nor, surely, did the experience in Massachusetts. But it is quite amazing how readily it is assumed that ordinary people, acting democratically, will be "tyrannical."[35]

On the other hand, while it is surely true to say that there is no guarantee that a popular majority will not attack property rights or act against the long-term interests of the community, why assume that a minority will not do this? As Dahl rightly remarks, "neither at the Constitutional Convention nor in the 'Federalist Papers' is much anxiety displayed over the dangers arising from minority tyranny."[36]

Yet, history abounds in instances in which minorities have both violated rights and acted against the best interests of the communities which they ruled. Finally, all elitist arguments seem to assume that there is some notion of "rights" and the "permanent interests of the community" which may be discovered *independently* of the views of the pertinent community; otherwise, it is hard to see why democracy is to be rejected. Historically, of course, it is exactly the assumption that some one or few know better than the many what the "permanent interests of the community" are which has been a license for tyranny.

Madison, like Plato and the entire antidemocratic tradition, sought a scheme by which a "worthy" minority would make decisions *for* the majority; and it is striking, not only that Madison's scheme presented a novel way of doing this, but that it came to be called "democracy"! Madison did not call his scheme "democracy," even "representative democracy," it is worth emphasizing. He was defending the idea of a "republic." The "turbulent democracies of ancient Greece, and modern Italy" are called "republics"; but, he protested, this is "a confusion of names" by which "it has been an easy task to transfer to a republic, observations applicable to a democracy only" (p. 84).

In the thirty-ninth paper Madison wrote, not unreasonably, that as regards the "distinctive characters of the republican form," if one looks at usage, "no satisfactory answer can be found." He then offers his "principled" definition: "We may define a republic to be, or at least may bestow the name on, a government which derives all its powers directly or indirectly from the great body of people; and is administered by persons holding their offices during pleasure, for a limited period, or during good behavior" (p. 251). The "good behavior" clause would make a hereditary monarchy or aristocracy functioning on Lockean principles a republic. Of course Madison would deny that England is a republic. But the only part of his definition which keeps it from being a republic is the requirement that the government "be derived from the great body of society, not from an inconsiderable proportion, or a favored class" (ibid.). Apart from the illusion of the "sovereign people," Montesquieu's analysis, ideologically unsuited to the American situation and two years later to the French, more nearly fits the facts, explaining, indeed, the deep similarities between the British and American systems of government!

Madison returned to the theme in the sixty-third paper, where, in contrasting the American system with earlier republics which had employed "representative" institutions, he wrote: "The true distinction between these and the American Government lies *in the total exclusion of the people in their collective capacity* from any share in the latter [that is, the American government] and not in the *total exclusion of representatives of the people* in the former [that is, previous republics]" (p. 428). Remarkably, in Greece and even in Rome "the people" did have some real "share" in government. Indeed, as Montesquieu had insisted, this was precisely what was wrong with them!

"Republics," then, could solve the problem of "internal stability." But could they be preserved from external threat? Indeed, could they be expansionist? These topics were the specialties of Hamilton and Jay and constitute the materials of Papers 2–8 and 15 and 16. Jay established the "nationalist" basis for the arguments that follow by noting in the second paper that "Independent America was not composed of detached and distant territories" and that

> Providence has been pleased to give this one connected country, to one united people, a people descended from the same ancestors, speaking the same language, professing the same religion, attached to the same principles of government, very similar in their manners and customs, and who, by their joint councels, arms and efforts, fighting side by side throughout a long and bloody war, have nobly established their general Liberty and Independence. (p. 9)

Some of this was manifestly false, of course. Even in 1787 America was emphatically not like Protestant Sweden, for example.[37] Some of it was true, however. True, and perhaps central, was the fact of the war. It had no doubt incited "nationalist" emotions; but it was by no means clear that these forbade a truly federal arrangement. Nor did the experience of the war entail, as Jay suggests, that the United States *was already* a nation-state, despite his assertions to the contrary: "To all general purposes we have uniformly been one people .... As a nation we made peace and war ...· as a nation we have formed alliances and made treaties, and entered into various compacts and conventions with foreign States" (p. 10). This move was brilliant. The Congress of the Confederation had managed the war and made foreign policy. Moreover, these were marks of "sovereignty" – indeed, they were normally the functions of a king, as we have seen. Jay put this fact to excellent polemical use. But obviously he knew that the

United States was not, *politically*, one nation. Indeed, it requires a simplistic notion of "sovereignty" to conclude that the United States under the Articles was *one* sovereign state.[38]

In the third paper Jay turned to Machiavelli's problem, that the first concern of "a wise and free people" is their "safety." There were two aspects to this problem in America: dangers from "foreign arms and influence" and dangers from contentions between the states. This last was reserved for Hamilton to discuss in papers 6–8.

Jay argued forcefully that a disunited America would provide more *just* causes for war than a united America. He gave a number of reasons: the "laws of nations" would be "more perfectly and punctually done by one national government"; they would be "expounded in one sense, and executed in the same manner"; and there would not be the problem that a part may be tempted to "swerve from good faith and justice." Similarly, "one good national government affords vastly more security against dangers" generated by *unjust* causes. In unity there is strength. Yet none of these considerations has any bearing on the difference between the United States as "united" under the Constitution and the states as they might have been "united" under the New Jersey Plan. But, of course, the New Jersey Plan was not now part of the consideration. Jay was correct in maintaining that the plan he was defending had distinct advantages over the Articles as they existed.

What Jay does *not* do here is argue that the new arrangement would have significant advantages for wars of aggression. We know that the government of one state can find good reason for such wars, reasons good enough to convince its citizens. Could the representatives of a state convince a congress of ambassadors from thirteen states to engage in a war of conquest? Could they then convince the citizens of thirteen states to do so? As Machiavelli and Montesquieu (and Washington, Elbridge Gerry, and others) had said, confederations are good for defense but not for offense. While one may reasonably infer that, to use Hamilton's phrase, the desire for "the grandeur and glory of America" had a high priority in nationalist thinking, we can also easily understand its absence in Jay's argument. Americans were "republicans." Perhaps, as Jefferson was later to argue, they would be proud of an "empire of liberty"; but an empire of liberty, as Jefferson appreciated, could be achieved only by "compact," not by conquest.

In the sixth paper Hamilton attacks the followers of Montesquieu and the "peaceful republic" idea. "The genius of republics (say they) is pacific . . . . Commercial republics, like ours, will never be disposed to waste themselves in ruinous contentions with each other" (p. 31). But, he responds, "have republics in practice been less addicted to war than monarchies?" Hamilton's counter-authority is Mably: "NEIGHBORING NATIONS (says he) are naturally ENEMIES of each other, unless their common weakness forces them to league in a CONFEDERATE REPUBLIC, and their constitution prevents the differences that neighborhood occasions, extinguishing that secret jealousy, which disposes all States to aggarandise themselves at the expense of their neighbors" (p. 36). Yet even if we agree that "neighboring nations" are "naturally" enemies and that a confederate constitution may prevent the "secret jealousy" which leads to aggrandizement, there would seem to be nothing in this which favors the old arrangement over the new. The key factor is the implications of "their common weakness." As the eighth paper makes clear, for Hamilton this means that the units must be deprived of a military force and that inter-unit disputes must be adjudicated and the verdict enforced by a third party, a national government.

He paints a horrifying picture of what will happen if the neighboring states remain disunited. Populous states, having the advantage of larger citizen militias, would "outrun their less populous neighbors." Moreover, as Greek history had so well shown, with citizen-armies, "conquests would be as easy to be made, as difficult to be retained. War therefore would be desultory and predatory. Plunder and devastation ever march in the train of irregulars." In the background of Hamilton's text is the specter of Athenians and Spartans burning crops and destroying cities but never able to conquer and dominate. But this desultory, predatory warring could not last indefinitely:

> Safety from external danger is the most powerful director of national conduct. Even the ardent love of liberty will, after a time, give way to its dictates. The violent destruction of life and property incident to war — the continual effort and alarm attendant on a state of continual danger, will compel nations the most attached to liberty, to resort for repose and security, to institutions, which have a tendency to destroy their civil and political rights. To be more safe they, at length, becoming willing to run the risk of being less free. (p. 45)

This is a remarkably prescient text, even though it is pure Machiavelli, of course. But the remainder of this argument is prescient in other ways as well.

Speaking for his time, he notes that the institutions which tend to destroy civil and political rights are standing armies. In a brilliant twist he argues that, of necessity, the weaker states would generate such. Since this requires, now following Montesquieu, that "the executive arm of government" be strengthened, these states would then tend toward monarchy. Moreover, by an obvious kind of logic, all the other states would be forced to have standing armies and thence to move toward monarchy. Thus, he concludes, "we should in as little time see established in every part of this country, the same engines of despotism, which have been the scourge of the old world" (p. 46).

Disunited, the United States faces "desultory, predatory war" and eventually the despotism of monarchy and those "engines of despotism," standing armies. Moreover, it is no objection to hold that standing armies did not "spring up out of the contentions which so often distracted the ancient republics of Greece." "The means of revenue ... the arts of industry, and the science of finance, which is the offspring of modern times ... have produced an intire [sic] revolution in the system of war, and have rendered disciplined armies, distinct from the body of the citizens, the inseparable companion of frequent hostility" (p. 47).

The answer follows: united into one nation, the United States will be free from that internecine strife which plagued the independent republics of Greece; but, as with England, "an insular situation, and a powerful marine, guarding it in great measure against the possibility of a foreign invasion, supercede the necessity of a numerous army." Here then was Xenophon's powerful picture of the Athenians, "able to annoy others," yet at the same time "out of danger of being annoyed," mediated by Montesquieu, now transformed by Hamilton.

Hamilton was to become critical in the "murder of the militias," his attack, a straightforward consequence of his analysis of Shay's Rebellion and his analysis here. For Hamilton, the Constitution was a compromise. One consequence of this, distasteful to him, was that in preserving the state governments, it kept alive the idea that they had a right to have a military force, an idea equivocally preserved in the Second Amendment to the Constitution. The upshot was the contradictory notion of "a national guard," a state militia under the control of a state governor. A further consequence, still with us, was the troublesome notion that "citizens" have a right to bear arms. Hamilton would rightly have asked, Is this Athens?

Nonetheless, his performance was brilliant. Where there is fear of being conquered, a people will relinquish its freedom in exchange for a promise of safety. Where wars of aggrandizement against states are likely, there will be "defensive" standing armies. Where there are standing armies, there will be powerful executives. By looking at the past, Hamilton has seen the future. But America would be favored. Not fearful of invasion, the states united could be powerful without either a "numerous army" or fear of being conquered. As he argued in the thirty-fourth paper, "If we mean to be a commercial people, it must form part of our policy, to be able to defend that commerce" (p. 211). Indeed, he hinted that "offensive" war, "founded on reasons of state," might also be necessary. "The support of a navy, and of naval wars must baffle all the efforts of political arithmetic admitting that we ought to try the novel and absurd experiment in politics, of tying up the hands of government from offensive war, founded upon reasons of state" (p. 211). It was not just regal republics like England that could have powerful executives without despotism. In this new model, a democratic republic could have a powerful executive, a powerful navy, *and* be an engine of war.

This perception of insular, republican America and the problem of war was to be critical as regards American understanding of itself in the first two decades of the new United States. It is no exaggeration to say that Hamilton's perception of this remained an essential aspect of American self-understanding until the bombing of Pearl Harbor. In the new climate, as "democracy" was redefined, it gradually came to stand in some new relations to the problem of war.

7

Politics and War in the New United States

At some useful level of abstraction, every president of the United States since Jefferson has been a Hamiltonian; and all of them, including Jefferson, have learned the lessons of Machiavelli. This is not surprising. Nor should it distress us. No modern statesmen can avoid learning these lessons. This is not to say that there were not differences between them which were real or important. On the contrary, seeing the differences between Washington, Adams, and Jefferson, and how each responded to the events of the first two decades of the new United States helps to explain how the American system of government was the first truly modern state, how there came to be a new set of relations between government and public opinion, how war and the threat thereof came to have new implications for domestic politics, how democracy got redefined, and how, despite the intentions of Jefferson and Madison, the Constitution proved to be the almost perfect basis for Hamilton's vision of a powerful commercial, aggrandizing republic led by a strong executive, without the "tyranny" of eighteenth-century despotisms.

The First Administration

In the months following the swearing of the oath by President Washington and Vice-President Adams, on 30 April 1789, a government had to be created. Jefferson, back in Virginia after five years in Paris, where he had experienced at first hand the dramatic beginnings of the French Revolution, reluctantly became Secretary of State. John Jay became Chief Justice; Edmund Randolph was appointed Attorney-General; General Knox, Washington's former Chief of Artillery, continued as Secretary of War, and Alexander Hamilton became Secretary of the Treasury. Robert Morris had been the obvious choice for the latter post but had declined. One can only speculate as to how things would have turned out had he accepted. Madison, elected from Virginia to the House of Representatives, quickly became its legislative leader.

Two problems became the immediate concern of the new government: the financial condition of the nation and how to pacify the Indians in the Northwest. Initially, neither was cause for much disagreement. Nobody wanted war with Indians. As Washington put it, "In a word there is nothing to be gained by an Indian War but the soil they live on and this can be had by purchase at less expense."[1] Knox agreed. An army would have to number at least 2,500 men, and a campaign would cost some $200,000, and this was not available.

In the new Congress, debate had begun on Hamilton's First Report on the Public Credit. Hamilton had proceeded cautiously, adapting to current circumstances the ideas of the previous period. The import of this in promoting confusion over what the Constutition had in fact wrought must not be underestimated. Hamilton had devised an intricate, conservative compromise, a new loan and the issue of federal "stock" in exchange for old securities. There were a variety of options for creditors: 4 percent stock, stock in Western lands, deferred 6 percent stock, and others. There would be no discrimination between original and present holders of public securities. The foundation of his plan was payment in specie of both interest and principal. This would be secured by an excise tax. In addition, the Government would assume the debts which the states had incurred during the revolution. Under the circumstances, Hamilton's proposal was reasonable; but it instantly ran into difficulties when all the arguments from the days of the Confederation returned. It provided the first occasion for a rift between Hamilton and Madison, a rift which was quickly to deepen.[2] In December 1790 Hamilton introduced his idea for a national bank. This produced Jefferson's first, albeit cautious, questioning of the drift of national policy.

The French Revolution

But between April 1789 and Jefferson's first intervention regarding the drift of national policy, revolution came to France. This is not the place to say much about the French Revolution; but it is essential to appreciate that every critical decision of the early years of the new American republic had the French Revolution as a deep, determining factor. Just as the American War of Independence had brought ideology into war and had re-posed the problem of democracy in the modern world, so the French Revolution quickly came to define an ideological chasm which, in alternative formulations, still divides the world.[3]

On the day after the July 1789 events in Paris, the Estates General became the "National Assembly." In August, as the popular revolution against the *ancien régime* spread rapidly, the Assembly adopted the Declaration of the Rights of Man and Citizen, surely one of the key documents of the modern world. It asserted not only that "men [sic] are born and remain free and equal in rights," but, inspired by recent developments in America, that "the source of all sovereignty is essentially in the nation," that "law is the expression of the general will," and that "all citizens have the right to take part personally, or by their representatives, in its formulation." The words were bold, and the ideas more explosive than perhaps anybody had supposed.

Indeed, they rapidly outran the aspirations of the men who had set them down. It quickly became clear that the Revolution was not to be contained within the strictures envisaged by the initial leadership of liberal aristocrats and articulate bourgeoisie. By the fall, the partisans of a bicameral system and an absolute royal veto — dubbed, significantly, "Anglomaniac or Monarchicals, or simply 'Englishmen'" — had failed to find sufficient support for their views.[4] In England, Edmund Burke was led to exclaim, "[The] old fanatics of a single arbitrary power dogmatized as if hereditary royalty was the only lawful government in the world, just as our new fanatics of popular arbitrary power, maintain that a popular election is the sole lawful source of authority."[5] Burke, of course, had not been unfriendly to the initial grievances of the colonies in America, believing that their claims were a test of Whig principles. Moreover, Burke tells us that his text was written in October 1789. It is easy to assume, but nevertheless of some importance to note, that Burke was not responding to the events of much later, the execution of Louis in January 1793, the Jacobin dictatorship, or the Reign of Terror of Spring 1793. Burke's horror at the idea that the only source of "lawful" authority was popular election suggests how rapidly ideas had moved.

The error, as Burke was well aware, had been picked up from the Americans, who had been encouraged by Thomas Paine. Paine remained an American hero, and in his *Rights of Man* was quick to respond to Burke. But while it is usually not made much of, John Adams's long, scholarly *Defense of the Constitutions of the United States*, published in 1787, was his own version of Montesquieu and thence of Burke, just as his *Discourses on Davilla*, published anonymously in 1790, was his own version of Burke's *Reflections on the Revolution in France*. But at this time, Adams's views, of which more anon, caused little stir.

Adams's views did not go entirely unnoticed, however. Without Jefferson's consent, a "preface" written by him appeared in the first American edition of Paine's *Rights of Man*. In a note intended for the publisher only, Jefferson had written that he was pleased "that something was at length to be publicly said against the political heresies which had of late sprung up among us, not doubting but that our citizens would rally again round the standard of Common Sense."[6] What were these "political heresies" which had lately "sprung up"? Were they being promoted by the new national government? Was Hamilton critical in this? And what of the Vice-President? or the President himself? It is fair to say that the minor episode of the unintended preface thrust Jefferson, just returned from France, into prominence as a defender of "republicanism." But "republicanism" was anything but a settled idea, and the recent events in France could only add to the confusion. Circumstances had conspired to produce the beginning of an ideological struggle between "Federalists" and "Republicans," or more polemically, between "Monocrats" and "Jacobins."

The Beginnings of Political Parties in America

One immediate consequence was the birth of political parties. Although we think of parties as essential to the health of "democracy," in America there were then no such things, and at that time no one wanted them. The point is important enough to pursue, if briefly. "Party" and "faction" were very nearly synonymous to eighteenth-century men. Parties represented special interests; they were therefore divisive and provoked "strife" – Greek *stasis*. As every eighteenth-century man knew, "strife" could not be a permanent condition of society. It would lead inevitably to anarchy or civil war.

Madison had railed against "faction" in the tenth of the *Federalist Papers*. But by now he was the leader of the "opposition" in Congress. He therefore needed to shift his ground. Indeed, he was very nearly ready to argue that a "faction" had secured power, and that he and the "republicans" represented the majority of Americans. Jefferson, by contrast, had always been committed to the view that the majority should rule; accordingly, he had no difficulty in his new role. The other side had a complementary picture. From their point of view, the behavior of the Republicans smacked of subversion. In 1792 Jefferson was furious with Hamilton "for daring to call the Republican party a *faction.*" It is hard to exaggerate the importance of this perception of "parties."[7] The *peaceful* transfer of power in the election of 1800 was a novelty in politics, critical in what we have come to call "democracy;" and it was a novelty which had much to do with Jefferson's perception that the election of the Republicans represented a "revolution."

In the elections of 1792, as Cunningham says, "there was little outward appearance of party organization." Nominations for elections were completely open, often the outcome of self-nomination and "freemen's meetings" in the towns or of self-generated committees of correspondence. Very little expense was involved. For New Hampshire's four seats in the House, there were eleven "principle candidates," for example. Under the system of indirect election of the president, twenty-seven candidates received votes for the five presidential electors to which Boston was entitled. Nevertheless, "tickets" began to appear along ideological lines. In Philadelphia, for example, voters were offered "The Ticket which will be supported by the Federal Interest," and "The Ticket which will be supported by the Anti-federalist Interest." But the absence of any party organization or "party platform" is suggested by the fact that seven of the thirteen names appeared on both "tickets."

Events in France were now clearly decisive. Hamilton's program, which by this time included a federal excise tax and a national bank (passed in Spring 1791), was being pictured by "Republicans" as evidence of unmistakable monarchic tendencies. By February 1792 Madison could write that the administration of Washington was "converting its pecuniary dispositions into bounties to favorites or bribes ... in a word [the government was] enlisting an army of interested partisans whose tongues, whose pens, whose intrigues, and whose active combinations, by supplying the terror of the sword, may support a real domination of the few under an apparent liberty of the many."[8]

Hamilton was justifiably angered. In a letter to Carrington in May 1792, he wrote that he had expected, as Treasurer, to have Madison's support, and that Madison's opposition had surprised him. Viewed from the perspective of the present, from the Philadelphia Convention on it had seemed that, on the question of the weaknesses of the Confederation and their remedy, they had seen eye to eye. Hamilton went on to say that

> It was not 'til the last session [the first session of the Second Congress] that I became unequivocally convinced of the following truth – That Mr. Madison, in cooperating with Mr. Jefferson, is at the head of a faction decidedly hostile to me and my administration and actuated by views in my judgment subversive of the principles of good government and dangerous to the union, peace, and happiness of the country.[9]

Indeed, as heads of state, "the Virginia dynasty" would later confirm that the policies which Hamilton had pursued were *exactly* those which "the union, peace, and happiness of the country" demanded.

In January 1793 Louis XVI was executed, and the French Revolution took an even more radical turn; but American enthusiasm for it did not wane. Indeed, a new wave of radical sentiment was unleashed as Americans claimed the cause of France as their own. "Democratic Clubs" popped up all over the country, clubs which, as Appleby writes, "attacked the forms of polite society by electing to drop conventional honorifics like 'sir' and 'humble servant' in favor of 'fellow citizen.'" An ominous turn for the established order, as Appleby writes, "it brought to the surface of public life opposing conceptions of society."[10] Confusion over just what was entailed in these opposing conceptions was important to the cause of "republicanism" and thence, as we shall see, to the redefinition of "democracy."

More immediately critical for decision-makers, in February the Convention of France declared war against England and Holland. Washington affirmed neutrality, a policy which generated a furor in the Republican press: "The present war in Europe is the cause of man, and neutrality is desertion."

The Newspaper War

We need to pause here, if much too briefly, to sketch a part of the history of the modern idea of democracy that is usually taken for granted. Prior to this time, various publications were available to literate "subjects of the realm" – the term is carefully chosen. These provided "news," political commentary, and other writings of interest. But with the idea of a citizen, all this took on new meaning and significance. If people were to be voters, they needed information. But different interpretations of the news were inevitable, and if there were to be differences over policy in Congress, then getting people on your side was *politically* necessary. Indeed, republican politics required newspapers. Jefferson fully appreciated this. In 1791 he and Madison acted to bring Philip Freneau to Philadelphia to establish a newspaper. John Fenno's *Gazette of the United States* had a quasi "national" character; but Jefferson wanted a truly national paper "which would give a more widespread circulation to the proceedings of the government and interpret events in a spirit more republican than that which seemed to guide John Fenno in editing the Gazette."[11] Freneau's paper was called, significantly, the *National Gazette*.

Initially, the editors professed impartiality; they would simply report the news. By the end of the 1790s, however, "editors were to be found who unhesitantly proclaimed their partisanship."[12] Everyone began to see, as Cunningham writes, that the Press was "a most important instrument for influencing the electorate." There can be no doubt that the first serious foreign policy issue of the new nation was the occasion for a newspaper war which enormously widened the ideological chasm which had begun to divide Americans. It also raised entirely new questions regarding "the free press" and its role in "republican" institutions. Thus, was "truth" a sufficient defense for a free press? Or was there perhaps such a thing as a seditious libel? The Sedition Act of 1798, to which we will return, gave the first Republican answer to this still unsettled question.

Trade, Rebellion, and Indian War

Meanwhile, in the Congress, Madison was continuing his struggle against Hamilton's commercial policies. For many — then as now — the division seemed to have more to do with domestic politics or ideology than the interests of the United States at large.[13] In Madison's view, "republican" France deserved favored status; since independence, the United States had been "dependent" in its trading relations on "monarchic" England. But Madison employed Hamiltonian political arguments: "We have the power to avail ourselves of our national superiority and I am for beginning with some manifestation of that ability, that foreign nations may be taught to pay us that respect which they neglected on account of our former imbecility."[14] Setting out the parameters of Jefferson's later embargo policy, Madison admitted that American prosperity depended on British trade and that interrupting this is any way would, at least initially, hurt Americans. Patriotic Americans, however, would make the sacrifice. Moreover, while Madison was arguing that the "national security" — an early use of the term — depended on making the United States autarchic, Hamilton was insisting that this was impossible for the time being.

In the summer and fall of 1794 the administration twice applied force successfully. Hamilton's excise tax was not always being collected. Riots had occurred in North Carolina, and the Administration had decided that it must do something; at the same time there was an attack on the estate of the whiskey tax collector in Western Pennsylvania. Washington concluded — on what evidence, it is unclear — that one of the Democratic clubs had instigated the "rebellion." But what to do? Would the use of military force restore order, or would it provoke a civil war? The Cabinet split. Hamilton wanted to use force immediately, but Jay wanted the President to wait until Congress convened. Washington saw that if force was demanded, it would be ideologically disastrous to use the Army, which had been created, presumably, for use against the Indians! Nothing would provide better proof to Republicans that the government was rapidly becoming a tyranny than the use of federal troops to suppress "insurrection."

The fear of "standing armies" had deep roots, as already noted; for they were seen as the instruments of kings. It is striking, however, that there was a genuine fear that the use of force would provoke civil war. In part, this was a reflection of the same paranoia which had made Shay's Rebellion so critical; in part, it was because this was the first test of federal power; and in part, it derived from eighteenth-century understandings of the ancient republics.

Yet state officials were utterly uncooperative. A peace commission was sent, with authority to grant amnesty to the rebels. Fearing that these steps reflected the weakness of the federal government, Washington resolved to use force. In September, he found grounds to justify his use of militia units to enforce the laws of the United States. With Washington and Hamilton themselves in charge, some 15,000 militiamen from New Jersey, Maryland, and Virginia converged on Carlisle and Cumberland. Just like Shay's even more famous rebellion, the famous "Whiskey Rebellion" ended quickly, without violence. Several men were arrested, and two were convicted of treason; but both received presidential pardons. "Domestic tranquility" was restored. Hamilton concluded: "The insurrection will do us a great deal of good and add to the solidity of everything in this country."[15]

It is striking here, as in the earlier episode in Massachusetts, that the lesson should have been that one hardly needed the new Constitution *or* a standing army in order to collect a federal tax, since, as Jefferson was then insisting, once informed of the facts, most reasonable people would respond reasonably.

In his annual message to Congress, in November 1794, Washington took the opportunity to justify his actions; but by assailing the Democratic clubs as "self-created societies," he undercut his otherwise even-tempered account. Hofstadter quotes Madison: "The game . . . was to connect the democratic societies with the odium of insurrection, to connect the Republicans in Congress with these societies, [and] to put the President ostensibly at the head of the other party in opposition to both."[16]

The second use of force that year was, perhaps, the United States's first undeclared war, a war which it quite literally stumbled into. All the evidence suggests that the Administration tried very hard to avoid it. During the first months of the Administration, it was hoped that militant Kentuckians could be restrained, and that escalating hostilities with the Indians could be contained. But it turned out that they could not. Then it was hoped that a show of strength by militia would suffice. After General St Clair landed his poorly disciplined army of militia units and short-term enlistments in a trap and the army was all but annihilated — 900 of the 1,400 were either killed or wounded — Washington decided that more must be done. He asked the Congress for a regular army of five regiments, some 5,000 men costing perhaps $1,000,000 per year. On 2 February 1792, Congress, now with the support of the earlier "republican" opponents, assented.

But negotiations with the Indians continued to go forward, even while hope of their success continued to diminish. In his notes of a Cabinet meeting a year later, Jefferson reported that he was then arguing for fixing a date for a negotiated settlement and for proceeding with military preparations "with the least relaxation." By 1794 the Army, with "Mad Anthony" Wayne in command, was ready. The British provided the excuse. With the news that the British, now at war with France, were seizing American ships and impressing American seamen, Washington was able to lay the blame on the British for the defeat of the protracted negotiations. He gave the go-ahead to Wayne. Wayne's campaign, to the delight of all, was a complete success. Theory had taught that a confederation of republics would not be imperial. It had said nothing about the new United States.

Washington, as the commanding general during the War of Independence, had been the natural choice for president; and initially, he had been enormously popular as such. It is remarkable, therefore, that toward the end of his term, he became subject to considerable abuse by publicists writing in Republican newspapers. When he decided not to run for reelection, the Republicans were delighted. At least they would not have to deal with the great war hero. One would have expected that Jefferson or Madison would have been anxious to take up the standard; but not so. While Jefferson was the unanimous choice of the Republican caucus, he persistently disclaimed interest and took no part in the campaign. His nomination, it is worth mentioning, was the first in which the party men in office had appropriated the function of nominating a presidential candidate. On the other side, it is probably true that, as Hamilton had it, the Federalists were in agreement that a "safe man" should be elected to succeed Washington. But, he continued, "it is far less important who of many men that may be named shall be the person." [17] Jay, held responsible for the treaty which bears his name, was a possibility, favored, wrote Madison, by "the British party." Hamilton schemed in favor of Charles Pinckney. But John Adams, who had never been identified with Hamilton's economic program but was a "safe man," became the majority choice of the presidential electors. Attesting to the continuing hope for unconflicted consensus, his old revolutionary friend Jefferson assented to be his vice-president.

The Politics of the Quasi-War with France

Adams was bequeathed the problem of a potential war with France, the background for which was Jay's Treaty. Jefferson and Madison were not wrong in insisting that the British had behaved badly in their dealings with the Americans. Nor did the Government want a war with England, even though there were economic issues at stake. The Federalists could use this argument, even if it was not clear how serious the threat was.[18]

Jay negotiated a treaty which he sent to Philadelphia. Hamilton and Randolph, then Secretary of State, had problems with the draft; but their criticisms did not reach Jay until after he had signed it. Secretly, the President submitted to the Senate the version that Jay had signed. It narrowly secured consent. This was proper procedure. Just as a king and his ministers were sovereign over matters of war and peace, so the "sovereign people," acting through its new Constitution, had acted with regard to such matters.

Madison, acknowledging that the Executive had acted within its constitutional province, nevertheless carried on the battle in the House. Putting aside the doctrine he had expounded in the tenth *Federalist Paper* and believing that "the popular will had been denied," he tried to stop the treaty. He got the House to pass a resolution "maintaining its power to pass on any treaty that required laws to put it into effect." Madison finally lost this battle, when on 19 April 1796 the House voted fifty to forty-nine to effectuate the treaty. Not only did this maneuver help widen the ideological chasm between "Monocrats" and "Jacobins;" it helped, as well, to further confound the nature of the American system of government.

The revolutionary government of France, the Directory, intent on harming the British wherever it could, responded. It turned privateers loose on American shipping, threatened — emptily — the Mississippi, and then, after the 1796 American elections, in the notorious X, Y, Z, affair — of which more in a moment — insisted on terms which were manifestly unacceptable. All these machinations were not uncharacteristic of "international" politics before this period, of course. What was different was the acknowledgment by "governments" that "public opinion" had become a serious problem and that it had, in some fashion, to be dealt with. In the new United States, where national electoral politics was getting its baptism, the problem was exacerbated, as already noted.

The point bears emphasis. The United States was the first polity with a national government but no king and king's household as its executive. Its chief executive, responsible for foreign policy, was elected. "Public opinion" had begun to assume importance in politics in England in the first decades of the eighteenth century. But because England was a "regal republic," the character of the relation between foreign policy decision making and domestic politics was different from what it was in the new United States. Indeed, until at least the time of Max Weber, writing in war-torn Europe, these differences were highly significant, much affecting the perceptions of writers sensitive to the Machiavellian imperative of modern politics: Namely, how an executive responsible for the national security was to deal with a recalcitrant, uninformed and voting public.

In his inaugural address, John Adams relieved everyone by promising that the United States would stay out of war with France. But, as Banning remarks, "The honeymoon was brief. On May 16, 1797, the President's address to a special session of Congress made it clear that new attempts to find diplomatic resolution of the differences with France would be accompanied by further preparations for defense. By June, Congress was debating bills to fortify the harbors and construct a larger navy."[19] This was good Hamiltonianism, of course, and it fueled the argument as to whether the real threat to "liberty" was princely aggrandizement or Caesarism. One side argued that the threat came from an executive with its standing army, the other that it came from demagogues who would manipulate "the people." What neither side noticed, hardly surprisingly, was that, looked at from the point of view of "the people," even representative governments were *governments*, and that they had enormous power to affect the fortunes of the people for good or for ill.

In July, Elbridge Gerry and John Marshall joined Charles Coteworth Pinckney as envoys to France. Everyone waited. The first dispatches from the envoys did not arrive until March 1798. The French were intransigent. The first inclination of the angry Adams was to seek an immediate declaration of war. But he feared for the lives of his envoys and evidently hoped that with more time he could secure popular support for a war against France. He contented himself, on 19 March, "with an announcement of a state of limited hostilities and a request for additional measures of defense." Banning continues, "To the Republicans, this shocking blow at the cause of liberty in the world seemed literally insane."[20] Whether or not this was "insane" or "a blow at the cause of liberty" need not be debated here. What should be noticed, however, is just how critical ideology had become. The Federalists saw Jacobin conspiracy everywhere; the Republicans believed that the Administration was lying about the progress of negotiations, and that it was committed to war. They insisted that the diplomatic correspondence be made public.

With knowledge of the outcome, it has been suggested that publication of the secret documents was a trap set by Adams to destroy his political opposition, and that this was part of his plan to bring public opinion around to his views. But neither thesis needs to be supposed or argued here. Sufficient that the event demonstrated, for the very first time, how in representative governments, matters of war and peace can be employed for domestic political purposes. It also proved, dramatically, how easily public opinion can be manipulated.

The diplomatic papers showed that the American ambassadors had waited for weeks for an audience. This explained much of the long delay between their arrival in France and the first dispatches. The papers also revealed that unofficial agents of Talleyrand, called X, Y, Z, in the dispatches, insisted on a bribe for Talleyrand before negotiations could begin. But more than this, the French demanded a large American loan – which surely would have brought England to war with the United States – and apologies for certain comments made by the President. Insult had to be added to injury.

The Republicans in government refused to accept this as evidence of *official* French policy. They argued that the whole business was a conspiracy by the Tories to bring Americans into a war with France. Although this contradicted the facts, more than one historian has noted that the Federalists needed not war, but at least the *threat* of war, if they were to deal effectively with the threat, real or imagined, posed by the Republicans. This is, perhaps, a perfect example of how accidents sometimes conspire to bring about what might otherwise not have been possible.

What followed was a dramatic shift in public opinion. As Banning summarizes it:

> Overnight, the public temper turned explosively against the French. New songs, "Hail Columbia"; and "Adams and Liberty" replaced the "Marseillaise" in theaters. Patriotic mobs attacked the homes and offices of republican editors . . . . A flood of patriotic addresses poured into Philadelphia and the bellicose replies of President Adams, who had suddenly become a hero to rival Washington himself, encouraged the rising hostility against the French and their domestic sympathizers.[21]

Taking advantage of the situation, the Federalists launched a limited naval war against France, the "quasi-war," quadrupled the regular army, and, with the specific intention of crushing domestic opposition, engaged in a fury of repressive legislation – the so-called Alien and Sedition Acts.[22]

Assault on Freedom?

Hamilton was again correct in saying that "safety from external danger is the most powerful director of national conduct. Even the ardent love of liberty will, after a time, give way to its dictates." The Alien and Sedition Acts form a critical episode in the history of democracies, too often vindicated or brushed aside by historians anxious to celebrate the genuine advances of the American system of government.[23] They also raise interesting and important theoretical questions, as regards both the doctrine of seditious libel and constitutional questions relating to the province of "state's rights." To the latter, we will return later. Here we will concentrate on the issue of free speech.

Everyone knows that the First Amendment to the Constitution of the United States asserts that "Congress shall make no law . . . abridging the freedom of speech or the press." But everyone also knows that this freedom is not absolute, and that all sorts of reasons have been adduced for reatricting both speech and the press. The idea at issue is that of seditious libel, the notion, roughly, that some utterances are defamatory, false, and, if directed at the government and its officers, subversive. The Sedition Act addressed such conditions. As Levy writes, "it required that criminal intent be shown; it empowered juries [in contrast to judges] to decide whether the accused's statement was libelous as a matter of law as well as of fact; and it made truth a defense against the charge of criminal libel."[24] Viewed in the light of the past, even the recent past, the Act was, "ostensibly a victory for libertarianism."

But under the new conditions – in a republic with partisan newspapers – it was clear to many that this older, hard-won doctrine was unnecessarily oppressive and, accordingly, that it would no longer do. The problem was in part epistemological. As one of the parties to the struggle, George Hay, put it, "There are many truths, important to society, which are not susceptible of that full, direct, and positive evidence, which alone can be exhibited before a court and a jury."[25] The problem was also in part political. Tunis Wortman put this aspect bluntly when he concluded that the idea of seditious libel could "never be reconciled to the genius and constitution of a Representative Commonwealth."[26] The Republicans were advocating an absolutist conception of the First Amendment in which seditious libel made no sense.

It would be well to emphasize here that this absolutist (Millian) interpretation of the First Amendment became pertinent only because, for the first time, "the people" were voters, the "opinions" of the people counted, and because the information on which those opinions were based would *of necessity* be mediated by a press with its *own* views and opinions. On this view, perspectives played a critical role in constituting information; in a republic, the formation of the public's opinions required a press which could not be vulnerable to the charge of sedition.

This left-wing libertarian view was not sustained; but it is striking that among the leading Republicans it was Madison, not Jefferson, who put it forward. Motivated by the passage of the Alien and Sedition Acts, Jefferson wrote the Kentucky Resolution; but his argument there, as is easily established, was about states' rights. It was not the libertarian argument which Madison, Gallatin, Nicholas, Wortman, Hay, and others had put forward.

Indeed, Jefferson saw a danger on the other side. If the Press could print whatever it pleased, who would believe anything it printed? As president, he was willing to go a long way to preserve the credibility of the Press. In a remarkable letter of 1803 to Governor McKean of Pennsylvania, he wrote that he sensed "a dangerous state of things." He continued:

> The press ought to be resorted to it's [sic] credibility, if possible. The restraints provided by the laws of the states are sufficient for this if applied. And I have therefore thought that a few prosecutions of the most prominent offenders would have a wholesome effect in restoring the integrity of the presses. Not a general prosecution, for that would look like a persecution; but a selected one.[27]

Jefferson's Machiavellian caution was no betrayal of his principles. On the contrary, he was responding to a genuine dilemma created by the institutions of representative democracy. It would not be many years before the real solution to this dilemma would be found. Self-censorship, even cooperation of the Press with the Government, would preserve its credibility *and* allow it to become the primary vehicle for molding public opinion in a democracy. We need not pause here to consider whether this is something which should be celebrated.

On the other hand, it is often said that Jefferson had an "idealistic and unrealizable" view of the role of the press. This is hardly the case as I see it. He was, evidently, more than satisfied with the performance of the second important national newpaper which he had a direct hand in creating, the *National Intelligencer,* instituted in Washington, D.C., early in his first administration. Indeed, a case can be made that this paper was an early *New York Times* or *Washington Post* and UPI combined. As Johnstone observes, its editor Samuel Harrison Smith, was selected to sit on the floor of the House. As "semi-official House reporter," the *Intelligencer* "came to serve ... as a kind of national news service, as provincial newspapers clipped and quoted liberally from its informed pages." Johnstone continues:

> There is little evidence that Jefferson sought to intervene in the daily operations ... or try to control its editorial policy. Even if he entertained the idea, *he had no need.* The two men, Jefferson and Smith, thought very much alike; besides, Smith knew quite well the sources of his own influence and was content to function as the semi-official barometer of administration thinking.[28]

In any case, the libertarian Republicans lost the argument; and whichever view is to be sustained regarding the justice of the 1798 Acts, there can be little doubt that they were enforced with *partisan* vengeance and that the rights of innocents were violated. One or two examples will suffice. Mederic Louis Elie Moreau had fled the Reign of Terror and in 1794 had established a bookstore in Philadelphia. When he was vice-president, Adams often frequented the shop, even exchanging copies of his own writings with those of Moreau. Fearful in view of the climate of hysteria, Moreau decided to leave; but before he could, the French consul warned him that "all those who have love for Robespierre had better get out and get out quick." Shortly thereafter he appeared on the President's list of persons to be deported. When Adams was asked what particular charges were, he replied, "Nothing in particular, but he's too French."[29] Under the Sedition Act, at least fourteen indictments were brought, and Secretary of State Timothy Pickering, taking on a novel role, became the chief enforcement officer. In 1799 he began a campaign to close down every newspaper which supported Jefferson's bid for the presidency.

Arming the Nation

But if there was a deep division regarding the role of a free press in a republic, there was a deep paradox regarding the Army. The Federalists had not been content to build a navy in defense of American interests. The threat of war had prompted perception of a need for an enlarged army as well. Successive attempts in 1798 to further enlarge the regular Army met with repeated opposition in the House. But by July, Republican opposition had broken, and a vote of sixty to eleven approved twelve new regiments and dragoons, some 12,000 new men in all. The paradox was this: that Adams, the "Federalist," now did everything he could to dead-letter the legislation! By fall he was telling McHenry, the Secretary of War, that keeping up an army "without an enemy to fight" would be disastrous domestically. He concluded that, "At present there is no more prospect of seeing the French army here than there is in Heaven."[30]

The domestic complications stemmed from complications produced by Hamilton. Adams had long since come to distrust Hamilton, who now retired from office, conspired with McHenry, a colleague and Washington's former aide, to become the leading general in America. He would do this by becoming second-in-command under Washington. Everyone knew, writes Kohn, that Washington would be but the figurehead for the new army, and that his second-in-command would have effective control. This led Adams into struggles with Washington over his role in the Army, particularly over the selecition and rank of its officers. Adams was outmaneuvered by his own Cabinet, and Hamilton succeeded in becoming Major General, second only to Washington. He then set out to recruit the officer core. Along with a host of his Federalist colleagues, Hamilton was convinced that an army was essential, not only for purposes of war, but in case of rebellion as well. He had argued as much at the Philadelphia Convention, but of course was more circumspect in public utterances. Accordingly, it was critical that politically reliable, that is, anti-Republican – anti-Jacobin – men be recruited. As Kohn tells us the story, Generals Washington, Hamilton, and Pinckney "approached every candidate with suspicion. For five hours a day they meticulously reviewed applications and recommendations, searching for talented men with suitable political leanings, attempting to assign to each the appropriate rank."[31]

Six months were consumed in this process. But administrative difficulties, contracts for clothing, shoes, arms, supplies, and so forth, reminded Hamilton "of the worst period of our revolution . . . over again . . . with caricature."[32]

So much for the cranking Congress under the Confederation! Adams, now fearful that the Hamiltonians were militarists bent on destroying the Constitution, refused to promote Hamilton to the rank of lieutenant-general when Washington died in December 1799.

Indeed, the army issue had divided the Federalist party itself. Here was Adams, firmly committed to the view that the Constitution had given the United States a "regal republic," now engaged in a struggle to the death with one of the leading proponents and theorists of the Constitution, himself an explicit supporter of the view that the English Constitution was the best in the world! One story will perhaps catch the flavor of the irony involved here. Jefferson recollected a dinner in April 1791 when Adams remarked that the British Constitution, purged of corruption, would be the most perfect. Hamilton thought otherwise: "Purge it of its corruption and . . . it would become an impracticable government; as it stands at present, with all its supposed defects, it is the most perfect government which ever existed." Jefferson, no doubt scandalized, decided that "Hamilton was not only a monarchist, but for a monarchy bottomed on corruption."[33]

Adams saw that if peace could be made with France, all the air would be taken from the Hamiltonian balloon. In April 1799, without consulting either the Cabinet or Congress, Adams asked the Senate to confirm William Van Murray as Minister. He would proceed to France to resume talks. Adams's gamble paid off. If the United States stumbled *into* its first undeclared war against native Americans, it seems to be have stumbled *out* of its second. The quasi-war with France never became a real war.

The election of 1800 was perhaps the most hotly ideological presidential contest every held in the United States; but oddly enough, Jefferson's victory was in part at least a result of the split within the Federalist ranks.[34] On the surface, at least, the two candidates seemed to give Americans an absolutely unequivocal choice (remembering, of course, that the decision would be in the hands of electors), for they appeared to be divided on all the major domestic and foreign policy issues. Moreover, their rhetoric would lead one to conclude that there were deep philosophical differences between them. But there was one gigantic paradox, in that *neither* of them seems to have seen in any clear way what the Constitution had wrought. In this the two of them, along with Madison and Hamilton, unconsciously conspired in redefining democracy. Adams's philosphy of government can be treated first.

The Philosophy of Government of John Adams

Though nominally a "Federalist," at least, Adams refused to accept the new categories which the proponents of the new Constitution had put forward in its defense. He saw in it a *traditional* "balanced constitution," which allowed the different orders in society a place in goverment. Society was comprised of the many, who were small property-owners or propertyless, and the few, the "aristocracy," "the rich, the well-born, and the able." Both groups were to be feared and both needed to be checked. The English had found the way to do this. As Adams said in the *Defense*, "I only contend that the English constitution, is, in theory both the adjustment of the balance and the prevention of its vibrations, the most stupendous fabric of human invention; and that the Americans ought to be applauded instead of censured, for imitating it as far as they have done."[35] They could not entirely "imitate" it, of course, since they had just fought a war against a king who had been "tyrannical." Nor did they have a hereditary aristocracy out of which to form a senate.

At the same time, he never felt that the Founders had come close *enough*. He feared, like Plato and Bolingbroke, that "corruption" − "the sacrifice of every national interest and honour, to private and Party Objects" − would some day be its undoing. In exact opposition to Madison's views, he saw this corruption as *spurred* by elections, not contained in them. In 1790, he explained that elections "cannot be long conducted in a populous, opulent and commercial nation, with Corruption, Sedition and Civil War."[36] Quite the opposite of Madison's famous doctrine of the tenth *Federalist Paper* Adams believed that the larger the compass of the government, the more extensive and divisive the factions. In the struggle for power, then, men and parties would resort to any means to realize their own interests. Eventually, the fundamental social division between rich and poor would bring on civil war. Adams's analysis, close to Montesquieu's, suggested the answer: *do away with the most dangerous of elections*, that of the president and the senate.

The president and the senate were elected by entire states, and the attractions were great. If they were made hereditary, the "aristocracy" − America's rich and well-born − would be denied the opportunity and necessity of interfering in elections. In Adams's view of "the balanced constitution," only the House was properly elective, the representative organ of "the people" − the poor.

These ideas, spelled out in both private and public made him no friends among "republicans," to be sure. He was accused, wrongly, of advocating that the changes be made at once, if necessary by force. But Adams was not so foolish. He believed that "the experiment [with the new Constitution] is made and will have a fair play." In 1789 he predicted that changes would be needed at "no very distant period of time." By 1813 he was projecting crisis "many hundred years" into the future. And he persistently argued that force would not be needed: "Thank Heaven! Americans understand calling conventions; and if the time should come, as it is very possible it may, when hereditary descent shall become a less evil than annual fraud and violence, such conventions may still prevent the first magistrate from becoming absolute as well as hereditary."[37] Adams hoped that acknowledgment of the "annual fraud and violence" of elections would keep Americans from Caesarism. But this would mean acknowledging a hereditary monarch constrained by a hereditary senate and a popularly elected representative body. That he should have believed this possible may appear stunning to us. Rather, it shows the enormous difference between 1776 and 1787!

In the interim, some small changes might help, including assigning to the president titles such as "His Highness" or "His most benign Highness." The title suitable for the office of president might be "His Majesty, the President." Such a title, he explained, "would be found 'indespensibly [sic] necessary' to maintain the dignity of the American people."

Nor was the new arrangement sensibly a federation. As Howe points out, for Adams it was properly called "national," "foederal" being "an improper word."[38] In Adams's view, by contrast with the new propaganda, either the central government was supreme or the states were. In his ten years as an American envoy to the capitals of Europe, Adams had had direct experience of the weaknesses of the Congress under the Confederation. He had gradually become convinced that Congress needed additional powers, but *only* as regards foreign policy and commerce. Through 1787, in full agreement with Jefferson, he believed that with some additional power, the Confederation would be entirely adequate. But in contrast to Jefferson, he believed that the real threat was "civil war," Greek *stasis*. This stemmed from weaknesses in the *state* constitutions, which he saw as insufficiently "balanced."

Howe points out that Adams had no interest in the conventions at Annapolis or Philadelphia, concluding that "Congress would have done as well, at a least Expense and in a shorter time."[39] But when he received from Jay a copy of the proposed Constitution, he quickly became an advocate of it. Congress would no longer be a "diplomatic assembly"; it would have genuine legislative power. He thus had no misgivings about the choice that had been made, but like those called "antifederalists," he was clear that it was a *fundamental* choice. Howe's summary of Adams's views of the central government showed that he grasped the critical point: "It operated directly upon the people and was intended to regulate many of their domestic affairs. Its officials were responsible to the people, not to the various states."[40]

This contributed to Adams's rejection of Madison's novel ideas about what a republic was. For Adams, a republic was *"[a] government whose sovereignty is vested in more than one person."*[41] In every republic, there is a *"first magistrate, a head, a chief,* under various denominations, indeed, and with different degrees of authority, with the title of stadtholder, burgomaster, avoyer, doge, gonfaloniero, president, syndic, major, alcade, capitaneo, governor, or king"; there is also a senate and a larger assembly which always represents the people and is usually elected by them. As he said to Samuel Adams, "Whenever I use the word republic with approbation . . . I mean a government in which the people have collectively or by representation, an essential share in the government."[42] Again, in distinct contrast to Madison, though usually unnoticed, on Adams's view of a proper republic, "the people" are not entirely excluded from having a share. They have a share, even it if it is only a small one.

Echoing the Federalist formula of power being "derived from the people," Adams now assented, as any Whig would, that "all power resides originally" in "the people, the nation," but that power delegated is power alienated. Power might be alienated, as Locke said, for one year or for life. Similarly, "the duration of our president is neither perpetual nor for life . . . but his power during those four years is much greater than that of an avoyeur, a consul, a podesta, a doge, a stadtholder" − nay, than a king of Poland; nay than a king of Sparta. Only the monarchs of England and Neuchâtel possess a constitutional dignity, authority, and power comparable to his."[43]

Finally, although the French preached that they had eliminated inequality, such was not the case. Nor can it ever be. In his *Defense*, Adams wrote: "In every country we have found a variety of *orders*, with very great distinctions," even if in America, there is no juridical nobility.[44] On Adams's view, the new "republics," American and French, had been incorrectly described by confused, if well-meaning, "republican" publicists.[45] He could accept the term "democratic republic," because "the people" did have "a share." But surely these polities did not implement democratic equality; nor, accordingly, were they democracies. Adams was too well versed in both history and ancient theory to think otherwise.

Liberté, égalité, fraternité had been a motto of the French. Moreover, as Palmer has noted, the *locus classicus* of the word "democracy" in the French Revolution is a speech by Robespierre of 5 February 1794. For him, democracy was "a state in which the people, as sovereign, guided by laws of its own making, does for itself all that it can do well, and by its delegates what it cannot." Robespierre had gone on to say: "The French are the first people in the world to establish true democracy, by calling all men to enjoy equality and the fulness of civic rights."[46] It is clear that for Adams this was unmitigated ideological nonsense. He asked, "Have they leveled all fortunes and equally divided all property? . . . Have the French officers who served in America melted their eagles and torn their ribbons?[47]

On the other hand, in any *good* government, there will be equality *before the law*, defense of natural rights, and trial by jury. On Adams's view, a good state was a liberal state; it need not be a democracy. Nor had the French constituted a just, well-ordered state. Indeed, the "delegates" of the people were, if anything, *tyrants*, precisely because, foolishly, the French had abandoned the sensible teachings of Montesquieu for the idiocracy of Turgot.

This was both perceptive and honest, certainly more perceptive and perhaps more honest than anything written by American "republicans" of this period. On the other hand, Adams's view of well-ordered polity was not what Americans had fought a war for. Adams was simply brazenly revealing his aristocratic aspirations, the same aspirations which were so manifestly evident in the policies of Hamilton, the sell-out by Jay, and the quasi-war with France. In its Declaration of Independence, America had established the "form" and the "principles" for which it had fought the war. It had recovered the idea of "self-government." Nothing was clearer to Jefferson. In the next chapter, we turn to Jefferson's philosophy of government and to his revolution of 1800.

8

Jefferson and the Revolution of 1800

Numerous writers have seen Jefferson as the American democrat *par excellence*. Surely, this is correct. All the "framers" were "liberals." All believed in the idea that persons had rights, that the right of property was a fundamental human right, that government had been instituted to secure rights, and that republican forms of government were the best guarantees of these rights. Yet these views do not define democracy. Jefferson certainly held these views, but he also had some distinctly democratic views.

Likewise, a great deal has been written about Jefferson's rejection of aristocratic values, his commitment to equality of opportunity, and his belief that the liberation of "the free and independent man" would be a sufficient guarantee of prosperity. Some of these positions contrast with those of Adams, for example; but, as with those views which define a liberal and a republican, they do not constitute the backbone of Jefferson's genuinely democratic philosophy. The latter can be brought out best, perhaps, by contrasting it as sharply as possible with the philosophy of government of the other republican from Virginia, Madison.

It is critical to notice right away that, unlike Adams, Jefferson wrote no systematic philosophy of government, no scholarly books on the topic, and that unlike even Madison, he penned no polemical essays. Nor, it seems, did he often enter public debate or ever give a campaign speech. This was, we must remember, an early time in the genesis of modern democracy. Indeed, aside from the Declaration of Independence, his two inaugural addresses, annual messages to the Congress, the Kentucky Resolution, and his autobiography, what he wrote and said was not offered for public consumption. (Indeed, he was careful not to let it be known that he authored the Kentucky Resolution.) He did write letters, of course, thousands of them. As he put it, letter writing was "the burden of my life." It is mainly from these letters that scholars have attempted to piece together his philosophy and his vision. That this should give rise to interpretative difficulties is plain enough. Not only are the letters not systematic, but we may wonder to what extent he wrote to please those to whom he was writing, or at least not to offend them. Moreover, once we leave behind "glittering generalities" – his own expression – such as "self-government," "freedom," and "the rights of man" and brilliant dicta such as "The boisterous sea of liberty indeed is never without a wave," and "To appoint a monarchist to conduct the affairs of a republic is like appointing an atheist to the priesthood," we may well wonder exactly where Jefferson did stand in relation to the philosophy of his contemporaries. Indeed, the fantastic symbolic power of Jeffersonian republicanism *required* that more than one answer be given to this question.[1]

Jefferson's Philosophy of Government

Everyone agrees that Jefferson was a localist. He also seems to have been "anti-statist." We begin to get at the meaning of this by acknowledging his repeated praise of the Indian mode of social organization. "It will be said," he wrote in *Notes on Virginia* (1783), that "the great societies cannot exist without government. The savages, therefore, break them into smaller ones."[2] And in a famous letter to Madison, he pursued this idea by means of his often quoted classification of societies. There were three types: those "without government, as among our Indians," those "under government, wherein the will of everyone has a just influence; in England in a slight degree, and in our states, in a great one"; and finally, those "under governments of force." "It is a problem," he continued, "not clear in my mind, that the first condition is not the best" (VI. letter to Madison, 30 January 1787). That same month, Jefferson noted that were it left to him to decide "whether we should have a government without newspapers, or newspapers without a government, I should not hesitate a moment to prefer the latter." He continued: "Those societies (as the Indians) which live without government enjoy in their general mass an infinitely greater degree of happiness than those who are under the European governments ... Among the latter, under pretence of governing, they divided their nations into two classes, wolves and sheep" (VI. letter to Carrington, 16 January 1787).

These texts suggest an anarchist reading.[3] According to Jefferson, the Indians had never "submitted themselves to any laws, any coercive power, any shadow of government." This did not mean that they were la*wless*, only that *statutory* law did not govern their transactions. "Their only controls are their manners [customs, mores], and that moral sense of right and wrong, which, like the sense of tasting and feeling in every man, makes a part of his nature." Jefferson discerned that among the Indians this was a powerful force for lawfulness, and that "crimes are very rare among them" (II. *Notes on Virginia*, pp. 128–9).[4]

Jefferson, of course, was no anarchist, in that he did believe in government, in part at least because, in his view, the first condition of societies, "as among the Indians," was "inconsistent with any degree of population." The second type of society, "under government, wherein the will of everyone has a just influence," was what he aimed at. But this raises two questions. First, did this mean the less government the better, the standard interpretation? Or did it mean that whatever government there is must be under the direct control of the governed? Or both? It seems clear enough that, for Jefferson, it meant both. That is, if Jefferson saw no need for extensive government, in part because he believed that people were governed by norms which were independent of government and in part because he believed that people could act for themselves, he also believed that when government was necessary, when it made law, that law should be made as far as possible by the people who would live under it. "Get the government off our back's" has persistently been part of "Jeffersonian" rhetoric, usually as part of libertarian philosophy; but the *radical democratic* part of the Jeffersonian philosophy has been largely lost, even in scholarly interpretations.[5]

The ideas of minimal government and strong democracy need not go together. In the eighteenth century they did not, precisely because with the obvious exception of Rousseau, perhaps Paine, and on the present view Jefferson, no other leading modern writer had a very strong sense of democracy. Moreover, because it was possible for Jefferson to believe that civilization was simple enough to allow for informal control of the everyday transactions of life, the combination could be both plausible and uncritically assumed.[6] Local needs could be satisfied with a minimal civil apparatus; and as new needs arose with larger groupings and additional mechanisms were demanded, such "governments" could be "representative."

Our second question is then: What did Jefferson take "representative" to mean? His utterances about "representation" are perfectly consistent. He persistently avoided the Federalist formula of power "originating in" or "deriving from" the people. He always spoke of representatives as delegates, deputies, servants, functionaries, or agents. His own novel, most formal definition of a republic, in sharp contrast to that of Madison, may be this: "I would say, purely and simply, it means a government by its citizens in mass, acting directly and personally, according to rules established by the majority; and that every other government is more or less republican, in proportion as it has in its composition more or less of this ingredient of the direct action of its citizens" (XI. letter to Taylor, 28 May 1816). This famous text continues with Jefferson's acknowledgment that "such a government is evidently restrained in very narrow limits of space and population" – "the extent of a New England township." Accordingly, we must take "the first shade from this pure element": "The powers of government being divided, should be exercised each by representatives chosen either *pro hac vice*, or for such short terms as should secure the duty of expressing the will of their constituents."

This "first shade" could *not* be the sense of representation which Madison had defended in the tenth *Federalist Paper*. In the latter, it was the function of the representative "to refine and enlarge" the public view, not to express "the will of his constituents." On Madison's view, a representative might listen to those whom he represented, of course; but if the public was wrong, he was not obliged to abide by its view. Indeed, he might go directly against the public's will. Jefferson's practice suggests that he could never have accepted this view, and that a good part of his "Revolution of 1800" was designed to get back to the sense of representation as "attorneyship." The "first shade" had to be either the sense articulated during the Revolution, and more sharply in the Maryland debates, or something very close to it. Either representatives acted on "instruction," subject to "the direct and constant control by the citizens," as Jefferson wrote, or they were in some sense obliged to discover the will of their constitutents and to act on it. In a perfectly clear sense, they had to represent it. Of course, this would not be easy, especially if a representative had to act for relatively large numbers of people. In the letter just quoted, as in many others, he complained that "it must be agreed that our governments [note the plural ending] have much less of republicanism than ought to have been expected." His point of reference here, as elsewhere, is "the *State* Constitutions," not the federal Constitution.

To be sure, we have totally lost sight of the ratios that Jefferson could so easily take for granted. Pole points out that during the colonial period, the British Parliament had one member for every 14,300 people, whereas in the American colonies there was one representative to every 1,200. Even in the national election of 1800, only 12,000 Pennsylvanians actually voted. Cunningham, from whom these figures are taken, also points out that John Beckley, taking charge of the Republican campaign, scattered 30,000 tickets in Pennsylvania, where the total number of eligible voters was only 90,000.[7] As Jefferson saw it, far more "direct control" could have been expected.

Moreover, while Jefferson seemed to believe that the Montesquievian problem of size had been solved by the new "federalism" of layered jurisdictions, from the local to the national, it seems that he was never quite clear on this. Most critically, he persistently spoke as if the United States was a traditional confederation and as if no *fundamental* change had been wrought by the Constitution. His reading, we should emphasize, was exactly the opposite of the (still influential) "nationalist" understanding. That is, it was not that the Confederation was *already* a national government, but that under the Constitution, the states were still in confederation! On this view, the Congress "represented" the "nation," but only because "national" policy was the outcome of negotiation and compromise by the representatives of the several states, each representing the will of the people of those states. Thus, advancing the cause of republicanism meant making the *state* constitutions more "republican" (in his novel sense).

Hence he repeatedly spoke of the states as the basis of the United States government and insisted that they were "single and independent as to their internal administration." In August 1800 he spoke of "the true theory of our Constitution" and said, "Let the General Government be reduced to foreign concerns only . . . and our General Government may be reduced to a very simple organization and a very inexpensive one." He repeated this in a remarkable letter of 1811 to Destutt de Tracy, in which he instructed his friend as regards the "true barriers of our liberty." De Tracy had argued that they resided in the principle of frequent elections and a plural executive. Jefferson countered that this was not the case, that "the true barriers were our State governments; and the wisest conservative power ever contrived by man, is that which *our Revolution* and *present* government found us possessed. Seventeen distinct states, amalgamated into one as to their foreign concerns but singly and independent as to their internal administration."[8] And as late as 1826, he could still write, "The Constitution of the United States is a compact of independent nations subject to rules acknowledged in similar cases." (XV. letter to Everett, 1826).

These startling remarks are easily joined both to his increasingly strident criticisms, after he left office, of the direction of American politics and to his conviction, expressed in 1823, that the problem had begun at the convention in Philadelphia, where the Federalists had "endeavored to draw the cords of power as tight as they could obtain them" — indeed, as Madison had all but said in the tenth *Federalist Paper* — "to lessen the dependence of the general functionaries on their constituents" and "to weaken the means of maintaining a steady equilibrium which the majority of the convention had deemed salutary for both branches, general and local" (XV. letter to William Johnson, 12 June 1823). These were the words of a man who did not accept Madisonian arguments against democracy or Madisonian views of "federalism."

Jefferson's despair over the problem that had begun in Philadelphia is easily joined with his 1816 positive discovery of "pure, elementary republics — all together making the state of democracy." On this purely confederal view, "We think experience has proved it safer, for the mass of individuals composing society, to reserve to themselves personally the exercise of all rightful powers to which they are competent, and to delegate those to which they are not competent to deputies named, and removable for unfaithful conduct, by themselves immediately" (XIV. letter to Dupont de Nemours, 1816). These are the words of a classic democrat.

It is hard to know when he arrived at this view. While still in Paris in 1787, Jefferson had had problems with the proposed new Constitution; but he had been ambivalent as to whether the needed changes should be made after ratification, by amendment, as Madison was urging, or by sending the document back to specially elected "deputies." These were very different processes. As Madison understood perfectly well, sending the document back to deputies would surely have risked losing it altogether. In 1791, then, after Jefferson had got his Bill of Rights, he was still unhappy that there was too much federal power and too little republicanism. He wrote:

> I would rather be exposed to the inconveniences attending too much liberty, than those attending too small a degree of it. Then it is important to strengthen the State governments; and as this cannot be done by any change in the federal constitution (for the preservation of that is all we need contend for), it must be done by the States themselves, erecting such barriers at the constitutional line as cannot be surmounted either by themselves or by the General government."
> (VIII. letter to Archibald Stuart, 23 December 1791)

The point is easily missed. Greater "liberty" required *stronger* state governments, because as levels of concern become more local, the greater the possibility of *increasing* direct participation.

A letter of 1824 provides more evidence that Jefferson believed that the problem of insufficient republicanism (in his sense) centered on the constitutions of the states, not on the relation between "the General Government" and the states, and that greater democracy was possible. Jefferson hoped that a proposal for a convention to amend the Virginia Constitution might adopt his plan for subdividing counties into wards. "Each would thus be a small republic in itself, and every man in the State would thus become an acting member of the common government, transacting in person a great portion of its rights and duties within itself, subordinate indeed, yet important, and entirely within his competence." He went to argue that,

> with respect to our State and federal governments, I do not think their relations correctly understood by foreigners. They generally supposed the former subordinate to the latter. But this is not the case. They are coordinate departments of one simple and integral whole. To the State governments are reserved all legislation and administration, in affairs which concern their own citizens only, and the federal government is given whatever concerns foreigners, or the citizens of other States. (XVI. letter to Cartwright, 5 June 1824)

It was easy enough for Jefferson to believe that his distinction between what concerns a state's own citizens and what concerns others sufficed, since, as everyone knew, foreign policy and commerce concern others. Indeed, *that* had been his problem as president. But, as at Philadelphia, to ask whether state governments were "subordinate" or "coordinate" was to misstate the problem. The "foreigners" he had in mind, as well as Adams and the whole of the anti-Federalist opposition, understood that the capacity of the federal government to legislate over individuals had compeltely altered the old arrangement.

The Kentucky and Virginia Resolutions

There may still be doubt as to whether Jefferson had a proper grasp of the Constitution. An account of his Kentucky Resolution may settle this. As is well known, to the horror of "nationalists," later secessionists were to draw on Jefferson's Kentucky Resolution of 1798.[9] But it is easy to see that it is inconsistent with the Constitution. Jefferson's "compact" arguments and his thesis that each state had a right to judge for itself infractions incurred by the federal government against its delegated authority are patently *subversive*, as Madison, author of the very different Virginia Resolution, must surely have known. Of course, in a classic federation, the arguments and their conclusions are just what one would expect.

We can go directly to the source of the critical confusion by looking at a famous gloss by Madison.[10] After the hysteria had passed, Madison claimed that in his text the word "states" had been used ambiguously. He had meant it to refer to "the people composing those political societies in their highest capacity." The phrase "it views the powers of the Federal Government as resulting from the compact to which the states are parties" did not mean that "the societies organized by particular governments" make a compact, but that "the people of the United States" do so. The difference was critical, since on the latter view of the matter, the "states" drop out. The compact which authorized the powers of government was given by individuals in, effectively, a state of naturre. If so, each state was bound by the principle of majority rule of the *whole* people of the United States; hence, if the national government usurps power, then recourse to these same people is possible by any of the modes included in the Constitution, the vehicle of the original compact of "the people." This was consistent with his doctrine in the thirty-ninth *Federalist Paper*, even though it left a fundamental tension for his "federalism."

In this paper Madison had offered:

In order to ascertain the real character of the government it may be considered in relation to the foundation upon which it is to be established; to the sources from which its ordinary powers are to be drawn; to the operation of those powers; to the extent of them; and to the authority by which future changes in the government are to be introduced. (*Federalist Papers*, p. 253)

The first and last considerations are pertinent here. As regards the first, he writes:

It appears on one hand that the Constitution is to be founded on the assent and ratification of the people of America, given by deputies elected for the special purpose; but on the other that this assent and ratification is to be given by the people, not as individuals composing one entire nation; but as composing the distinct and independent states to which they respectively belong. (pp. 253–4)

The first part appears to be "national" – as required by his gloss – but the second is unequivocally a "compact doctrine," confirmed by his summary remark to the effect that "The act therefore establishing the Constitution, will not be a *national* but a *federal* act." With regard to the last consideration, the problem is even more vivid. Thus, as the regards the amendment process, he says: "We find it neither wholly *national*, nor wholly *federal*. Were it wholly national, the supreme and ultimate authority would reside in the majority of the people of the Union .... Were it wholly federal ..., the concurrence of each State in the Union would be essential to every alteration that would be binding on all" (p. 257) Put in other terms, can one square the wholly federal "foundation" with the partially national amendment procedure? This was the problem of the Virginia Resolution.

The contrast between Madison and Jefferson is fundamental. Jefferson held that the Constitution was a compact to which "each state acceded as a State, and is an integral party, its co-states forming, as to itself, the other party." Thus, "as in all other cases of compact among parties having no common judge, each party has a right to judge for itself, as well of infractions as of the mode and measure of redress." This is as clear as it can be, and, contrary to Jaffa, perfectly consistent. Indeed, it is a consequence of the classic notion of confederation. Each state had a compact with every other, and there was no "third party" with authority which superseded the authority of the compacting parties. As already noted, from the beginning Jefferson had been concerned with flaws in the proposed Constitution. When Madison sent him a draft, he was displeased that there was "no declaration of rights," a point presumably settled by the new understanding of sovereignty. But Jefferson argued:

... in a constitutive act which leaves some precious articles unnoticed, and raises implications against others, a declaration of rights becomes necessary, by way of supplement. This is the case of our new federal Constitution. This instrument forms us into one state, as to certain objects and gives us a legislative and executive body for these objects. It should therefore guard us against their abuses of power, with the field submitted to them. (VII. letter to Madison, 15 March 1789).

In a classic confederation, states would alienate certain powers with regard to "certain objects." But what if the central government then infringed on the rights of states or individuals? A bill of rights directed at the central government could provide legal machinery for redress short of nullification. On this view, an independent "federal court" might also serve to arbitrate such matters. But if Virginia, say, judged that the Congress had usurped power and it could not by any constitutional means secure redress, then who was to decide but Virginia?

It is clear from Jefferson's activities vis-à-vis the Court after he became president (see below) that he continued to believe in the need for an "independent" judiciary, so as to put "a legal check in the hands of the judiciary" (letter to Madison, 1789). But, of course, he strongly objected to the "independence" of the judiciary insofar as its members were not *elected* by anybody and had lifelong tenure. Indeed, his views on the Court are bound to be thus if, as surely seems to be the case, Jefferson never accepted the Madisonian and Hamiltonian view that the sovereignty of the people was embodied in the Constitution, that it was therefore "sacred," and that therefore the Court could speak *ex cathedra* in defense of it. As Jefferson said, this was "dangerous doctrine indeed, and one which would place us under the despotism of an oligarchy" (XV. letter to Jarvis, 28 September 1820). It is in this context too that we must appreciate his famous remark that "some men look at constitutions with sanctimonious reverence and deem them like the ark of the covenant, too sacred to be touched" (letter to Kercheval, 1816). It was not merely that looking at the Constitution "with sanctimonious reverence" froze institutions, but that doing so deprived the people of their capacity to determine their fates. On the Madisonian-Hamiltonian view, it was not the people who were sovereign; it was the judges![11]

One might argue here that Jefferson's compact view was the Achilles heel of a traditional confederation, showing that it could not work. But that would surely be presumptuous. As already noted, the dire prediction that the Confederation would degenerate into "anarchy" did not occur despite the very weak Articles. Yet, with the greatly strengthened "federal system" of the Constitution, with a Supreme Court, with a fully spelled-out amendment procedure which did not require unanimity among the states, and with no existing state standing armies, the issue of slavery utterly broke down the system. More generally, whether a confederation will be stable or not depends upon the objects it is designed to serve and the extent to which the parties share in acknowledging these to be proper objects.[12]

As regards the use of force against states, Jefferson is quite clear in a letter to Colonel Carrington that he believed that under the Articles, the Congress had a right to coerce contributions of money and to use compulsion to secure other legitimate − that is, authorized − ends. As he noted, "it was not necessary to give them that power expressly; they have it by a law of nature. When two parties make a compact, there results to each a power of compelling the other to execute it" (VI. letter to Carrington, 4 August 1787). To will the ends is to will the means. What was at stake as regards the Kentucky Resolution, in no way simplified by the Constitution, concerned what in fact had been authorized by the parties, not whether force could be used. The differences between Jefferson and Madison are fundamental, and it may be wondered how in those first years of the United States, as well as since, they could have been seen as a minor quarrel between essentially like-minded men.

Jefferson had been in Paris for the five years between the end of the war and the ratification struggle. He had seen French revolutionary activity and heard its rhetoric. He recognized that there were "weaknesses" in the Confederation but, like Adams, believed that they were easily remedied. Unlike Adams and Madison, he was not at all concerned that "faction" or "civil war" was a problem. As Merrill Peterson points out, while still in Paris, Jefferson feared that the document was the result of "overzealous reaction to . . . democracy" − to Shay. And as soon as he saw it, he wrote to Adams: "I confess that there are things in it which stagger all my dispositions." The good in it, he continued, "might have been couched in three or four new Articles to be added to the good, old, and venerable fabric," the Articles.[13]

For reasons which remain conjectural, Madison, who had worked so hard in Philadelphia for a document to remedy the "imbecility" of the Confederation under the Articles, not only attacked just those policies which everyone agreed were essential to overcome its "imbecility," but, despite differences in their "republican" philosophies which should have been evident, he quickly became an ally of Jefferson against his former allies. Indeed, he used arguments which did not square with his arguments in the *Federalist Papers*! Of course, the development of ideas in the decade and a half which preceded ratification had been both rapid and extraordinary. Just as Adams's vision of the new United States made him seem like a reactionary, so Jefferson's vision makes him seem like a radical. And perhaps if Jefferson had not become president, the differences between the two Virginians on this issue, as well as on others even more basic to the problem of democracy, would have emerged more clearly and been more critical in the ensuing development of the philosophy of democracy.

The Revolution of 1800

Peterson has remarked that "men like Jefferson, deceived by the French Revolution, . . . taught the people to think of their government as a democracy rather than a balanced republic after Adams' vision."[14] This is absolutely correct. Moreover, the implications were enormous. The Republican administrations of Jefferson and Madison played a critical role here.

As noted, the election of 1800 was hotly ideological. And it was close. When all the returns were counted, it was found that "Republican" electors had split their votes evenly between Jefferson and Aaron Burr, the New York leader of the Virginia/New York "Republican axis." Adams was not far behind. The decision was in the hands of the House, voting by states. In thirty-five successive votes, a majority could not be achieved. Finally, after three Federalists cast blank ballots, Jefferson was elected.

Jefferson called his election and administration "the Revolution of 1800"; it was, he said "as real a revolution in the principles of our government as that of 1776 was in its form." But in fact it was nothing of the kind. No matter; Americans believed what he said. The victory of Jefferson, the first of a long series of "republican" victories, was a revolution in neither form nor principles. It was a revolution in ideology.[15]

This is not to charge Jefferson and the Republicans with apostasy, for this would presuppose what was not true; namely, that there was some clear, consistent set of "principles" shared by Jefferson and the Republicans, principles which they cynically abandoned once they achieved power. What *was* true was that different Republicans had different "principles," and that some of these were *shared* by Federalists. Moreover, while some of the principles were abandoned, others which were even more important were not.

Indeed, here was a party which promulgated ideas which allowed it to attract both northern farmers and southern planters who feared merchants and the commercial policies of the Federalists, westerners who hated excise taxes which were used to pay off eastern bond-holders, land-hungry speculators, antidemocratic states' righters who feared federal power and sought to alter the Constitution, democratically inclined states' righters who feared federal power and sought to alter the Constitution, civil libertarians horrified by the Sedition Act, fierce defenders of American autarchy, Jacobin-inspired members of Democratic clubs, and Quaker pacifists! Many of these were ordinary people: the disinherited, the "mechanics," artisans, and small farmers who believed that the Revolution had been fought to establish forms of democracy which the rhetoric of republicanism so warmly promoted. These were the people who had provided the army for Washington and his officers. These were the people who, during the Revolution, in "committees" and "conventions," had overwhelmed the duly constituted vehicles of government and who, symbolized (and *only* symbolized!) by Shay, had caused such anxiety among the leading elites. Indeed, it was this that gave them an additional incentive to define a new course for American history.[16]

The *image* of Jefferson, author of the Declaration of Independence, opponent of the Monocrats and the eastern big-money men, was critical, both in holding together the Republicans and, during his two terms as president, in obscuring the reality. The *real* United States, as Adams saw, had a consolidated government and was a "balanced republic." Yet because there were state governors and assemblies, because no one denied that the central government had responsibility for foreign affairs and interstate commerce, and because the new arrangement preserved the states' responsibility for "internal" affairs, it was easy to feel that the "form" for which the Revolution had been fought was still firmly in place. People could vote, and their votes still counted. On his view, the United States had been sidetracked. He would put it back on the road to "true" republicanism.[17]

Jefferson surely believed in a strong form of democracy which he sincerely wanted to promote. But, caught in the institutions which the new Constitution had created and given his particular set of ideas, he responded much as would be expected. Indeed, he was America's first imperial president in the twofold sense that he acted decisively to enlarge "the empire of liberty" and took to himself not only more executive power than his predecessors, but more than any president until the twentieth century! Moreover, he did these things because he believed that in a republic there was not merely a sacred trust to preserve the republic, as Machiavelli had taught, but that his *executive* responsibility was to implement the *people's* will. This was the novelty of his administration; for not only did this view motivate him personally, but, remarkably, people came to believe that this was the substance of democracy.

There are four problems in Jefferson's two administrations which rightly command our interest, the question of the national bank, the Louisiana Purchase, his attitudes and activities vis-à-vis the federal courts and Aaron Burr, and most interesting, the embargo of 1807–9. All can be better understood if we take seriously the fact that the United States was a modern republican state in a world of states. The point here is not to either praise or condemn Jefferson's policies. It may be that others would have done worse. The point is to get a clear view of the new relations between war and "representative democracy" in the era of modern state.

Hamiltonian Finances

The continuation of Hamilton's fiscal innovations is the easiest to deal with. Jefferson continued them because there were no viable alternatives and the Government needed resources. It is true that under his administration (and Madison's to follow), the debt was reduced; but Jefferson did not act to undermine the national bank, nor did he hesitate to borrow more for the Louisiana Purchase. When faced with war in 1812, Madison, the arch-enemy of those policies in 1792, did the same. In a sense, of course, the problem of guaranteeing the financial capabilities of the central government had been, since the Confederation, a red herring. It had been stimulated by the extraordinary circumstances which had propelled the colonies into war and by the assumptions of the leaders of some states who could not see how the Congress could be made fiscally viable without threatening state sovereignty. It was a central feature of the argument in chapter 6 that, as the defenders of the New Jersey Plan argued, this was entirely possible. Moreover, as argued in chapter 7, it would have been desirable; and, as argued in this chapter, the federation it envisioned was essential to the prism through which Jefferson looked at America. In fact, the purchase of Louisiana was designed precisely to promote Jefferson's distinct *republican* vision.

The Louisiana Purchase

There is a double paradox here. First, as Hofstadter says, Jefferson's achievement "was an accident, the outcome of the collapse of Napoleon's ambitions for a Caribbean empire — the inadvertent gift of Toussaint L'Ouverture and the blacks of Haiti to this slaveholding country."[18] Second, given that the United States was a consolidated state, there were obvious reasons for acquiring Louisiana, peacefully if possible, but by war if necessary. Thus, everyone accepted the Machiavellian imperative that, to be secure, one must be powerful, and that extensive territory was indispensable to power. It seems undeniable that "consciousness of empire" was widespread among America's leading elites.[19]

The second paradox is that, as regards continental expansion, it was Jefferson, not Hamilton, who was at this time interested in aggrandizement, preferably by peaceful means, but if necessary by force. To be sure, both were interested in the "future grandeur and glory of America"; but they differed enormously on what this meant.

Hamilton was a Machiavellian, and he was informed by Jefferson's intellectual *bête noire*, Hume. According to Jefferson, Hume was "an apostle of Toryism" and "a degenerate son of science." The issue for Jefferson concerned the content of Hume's brilliant "Of Commerce" (see chapter 5 above), which Hamilton had developed in the American setting in his incisive "Report on the Subject of Manufactures" of 1790. Equally reprehensible in Jefferson's view were those Humean views which undercut the entire logic of the "compact" so dear to Jefferson. On both, Hamilton was a Humean. These views found expression in the context of the Purchase.

According to Hamilton, westward expansion would be premature. It could not be controlled, and it would be counterproductive. By scattering the already small population, it would "hasten the dismemberment of a large portion of our country" and thus lead to "a dissolution of the government." By encouraging an agrarian society, it would discourage the economic development vital to the future grandeur of the nation. At such time as the United States achieved sufficient economic power, it could *then* engage in the rapacious struggle for hegemony. For the present, it was essential only that the mouth of the Mississippi be controlled by the United States.[20]

Jefferson and Hamilton agreed on some of the facts; but since their visions were so different, the contrast was stark. For Jefferson, westward expansion meant maintaining conditions for the free, independent farmer, whom he saw as the lifeblood even of a commercial society. Second, it meant keeping "the intrigues of foreign nations to a distance from which they can no longer produce disturbance between the Indians and us." By keeping Europe at a distance, there would be, *contra* Hume, no need for a large army, and America could carry on without fear. Jefferson thus internalized the Montesquievian ideal of a "peaceful republic," autarchic, democratic, and egalitarian. As he wrote to Barbé de Marbois, "I have confidence that we shall proceed successfully for ages to come, and that, contrary to the principles of Montesquieu, it will be seen that the larger the extent of the country, the more firm its republican structure, if founded, not on conquest, but on principles of compact and equality" (XV. letter of 14 June 1817). As an "empire of liberty," the United States represented an innovative improvement on Montesquieu, not a rejection of his view of peaceful republics. American "federalism" was unique, and the United States was not a "republic" in the sense of either Rome or Venice. Expansion by "compact" made the "empire" infinitely expandable *and* stable at the same time. From thirteen "states," to sixteen to fifty! The new territories would one day become "states," but not by conquest. They would be joined as the others had been, by compact.

It turned out, of course, that as regards Louisiana, Jefferson was right and Hamilton wrong — but for none of the right reasons. Jefferson did not get the empire of liberty which he had envisaged; economic development was *not* slowed, and America *was* ready to embark on a quest for Hamiltonian "glory and grandeur." Although republican designs on Canada were not abandoned until the war of 1812, it is no accident that James Monroe, "the legitimate heir of the Virginia dynasty," issued the "momentous declaration of American foreign policy" which asserted the right of the United States to secure its hegemony over *both* hemispheres of the New World. By this time, needless to say, the republican motif of the "empire of liberty" had been thoroughly absorbed into the Hamiltonian vision.[21]

As regards the Purchase, Jefferson worried about whether he had acted within his own understanding of the Constitution. Indeed, he argued: "The executive in seizing the fugitive occurrence which so much advances the good of the country, have done an act beyond the Constitution." (X. letter to Breckenridge, 12 August 1803).[22] As to the role of the legislature, "The Legislature in casting behind them metaphysical niceties, and risking themselves like faithful servants, must ratify and pay for it, and throw themselves on their country for doing for them unauthorized, what we know they would have done for themselves had they been in a situation to do it" (ibid.). Of course, the people were not "in a situation to do it," precisely because the new republic was a modern state. On the other hand, Jefferson here suggests not merely that it was the right thing to do, but that had the people been asked, they would have agreed. Jefferson acted in line with an ancient analogy: "It is the case of a guardian, investing the money of his ward in purchasing an important adjacent territory; and saying to him when of age, I did this for your own good." We may easily grant that Jefferson and the Congress were acting as the "guardians" of the people, but did this imply, following now a Platonic perception, that the people were but "children," or, more generously, that had the people his "vantage point," they would have done what he did? Since future generations would profit, the Purchase was like a long-term insurance policy and plainly it involved but a minimum of expense on the part of those then living. Louisiana was a real bargain, even if, in fact, the people were not asked.

The Court and the Attack on Burr

Jefferson's attack on the Court was directly justified by "democratic" arguments. It is sometimes forgotten that it was John Taylor, Gideon Giles, John Breckenridge, and those who were still strongly anti-Federalist who pushed Jefferson for radical reform of the Court. More important, if they felt betrayed, they had good reasons, for no structural changes were even attempted.

Johnstone points out that initially Jefferson sought ways "to curb the excesses of the federal judges without altering the Constitution or jeopardizing the essential independence of the judiciary." In this he was acting in accordance with the beliefs with which he entered public life, in this instance, belief in the viability of a balanced constitution. While it seems that he never quite gave up this belief, his experience as President, especially regarding the Burr affair, led him to believe that "the people" would be better served if judges, like other "representatives" of the people, were elected.

The business with Burr is a remarkable case study of a deep tension in "representative democracies." Everyone agrees that, at the very least, Jefferson committed a series of serious "indiscretions" in his wish to see Aaron Burr convicted of treason. Although the custodian of the Court, John Marshall, also behaved badly, he tried to block Jefferson. But what is most critical for present purposes is not whether Jefferson − or Marshall, for that matter − was justified in what he did or even whether Burr, no doubt a scoundrel, should have been convicted of the "crimes" of which he was accused.[23] What is important here is the reasons and arguments.

In Jefferson's opinion, Burr's activities threatened the safety of the republic. Even if Burr did not have the capacity to carry out a rebellion, there was a potential gravity to his activities which threatened the safety of the republic. This was quite sufficient. Those who stood on legal niceties or worse were deliberately obstructionist and failed to appreciate this. Thus, he sarcastically congratulated the Court for its "new-born zeal for the liberty of those whom we would not permit to overthrow the liberties of their country." Jefferson was perfectly willing to bend, if not break, the laws; but he seems to have believed that in any case his actions had the full support of "public opinion." In fact, his faith in the democratic process made it *easier* for him to risk illegality. He wrote:

> The nation will judge both the offender and the judges for themselves. If a member of the executive or legislature does wrong, the day is never far distant when the people will remove him. They will see and amend the error in our Constitution which makes any branch independent of the nation .... If [the Court's] protection of Burr produces this amendment, it will do more good than his condemnation would have done. (XI. letter to William Giles, 20 April 1807)

In a letter to Governor Claiborne in the same year, he used a Hamiltonian argument and was quite candid regarding his willingness to risk infringing liberty:

> On great occasions every good officer must be ready to risk himself in going beyond the strict line of law, when the preservation justifies it. ... On the whole, this squall, by shewing with what ease our government suppresses movements which in other countries requires armies, has greatly increased its strength by increasing the public confidence in it. It has been a wholesome lesson, too, to our citizens, of the necessary obedience to their government. The Feds, and the little band of Quids, in opposition, will try to make something of the

infringement of liberty by military arrest and deportation of citizens, but if it does not go beyond such offenders as Swartwout, Bollman, Burr, Blennerhassett, Tyler, etc., they will be supported by the public approbation. (XV. letter of 3 February 1807)[24]

This text confirms an emerging perception of how "representatives" can justify policy. It also reveals, dramatically, a new and serious problem: *not* what are the rights of a majority against the rights of citizens, but what are the rights of a "representative" acting in the name of the majority of the people against the rights of a citizen and, more generally, in the interests of the "safety of the republic"?

Americans can surely be thankful that Jefferson and American governments since then have not been anything like as ruthless in this regard as Robespierre or later "representatives" who have claimed authority in the name of "the people." Still, it must be emphasized that the problem is a distinctly modern, "republican" problem. Traditional rulers did not act in the name of the people; accordingly, they could not justify acts by arguing that a majority of the people really did support their policies or, worse, that had they had the chance, they would have supported their actions! In representative regimes, the opportunities are truly stunning. Not only are there serious questions about what "the will of the people" might mean, but there is also the problem of how it is to be determined. In justification of his embargo, Jefferson seemed willing to accept as decisive the evidence of letters written to him! But more than this, suppose that the Executive does wrong and that what was done cannot be undone? Suppose he commits the nation to war?

In general, it has been easy for historians, as others, to fudge the genuine dilemmas to which this innovation gave rise. It has always been easy to applaud governments when, in violating rights, the consequences seemed worthwhile, even "necessary." It is even easier to justify them when they are judged to represent the "will of the people." Perhaps even more important, it is common to condemn acts and policy when they seem to us to be the policy of "a willful minority." The contrast to the ancient world is striking; democratic assemblies surely did make mistakes and commit injustices. But now we can condemn or applaud a government's acts on the grounds that in some vague sense, it either did or did not act in accordance with "the will of the people."

The Embargo

The episode of the embargo further illustrates this deep problem. It also raises some additional interesting questions as regards the problem of war and democracy and deepens our understanding of the Jeffersonian vision.

Relations with Britain continued to deteriorate. At the same time, British seamen had been deserting British vessels to sail American ships. The American vessel *Chesapeake* was hailed at sea by H. M. S. *Leopard*. The captain of the *Chesapeake* refused to heave to, whereupon the *Leopard* fired three broadsides, killing three and leaving the *Chesapeake* defenseless. The *Leopard* found one British deserter, one Marylander, one American black, and one Indian. All four were impressed.

The Republican Press responded with outrage. Jefferson, hoping to avoid war, decided on an embargo. American ships would not be allowed to sail to foreign shores; exports by sea or land would be prohibited. The idea was not merely to force recognition by the British (and the French) of the sovereign rights of the United States or to give time to prepare for war or temporarily to punish the British homeland. The policy was intended to coerce Britain into acknowledging the sovereign rights of the United States in *all* future relations, economic and political. Jefferson had decided that it was time the United States was taken seriously. It is easy, in retrospect, to say – as historians all do – that the policy did not have a ghost of a chance of succeeding. That may well be true; but focusing on this aspect may distract us from other more fundamental issues.

The country was in no danger, politically or economically. Worse offenses had been committed against the flag. Jefferson would have had no difficulty in pacifying the militant voices in the Press and elsewhere. It is striking, indeed, that earlier, Hamilton and Adams, the "Anglophiles," had been willing to take Republican heat to avoid war with Britain. The argument that Jefferson realized that "the new country" needed time to get on its feet and so should avoid war is both good Hamiltonianism and relevant to the defense of the embargo only if war and the embargo were exhaustive alternatives.

But there were other alternatives. He might, first of all, have done nothing except bluster a bit. Or, since the nation was in no immediate danger, he could have ordered that warships to protect American commerce be built, or that merchantmen be armed. These policies would have increased the risk of war, it is true. But the embargo itself was not beyond the risk of war. Still, the United States was ill prepared for war, and all three policies would have bought time. Moreover, since the British, who were already fighting the French, would not themselves have favored a war with Americans at that time, it would not have been unreasonable to build warships or arm merchantmen. Further, these policies could have been reassessed as time went on. But the evidence suggests that Jefferson gave no serious consideration to any of these ideas.

What is perhaps most striking is that the second and third possibilities, greatly enlarging the Navy or arming the merchant marine (or both) were options fully consistent with republican theory. Standing armies were the *bête noire* of republicans, not navies. In 1786, in a letter to Monroe, Jefferson had himself asserted that "a naval force can never endanger our liberties, nor occasion bloodshed; a land force would do both." Jefferson's "republicanism," unlike Hamilton's or Adams's, was built on an image of the United States as "a peaceful republic," consisting of "states" bound together for mutual concerns but otherwise independent and serene.

On the other hand, in his refusal to see much "republicanism" in Britain, he may have seen no point in the lesson that Montesquieu had derived from Xenophon. The United States needed no standing army; nor, because it would be autarchic, did it need a navy. Indeed, on Jefferson's view, the embargo would have the additional good consequence of forcing Americans toward a Spartan-like autarchy. In the meantime, Jefferson was perfectly willing to abandon some other "republican" principles to make the embargo work.

In 1787 he had written that "information to the people" is "the most certain, and the most legitimate engine of government. Educate and inform the whole mass of the people . . . . They are the only sure reliance for the preservation of our liberty" (VI. letter to Madison, 20 December 1787). And in the same year, "I am persuaded that the good sense of the people will always be found to be the best army. They may be led astray for a moment, but will soon correct themselves . . . . The way to prevent these irregular interpositions of the people, is to give them full information of their affairs through the channel of their public papers" (VI. letter to Carrington, 16 January 1787). But Jefferson did not try to communicate his understanding of the embargo and his reasons for it, either to the people, or to their "representatives." After the Administration asked for a third embargo Act — there were five altogether, each of which cast the net wider and added new teeth — Representative Barent Gardenier of New York offered an objection which, to this day, has been a recurring congressional argument:

Why we passed the embargo law itself, I have been always unable to tell . . . . It does appear to me, sir, that we are led on, step by step, by an unseen hand . . . . Darkness and mystery overshadow this House and the whole nation. We know nothing, we are permitted to know nothing. We sit here as mere automata; we legislate without knowing, nay, sir, without wishing to know, why or wherefore . . . . If the motives and the principles of the Administration are honest and patriotic, we would support them with a fervor which none could surpass. But, sire, we are kept in total darkness. We are treated as the enemies of our country.[25]

Historians agree that his complaint is very well taken. It did not speak well for the represntative body of the people that they so willingly sat like "mere automata"; but then, as Gardenier suggested, they did not desire to be execrated as lacking "confidence" in the Executive or, worse, as themselves harboring treasonous impulses! Important then perhaps, although not now, the Congress had had experience with kings, but not with presidents, and everyone accepted that foreign policy was an *executive* responsibility.

As noted, the policy had no chance of succeeding, for two reasons. First, it assumed that the English *nation* would feel the pinch, and that, accordingly, the English *government* would be forced to come to terms. But, in the modern state, "the nation" and "the government" are not the same thing. In particular, while prices on tobacco, rice, and cotton rose, those in Britain who suffered most, textile workers who depended on cotton imports, had no voice. George III and his Cabinet had plenary war powers and could carry on with impunity, without concern for the vagaries of electoral politics and without undue fear of civil war or disorder.

Second, for the plan to have any chance whatever of succeeding, the citizens must understand the reasons for the sacrifices they were being asked to make and the extent of these. As noted, Jefferson made little effort to aid citizens in understanding. Ironically, his failed embargo policy established that if, in a republic, one sought to implement a policy which demanded sacrifices by the people, then one had to do it in terms of war, present or potential – millions for defense, not a penny for tribute. Not only could such a sacrifice then be passionately motivated; but, as everyone knew, such judgments were best left to experts and those who had a view "from the vantage point." The citizens of Athens would rightly have been amazed – just as any eighteenth-century king would have been amused.

The sacrifices were considerable.[26] Even more considerable was the preemption of presidential authority and the extent of the repression which Jefferson managed to justify in order extract these sacrifices. The Constitution had authorized the Congress to regulate commerce; but, putting aside the question of whether it had authorized the Congress to stop it altogether, Jefferson and the Republican Congress had made a mockery of Republican principles.[27] They had protested Washington's use of milita to enforce the whiskey tax and would have been appalled at the suggestion that regulars be used to put down domestic violence. Yet they now employed the regular army and navy as enforcers of statutes which totally disregarded Fourth Amendment constraints on unreasonable search and seizure. Jefferson had zealously guarded the division of powers and the authority of the states; yet he now asked for, and got, presidential authority to call into service whenever he deemed it necessary "any part or the whole" of 100,000 militiamen. He had feared that the Constitution was a quixotic response to Shay and had written, "God forbid that we should ever be twenty years with such a rebellion"; but now he was ready to redefine "insurrection" so as to include attempts to avoid customs men! Writing in 1963, Leonard Levy could say of the fifth embargo Act that "[t]o this day it remains the most repressive and unconstitutional legislation ever enacted by a Congress in time of peace."[28]

As with the attack on the Court, Jefferson believed that he was justified insofar as he had "the approbation of the people." During the long period in which he tried to make the policy work, he was able to convince himself of this, in part because it seems that the majority of the letters he received supported the policy.[29] We know that scientifically conducted public opinion polls are dangerous enough measures of the "popularity" of any policy, never mind inferring support on the basis of correspondence.

When Jefferson left office, after the plan had been abandoned, he was not misguided in thanking God "for the opportunity of retiring from [the "shackles of power"] without censure" (XII. letter to Dupont de Nemours, 2 March 1809).[30] His letters may have given him "most consoling proofs of public approbation"; but even if he was correct in thinking that a majority did support the policy – and this was almost certainly not true – it was a most dubious ground for its justification. His belief in "the first principle of republicanism, that the *lex-majoris partis* is the fundamental law of every society of individuals of equal rights," articulated to Humboldt in 1817 – paradoxically, in explicit criticism of the French Revolution – made obvious sense in a *classic* democracy, although even there, it was not without its problems. But in a "representative democracy," it could be downright dangerous to justify policy on the *surmise* that a policy had the support of the majority. The widespread, ongoing disobedience and the fact that the New England states were being provoked into making plans to secede from the new United States should have been all the proof he needed that opposition was coming from no small minority of criminals, ill informed and intransigent.

This is not to charge Jefferson with tyranny, for surely he was no "tyrant."[31] Still, if we are to get a better grip on the problems of republicanism in the era of the modern state, we must acknowledge that because American republicanism played a critical role in getting republicanism redefined as democracy, it also played a role in generating and promoting new kinds of arguments for dubious – even evil – uses of centralized executive power. The "conservatives" of the modern period who denied that *vox populi vox Dei* were surely not wrong; but after the Americans invented the idea of a sovereign people who themselves lacked the resources, the responsibility, and the power to make law and policy, *vox populi vox Dei* took on an entirely new meaning.

Similarly, it is too easy to miss the point and to argue that Jefferson was not a "philosopher" but a public man, and that his responsibility as

President meant that he had to deal with concrete problems, not philosophical abstractions. Whether philosophers *can* properly deal with "philosophical abstractions" is another question, of course, and not one that can be dealt with here.

There are two other issues. Public men, like others, need ideas in terms of which to deal with concrete problems. Surely, in each of the episodes reviewed in this chapter, there were great differences in the stock of ideas which might have guided decision making, just as there were different policies to which these differences might have led. Jefferson's particular vision of republicanism figured hugely in the decisions he made; and the consequences, intended *and* unintended, were significant. *As* important was the manifest Machiavellian assumption of Jefferson's republicanism in the era of the modern state, his acceptance of the two moralities, of the public man and of the private man. It was the assumption on which all else depended. In a remarkable letter to John Colvin written just after he left office, Jefferson said:

A strict observance of the written laws is doubtless *one* of the high duties of a good citizen, but it is not *the highest*. The laws of necessity, of self-preservation, of saving the country when in danger are of higher obligation. To lose our country by a scrupulous adherence to written laws, would be to lose the law itself . . . thus absurdly sacrificing the end to the means. . . . It is incumbent on those only who accept great charges, to risk themselves on great occasions, when the safety of the nation, or some of its very high interests are at stake." (XII. letter of 20 September 1810)

No modern chief executive has rejected this Machiavellian imperative. Antidemocrcy and war have been its consequence. So far, at least, humanity has survived this. Whether, in the era of nuclear war, it will continue to do so remains to be seen.

Part IV

Absolute War and Social Democracy

Introduction

In the years between Montesquieu's *Spirit of the Laws* (1748) and Tocqueville's *Democracy in America* (1830) the world was dramatically transformed. The Americans achieved a large, powerful state and, to boot, invented modern democracy; Spanish, Portuguese, and French colonies in Latin America and the Caribbean fought wars of independence, and Greece fought a war of independence against the Ottomans; and France threw the whole of Europe into a turmoil which lasted for nearly two and a half decades. Although this uproar was precariously contained by counter-revolution and reaction, nevertheless, a new agenda for civilization had been outlined. It was the agenda of Social Democracy set, tragically, in the epoch of "absolute" war.

To the modern mind, the legacy of revolution in France remains ambiguous. On the one hand, as regards historical significance, the Declaration of the Rights of Man and Citizen preempts the American Declaration of Independence. On the other, the French Revolution is very nearly the paradigm of that movement of history which Plato depicted in the *Republic*. Failing to achieve "the just state," the arrogant oligarchic regime of France collapsed into the anarchy of "extreme democracy," and thence into the tyrannies of Robespierre and Napoleon Bonaparte. From this perspective, all the fears unrealized in the American Revolution were realized in the revolution in France and in the wars to which it gave rise. The result, as everyone knows, was the elimination in continental Europe of democracy — in the new sense — for nearly a century.

Yet this perspective distorts the facts, for it both denies the betrayal of democracy by the "middle" and ignores the crucial role of the war. As Godechot wrote, "The war profoundly altered revolution."[1] Indeed, from the point of view of the argument of this book, there were two clear, world-historical consequences of the revolution in France.

First, because the French connected the idea of democracy with an egalitarian ideal, they introduced to the world the idea of Social Democracy. The democratic movement in France shared with the movement in America the idea that people ought to govern themselves; but it went beyond this in holding that inequalities of status and wealth were unjustified and must therefore be eliminated. Henceforth, "civic equality," equality under the law, was not enough. In France, unlike America, there were no slaves; nor were there serfs as in the monarchies and empires east of the Elbe. There were obviously plenty of free poor people, who had been made even poorer by the economic crisis which had been building since the Seven Years' War. Their intervention in the Revolution caused as much concern among the bourgeois as among the aristocracy in France. But if the center, the bourgeois and "constitutionalists" like Lafayette, did not want an Athenian-style ochlocracy, they did want a republic, nevertheless. This was not the wish of the right quite clearly. Before an American-style "republic" could be instituted, the power of the traditional nobility would have to be broken. The war which altered the course of the Revolution was counterrevolutionary war. This, then, became the primary condition for the failure of any sort of democracy, and subsequently of the violence which, by its own logic, became the Terror.

In France, the idea of a radical democracy did not have a ghost of a chance of succeeding, a fact of enormous historical significance. But the two ideas, self-government and the elimination of unjustified inequalities between persons, held by only a small minority, did put genuine fear into the hearts of the men and women of the center and the right, both in France and, as important, in the ruling classes in the rest of Europe. This was the crucial social fact about the Revolution. Viewed from the side of the center and the right, the people in the streets were "*canaille*," "fishwives," "bullies," "the criminal scum," "brigands," and, more descriptively, "sans-culottes." Surely they could not be trusted to rule; they could not be trusted to rule even themselves, still less others. After 1792, these "revolutionaries" could not be labeled "terrorists," "anarchists," or, more dramatically, "drinkers of blood." After the Restoration and throughout the remainder of the century, they and their revolutionary leaders would be called "anarchists," "socialists," and "communists."

Since the failure of "democracy" was attributed to the "excesses" of the Revolution, the tragic outcome of the Revolution reinforced ancient prejudices about "the people," thereby underlining the ideological power of the new "experiment" in America. It is not too much to say, perhaps, that after 1793 there came to be but two "parties" in the world, those who would defend the French Revolution and those who would not. The revolutionaries of the world — anarchists, Marxists, social revolutionaries, Social Democrats, and "left" Republicans of this stripe or that — are just those who have struggled and continue to struggle to complete the French Revolution, to complete the struggle for radical democracy. For other people, American-style democracy, if not the best of all possible worlds, is, at any rate, the best in this world.

The French Wars of Liberation gave rise to the second world-historical theme to emerge from the French Revolution. As Clausewitz so brilliantly discerned, these wars involved a totally new understanding of war, its means, its objects, and its role in the relations of states. In crucial ways, all modern statesmen are Clausewitzean, even if they are less than clear — or honest — about what this commits them to. Clausewitz's philosophy of war and politics is inconceivable prior to the French Revolution. To be sure, insofar as the American War of Independence was "an affair of the whole Nation," the Americans had taken a giant step in realizing the new form of war. Still, the number of people involved was relatively small; the United States, after all, was only sparsely populated and it was an ocean away from its enemy. The Thirty Years' War in Europe had involved bigger armies and far greater violence. France's population alone was twelve times that of all the colonies combined, and by 1793 France was at war with most of Europe!

As Clausewitz saw, the changes in war brought war nearer to its "absolute form." These changes were not the result of new technologies and methods, but "were caused by the new political conditions which the French Revolution created both in France and in Europe as a whole."[2] The point is central, and it is a central theme of the chapter which follows. Modern historians are correct in emphasizing that war utterly altered the French Revolution. But it is as important to grasp the deep cause and implications of this, fully recognized by Clausewitz. As he said, the critical fact was "the participation of the people in this great *affair of State*"; and he went on, rightly, to insist that "this participation arose partly from the effects of the French Revolution on the internal affairs of other countries, partly from the threatening attitude of the French towards all Nations." From the point of view of the ruling aristocracies of Europe, the problem was "to contain the revolutionary forces" in

France. This was the logic of the campaign of 1792, and it was this which, by its own logic, "set in motion new means and new forces." "War, freed from all conventional restrictions, broke loose, with all its natural force." Although the Revolution was "contained," the world which resulted was, in many ways, very, very different.

In addition, then, to identifying the radical character of the French Revolution, chapter 9 considers how, in the light of the new republican ideas, but *before* the Wars of Liberation, enlightened opinion, beautifully represented by Turgot and especially by Kant, envisioned the future of the emerging republican order and of war; and how, *after* these wars, Clausewitz and Hegel totally revised this vision. In chapter 10, we consider, against this background, the revolutionary thought and practice of Marx and Engels. But, in contrast to most authors, I take seriously their views on war and democracy.

9

The Revolution in France and the Revolution in War

In the European state system as it had been since the end of the Thirty Years' War (1648), foreign policy was in the hands of the monarch, as it had been for centuries. Kings and queens had interests which were as clear to them as the interests of the owner of a large business are to him. In pursuit of these ends, the monarch engaged in time-tested means: diplomacy, intrigue, bargaining, the making of coalitions, sometimes by marriage, and, if the benefits looked as if they would outweigh the costs, the making of war. Wars were the prerogative of the sovereign, fought with professional armies under the command of generals who, like the men they commanded, had but limited allegiances. As a profession, war was a way of life not death. While the objects of war were limited by the means, changes, particularly in technology, had made wars increasingly expensive and increasingly violent. Accordingly, their "rationality" was increasingly called into question, especially by those who saw changes in society which suggested that war might be a thing of the past. Indeed, before the French Wars of Liberation, enlightened European opinion could believe that, with the advent of republican institutions, war might be eliminated altogether.

We find the idea in Montesquieu's notion of "peaceful republics" and in his hope that "commerce" had undercut the possibility of war. But Montesquieu's paradigm of a republic was a tiny commercial republic. He had not envisaged the possibility of an extended republic; this was an American invention. But the Frenchman Turgot and the Prussian Immanuel Kant could now assume that large republics would be the order of the future.

The "Interests" of Individuals and the "Interests" of "Nations"

Anne Robert Jacques Turgot (1727–81) had been Controller-General of Finances when the colonies of North America declared their independence.

An economic and political liberal, he is introduced here because there is probably no one who had greater hopes that "men [sic] can be both free and peaceful and can dispense with the trammels ... which tyrants ... have presumed to impose under the threat of public safety."[1] For Turgot, the Americans were "the hope of the human race," and America "should be the model."

His argument is quite remarkable – at least from the point of view of the present. Turgot disapproved of the Confederation of American states, but for surprising reasons. For him, the idea of the Confederation, like that of "nation," rested on "a very ancient and very vulgar policy," specifically "on the prejudice that nations and provinces have an interest as nations and provinces other that the interest of the individuals composing them." It was perfectly plain to Turgot that all people want to be free, and that government has as its *sole* aim "sacred respect for the liberty of persons and of labor ... the inviolable maintenance of the rights of property." Securing the liberty of persons and property defines "justice between all." Individuals have an interest "in buying and selling merchandize," but none in "compelling the foreigner to consume their productions." Nor do individuals have an interest in expanding the territory of the state or in "gaining an ascendancy over other peoples." The "ambitions of princes" and the irrational rivalries between European states have "obliged all States to hold themselves armed ... and to regard the military force as the principle object of government." But, Turgot insists, "America has the happiness to have no enemy to fear" – unless, indeed, "she creates a division within herself."[2]

This was a remarkable insight into the peculiar condition of the new United States. As he saw, slavery in the South was "incompatible with the good political institution." Anticipating a fundamental goal of the Revolution in France, he argued strongly that "uniform codes and conditions be advanced." Persons, as persons, should be subject to the *same* laws. Slavery, like serfdom, was a blight because it falsely and wrongly discriminated between humans. Remarkably, he went on to argue that unless equality was accomplished soon "even when the liberty [of black persons] is granted, [it] will cause embarrassment by forming almost a second nation in the same state."[3]

Turgot was correct in saying that if the United States could overcome "division within herself," then, being blessed by freedom from invasion, she need not suffer war. Apart from the blustering of the war of 1812, the only war *ever* fought on American soil was the American Civil War, a terrible introduction to the horrors of "absolute war," fought precisely because America had not succeeded in overcoming "division within herself." Turgot was further correct: the legacy of the early failure to overcome the "division within herself" remained.

But the main premise of his argument that war might be a thing of the past is even more astounding. According to Turgot, if there are no *sui generis* national interests, war *cannot* be rational. Thus, "by the sacred principle of freedom of commerce ... the presumed interest of national commerce disappears, also the interest to possess more or less territory will vanish, by the principle that territory belongs not to nations, but to individual proprietors." Even the question of the boundaries of the state had been misconceived; for "whether such a canton, such a village, ought to belong to such a province, to such a state, ought not to be decided by the presumed interest of that province or State, but by the interest of the inhabitants of that canton or village themselves."[4]

Turgot has gone far beyond Montesquieu's hope that "commerce" might mitigate the irrationality of war and has totally rejected the paradigm of tiny Montesquievian "peaceful republics" existing precariously in a world of massive, aggrandizing monarchies and despotisms. In these remarkable passages, he expresses a radical cosmopolitanism in which the state does not disappear, but in which it is not in the least a machine of war. Rather, it is merely (to use a current formulation) "the dominant protective agency," the arm of internal justice defined in the individualist terms of the classic liberal state! Nor was Turgot alone in this vision. Kant's much misunderstood "Perpetual Peace: A Philosophical Sketch" is continuous with Turgot's most basic insights — and suffers, as we shall see, from the same fatal flaws.

Perpetual Peace: The World Republics

Like Plato and Machiavelli, Kant saw that the problem of how to establish a perfect constitution could not be separated from the problem of war. As he put it, "the problem of establishing a perfect civil constitution is subordinate to the problem of law-governed external relations with other states, and cannot be solved unless the latter is also solved."[5] This realization put him in the distinguished company of Plato, Machiavelli, and Montesquieu, who unfortunately form only a tiny minority of thinkers on politics. Indeed, one goal of the present book is to reconnect what the mainstream of theory has put asunder. Kant disagreed with Plato and Machiavelli, however, in believing that war could be eliminated. For Kant, as for Turgot, the "fortress state" of the Greeks and the Florentines was based on a misconception of the proper aim of government. Kant's theory was thoroughly in keeping with liberal political thought, and no writer has given us a deeper analysis of the alternative he envisioned.

Kant wrote little political philosophy and wrote even less aimed at a wide reading public. His "Perpetual Peace" is unique in this respect. It was, as Gallie says, a political act, written in express criticism of the Treaty of

Basel, which was signed when, in 1795, Prussia decided to retire from the coalition against France.[6] The date and motivation are important. Kant could not have written such a tract before 1776, and perhaps not before 1787 or 1789. Moreover, given his acumen, it seems unlikely that he would have written it after 1799 or so, since by then he would almost certainly have abandoned his hopes that a world of republics would be a peaceful world.

The argument in "Perpetual Peace" has two main sub-arguments. The first depends upon the emergence of states with "republican" constitutions. It is important to gloss this is some detail. It has been said that Kant was "the philosopher of the American and French Revolutions," and, to be sure, he did express enthusiasm for both. But it is terribly important to be clear why. As noted, Kant was a thoroughgoing liberal. What he saw emerging in the American and especially the French Revolution was the possibility of a world governed by consistent liberal principles. But this does not mean, as he was clear to point out, a world of democracies.

In "Perpetual Peace" he gave a succinct definition of the "principles" of a liberal republic. He wrote:

> A republican constitution is founded on three principles: first, the principle of freedom of all members of society (as human beings); secondly, the principle of dependence of everyone upon a single common legislation (as subjects); and thirdly, the principle of legal equality for everyone (as citizens).[7]

All had been expressed, of course, in the 1791 Declaration of the Rights of Man and Citizen. All three strike at the core of feudalism – indeed, of despotism and tyranny in any form. The second is more expressly "republican"; and, so that we do not confuse a republican constitution with a democratic constitution, he glosses "republican."

There are two ways to classify states, he writes. The first depends upon who exercises power ("sovereignty"): an individual, several persons, or "*all* those who constitute civil society." Though he does not say so, this is plainly the ancient way of classifying "constitutions," the way abandoned by Montesquieu, but one that still lingered in the brains of theorists. The second way is thoroughly modern. It "depends upon the form of the government," which is either republican or despotic. This is quite remarkable, because it may be the first occurrence of a dichotomy which remains in use today. Monarchy has dropped out of Montesquieu's trichotomy altogether, leaving only the two forms. Although the labels are different, understandably, Kant's dichotomy corresponds exactly to the current dichotomy of governments as either "democracies" or "tyrannies." With Kant, we can be sure that the modern state has been acknowledged.

In republican forms, "the legislative power can belong only to the united will of the people" — that is, to "citizens" who act through "representatives." In tyrannies, the legislative power "belongs" to something less than "the united will of the people." This yields part of the argument for peace. "Since the consent of the citizens is required to decide whether or not war is to be declared, it is very natural that they will have great hesitation in embarking on so dangerous an enterprise." The decision to make war means "calling down on themselves all the miseries of war, such as doing the fighting themselves, supplying the costs of war from their own resources," and much else besides. The contrast is clear. When the "head of the state is not a fellow citizen, but the owner of the state," "it is the simplest thing in the world to go to war." Not only will a war "not force him to make the slightest sacrifice," but he can "unconcernedly leave it to the diplomatic corps ... to justify the war for the sake of propriety."[8]

It is pleasant to read this as contrasting the "philosophies" of "peace-loving" "democracies" and warmongering tyrannies; but it is quite plain that for Kant (as for Adams, Madison, Lafayette, Sieyès, and others), not only was it not necessary that most "subjects" be "citizens" who vote for "representatives," but it was quite alright that most "citizens" be "passive," with no right to vote at all! Nor was it necessary that the chief executive of the state be elected. A hereditary king could function very well in a constitutional republic.[9]

Kant's Model of Republican Government: The Constitution of 1791

The distinction between *citoyen actif* and *citoyen passif* stems from the French Revolution, and some context here may be useful. The impetus for the Revolution in France paralleled that of the Revolution in America in having relatively modest goals. It began with the "Revolt of the Notables" in May 1787, came to a head with the opening of the Estates General in 1789, and was consummated with the intervention of the poor people of Paris in July and October of 1789. The Crown yielded to the demand that, as the Americans had it, there be no taxation without representation; but by July, Louis had also yielded in effect to the end of the *ancien régime*.[10] In the French context, this meant the end of feudalism, the unification of the "orders" into a "National Constituent Assembly," and the acknowledgment that "privilege" be eliminated. In accordance with Kant's second principle, there would be *one* law for *all* the French. The Revolution did not at the time involve the destruction of the aristocracy; nor was it clear in denying the king an authority vested in him by God and tradition. His authority was special, even if for some republicans, that authority, like the authority of any of France's ministers of government, was not independent of "the sovereignty of the people." What the Revolution did mean had been more than enough for Burke, thereby distinguishing him from Kant. Burke, as noted, had no patience with the "new fanatics" who insisted that "popular election" was the sole source of authority. Still, had matters ended there, the trajectory of French history might well have paralleled that of American history. France might have settled for an American-style liberal state, closer, probably, to Burke's favored form of polity, a "republic disguised as a monarchy."

The men of the Assembly, now called "Constituents," passed, on 4 August 1789, the Declaration of the Rights of Man and Citizen, "the death certificate of the old regime." While too little is usually made of it, on 14 December the Assembly began to implement, in accordance with Turgot's 1775 *Sur les municipalités* a radical decentralization of power in France. There were to be eighty-three departments, subdivided into districts and thence into cantons and communes, formerly parishes; and the latter were to be the basic administrative units. (The revolutionary significance of the Paris Commune stems from this). As in America, the whole was to be a thoroughly federal arrangement — in the *new* sense in which each division would be administered by elective representatives. Each commune, district and department would elect a council, which would serve a legislative function, and for each there would be an elective executive, a "directory" for the district and the department and a mayor for the commune. Moreover, each division would have a court with a sharply limited jurisdiction.

It is worthwhile pausing here to emphasize a difference between France and the United States in Confederation. Whereas the United States had to *create* a central government in order to fight a war, France already had a central government which, by eighteenth-century standards, was effective. The Assembly attempted to decentralize government by creating federated layers of government. In his report to the King, Turgot complained that France was barely governable, being so large and composed of "different orders ill-suited." Everything had to await the king's "special orders," since he was "compelled to decree upon everything."[11] It is a major tragedy of the Revolution, as we shall see, that the system did not have time to take root. With the war, France was subjected to a centralization of power which far exceeded anything that any absolutist state had ever had.

The Constitution of 1791 had created the form of a modern state; but it would be an enormous error to suppose that it had created either a democracy or universal suffrage. In the first place, as in America, the idea of universal suffrage was never broached. While in some states of the United States, though by no means all, there were, as compared with France, proportionately more males who were propertied and who, by virtue of this, gained suffrage rights, the principle restricting suffrage was the same. Of some 25,000,000 French, perhaps 4,300,000 had full suffrage rights — that is, were *citoyens actifs*. The rest were *citoyens passifs*, which would have been an incoherent notion to an ancient Greek. Indeed, although he heartily approved of the idea, the sensitive Kant commented that the concept "seems to contradict the definition of a citizen altogether" (p. 139). The argument that many were "unfit" to vote, still less hold office, had its origins in antiquity, of course. As Kant argued: "Apprentices to merchants or traders, servants who are not employed by the state, minors, women in general and those who are obliged to depend for their living ... on the offices of others — all these people have no civil personality" (ibid).

Second, also as in America, most authorities were elected indirectly. Moreover, in France the basis was even narrower than in America. Electors chose officials from among the wealthiest Frenchmen, perhaps some 50,000 citizens. Article VI of the Declaration of the Rights of Man and Citizen asserted that "all citizens have the right to take part, in person or by their representatives" in the formation of law. Similarly, Article XIV said that "all citizens have the right to ascertain by themselves or by their representatives, the necessity of a public tax." As Sieyès, Lafayette, and the members of the Assembly recognized, the Americans had proved that governments could be fully "representative" in the absence of direct election. Even more, after Madison had "clarified" matters in his remarkable *Federalist Paper* no. 10, the whole point of "representative" institutions was to *prevent* implementation of the "majority will." Although few were as ready as Madison to say it, the "will of the people" was now to mean what the representatives of the people believed was best for the people. It was to be government *of* and *for* the people. There was, accordingly, no inconsistency between the Declaration of the Rights of Man and Citizen and the "representative" institutions which were being created — even if, as in America, there were some who took the idea of democracy far more seriously. It was just those people, of course, who would cause trouble for the liberal center. Indeed, they caused trouble even for Robespierre and the "radical" men of the Mountain.

"The people" might well be "sovereign;" but neither Kant nor Robespierre believed in government *by* the people, even if Robespierre did believe in universal male suffrage. Given the respective reputations of the two men, the "tyrant" Robespierre and the "gentle" liberal from Königsberg, it may seem paradoxical that they should have agreed on the implications of the new concept of the "sovereign people." Robespierre had this to say on the matter:

True democracy is not a state in which the people, continually assembled, itself directs public affairs; still less is it a state in which a hundred thousand fragments of the people, by contradictory, hasty and isolated measures, should decide on the destiny of society as whole. Such a government has never existed, and if it did could do nothing but throw the people back into despotism.

Kant went even further. He asserted that democracy "in the truest sense of the word, is *necessarily* a despotism" (p. 101; my emphasis)! But even more, he can say with Robespierre that "since all right is supposed to emanate from this power, the laws it [the representative regime] gives must be absolutely incapable of doing anyone an injustice" (p. 139)!

Although the source of this bizarre, frightening conclusion in Robespierre and Kant is perhaps a bad distortion of Rousseau, it is manifest that both men quite happily ignored Rousseau's most fundamental dictum, that legislative power cannot be alienated, to a king or to "representatives" for whom one votes or to anybody! Rousseau had the temerity to hold that true democracy could exist; further that it was the only *rightful* form of rule.[12]

The Argument for Perpetual Peace

We can now complete the argument for perpetual peace. If one or more states achieve republican institutions (in the foregoing clear, concrete sense), they will simply agree among themselves not to engage in war. Instead, they will voluntarily submit whatever disputes they may have to peaceful adjudication. Each will recognize the absolute sovereignty of the other and will promise noninterference. This is a "pacific federation," a kind of "federalism" which has "a practicable and . . . objective reality," extendable "gradually to encompass all states and thus lead to perpetual peace" (p. 104).

We need to be clear about what the "pacific federation" is not. In the first place, it is not a defensive league. The idea is not to secure peace for the signatories against *other* noncompacted states, but to secure peace among themselves. Second, this was no pacifism. States reserve the right to defend themselves against aggression. It was Kant's view that if republics came to see the truth of his vision, they would gradually abolish standing armies, leaving in their stead militias. Standing armies, he insisted, created the need for war and made men into "mere machines and instruments in the hands of someone else (the state)"; whereas militias were not only consistent with "the rights of man in one's own person," but in his view were adequate "to secure themselves and their fatherland against attacks from outside" (p. 95).

This was not the first time, or the last, that the argument was offered that regular armies should give way to militias. General George Washington had urged this at the end of hostilities with Britain. Frederick Engels was to make it the center of his remarkable argument at the end of the nineteenth century. Everyone agreed that militias were ineffective machines of *conquest* and that militias could be effective as defensive forces.

Third, this is not a federation in which some third party has coercive power to enforce the agreements of the signatories. Nor is it a "world republic," something akin to the United States after the Constitution, but on a larger, ultimately all-inclusive, scale. Kant is not altogether clear whether he believes that some such arrangement would be desirable; but regardless, he finds it practically impossible. Such an arrangement would require that sovereignty be alienated. There is, evidently, a radical symmetry betwen "contract" arguments for law between individuals and "contract" arguments for law between states. Since people live in states under law, the juridical fiction of a contract between individuals by which each relinquishes sovereignty, as Hobbes had argued, could be made plausible. States are not similarly situated, and Kant seems to have believed that they would not relinquish sovereignty — what he termed, in a Hobbesian mode, their "savage and lawless freedom" (p. 105).

There is a sense in which Kant was firmly "statist" in believing that a "republic" was not only the best form of human association, but the ultimate form. For him, as for all liberals, a generally recognized government enforcing law uniformly was the indispensable condition of human life. This is not surprising. What *is* surprising, although it tends to go unnoticed, is his assumption that it is inconceivable that a state would yield any part of its sovereignty.

In accepting the American Constitution and in abandoning the idea that they should maintain effective militias, the states of the United States did in fact alienate both the right and the power to make war on one another. These circumstances were very special, of course, and the point is not to argue, *contra* Kant, that one could expect this example to be repeated, still less to issue ultimately in a "world republic." In finding the solution to the problem of "divided sovereignty" in the idea of "the sovereign people," the American experience had thoroughly muddled the concept of sovereignty.

But while Kant did not require that states abrogate their sovereignty, he rejected the view, held by Machiavelli, Hobbes, and Vattel, that "the concept of international right becomes meaningless if interpreted as a right to go to war." If this were the case, it would be "perfectly just for men . . . to destroy one another, and thus to find perpetual peace in the vast grave where all the horrors of violence and those responsible for them would be buried" (p. 105). That is, since in his view, states lacked the right to make war against any other state, it was no restriction of their sovereign rights to agree to peaceful relations.

More important certainly, and in agreement with Montesquieu and

Turgot, Kant believed that the breakdown of monarchic and feudal assumptions regarding territorial rights, the articulation of private property based on "consent," and the internationalization of commerce would provide conditions for genuine internationalization. "No one," he wrote, "originally has any greater right than anyone else to occupy any particular portion of the earth." Moreover, "the ship or the camel ... make it possible for them to approach their fellows over these ownerless tracts, and to utilize as a means of social intercourse that right to the earth's surface which the human race shares in common" (p. 106). "The peoples of the earth have thus entered in varying degrees into a universal community, and it has developed to the point where a violation of rights in one part of the world is felt everywhere. The idea of a cosmopolitan right is therefore not fantastic and overstrained" (pp. 107−8). This powerful idea was to leave it mark on the thought of a number of people, including of course, "internationalists" who were also socialists.

In sum, while there were no guarantees, the idea was that citizens in republican states could have no valid motives for wars of aggrandizement. If several sufficiently large republics could show that war was a horrible waste and that it was irrational, then it was possible that such a pacific federation could grow until it included all the states of the world.

This was not the utopian fantasy of a moralist, even if the analysis was flawed and the project doomed − at least to date. There was, I believe, a profound truth in Kant's notion that if perpetual peace was to be achieved, it would be a slow process bilaterally − or unilaterally! − initiated by governments whose interests were fully coincident with the interests of their citizens. But unfortunately, as with Turgot's argument, there were two, profoundly related, fatal flaws in Kant's argument.

In allowing that government and people were distinct − that is, in rejecting democracy − Kant allowed that there could be a wide disparity between the interests of the one as against the other. Moreover, as perhaps no one could have seen prior to the French Wars of Liberation, he did not see that "nations" could go to war for reasons utterly unrelated to the *rational* interests of the people who comprise them.

Kant knew of mass invasions and "of wars of whole peoples or cities, driven to exterminate or enslave one another by economic, demographic, religious or ethnic causes."[13] But he believed that these were things of the past, long gone. Second, he was writing on the edge of an entirely new situation. How could be know that "republican" states would engage in unlimited wars in which poor men would die to preserve the interests of rich men and in which both would die for reasons of ideology?

One could take the opposite tack, of course, and still argue against Turgot and Kant. One could simply *assume* that nations have rational motives for going to war, and that those who decide to make war, those who fight, and those who suffer the sacrifices and horrors of war share an interest in the war. This is an easy assumption to make. It is a basic assumption of a Prussian of the next generation, a philosopher of war with no articulated philosophy of the state, General Carl von Clausewitz. Indeed, it is the assumption of *all* those who make decisions about war and peace today.

The State and War: The Philosophy of Clausewitz

Clausewitz was born in 1780, the third son of a middle-class Prussian family. He enlisted in the infantry in 1792 and saw action before he was thirteen.[14] In 1801 he became an officer cadet in the new Berlin War School (the *Allgemeine Kriegsschule*), which he was to head in 1818. He took part in the campaigns at Auerstadt and Jena, where he was captured by the French. After his release, by which time he had attained a majority, he was at last able to marry the countess Maria von Bruhl, in 1810. When Frederick William decided to align Prussia with Napoleon, committing 20,000 men to the Grand Armée, Clausewitz left Prussia to serve with the Russian forces against Napoleon. The decision was a risky one; but he was correct in foreseeing that his king would again change his mind. From 1812 to 1815, as a lieutenant-colonel and then a colonel, in a Russian uniform, Clausewitz participated in the final destruction of Napoleon, played critical roles in three battles, helped to persuade the Prussian General von Yorck to join the anti-Napoleonic cause, and helped to organize a *Landwehr* (militia) of 20,000 East Prussians. His unfinished *magnum opus, Vom Kriege,* was published by his wife after his death in 1831. He was a victim of the same cholera epidemic which took the life of countless others, including the philosopher Hegel.

These brief biographical facts are intended to locate the man and his ideas. Clausewitz was a soldier who understood war; but he was much more than a strategist or a technician of war. He was a philosopher of war in the sense that he sought to grasp its "essence" and to situate it within the nexus of politics and society. Yet it is important to see that while his philosophy was based on assumptions about politics and society, he did not develop any sort of political philosophy. His remarks on this score are suggestive, but sketchy, and they leave much room for speculative inference. We can best begin by quoting liberally from his brilliant sketch of the history of war, in Book VIII.

Clausewitz writes that "half-civilized Tartars, the republics of ancient times, the feudal lords and commercial cities of the Middle Ages, kings of the eighteenth century, and last, princes and people of the nineteenth century, all carry on War in their own way, carry it on differently, with different means and for a different object."[15]

"The Tartars seek new abodes." Accordingly, "they march out as a nation with their wives and children." Yet their form of war is not consistent with "a high degree of civilization." The ancient republics, excepting Rome, were small, and "still smaller their Armies, for they excluded the great mass of the populace." Because the ancient republics were numerous and close together, none could overwhelm the others. Their wars, therefore, "were confined to devastating the open country and taking some towns" in a game of agricultural chess. Rome became the exception – in this he agrees with Machiavelli – because she was able to amalgamate her neighbors and conquer territories "into one great whole." Rome was extraordinary and almost unique.

"The Great and small monarchies of the Middle Ages carried on their Wars with feudal levies," with knights organized through vassaldom. But since these were weak confederations, temporary and fluid, wars were combats. They were brief, and their object was "generally only punishing, not subduing the enemy." The "commercial towns" employed expensive and, echoing Machiavelli, unreliable *condottieri;* and their wars were "sham fights." "In a word, hatred and enmity no longer roused a State to personal activity, but had become articles of trade." "The feudal system condensed itself by degrees into a decided territorial supremacy; the ties binding the State became closer ... and feudal levies were turned into mercenaries," an army with "its base in the public treasury." This reached its zenith with Louis XIV (1643–1715). At this point, "three new Alexanders" appeared: Gustavus Adolphus, Charles XII (the first European ruler to experience disaster in invading Russia), and Frederick the Great. These men aimed with "small but highly disciplined Armies, to raise little States to the rank of great monarchies." Indeed, "had they only to deal with Asiatic States they would have more closely resembled Alexander in the parts they acted." At this point, Clausewitz summarizes the condition of both eighteenth-century states and eighteenth-century war:

> Armies were supported out of the treasury, which the Sovereign regarded partly as his private purse, or at least a resource belonging to the government, and not to the people. Relations with other states ... mostly concerned only the interests of the treasury or of the Government, not those of the people .... The people, therefore ... were in the eighteenth century absolutely nothing directly .... The consequence of this was that the means which the Government could command had tolerably well-defined limits, which could be mutually estimated, both as to their extent and duration ...
>
> This restricted, shrivelled up form of War proceeded ... from the narrow basis on which it was supported ....
>
> Thus matters stood when the French Revolution broke out ....
> Whilst, according to the usual way of seeing things, all hopes were

placed on a very limited military force in 1793, such a force as no one had any conception of made its appearance. War had again suddenly become an affair of the people, and that of a people numbering thirty millions, every one of whom regarded himself as a citizen of the State .... By this participation of the people in the War instead of a Cabinet and an Army, a whole nation with its natural weight came into the scale. Henceforward, the means available — the efforts which might be called forth — had no longer any definite limits.

The foregoing contains the heart of Clausewitz's incisive analysis. It can be discussed in two parts. First, developed extensively, if not altogether clearly, in the body of *On War*, there is the treatment of "absolute war" and "real war." Second, there is an implicit philosophy of international politics. Our discussion concludes by inserting into Clausewitz's account some premises best articulated by his contemporary Hegel.

Like Montesquieu and Herder, Clausewitz had a holistic, concrete, historical view of society.[16] For him, differences in geography, in the mode of production and in culture and religion were causal factors which shaped politics and war, and which then, had effects on society. It is not my intention to try to infer how he saw these differences operating in the history just sketched, or even as regards the critical juncture which is his central interest on *On War*. Still, it is a major error to detach what he said about war from the concrete historical situation which prompted his reflections. In particular, his concept of "absolute war" has been victimized by abstracting it from its concrete context and treating it as if it were an early anticipation of a strategic game theory. It is not unreasonable to suppose that Clausewitz would have been appalled by this.[17]

To be sure, "absolute war" is an illuminating idealization as far as it goes. Briefly, since for Clausewitz the distinguishing feature of war is the violent clash of two parties, we can think of it as "a duel on an extensive scale." Second, since neither side is wholly in control of the other, and war is "an act of force," "there is no logical limit to the application of that force." Thus in (ideal) war, there is "a clash of forces freely operating and obedient to no law but their own." The limit of this freely operating clash of forces is absolute war, as Paret paraphrases Clausewitz, "absolute violence ending in the total destruction of one side by the other."

This is, if you will, the "law" of war; but, like falling bodies which never fall at exactly $\frac{1}{2} at^2$, no *real* war, to date, has been "absolute," even if, since Clausewitz wrote, we have come horrifyingly close to realizing absolute war, and even if, with nuclear weapons, absolute violence would almost certainly result not merely in the annihilation of one side by the other but in the destruction of every human being alive.

To date, at least, other forces have been at work constraining the outcome of war. To fill out this picture would be, of course, to complete Clausewitz's sketch of the history of war, to see in specific terms what economic, social, and political forces constrained war in human history. But Clausewitz did not do this; nor has it been done since. Still, a bit more needs to be said about the juncture which prompted his concept of "absolute war." We need to see more clearly why "absolute war," like capitalism, to take an obvious example, is an entirely modern idea.

There were three concepts on which Clausewitz constructed the core of his theory of war: "the people," "the government," and distinctly, "the army." Thus, (real) war is "chameleon-like" in that "it changes its colour" according to the relations in "a wonderful trinity." The "trinity" may be identified. First, there are the "blind instincts" which break forth in War" and which "must already have a latent existence in the peoples." Second, there are the "political objects" which belong to the Government," the aims and goals of a war. Third, there is "the range which the display of courage and talents shall get in the realm of probabilities and of chance," and this "depends on the particular characteristics of the General and his Army" (I. 1). The last, as might be expected, is of enormous interest to Clausewitz as it has been to all military readers of *On War*. In particular, it is precisely here that Alexander and Napoleon take their rightful place. But our primary interest is the relation of the "wonderful trinity," both prior to the revolutionary wars and in them.

It is easy to see that in eighteenth-century war, since "the people" were only marginally involved "the blind instincts" which have "latent existence in the people" came into play hardly at all. In the French wars, this changed fundamentally. All the "blind instincts" of the mass of people came into play, releasing energies which had never before been so completely let loose. Similarly, because, prior to the French wars, the people were not involved, the "political objects" of war were distinctly limited, involving only dynastic interests, new territories, and new wealth. Until the nation had the capacity to become directly involved in war, war had to be "restricted" and "shrivelled-up." Involving the nation meant reinventing citizen-armies. But these were massive armies mobilized by "governments" that were distinct from "the people," in marked contrast to the ancient armies. These governments had interests which were different from the "limited" interests of eighteenth-century sovereigns. Now, for example, the nation could fight for "freedom."

But in these new social and political conditions, the character of the general and his armies was also different. The bourgeois general Napoleon and his citizen-armies must be contrasted with the aristocratic generals who headed mercenary armies. Finally, then, and because of this, both strategy and tactics could differ fundamentally. For example, because he was able to draw on an almost unlimited pool of replacements, Napoleon could adopt as his aim the destruction of the enemy's force, rather than mere occupation of his territory. The price of this aim was huge casualties. Perhaps 600,000 died between 1792 and 1799. By 1815, another 700,000 −900,000 must be added − perhaps 20.5 percent of all French males! As Clausewitz commented, "Let us not hear of Generals who conquer without bloodshed. If a bloody slaughter is a horrible sight, then that is a ground for paying more respect to War" (IV. 9).

How War was Altered and How it Altered the Revolution

What was achieved in July and August of 1789 could not have been achieved without the intervention of the poor of France; nor could it have been achieved had the King's army not crumbled. Geoffrey Best (summarizing Scott) gives the picture.[18] By mid-June, the men of the elite of the army, the French Guards, were "fraternizing with the crowds and agitators at the Palais Royale"; they refused police duties from 23 June. On 30 June, ten who had been jailed for insubordination were "liberated" by a large, enthusiastic crowd. By 6 July, they were picking "patriotic" quarrels with German-speaking Hussars; and on 12 July, against loyal cavalry, they took the demonstrators' side. By 14 July there were huge defections, and in the end the elite French Guardsmen were part of the assault on the Bastille!

This was not to be the last time a revolution became possible because the Army was unwilling to suppress popular insurrectionary activity. Indeed, the converse also holds. What is most remarkable, perhaps, is the ease with which citizens in arms have been willing to kill fellow citizens, a critical point with regard to the Paris Commune and to Engels's later thinking on revolution.[19] Of the day that the revolutionaries, surrounded in the Faubourg St.-Antoine, capitulated to the Army, George Lefebvre remarks with disarming matter of factness: "This is the date which should be taken as the end of the Revolution." By then, the Army was a citizen-army with allegiance to France, not the king of France. Who controlled that army indeed controlled France.

One of the early acts of the Constituent Assembly was to legalize the militias which had grown up in July and August. They became a National Guard − initially not armies, but designed, as in England and elsewhere, for defense and the maintenance of internal order. But the new order had immediate effects on the Army as well. By the end of 1791 perhaps half the officer core had become emigrés; noncommissioned men filled their places, and the officer core was no longer the preserve of the nobility. The consequences of this were to be critical, since not only was the pool of able men enormously enlarged, a requirement for a large army, but with bourgeois officers securing command, its character was dramatically altered. Indeed, this was one of the conditions which made the rise of Napoleon possible.

The next development was precipitated by Louis XVI's abortive flight to Varenne on 21 June 1791. The day after, the Assembly called for volunteers. By August, France had a genuine citizen-army of 100,000 to serve alongside the already existing "line" army of France. Recruited locally and organized democratically — the officers were elected — this army was drawn directly from the bourgeois and artisan classes, members of the *citoyens actifs*. As in Athens, the poor were not yet part of the citizen-army.

Counterrevolution remained a likelihood, and the emigration of nobles accelerated. Leopold II, Habsburg head of the Holy Roman Empire, refusing the appeals of Louis and Marie Antoinette to intervene, continued a policy of bluff. By spring of 1792, the Assembly was convinced that something had to be done. Responding to a virtual ultimatum from Francis II (who upon Leopold's demise, had succeeded his father), on 20 April 1792, war was declared, not against the Empire but against "the King of Bohemia and Hungary" — that is, against Austria. France had taken the fatal step that was to put her in the position of fighting ultimately, all of Europe.

The question of who bears responsibility for the outbreak of war has always been both interesting and problematic, and we can see why. Because the war, which escalated in accordance with Clausewitz's law of absolute war, was such a critical fact in the development of the Revolution and then in the reshaping of Europe, historians have spilled more than the usual amount of ink in arguing about its causes. It has been easy to blame the left, but Clausewitz and his near-contemporary Ranke no doubt came nearer to the truth. As Ranke put it, "to contain the revolutionary forces [in the European states-system] was the true objective of the campaign of 1792."[20] This Thucydidean formulation suggests that the circumstances were such that, as Thucydides might have said, it is hard to imagine how war could have been avoided!

On the one hand, it can hardly be doubted that the kings and the aristocracies of Europe had a "passionate desire to crush the Revolution," and that, as in the American case, they all believed that with some sort of coalition, victory could be achieved without too much difficulty. On the other hand, and remarkably, the King, Lafayette and his constitutionalist friends, and the Girondist bourgeoisie, who, in the intervening winter months, had emerged to lead the Assembly, all wanted war. Their reasons were not only different, but actually opposing. The King believed that with French defeat, his monarchy would be restored. Lafayette believed that he would command the Army, which he could then use to bring France under control, whereupon an American-style republic could be secured. The

Girondists thought that war would dethrone the King and thereby allow them to achieve their own vision of the republic! There is huge irony in the fact that only Robespierre and some of his Jacobin supporters *opposed* the war. Although the Jacobins were the immediate beneficiaries of the war, Robespierre's prediction, that the different dreams of the republic would be shattered by despotism, was remarkably prophetic.[21]

The first engagements, on the frontier of Belgium, were French disasters. Fear spread throughtout France. The Assembly voted decrees which dissolved the King's guard and called for the deportation of refractory priests. Some 20,000 "federates," volunteers from the National Guard, were ordered to defend Paris. En route they sang the newly composed "The Army of the Rhine," what we now know as "The Marseillaise." Encouraged by the successes of France's opponents, Louis vetoed the decrees. On 20 June 1792, the Tuileries was invaded by an angry mob. The King refused to budge. Instead, he instigated a proclamation signed by the Duke of Brunswick, the leading general of the Prussian army. Published in Paris on 1 August, it threatened the city with "a military execution and total destruction" if there was any harm done to the King or his family. The upshot was the coup of 10 August, the emergence of Danton, Robespierre, and the Commune of Paris as the new leaders of the Revolution, and following the example of the United States, the calling of a Convention whose task it was to draw up a new, democratic constitution for France. For the first time anywhere, *all* adult males were given the right to vote. Year I, the year of the Second French Revolution had begun.

The war gave rise to two contradictory processes. On the one hand, the ideology of democracy became the natural means of mobilizing the nation. With the exhaustion of bourgeois volunteers for the Army, poorer citizens – the *citoyens passifs* of the Constitution of 1791 – were pressed into service. In 1793 conscription of able-bodied unmarried males between eighteen and forty became necessary. But in "republican" France this could have a rationale which it could *not* have in the absolutisms of the remainder of Europe. Chateaubriand put the matter precisely. Conscription, he said, was

at the same time naturally suited to despotism and to democracy; to the former because it enlists men by force, violates political and individual rights, and necessarily is arbitrary in its implementation; to the other because it is concerned only with the individual, and establishes a metaphysical equality that does not exist in wealth, education and manners.[22]

Moreover, republican France had the advantage that it need not fear arming the people. Clausewitz summarized what Monarchs and Aristocrats all knew: that in an era "characterized by unquiet aspirations and a spirit of dissaffection with government ... *it [was] now doubly dangerous to place weapons in the hands of the people.*"[23]

On the other hand, the organization for war against the formidable forces of the Coalition demanded extraordinary centralization, perhaps the suppression of everything associated with those ideals of democracy which had just been articulated but which had not yet had chance to take root. Indeed, lack of historical imagination has allowed many to utterly ignore this fairly obvious truth. The American War of Independence was the last "revolution" to have been largely spared this, primarily because it occurred in isolated North America before the age of unlimited war.

As has become typical in the modern world, here was a clash of "governments" with interests radically unlike the interests of earlier eighteenth-century governments. On the one side, the republican government of France was going to war with a national army to preserve a revolution. On the other, the governments of Austria, Prussia, and the First Coalition were going to war with eighteenth-century armies to restore a monarchy, and thus to extinguish a fire which might consume them all.

This explanation of the destruction of democratic aspirations – indeed, of the Terror which attended it – is not intended as a *justification* of what occurred. Still, if one assumes the same Machiavellian posture that has characterized the stance of all modern statesmen, a justification can easily be provided. Thus the important French historian Godechot:

> Until 1792 the French Revolution had scarcely known violence; a few assassinations, inseparable from strong popular emotion, in July and October, 1789, and a few demonstrators shot in July, 1791...The clergy alone had suffered great losses, and even at that, France had only imitated on a larger scale what had been done for a long time in other countries, even in the papal states; moreover, the clergy were indemnified.... The possessors of feudal rights in land also received, in accordance with the terms of the Declaration of the Rights of Man, a "just and preliminary indemnity." The war changed all that.
>
> The war suddenly jeopardized the very existence of the country. To save the liberty and independence of the nation – the provider and defender of individual liberty – it was necessary provisionally to suspend individual liberties and to impose political, economic, social and economic constraints. The war also made clear the attitudes of the King.... And if treason and conspiracy multiplied, was it not indispensable to inaugurate a reign of terror to save both France and the revolution? Had it not been for the war, there would probably never have been a reign of terror, and without the terror, victory would not have been possible.[24]

Most of what Godechot says here is probably true. But the second paragraph makes some assumptions which should be made explicit. Like all modern republicans, he assumes that the "nation" is "the provider and defender of individual liberty." In this case, in order to preserve the goals of the Revolution – individual liberty – the nation had to be secured against counterrevolutionary invasion. But, Godechot knows that if the resources of a nation are needed for its defense in the modern epoch, then the government must act in the *name* of the nation. The head of the government, the King, was in effect a traitor – hence the coup.

Once one accepts the idea of government (in the modern sense) and the fact that its officials have a right to act so as preserve the nation – in this case, so as to preserve the condition for the preservation of individual liberty – then the remaining questions are *technical*. One can then argue about whether the *means* adopted by the Committee of Public Safety were justified. Given the premises already adduced and given the war, then, *if*, as Godechot says, the suspension of individual liberties and the endorsement and organization of the Terror were *necessary* means, then the actors were justified.

To answer the question of whether they were in fact necessary, one must take note of Thucydides' frame. Were the actors really "compelled"? The issue does not concern the philosophical chestnut of whether their will was free or whether they were "fated" to act as they did. Rather, it concerns whether there were alternatives consistent with the imperative to defend the nation. And plainly, to answer this question, one must engage in counterfactuals. What would have happened had they not done what they did? What would have been the outcome had the Committee *not* silenced the Press, for example, *not* closed the tollgates, *not* ordered the arrest of refractory priest and aristocratic nobles, and *had* used the *federates* to quell the murderous riots which broke out, and so forth.

It may be countered that this is the idlest of speculation; and no doubt, it is difficult – perhaps impossible – to answer these particular questions. But if they are utterly unanswerable, then one had best retreat to one's premises. By denying the usefulness of counterfactual judgments about the consequences of alternative possibilities, *all* judgments on the technical questions are disallowed. One can neither condemn nor approve. If this displeases, then one must reject the Machiavellian imperative which makes the actions of public men assessable only by appeal to judgments on technical questions. It is a fundamental point of this book that few among us are willing to do that. How to preserve the republic? How to preserve its ends? Rather, it becomes easy to defend acts as necessary and hence justified, perhaps because we favor the goals, the outcome, or the actor – for whatever reason. It is not too much to say here that those who judge the acts of 1792 to have been necessary need not admire the actors or approve of the outcome. It is sufficient to believe passionately in the goals; those who condemn those acts do so because they reject the outcome, the men, or the goals – or all three.

Within a year there were one million men on the army rolls of France, an unbelievable total. But this was not the whole of it, since the famous *leveé en masse* was aimed not only at fielding a huge army but in mobilizing every man, woman, and child in France in defense of the Revolution. The Committee of Public Safety put the matter squarely:

> Until the enemies of France shall have been chased off the territory of the Republic, every French person must stand ready to serve and support our armed forces. Young men will go to fight, husbands will forge weapons and manage the transport of services; wives and daughters will make tents and uniforms and will serve in the hospitals; old men taking their stand in public places will inflame the bravery of our soldiers and preach the hatefulness of kings, the unity of the Republic.

The ideological component of this is strikingly put and cannot be overstated; nor, perhaps, the commitment that had been engendered. Indeed, the Committee of Public Safety could not keep women from the ranks. Their role in the Revolution had been critical from the very beginning, a fact of some importance; but there was some novelty in finding women in the revolutionary army. The commander of the 1st Battalion of the Saint-Denis, the Army of Belgium, wrote a final leave of absence for Felicité Duquet, "whose zeal had induced her to take up arms when the country was in danger and who since has been serving in our battalion." In granting her leave, the Lieutenant Colonel publicly declared "that said Duquet conducted herself with valour and courage in all the actions in which the battalion was engaged."[25]

As Clausewitz saw, the republic of France had been able to field an enormously large army and to tap the resources of the entire nation. This changed everything; for "the people," "the army," and the "government" were now effectively one. Could a coalition of eighteenth-century armies defeat the French, especially when passion and numbers were joined with the brilliance, boldness – indeed, recklessness – of a Napoleon?[26]

War, State and Nation

As it happened, the answer was yes, and this points to an easily overlooked feature of Clausewitz's analysis. While "people," "government," and "army" are so obviously independent ideas, it is nevertheless amazingly easy to forget this, when, for example, we talk about "Prussia" or "The French

Republic," or "the state" or "the nation." Prussia was a state, but only dubiously a nation; it had both a government and an army. The *armies* of the Second Coalition did defeat the *armies* of France, but it was not the Prussians and the Russians themselves, for most of the people remained nothing, as Clausewitz so bluntly put the matter.

Clausewitz knew this, of course. Still, he regularly and uncritically wrote as if "governments" — republican, monarchic, or despotic — unproblematically "represented" "nations"; and that when it came to war, any government worth its salt should, unproblematically, be able to call for the exceptional energy and resources which the French had been able to mobilize. Thus, after completing his "galloping" historical survey (sketched above), he wrote:

> Whether all Wars hereafter in Europe will be carried on with the whole power of the States, and consequently, will only take place on account of great interests closely affecting the people, or whether a separation of the interests of the Government from those of the people will again gradually arise, would be a difficult point to settle. (VIII. 3)

This text is frequently quoted, but no one seems to have noticed that it is unmitigated nonsense. It plainly assumes, against all evidence, that the wars of the period were fought because of "great interests" which "closely affected the people," and that in each of these states, including presumably Tsarist Russia, the "interests of the people" were largely coincident with the "interests of the Government."

This was not true even of France. Indeed, the internal politics of France, the vigorous intervention of the sans-culottes, the repression, the Terror, the Vendée, the treason of Dumouriez, and much else besides would be utterly unintelligible if we assumed some unproblematic relation between "people" and "government." To be sure, the successive regimes of France — the Committee of Public Safety, the Directory, and after 10 November 1799 ("the 18th Brumaire") the regime of Napoleon — were "governments" which could with some plausibility claim to "represent" "the nation"; for in France republican ideas and institutions had come into existence, and there had been a revolution which put Social Democracy on the historical agenda. The "orders" had been shattered, and *égalité* had gone beyond civic equality to full suffrage. In addition to the "metaphysical" equality justly named by Chateaubriand, there was a "metaphysical" *unity* that one could attribute to the French "nation."

But, surely, as much cannot be said of the remainder of Europe, including Britain. These other states fought with eighteenth-century armies and did so precisely to maintain a status quo in which "the people" were nothing —

as Clausewitz well knew.[27] These states, combined against the audacious armies of France, did "contain" the Revolution, even though as Tocqueville was later to write, the *idea* of democracy, once unleashed, would prove to be irresistible.

Nevertheless, what is most remarkable perhaps is how ready modern writers on war and international politics are to treat states as homogeneous entities with certain "interests," to assume, as above, that "national interests" are coincident with the interests of "the people" and that "governments" more or less represent the nation's interests. The contrast with Turgot is stunning.

These assumptions depend on two critical ideological elements, both born between 1787 and 1792. The modern idea of "representative government" is one. Once "the people" are "sovereign" and sovereignty is "represented," the battle is half won. But the modern idea of a "nation" is also critical. Once the older concept of *patria* could be used to mobilize those who might share little more than a written language, then the idea of a nation-state became possible. This is an entirely modern invention; and we need to pause here to consider, all too briefly, what it involves.

The preconditions of the modern nation reach well back into history and include the secularization of knowledge, "print-capitalism," and through this the standardization of vernacular languages in writing.[28] Variety in the countless French, English, German, and Spanish dialects which made it difficult – if not impossible – for one local group to understand another not too far away was now overcome in print. The upshot was "unified fields of exchange and communication," and a new language of power, the "official" languages of secular authority. By the eighteenth century, sense could be made in Europe of the idea of nations, imagined communities of "peoples" linked by no more than a common script perhaps. But, as Benedict Anderson rightly sees, the catalysts for the emergence of the modern concept of "the nation," the nation as a nation-state, were the independence movements of the New World. He writes:

> Out of the American welter came these imagined realities: nation-states, republican institutions, common citizenships, popular sovereignty, national flags and anthems, etc., and the liquidation of their conceptual opposites: dynastic empires, monarchical institutions, absolutisms, subjecthoods, inherited nobilities, serfdoms, ghettos, and so forth.[29]

With this giant step, the idea that individuals have interests in common with others merely by virtue of being members of the same "nation" now made sense.

The idea of the nation-state, once created, could not be stopped. Shipped to France in the French Revolution and empowered by the French Wars of Liberation, it took on a potency which it could never have had in the relatively unpopulated, already polyglot, isolated states of the Americas. Given the circumstances in Europe, war, symbolized by the unfurling of tricolors, was the critical fact. In the environment created by the Revolutionary French armies, the idea of a nation worked hand in hand with republican ideas, propelling them and being propelled by them. Thus the confrontation of German speakers with Napoleon's armies stirred German "nationalism." With good reason, the Prussian ruling class associated this new nationalism with liberalism, a fact of some historical importance. Fichte's Berlin "Addresses to the German Nation" of 1807–8 were given just after Napoleon's dreams of the Grand Empire had forced a break with Prussia. They are the background for Hegel's influential theory of the nation-state, to be developed next.

Clausewitz and Hegel: The Philosophy of International Relations

As noted, Clausewitz had an implicit philosophy of international relations. It is compressed in his famous dictum that "War is not a mere act of policy but a true political instrument, a continuation of political activity by other means." It is fair to say that Clausewitz took for granted a philosophy of international relations which derived from the new environment of warring nations. And, with good reason, it was deeply indebted to Machiavelli.[30] This philosophy may be summarized in the five following propositions:

1 The actors in international relations are nation-states. Like individuals, nation-states have definable interests and goals.
2 It is the object of foreign policy to realize these.
3 The state is sovereign in that it recognizes no authority above itself.
4 Since at any time it may be in the interests of a nation-state to increase its power at the expense of other states if it is to preserve its independence, there is a persistent need to have offensive and defensive strength.
5 Since war is but an extension of foreign policy by other means, it is the normal condition between states.

Now it seems true enough that, at least as regards modern war, as Clausewitz saw, the "actors" in international relations are whole "nations" mobilizing the resources, skills, and passions of entire populations. In a certain sense, this is the definitive feature of modern war. Yet it is even more obvious − even if it is ignored by Clausewitz and most writers on the topic

— that decision making regarding war, its initiation and conduct, is in the hands *not* of the "nation," but of its government.

Moreover, there is the matter of "national interests." This raises a number of questions. First, do "national interests" transcend the interests of members, or are they merely the interests of the members of a nation, taken distributively? Second, either way, what are these interests, and how are they to be determined? Third, are there interests which override all others — for example, "national security" interests? And if so, why? Even if Machiavelli is correct in saying that it is the responsibility of a government to guarantee the freedom and security of the state, is this always in the interests of all the members of the state? Finally, connecting these concerns with the foregoing, in what sense are national interests, assuming this idea can be made intelligible, "represented" by governments who have the responsibility of carrying them out?

It will take some powerful arguments to answer these difficult and important questions, I believe. Yet they need to be answered if this philosophy of international relations is to have any plausibility. We need to establish that the nation — not merely the government, the ruling class, or this or that group — has interests. We need to be able to determine what these interests are, so that they can be represented and acted upon; and we need to have mechanisms for assuring that the government is, in fact, acting to realize these interests.

Yet difficult and important as these issues are, there are, it seems, but two general lines of argument which can be used in responding to them. One requires the idea of democracy in some sufficiently strong, interesting sense. It requires that individuals with interests are able collectively to define interests which as individuals they share. It can hardly be doubted that there can be collective interests, even "national" interests, in this sense. But whether such interests can be articulated in a representative democracy is a difficult question, not to be argued in this chapter.

The other line of argument does not require the idea of democracy. This argument is metaphysical and moral and was developed in extraordinary, if abstruse, detail, by an exact contemporary of Clausewitz. It is fair to say, however, that if the argument is abstruse, the conclusions are taken for granted in all modern nation-states. The theory and argument are part of the complicated philosophy of Hegel.[31]

Hegel's argument is not easy to grasp and, accordingly, it is not part of the common understanding; but by now his conclusions seem so intuitively sensible that they are widely shared. Hegel held that members of nations — or more strictly, nation-states — are members of particular, idiosyncratic unities. Anything which affects such a unity affects all. Accordingly, individuals have a duty to defend it, for in so doing, they are defending its special character, institutions, way of life, and so on. Insofar as it is constitutionally organized, its government is its mind and its will. Thus the constitutionally organized nation-state is like a person in a world of other persons, each with his or her own individuality and interests. Clausewitz put the matter clearly in describing, in the terms of Thucydides, the decision to go to war. He wrote: "If we regard the State policy as the intelligence of the Personified State, then amongst all the constellations in the political sky whose movements it has to compute, those must be included which arise when the nature of its relations [to other Personified States] imposes the necessity of a great War" (I. 1).

Hegel gives a profound argument for this view; but unfortunately, this cannot be developed here in any useful way.[32] Hegel wanted to show that the idea neatly captured by Clausewitz's remark rests on conditions which are wholly *rational*. Indeed, we can say that the philosophy of international relations summarized in the five propositions above is the most rational thing in the world, rooted, for Hegel, in a grand, inclusive, metaphysical vision of history. But his argument is not convincing, even if, as Marx saw, it contains some undeniably true elements. No matter. Nobody who believes in the truth of his conclusions believes them because they were led to them by his argument. What follows is meant only to expose the heart of his influential philosophy of international politics.

Hegel writes: "A nation does not begin by being a state. The transition from a family, a horde, a clan, a multitude &c, to political conditions is the realization of the Idea in the form of that nation" (para. 349). The Idea, as we shall see, is the Idea of Freedom. The key development for Hegel was the emergence of the constitutionally organized nation-state. "So long as [the nation] lacks objective law and an explicitly established rational constitution, its autonomy is formal only and is not sovereignty" (para. 349). That is, once "a nation," a people united by ties of "speech, mores and customs [*Sitten und Gewohnheit*] and culture [*Bildung*]" is constituted as a "society of persons [*Menschen*] under juridical conditions," it becomes a nation-state.

Hegel saw that it was no longer possible to hold that monarchies were kingdoms, because in no way could it be maintained that the monarch's "domain" was his *property*. Hegel agreed here with Kant. Nor, for the same reasons was it possible to legitimate a king and his "government" – no longer his "household" – in terms of "tradition" or "Divine Right." Capitalism and the invention of "civil society," from Hobbes to Locke to Kant, guaranteed this. On the other hand, it was still possible to deny that any sense could be made of the concept of a "sovereign people," the alternative which has become available only in the last decades of the eighteenth century.

In a section of *The Philosophy of History* entitled "The Eclaircissement and Revolution," Hegel posed the problem of the sovereign people and provided his explanation of the Terror. With Rousseau clearly in the background, Hegel asked, "How does Will assume a definite form?" In Germany it received a "speculative," "formal," "tranquil" expression in Kant. But with the Revolution, the French gave it "practical effect." Unfortunately the Constitution of 1789 "involved from the very first an internal contradiction; for the legislature absorbed the whole power of the administration."[33]

With the king and aristocracy "under suspicion," ruin was inevitable. A government of some kind however is always in existence. The question presents itself then, Whence did it emanate? Theoretically, it proceeded from the people; really and truly from the National Convention and its Committees. The forces now dominant are the abstract principles — Freedom, and, as it exists within the limits of the Subjective Will, Virtue.[34]

Robespierre, of course, was "Robespierre the virtuous." He erected "the principle of Virtue as supreme, and it may be said that with this man Virtue was an earnest matter." But "Subjective Virtue, whose sway is based on disposition only, brings with it the most fearful tyranny."[35]

Hegel, unsurprisingly perhaps, found the solution in "constitutional monarchy." "In the Crown, the different powers are bound into an individual unity which is thus at once the apex and basis of the whole, i.e., of constitutional monarchy" (para. 273). Hegel is a committed constitutionalist, republican in the sense that rule of law and the Rights of Man and Citizen are critical modern innovations. But unlike Kant, he takes very seriously the idea of a nation which, taken together with its rational Constitution, forms a substantial unity which is the nation-state.

Although this difference between Kant and Hegel is absolutely fundamental, it is fair to say that it constitutes a deep, but easily accommodated, tension of liberalism in the era of the national state.[36] In Kant's cosmopolitan conception, people live in "civil society," indifferently in states. For Hegel, as for Marx, "civil society" is an improverished abstraction which involves "a loss, destruction, or privation of ethical life" (*Verlust der Sittlichkeit*). For him, the state as nation is "the actuality of the ethical Idea." Moreover, the nation is internalized in individual consciousness: "The state exists immediately in custom [*Sitten*], mediately in individual self-consciousness, knowledge and activity" (para. 257).

But if a nation acts, it acts by means of somebody. The personification of the State in the person of the sovereign is explicit: "[T]he state has individuality, and individuality is in essence an individual, and in the sovereign an actual, immediate individual" (para. 321).[37] Finally, the nation-state is a sovereign entity: "The nation state is mind in its substantive rationality and immediate actuality and is therefore the absolute power on earth" (para. 330). Individuals "participate" in a larger whole. God is the absolute power; but the nation-state is "the absolute power on earth" in that it is sovereign vis-à-vis the earthly affairs of human beings.

For Hegel, the transition from family, horde, and clan to the constitutionally organized nation-state is part of the struggle to realize the Idea of Freedom. Indeed, the French Revolution had provoked Hegel into believing that "the History of the World is none other than the progress of the consciousness of Freedom."[38] But this realization presupposed, he insisted, the clash of autonomous nations. Thus, "[the] actual and organic mind . . . of a single nation . . . reveals and actualizes itself through the interrelations of the particular national minds until . . . in the process of world history it reveals and actualizes itself as the universal world-mind whose right is supreme" (para. 33). This is a profoundly eschatological vision of history, of course. Indeed, it is a theodicy.

Each such sovereign unity has as its aim and object the "welfare" of the whole. But this is inconsistent with peace. "Since states related to one another as autonomous entities . . . and since the particular will of the whole is in content a will for its own welfare pure and simple, it follows that welfare is the highest law governing the relations of one state to another" (para. 336). "If states disagree and their particular wills cannot be harmonized, the matter can only be settled by war." To be sure, "a state through its subjects has widespread connections and many-sided interests, and these may be readily and considerably injured; but it remains inherently indeterminable which of these injuries is to be regarded as a specific breach of a treaty or as an injury to the honor and autonomy of the state" (para. 334). Because the nation-state is sovereign, only it can decide when there is an injury to its "honor" or autonomy. In a constitutional monarchy, of course, the "ultimate decision," "the will with the power of ultimate decision," is the Crown (para. 273).

As for subjects, "sacrifice on behalf of the individuality of the state is the substantial tie between the state and all its members and so is a universal duty" (para. 325). Finally, then:

> War has the higher significance that by its agency, as I have remarked elsewhere, "the ethical health of peoples is preserved in their indifference to the stabilization of finite institutions; just as the blowing of winds preserves the sea from the foulness which would be the result of prolonged calm, also corruption in nations would be the product of prolonged, let alone "perpetual," peace. (para. 324)

That Hegel stands at the opposite pole to Kant is clear enough. Indeed, it is quite incredible that we should have such a stunning contrast in so short a span of history. Kant and Hegel were both Germans and both republicans; but no comparison can better show how much the

European world had changed with the Revolutionary Wars of France. For Kant, perpetual peace was possible precisely because republics are comprised of rational individuals, transacting business under a common law. The state simply serves to make the rules under which all are equally free. For Hegel, this defines "civil society," but not the state. In his view, republics are nation-states, comprised of "peoples" who live in community. But because these unities are "autonomous" and the effort to achieve their unique geniuses will inevitably put them in conflict, war is inevitable. Remarkably, war is also "healthy," solidifying the community, cleansing it, and tapping energies which would otherwise remain latent. There is no "moral equivalent" for war.

It is deeply ironical that Hegel, who struggled to comprehend what was happening in terms of Reason and Freedom, should provide materials for the nineteenth-century conception of *Weltmacht* and the twentieth-century irrationalisms which we call fascism and Nazism. But we make a gigantic error if we fail to appreciate the incredible vitality of his conclusions even in liberal democracies. At least as regards international relations, no one doubts that a nation-state is person-like, and that nations have a will and interests. No one denies that there is an ethical imperative requiring that participating members act to sustain the unity which is the nation-state, even in war. Indeed, these ideas are reinforced when they are joined, as they always are nowadays, with the equally fraudulent view that just because the authority of the representative regime derives from popular election, it is "the people" whose distributive will and interests are expressed and carried into action.[39]

So the arguments are fraudulent. Nevertheless, if the philosophy of international relations defined above remains eminently plausible and still defines the common assumptions of the present world, then, though we might profoundly regret this, it defines a "reality" which has to be lived with, not fantasized away.

Although we will go on to deepen our understanding of this historically constituted reality, we conclude this chapter by drawing an obvious implication of it. As Clausewitz taught us, "real war" risks "absolute war," and "absolute war" requires that entire nations have reasons to mobilize themselves against one another in war. But given the logic which propels arming a nation for war and which then propels the course of a war of nations against nations, victory means destruction not of the *armies* of the nations on the other side, but of the nations themselves. The two world wars of this century were constrained, but barely so. They did not run their course to the limit. But today, with nuclear weapons, "absolute war" would seem to mean the end of *homo sapiens*, a poor name perhaps for the human species, given its history.

10

War and Revolution: Marx and Engels

The period from the Congress of Vienna (1815) to the outbreak of World War I (August 1914) has been termed "the European century of peace." Everything, of course, is relative. The wars of the period, Crimea (1853–6), Italy (1858–9), the war between Prussia and Denmark (1864), the Austro-Prussian war (1866), the Franco-Prussian War (1870–1), and the Russo-Turkish War (1877–8), were *limited* wars, fought for the most part as wars had been fought in the eighteenth century, with long-term professional armies for limited goals. Overshadowing these were the revolutions of the period: a small wave, first in Spain and Naples (1820), then Greece's War of Independence (1821). These were followed by a second, more serious wave from 1829 to 1834. All Europe west of Russia was affected, most notably France with the ascension of the "Citizen King," Louis Philippe as constitutional monarch, Belgium in gaining independence from Holland, and Poland with its unsuccessful revolution. A still more potent wave started in 1848. It led to the creation of the Second French Republic and encompassed the whole of Italy and the German states. It affected most of the Habsburg Empire, as well as Spain, Denmark, Rumania, Ireland, and Greece, though less acutely. In the 1870s came the Paris Commune and the Third French Republic, the development of Russian populism (the Narod, or "Going to the People movement"), and elsewhere, especially in Germany and Britain, the dramatic growth of socialist labor parties and hence the threat of socialist revolution, real or imagined.

Marx and Engels

Most people, being born in this place or that, quickly come to accept the political and social system in which they grow up. But some of them become revolutionaries — for reasons which may be as different as are the individuals and their circumstances. Karl Marx was born in 1818 in Trier, then still predominantly Catholic. On both sides of his family there had been a long line of rabbis. His grandfather, Marx Levi — the Levi was later dropped — was a rabbi in Trier, but his father, Hirschel Marx, a lawyer, had converted to Christianity in 1824, taking the name Heinrich. Although Napoleon Bonaparte had given Rhenish Jews civic equality, Heinrich Marx both hated the conqueror and had an unshaken belief in the "genius" of the Prussian monarchy, anti-Semitic though it was. Karl Marx went to Bonn to study law and then, urged by his father, to the new University of Berlin. There he decided on an academic career. After writing a dissertation on Greek philosophy entitled "The Difference between the Democritean and Epicurean Philosophy of Nature," he was awarded a doctorate in 1841, *in absentia*, by the University of Jena. Academic infighting between the "young Hegelians" and the conservative establishment at Berlin had made this the wisest course.

Frederick Engels was also bourgeois, born in Barmen, Westphalia, the son of affluent, conservative, religiously orthodox Pietist parents. He went to college in Elberfield but left before taking his final examinations to enter his father's firm, which he described as "this damned business." The year in which Marx became editor of the *Rheinische Zeitung* and began his battle with Prussian censorship, 1842, Engels was in "the King's uniform," fulfilling his duty as a conscript in the Prussian artillery. En route to Berlin, he had met Marx, but the meeting was cool. By the time they met again, after Engels's twenty-one months in England and Marx's exile in Paris, they had both became revolutionaries.[1]

Today, of course, the majority of the people of the world are educated in schools in which the names of Marx and Engels stand in much the same relation as the names of Locke, Adam Smith, Voltaire or Jefferson stand in schools this side of "the iron curtain;" and moreover, in many places, the struggles between these two great ideologies are surely not over. In this chapter the focus is on the thought and action of Marx and Engels. I do not intend to be comprehensive, as regards either the many issues of historical significance or the particular problems of Marxist exegesis. My main aims are to combat anachronism; to fight the all but overwhelming tendency to read history backwards, either by fantasizing about "revolution" or by finding the "seeds" of existing forms of socialism in the "logic" of the thought of Marx and Engels. Existing forms are light-years away from even the least of the hopes of Marx and Engels, and this needs to be explained. But Marx and Engels were nineteenth-century thinkers. The modern state was new; "democracy" was not a utopian vision; and Clausewitz's insights about "nations" armed to the teeth and ready to annihilate one another had not yet become the reality of World War I.

There can be little doubt that a misread Marx and Engels powerfully engendered confusion as regards the 1917 revolutionary situations in both Russia and Germany and then as regards "socialist" development in Russia, especially after 1927. Getting closer to the real Marx and Engels is a struggle, requiring an act of historical imagination as well as the usual tools of scholarly exegesis. We begin with the "young" Marx.

Uncivil Society

Because the modern state emerged on a foundation of capitalist social relations, it arose as the liberal state. In the eighteenth century, "civil society" and "political society" were synonymous, as evidenced in the title of the seventh chapter of Locke's *Second Treatise,* "Of Political or Civil Society," the chapter which takes persons from "the state of nature" to that of "civil society."[2] The key feature of this transition was the existence of statutory law. The same idea is found in Kant, who believed, contrary to fact, that therein were the makings of a peaceful world. But with the advantage of hindsight, Hegel saw more clearly what had happened. On his view, if "civil society" (*Bürgerliche Gesellschaft*) is the state, then there is no state; there are only individuals standing in voluntary exchange relations under the protection of a system of law, just as Kant had implied. In contrast to Kant (and nearer to Hobbes), for Hegel, "civil society is the battlefield where everyone's individual interest meets everyone else's, so here we have a struggle (a) of private interests against particular matters of common concern and (b) of both of these together against the organization of the state and its higher outlook."[3] Marx liked the battlefield metaphor. As he put it, "*Security* is the supreme social concept of civil society, the concept of the police, the concept that the whole society exists only to guarantee to each of its members the preservation of his person, his rights, and his property."[4]

Hegel had sharply distinguished between civil society and the state. Once "a nation" became a constitutionally organized society, it was a state – or better, a nation-state. Civil society was but an abstract, limited conception, which entailed a "loss, destruction, or privation of ethical life." In words powerfully recalling Aristotle's, the state was a unity, but not a "partnership" existing for the sake of exchange, as Lycophron had it. It was a "substantial unity," and membership in it was not, as contract theory implied, "something optional." It was thus, also, that the *bourgeois* was raised to the status of a *citoyen*. In the state, "personal individuality and its particular interests not only gain explicit recognition ... but they pass over of their own accord into the interest of the universal and, for another thing, they know and will the universal" (para. 260). In the state, persons participate in a common life. This participation includes the duty to preserve this common life, which itself includes the duty to defend, in war, the national state. A true state needs a mind and a will as well as a soul. Hegel ´ held that the French Revolution had raised the problem of sovereignty in a critical way, and he was altogether correct in judging that it was this problem with which "history is now occupied, and whose solution it has to work out in the future."[5]

Marx fully agreed with Hegel's characterization of "civil society" and was thoroughly familiar with Hegel's difficult philosophical argument for his preferred solution to the problem of the modern state, a constitutional monarchy. But Marx also saw that Hegel's solution was already reactionary. We can begin with Marx's 1843 critique of the solution developed by Hegel in his *Philosophy of Right*, especially the sections on sovereignty.

The Sovereignty of the People

Marx quotes Hegel: "'The sovereignty of the people' is one of the confused notions based on the wild idea of the 'people.'" Hegel had continued: "Taken without its monarch and the articulation of the whole . . . the people is a formless mass and no longer a state" (quoting para. 279). For Marx, the "confused notions" and the "wild idea" are *Hegel's* confused notions. Just as Hegel had returned to Aristotle, so did Marx, except that Marx rejected Aristotle's untranslatable *politeia* − "the generic constitution" − for democracy. For Marx, "democracy is the generic constitution." "Democracy can, monarchy cannot, be conceived in its own terms . . . . [I]n Monarchy a part determines the character of the whole."

> Democracy is the solution of the *problem* of all constitutions. In democracy the constitution is always based on its actual foundation, on *actual man* and the *actual people*, not only *implicitly* and in its essence [as Hegel would have it] but in its *existence* and actuality. Here the constitution is man's and the people's own work. The constitution appears as it is: the free product of man. (p. 173)

But a democracy is *not* a republic (the word often used, misleadingly, as has already been pointed out, to translate *politeia*). The modern republic is "only a particular form of state," and in the modern state "political man," as Hegel had argued, "has his particular existence alongside unpolitical man, private man," in Hegel's terms, *Bürger als bourgeois*. Thus, "the struggle between monarchy and republic is itself a struggle inside the abstract state." "In North America," Marx's paradigm of a republic, "the *republic* is thus a mere form of the state as monarchy is here [that is, in Prussia]. The content of the state remains outside these constitutions." It is thus that "*political life* in the modern sense of the word is the *scholasticism* of a people's life. *Monarchy* is the completed expression of this alienation. The *republic* is the negation of alienation within alienation."

This Hegelian language should not deter us. Having relinquished all power to the monarch who "represents" his subjects, with the American and French revolutions, monarchy is "negated." But in denying the "sovereign" in favor of the "sovereign people," people in their everyday lives are still members *only* of civil society, in that they do not rule. Indeed, "the abstraction of the *state as such* belongs only to modern times because the abstraction of private life belongs only to these times. The abstraction of the *political state* is a modern product." This "abstraction" is not possible in the ancient republic, for in the ancient republic, there is no bifurcation of the public (and political) and the private. Hegel is not wrong, accordingly, in his diagnosis of the *problem* of the modern state, even if, from Marx's point of view, he fails to take the obvious, if radical, step toward democracy.

Hegel sees as well that states have governments and that the key feature of government is bureaucracy: "service of the state," "offices" which require "renunciation of selfish and capricious purposes," tasks in which there is "satisfaction in dutiful achievement, and only in that." Indeed, for Hegel, "here lies the link between universal and particular interests, constituting the concept of the state and its inner stability" (pp. 177–90, *passim*).

Marx draws different conclusions. In a chilling remark he alludes to the Kantian conception of universal duty: "Bureaucracy makes the 'formal state spirit' or the *actual* spiritlessness the categorical imperative." Do your duty. Do it whether or not it pleases you, whether or not *you*, in your individual will, think it right. The member of the bureaucracy is "compelled to pass off what is formal for the content and the content for what is formal. The purposes of the state are changed into the purposes of the bureaus and vice versa." Now offering a Kafkaesque metaphor, "bureaucracy is a circle no one can leave." "Its hierarchy is a hierarchy of information. The top entrusts the lower circles with an insight into details, while the lower circles entrust the top with an insight into what is universal, and thus they mutually deceive one another" (pp. 185–6). This is the alienation of the modern state. As hinted, the defining institutional feature of the modern state is the location of legislative power in a representative body, either in a constitutional monarchy as Hegel would have it, or in a pure republic, as in North America. But "the participation of civil society in the political state through deputies is precisely the expression of the separation and merely dualistic unity." "If all were to be legislators, civil society would have to abolish itself." Accordingly, direct democratic control, if realized, is "also the abolition and transcendence (*Aufhebung*)" of the "abstract" state. It is "the dissolution of the state, but likewise the dissolution of civil society" (pp. 190–202).

This line of argument informs everything that Marx ever wrote on the modern state. In the next year, in "The Jewish Question," a review of treatises by his former mentor, Bruno Bauer, Marx returned to these themes, deepening his analysis. In this essay, Marx distinguished "political emancipation" from "human emancipation." Fresh from a reading of the French Revolution and American society, he again clearly catches the significance of the use to which the Americans had put the concept of "the sovereign people." But now, he seems to have discerned that the *fully realized* modern state would be a *democratic* state. With the creation of the United States, the term "democratic state" was no longer a *contradictio ad adjectivo*.

Political emancipation − "a great step forward" − would be fully realized when "distinctions of birth [including race and gender], rank, education and occupation" are no longer political distinctions, when "every member of a community equally participates in popular sovereignty without regard to these distinctions" (pp. 224−5). This achievement required, however, that in the fully realized modern state, the republic with universal suffrage, alienation be fully obscured; indeed, this was exactly the upshot of "the negation of alienation within alienation." Exclusion from the state was the mark of political powerlessness. Thus women and blacks were not citizens. They knew themselves to be nonmembers. But when everyone is equally a citizen, then each is equally potent − or impotent. It was thus that even if political emancipation was "the final form *within* the prevailing order of things," political emancipation could not be "the final form of universal human emancipation" (p. 227).

Marx's analysis parallels exactly Feuerbach's criticism of Christianity. In the Christian community, all humans, as the children of God, are brothers and sisters, equal members of the Christian *ecclesia*. But this is the "*fantastic* [meaning in fantasy, not "marvellous"!] *realization* of the human essence inasmuch as the human essence possesses no true reality" (p. 250). The human becomes human not on earth but in heaven. Just as that critique had "unmasked human self-alienation" in its "holy" form, the task now was to unmask it in its "unholy form." It is thus that "the criticism of heaven turns into the criticism of the earth, the *criticism of religion* into *the criticism of law*, and the *criticism of theology* into the *criticism of politics*" (p. 251).

In a republic, each citizen is "an imagined member of an imagined sovereignty, divested of his actual life" − divested of gender, race, class, occupation, religion, and of his or her unique and individual qualities. Instead, each is "endowed with an unactual universality" − the Rights of Man and Citizen. But who is this Man and Citizen?

Political democracy is Christian in that it regards [humans] − not merely one but every human − as *sovereign* and supreme. But this means man in his uncivilized and unsocial aspect, in his fortuitous existence and just as he is, corrupted by the entire organization of our society, lost and alienated from himself, oppressed by inhuman relations and elements. (p. 231)

To say that in the democratic state individuals are "uncivilized" and "unsocial" and that they have "fortuitous existences" is not to say that individuals are barbaric or nasty or motivated by greed — though this may also be true. The point has nothing to do with "human nature." It is to say, rather, that they are isolated, that they relate anonymously, that their situations are "accidental," like their sex or race, and that, in consequence, their distinctly human, individual, and social powers are unfulfilled. This is the result of "the entire organization of society," but in particular of the market structure of bourgeois society and the alienating structures of the modern state. As Paul Thomas points out, "the state becomes a fetishistic personification of political potential, very much as the concept of capital designates the separation between the conditions of labor and the producer. Both are the members of society's own, real force set up against them, opposed to them, and out of control."[6] "The people" are sovereign, but they have no power over the conditions of their lives. As sovereign in an illusory community, they are in reality controlled by "inhuman relations," by the "laws" of the market, by the imperatives of the bureaus and offices of the state.

The problem of democracy is not solved by the institutionalization of abstract rights, however much acknowledgment that people have equal rights is a monumental step in both consciousness and law. Rather, the problem of democracy is the problem of establishing a way in which people can control the conditions of their lives and so end alienation. This is the problem of democracy exactly because these conditions, excepting those determined by "nature," are in general the unintended consequences of deliberate human action.[7] People make the social world, but they do not make it with materials of their own choosing; nor, except in democracy, is the world they make subject to their control. Just as the social world is the unintended product of the activities of countless anonymous, isolated individuals, creating conditions which in turn control the creators, so controlling the conditions of life can only be a conjoint effort.

A number of critical implications flow from Marx's analysis. First, the problem for Marx is first and last *political*; it concerns what has to be done and what has to happen if people are to gain control of the circumstances which structure their lives. This problem is not to be solved "economistically" or by perfecting the instrumentalities of the democratic state. This distinguishes Marx's view from, for example, that of Proudhon on the one hand, and republicans on the other. For Marx, human emancipation could not be arrived at by a more just distribution of the social product, even though people obviously need bread to live; nor could it be achieved by perfecting the machinery of statist politics. The end of alienation meant, rather, the realization of the human capacity for self-determination. This meant gaining control of the *means* of life, which in turn meant gaining control of the means of *organizing* life.

Second, to achieve this goal is to overcome the *duality* of civil society and the state. But this means, as Marx writes, that "in true democracy, the political state disappears *(untergeht)*." This view has its Rousseauian intimations, of course, and suggests the critical point of comparison to nineteenth-century anarchisms and to later Social Democracy. Although a great deal more could be said about what this might mean, there can be no doubt that it is the most historically troublesome feature of Marx's analysis. It will haunt both Lenin and the Social Democrats of revolutionary Germany. Viewed from the vantage point of today, it seems hopelessly naive and utopian. But whether it is to be written off entirely depends, perhaps, on the use to which this vision is put, whether to constrain programs and politics, thereby keeping them aimed toward increasing democracy or whether, as in contemporary states, to justify antidemocracy, either by discrediting all attempts at increasing democracy as an illusory ideal or by pretending that the democractic state is already the realization of the most democratic of possible political forms.

Third, if state power was to be broken, it had to be done by an agency which did not reflect the alienated relations of private property. As Marx wrote, the task of breaking state power had to be that of "a class with *radical chains*, a class in civil society that is not of civil society, a class that is the dissolution of all classes, a sphere of society having a universal character because of its universal suffering" (pp. 262–3).

This is an early statement of what, for most people, is the most distinctive feature of Marxian politics: the *inevitable* revolution of the proletariat.[8] It takes us straight to the most famous of the tracts written by Marx and Engels, the *Communist Manifesto* of 1848.

Revolution and Class Democracy: The Communist Manifesto

The predictions of the *Manifesto* are wildly optimistic, to be sure. Marx and Engels assume, on the basis of the "forces" at work, that capitalism is forging the weapons that will bring "death to itself." Moreover, in a marvelous "dialectical" twist, these forces are calling into existence "the men who are to wield those weapons." World revolution is just around the corner.

What goes unnoticed about the *Manifesto*, however, is that the idea of the proletarian revolution is not in the slightest fleshed out; while at the same time, the program for transformation *after* the revolution could not be more concrete and hard-headed. Indeed, if we· look at it historically, without jumping to conclusions, there is nothing in it which is antidemocratic, still less totalitarian.

It is of greatest importance to notice that the idea of "revolution" can *not* be taken for granted, even if a number of features of the idea in the writings of Marx and Engels are both clear and highly significant. These may be summarized as follows. First, "revolution" always refers to social transformation. Thus, in the *Manifesto* Marx and Engels oppose "Conservative, or Bourgeois, Socialism." Conservative socialists — "economists, philanthropists, humanitarians, improvers of the condition of the working class, organizers of charity, members of societies for the prevention of cruelty to animals, temperance fanatics, hole and corner reformers of every imaginable kind" — are but "desirous of redressing social grievances, in order to secure the existence of bourgeois society."[9] But, second, a social revolution, if it is to be a *revolution,* is also and necessarily political. Revolutions require "the conquest of political power." But the converse does not hold: not every such "conquest" is "revolutionary." A *coup d' état* is, as such, not revolutionary. This suggests a third feature. A conquest is revolutionary when it is made by a revolutionary class. In securing political power and destroying feudalism, the bourgeois were a revolutionary class. Likewise, the proletariat constitute a revolutionary class, who, according to Marx and Engels, have "nothing to lose but their chains."

Fourth, all the emphasis in the *Manifesto* (as in the corpus as a whole) is on the formation of a revolutionary *political party,* a working-class party distinct from other parties which, once it attained power, would "revolutionize" society. As Hobsbawm points out, neither Marx nor Engels paid any attention to questions about the nature of that party; nor did they ever suggest that it was to be sectarian or conspiratorial. Indeed, they frequently asserted that it could *not* be either of these things. Nor did they ever deviate from the assertion in the *Manifesto* that "the Communists do not form a separate party opposed to other working-class parties," or that their immediate aim is "the same as that of all other proletarian parties: formation of the proletariat into a class, overthrow of the bourgeois supremacy, conquest of political power by the proletariat." As Hobsbawm remarks, "it is thus vain to seek in Marx for the anticipation of such later controversies as those between 'reformists' and 'revolutionaries' .... He recognized no conflict in principle between the everyday struggle of the workers for the improvement of their conditions under capitalism and the formation of political consciousness which envisaged the replacement of capitalist by socialist society."[10]

Fifth, there is the question of violence. Almost everything that Marx and Engels wrote suggested that the *transformation* would involve violence; but their writings are not clear on the question of whether the *conquest* of political power would require violence. The two terms which are most useful here are perhaps "insurrectionary accession" and "accession constitutionally."[11] Marx and Engels always insisted that "the workers will have to win political supremacy in order to organize labor along new lines, . . . to defeat the old policy supporting old institutions;" it is also fair to say that they always insisted as well, to continue this text, that "we have by no means affirmed that this goal would be achieved by identical means." And at least by the time of this text, a speech by Marx in Amsterdam in 1872 – though perhaps much earlier, in the fifties – they held that the conquest of political power could be by peaceful means. Marx wrote: "We know of the allowances we must make for the institutions, customs and traditions of various countries; and we not deny that there are countries such as America, England, and I would add Holland if I knew your institutions better, where the working people may achieve their goal by peaceful means."[12] Marx was nevertheless quick to point out that "in most of the continental countries it is force that will have to be the lever of our revolutions; it is force that we shall some day have to resort to in order to establish a reign of labour." Most of the continental countries, of course, were not democratic republics in any useful sense. The problem was to sharply confront both German and Russian Marxists in 1917–18.

Still, in the *Manifesto*, there is one paragraph – and *only* one – which anticipates an insurrection: "In depicting the most general phases of the development of the proletariat, we traced the more or less veiled civil war, raging within existing society, up to the point where that war breaks out into open revolution, and where the violent overthrow of the bourgeoisie lays the foundation for the sway of the proletariat." The model here is almost certainly Paris, but was it Paris in 1789 or 1792 or later? What happened in Paris in 1789 was relatively nonviolent; in 1792 it was not. And, critically, the violence of 1792 was incited by the threat of war and counterrevolution. Counterrevolution is *always* violent, and Marx and Engels were never pacifists. Even if the conquest of political power did not require violence, they never doubted that the encounter with counterrevolutionary forces would be violent.

Finally, we know that for Marx and Engels both the conquest of power and the movement toward transformation would constitute an extended process involving problems which could hardly be predicted. Even if there were "a crucial moment," it would not be, to quote Hobsbawm, "a once-and-for-all transfer of power to be followed by some sectarian Utopia." Nor could this "moment" be simply "decided." Rather, it was conceived as the outcome of long, often disappointing struggle. Indeed, this was the source of the rift and the debates in the First International with the anarchists and other more apocalyptically inclined revolutionaries.[13]

Perhaps the clearest statement of Marx's unwavering position is his 1850 speech, given in response to a deep rift regarding strategy among the members of the Central Council of the Communist League:

> The materialist standpoint of the *Manifesto* has given way to idealism. The revolution is seen not as the product of realities of the situation but as the result of effort of *will*. Whereas we say to the workers, "You will have 15, 20, 50 years of civil war to go through in order to alter the situation and to train yourselves for the exercise of power," it is said" We must take power *at once*, or else take to our beds.... Just as the democrats abused the word "people," so now the word "proletarian" has been used as a mere phrase.[14]

Revolutionary "catchwords" were no substitute for revolutionary process. Marx and Engels may have been persistently forced to readjust their calenders, but they appreciated that any conquest of power worth the name of a proletarian revolution would be by politically conscious proletarians who were ready to exercise power.

Recurring, then, to the Aristotelian lineage of the idea that democracy was class rule by the poor, Marx and Engels wrote that "the first step in the revolution by the working class, is to raise the proletariat to the position of ruling class, to establish democracy." In *this* democracy "the political state" does not disappear for, as a *statist* form, *it* is still a "dictatorship," albeit a dictatorship of the majority, the proletariat, against the minority, the owners of the means of production. This democracy was exactly what Madison, in the tenth *Federalist Paper* had feared: the "party" of the poor governing in the interests of the poor.

The *Manifesto* is not clear about how the proletariat would get this power, but it is perfectly clear about how it would use the power once it got it. The general aims are summarized thus: "The proletariat will use its political supremacy to wrest, *by degrees*, all capital from the bourgeoisie, to centralise all instruments of production in the hands of the State, i.e., of the proletariat organized as the ruling class; and to increase the total of productive forces as rapidly as possible" (my emphasis).

It will pay to look more closely at what this means. A ten-point program is involved, as follows:

1 Abolition of property in land and application of all rents of land to public purposes.
2 A heavy progressive or graduated income tax.
3 Abolition of all right of inheritance.
4 Confiscation of all property of all emigrants and rebels.
5 Centralization of credit in the hands of the State, by means of a

national bank with State capital and an exclusive monopoly.

6 Centralization of the means of communication and transport in the hands of the State.

7 Extension of factories and instruments of production owned by the State; the bringing into cultivation of waste-lands and the improvement of the soil generally in accordance with a common plan.

8 Equal liability for all labour. Establishment of industrial armies, especially for agriculture.

9 Combination of agriculture with manufacturing industries; gradual abolition of the distinction between town and country, by a more equable distribution of the population over the country.

10 Free education for all children in public schools. Abolition of children's factory labor in its present form. Combination of education with industrial production, etc., etc.

Items 1, 5, 6, and 7 taken together give more concrete meaning to the idea that "the proletariat will use its political supremacy to wrest, by degrees, all capital from the bourgeoisie." As Adam Smith had argued, "as soon as the land of any country has all become private property, the landlords, like all other men, love to reap where they have never sowed." Item 1 proposes to end this, cheerfully acknowledging the step as one of the "despotic inroads on the rights of property." From the Greeks to Marx's day, democratic attacks on private property constituted the very definition of tyranny. Indeed, up to the 1830s and perhaps later, capitalism was thought to be incompatible with democracy! Liberalism, yes. But democracy?

Item 1 does not demand that enterprises which formerly paid rent to rentiers be state-owned or managed, however. Items 2, 6, and 7 imply that, except for communications and transportation, businesses and industries which are privately owned will, at least initially, remain that way. Had Marx and Engels intended otherwise, presumably they would have said so. Item 7 does not call for the expropriation of the existing private industrial sector, either all at once or gradually. Rather, it calls for the creation of a public sector alongside it. Presumably, capitalist relations of industrial production will gradually give way to the new socialist relations, simply because capitalist "rationality" is in fact irrationality. The point is critical as regards the claim (below) that "in the course of development," "class distinctions will disappear." Similarly, one must be wary of the remark that the aim is "to centralise all instruments of production in the hands of the State, i.e., of the proletariat organized as the ruling class." This surely means that, as with property in land, eventually the instruments of production will be "in the hands of the State"; but, as the text says, "the state" is here considered not as something over and above the proletariat, but as the proletariat politically in control.[15]

There are at least two cautions regarding of the picture sketched so far. But these stem from what we *now* know, not from theoretical inconsistency on the part of Marx and Engels. We would doubt that, if put side by side, businesses in the public sector, whether under workers' control or state control, would put businesses in the private sector "out of business." Second, we know that "socialism" subsequently came to mean antidemocratic state control. Neither Marx nor Engels, of course, could foretell the future.

Similarly, item 5 does not call for the confiscation of deposits – what would amount to the elimination of private capital as such. Its purpose, as Bender notes, is to transfer the power of credit, a step which might well have been endorsed by Alexander Hamilton! All modern industrial societies have some version of items 2, 6, and 10, even if the United States is unique in leaving communications and transportation mostly to private monopolies. Item 4, confiscation of the property of rebels and emigrants, is by definition, "despotic;" but there is nothing particularly Communist about it. It has a long history, from ancient times to the American and French revolutions. Item 8, the "equal liability for all labor" seems to mean "no work, no eat;" and though when we think of "industrial" and "agricultural armies," we think of Stalin, Marx and Engels's reference is to the idealized work-place democracies of those "utopians" who "by the force of example" hoped, mistakenly in the view of Marx and Engels, "to pave the way for the new social Gospel." That is, Marx and Engels rejected not anarchist and utopian views of work and community, but anarchist and utopian views of what had to be done to bring these to reality.[16] Perhaps item 3 is the most radical measure, though it should be compared to Jefferson's remarkable idea that every forty years all inheritances should be abrogated!

The "dictatorship of the proletariat," a democratic class state, was, however, but "a first step in the revolution of the working class," as was stated in *The German Ideology* of the same year: "The reality that communism creates is the actual basis for making it impossible that anything should exist independently of individuals, insofar as this reality is only a product of the preceding interaction of individuals themselves" (*Writings*, p. 456). And found expression in the *Manifesto*:

When, in the course of development, class distinctions have disappeared, and all production has been concentrated in the hands of a vast association of the whole nation, the public power will lose its political character.... In place of the old bourgeois society, with its classes and class antagonisms, we have an association, in which the free development of each is the condition for the free development of all. (*Works*, vol. 6 pp. 505–6)

Marx and Engels did have a deep critique of the democratic republic, but as Lenin put it, they never wavered from "the idea which runs like a red thread throughout all of Marx's work, namely that the democratic republic is the nearest approach to the dictatorship of the proletariat." But this was not because (or only because) in the democratic republic, there would be a well-developed economy, but because in that form of polity, the realization of political emancipation could give way to the task of realizing human emancipation. Individuals, now alive to their collective power, would be ready to take control of the conditions of their lives.

Similarly, the text just quoted anticipates Engels's much later "withering away" metaphor. *We* know that in actually existing socialisms, the state has not "withered away." We also know − *a priori?* − that regimes, with the police and an army at their disposal, do not put themselves out of business. But if the democratic class state of the *Manifesto* is not a warfare state with a centralized planned economy, self-reproducing bureaucracy, and all the other now taken for granted elements of a modern national state, the vision is not far-fetched. The army, for example, might well be a militia. Indeed, initially the new class state might be quite a *minimum* state, something like the United States in 1848, except that its elected central government, in representing the politicized proletarian majority, will be asked − that is told! − to do less and less. "In the course of development," as production is put into the hands of producers, "public power" *loses* its "political character," loses, that is, its repressive character. As the producers increasingly take control of decisions which affect them, in the workplace and in their communities, the "state" ceases to have critical functions. If this vision is utopian, as well it may be, it is nevertheless hard to see how it is antidemocratic.

In part, this vision of the economy in transition explains the failure of Marx and Engels to address what *we* know to be critical *constitutional* questions regarding the democratic class state. What about the problem of usurpation? What about civil liberties? In terms of the sketch just offered, the optimal case is surely that the conquest of political power would take place in a modern state, preferably a republic, with all that this implies: representative institutions, freedom of speech and the press, regular elections, and so forth. The objection to the hard-won idea of the republican state was that in the *bourgeois* class state, the Rights of Man and Citizen were both abstract and sharply restricted, that they gave persons only an *imagined* freedom and an *imagined* sovereignty. Concretely one had the right to choose among one's exploiters, the right to own what one could never afford, the right to say what one pleased unless it threatened the status quo, and the right to vote for candidates who represented the interests of the rich and the powerful. But everything Marx and Engels ever said on the subject shows that they appreciated that you cannot get to democracy undemocratically.

Marx's "Critique of the Gotha Program" of 1875 is pertinent here.[17] Despite "their motley diversity of form," modern states are "based on modern bourgeois society." Between capitalist and Communist society "lies a period of revolutionary transformation of the one to the other. Corresponding to this is also a political transition period in which the state can be nothing but the revolutionary dictatorship of the proletariat." The problem with the Gotha Program is precisely that "it does not deal with this nor with the future state of communist society." In a word, it was not revolutionary. Its *political* demands, "universal suffrage, direct election, popular rights, a people's militia," were certainly excellent; but in the German context, they were utterly meaningless. The German workers' party has "forgotten the chief thing, namely that all those pretty little gewgaws rest on the recognition of the so-called sovereignty of the people and hence are appropriate only in a democratic republic." The German workers' party would make a revolutionary demand if it demanded a democratic republic, as did the French under Louis Philippe or Louis Napoleon. Instead, lacking the courage to do this, they resort to "subterfuge." They *pretend* a democratic republic and then make demands from "a state which is nothing but a police-guarded military despotism, embellished with parliamentary forms, alloyed with a feudal admixture, already influenced by the bourgeoisie and bureaucratically carpentered."[18] In the bargain, they "assure this state" that "they will be able to force such things upon it 'by legal means.'" Worse, its vaguely asserted economic demands – a progressive income tax and "fair" distribution of the proceeds of labor – could be endorsed by "Liverpool financial reformers, bourgeois headed by Gladstone's brother"!

Phrases like "pretty little gewgaws" may encourage the view that Marx disdained universal suffrage and what not; but as the foregoing should have made clear, for Marx, the German workers' party could not accede to political power and begin the transformation of society as long as Germany was "a police-guarded despotism, embellished with parliamentary forms." The road to "true democracy" required the smashing of the Bismarckian state and the constitution of something closer to democracy, perhaps a bourgeois republic as in Britain or perhaps, better, a proletarian republic, as Rosa Luxemburg was later to suggest.

It was thus that the Chartists, who "contend for nothing but the demand for *Universal Suffrage*," are revolutionary.

Universal Suffrage is the equivalent for political power for the working class of England, where the proletariat forms the large majority of the population, where through underground civil war, it has gained a clear consciousness of its positions as a class .... The carrying of Universal Suffrage in England would, therefore, be a far more socialist measure than anything which has been honored with that name on the continent.

That Marx mistakenly believed that a workers' party in England would be revolutionary should not keep us from seeing his point. To emphasize, this is not merely an endorsement of a "peaceful" conquest. It also presupposes that this conquest achieves a form of republic in which the ruling class is no longer the bourgeois, but a political organized proletarian majority ready to transform the social relations of society and move toward "true democracy."

One final point regarding "the dictatorship of the proletariat." It has been pointed out that the use of the Roman *dictatura* in the *Manifesto* implied delegation of power in cases of temporary emergency and that, given the failure to include consititutional guarantees, this was an "invitation to permanent usurpation of the dictatorship and destruction of proletarian democracy." Yet, even if it be granted that "dictatorship" was meant to carry the connotations of Roman *dictatura*, there is no reason not to grant as well that in the proletarian conquest of power, the proletariat would be less interested than their bourgeois predecessors in such safeguards. But in fact the use here of the term "dictatura" is far from clear. From Marx's point of view, wherever there is a state, there is a dictatorship, precisely because states are repressive. Still, there is no doubt that Marx and Engels ignored constitutional questions vis-à-vis the democratic class state, and that it has therefore been easy – though not all *that* easy – to find in their texts justifications for the later antidemocratic acts of Marxist revolutionary parties.[19]

But it is the Paris Commune of 1871 which, perhaps paradoxically, gives us the best perspective on how they saw democracy in the real world. The Commune gave Marx and Engels a paradigm of the "dictatorship of the proletariat," a paradigm which prefigured – albeit prematurely – the earlier intimations of "true democracy." But before discussing this, we need to see how war comes into the picture, how the Franco-Prussian War promoted the Commune, and how, with the disaster of the Commune, Marx and Engels came to change their minds about the relations of war and revolution.

The Question of War

It is surely true that neither Marx nor Engels provided any sort of analysis of the pertinence of nationalism in the modern world, and that this constituted a huge, critical lacuna in Marxist theory. Marx and Engels were internationalists, clearly; but if they lacked an adequate analysis of the phenomenon of nationalism, they nevertheless were students of Hegel and there fully recognized that the nation-state was, for the foreseeable future, a permanent part of the landscape, and that war was a fact of life and a critical variable in the cause of revolution. Finally, they recognized that chauvinism (after Paul Chauvin, the hyperpatriot of the French Revolution) might well be a serious problem. As Engels came to conclude, war would surely lead to "the recrudescence of chauvinism in all countries."[20]

But Engels did not begin with this view. His first "model" of the relation between war and revolution was certainly the 1792 (or 1793) model. War would create the conditions for revolution; for not only did it destabilize existing regimes, but it brought ordinary people under arms, inspired them to military triumph, and presumably, by politicizing them, intensified a revolutionary consciousness, as had allegedly occurred in France's "second" radical revolution. This model continued to have its attractions; and indeed, for many it still does. But the events of 1848–9 caused Marx and Engels to rethink their position.

Engels was directly involved in several of these events.[21] In May 1849 the *Landwehr* of Elberfield, Engels's old college town, refused Prussian orders to march against Baden for having accepted the Frankfurt Assembly's Constitution. Two companies of Prussian regulars arrived but refused to fire on the recalcitrant militiamen. Barricades went up, and swarms of helpers arrived, including "the Cologne writer, Engels, from Barmen." Engels "did find some military employment" but created new problems in advising that a volunteer *Bürgerwehr*, armed to protect property, be disarmed. We shall never know whether he was actually responsible, but he was accused of replacing the black-red-gold flags – liberal nationalist – on the barricades with red flags, symbol, of course, of the socialists; and he was asked to leave.

Engels and Marx then went to Baden, where a republic had been proclaimed. They were rebuffed and promptly arrested. After their release, Marx went to Paris, and Engels took a position as August Willich's adjutant. Willich's *Freischaar* (volunteer corps) had performed nobly in the next to impossible task it had taken on. It would bring on the revolution by force of arms.

From the start, Engels believed that Willich could not succeed, and as Berger notes, there is "more than a hint of embarrassment in Engels's explanation of his motives for enlisting."[22] He would represent the *Neue Rheinische Zeitung* "*honoris causa*," because "the whole motley pack of democrats were in Baden and the Palatinate and now congratulate themselves on their imaginary exploits."[23]

These episodes have two features that are pertinent here. First, these "imaginary exploits" form the background of the 1850 split in the emigré-dominated Communist League, alluded to earlier, in which Willich and Marx found themselves on opposite sides. On Marx's view, the idea that a revolution could be instigated by "a small, well-armed band, amply supplied with money" was a version of Blanqui's politics and pure nonsense. As what had happened in the Germanies had confirmed and as Marx and Engels had insisted from the *Manifesto* on, a putsch, assuming, contrary to fact, that Willich's courageous warrious could have succeeded, was not the sort of "revolution" they had in mind.

Second, the experience may well have raised in Engels's mind the question of the difficulties of repeating the experience of 1792, and this in two senses. First, as he later came to see, the population was not politicized in anything like the appropriate way; and second, the capabilities of militia in Elberfield and volunteers in Baden suggested that, judged from a strictly military point of view, there were some problems which needed to be thought through.

Still, it seemed that other events were confirming the 1792 model. In the Prussian-Danish war, at first a patriotic and reactionary effort (according to the *Neue Rheinische Zeitung*, "Schleswig-Holstein-meer-umschlungenen Strohenthusiasmus," ["Schleswig-Holstein sea embattled enthusiasm,"] a pun on the anthèm of Schleswig-Holstein), the struggle against the Danes had driven the Schleswig German leadership to more radical measures. Engels hoped that it would trigger a larger conflict, and that the armistice would be repudiated and would bring Russia and England, aligned with Denmark, to war. This would provoke, as in 1792, a genuine revolution: "Only war with Russia is a war of revolutionary Germany," Engels wrote. Marx added that "the old England [would] be brought down only by a world war, which alone [could] offer the Chartists the conditions for a successful uprising."[24] Marx suggested that an *unpopular* war might lead to revolution in England. In the event, the armistice was ratified, and the *Landwehr* and the republicans knuckled under. No German revolution was in the cards.

Similarly, Engels was writing that the Austrian war was promoting revolution in Rome, Tuscany, and Piedmont. But three days after writing this, he changed his mind, noting that "it was a great blunder from the beginning for the Piedmontese to oppose the Austrians only with a regular army that would fight an ordinary, bourgeois *honetten Kreig* [genteel war]"[25]

Perhaps a limited, eighteenth-style war was useless. This suggested, ominously, that what was needed was not merely war; it was a war like that in 1793, a war which was republican and unlimited. Engels exclaimed: "[A] mass uprising, general rising of the people — these are the means from which the kingdom shrinks in terror. These are the means which only a republic can employ — 1793 proves it."[26] The already mythological Hungarian situation was evidence for this. Inspired by Kossuth, here was a nation which dared "to oppose skulking counterrevolution with revolutionary passion, to oppose white terror with red terror." "All the principal features of the glorious year 1793" were there: "mass rising, the manufacture of weapons on a national basis, assignats, swift justice for those who impede revolutionary movement, the Revolution in Permanence."[27]

On the other hand, by 1851 Engels was clear about an issue which pulled in the opposite direction. Could volunteers and militiamen, even given a radicalized population, win a war against a determined, professional army? After all, there had been *no* successes. At this juncture, even the apparent French successes of 1793 and the following years came in for reappraisal. Valmy was a trivial duel. The *levée en masse* was no panacea. Indeed, Engels was now led to confess that "precisely the factor that enabled Napoleon to form gigantic armies rapidly, namely good cadres, is necessarily lacking in any revolution (even in France)."[28] Finally, the successes of Napoleon were due as much as anything to the indecision and incompetence of his opponents, as Clausewitz and the Prussian military reformers had judged.

For Engels, there were two sides to the coin: "It is a plain fact that disorganization in the armies and the total disorganization of discipline have been conditions as well as results of every successful revolution to date." On the one hand, nothing guaranteed that regular armies would refuse orders, fraternize with the enemy, or fall apart. On the other, "national enthusiasm ... is a capital thing to work upon, but until disciplined and organized, nobody can win battles with it."[29] The Franco-Prussian War would prove the point. Indeed, it would prove to Marx and Engels beyond any doubt that Marx's words of 1852 ought not ever to be forgotten:

> The social revolution of the nineteenth century cannot draw its poetry from the past, but only from the future. It cannot begin with itself, before it has stripped off all superstition in regard to the past. Earlier revolutions required world-historical recollections in order to drug themselves concerning their own content. In order to arrive at its content, the revolution of the nineteenth century must let the dead bury their dead.[30]

But, of course, this was easier said than done.

The Paris Commune, War, and Democracy

Louis Napoleon described his foreign policy as "*L'Empire, c'est la paix.*" But like others before and after him, he used war to encourage chauvinism and to shore up his popularity. He encouraged the Crimean War for reasons that would have been intelligible to an eighteenth-century monarch: Nicholas I had slighted him; the Italian war was prompted by a failed assassination attempt; and dynastic motivations prompted the failed effort in Mexico, with Archduke Maximilian of Austria. With liberal opposition growing, he came to believe that war would be the solution to the problem of assuring the accession of a Napoleon IV. Bismarck could not have been more pleased.[31]

The Franco-Prussian War, like all wars, had unintended consequences. One was was the end of Louis Napoleon's Second Empire; another was Bismarck's successful unification of the German states. A third, following on the first, was the Paris Commune. With the Army at the front, General Trochu was sent back to Paris to defend the city.[32] The prospect of invasion had roused the left, and republicans feared revolution. Still, there was no choice but to reconstitute the National Guard in defense of Paris. Sixty new battalions were created, making a total of 300,000 Parisians in the Guard. The original sixty "good battalions" – that is, safe, reliable battalions – had been drawn from the bourgeoisie. On 3 September, at Sedan in Belgium, MacMahon's entire army, along with the Emperor, was captured. A provisional government composed of Paris deputies was declared. Leon Gambetta convinced the festive crowd which had gathered at the Hôtel de Ville that the tricolor, not the red flag, should be the flag of the Republic. No one in the crowd had any way of knowing, however, that this would not be a Government of National Defense, but a "Government of National Defection."[33]

The *Gazette de France* of 5 September, however, rightly diagnosed the problem. The government, it wrote, was caught between the Prussians and the Reds. The writer did not know, however, "which of the two evils the bourgeoisie most feared; they hate the foreigner most, but were more fearful of the Bellevillois."[34] Belleville was the most notorious working-class quarter of Paris, the place where, appropriately, the Commune was to make its last stand in May 1871.

After four months of siege, on 28 January 1871, the Government of National Defense capitulated. Paris now had to be disarmed, but this proved to be far from easy. Indeed, the elected central committee of the National Guard, acknowledging only an armistice, itself became a rump government. When on 18 March, Prussians moved to take National Guard artillery, Parisians mobilized. On 30 March the Paris Commune was elected, and an entirely new experiment in democracy had begun.

The Commune remains, for most, an anachronism, a throwback to some nostalgic, idiotic past. Indeed, as Marx noted, "it was generally the fate of completely new historical creations to be mistaken for the counterpart of older and even defunct forms of social life, to which they bear a certain likeness" (p. 73). But for Marx, the democracy of the Commune was a "historically new creation" and "the glorious harbinger of a new society." In what sense, then, was the Commune "a completely new historical creation"?

On the one hand, it was anarchist in that it broke state power. As Marx wrote, "The unity of the nation was not to be broken, but, on the contrary, to be organized by the Communal Constitution and to become a reality by the destruction of the State power which claimed to be the embodiment of that unity independent of, and superior to, the nation itself, from which it was but a parasitic excrescence" (*ibid.*). But it was not anarchist in the sense of Stirner, Proudhon, or Bakunin. Marx took these writers seriously – with good reason – but because, on his view, they lacked an adequate understanding of political economy, he saw them as mistaken as regards both their vision of a good society and the means of attaining it. In a nutshell, Marx saw anarchists as inverted statists. Since on their view the state was the problem, once ride of it, all would be well. Because for them there was little point in discriminating between forms of the state, transformative activity, whether the anti-revolutionary activity of Proudhon or the conspiratorial activity of Bakunin, must wash its hands of the state. As Proudhon said, "To indulge in politics is to wash one's hands in dung."[35]

Marx saw the matter very differently. His view of the Commune gives us a start in seeing how. In the first place, the Commune was "a thoroughly expansive political form, while all previous forms of government had been emphatically repressive. Its true secret was this. It was essentially a working-class government, the product of the struggle of the producing against the appropriating class." (p. 75). Marx was surely overstating his case here, as he himself admitted later. But we must be clear what this means. The Commune had fashioned the first "government" – the word must be used gingerly – to aim at realizing full control over the circumstances of life by ordinary citizens. It was thus "expansive" by contrast with those previous forms which took for granted the conditions of ordinary life. Even the best of previous forms – for example, the democracy of ancient Athens – took these for granted. Previous democracies, like nondemocracies, were "repressive" in that they aimed only to replace the rule of one class by that of another – without altering the alienating conditions which called for class rule in the first place. For these democracies, the mode of production was "given," a "natural," unalterable fact.

Thus, in the ancient *polis*, "politics" concerned the struggle between rich and poor over decisions of law and war; but the poor were not social revolutionaries in the sense that they either did or could aim at reconstituting society. This latter idea, which derived from the French Revolution, was based on the perception, now familiar largely through the thought of Hegel and Marx, that human history was radically *unlike* natural history in being the product of human activity. As Marx and Engels had said in *The German Ideology*, "Communism differs from all previous movements in that it overturns the basis of all earlier relations of production and intercourse, and for the first time consciously treats all natural premises as the creatures of hitherto existing men, strips them of their natural character and subjects them to the power of united individuals" (*Writings*, pp. 460–1).

A second point of comparison between Marx's understanding of the Commune and anarchist thought regards the question of "government." For us, either there is some form of government or there is "anarchy" – meaning no authority, no coercive organization. Indeed, this idea is reinforced by a great deal of anarchist polemics; but the confusion goes deeper and depends on the eighteenth-century identification of rule with government.

In the ancient *polis*, there was, strictly speaking, no government; but there were rulers, either one, few, or many. Political power was *unmediated*, In the modern state, however, there are always governments, the executive, a parliament, bureaucracies, and the police; and they always claim to "represent" the "governed." It has therefore been easy to suppose that the middle ground between self-rule and rule by others is modern political democracy, "representative government." But, if we look more critically, we will be inclined to say that power is exercised by *governments*, even if it is exercised on behalf of "the people" or , with Marx, on behalf of a "ruling class." But for Marx, the form of a republic was not the only alternative, and the institutional novelty of the Commune lay precisely in this.

There were "functionaries" of the people, "agents" in the strictest sense, and these were under strict "instructions" from those whom they represented. These functionaries were not, as in bourgeois democracy, merely "authorized" to rule those who elected them; they were ambassadors or military commanders, "responsible" and "revocable" at the pleasure of those who elected them. "Sovereignty" was *not* alienated, just as Rousseau had insisted. As Marx wrote:

> Instead of deciding once in three or six years which member of the ruling class was to misrepresent the people in Parliament, universal suffrage was to serve the people, constituted in Communes, as individual suffrage serves every other employer in the search for the workmen and managers in his business. And it is well known that companies, like individuals, in matters of real business generally know how to put the right man in the right place, and, if they once make a mistake, to redress it promptly. On the other hand, nothing could be more foreign to the spirit of the Commune than to supercede universal suffrage by hierarchic investiture. (*Commune*, p. 73)

It is hard to know how to classify such an arrangement. Is it a "government" with power but no authority, or with authority but no power? It would "manage," but, like the police and the courts — which are not to be abolished — it would be "elective, responsible, and revocable."[36] Marx's analogy is almost perfect. A "company" could be "operated" by "workmen and managers," and no one would suppose that the owner of the company had lost his "sovereignty." It was but elitist propaganda to believe that the same principles could not apply to a commune.

It is also clear that if "the unity of the nation" was not to be broken, then some sort of federation must be involved; but while this was not to be a "federation of small States, as dreamt of by Montesquieu and the Girondins," it is not clear what exactly Marx had in mind. The point is critical and is usually passed over too quickly.

Neither Marx nor Engels had much to say about "federalism." Yet, as seems clear enough from this context and the few others that we have, the objection to the federalism which they attributed to Montesquieu and the Girondins — and even more to anarchists like Proudhon and Bakunin — was that their "federalist" views were strikingly ahistorical. They believed that "nations" were entirely dispensable unities sustained *only* by the coercive force of the state, and that, as Proudhon had arued, a modern economy could be reduced to simple contractual relations between individuals. This was, accordingly, the federalism of Turgot and Bakunin.[37] Marx, the internationalist and student of Hegel, believed that "the nation" was, as Bloom writes, "an individual society which functions with a considerable degree of autonomy, integration and self-consciousness."[38]

Contra Hegel and his "nationalist" predecessors, Marx is clear that a "nation" is not to be understood as an entity defined by a common language. German speakers who lived in Poland or Hungary or America were members of the Polish, Hungarian, and American nations, not automatically or "naturally" members of the German nation. Marx evidently accepted the *de facto* territorial boundaries of "advanced countries" as "nations." The basis of such "unities" as suggested, was the fact that they had more or less unified economies. Accordingly, not all historically generated territorial boundaries qualified as nations. Marx and Engels seem to have held that, in the *modern* world (and for the indefinite future), not only were "large members and compactness of territory" necessary to ensure the economic viability of a "nation," but that there were broader requirements having to do with resources, the level of social development, and the degree of scientific advance which had been attained.[39] Just after saying that the Communal Constitution was mistaken "for its attempt to break up into a federation of small States," Marx says that "the unity of great nations which, if originally brought about by political force, has now become a powerful coefficient of social production" (*Commune*, p. 74). It was thus that, as everyone notices, Marx and Engels never supported national "self-determination" as desirable in itself. If it served to advance the cause of socialist revolution, it was desirable; otherwise, not.[40]

Finally, as part of this, if we are to move progressively toward the future and to be realistic, we need, in a world of aggrandizing nation-states, to think in terms of those unities which we call nations. Modern war became industrialized and came to involve perhaps millions of troops. Only large, integrated, well-developed nation-states could not succeed in war. However much that was to be regretted, it was a plain fact.

The organization of the Commune required some sort of federalism if the unity of the nation was not to be broken. The Commune was "to be the political form of even the smallest country hamlet," and these units "were to administer their affairs by an assmebly of districts in the central town." But in addition, "these district assemblies were ... to send deputies to the National Delegation in Paris, each delegate to be at any time revocable and bound by the *mandat imperatif* (formal instructions) of his constituents" (*Commune*, p.72). France was to remain a unity, not a federation of tiny "republics," each an individual society functioning with a considerable degree of autonomy, integration, and self-consciousness. The idea of a federation of tiny republics, from Marx's point of view, was utopian.

Consideration of war in the modern world was, I believe, the decisive fact. Marx's conclusion that, had the Commune shown "a modicum of common-sense," it would have tried to reach "a compromise with Versailles" powerfully reinforces a host of evidence that if Marx's democratic vision of integrated, self-managed communes was utopian, his politics were always realistic. This means that the best one could have hoped for in these circumstances was the best possible compromise consistent with the continuing existence of the French state. To suppose that the Communards could have mapped out and realized the future is the worse kind of utopian thinking.

It became tragically clear to Marx and Engels that the Commune could not have succeeded, for two quite independent reasons. "Apart from the fact that this was merely the rising of a city under exceptional circumstances, the majority of the Commune was in no way socialist, nor could it be."[41] First, as regards the "exceptional circumstances," the government at Versailles still had a large, professional army. Writing of the French defeat at Metz, just after the Sedan capitulation, Engels said that "it is extremely difficult in turn crowds of men into companies and battalions into soldiers." He continued:

Whoever has seen popular levies on the drill-ground or under fire – be they Baden Frieschaaren, Bull-Run Yankees, French Mobiles, or British Volunteers – will have perceived at once that the chief cause of the helplessness and unsteadiness of these troops lies in the fact of the officers not knowing their duty; and in this present case in France who is there to teach them their duty?[42]

The beleaguered Parisians were surely in a far worse situation than Baden Frieschaaren or Bull-Run Yankees. "National enthusiasm," even coupled with boundless courage, may be "a capital thing, but until disciplined, and organized, nobody can win a battle with it." Worse, this was a commune, isolated from the rest of the countryside and from the spontaneous communes which had sprung up in Lyons and elsewhere. Unlike the situation in the American War of Independence, there was no way to confederate, and as Marx said, the "rough sketch of national organization . . . had no time to develop." Indeed, the situation here was almost the reverse of the process at the time of the American War of Independence. In France, there was a nation-state and a central government; in the North American situation, a government had to be created. War could do this. War had given Paris a chance to free itself from the apparatus of the state, but state power had not been "shattered" except in Paris. Meanwhile, the French army awaited orders.

Second, as regards the fact that "the majority of the Commune was in no way socialist, nor could it be," the point is important. It is also important to see what difference this made. Because the Communards were not organized, politically active workers, their political capabilities were undeveloped. The problem was not that they lacked revolutionary consciousness, for they certainly knew how to die on the barricades; nor was the problem economic, a matter of their incapacity at the existing stage of economic development to conquer scarcity. The problem was that an alienated citizenry was in no position to reabsorb its alienated social powers. The citizens were still isolated, "private" persons who, not yet thoroughly interdependent, could not organize themselves so as to fully realize the powers which they had. The bifurcation between civil society and the state which had to be surmounted if democracy were to be possible had not yet been overcome. As an alliance of artisans, workers in craft industries, petty bourgeois shopkeepers, lawyers, and journalists, it was quite impossible for them to overcome "the conflict between *general and private interest*" (*Writings*, p. 226).

The anarchists saw and celebrated the fact that the Commune was not made by "the proletariat" but was instead an alliance of "the people." They saw and celebrated the spontaneity and disorganization which were its critical characteristics. But they failed to see that unless the Communards were to have a long period for self-education in self-rule − an impossibility in circumstances of civil war − the Commune was bound to fail. "True democracy" was not a throwback to the conditions of the ancient *polis*; nor in the conditions of the capitalist modern state could it be created by an act of revolutionary will. It was thus that "with a modicum of common-sense . . . [the Commune] could have reached a compromise with Versailles useful to the whole mass of the people − the only thing that could have been reached at the time" (*Commune*, p. 293).

Paris "bristled with barricades," but under the circumstances it could not be defended. The response to the "invasion" by the troops of Versailles, like everything else, was spontaneous. Many Communards had believed that the entering army would fraternize with them. Perhaps no one anticipated the violence which would occur. The Versailles troops had been kept away from the population, and evidently they had little idea of what the Commune was about. Instead, as Edwards writes, "they had been carefully nurtured on a diet of patriotism against those who had dared to dishonor France any further."[43] Unlike 1793, there were no officers from the lower ranks of society who had been promoted from NCO status. Instead, they were sons of "good families," trained at St Cyr and the Ecole Polytechnique.

The Communards fought for their own districts. The Versailles army, with cannon and rifled guns, grouped their forces and assaulted the barricades one by one. The troops of Versailles were totally unforgiving as they engaged in indiscriminate slaughter, and neither the Government, General MacMahon, or his officer core interceded. "Paris was put to the sack by the French army, 130,000 troops − or to adapt a contemporary term, it experienced an army-riot." According to Edwards, more died in one week that May than had died in any battle in the Franco-Prussian War or in any previous "massacre" in French history, more than in the Terror of 1793−4 and the White Terror of 1815. Perhaps 25,000 Parisians were killed. Versailles losses were 877 dead and 6,454 wounded.

The Commune was justifiably "enshrined" in the ideology of revolution; but because "it symbolized everything that was frightening and revolutionary about the lower classes," the memory of the commune created new problems for Social Democratic parties. Not only did such parties experience severe repression, especially in France; but the perception of the aims and consequences of the revolutionary Commune made it more difficult for revolutionary parties to be political vehicles for European labor movements, a consequence exacerbated by the stimulus given to anarchist views and movements. The repression was surely the decisive cause of the demise of the First International (in 1872, formally in Philadelphia in 1876) and the shift in the focus of revolution from France to Germany. Out of this was born the Second International, comprised of new men with new ideas, men and ideas which, though avowedly Marxist, would diverge in more than one way from the Marxism of Marx and Engels. But this is a complicated story, not to be told here.[44] Instead, we conclude this chapter with Engels's last thoughts on war and revolution.

A New Model of War and Revolution

Engels rethought the Paris 1793 model, yet again. As Berger points out, from time to time in the past, Marx and Engels had said that war might be a threat to the progress of socialism. After the Commune, they became sure of this, consistently arguing that "struggles for national survival" would produce nothing but chauvinism and reaction. Even in Russia, so long considered the most reactionary of places, war would set back socialism.[45] Marx and Engels could not know, of course, how in 1914 the ruling classes of Europe would put this idea to work on their own behalf.

Engels also rethought the idea of insurrection. In 1852 he had written that "insurrection is an art quite like war," and, continuing in a distinctly Clausewitzean mode, he noted that it is

> subject to certain rules ... which when neglected, will produce the ruin of the party neglecting them .... Firstly, never play with insurrection unless you are fully prepared to face the consequences of your play .... The forces opposed to you have all the advantages of organization, discipline and habitual authority; unless you bring strong strong odds against them you are defeated and ruined. Secondly, always act with the greatest determination, and on the offensive. The defensive is the death of every armed rising ... in the words of Danton, the greatest master of revolutionary policy yet known, *de l'audace, de l'audace, encore de l'audace!*[46]

By 1895 revolutionary audacity no longer included insurrection: "Rebellion in the old style, the street fight with barricades, which up to 1848 gave everywhere the final decision, was to a considerable extent obsolete" (ibid.).[47]

There were two aspects to this conclusion, one political, the other military. The first was the outcome of four decades of industrial growth, especially in Bismarck's recently unified German "hothouse." This had spawned a remarkable growth of labor parties. In Germany, the Social Democratic Party was "the strongest, best disciplined and most rapidly growing Socialist Party," a fact acknowledged by nearly everyone. At the same time, as the Commune had taught Engels, "an insurrection with which all sections of the people sympathize, will hardly ever recur." "The 'people,' therefore, will always appear divided" (ibid., p. 24). The second aspect concerned changes in the military, especially since the almost mythological days of 1793. "The chances ... were in 1849 already pretty poor .... The spell of the barricade was broken; the soldiers no longer saw behind it 'the people,' but rebels, agitators, plunderers, levellers, the scum of society" (ibid., p. 23). Here again the experience of the Commune was surely pertinent. But this was not the whole story. Engels noted further that, not only does the barricade lack the "moral effect" it once had, but "by means of the railways, the garrisons can, in twenty-four hours, be more than doubled, and in forty-eight hours they can be increased to huge armies" (ibid., p. 23). Even former soldiers who come to the side of an insurrection will be poorly armed. Finally, the cities have been transformed, "laid out in long, straight, broad streets" — as in Haussmann's deliberate plan of Paris — so as "to give full effect to the new cannons and rifles" (*ibid.*).[48]

All this may seem painfully obvious to us. Nevertheless, if, as seems to be the case, in an economically and politically advanced state, insurrection is now almost hopeless, we need to emphasize two critical assumptions of Engels. First, he remained confident that a socialist party would be revolutionary, not reformist. Second, given the military problem he had identified, how could one be confident that after a revolutionary party had attained political power, it would be secure against counterrevolution? For, would the army not be a force of reaction?

Engels never gave up the first of these assumptions, and, of course, he could not predict the future. He could not know what the German Social Democrats would do after his death in 1895, still less in 1918. However, he did offer an argument in support of his second assumption. Berger calls it Engels's "Theory of the Vanishing Army."[49]

The main strands of the theory are clear. Modern war has forced universal conscription on states, and this has had unintended consequences. Since "it was precisely the younger generation which provides our party with the most recruits, it follows that a German army is more and more contaminated by socialists." Engels went on: "Today we have one soldier in five; in a few years we shall have one in three, and in about 1900 the army, formerly the most Prussian element in the land, will be socialist in its majority. This is coming, as inexorably as a decree of fate. The Berlin regime sees it coming just as clearly as we do, but it is powerless."[50]

While Engels is hardly clear, it seems that there are two possible consequences. One, emphasized by Berger, is that "a revolution could be made *with* the army," where this means not just that the army will support revolution or at least not oppose it, but that the army would itself be the revolutionary force. Thus Engels wrote to Lafargue that "*demoralization* (from the bourgeois standpoint) must spread precisely in the ranks of the army; under the conditions of modern military technology (rapid-fire weapons, etc.), the revolution must begin in the army."[51] The other possibility is in line with the older idea that proletarian voters would achieve the conquest of power, but adds the notion that soldiers would have to defend it. Thus revolution and counterrevolution cannot be separated.[52]

Either way, the transformation of the army to the point where it would have socialist sympathies would take time; accordingly, it was critical both to avoid a premature confrontation with the army and to avoid war. Engels was not succumbing to "reformism;" but his new view of the possible role of the army in any conquest of power, coupled with his increasingly gloomy — and prophetic — picture of the next war, forced a new caution on both Marx and Engels.

Modern industry had developed powerful new instruments of war and had called into existence the need for huge conscripted armies. This is why the Berlin regime was powerless to stop the process which Engels counted on. On the other hand, a war under these conditions would be terrible. In 1878, Marx had observed:

> No war is any longer possible for Prussia-Germany except a world war and a world war indeed of an extension of violence hitherto undreamt of. Eight to ten millions of soldiers will mutually massacre one another and in so going devour the whole of Europe until they have stripped it barer than any swarm of locusts has ever done . . . .
> We will see famine, pestilence, general demoralization both of the armies and of the mass of the people; hopeless confusion of our artificial machinery in trade, industry and credit, ending in general bankruptcy; collapse of old states and their traditional state wisdom to such an extent that the crowns will roll by the dozens on the pavement and there will be nobody to pick them up; absolute impossibility of foreseeing how it will all end and who will come out of the struggle as victor; only one result is absolutely certain; general exhaustion and the establishment of the conditions for ultimate victory of the working class.[53]

The *optimistic* predictions of Marx and Engels were often wrong. But most of the foregoing, tragically, was remarkably on target — except the one thing of which they were absolutely certain. One might say that this was merely a "mechanically dutiful claim." Or one might say that they were partly right even in this. It implied another model of revolution, which very nearly fit Germany and did fit militarily invulnerable, reactionary Russia. After all, it was the general exhaustion of World War I which led the last imperial chancellor to turn the government over to Frederich Ebert, the SPD leader who betrayed democracy, just as in Russia, the disintegration of the old order made possible the coup of the Bolsheviks. Of course, if Germany then had a genuine chance to take a giant step toward democracy, Russia was the last place that anybody — including Engels — would have predicted an effort at a "socialist" revolution.

Even so, this ultimate "certainty" gave Engels no comfort. Quite the contrary. He persistently warned against a new war and did everything he could to prevent one. Indeed, this seems to have been the most subtle part of the "vanishing army" theory. His gloomy prediction presupposed that national armies, socialist or otherwise, would not hesitate to annihilate one another. Nor did he fantasize that nations would disarm. Although invented only in the French Revolution, the idea that all must be committed to the defense of the "nation" was by now a clearly acknowledged general fact, and there was no turning back. Still, there was the possibility − *less* urgent in the 1890s than today − that, faced with the threat of a "general war of annihilation," nations would restrict themselves to *defensive* arms and armies. Indeed, it was Engel's view that Social Democrats should make this their policy in regard to war. They should take the initiative in arguing that the survival of the nation demanded its defense by socialists; accordingly, socialists should work for universal conscription, but nevertheless insist that conscripted armies be strictly defensive, adopting the Swiss model of thoroughgoing citizen militias, highly trained and quickly mobilizable. In a series of articles entitled "Can Europe Disarm?", published in *Vôrwarts* in 1893, Engels concluded: "From the purely military point of view there is nothing to prevent the gradual abolition of the regular army; and if the regular army *is* still maintained, it is maintained not for military but for political reasons − in a word, it is meant for defense, not against a foreign enemy, but against a domestic one."[54]

We must be clear that at this point in history, the nature of the army was the key issue regarding the question of offensive versus defensive wars. This was before tanks, bombers, and missiles. Technology had put new, more deadly weapons in the hands of armies, but armies still fought armies. Engels, like Kant, believed that citizens in arms, nonprofessionals, would fight a war in defense of their homeland, but that they were not likely to engage in foreign adventures instigated by governments whose interests might well be different from their own.[55] This may have been a vain hope. Moreover, it will surely be contested that a conscripted militia, nationally organized and disciplined with trained cadres, would be adequate, even for purposes of defense. But Engels was in no way militarily naive, as I have already indicated. If he was wrong, we shall never know, since his ideas, of course, came to nothing.

To many, he sounded defeatist, and in a world full of fear he certainly assumed too much. Moreover, were not socialists internationalists? And if so, why was not Engels's call to socialists to prepare to defend their country as jingoistic as the views of Bebel? Indeed, how did Engels's view really differ from the views of the "nationalist" liberals or reactionaries? Socialist parties should disavow war; socialist conscripts should refuse to fight a capitalist war; and socialists everywhere should, in case of war, commit themselves to a general strike. He did not live to see it, of course, but when the German Social Democrats voted war credits for the war which began in 1914, his worse fears were realized. Socialists rushed to annihilate socialists in the trenches of France.

Part V

War and Mass Democracy

Introduction

For most people, World War I seems a very long time ago. But it was "the Great War" nonetheless, a war which almost realized Clausewitz's notion of "absolute war." It was the first international war in which very nearly the full resources of many nations were thrown into a duel to the death. It was the first war in which generals could define victory as a condition in which the enemy, not defeated or even dislodged, had bled more, in which at the end of the "battle," "we" had marginally more fit fighting men than "they." In the nine-month battle of Verdun, some 500,000 men on each side died. Both sides could find satisfaction in the fact that neither could claim a significant advantage in the daily roll call, and that the battle lines remained more or less where they had been at the beginning of the carnage. It was the first war which proved the efficacy of a command economy which could produce and mobilize tons of materials, arms, bread, and shoes for millions of uniformed fighters. It was the first war fought with airplanes and poison gas, the first in which cities were attacked by air (by zeppelins) and ships were sunk by submarines.

After nearly three years of evidently fruitless slaughter, a war which nobody doubted was an imperial squabble for markets and for slices of the world, became, magically, a war to end all wars, a war to make the world "safe for democracy." The reason for this change was clear enough to many. As Walter Lippmann neatly put the matter, the war was "dissolving into a stupendous revolution. The whole perspective is changed ... by the revolution in Russia and the intervention of America. The scale of values is transformed, for the democracies are unloosed."[1] These two facts, the revolution in Russia and the intervention of America had made imperialist war a war to make the world safe for democracy.

The men who decided to begin the war clearly had imperial problems and designs; and if they had democracy on their minds at all, it was only that they shared in thinking that there was altogether too much of it. A successful imperial policy, they believed, would go some way toward resolving a host of social tensions which liberals and socialists had been exploiting so successfully. As an important historian of Germany put the matter, "By involving the masses in the great struggle, those parts of the nation which had hitherto stood apart would be integrated into the monarchial state."[2]

The men whose decisions led to the war would barely have sufficed to fill three tables of contract bridge: Kaiser Wilhelm II, Chancellor Bethmann Hollweg, and Field Marshal Helmuth Graf von Moltke, the Emperor Franz Joseph and his Foreign Minister, Count Berchtold, his Chief of Staff, Baron Conrad von Hoetzendorf, and Stephen Tisza, the Hungarian Prime Minister; and on the other side, the Serbian Prince Regent, Alexander, and his Prime Minister, Nicholas Pasic; and, critically, Tsar Nicholas II, his Foreign Minister, S. D. Sasanov, and General Yanushkevich, the Chief of Staff of the Russian Army. The whole business might have been inconsequential had the French failed to satisfy promises made to Russia – promises made in a secret, fateful alliance of 1894 – and had Lord Grey then, resisted committing Britain to war.[3]

Although they were experiencing domestic "strife," as Halévy put it, France and Britain were democracies. Still, even if we include the February–October 1917 period, from the overthrow of the Russian Tsar to the demise of the Provisional Government, this was no war of democracies against autocracies. Nor was it fought to bring democracy to the world, whatever the dreams and illusions of some may have been. Moreover – and usually ignored – neither Lord Grey nor President Poincaré needed consent to engage in war either from their respective parliaments or, more obviously, from the citizens of their respective nations. For what turned out to be a monumental decision which profoundly affected the lives of hundreds of millions, a majority in their respective Cabinets was quite sufficient.[4] In France and Britain, as in Germany, syndicalist agitators, striking miners, and transport workers, not asked if they wanted war, responded soon enough to the patriotic call.

Nonetheless, if war did dampen "strife" in France and Britain, Lippmann was correct in judging that by 1917, at least in the autocratic states, the war was dissolving into "a stupendous revolution." In Russia the war finally undid the Tsar. In 10 short days, 300 years of Empire collapsed. The regime led by Lvov and Kerensky was quickly replaced by the Bolsheviks, who as quickly sued for an independent peace with Germany. In Germany, Bethmann Hollweg's worst fears were realized. He had argued that the ruling classes of Germany had "expected a war to turn domestic politics in a conservative direction." Yet, he went on, it might also be that "a world war with its unforeseeable consequences will greatly strengthen the power of social democracy since it preaches peace and will topple many a throne."[5] Nor, of course, did the empires of the Habsburgs or the Ottomans survive the peace. Indeed, with the distintegration of empires, millions — including the peoples of Imperial Russia — were for the first time acquiring a taste for self-government. As in 1848, once unleashed, the spirit of democracy seemed irresistible.

On the other hand, and with considerable irony, as Gordon Craig has said, "the war opened a new and difficult era for liberal democracy even where ... [it] was being fought in its name."[6] The process was complex, of course. The war plainly involved the centralization of authority and the suspension of the most elemental civil liberties. It also brought into being something new, the characteristic form of the modern state, a *Kriegswirtschaft* (war economy), the accession of soldiers, organizers, and new technocrats in new state bureaucracies, which, as an unintended consequence, set out the elements of the contemporary "welfare state." But perhaps as important, though much less obvious, there emerged a new need, willingness, and capacity to manipulate collective passions — "the mobilization of enthusiasm," including the mobilization of hatred, as Craig says. What had been discovered in the wars of Revolutionary France became, with the full maturing of the nation-state, a key feature. In a word, the liberal order which had been the vision of the Enlightenment was replaced by highly centralized, bureaucratized mass states. Mass democracy, of course, was only one of the new possibilities.

In the next three chapters, some of the consequences will be discussed. We begin with the defining revolution of the twentieth century, born in war, the Bolshevik Revolution in Russia, and consider a number of questions regarding the consequences of war and the possibilities for democracy in Russia. As everyone knows, there are no "republics" in the Union of Socialist Soviet Republics, and, like the United States, it is no federation. The reasons for this will be explored in what follows. Whether there is no socialism either, as many would argue, depends on whether we insist that socialism be democratic. Surely there is no democracy, even if, as it will be argued, the "Old" Bolsheviks were democrats.

To make my case plausible, if not convincing, a fairly full-blown sketch of the conditions and history of the Bolshevik Revolution will necessary. Although this revolution is understood well enough by scholars of the period, the terrible fragmentation of the disciplines and specialties, including here political and social theory, political history, social history, and international relations, has made it difficult to get an adequate grasp of what was, to be sure, an extraordinarily complex phenomenon. The sketch given in the next chapter could easily be filled in and, in all likelihood, corrected by scholars in the pertinent specialties. The main outline, I hope, can be sustained. Against this background, the ideas and aims of Lenin and Bolshevism will be examined. Events moved quickly, and people with ideas responded to these events. On the present view, Lenin grasped, rightly, that socialist revolution as codified by their doctrinaire texts was not possible; but neither was a liberal revolution possible. The Bolsheviks would make the attempt to find a third way, a democratic revolution of workers, soldiers, and peasants. They failed in this. But the failure was less a failure of ideas than the outcome of events and conditions beyond their control. The consequences were tragic. Instead of saving from the ruins of war some sort of severely compromised socialist democracy, the Bolsheviks created a monster state and, in so doing, established the conditions for the twentieth-century's first totalitarian mass state.

In the second chapter of this part of the book, we will turn out attention to Germany in 1918, with Rosa Luxemburg, the leaders of the Independent Socialists, and Max Weber as the theoretical foci. Again, the problem is war and the possibilities for democracy, and again there is the question of a "third way." If we put aside Hitler, the Weimar Constitution was a great success; but, of course, we cannot put aside Hitler. In the third chapter of this part, we turn to the United States, already a democracy, even if, on the varying accounts of Walter Lippmann and John Dewey, it was in need of considerable attention. The American intervention in the Great War provides a case study in the problems of representative democracy in the era of the mass state. Further, the peace which came about as a result of the American entry was surely very different from what it might otherwise have been. The intended and unintended consequences of this have contributed mightily to our present situation.

11

Bolshevism and the Question of Democracy

The Consequences of War

Bolshevism is utterly unintelligible apart from a consideration of war. It is not just that the critical difference between the unsuccessful revolution of 1905 and the successful revolutions of February and October 1917[1] was world war, but that what is somewhat misleadingly called the "Civil War," from the spring of 1918 to the spring of 1921, profoundly affected everything: the possibilities which were available to the new regime, the beliefs in terms of which they made their decisions, some fateful, and the historical memory which later Bolsheviks, especially Stalin, drew upon in constructing the Soviet system.

For most of us living in Western democracies, including those who have experienced directly the death and dislocation of war, it takes a monumental effort of historical imagination to grasp the significance of seven years of war in Russia. Moshe Lewin writes that "the period 1914–21 was unquestionably a demographic earthquake."[2] Some sixteen million deaths were direct consequences of war. But if we add the calamities that befell potential parents, then by 1921 Russia's population was thirty million less than it would otherwise have been. Imperial Russia was huge, of course, and it was backward. Before the war, significant advances had been made in industrialization, and the cities had begun to grow faster than the total population. Still, the whole urban sector, the locus of the educated, the workers, the bureaucrats, and the technical elite comprised no more than 18 percent of the population. As compared to the 11.6 per 100 employed in manufacturing in the United States at that time, only 2 per 100 were so employed in Russia. The outcome of decades of serfdom, rural Russia's immense peasantry already lived on the edge of survival.

War began the process of undoing what gains had been made but it was the civil war which followed on its heels which "brought economic life almost to a standstill and destroyed the old social structure."[3] Moscow lost half its population, Petrograd (St Petersburg) two-thirds, declining from some two and a half million to about three-quarters of a million. The working class was halved, depriving the Bolsheviks of immense numbers of precisely those on whom they had rightly counted. Of the 600,000 who served in the Red Army, 180,000 were killed. Because industry had all but collapsed, many more returned to the countryside in order to survive. By August 1920 Petrograd had only a third of the nearly 300,000 factory workers it had in 1917.

The figures regarding industry are even more incredible. Overall, it shrank to about one-fifth of its 1913 levels; cast iron output was less than 3 percent, the production of copper had ceased, and only one out of every twenty textile spindles remained in production. Russia's already feeble transportation network was tattered. Bridges had been destroyed and railway track torn up as armies retreated. Trains ran on wood. Even when food for the hungry in the cities was available, it could not be delivered. All this was greatly exacerbated by the Allied blockade, imposed after the Brest –Litovsk Treaty of 1918.

During the civil war the peasants fared somewhat better than the people in the cities. It had been clear enough to the Bolsheviks that nothing could be done without the support of the peasants. The Bolshevik land decrees of October 1917 and February 1918, in effect the program of the Socialist Revolutionaries (SRs), institutionalized what the peasants had themselves begun during the summer of 1917, a division of the land. By 1920 there were more than twenty million small holdings worked by families. But at the same time, "war communism" – the response to the civil war – had as its "essence," the coerced expropriation of the peasant product. Indeed, Lenin admitted, "We actually took from the peasant all his surpluses and sometimes not only the surpluses but part of the grain the peasant needed for food."[4] The consequences of this contradictory situation were absolutely critical.

On the one hand, the Bolsheviks created an entirely novel situation. As Lewin says, "the peasantry lived in an entirely different social setting – without capitalists, without any important merchantry, without the gentry, without as yet a strong supervisory administration ... without the powerful kulaks but with a strong, reinvigorated (for a time) commune."[5] He continues, "What it all meant was the peasants came out of their redistributive frenzy – and frenzy is the right term here – looking more *muzhik*, as it were, than even before, more sui generis, more family consumption-oriented, less 'farmers' than ever since the emancipation [of 1861]."[6] This, plainly, was not an ideal condition for building socialism!

On the other hand, the war communism policy had inevitably and profoundly alienated the peasants. One might argue here about whether either the land policy or the policy of compulsory requisition were necessary, whether there were not other choices. But all the evidence suggests that there were no other choices. The Russian peasantry was not to be denied; indeed, it is doubtful whether either the Provisional Government or the Bolsheviks had the power to prevent the "redistributive frenzy," even if they had wanted to. The latter policy seems the more contestable of the two; yet one knowledgeable historian has concluded that "there is little doubt that compulsory requisitioning (in Russian *prodrazverstka*) saved the Bolshevik regime from defeat, for without it neither the army nor the urban population, from which the government drew its main support, could have survived."[7] In any case, the Army and the urban population needed to be fed. Still, in assessing the Revolution, we should consider whether some *other* regime might have had other choices. Of course, this will hardly be a matter easily accessible to convincing answers.

But more needs to be said about the civil war. Plato had held that between "internal" and "external war," "internal war" was the greatest of evils. But after the experience of the American Civil War, the first modern civil war, it is perhaps even easier to appreciate the force of this. Even so, it is not uncommon in discussions of the Russian revolutionary situation to treat the concept of "civil war" rather uncritically, to suggest — if not to argue — that it was the result of a militant Bolshevik minority using force of arms in an attempt to dominate Russia and the vast territories which had been part of the Empire, that it was a war of an armed, ideologically fanatic few against the freedom-loving population of Russia, Greater Russia, and the huge non-Russian borderlands. But the reality, not easy to grasp, is quite otherwise.[8]

Three factors combined in making the civil war what it was. First, there were historically rooted nationalisms, unleashed by the disintegration of the Empire. Second and more obviously, there was class war, especially versus those elements of the Army whose allegiance was to the social system of Imperial Russia. Finally, and not insignificantly, there was the fact of Allied intervention. Indeed, as Chamberlin concluded: "Had there been no intervention, had Allied aid to the Whites stopped after the end of the war, the Russian Civil War would almost certainly have ended much more quickly in a decisive victory for the Bolsheviks. Then a triumphant revolutionary Russia would have faced a Europe that was fairly quivering with social unrest and upheaval."[9] Chamberlin's unrealized counterfactual was subsequently realized in the aftermath of World War II, a fact not lost on the more perceptive of those who have formed foreign policy since that war.[10]

Revolution, Counterrevolution, and the Disintegration of Empire

The exultation of the February revolution did not last. The Provisional Government soon faced a spontaneous insurrection in the streets of Petrograd

– the "July days." This was probably triggered by soldiers of the First Machine Gun Regiment; but no doubt Bolshevik agitation also contributed to it. Further, the fury heaped at the party by the liberal newspapers and, perhaps surprisingly, by *Izvestia*, the paper of the Petrograd soviet, was enough to justify the new round of repression directed at its leadership. It seemed at first that the new government had stemmed "the anarchy and disorder," which it attributed, characteristically, to "insurgent lackeys" and "drunk helots." While the Right gained enormous encouragement from what seemed like a shift in the public mood, the disintegration of society continued. For increasing numbers among the well-established groups, by August "the lone remaining hope of restoring order at the front and arresting chaos in the rear seemed to be an alliance of anti-socialist liberal and conservative forces and the establishment of a strong dictatorship."[11]

General Denikin, subsequent leader of the counterrevolutionary White Army perceptively remarked, "Kornilov became a banner. For some of counter-revolution, for others of the salvation of the Motherland,"[12] Kornilov's counterrevolution failed; but it is important to see that it did not fail because the Provisional Government had secured itself and was able to mobilize resistance.

It was "a matter of record" that Kornilov had "a predilection for the application of massive military force to curb disorder at home and at the front."[13] Accordingly, it is not likely that Kerensky made Kornilov commander-in-chief for the reasons he later gave: his battlefield record, which was undistinguished, and, less plausibly, because Kornilov favored democratic reform of the Army. Kerensky was convinced that only a strong unified Directory could "save Russia." He did not foresee, evidently, that Kornilov would be his competitor for the role of leader. When Kornilov began the execution of his planned coup, the Government vacillated, in part because so many officials were sympathetic to Kornilov, in part because they knew that they lacked all authority over the masses. But ordinary people were not sympathetic to Kornilov, and they did not vacillate.

Rabinowitch summarizes the situation thus:

> Spurred by the news of Kornilov's attack, all political organizations left of the Kadets, every labor organization of any import, and soldier and sailor committees at all levels immediately rose to fight against Kornilov. It would be difficult to find, in recent history, a more powerful, effective display of largely spontaneous and unified mass action.[14]

Although it would have taken very little cooperation among soldiers, tele-graph operators, railroad workers, and others for the counterrevolution to have succeeded, Kornilov was unable to generate *any* useful cooperation. Indeed, the bloodless character of the Bolshevik coup six months later makes the case.

Lenin, now recognizing that he had been wrong in saying that the soviets would not be revolutionary, reconsidered the "peaceful" pre-July tactical plan. By September, however, he was convinced that the masses of Petrograd were more radical than the Right Wing of his own party. The memories of failed insurrections haunted Zinoviev and the others. Lenin wrote: "Comrade Zinoviev made a mistake in writing about the Commune ambiguously, to say the least, so that it appeared that the Commune, although victorious in Petrograd, might be defeated, *as in France in 1871*. This is absolutely untrue. If the Commune were victorious in Petrograd, *it would be victorious throughout Russia*."[15] Red Guards in Petrograd, factory workers organized by the Bolsheviks after the defeat of Kornilov, numbered perhaps 12,000. Russia had then in uniform some nine million men. But "the greatest mutiny in history" made it possible for the Bolsheviks, in cooperation with workers in critical locations, to seize power. War, the complete collapse of authority, and the fact that the Bolsheviks were organized and were "the only significant political force consistently voicing and supporting the radical mass opinion of 1917" made a Bolshevik success possible.

Yet we need to distinguish here between the capacity of the Bolsheviks to seize power and their capacity to hold it. In addition, we must also acknowledge that having power and having the capacity to *rule* are not the same thing. For reasons already noted, the Bolsheviks were in no position to use force against the population. No more than Kerensky could the Bolsheviks hope to appeal to the army to carry out their will. At the same time, we have no way of knowing how much actual support they had, how willing people were to acknowledge their claim to authority. It was plainly considerable. There were perhaps 300,000 Bolshevik party members at the time of the October Revolution, a not insignificant number. On the eve of the coup, the Bolsheviks had acquired an absolute majority in the Second All-Russian Congress of Soviets, and in the elections for the Constituent Assembly the next month, the party won nine million votes, some 25 percent of the total. Moreover, we can guess that many who voted for left SRs and others were not hostile to the Bolsheviks. Thus, even if the coup was the work of a relatively small number, the Bolsheviks' slogan of "Peace, Land, Bread" had gained for them a very wide base of support.[16]

But if the Petrograd and Moscow Bolsheviks held the reins of power, they were certainly not in control. Within weeks of the Bolshevik coup, it became clear that the condition of Russia was anarchy. "Russia" was without a state and was not in any sense a nation. The leading student of the nationalities problem in the period under study, Richard Pipes, summarizes the disintegration of the Empire thus:

The separation of the borderlands previously under the control of the Provisional Government [viz., the several "nations" of Transcaucasia] was accompanied by the loss of other Russian territories, some under enemy occupation. Lithuania and Finland proclaimed their independence in December 1917; Latvia followed shortly afterwards. Poland, which was entirely occupied by German troops, enjoyed de facto independence, recognized officially by the Soviet delegation to the Brest Litovsk Peace conference. Estonia severed its bonds with Russia in February 1918. In addition, vast areas, inhabited by Russians who did not desire to be subjected to the Soviet Regime, formed their own governments and proclaimed statehood. Most important in this category was the Siberian Republic created by the SR's [Social Revolutionaries], and the Southeastern Union, embracing the Cossack regions of the Northern Caucasus and the Urals, both established in January 1918.[17]

The Bolsheviks were, as Lenin put it, willing "to concede space ... in order to win time." There was never any doubt that Lithuania, Courland, Estonia, Livonia, and the Turkish frontier districts of Kars, Ardhan, and Batum would become disconnected from Russia.[18] But as Pipes says, "deprived of its borderlands, Soviet Russia had neither sufficient food, nor fuel, nor raw materials."[19] There were two questions. Pipes identifies the first: Could the Bolsheviks "reconcile the slogan of national self-determination with the need for preserving the unity of the Soviet state [?]."[20] The notion of federation was critical here. This would not have been easy under the best of circumstances. (We might compare here the founding situation of America.) But there was another plain question, that of how to prevent national self-determination from becoming a force for counterrevolution. This question, it should be emphasized, would have confronted any form of revolutionary government committed to destroying the regime of the Tsar, including the liberal Provisional Government of Lvov and Kerensky.

In the Ukraine and North Caucasus, as in most of the regions outside the core of Greater Russia, Bolshevik efforts to vest authority in soviets of workers', soldiers', and peasants' deputies met with difficulties. In the Ukraine (including here the provinces of Khardov, Kherson, Ekaterinoslav, and Taurida) there was a central Rada which, after the February Revolution, claimed to be the national soviet for the territory. On 17 December the Government in Petrograd dispatched an ultimatum to the Rada, demanding that it not permit troops abandoning the front to pass through its territory to the Don and Urals without consent of the Commander-in-Chief, that it stop disarming Red Guards in the Ukraine, and that it cooperate with the government in fighting the counterrevolutionary Ataman of the Dons,

General Kaledin (see below). If it refuses these demands, "the Council of People's Commissars will regard the Rada as in a condition of open war against the Soviet Power in Russia and the Ukraine."[21] The Secretariat of the Rada responded by asserting, consistent with Soviet acknowledgment of the Ukraine's right to self-determination, that it had a perfect right to make decisions affecting its own territories.

But the Ukraine was not the only place where disintegration was accelerating. Sixteen million Moslems lived in areas which were part of the Empire. Moslem liberals, breathing the new air of democracy, instigated the All-Russian Moslem movement, which had its first congress on 1 May 1917. But if the sixteen million shared a religion, they did not all share "nationalist" aspirations. The congress voted for a federalist scheme by which many "nations," Volga Tartars, Azerbaijani, Crimean Tartars, Bashkirs, Kazakh-Kirhiz, and others would have territorial self-rule. In Turkestan, the Caucasus, and Transcaucasia, there were similar developments, albeit with differences.

In Turkestan, the last of the important territories subjected by Tsarist Russia (in the 1860s), the new Bolshevik regime had resolutely – and counterproductively – denied the right of Moslems to enter "into the higher organs of the regional revolutionary authority." The response should have been anticipated. The Fourth Regional Moslem Congress of Kokand declared "the territory of Turkestan to be autonomous but united with the Russian democratic federative republic."[22] In the Caucasus, where there were 614,194 indigenous mountaineers (*Gortsy*) and only 412,489 Russians, along with 24,012 Armenians and 35,152 Kalmyks, mountain-dwelling Chechens and Ingush left the hills to attack Cossack settlements, including Valdikavkaz and Groznyi.

In Transcaucasia the political parties of the three principal ethnic groups, the Georgians, the Azerbaijanis, and the Armenians, reorganized very quickly and soon became forces to be reckoned with. The Georgians did not have national aspirations, but the Moslems, led by the liberal Turkish federalist party Mussavat could secure twice as many votes as the Bolsheviks.[23] The 1915 massacre of one million Armenians, more than half the population of Armenia, by Ottoman Turks had left the Armenians in Russia loyal to the Provisional Government; but the Seim (Parliament) in Tiflis, created to maintain order until the All-Russian Constituent Assembly had established government for all of Russia, was faced in April 1918 with a tragic dilemma: "either to proclaim themselves at present an inseparable part of Russia, and in this manner repeat all the horrors of the Russian Civil War and then become an arena for foreign invasion, in this case Turkish; or to proclaim independence and with their own powers defend the physical existence of the whole country."[24] Over the protests of Kadets (from the acronym Ka De, for Russian "Constitutional Democrats") and SRs, they proclaimed an independent Transcaucasian Federative Republic. Pipes concludes: "It is not farfetched to assert that at the beginning of 1918 Russia, as a political concept, had ceased to exist."[25]

The Class War

The first signs that the disintegration of authority might turn into civil war came from the Don River city of Rostov, some miles from Bolshevik-controlled Petrograd. General Kaledin, who had been critical in the Kornilov plot, was the ataman of this territory. Within weeks of the Bolshevik coup, a Bolshevik-led military revolutionary committee had demanded the resignation of his government. Kaledin had Cossack troops loyal to him, so he decided to fight. While the Cossacks were a premier fighting force, better trained and better disciplined than other units of the Tsar's army, they fought with so little enthusiasm that the Red Guards who supported the Committee succeeded in disarming them. The Bolsheviks thereby gained control of the city of Rostov. But five days later, the city fell to a force of "Volunteers." This force of not more than three or four thousand became the nucleus of the White Army which, by the fall of 1919, very nearly succeeded in destroying the Revolution.

As noted above, any government would have had to respond to the disintegration of authority, just as any government would have had to face counterrevolution. There was surely opposition to the Bolsheviks, from Mensheviks, SRs, and Kadets. But the *armies* of the counterrevolution had a distinct class base. The organizers of the counterrevolution, General Alekseev and the five generals who had been most active in the Kornilov affair, had a loyal core of several thousand officers, and unsurprisingly they chose the Southeast as the place to begin their counterrevolutionary struggle.

The Cossacks of the Don and Kuban were "a privileged estate," the descendants of those who had conquered the native peoples of the area and appropriated their land. Cossacks were traditionally trained for service in the Tsar's armies, serving terms of twenty years. In compensation, they received tax and land privileges. Peter Kenez, in the most recent study of the civil war, summarizes the situation neatly: "The Volunteer army was an organization of officers .... However, it was neither officers nor Russian soldiers but Kuban and Don Cossacks who made up the majority of the fighting men. The Cossacks, men who differed in background and ideology from the officers, came to fight the Bolsheviks for reasons of their own."[26] For them, "Civil War was a struggle against the non-Cossack peasants, the so called *inogorodyne*, who looked covetously at Cossack lands."[27] Not only did Cossacks not want to fight outside their own territory, but it was almost impossible for the White generals to develop a positive ideology which could attract mass support. Indeed, Chamberlin concludes, not without reason, that "herein lay the secret of its ultimate defeat."[28]

On the other side of the struggle was the Red Army, initially a genuinely motley aggregation of workers, sailors, and criminals, mostly untrained, undisciplined, and ill equipped. Chamberlin observes that "in general the characteristics of this early phase of the civil war were the small number of troops engaged, the lightness of the casualties, the ease with which both sides succumbed to panic and the general atmosphere of confusion and disorganization."[29]

We need to be reminded, perhaps, that most people will not eagerly join in armed struggle against a regime, even when they are not already thoroughly war-weary from three years of struggle and death, as was the case in the Russian Empire. Nor, given the disintegration of civil authority, could governments easily coerce men to fight. But perhaps even more important, the vast majority of the people tolerated − even if they did not favor − the Bolsheviks. The overwhelming mass of peasants had achieved what, in their view, the Revolution had set out to achieve. Their disillusionment came later, with the defeat of Wrangle's White Army in the fall of 1920. As Avrich writes, "The bulk of the peasants, for the duration of the Civil War, continued to tolerate the Soviet regime as a lesser evil than a White restoration." But with the evaporation of the White danger, "peasant resentment against *prodrazverstka* and the state farms flared up out of control."[30] Likewise, the majority of the workers had supported the Bolshevik regime. Indeed, they constituted the core of the Red Army so hastily built under the guidance of Trotsky.

A decree of January 1918 called for recruitment of a volunteer "Workers' and Peasants' Red Army," with men committed to three months' service. There were perhaps 5,500 in the initial force in Petrograd, surely the place where revolutionary ardour was strongest. By April, with civil war and foreign intervention now manifest, it was clear to Trotsky that this would not do. As War Commissioner, he called for the creation of a new kind of army. But he gradually − if quickly − came to see that, as Carr put it, "to organize the Red Army from scratch, without taking advantage either of the accumulated experience or of the surviving machinery of the old Russian army, was a task of herculean proportions."[31] Late in April, conscription was reintroduced, and the practice of electing officers was abolished. It is worth noting here that this was the first step in the process which destroyed hopes for Soviet democracy.

The Red Army numbered 800,000 by the end of 1919, and by 1920 there were, on paper, some 3,000,000 troops, scattered across the vast territory of the emerging Soviet state. Still, we should note that, according to official Soviet figures, there were 2,846,000 deserters in the years

1919–20. Conscription is one thing; but mobilizing troops and maintaining discipline are something quite different. During the last seven months of 1919, of 4,112 deserters who were sentenced to death, 612 were executed. One gets a better sense of things by noting that in General Yudenitch's critical White offensive against Petrograd, there were but 18,500 men in his Northwestern Army pitted against 25,000 troops of the Seventh Red Army. In the decisive campaign on the 700-mile southern front in the fall of 1920, some 186,000 Reds faced 112,600 Whites.

The Intervention

But, since modern war involves not simply armies fighting armies, and the effects of war are not only the deaths of troops, the Russian civil war was tremendously complicated by the continuing advance of Germans in the West until the "peace" could be secured. This came about by a remarkable historical accident which put into Siberia a brigade of Czecho-Slovak troops; by the intervention, in April, of the Japanese, who sought territory, and finally, by the intervention of the Allies, who aimed, at the very least, to destroy the Revolution.

Initially, it was easy enough for the Allied governments to justify the intervention on the grounds that the Red regime had chosen not to pursue the war against the Kaiser. The counterrevolutionary generals were not only anti-Bolshevik, but they could be trusted to continue the fight against the Germans. It was true that German armies had penetrated into the Ukraine, the Crimea, and Georgia, and that further penetration seemed likely. On the other hand, it was quite clear before the end of the war that the Allied interests in Russia were not simply interests in defeating Germany. Indeed, it was by now clear that the confidence placed in the Russian generals was not misplaced. Like so many in the West, some of them, at least, seemed to hate Bolsheviks as much as they hated the Germans – perhaps more.

The Germans had established puppet regimes in the territories they controlled; and while they were negotiating with the Bolsheviks, they were not adverse to using local forces in pursuit of their strategic and imperial interests. But neither were counterrevolutionary forces adverse to making use of German assistance. In June, the "National Center," led by Professor Paul Milyukov, Foreign Minister of the fallen Provisional Government, made an effort to secure an alliance with General Hase of the German High Command, on grounds of "mutual need."[32] He failed, perhaps because the Germans had no confidence in his ability to deliver. Such was not the case in the Don, however. The new ataman, General Krasnov, had an army, and despite the objections of Denikin, he happily accepted

German cooperation in the fight against the Bolsheviks. During the summer of 1918, the Germans supplied Krasnov's Cossack army with some · 11,000 rifles, 46 cannons, 88 machine guns, and 11 million rounds of rifle ammunition.[33]

During the fighting against the central powers, Czech nationals resident in Russia had been formed into a brigade and attached to the Russian army. Masaryk and Bênes, the Czech nationalist leaders, encouraged war prisoners and deserters to join this group, which was in the vicinity of Kiev. In order to strengthen his nationalist cause, Masaryk threw in his lot with the Allies. It was the hope of Masaryk to get this army, which was eventually to number some 60,000, to France. Incredibly, perhaps, it was decided to transport them almost around the world, from the region of Kiev to Vladivostok, through the Panama Canal, and thence to France.

In March 1918 the Bolsheviks agreed to allow the Czechs to travel "not as fighting units, but as groups of free citizens, who carry with them a specified number of weapons against counterrevolutionary attacks."[34] But neither side trusted the other; and under complicated circumstances of misunderstanding and miscommunication, a small incident between Hungarian war prisoners and a Czech detachment erupted and subsequently led to open hostilities between Red Army units and Czechs.[35] The consequence, unintended on both sides, was the establishment, first of the West Siberian Commissariat, headed by an SR, which declared an autonomous Siberia, then of the Committee of Members of the Constituent Assembly in Samara, all SRs, followed by the emergence of a third anti-Bolshevik regime in the capital of the Urals (headed by the president of the Ekaterinburg stock exchange), then by a Directory of five persons which claimed authority to act without consent of the Duma. Neither democratic, nor left nor right, the short-lived Directory satisfied no one. "With the willing acquiescence of the local representatives of the Allied powers," Admiral Kolchak, taking command of the complex array of anti-Bolshevik forces fighting in Siberia and European Russia, then made himself a military dictator. He did this on 17 November 1918, just three days after the formal end of the war that was to make the world "safe for democracy." Indeed, by July at least, the original plan for evacuating Czechs to fight Germans on the Western front had been effectively abandoned, and instead, as Kennan writes, "in alliance with White Russian forces," the main body of Czechs "had thrown themselves with vigor and with initial enthusiasm into the struggle against the Bolshevikii in the Urals-Volga area .... They were now confidently awaiting the Allied help that was never to come."[36]

But it was not that the counterrevolutionary forces got no help, even if, as Kennan says, they never did get the help they needed or expected. Some detail is essential here. Between April 1918 and the winter of 1920–1, Japan, France, Britain, Greece, Canada, Poland, and the United States each sent sizeable military units to Russia. Britain, whose armies had been horribly depleted by the Great War, included in its force many Indians. Still, among all the Allies, Britain, with its imperial and naval concerns, was surely the most heavily involved in the intervention. In addition to its continuous diplomatic involvements and active leadership, it was most generous in sending material aid. This totaled the not inconsiderable sum of £100,000,000.

The Japanese landed first, at Vladivostok, one month after the Czech uprising. Though this initial force was small and the pretense reasonable – a response to the murder of three Japanese in a shop in Vladivostok – the news was naturally received with considerable alarm in Moscow. Lenin instantly concluded that "it is probable, in fact almost inevitable, that the Japanese will advance." He went on, "Undoubtedly, the Allies will help them."[37] He was not mistaken. Sometime that same month, a joint French-British scheme "envisaged the advance of an Allied expeditionary force from Vladivostok to the area of the Urals, and possibly the Volga." Kennan continues: "The Japanese were to form the 'mobile base or nucleus' of this force; but were to enjoy, it was envisaged, 'the eventual assistance of *Czech and other elements which can be organized on the spot.*' "[38] The French and British tried desperately to convince the Americans, with their superior resources and abundant manpower, that they should provide the substance of this expeditionary force. President Wilson, aware of popular skepticism regarding European imperial dreams, resisted this; but remarkably, on grounds that Americans would support Czechs against the Germans, in July 1918, he dispatched troops to Siberia – numbering eventually almost 9,000. Much to Wilson's chagrin, instead of restricting themselves to the promised 7,000 troops, the Japanese landed 72,000, and before long they controlled the entire area from Vladivostok to Irkutsk.

Further north, the hapless General Graves, commander of the Americans, who had been instructed to "steady" Russian efforts at "self-government," could not share the benevolent attitude of his Washington superiors toward Kolchak's tyranny and finally forbade American troops "to engage in any military actions against the partisan bands which were beginning to harass Kolchak's lines of communication."[39] Indeed, Kennan reports the supremely ironical fact that the only election in Siberia that summer, held in Vladivostok under the aegis of Czechs and Americans, "yielded an unquestionable Bolshevik majority."[40]

Like the American intervention, French efforts were also luckless. The French were at first part of an Allied force which included British and Americans and which succeeded, in August 1918, in putting Archangel under White control. A poster identified the enemy as Bolsheviks, "soldiers and sailors who, in the majority of cases, are criminals," and Germans, who "usually appear in Russian uniform and are impossible to distinguish."[41]

The closest Germans "were actually four to five hundred miles away." In December a large French command, consisting ultimately of four full divisions of French and Greeks (some 48,000), supplemented by 4,000 Poles and a number of Algerians and Rumanians, landed at Odessa. They had hoped to give "the healthy and patriotic elements" the upper hand; but they found "a great many disputing politicians, but very few organized Russian troops."[42] In their first skirmish with the Reds, "the French, Greek and Polish soldiers discovered with dismay, that the population which they were supposed to protect actually sided with the Bolsheviks during the fight."[43] Before very long, the French had managed a "united front" of sorts: all the very conflicted political groups in Odessa were *against* them! Aided by what common sense could teach, Bolshevik propagandists succeeded in convincing these recaciltrant warriors that this was not their war to fight. Interestingly, a shortage of Greek-speaking Bolsheviks hampered Bolshevik efforts with the Greeks. With supplies short and the city on the edge of anarchy, in April 1919, an evacuation was ordered.

A third, much smaller French force in the Crimea was similarly without effect. When the Germans withdrew, liberal Kadets acceded to power; but the regime faltered because it utterly lacked indigenous support. White troops, persistently at odds with the population, committed atrocities against them. After a brief exchange with approaching Reds, the French negotiated a truce and on 30 April evacuated Sevastopol.[44]

But for all their lack of success, it would be an error to suppose that the interventions of the Allied troops were of no consequence. If nothing else, they gave impetus to White beliefs that more help was on the way, and that, ultimately, they would conquer. If one errs in judging the significance of this, then it seems wiser to err on the side of overestimation; for men with no hope are not likely to persist. Further, in addition to this false hope, there was all the British material assistance: food, weapons, financial credits, and instructors. The British had actively supported the newly formed Estonian army and the efforts of the new republics of the southern Caucasus. But more important was the material provided to Kolchak in Siberia, to Denkin in South Russia, and to Yudenitch, who, as noted, was able to launch two serious attacks on Petrograd.

As to British motivation, Chamberlin comments that "the lively British interest in the security of Georgia, Azerbaijan and Armenia can scarcely be attributed to abstact zeal for the rights of small nations. Some of the richest oil deposits in the world are in the neighborhood of Baku."[45] Indeed, a meeting of the Bibi-Eibat Oil Company in London in December 1918 had noted that, despite "the feeble voices of our politicians, under the heel of democracy," "never before in the history of these islands was there such an opportunity for the peaceful [sic] penetration of British influence and trade, for the creation of a second India or a second Egypt."[46] The redoubtable

Winston Churchill put the matter with his characteristic irony:

> Were they [the Allies] at war with Soviet Russia? Certainly not; but
> they shot Soviet Russians at sight. They armed the enemies of the
> Soviet Government. They blockaded its ports and sunk its battleships.
> They earnestly desired and schemed its downfall. But war − shocking!
> Interference − shame! It was, they repeated, a matter of indifference
> to them how Russians settled their own internal affairs. They were
> impartial − Bang! And then at the same time: parley and try to make
> trade.[47]

There is argument, of course, about the ultimate significance of the intervention. One view suggests, implausibly on the evidence, that when pluses
are added to minuses, it finally made little difference to the course of the
civil war.[48] On the other hand, if, as Chamberlin suggests, in the absence
of intervention, the struggle would have ended much much sooner, then it
seems safe to infer that the course of "war communism" would surely have
been different, if indeed, necessary at all. The British agent on the scene,
Bruce Lockhart, seems nearer to the truth in holding that the intervention
"was a blunder . . . comparable with the worse mistakes of the Crimean
war . . . . It raised hopes which could not be fulfilled. It intensified the civil
war and sent thousands of Russians to their deaths. Indirectly, it was
responsible for the Terror."[49]

No friend of Bolshevism and himself, in the end, on the side of intervention, Lockhart also saw Bolshevik gains. He continued: "Its direct effect
was to provide the Bolsheviks with a cheap victory, to give them new
confidence, and to galvanize them into a strong and ruthless organism."[50]
No doubt. The victory was cheaper than it might have been had the voters
of France, Britain, but especially America been convinced that they had to
make the sacrifice to destroy the Revolution. This was surely one of the
many ironies. The Revolution was "saved," finally, because, after defeating
the Kaiser, no politician in the West could risk demanding of its population
what would have been necessary to destroy Bolshevism. Perhaps we can
take some comfort in this − but perhaps not. No doubt the Bolsheviks did
create a powerful, ruthless state. Yet was this their wish and intention?
Indeed, did the civil war, extended by intervention and accident, play into
the hands of Bolshevik ideology? Or, quite the opposite, was the outcome a
monumental tragedy of distortion? To this question we now turn.

Was Democracy Possible?

The Provisional Government lasted from February to October. It is easy to
say that the regimes of Lvov and then Kerensky were short-lived because

the leadership was incompetent or because Bolshevik power was overwhelming. No doubt the leaders of the Provisional Government made some huge mistakes, especially in being unwilling to relinquish what was a manifestly untenable war policy. And no doubt the Bolsheviks did manage a coup. Yet the question of whether democracy was possible is far more complicated.

First, there is the question of whether any sort of parliamentary form of democracy was possible. We can say at once that it is hard to deny that the Provisional Government collapsed because "it had no solid foundation, because Russia was conspicuously lacking in all the conditions which historical experience indicates as essential to the effective functioning of parliamentary democracy: a general literacy; a numerous, well organized middle class, a long tradition of settling internal differences by peaceful methods; a keen sense of personal and property rights."[51] But this does not satisfactorily answer the question, since it is possible that a more left-oriented regime adopting a peace policy could have survived.

Any genuinely representative body in Russia at this time would have found itself in complete disarray; accordingly, no coalition government would have had an easy time of it. The root of the problem was the fragmentation of the population. Indeed, as Weimar Germany perhaps proved, in the absence of a mass base, no republic can survive in the twentieth century. One must here emphasize "in the twentieth century;" for in the eighteenth century and most of the nineteenth, republics did not need a mass base.

There are several things at work here. First, the period between the birth of the first republics and the Great War was one of transition to mass democracy, during which extended rights of suffrage became the focus of political struggles. As we saw, even Marx believed that in republics, at least, achieving this would be revolutionary. Gradual success in extending suffrage rights was precisely what made the problem of a mass base increasingly urgent, as was seen by Max Weber and by elites in all the parliamentary republics. The republics of the twentieth century had no choice, of course. The epoch of revolution had left many marks, not least the idea that every person had a just claim to full rights of citizenship. The new republics had to accept this.

Second, not only were people insisting on suffrage rights, but the people doing so had been radicalized by the epoch of revolution. There had been nothing quite like this when republican institutions were being created in England and the United States. France had failed to achieve a stable republic. Russia lacked a sufficiently large, coherent bourgeoisie, and the Russian masses, far more than the French masses, could not be easily constrained by the ideals of bourgeois democracy. They wanted the vote, certainly; but they also wanted land, a redistribution of social wealth, and even more than the Americans, institutions which would give them a strong form of democracy.

Third, Russia was unevenly developed. Accordingly, the Russian parties of the left, the only ones that had any chance of achieving a mass base, had bases each with widely different interests, aspirations, and demands. Many people, especially peasants, identified with the program of the Social Revolutionaries. Indeed, as noted, in adopting what amounted to the SR program of land reform, the Bolsheviks in power quickly acknowledged this. SRs were, by definition, revolutionaries; but not only did they split into a left and a right, but as a party, they had little affection for Mensheviks or Bolsheviks, who, after all, were advancing Marxian views which were rooted in the entirely different social setting of a Western European urban, industrialized society.[52] The Menshevik and Bolshevik parties, deeply at odds even before the formation of the Bolshevik party in 1912, each had significant bases in urban centers. The Mensheviks divided over the war between "Defensists" who persisted in demanding victory as the only sure defense and a "left" wing which held to the idea that the socialist parties of Europe could force a general peace. And, not to be underestimated, anarchist ideas of various sorts were rampant throughout the population.[53]

Some writers have suggested that a "coalition of socialist parties, based primarily on the soviets, would have been possible if Martov and the left Mensheviks had been able to act decisively on their positions," that

> if there ever was a chance for the establishment of a relatively democratic and pluralist socialist government in Russia, its best opportunity would seem to have been after the Kornilov affair and before the formation of a third coalition government with the Kadets on 25 September, and the subsequent decision on insurrection taken by the Bolshevik Central Committee.[54]

This is possible, but doubtful. Likewise, and of some importance, is the possibility expressed by the left Menshevik N. N. Sukhanov. In his memoirs, he wrote that, in walking out of the All-Russian Congress of Soviets, on 25 October,

> we completely untied the Bolshevik's hands, making them masters of the entire situation and yielding to them the whole arena of the revolution. A struggle at the Congress for a united democratic front *might* have had some success .... By quitting the congress, we ourselves gave the Bolsheviks the monopoly of the Soviet, of the masses, and of the revolution. By our irrational decision, we ensured the victory of Lenin's whole "line"![55]

It is impossible to say how significant this move was, even if there can be little doubt that by walking out, moderate socialists made it impossible for Bolshevik moderates, left SRs, and internationalist socialists to construct a compromise. As Rabinowitch argues, in this they played exactly into Lenin's plan for an unencumbered Bolshevik-led revolution.

But the question as to whether democracy was possible raises a second question: Could there have been Bolshevik democracy? Many readers will doubtless say that the question is misplaced, that the Bolsheviks had no interest in democracy, and that from the beginning Bolshevism preached the virtues of a one-party state, that the "seeds of totalitarianism" were already in Marx and Engels, only to be made explicit in Lenin, especially in his famous "What Is to be Done?" of 1902. They would see this anti-democracy as confirmed by the fact that the Bolsheviks quickly abolished the Constituent Assembly and from 1921 not only brutally destroyed the anti-Bolshevik opposition, but eliminated Communist party factions as well. These issues are not only heavily freighted with political and ideological implications which are still profoundly pertinent; they are also enormously complicated. Plainly, this chapter cannot do them justice; still, it may be possible, following the recent work of "revisionist" historians, to stimulate reconsideration of the texts and arguments.

The aim here is to emphasize what is too often overlooked, that statist forms of liberal democracy were not the only conceptual possibilities, that Lenin had arrived at a consistent vision of a quasi-socialist, decentralized yet integrated federation of democratically organized units. When they seized power, Lenin and the Bolsheviks counted on revolution in Germany. Whether this was mere wishful thinking is not easy to judge; that is the topic of the next chapter. When this revolution failed to materialize in the condition of civil war, aided and abetted by the Allies, they realized that their situation was desperate. Indeed, under these conditions the vision which is quite clearly articulated in *State and Revolution* of an anti-statist – anarchistic – decentralized association of soviets had absolutely no chance of succeeding. Whether the choices they then made were correct is another matter, as is the question of whether those choices "determined" the Stalinist outcome.

"What Is to be Done?"

We can best begin with an account of the tract which is rightly seen as Lenin's first significant departure from what had become orthodox Marxist Social Democracy. It has also been seen, wrongly, as a vindication of antidemocracy. The occasion of What Is to be Done? was a response to Lenin's article "Where to Begin?" of 1901 in *Iskra* ("The Spark") by the editors of *Rabocheye Dyelo*. Both were Russian-language journals published outside Russia. In his *Iskra* article, Lenin had put forward a plan for an all-Russian organization to be linked up with an all-Russian newspaper. The editors of *Rabocheye Dyelo* argued that this was merely a means to "propagate armchair ideas and armchair work," and that such an organ would be "an uncontrolled autocratic legislator for the whole of the practical revolutionary struggle." In What Is to be Done?, Lenin answered this charge and did so by claiming that the argument against an all-Russian newspaper is best seen as continuous with a "'new' tendency," an "opportunist" tendency which "adopts a 'critical' attitude towards 'obsolete doctrinaire' Marxism," a tendency "*presented* with sufficient precision by Bernstein, and *demonstrated* by Millerand."[56] This "tendency" − "revisionism" − is accurately characterized by Lenin thus: "Social-Democracy must change from a party of the social revolution into a democratic party of social reforms" (V. 353).

It is this, of course, which is latched on to by both the later supporters *and* critics of Lenin (and "Leninism"). The supporters, insurrectionaries of this stripe or that, applaud Lenin's rescue of revolutionary Marxism. The critics find in his critique an early statement of what they see to be Lenin's fanaticism and failure to adjust practice to a changing reality. These more recent "Leninists" are correct in judging that Marxism must be revolutionary in the sense that, with the conquest of power, the Communist regime would need to be "a dictatorship of the proletariat" − as argued in the *Manifesto*. Nevertheless, these more recent writers too often not only fail to see that "revisionism" was a minority tendency within pre-World War I Social Democracy, but also they share with the critics of "Leninism" what can usefully be called a "Second International" understanding of some of the critical theoretical premises of Marxism.[57]

First, the parliamentary tactics of Bernstein were not the problem. As Engels had argued (in the 1895 introduction to *The Class Struggles in France*), insurrectionary politics had to be rejected for "slow propaganda work and parliamentary activity." But for Kautsky, Luxemburg, *and* Lenin, this did not call for a revision of the Marxist theoretical view that a revolution demanded a transformation of the social relations of production. Socialism, on this view, was the end of exploitation, the end of classes and class rule. Lenin, like Kautsky and Luxemburg, argued that Bernstein was mistaken in believing that the recent changes in capitalism and the development of republican institutions had made this unnecessary. He was wrong in believing that where a working-class party dominated a parliamentary democracy, socialist redistributive justice was tantamount to the overcoming of exploitation and class antagonism. This was the central point of the debate regarding "revisionism."

But there was another critical theoretical question. It regarded the general question of the level and quality of *political* consciousness among the workers. This is the central theoretical question of Lenin's tract. Lenin's position on this marks the beginning of his departure from the basic premises of Second International Marxism.

Marx and Engels had said precious little about the nature of a revolutionary party. It was to be a political party (in our ordinary sense); it was to be the party of the proletariat (as the revolutionary class); and it was to engage in all the activities which any political party engaged. Thus, it was to spread its ideas, gain new members, and, if it could, gain power. By the turn of the century, the Marxist parties of Europe had attained the status of mass parties. The most successful of these, the German Social Democratic Party (SPD), was in 1912 the largest party in the Reichstag, with 110 deputies and 34.7 percent of the vote. It had, at that time, 90 daily newspapers and assets of 21.5 million marks.

Yet, by the turn of the century, although economic development was creating the conditions for "socialist production," it was not as clear that the optimistic predictions about "revolutionary consciousness" among the workers were being realized. Bernstein's criticism of the gap between the rhetoric and the practice of the SPD was in part, at least, a response to this. Not only were the policies of the SPD cautious, even "reformist," but there was little evidence that the workers were caught up with revolutionary fervor. On this there was full agreement. Thus, Lenin quotes Karl Kautsky: "Many of our revisionist critics believe that Marx asserted that economic development and the class struggle create, not only the conditions for Socialist production, but also, and directly, the *consciousness* [emphasis original] of the necessity [of socialist production]." While Kautsky insisted that "this is absolutely untrue," Bernstein was not wrong in believing that this assumption was at the center of the theory *and* rhetoric of Second International "revolutionary" Marxism. After all, in his comment on the Erfurt Programme (1891–2), Kautsky had himself insisted that "economic development creates with a *natural necessity* conditions which *force the exploited to strive against private property.*"[58] To be sure, no Marxist denied that *people* would make the revolution. The question was: Would workers be "forced" to become revolutionary? Bernstein was correct in thinking that Marxists were disabled by their commitments to apriorist materialist history. Indeed, what is striking here is that while "What Is to be done?" does take aim at "revisionism," Lenin and Bernstein both rejected the materialist version of eschatological history. But to understand Lenin's tract, one further fact is critical. It is that some of the revolutionary parties of Europe operated legally, and some, as in Russia, did not.

Lenin's response to his opponents in *Rabocheye Dyelo* is both "theoretical" and concrete, with attention to the particular conditions of Russian Social Democracy. We need to be reminded that Lenin's primary audience consisted of Russian Marxists who, like him, had been students of Plekhanov, but who, unlike him, were still operating with assumptions which scarcely pertained to Germany, never mind Imperial, peasant Russia.

Lenin cut to the theoretical problem of his essay by observing that "'everyone agrees' that it is necessary to develop the political consciousness of the working class." "The question was," he continued, "how is that to be done and what is required to do it?" (V. 421). As Lenin sees it, *Rabocheye Dyelo*, Bernsteinism, the English Fabians, the French Ministerialists, and, on the other side, those revolutionaries who adopt terrorist tactics, have a "common root." They are all "subservient to spontaniety" and hence *apolitical*. "The Economists and terrorists bow to different poles of spontaneity: The Economists bow to the spontaneity of the 'pure and simple' labour movement while the terrorists bow to the spontaneity of the passionate indignation of the intellectuals who lack the ability or opportunity to connect the revolutionary struggle and the working-class movement into an integral whole" (V. 418). "Terrorism," of course, especially identified anarchists as revolutionaries influenced by the apocalyptic philosophies of Bakunin and Nechaev. Like Marx and Engels, Lenin had no patience with this version of romanticism.

On the other hand, there is, he insists, an enormous difference between "trade union consciousness" and "Social-Democratic consciousness." The former, the demand for increased wages, shorter hours, and so forth, is generated spontaneously by the workers, whereas the latter is not (V. 384). The former may be a class consciousness; but it is a narrow, self-interested consciousness (V. 413). Indeed, as a spontaneous movement "along the line of least resistance," it will lead "to the domination of bourgeois ideology" (V. 384–5). Because bourgeois ideology is far older than Social Democratic ideology, "it is more fully developed and ... possesses immeasurably more opportunities for becoming widespread." It was hardly surprising, therefore, that workers, responding "along the line of least resistance" would reproduce it! Social-Democratic consciousness, by contrast, is a *democratic* consciousness, and this is something which does not come about spontaneously:

> The workers can acquire class political consciousness *only from without*, that is, only outside the economic struggle, outside of the sphere of relations of workers and employers. The sphere from which alone it is possible to obtain this knowledge is the sphere of the relationships between all classes and the state and the government – the sphere of the inter-relations between all classes. (V. 422)

Accordingly, the task of the party is educational:

> To bring political knowledge to the *workers* the Social-Democrats must *go among all the classes of the population*, they must dispatch units of their army *in all directions* ....

The Social-Democrats' ideal should not be a trade-union secretary, but *the tribune of the people*, able to react to every manifestation of tyranny and oppression, no matter where it takes place, no matter what stratum or class of the people it affects; who is able to group all these manifestations into a single picture of the police violence and capitalist exploitation; who is able to take advantage of every petty event in order to set forth *before all* his Socialist convictions and his democratic demands. (V. 423)

But if the primary task of the revolutionary party is pedagogic,[59] there is still the question of the nature of the party, of the sense in which it is a "vanguard."

Lenin did not depart from the Marxist tradition in holding that a social revolution must have as its center the working class. But writing with Russia as the focus of his attention, he was clear that instigating a revolution there would require the support of many classes of the population. Accordingly,

We must find ways and means of calling meetings of representatives of all and every other class of the population that desire to listen to a democrat; for he is no Social-Democrat who forgets in practice that "the communists support every revolutionary movement", that we are obliged for that reason to emphasize *general democratic tasks before the whole people*, without for a moment concealing our Socialist convictions. (V. 425)

This hardly sounds like the antidemocratic, conspiratorial, class-reductionist Lenin of the popular imagination – or even of the literature. Yet, this does not deny "the need for a strong revolutionary organization"; on the contrary, it makes it all the more necessary (V. 474).

The oldest revolutionary party, the German SPD, certainly had its organizational birth pangs and its period of underground activity; but no one denies that it was a strong organization or that its publication, *Vorwärts*, played a vital role in developing German Social Democracy. But the SPD was a legal party, whereas the revolutionary party in Russia was not.

Everything that Lenin urges as regards his "plan" for a unified all-Russian party follows from this. As he remarks, "only an incorrigible utopian would have a broad organization of workers, with elections, reports, universal suffrage, etc. under an autocracy" (V. 459; and also V. 478–9). As is well known, Lenin calls for "a small, compact core, consisting of reliable, experienced, and hardened workers, with responsible agents in the principal districts and connected by all the rules of strict secrecy with the organizations of revolutionaries" (V. 112). It was Lenin's idea that such an organization of "professional revolutionaries" guided by theory might be able, "despite the gendarmes," to build a socialist mass movement which would include not only workers but "aroused students, the discontented Zemstov [united self-government bodies], the incensed religious sects, the offended elementary teachers, etc., etc." (V. 428). This, he insists, is "the role the revolutionary 'vanguard' must really play." But if in Russia this requires secrecy, it is nevertheless not conspiracy (V. 465). Thus, "centralization of the secret functions of the organization by no means implies centralization of the functions of the movement" (V. 465). Still, there is no pretense that a secret organization can be democratic: "We call the German Socialist Party a democratic party organization because all it does it does publicly; even its party congresses are held in public. But no one would call an organization that is hidden from every one but its members by a veil of secrecy, a democratic organization" (V. 477). That is, if in an autocratic country, the form of the organization is "conspirative" on pain of making itself readily available to the police, it is not thereby Blanquist.[60]

Blanqui, of course, had held that an active *minority* of revolutionaries, if sufficiently well organized, could seize power and make a revolution. *None of the Bolsheviks accepted this.* On the contrary, they assumed, fully in keeping with the views of Marx and Engels, that only a majority of the people could make a social democratic revolution. They did not, however, deny the need for a party, nor, in the conditions of Russia, for a highly disciplined secret party. A revolutionary mass would still need organization and leadership.

On the other hand, Rosa Luxemburg's charge that Lenin's views of the party are "a mechanical transposition of the organizational principles of Blanquism into the mass movement of the socialist working class," makes a vital point.[61] Luxemburg was in full sympathy with Lenin's diagnoses of the particular problems of party organization in Russia. As she said, not only is the party illegal, but in Russia, unlike Germany, there was the additional problem of "how to create a Social Democratic movement when the state is not yet in the hands of the bourgeoisie." Her argument versus Lenin's "centralism" is that Russia at that time lacked not just "the possibility for the workers to develop their own political activity through direct influence on public life, in a party press, and public congresses, etc," but that it *also* lacked "the existence of a large contingent of workers educated in the political struggle." Lenin was correct, as it happened, that the masses could be politicized behind the revolutionary vanguard of workers; but he was sadly in error in believing that the "contingent of workers" was sufficiently large to make a social democratic revolution, given the frightful conditions produced by war.

Lenin's tract concludes, then, with a series of arguments in favor of what for Lenin was a key element in establishing an effective, militant, all-Russian organization, an all-Russian political newspaper!

No doubt, there are serious difficulties with "What Is to be Done?" Perhaps most fundamentally, there is Luxemburg's question of whether a secret party, operating in an illiberal state can ever achieve the mass base which would make possible a revolutionary transition to social *democracy*. Lenin assumes that when such a party takes power, it becomes the instrument of the masses who are solidly behind its programs; that, to recapitulate the words of the *Manifesto*, a dictatorship of the majority will replace a dictatorship of the minority. Organizationally, Lenin did construct, in Russia, something much like the party he wanted.[62] Indeed, had he not done so, there would have been no Bolshevik Revolution.

The Situation in 1917

In the late summer of 1917, Lenin sat down to write what we call *State and Revolution*, an incomplete tract which ends with the title of a planned chapter 7. As he wrote in December of that year in the first Petrograd edition, "I did not succeed in writing a single line of the chapter, what 'interfered' was the political crisis – the eve of the October Revolution of 1917." Of course, "such 'interference' can only be welcomed." No doubt the tract contains Lenin's best theoretical treatment of the revolutionary state, despite the redundancies and infelicities which editing might have removed. While I believe that it contains the core of Lenin's consistent thoughts on democracy, it is by no means easy to comprehend. There are two main reasons for this. First, its ideas were unquestionably designed to boost Lenin's call to seize power, even if one could argue that, if anything, they should have done just the opposite! Second, it is well-nigh impossible not to read *State and Revolution* in the light of the Bolshevik Revolution and its aftermath. Put briefly, the usual interpretation has it that *State and Revolution* promises some utopian notion of democracy in some indefinite future but utterly divorces such an end from any sort of democratic means.[63]

An alternative view is possible if we put at the center of our analysis, first, the World War, and second, the critical developments in Russia from February to October of 1917. In *State and Revolution*, Lenin held that the war had created revolutionary conditions in the *whole* of Europe, that the revolution in Russia, under way since February, "can be understood in its totality only as a link in the chain of Socialist proletarian revolutions called for by the imperialist war." The critical developments in Russia concerned the remarkable radicalization of the mass – for the most part way beyond that of the radicals in the left parties – and the generation of "soviets" – literally councils.

The remarkable idea of "soviets" had been created by workers and intellectuals in a hall in the St Petersburg Technological Institute during the revolution of 1905. During the February Revolution, soviets had been reinvented as "Soviets of Workers' and Soldiers' Deputies." Within a month of the fall of the Tsar, 479 deputies from 138 local soviets, 7 armies, 13 rear units, and 26 front units convened the first All-Russian Conference of Soviets. It was not long, indeed, before every town of any size had its soviet.[64]

The judgment regarding the war's consequences and the idea of soviets is evident in the first of Lenin's "Letters from Afar," written in March while he was still in exile in Zurich.

[T]he first stage of this first Revolution, namely of the Russian Revolution ... has ended. This first stage ... will certainly not be the last .... The imperialist war was bound, with objective inevit-ability, immensely to accelerate and to intensify to an unprecedented degree the class struggle of the proletariat against the bourgeoisie; it was bound to turn into a civil war between the hostile classes. (XXIII. 297–9)

The Russian Revolution (of February) would enter its second stage, its proletarian stage, as part of the chain of revolution in Germany and elsewhere. Russia hardly fits the "classic" image of socialist revolution; but the Russian working class has allies. First, there is "the broad mass of the semi-proletarian"; but more important is "the small peasant population [of Russia], who number scores of millions." "This mass must have peace, bread, freedom and land." The letter continues:

The cruel lessons of the War, and they will be all *the more* cruel the more vigorously the war is prosecuted by Guchkov, Lvov, Milyukov and Co., will *inevitably* push this mass toward the proletariat, compel it to follow the proletariat. We must now take advantage of the relative freedom of the new order and of the Soviets of Workers' Deputies to *enlighten* and *organise* this mass first of all and above all. (XXIII. 307)

In a third letter, dated 14 March, Lenin combined the themes of war and the soviets by offering a militia scheme, involving adults of both sexes. The image of the Paris Commune was in the forefront of his consciousness. The militias would be the executive arm of the soviets and would bring the whole population into active administration. Lenin wrote: "Such a militia would transform democracy from a beautiful signboard ... into a means of actually *training the masses* for participation in *all* affairs of state" (XXIII. 328). The militias would see to it that "*every* toiler should *forthwith* see and feel some improvement in his life [,] that every family should have . . . bread that not a single adult in a rich family should dare take extra milk until the children are provided for [,] that the palaces and rich apartments abandoned by the Tsar and the aristocracy should not remain vacant, but provide shelter for the homeless and destitute," (XXIII. 329).

Upon his return to Russia, Lenin offered the famous April Theses, which scandalized the leading members of the Bolshevik party. We need to pause here to emphasize why, as Bukharin said, a "part of our party, and by no means a small part of our own party, saw in this almost a betrayal of Marxist ideology," and why Trotsky could say that the Theses were met with a "hostility softened only by bewilderment."[65] The "Old Bolsheviks" were scandalized, because in their view, in the conditions of the time, the very idea of a dictatorship of the proletariat was quite insane. They saw Lenin as having utterly abandoned the "classic" scenario for a "proletarian revolution." His program would thoroughly isolate the party, so they believed. On this they were wrong. But, like the Social Democrats of Germany, looking at events from afar, those who could not foresee a happy outcome, even with success, would tragically be proved to be correct.

Lenin's departure was a *radical* departure from a common assumption of Second International Marxism, "the fundamental idea which runs through all of Marx's works, namely that the democratic republic is the nearest approach to the dictatorship of the proletariat (XXV. 445). Lenin may not have been wrong in not waiting for the creation of a democratic republic, yet wrong in saying that "the objective conditions" called for a "dictatorship of the proletariat." We know the outcome of the successful coup of the Bolsheviks, a success which has fundamentally shaped the twentieth century. Perhaps we can say that, had the Bolsheviks not acted, it is very likely that the Provisional Government would have given way to some form of reactionary order. But we cannot even guess what the consequences of this might have been.

Still, as the content of the April Theses demonstrates, if Lenin was not at this time entirely clear on his theory, his concrete program was not at all far-fetched. He called not only for an immediate peace, but also for "no support to the Provisional Government," (XXIV. 22). But he did not at that time call for insurrection. He wrote, "As long as we are in the minority we carry on the work of criticism and exposing errors and at the same time we preach the necessity of transferring the entire state power to the Soviets." The soviets were the key. The Bolsheviks would need to achieve a majority in them. It was thus that he rejected a parliamentary republic. "To return to a parliamentary republic from the Soviets of Workers' Deputies would be a retrograde step." Instead, there would be "a republic of Soviets of Workers', Farmhands' and Peasants' Deputies throughout the whole country" (ibid.). Supporting the actions of peasants who did not wait for a program,

he endorsed "confiscation of all landlords' estates" and called for nationalization of all land, with the establishment of model farms under the control
of Soviet Farmhands. In addition he called for "the immediate amalgamation
of all banks in the country into a single national bank," which in his view
was the most purely socialist step in the program. He saw it as not "our
immediate task to introduce socialism, but only to bring social production
and the distribution of products at once under the *control* of the Soviets"
(XXIV. 24). Capitalist relations could remain, as long as production and
distribution were democratically controlled.

All these ideas are given a full-blown theoretical treatment in *State and
Revolution*, to which we now turn.

State and Revolution

Taking his clue from the last preface signed by Marx and Engels, dated 24
June 1872, Lenin argued that "the programme of the *Communist Manifesto*
is now 'in places out of date'" (XXV. 414). Again, including a quote from
Marx and Engels, "one thing especially ... was proved by the [Paris]
Commune, viz., that 'the working class cannot simply lay hold of the ready-
made state machinery and wield it for its own purposes'" (ibid). Thus
Lenin insists that "Marx's idea is that the working class must *break up,
smash*, the 'ready-made machinery,' and not confine itself merely to taking
possession of it."[66]

It will be well to recall here our earlier account of the *Manifesto* (in
chapter 10 above). As we saw in the *Manifesto*, the idea of the proletarian
revolution is not at all filled in, whereas the program for transformation
after the seizure of power could not be more concrete. Indeed, a proletarian
party representing a politicized proletarian majority carrying out the ten-
point program in a well-advanced democratic republic would, from a
contemporary stance, look "reformist"! Similarly, in the *Manifesto* (as elsewhere), the "dictatorship of the proletariat" was a class state, and this class
state was but "the first step in the revolution of the working class;" for, "in
the course of development," as production is put into the hands of producers, "public power" loses its "political character." That is, as an instrument of repression, the state increasingly loses those functions required by
the capitalist state; thus, to return to Engel's metaphor, it "withers away."

In what respects, then, do the views of the *Manifesto* need to be rejected,
amended, or supplemented? According to Lenin, in the *Manifesto*, Marx
and Engels did not answer the question of what was to replace the democratic state or how democracy was to be achieved.

Without resorting to Utopias, Marx waited for the *experience* of a mass movement to provide the reply to the question as to the specific forms which this organization of the proletariat as the ruling class will assume and as to the exact manner in which this organization will be combined with the most complete, consistent "winning of the battle of democracy." (XXV. 417; see also XXV. 409)

This "experience" was provided by the Paris Commune and then, for Lenin, by the workers', soldiers', and peasants' councils, the soviets. If we grant — as I think we must — that "this organization of the proletariat as the ruling class" refers to a proletarian *party* leading a mass movement, then Lenin's analysis seems to be entirely sound. Even so, it is not at all clear how it relates to the idea that the state machinery must be "smashed."

We can get clearer by noting that, for Lenin, the "machinery of the state" reduces to the standing army and the bureaucracy (XXV. 407). Lenin observes that with *The Eighteenth Brumaire*, "Marxism takes a tremendous step forward in comparison with the position of the *Communist Manifesto*;" for the question of the state is now "treated in a concrete manner." Marx had seen that the process of perfecting the machinery of the state had begun with the French Revolution. But in 1871 he had restricted his conclusions to the Continent and had excluded both England and America. "This was understandable in 1871, when England was the model of a purely capitalist country, but without a militarist clique and, to a considerable degree, without a bureaucracy" (XXV. 415).

But between 1914 and 1917, he writes, it is exactly these democratic republics which have brought the machinery of the state "to general 'European' imperialist perfection." "Both Britain and America, the biggest and last representatives — in the whole world — of Anglo-Saxon 'liberty' . . . have completely sunk into the all-European, filthy, bloody morass of bureaucratic-military institutions which subordinate everything to themselves and which trample everything under foot" (XXV. 416).

Lenin's equation is simple enough. The capitalist state equals the perfected modern state equals the warfare state equals an executive power with a huge bureaucratic and military organization — to use Marx's words, a "frightful body of parasites wound like a caul about the body of . . . society and clogging its every pore." It is *this* state which needs to be "smashed" and replaced. Lenin tries to be specific regarding what will replace it. Much of what he says differs not at all from what Marx and Engels, in one place or another, had already said. Nevertheless, since the message has not got through, for whatever reason, summarizing it here may be useful.

First, "representative institutions remain, but parliamentarianism as a special system, as a division of labour between legislative and the executive functions, as a privileged position for the deputies, no longer exists." Representative institutions require mechanisms for assuring the responsibility of representatives, and they require free communication. But there are representative institutions of all sorts. Parliamentarianism is a special type characterized most distinctively by the view of representatives as authorities, not "agents," and by separation of function. Lenin asserts: "We cannot imagine democracy, even proletarian, without representative institutions, but we can and *must* imagine democracy without parliamentarianism" (XXV. 424).

This does not mean the abolition of bodies of representatives (soviets) or of the "elective principle." What it does mean is that these bodies be comprised of persons whose decisions are mandated by the persons they represent, and not be mere "talking shops," but "working bodies," "executive and legislative at the same time."

In calling the parliamentary bodies of America and England "talking shops," Lenin both endorses J. S. Mill's view of them and overstates his case. He was not wrong that in these countries, "the actual work of the 'state' . . . is done behind the scenes and is carried out by the departments, the offices and the staffs." On the other hand, he seems to have no appreciation of the problems of getting things done in what he ironically calls a "primitive democracy." This, perhaps, is the greatest theoretical weakness of his position in *State and Revolution*, one that has direct bearing on the party's practical problems in the period of the civil war.

This is not unrelated to his optimistic remarks regarding the second feature of the democracy which will replace the warfare state, the gradual elimination of specialized bureaucracies. Against both nostalgic anarchists and those who jeer at "primitive democracy" he writes:

Capitalist culture has *created* large-scale production, factories, railways, the postal service, telephones, etc., and *on this basis* the great majority of functions of the old "state power" have become so simplified and can be reduced to such simple operations of registration, filing and checking that they can easily be performed by every literate person, and it will be possible to perform them for "workingmen's wages", which circumstance can (and must) strip those functions of every shadow of privilege, of every appearance of "official grandeur." (XXV. 420–1)

Given that the Soviet state became a bureaucratic class state, this is supremely ironical, to say the least. And plainly, it needs to be explained. Lenin later came to argue that it was the absence of "capitalist culture" in Russia which so profoundly undermined his hopes for the Soviet state.

Third, there is the question of "national unity." His account of this has given rise to much confusion; yet this is easily explained. As everyone knows, Lenin counterposes "federalism" with "centralism" and rejects the former. This has led a host of writers to gloss "democratic centralism" as a unitary state in which power is located at the top and officials at lower levels in a structured hierarchy provide advice and information but are themselves merely instruments of the central authority. This, surely, is what the Soviet state became. It is thus easy to read history backwards. Nevertheless, it is clear that the federalism which Lenin rejects is the classical — pre-American — idea of it. This is "the Federalism of Proudhon," the notion that arises, he says, "from the petty-bourgeois views of Anarchism" (XXV. 429). Lenin, like Marx and Engels (in their writings on the Paris Commune), defends "democratic centralism, the republic — one and indivisible" (XXV. 426). He asks rhetorically:

Now if the proletariat and poorest peasants take state power into their own hands, organize themselves quite freely in communes, and *unite* the action of all the communes in striking at capital, in crushing the resistance of the capitalists, and in transferring the privately owned railways, factories, land, and on, to the *entire* nation, to the whole of society, won't that be centralism? Won't that be the most consistent democratic centralism and, moreover, proletarian centralism? (XXV. 429–30)

Bernstein and the "social chauvinists" "cannot conceive the possibility of voluntary centralism, of a voluntary union of the communes into a nation . . . . Like all philistines, Bernstein can imagine centralism only as something from above, to be imposed and maintained solely by means of bureaucracy and militarism." *Coerced* centralism — the centralism of the modern state — is both required by militarism and bureaucracy *and* made acceptable by means of them. Once eliminated, the "unity" of the nation may be preserved, voluntarily.

The arrangement hinted at here (and expanded more fully in his account of Engels's discussion of the Erfurt Programme) is both federalist — in the new American sense — and anarchist, with the vital difference that for Lenin, as for Marx and Engels, the smashing of the state presupposes the smashing of capitalism. Lenin argues that the state, as a special organization of force, is needed by the proletariat precisely because it will need to use force "to break the resistance of the capitalist exploiters." Under any circumstances that one might reasonably conceive, the proletarian class state once established, can expect counterrevolution. This is not at all obvious to the "opportunists," because they are not revolutionaries, in that they have no intention of smashing capitalism. Moreover, capitalist organization is "national," and no modern state could exist without a unified economy. That this is not obvious to the anarchists reflects their misunderstanding of a modern economy.

The arrangement hinted at is "federalist" in that centralism does not, in Engels's words, "in the least preclude such broad local self-government as would combine the voluntary defense of the unity of the state by the 'communes' and districts with the complete elimination of all bureaucratic practices and all 'ordering' from above' (XXV. 447). This is not "empire minus the Emperor." Rather, it demands "complete self-government for the provinces, districts, and local areas through officials elected by universal suffrage." Indeed, "How self-government is to be organized and how we can manage without a bureaucracy has been shown to us by America and the first French Republic" (XXV. 447). Lenin is making a number of critical assumptions here, needless to say; not least that imperialist war has at least abated, and that a proletarian party leading a mass movement which acceded to state power would have the chance to begin to build, on the foundation of workers', soldiers', and peasants' councils, a new form of "republic," democratic and socialist.

We can now look at this argument in terms of the circumstances of August and September 1917. Lenin was prepared to seize power in backward Russia precisely because he believed that the government of Russia was a government in name only, in that real power lay in the soviets; that the Bolsheviks would constitute a majority in the soviets; that counter-revolution could be defeated by the organizations being created in the revolutionary process, especially the newly constituted Red Guards; and that the embryonic "proletarian" revolution would soon have the support of at least some proletarian states in Western Europe. Sick of imperialist war, the working classes would force revolutionary war.

Admittedly, Russia was not advanced and could not meet the classical Marxian conditions of a proletarian revolution; but if it were a link in the chain of proletarian revolutions, it could still succeed. It could go directly to the "second stage," since the Tsarist, bourgeois state was already smashed and was being replaced by new democratic forms. As Lenin said, this second stage would not be socialism in the strictest sense. But with good fortune, it would be a stronger form of democracy than the world had yet seen.[67]

Lenin proved to be correct in judging, *contra* many in his own party, that the Bolsheviks could seize power and hold it. Right up to the coup, Kamenev, Zinoviev, Gorky, Lunacharsky, and others continued to argue that any attempt at a coup would be crushed, and that their only option was to attempt to strengthen the party by peaceful means. In their view, the best that might be hoped for was "the Constituent Assembly plus Soviets," with Bolsheviks holding a third of the seats in the Assembly. Lenin's confidence was expressed in an essay written in response to arguments advanced in Maxim Gorky's *Novaya Zhizn* (*New Life*). In "Can the Bolshevikii Hold State Power?" written just prior to the coup, Lenin insisted: "Since 1905,

Russian has been governed by 130,000 landlords who have perpetuated endless violence against 50,000,000 people .... Yet we are told that the 240,000 members of the Bolshevik Party will not be able to govern Russia in the interests of the poor against the rich" (XXV. 111). He believed, of course, that the "poor" would be the mass base consenting to "government" by his party.

Even though most of the argument about "dual power" is misleading at best, it is true that the soviets were the locus of whatever power remained, and that Bolshevik majorities existed in the most critical of these. The Bolsheviks attained their first majorities in the Petrograd and Moscow soviets just after the Kornilov affair. Trotsky offered the characteristic dichotomy: "Either the bourgeoisie will actually dominate the old state apparatus, altering it a little for its purposes, in which case the soviets will come to nothing; or the soviets will form the foundation of a new state, liquidating not only the old governmental apparatus, but also the dominion of those classes which it served."[68] But it was quite clear that even if the bourgeoisie could dominate the old state apparatus, they could not rule.

In March, War Minister Guchkov wrote to General Alekseev: "The Provisional Government possesses no real power and its orders are executed only in so far as this is permitted by the Soviet of Workers' and Soldiers' Deputies which holds in its hands the most important elements of actual power, such as troops, railroads, postal and telegraph services."[69] According to Francis Carsten, Sukhanov, "one of our most reliable witnesses of the Russian Revolution," offered that "all power and authority was in the hands of the Soviets."[70]

As Cohen argues, the like-mindedness of Lenin and Bukharin, along with Trotsky, was at this juncture critical. Significantly, like Lenin, Bukharin had just returned from exile to take over leadership of the critical Moscow unit of the party, and Trotsky did not join the Bolsheviks until July 1917. It is unlikely that the coup would have been attempted had there not been a convergence in the views of the three on the critical assumption that there would be revolutionary war in Europe. Bukharin's confidence is clear. As he put it, "There is no doubt whatsoever that the Russian revolution will spread to the old capitalist countries." Similarly, he was clear that "a lasting victory of the Russian proletariat is ... inconceivable without the support of the West European proletariat."[71] Trotsky agreed. As he said, "If the peoples of Europe do not arise and crush imperialism [N. B., not "capitalism"], we shall be crushed — that is beyond doubt." Of course, all three dreamed that these peoples, at least in Germany, would arise and crush *capitalism*; but short of that, there was the hope that enlightened opinion in the capitalist democracies would forbid intervention, and that the growing sentiment of bourgeois organizations like the British Union of Democratical Control (UDC) could be tapped to prevent this.

The Imperatives of Revolution

But because they were wrong in their assumption about European revolution, because the first imperative of the Revolution was to preserve it against interventionist-supported counterrevolution, and because in conditions of modern war, soviets were utterly insufficient, the Bolsheviks acted contrary to their vision of democracy. The dictatorship of the proletariat, never a reality, became, because of isolation, capitalist encirclement and civil war, a dictatorship of the party and then of the few.

Lenin quickly came to realize where things had gone wrong. Having grasped the tail of the tiger, the Bolsheviks waited for the European revolution which never came. As early as March 1918, Lenin noted that "there is much that is crude and unfinished in our Soviets," so that, as regards the soviet system – in the literal sense – "this has scarcely begun and has begun badly" (XXVIII. 132–3). In *Pravda* of 23 January 1921, he wrote: "I was wrong and Comrade Bukharin was right. What I should have said is: 'A workers' state is an abstraction. What we actually have is a workers' state, with this peculiarity, firstly, that it is not the working class but the peasant population that predominates in the country, and secondly, that it is a workers' state with bureaucratic distortions'" (XXXII. 48). By March 1922 Lenin was prepared to concede that "the proletarian policy of the Party is not determined by the character of the membership but by the enormous undivided prestige enjoyed by a tiny group which might be called the Old Guard Party" (XXXIII. 257). And that month, in his address to the Eleventh Party Congress, he argued that the past year "showed quite clearly that we cannot run the economy." This was "a fundamental lesson. Either we prove the opposite in the coming year, or Soviet power will not be able to exist" (XXXIII. 274).

Martin Buber remarked that "the operative law is that strictly centralist action is necessary to the success of the revolution, and obviously there is no small truth in this." But he continued, correctly, "what is wanting is the constant drawing of lines of demarcation between the demands of this action and – without prejudicing it – the possible implementation of a decentralized society ... between the claims of revolutionary politics and the rights of an emergent socialist life."[72] Still, assigning reasons for the Bolsheviks' failure to achieve anything like what they had envisioned will not go without argument.

For many, the fault was in the ideology of Marxism. But we need here to keep chronology in mind. It is tempting to argue that, prior to the civil war and intervention, the idea that Marxism was alone a "scientific" socialism had its direct ill effects, especially in the idea that the soviets could control production and distribution in a rational and humane manner. This now seems to us to be naive, perhaps worse. But the Bolsheviks knew full well that they could not go immediately to socialism – even if they had not been at war.

More problematical is Buber's suggestion that part of the cause of the Bolshevik failure was the Marxist idea that there was only one true doctrine and program. It is often said that it was this idea which propelled the authoritarianism and centralism which were realized so quickly. Marxists had a doctrine, a theory, which was in many ways unlike the theories (doctrines!) of, for example, liberals. In responding to concrete situations, people apply ideas. But not only is there an inevitable gap between abstract theories and the implementation of a policy in a concrete historical situation, but these ideas also become transformed in being applied concretely. Marx had never failed to recognize the need for fresh analyses of changing situations; the same is true of the Old Bolsheviks. However, and inevitably, Marxists from Marx to the Old Bolsheviks had never agreed on just what this "truth" might mean concretely. As everyone agrees, up until 1921 or perhaps later, there was open debate and disagreement among Bolsheviks on both doctrine and program. Indeed, Rabinowitch attributes Bolshevik success in 1917 to the nature of the party, concluding, significantly:

> Here I have in mind neither Lenin's bold and determined leadership . . . nor the Bolshevik's proverbial, though vastly exaggerated, organizational unity and discipline. Rather, I would emphasize the party's internally relatively democratic, tolerant, and decentralized structure and method of operation, as well as its essentially open and mass character – in striking contrast to the traditional Leninist model.[73]

Rabinowitch's book provides a wealth of evidence for this, but the critical issue of the Constituent Assembly is a pertinent case in point.

It is true that Lenin and Trotsky polarized the alternatives, "Constituent Assembly" or "Soviet Republic;" but, as Anweiler writes, Kamenev and Zinoviev wanted to combine these forms.[74] There was nothing in Marxist theory which, in those particular circumstances, spoke to the correctness of either stance. Indeed – and nobody says otherwise – it was Bolshevik inability to secure a majority and the crassest political expediency which motivated the decision to dissolve the Assembly. Lenin's claim, in his "Theses Concerning the Constituent Assembly" of 26 December, that "the republic of soviets is a higher form of democracy than an ordinary bourgeois republic with a constituent assembly" was not a lie. Nor was he wrong in judging that at this time the Assembly did not accurately reflect the sentiments of the population, which had quickly become radicalized. Given this, Rosa Luxemburg, writing from prison in Germany, was no doubt correct in judging that the wiser course would have been to delay elections until the Bolsheviks could secure a majority – or at least a stable revolutionary coalition. Had they done so, it could have turned out that the state which was created might have been less centralized, much less party-centered.

To be sure, the Bolsheviks invented neither hierarchy nor modern bureaucracy, although the idea of a one-party state was, no doubt, a Bolshevik invention. Further, Lenin's rejection of parliamentarianism certainly made it easier to justify a revolutionary one-party state. But the reasons produced to justify what has happened need not be the reasons which motivated actors to do what they did; nor is it the case, surely, that what happens is what was intended.

For Lenin, parliamentary politics was party politics, whereas soviet politics was democratic politics. As Anweiler points out, in the first months of the Revolution, the Bolsheviks worked energetically to institutionalize power in the soviets. He quotes an official circular of 5 January 1918:

> The whole country must be covered with a network of soviets, and they must maintain close relations. Each of these organizations, down to the smallest, is completely autonomous in local matters, but it coordinates its activities with the general decrees and regulations of the centralized supreme soviet. In this way a coherent and fully integrated soviet republic will emerge.[75]

This was not ideological hot air. Literally hundreds of soviets *were* created, 500 in Perm province, 84 in Voronezh, and so on. The "state" was "smashed" and was being replaced! Yet, beginning in the summer of 1918, with the disintegration of Russia, the civil war, and the continuing inability of the Bolsheviks to gain majorities in all the soviets of Russia, the non-Bolshevik parties were gradually crushed.

Doctrine was not to blame for this.[76] The Bolsheviks, like revolutionaries in the American colonies and France, did what they saw as necessary in order to secure the Revolution. One can, obviously, argue that what they did was not necessary, that there were alternatives. Perhaps there were. Still, as Lewin points out, "the formidable administrative machine created from scratch in the course of the civil war was a decisive factor in the Bolshevik victory."[77]

What then of war communism? In the effort to achieve military victory, the party state had subordinated everything toward its end. The result was "statization," a word widely and accurately used by the Bolsheviks. Here ideology did come to play a crucial role. As Cohen writes, "Having come to office with no preconceived economic program, Bukharin, and the Bolsheviks generally, embraced the first one that appeared to arise out of and correspond to actual events. An internal logic − what Marxists called lawfulness or regularity − seemed discernible in the kaleidoscopic developments of 1918−20."[78] The Bolsheviks had found a new road to socialism.

Within months, what had been necessary became desirable, as Luxemburg prophetically saw.

But in 1921, with victory in hand, the Bolsheviks had to confront the almost complete alienation of the regime from the masses. A new and more dreadful kind of civil war threatened, and there was little clarity or agreement about what steps should be taken. As Cohen writes, the Bolshevik response went from "spurts of boldness" to "semi-paralysis."[79] During the next six months, July 1920–February 1921, peasant uprisings accelerated and the trade unions rebelled against their "militarization." Wildcat strikes swept Petrograd, and a rebellion erupted at Kronstadt, which, since the beginning, had been the bulwark of Bolshevism.[80] As the rebellion was being suppressed, the Tenth Party Congress convened.

The demise of war communism was undramatic. Although it was debated for a month in the Politburo, almost no debate followed Lenin's announcement at the Congress that grain requisitioning would be replaced by a fair tax in kind. All eyes were on Kronstadt. But more than this, as Cohen writes, "no one apparently understood that the decision would quickly lead to a radically different economic system – to the restoration of private capital, market and monetary exchange, the denationalization of many enterprises, and thus the diminishing of the socialist or state sector."[81] The Bolsheviks had returned to the "state capitalism" from which they had started, to a transition scenario not unlike that of the *Communist Manifesto* – but with one extraordinary difference. The difference was that the state which had been created and which was to begin to rebuild socialism was not at all the republic that Marx and Engels had envisaged. It had not been so in 1917; nor was it so in 1921. By 1921 it was neither a parliamentary republic nor a republic of soviets. It was, rather, as Lenin all but acknowledged, a one-party dictatorship of the few over the many.

Lenin knew that they had failed, just as he knew, as Lewin notes, that "however often and however strongly he criticized [the formidable state machine which was created], he was obliged to admit that it was itself a success."[82] Could the damage to the vision now be undone? Could Russia now be put back on the track set out in *State and Revolution?*

Lenin's Last Struggles

The shift from war communism to the New Economic Policy did not address "statization." As Lenin later admitted, there were two questions which "almost completely" escaped his attention, that of the party and the bureaucracy and that of the proper nature of the "union" of soviet republics.

The Union of Soviet Republics did not exist until 30 December 1922.[83] (Ratification of its Constitution came in January 1924, on the day Lenin died.) During the years 1920–2, there were six national republics: the Russian Soviet Federative Socialist Republic (RSFSR), the Ukraine, Georgia, Byelorussia, Azerbaijan, and Armenia. Their relations were established by a series of bilateral treaties which established cooperation on matters of the economy, defense, and foreign policy. Each republic had a government like that of the Russian government. The state had more unity that it might appear, however; since not only was the Army centralized, but the Central Committee of the Communist Party sought, through its various sub committees, to control the various organs of government.

A commission headed by the Commissar for the Nationalities, Stalin, offered what is known as the "autonomization plan," the inclusion of the "independent Republics" in the Russian Federation. It was approved by the central committees of Azerbaijan and Armenia, which were "now in the hands of safe men," but rejected elsewhere. One consequence of the troubled struggle was "the clandestine affair," the decision by Lenin "to crush Stalin politically."[84]

Deep personal and political differences between the two men had emerged over the nature of the Constitution of the Soviet Union. During these months, as a paralyzing stroke continued to undermine his health, Lenin declared a war "to the death on dominant-nation chauvinism." As Kamenev communicated to his colleagues, "Ilich is going to war to defend independence."[85] Lenin argued that it was inconceivable that the Bolsheviks should struggle against imperialism and then "ourselves fall – even in trivial matters – into something like imperialist relations toward the oppressed nationalities." Therefore, the Communists ought to defend the use of national languages. Abuses "under the pretext of unity of the railroad service, under the pretext of fiscal unity and so forth" must end. Plainly, there had to be centralization in the military and diplomatic spheres; but "in all other respects" the "full independence of the separate commissariats" should be maintained. Indeed, "the harm which can befall our government from the absence of unification between the national apparatus and the Russian apparatus will be incomparably smaller, infinitely smaller, than that harm which can befall not only us but also the whole International, the hundreds of millions of the peoples of Asia who in the near future are to enter the stage of history in our wake."[86]

If Lenin's words were prescient, Stalin's posture had the merit of simplicity – along with, one must add, the power of arguments long identified with the Marxist tradition, here including the younger Lenin. According to customary Marxist arguments, nationalism was but a reactionary residue. Moreover, for Stalin, whatever may have been the aspirations of the party, if the Soviet state was to be a unity and if the Politburo, the Central Committee, and the government of the RSFSR constituted the *de facto* ruling authority, then why not translate the *de facto* status into a *de jure* one?

After all, the niceties of bourgeois representative machinery were hardly to be taken seriously, as everyone in the party knew.

Within European Marxism, the debate on the national question had a longer history. In 1913 Lenin had tried to mark out a course between the followers of the Austrian socialists Karl Renner and Otto Bauer and the majority who either largely ignored the problem or subscribed to Rosa Luxemburg's more nuanced view. Renner and Bauer had given nationalism an independent, enduring role in the modern world; but the mainstream view was that this was merely a passing phenomenon. It is easy to say that "the fundamental weakness of Lenin's new approach was his endeavor to reconcile two sets of mutually exclusive premises, those derived from Marxism and those supplied by political realities."[87] But it is hardly clear that Lenin "never shared Renner's and Bauer's faith in the intrinsic values of nationality, or in the desirability of preserving the cultural heterogeneity of the world."[88] On the contrary, Lenin's rejection of the Austrian plan for extraterritorial cultural autonomy was based on what he considered to be "a faulty concept of 'national' culture." As Pipes writes, "it strove artificially to preserve all those ethnic differences which capitalism was already sweeping away." But Pipes then ignores his own words. It was hopeless to try to preserve those differences which capitalism was sweeping away, but there were some which were being preserved and which could be preserved in a socialist world order. Lenin was surely a good Marxist, and, as Pipes notes, he appreciated full well that the nation-state was not about to go away, that as Luxemburg had argued, any revolutionary politics had to work with that fact. In keeping with his understanding of history, Lenin had insisted that the "right to self-determination" "cannot be interpreted in any other way, but in the sense of *political* self-determination, that is, as the right to separation and creation of an independent government."[89] But he also hoped, perhaps naively, that, as Pipes puts it, "minorities would find it advantageous to remain within the larger political unit, and thus a lasting foundation for the emergence of large states and an eventual united states of the world would be created." This was exactly the position of *State and Revolution*. By the time of the Bolshevik conquest of power, of course, Luxemburg could correctly point out that "the Bolsheviks are in part responsible for the fact that the military defeat was transformed into the collapse and breakdown of Russia."[90] Luxemburg argued, rightly, that self-determination as understood by Lenin permitted a bourgeoisie in power to use it as an instrument of counterrevolution. But by the spring of 1918 they did not need Luxemburg to tell them this.

Stalin's machinations had also led Lenin to conclude that "Comrade Stalin, having become Secretary General, has unlimited authority concentrated in his hands, and I am not sure whether he will always be capable of using that authority with sufficient caution." As Lewin notes, the post of

Secretary General had existed only for eight months, and Stalin had been able in this very short time to acquire a surprising amount of power. Weeks later, Lenin suggested that Stalin was unsuited to the role of Secretary General and that, accordingly, he be removed. In subsequent notes, he accused Stalin, the Georgian, of acting like a "Great Russian bully" and of being a "deviationist." Three months later, a third stroke paralyzed half of Lenin's body, leaving him without the power of speech.

As Lewin notes, Lenin's ideas on the Constitution required, if they were to be coherent, reform of the party and especially that local Communists be permitted to develop their positions on matters of local importance. Lenin clearly had some critical changes in mind.

Multiparty government was an invention of the parliamentary democracies of the West; one-party government was an invention of the Bolsheviks. At the time of the October Revolution, the Constituent Assembly was the ostensible all-Russian representative body.[91] The All-Russian Congress of Workers' and Soldiers' Soviets, an instrument which the Bolsheviks hoped to employ, created the All-Russian Central Executive Committee of the Soviets (using the Russian initials of its title, VTsIK). Comprised of sixty-two Bolsheviks, twenty-nine left SRs, and ten other socialists, it was to be the supreme organ of power. The right SRs and the delegates of the other parties had refused to participate as a protest against the Bolshevik insurrection. The VTsIK was subsequently enlarged by the addition of peasant deputies elected by the Congress of Peasants' Soviets, a hundred delegates from the Army and the Navy, and fifty from the trade unions.

The All-Russian Congress also created a Council of People's Commissars (in Russian, Sovnarkom, for short), composed exclusively of Bolsheviks. Lenin held the chair until his death. Within days of its creation, the Sovnarkom gave itself legislative powers – fully in the spirit of Lenin's organizational views. Predictably, it quickly came to predominate over the larger body which had presumably given it authority.

Bolshevik party organization was also hierarchical, with a central committee and a political bureau (Politburo) with decision-making power. It picked the members of the Sovnarkom. Thus, effective power was lodged in the hands of a Bolshevik elite. The divisions which would have prevented a stable republic from being established also made it impossible for the Bolsheviks to lodge power in a truly representative Constituent Assembly or Congress of Soviets. Not only did Mensheviks and SRs still have a considerable base in the soviets, but the bourgeois parties would also have made themselves felt. Only if the soviets had themselves been what Lenin had hoped they would be was any alternative possible.

It is of more than marginal interest to observe that the Constitution of RSFSR says that "all authority within the Russian Republic is invested in the entire working population of the country, organized in the urban and rural soviets," and that this formulation would be *inconceivable* without the American invention of the "sovereign people." That is, if in parliamentary democracies, the sovereign people vests power in the successful party in a competition for the vote, in the new Soviet [sic] Republic, the sovereign people, organized into soviets, vested power in the Bolsheviks, without the need for such competition. As Marshal Tito is said to have quipped, "The only difference between the two systems is one party!"

As in any modern militarized state, effective power was located in a ruling elite; but it hardly seems necessary to say that, after the suppression of competing parties (in the summer of 1918), the Soviet state could not be regarded as a democracy in any meaningful sense.[92] And this is true, even if, within the party, there was still a considerable measure of open debate and something of what can be called intraparty democracy.[93] Nevertheless, Rosa Luxemburg was entirely correct in judging that, despite their limits, the representative bodies of parliamentary democracies possess "a powerful corrective," and that, as she predicted, with the abolition of the Constituent Assembly, "life in the soviets must also become more and more crippled" and "only the bureaucracy remains an active element."[94] It seems clear that Lenin never came to accept this analysis, even while he recognized that the state machine was just that, an unthinking, unresponsive mechanism of sheltered irresponsibility.

The Sovnarkom tried to establish its own administrative machinery, again in keeping with the ideas of *State and Revolution*; but it quickly became apparent, not merely in the Army, but in every area of government, that the peoples' commissariats *had* to use the old administrative machine. The state had been smashed; but the supreme irony was that, if the Revolution was to be preserved, it had to be rebuilt with the materials, both persons and practices, of the old Tsarist state.

As Lewin argues, the degree of capitalism had been highly exaggerated by "impatient revolutionaries," so the work of preparation which *State and Revolution* assumed had not taken place. The dictatorship of the proletariat had assumed a large, capable proletariat. In Russia, this had not been the case even at the beginning; but the situation was far worse after the civil war. Lewin summarizes the situation thus:

> Not very numerous and barely educated, this class was not capable of managing or even co-managing the factories, and it could not supply enough cadres to manage the state. It was too weak to bear up under the combined devastations of the war, the burden of service and losses in the Red Army, depletion at its core ..., and at the same time to survive the destruction of industry, unemployment, and famine.

Toward the end of that fateful civil war, we hear Lenin utter a cry of alarm: "The working class, devastated, declassed, dispersed in the countryside in search of bread, has disappeared!"[95]

The managerial and professional classes of the old order, often hostile or indifferent, were increasingly being supplemented by new party members, drawn from the "popular classes." But not only were these persons not usually immersed in Marxist ideology; they were "badly prepared for their new positions, in fact, for the most party purely uneducated, if not semi-literate." Given that the Army, the police, and the bureaucracy had become the only effective instruments of governance, Bolshevism acquired a state-created social base which it did not want and almost certainly did not understand.[96] Having acquired power, the Bolsheviks quickly learned to use it, but as Lewin writes, not always in the most palatable of ways.

In his remarkable "Better Fewer, But Better" (published in *Pravda*, 4 March 1923), Lenin remarked that "our state apparatus is so deplorable, not to say wretched, that we must first think very carefully how to combat its defects" (XXXIII. 487). These defects were "rooted in the past," he said; but this seemed to refer at least as much to the more distant past as the recent past. Moreover, the problem went deep: "The most harmful thing would be to rely on the assumption that we know at least something, or that we have any considerable number of elements necessary for the building of a really new state apparatus, one really worthy to be called socialist, Soviet, etc." On the contrary, "we are ridiculosly deficient of such an apparatus, and even the elements of it." He saw that only two such elements existed. First there are "the workers who are absorbed in the struggle for socialism." But "these elements are not sufficiently educated. They would like to build a better apparatus for us, but they do not know how. They cannot build one. They have not yet developed a culture required for this." Second, "we have elements of knowledge, education and training, but they are ridiculously inadequate compared with all other countries" (XXXIII. 488).

The discovery of this basic problem was tragically belated. Yet, given the extent of "statization" and the new social base that it had created, how could a *cultural* campaign be a sufficient remedy? That is, in the absence of structural changes in the state, would not increased education and training tend merely to create a technocracy? Again, Luxemburg seemed closer to the truth in arguing that "the only rebirth is the school of public life itself, the most unlimited, the broadest democracy and public opinion."[97]

Lenin was not insensitive to the institutional problems. But his specific proposals, the reform of the Workers' and Peasants' Inspection (RKI) by enlisting "irreproachable Communists" who "pass a test for knowledge of our state apparatus," repeat the error of thinking that one can create a bureaucracy to combat bureaucracy. His earlier idea, reform of the Central Committee, at least had the merit of increasing the opportunity for intra-party democracy. The Central Committee, he hoped, would be increased from 27 to 100; in addition there would be a new Central Control Commission of 75–100 members, which, with the Central Committee, would form a new Central Committee, an assembly that would meet six times a year.

The Bolshevik coup was premature, not so much because of the under-developed nature of the economy outside the cities of the core, but, as Lenin saw, because of the absence of democratic culture in the era of the modern nation-state. The Bolshevik elite might well have internalized the values requisite to democracy and had the skills to lead. Similarly, Lenin (and the Bolsheviks) were not wrong in placing great faith in the workers as the vanguard, precisely because some of them at least had achieved the political consciousness requisite to democratic control. But Russia was vast and amazingly heterogeneous; its population was largely illiterate, and its peasantry too deeply *muzhik* in its attitudes.

At the same time, 1917 was no longer the era of the *polis*, which meant that it was no longer possible for farmers or tribes or cities to establish autarchic communitites. As Machiavelli had seen, in the modern world, "to be secure, one must be powerful," and this meant that a viable political entity had to be large, unified, and centralized, as least as regards its capacity to make war.

The Bolsheviks obviously had to adapt to their situation, domestic and international, cultural and economic; but the problem was theirs only because the coup of October had succeeded, the hopes of international revolution had been dashed, and the capitalist powers of the world had sought actively to crush the Revolution. Both the policies of the years following and, at the end of the civil war, Lenin's recommendations for reform were responses to a situation which allowed few alternatives. As Lewin writes, "Political power, especially under the NEP, seemed practically the only instrument of action left to the Bolsheviks." Given this, Lenin had to opt for what was a pathetically inept solution to the problems which statization had created: that of trying to use the existing elite "in such a way that it would initiate the process of social transformation throughout the whole country."[98]

Yet, as Lewin argues, Lenin's program was not "socialism in one country," because he realized that, like the nations of the East, "we, too, lack enough civilization to enable us to pass straight through to socialism." His plan was one of merely holding on: "Shall we be able to hold on with our small and very small peasant production, and in our present state of ruin, until the West-European capitalist countries consummate their development toward socialism?" (XXXIII. 499). Or, if this were delayed, would Russia be devoured? Lenin seemed to see more hope in the East. "Russia, India, China, etc. account for the overwhelming majority of the population of the globe. And during the past few years it is this majority that has been drawn into the struggle for emancipation with extraordinary rapidity." Socialism would be victorious; he had no doubts about that. But, as the foregoing suggests, his reason was less the dialect of "forces" than the fact, observed by Tocqueville in 1848, that the idea of democracy was irresistible.

There is no way of knowing what might have happened had Lenin lived. Nonetheless, deplorable as it was, the Soviet state apparatus could have been reformed to become more democratic. Surely, the Soviet state was not yet totalitarian, not yet what it became under Stalin. The state under Stalin was the outcome of a series of new contingencies, the events between 1921 and 1928 which eroded the remaining institutional checks against tyranny, the grain crisis and the threat of famine, and the capacity of Stalin to communicate with the masses "over the heads of the bureaucracy as well as with the bureaucratic mass itself, over the heads of their bosses in party and state."[99] With Stalin, as with Hitler, one of the most original characteristics of our time reached full realization: the capacity of a "leader" to pacify, even enjoin, a mass in support of state terrorism.[100]

12

War and the Weimar Republic

The Weimar Republic is a troublesome episode in world history. War had forced the Kaiser to resign, and, as in Russia, a Provisional Government of liberals and socialists had been established. But unlike Russia, and perhaps because of fears of a German Bolshevism, revolution by the left failed in Germany. Instead, with the Weimar Constitution, Germany joined the ranks of Western liberal democracies. One might suppose that some satisfaction would be taken in this. But for most people, at least, it is spoiled — if this is not the wrong word — by the regime of the Nazis. This is striking. Bolshevism gave way to Stalin, Weimar to Hitler. Neither transition was inevitable, even though both derived from their country's past. As in Russia, so in Germany, the war and the decisions made had unintended consequences. There is an additional parallel, in that in both cases a "third way" might have avoided the disasters which in fact occurred. In this chapter, the focus is Weimar and the possibilities of an alternative to what actually happened. In discussing this, we will focus on two of the most penetrating theorists of democracy writing in Germany during this period, Max Weber and Rosa Luxemburg.

The Second Reich

Writing contemporaneously, Max Weber summarized the genesis of Germany's 1917 situation as follows:

The present condition of our parliamentary life is a legacy of Prince Bismarck's long domination and of the nation's attitude toward him since the last decade of his chancellorship .... As often before, epochal events such as those of 1866 and 1870 have had their greatest impact upon the generation for which the victorious wars were an indelible experience of its youth, but which had not clear comprehension of the serious domestic tensions accompanying them.[1]

Perhaps it is not too much to say that "the epochal events" of this, the second Reich (Empire), remained in the historical memory of Germans, for decades afterwards. But however that may be, the Second Reich itself grew out of the misfired revolution of 1848. This revolution had sought national unification and liberal reform. The failure of the middle class to carry this through had left Bismarck and the Prussian Junkers with the task of unifying the "nation" and making Germany a world power.

Bismarck was appointed chancellor of the Reich and the Kaiser Wilhelm, the monarch, was sovereign.[2] Germany was a "federated" empire, composed of twenty-four member states: four kingdoms (of which Prussia was the largest, comprising five-eights of the whole territory), six duchies, six principalities, and three free cities (Hamburg, Bremen, and Lubeck). In the German Reich, the chancellor was the only imperial official, "responsible" to the Reichstag to the extent that he had to defend imperial policies before it. The Reichstag had the authority to adopt budgets and consider imperial legislation, but its power was nominal. The paradigm of a "talking shop," it had no independence and no say in the appointment of the chancellor. Although carried out through the chancellor, foreign policy and the prerogatives of war and peace were in the hands of the monarch, who directly headed the Army and the Navy. There was no collective Cabinet responsibility, even though a changing set of intimates was close to the Kaiser. The Prussian government in Berlin was the center of the quite excellent civil bureaucracy.

The society and state of the Reich were dominated by the "aristocracy," centered in the Officer Corps and senior civil servants, who, like the Officer Corps, were predominantly from Prussian Junker families.[3] Capitalist industrialization had created both an urban working class and rich industrialists, bankers, and merchants: men like the industrialist Krupp, Gwinner and Helfferich of the Deutsche Bank, von Schinckel, and the brothers Stumm. These men had easily made themselves part of the Emperor's entourage. On the outside were very rich, assimilated Jews, men like Walter Rathenau and Max Warburg, who were received by the Emperor but were in no sense social equals of the Christian aristocracy. Utterly outside were the lesser bourgeois, the rapidly expanding class of industrial workers, and, finally, the farmers, neither peasants as in Russia, nor independent yeoman as in the image of Jefferson.

There were four main parties in the Reichstag: two "conservative" parties, the *Deutsch Konservative* and the *Reichspartei*, so-called the National Liberal Party, "the party of the Founding," the Catholic Center Party (*Zentrum*) and the Social Democratic Party (*Sozialdemokratische Partei*

Deutschlands, the SPD). They had very different constituencies and very different interests. The bourgeois parties had little reason to fight for parliamentary rights. This was true even of the National Liberals. They recognized a need for a strong parliament but knew also that "such a conflict would paralyze for a long time Bismarck's policies as well as the work of parliament."[4] Weber, who attended dinner parties with these men, tells us that "time and again I heard from their leaders that they would consider caesarism – government by a genius – the best political organization for Germany."[5] The absence of a liberal Constitution had been the concern of socialists since the days of Lassalle and Marx.

Bismarck had begun his war against Social Democracy in 1878 by making the party illegal. It remained illegal until 1890. But the party continued to make its presence felt among the workers. In 1897 Bismarck's anxiety deepened, and unwittingly or not, he used one of Plato's best metaphors in advising the "'bees . . . whether they produced grain, cloth or metal' to join forces against the mass of the people, the 'drones' who 'do all the talking in parliament.'" Fischer, here quoting Bismarck, continues: "The aim of that coalition of interests must be to counter the threat of 'latent parliamentary rule' and that was best achieved by 'fighting social democracy and getting it out of the way.'"[6]

This view was shared by all the bourgeois parties. To the conservatives, for whom Jews and the stock exchange were the root of all evil, anti-socialism went with anti-liberalism. They had support not only from the Farmers' League, but also from the "new" middle classes, the white-collar workers who were part of the National Association of Commercial Employees. Anti-Semitism undoubtedly played an important role in this alignment. Support of the right wing of the National Liberal Party came from heavy industry, which felt threatened by the rise of organized labor. The center of this party, led by Stresemann and Bassermann, represented the interests of the banks and the export industries. There were continuing tensions over tariff and trade policy between them and the big industrialists; but they shared in hoping that if Social Democracy could not be destroyed, it might at least become something akin to the British Labour party. In accepting imperialism, socialists might acknowledge the "social problem" as something that could be exported. The left wing of the National Liberal Party, the so-called Young Liberals, favored limited cooperation with "the party of revolt;" but they had no influence in the party overall. The Center Party had survived Bismarck's *Kulturkampf* and become a power base of the Kaiser. Still, its leadership could agree with the Social Democrats on some social policy issues, even if it could never agree on economic and ideological issues.

Yet the influence of the SPD in the Reichstag continued to grow. In 1912 there were nearly a million SPD members; in the Reichstag elections, the party polled 4,250,000 votes, some 35 percent of the total cast. The elections suggested that the threat to the status quo had reached alarming proportions: The *Sammlungspolitik* ("politics of alliance") of "World Policy" between Junkers and industry was shaken. As Fischer comments, "A new attempt was made to rally the bourgeois parties with anti-socialist slogans."[7] The "Kartell of the productive classes" – for the Social Democrats, the "Kartell of the grasping hand" (*raffende Hände*, in place of *schaffende Stände*) – was revived, and there was an all-out attack on "the insurance epidemic," Bismarck's breakthrough toward the "welfare state," a call for an imperial upper house to guarantee aristocratic control, and a demand for a further restriction of the franchise in order to combat the "dictatorship of democracy [sic]." Matthias Erzberger, on the Center Party's left as regards parliamentary rights and social policy, had this to say:

> The biggest problem facing the domestic policy of the Reich is the destruction of the tremendous power of social democracy; compared with this central issue of domestic politics all others pale into insignificance .... The Right, the Center Party and the National Liberals must take up the fight against social democracy ... and fight it united with determination and resolution – in the interests of the state as a whole. There exists at present [May 1914] no more necessary task than this and the next generation will never acquit us of the offense of party egoism, of the just accusation of political shortsightedness and ineptitude, if these parties fail.[8]

By 1914, the German Reichstag, though still only a "talking shop," was perceived to be a serious threat, at least potentially, to the plans of the ruling aristocracy. The social tensions in Germany were approaching a breaking point.

Although it cannot be said that this was the motive for the war, war nevertheless solved the problem – at least temporarily. Since 3 August 1914, socialists (with no hopes of achieving power?) have condemned the decision of seventy-eight members of the SPD, who in their caucus voted to support the Government's request for war credits. Hugo Haase, one of the fourteen who opposed credits, offered the party's decision the next day. He said: "For our people and its future freedom much, if not everything, is at stake in a victory of Russian despotism which has sullied itself with the blood of the best of its own people (tumultuous applause). We must ward off this danger, we must safeguard the civilization and independence of our own country (enthusiastic applause)"[9] He concluded with the words: "Here we make good what we have always emphasized: In the hour of danger we will not abandon our own Fatherland."

No doubt the Government had made a good show that the war was "preventive" and that the real threat was huge, backward Russia, a theme which, since the days of Marx, Social Democrats had been primed to accept (see chapter 10 above). And no doubt members who voted affirmatively believed that to do otherwise would separate them from the workers whom they presumably represented, and that they were therefore fearful that a negative vote would doom the party to irrelevancy. Indeed, politicians in representative governments, even with the availability of regular, putatively accurate polling techniques, persistently take a "safe" position, sometimes against sentiments which, though widely held, represent a radical break from the uncritically voiced platitudes of the governments in which they serve. Still, it is probably the case that with this vote the SPD "leadership" expressed the sentiment of many workers, even if at this juncture, as Barrington Moore points out, sentiment among the German working class to pursue a war was by no means a foregone conclusion. "Up to the last moment there were counter-currents." Indeed, "after the Social Democratic faction had come out in support of the government, the tension snapped .... A wave of tremendous relief swept much of the nation and affected many ordinary workers. The sharp pain of divided loyalties had come to a close."[10] This suggests that had the party acted otherwise, it might well have made the war quite impossible. We know that Chancellor Bethmann Hollweg had feared initially this, but that in July "he believed himself entitled to conclude from his conversations with the deputy Südekum that there was no reason to fear any particular trouble from the Social Democrats or their party leader. There would be no question of a general strike or of partial strikes or sabotage."[11] Of course, we shall never know.[12]

As Moore notes, at that moment — though the passing of the months would alter this — "the workers seemed to have achieved the dream of full acceptance into the social order." Even workers in Red districts could break out in the song "Deutschland, Deutschland über Alles!" The years of war soon eroded this, however. The losses at Verdun and on the Somme, the hard third winter of the war, and the effort at total mobilization, together with the Hindenburg Program, "had produced a material and physical crisis such as the nation had never known."[13] On top of this came the February Revolution in Russia. Fischer suggests that there were two effects. On the one hand, it seemed to Germans that this was a step toward "the long desired peace on the east." On the other, the Petrograd soviet's slogan of peace "without annexations and indemnities" made it almost impossible for the SPD leadership to convince the workers that German war aims were not imperialist. Indeed, on the issue of German war aims, the official Social Democratic leadership had been utterly irresponsible.

Some in the party, at least, had wanted Haase's initial endorsement of the war credits to include a firm statement that the Social Democrats would oppose any efforts to make a war of conquest out of the conflict. But the leadership retreated and "contented themselves with a vague remark that peace must be restored after the security of Germany's frontiers against foreign enemies had been established."[14] The "civic truce" (*Burgfrieden*) allowed the Chancellor to leave unvoiced German war aims. Indeed, it was a taken-for-granted feature of the diplomacy of the old order that such matters were not for public debate. Of course, by this time in German history, not everyone was so willing to accept this; nor was everyone by then so much in tune with the *Weltmacht* policy of the German ruling class. Karl Liebknecht, one of the original fourteen SPD dissenters and the only member to vote openly in the Reichstag against further credits, grasped exactly what had happened. In the first *Spartacusbrief* ("Spartacist Letter") of December 1914, he wrote:

This war which none of the participating nations itself has wanted was not started for the welfare of the Germans or any other people. It is an imperialist war, a war for capitalist control of world markets, for political control of important settlement areas for industrial and banking capital. From the point of view of an armaments race it is a *preventive war* brought about by the German and Austrian war party together in the darkness of semi-absolutism and secret diplomacy.[15]

By 1915 Liebknecht's "radical" circle had been joined by Georg Lebedour and others from the "left-center" of the party, and then by the party's senior chairman, Haase, and two of its most respected theorists, Karl Kautsky and Eduard Bernstein. At that point the question of Germany's war aims threatened to split the party.[16] In January 1916, Liebknecht, Rosa Luxemburg, and many of the "Spartacists" who would later comprise the nucleus of the German Communist Party (KPD) were expelled. Refusing to accept the censors, Liebknecht and Luxemburg continued their anti-war agitation, encouraged the strikes and food riots, and soon found themselves in jail. In March another group was expelled and formed the Social Democratic Alliance (SAG). Finally, in April 1917, a large group which included Ledebour, Kautsky, and Bernstein, split from the SPD and formed the German Independent Social Democratic Party (USPD), now joined by the "Spartacists." The war had served to divide German Social Democracy into two large, fundamentally opposed groups. Indeed, the next year, Germany experienced a Social Democratic revolution which was suppressed by the leaders of the SPD, "a process hardly paralleled in the history of the world."[17] But this is to jump ahead.

"Democratization From Above"

There were two stages in the remarkable German "democratization from above," and although they are part of the same process, it may be best to keep their consequences distinct analytically. The first was initiated by chancellor Bethmann Hollweg and ultimately cost him his job. In November 1916, the ban on public discussion of war aims was lifted. It brought forward a flood of annexationist propaganda, which made perfectly clear what Bethmann Hollweg had been content to fudge. The split of the USPD from the SPD propelled the disintegration of the civic truce. The Scheidemann Peace, so called after the man who replaced Haase as co-chair of the SPD, offered a return to the *status quo ante bellum*, modified by "self-determination." The impetus for this was the Russian Revolution, especially the Petrograd soviet's formula "no annexations, no indemnities." Meanwhile, America had entered the war. As Bethmann Hollweg saw it in April 1917, "a big gesture" was necessary if the regime was to be saved to carry on the war. Accordingly, he called for the end of the Prussian three-class franchise and its replacement by a general Reichstag franchise. But the German people did not get what they had thought they would get. As Fischer writes:

The Easter Message is usually extolled by German historians (or blamed, according to their views) as the first break-through of democracy. In reality, its pre-history reveals it as little more than a miserable remnant of what had been a grandiose attempt to place Prusso-Germany on a new basis of initiative from above, that of the monarch's government.[18]

In addition to vague promises of constitutional reform *after* the war, the franchise was to be "secret" and "direct," but not "general." The right, paranoid as always, was angry. Arguing that the call for a "peace of understanding" was in reality a call for a "peace of renunciation," it geared up for an all-out struggle against democracy as inconsistent with "the special nature and historic past of the German state." The SPD, vying with the new USPD for prestige, did get a Constitutional Committee. Bethmann Hollweg's ploy had produced at least some temporary benefits for the regime.

The second step in "democratization from above," overlapping the first, depended on some extraordinary, but not unrelated contingencies: the collapse of Tsarism in Russia and the decision of the United States to enter the war, already mentioned, and the Bolsheviks' accession to power and their desperate need to make peace. We need to pause here to link these contingencies.

The New Diplomacy

The end of America's "time of hesitation" and entry into the war, formally on 6 April 1917, stemmed from a number of causes, but surely the collapse of autocracy in Russia played a large role. If Woodrow Wilson, the elected president of the "classic" modern democracy, could not decide earlier on whether either side had sufficient right on its side, a case could now be made for a war to make the world safe for democracy.

Both the Pope and the Bolsheviks contributed to this possibility. In his Easter message, the Pope called for "Peace without Victory." Walter Lippmann offered Wilson a sharp distinction between the German people and their government. In August 1917, Wilson told the Pope that "the object of the war" was "to deliver the fine peoples of the world from the menace and the actual power of the vast military establishment controlled by an irresponsible government . . . . This power is not the German people but the masters of the German people."[19] As Lippmann had put it, the objective of the war was "a union of peoples pledged to cooperate in the settlement of all outstanding questions, sworn to turn against the aggressor, determined to erect a larger and more modern system of international law upon a federation of the world."[20] The United States would make war against "autocracy" to achieve a lasting peace: the Kantian project with a twist. The *status quo ante* was no longer sufficient: Wilson and the Allies would pursue the war until "German autocracy" was crushed.

When the Bolsheviks captured the government of Russia, they further confused things, not only by affirming the Petrograd soviet's appeal for peace without annexations or indemnities, but by denouncing all secret treaties and, then, by taking the further unprecedented step of making public all the treaties which had been signed by the Tsar with the Allies.[21] France would recover Alsace and Lorraine and gain parts of the Saar; Britain would take Germany's African colonies; Italy would acquire Istria and Dalmatia from Austria; and Japan would have the Shantung peninsula.

The publication of these documents (first in the *Manchester Guardian*, beginning on 12 December 1917) surely had a profound effect on President Wilson. Not only did the treaties display the Machiavellian character of traditional diplomacy, but they showed that they were part of the problem which had produced the international war which had taken millions of lives. Wilson responded with his famous Fourteen Points (delivered on 8 January 1918). He had not consulted the Allies first, since he knew that they could not affirm them. Still, if in pursuit of a just peace, Wilson was prepared to go further than his British cousins and French friends, the former burdened at home by the "Irish problem" and both burdened abroad by vast empires, the document was anything but clear. Article V, for example, offered "a free, open-minded, and absolutely impartial adjustment of all colonial claims," giving "equal weight" to "the interests of the populations concerned" and "the equitable claims of the government whose title is to be determined." There were, of course, a number of touchy problems, such as Alsace-Lorraine. While the French were determined to annex the entire area, in a plebiscite most people in the Saar would have chosen alignment with Germany. Surely the Germans were aware of this. As for Austria-Hungary, Wilson offered internal autonomy "within the Empire" for the national groups, Czechs, Serbs, and so forth; but in a separate message, Vienna was assured that "no dismemberment of the Empire is intended." An independent Albania, for example, was "an undesirable political entity." The messages of the Fourteen Points were thus mixed, giving even the Germans reason to believe that something of their plans might be rescued.[22] This last fact was not only to influence the decisions which led to the armistice, but to leave a bitter taste in the mouths of Germans for decades afterwards. In his effort to bring about a just peace, over the heads of the respective governments if necessary, Wilson had also brought a new factor into international politics. It has been called the "new diplomacy," and it is worth summarizing here.[23]

As used here, the term "the new diplomacy" included three elements: First, it took the position that just as the old diplomacy was a diplomacy of the old order of absolutism, whereas the new order was to be democratic, so foreign policy like domestic policy, must be under the control of the sovereign people. On this view, the practice of secret diplomacy, unchecked by parliamentary bodies, had been one of the most critical causes of the war. The argument for this view assumed premises already articulated by Kant: namely, that democracies did not engage in expansionist wars. Although no regime has ever acted on the belief that it was within the province of "the sovereign people" to make foreign policy, since the Great War the idea has become a key feature of the *ideology* of democracies.

Second, there was the idea that it ought to be the aim of democracies to support self-determination for the peoples of the world. Thus, in 1914 the UDC had already included among its planks the formula "No Province shall be transformed from one Government to another or without the consent of plebiscite or otherwise of the population of such Province."[24] The formulation was weak-kneed enough. Any consistent application of the idea of self-determination, now so much taken for granted, undermines not only empire, empires in existence and those dreamed of, but also the territorial integrity of *all* existing states. The Bolsheviks, as we saw, had begun to experience the difficulties inherent in this idea. Their successors in the Soviet Union are still experiencing them.

Third, "democrats" discovered that one could argue that, since the interests of *autocratic* governments and those of the peoples they govern are not the same, democratic diplomacy might well appeal to – and seek to manipulate! – the sentiments of the masses. Motivated by a need to buy time, this idea had already been taken to its extreme by the Bolsheviks. A democracy does not need to recognize governments or carry on diplomacy with them at all; it can deal only with "the people." Trotsky, the new

People's Commissar for Foreign Affairs, declared, "I will issue a few revolutionary proclamations to the peoples of the world and then shut up shop."[25]

These events seem to have had two major effects on the deliberations of the German regime. The German High Command came to believe that a "Hindenburg Peace" — that is, a peace *with* victory — was probably not to be achieved. Second, these events allowed the chance that Germany might salvage *some* of its war aims, or at least the possibility of preserving both its army and its monarchy. Briefly, Germany might achieve a satisfactory *Wilsonian* peace if it could show the world, especially America, that it, too, was prepared to join the march for democracy! Indeed, it might even take advantage of its strategic position as a bulwark against the frightening spread of Bolshevism!

The Reconstruction of German Politics: Max Weber

It was this situation which Weber's remarkable 1917 essay entitled "Parliament and Government in Reconstructed Germany" addressed. Mainly written and published in the summer of 1917, just after the Russian Revolution had begun, and subsequently enlarged and revised for publication in 1918, well after the Bolshevik coup, it was intended as a contribution to the serious substantive and ideological debates just sketched. The essay brings together much that is familiarly "Weberian," has some stunning prophetic aspects, and is one of the great statements of the modern theory of democracy — or, perhaps better, of the modern theory of antidemocracy.

The fundamental insight of Weber's tract concerns the emergence of "the mass state," a state for which "there are only a limited number of alternatives."[26] Weber does not define "the mass state," but his meaning is clear. The mass state "comprises masses of people" and is dominated by a bureaucratic administration:

> The democratic state no less than the absolute state eliminates administration by feudal, patrimonial, patrician or other notables holding office in honorary or hereditary fashion, in favor of employed civil servants. It is they who decide on all our everyday needs and problems. In this regard the military power-holder, the officer, does not differ from the civil official. The modern mass army, too, is a bureaucratic army. (p. 1393)

The mass state *is* the bureaucratized state. "The present world war means the world-wide triumph of this form of life, which was advancing at any rate" (p. 1400). "The future belongs to bureaucratization" (p. 1401).

"Universal bureaucratization" is "behind the so-called 'German ideas of 1914,' behind what the literati euphemistically call 'the socialism of the future,' behind the slogans of 'organized society,' 'cooperative economy,' and similar contemporary phrases" (p. 1400).

This is familiar — and perhaps overstated. Nonetheless, it is critical to identify what is taken for granted in this "inevitable" advance of the mass state. Immediately after telling us that "for a mass state, there are only a limited number of alternatives," Weber writes: "For a rational politician the form of government at any given time is a technical question which depends upon the political tasks of the nation" (p. 1383). He does not stop to fill in "the political tasks of the nation." He did not have to. He was addressing an audience which had accepted the idea of German "World Policy." Indeed, that Weber had grasped the import of German unification and the success of 1866 and 1870 is clear. In his inaugural address in Freiburg in 1895, he had said: "We must appreciate that the unification of Germany was a youthful prank indulged in by the nation in its old age and that because of its costliness it would have been better left undone if it was meant to be the end and not the starting point of German policy of world power."[27] And, as Fischer points out, Weber had not changed his mind in 1916 when he wrote: "If we had not wished to risk this war we could have left the Reich unfounded and continued as a nation of small states."[28] Indeed, the bureaucratized state is the modern state in the era of imperialist war.

But let us press the Weberian implications of the mass state. Given what was happening, three questions "about the future forms of political organization" may be asked. The first, not answered in his essay, is this: "How can one possibly save *any remnants* of 'individualist' freedom in any sense?" The second, to which we will return, is: "How will democracy even in [a] limited sense be *at all* possible?" The third, and for Weber the most important of all, is raised "by a consideration of the inherent limitations of bureaucracy proper" (p. 1403).

A person can be an excellent bureaucrat, be knowledgeable, serious, imaginative, engaged creatively in "intellectually demanding tasks," and be apt at problem solving, but be politically inept. A bureaucrat is not responsible in the way that an entrepreneur or "politician" must be, for different things are expected and a different sort of character is required.[29] This means that though he may be capable of doing his job and doing it extremely well, he will not be capable of *leadership*. Weber writes:

Since the resignation of Prince Bismarck Germany has been governed by "bureaucrats," a result of his elimination of all political talent. Germany continued to maintain a military and civilian bureaucracy superior to all others in the world in terms of integrity, education, conscientiousness and intelligence. The military and, by and large, also the domestic performance during the war has proven what can be achieved with these means. But what of the direction of German [domestic and foreign] policy during recent decades? The most benign thing said about it was that "the victories of the German armies made up for its defeats." (p. 1404–5)

Weber is not saying here that Germany is ruled by its bureaucracy, even if in every mass state, "power is exercised neither through parliamentary speeches nor monarchical enunciations but through the routines of administration" (p. 1393). Rather, power is exercised by its bureaucracy, and Germany is ruled by bureaucrats. Its "leadership" is comprised of men socialized in Germany's "excellent" bureaucracies, *not*, as in England, in the cauldron of party politics. Bismarck's successors, "who were no Caesars but sober bureaucrats," have hidden behind "the legitimacy of the Monarch" (p. 1413). Bismarck's "worst legacy" is that he left Germany "politically unsophisticated."

Evidently with Wilson's ideological politics in mind, he writes that "abroad it is fancied that German 'autocracy' is at fault." The "hypocritical phrase" "the 'liberation' of the Germans is employed," just as at home "the vested interests . . . manipulate the equally hypocritical slogan of the necessity to protect the 'German spirit' from contamination by 'democracy,'" or perhaps, thinking of the uses of anti-Semitism, "they look for other scapegoats" (p. 1405).

Both sides are wrong. Germany's failure is fundamentally a failure of leadership. Short of finding another "genius," it lacks political institutions which could provide competent leadership. In the era of the mass state, this, indeed, is the main argument for the necessity of a "strong parliament."

> Wherever parliament is so strong that, as a rule, the monarch entrusts the government to the spokemen of a clear-cut majority, the power struggle of the parties will be for a contest for this highest executive position. The fight is then carried on by men who have great political power instincts and highly developed qualities of political leadership (p. 1409)

"The essence of politics . . . is *struggle*, the recruitment of *allies* and of a *voluntary* following." One cannot get training for this in a bureaucratic career system. "Only a *working*, not merely a speech-making parliament can provide the ground for the growth and selective ascent of genuine leaders, not merely demagogic talents" (p. 1416). In the Reichstag, even the speech making is perfunctory: "The speeches of the deputies are today no longer personal professions, still less attempts to win over opponents. They are official statements addressed to the country ('through the window')."

The distinction between a "strong" and a "weak" parliament bears also on the second question, that of the sense of democracy in a mass state.

> Modern parliaments are primarily representative bodies of those ruled with bureaucratic means. After all, a certain minimum of consent on the part of the ruled, at least the socially important strata, is a pre-condition of the durability of every, even the best organized, domination. Parliaments are today the means of manifesting this minimum consent. (pp. 1407–8)

The mass state needs a kind of legitimacy not required by the pre-modern state. It needs a mass base. Weber believes in universal male suffrage. He takes it for granted "as a fact that cannot be undone without grave repercussions" (p. 1442). But there is no mystification of hypocrisy in his view of the function it serves. The only possible "influence" of the mass, he says, comes through the existence of parties, a necessary condition for a strong parliament.

"[Parties] are today the most important political vehicles for those ruled by bureaucracy – the citizens" (p. 1395). But even in the most democratically organized party, there is a "hard core" which is "directed by a leader or group of notables," which "defines program and tactics and selects the candidates." "The voters exert influence only to the extent that programs and candidates are adapted and selected according to their chances of receiving electoral support" (p. 1396). Parties may be primarily ideological, offering differentiated, substantive, political ideals, or they may be primarily "organizations for job patronage," as in the United States (p. 1397). "The common voter, who does not belong to any organization and is wooed by the parties, is completely inactive; the parties take notice of him mostly during the elections, otherwise only through propaganda directed at him" (p. 1445).

Where there are strong parties and, as already hinted, the possibility of a clear-cut majority in parliament, then we can speak of "positive politics," parliamentary influence in the "direction of political affairs." But "nowhere in the world, not even in England, can the parliamentary body as such govern and determine policies" (p. 1414). Indeed, "in mass states, [the] caesarist element is ineradicable."[30]

Where the parliament is weak, it can engage only in "negative politics." This means that "it will confront the administrative chiefs as if it were a hostile power; as such it will be given only the indispensable minimum of information and will be considered a mere drag-chain, an assembly of impotent fault-finders and know-it-alls" (p. 1408). Where there is a weak parliament, the chief executive will be "dependent upon the reports of officials for the supervision of the work of other officials." As Marx had said, and as Lenin seems to have forgotten, "this is a vicious circle" (p. 1406).[31]

Weber sees a "democratic" alternative to parliamentary control, but before we turn to it, we should consider his attack on "the new diplomacy." Like the "hypocritical phrases" about "autocracy" and American "democracy," most of this talk is hypocritical, even if in the mass state, foreign policy must be conducted with an eye to mass attitudes. Weber writes: "One thing stand to reason: Everywhere, and particularly in a democracy, the big decisions in foreign policy are made by a small number of persons. At present, the United States and Russia are the best examples, and no literary phraseology can change the facts" (pp. 1439–40). Moreover, "the opinion widely held in democratic circles that public diplomacy is a panacea – and always work for peace – is in this very generalized form a misconception" (p. 1423). Indeed, as regards foreign policy and decisions of war and peace, Weber "certainly" remains "convinced of the utility of monarchic institutions in large states" (p. 1431). Rational foreign policy requires secret diplomacy and acknowledging what these days is forgotten: namely, that "it makes a tremendous difference whether a *politician* (the prime minister or even the president of a republic) issues a statement ... or whether he makes public a personal statement by the *monarch* and then 'assumes responsibility' for it by a dramatic but cheap gesture" (p. 1433). There is a big difference between public pronouncements of policy and *real* policy, between securing mass support and letting the mass dictate policy.

There are two aspects to this. On the one hand "at home and abroad, the monarch's words are taken as binding." This means that his commitments, public and private, can have force with the other side. Similarly, what he says publicly – or what he says that becomes public – cannot be taken back "even if he tries to do so in a new situation." "Passions and sentiments of honor are aroused, for now it is a point of honor to support the monarch." On the other hand, "a politician can and should resign if conditions change and new policies become necessary against which he has committed himself" (ibid.) With a monarch, there is the possibility of a coherent, steadily directed foreign policy. The "government" remains, but in the light of new circumstances, the policy can shift to accommodate the new circumstances, the goal staying intact. But this depends on maintaining the secrecy of critical diplomatic steps and decisions. Weber would not have been pleased with the changes since the Great War. Since in all modern democracies there can be no monarch who directs foreign policy, and since today all parliamentarians assume a right to know, the chief executives of all modern democracies have what may be an irresolvable problem on their hands.[32]

Weber condemns recent German practice. After reviewing in some detail a series of diplomatic disasters which, taken together, have brought about what from Weber's point of view is "the unnatural coalition"[33] against Germany, he concludes:

What is one to say about a state of affairs – unknown to any other major power – in which the monarch's personal cabinet, courtiers or news agencies publicize events [and statements] that are the utmost importance for international politics, with the result of getting our foreign policy bogged down and messed up for decades .... All that in a state, for whose *domestic* administration the "service secret" is (in the power interests of the agency chiefs) the crown jewel of civil service duty! (p. 1439)

The reference to the "service secret" is to the fact that the Reichstag "has been sentenced to *ignorance*, plainly not for technical reasons, but exclusively because the bureaucracy's supreme power instrument is the transformation of official information into classified material" (p. 1418).

Weber is unhappy with the "service secret." "There is no substitute," he insists, for parliamentary inquiry, "for the systematic cross-examination (under oath) of experts before a parliamentary commission in the presence of the respective departmental officials" (ibid.). But however valid this principle seems to Weber, it does not apply to foreign policy deliberations. He writes: "In direct contrast to the utility of public scrutiny in the realm of public administration, at the stage of foreign policy deliberation such publicity can most severely disturb the rationality and soberness of decision-making and hence even endanger or prevent peace" (p. 1424). The argument is by now familiar. Still, does this not depend upon the nature of the plans and projects hatched up in the inner circles of government? Are those who would insist that World War I would not have been possible had these "deliberations" been subject to full "publicity" fundamentally mistaken? Yet the advocates of the "new diplomacy" surely failed to see that, in the mass state, if masses cannot rule, they can be manipulated. Indeed, when foreign policy pronouncements and acts can be used to solve domestic problems, the danger of war may be even be greater! Foreign policy moves, like war, have a logic of their own. There are steps which, once taken, do not allow for retreat, as Weber and Clausewitz saw. Do we then have the worst of all possible worlds?

We can conclude this account of Weber's thought on parliamentary reconstruction with his views on the alternative to parliamentarianism, "plebiscitary leadership." This possibility, too, was immediately pertinent, and it contained some prophetic insights.

Even if it is true that "the citizen in the parliamentary state fulfills no other political function than putting a ballot, provided ready-made by the parties, into a box every few years," the democratic opposite, "plebiscitary democracy," suffers from enormous shortcoming. First, "the specific means of purely plebistary democracy: direct popular elections and referenda, and even more so the instrument of recall, are completely unsuitable in the mass state for the selection of trained officials and for the critique of their performance" (p. 1456). Moreover, in plebiscitary leadership, the political leader becomes a leader by gaining "the trust and faith of the masses . . . . In substance, this means a shift toward the caesarist mode of selection" (p. 1451). Indeed, "every kind of direct popular election of the supreme ruler and, beyond that, every kind of political power that rests on the confidence of the masses and not of parliament — this includes also the position of a popular military hero like Hindenburg — lies on the road to these 'pure' forms of caesarist acclamation" (p. 1543).[34]

Weber is not unsympathetic to the argument that "genuine parliamentarianism" is incompatible with "democracy" (p. 1442), precisely because "democratization and demagogy belong together." But at the same time, in the mass state, this problem is not altogether unavoidable. "After all, the road to demagogy has also been chosen, in their own manner, by the modern monarchies." This is a key problem of any mass state; for in the mass state "the masses can no longer be treated as purely passive objects of administration, that is, insofar as their attitudes have some active import" (p. 1450). Once their "attitudes" count — and count they must — they must be reckoned with.

For all his "genius," even Bismarck failed to see that "a state that wants to base the spirit of its mass army on honor and solidarity must not forget that in everyday life and in the economic struggles of the workers the sentiments of honor and solidarity are the only decisive moral forces for the education of the masses" (p. 1391). As part of Bismarck's effort "to create a positive attitude toward the state," he granted welfare benefits; but he did not get what he had hoped for. The working class was left out politically. As Weber sees, this is a fact of some importance as regards the "social tensions" which had been ignored by the generation following Bismarck. And, it should be added, it was a fact of some importance as regards both the German Revolution and the consequences of its failure.

Weber turns to those on the left who, from his point of view, may forfeit Germany's chance to achieve a strong parliament. "There are," he writes, "not only subjectively sincere 'socialists,' but also subjectively sincere 'democrats' who hate the parliamentary enterprise so much that they advocate 'socialism without parliament' or 'democracy without parliament'" (p. 1453). What, however, would be the practical consequence "in a state with our monarchic constitution?" Could there be "a democracy without any parliamentarianism in the German political order with its authoritarian bureaucracy?" It would be "a merely passive democratization," he predicts, and thus "a wholly pure form of uncontrolled bureaucratic domination" (p. 1453).

There were many on the left — the "sincere socialists" who were also sincere democrats — who would have agreed with this. On the assumption that the authoritarian bureaucracy, including here the Army, was not smashed and that the fundamental power relations in society were not altered, then, · in the absence of a strong parliament, surely Germany would be in for profound difficulties.

But suppose, contrary to Weber, that a strong parliament cannot emerge short of revolution? Indeed, Weber's text itself provides good reasons for thinking that it cannot. These reasons turn on the fact, repeatedly acknowledged by him, that in fundamental ways the parties and the nation are divided. "At least four, and probably five, large parties will therefore permanently exist in Germany; coalition governments will continue to be necessary and the power of prudently operating monarchy will remain significant" (p. 1443).

Weber believed that a strong parliament could be attained most easily in a two-party system; hence the success of England. But the "advance of the Socialists" confounded this. Indeed, on his view, "two-party systems are impossible in industrialized states, if only because of the split of the modern economic strata into bourgeois and proletariat and because of the meaning of socialism as a mass gospel. This creates, as it were, a 'denominational' barrier, especially in Germany" (p. 1443). The point is critical. The older liberal states would survive this and overcome the "denominational barrier"; but we must not underestimate the strain that was put on them, especially at the time of the Great War. Having survived this, of course, the liberal societies of the West are today a long way from the conditions of 1914!

In Germany in 1917, the "denominational barrier" was huge. What, then, if the monarchy fails and no "clear-cut" majority can accede to power in the hoped-for "reformed" Reichstag? Will there not be misdirection and persistent instability? Will there not be a real possibility that with a failure to break this barrier and in the absence of a monarch, conditions will be exactly right for the emergence of some form of authoritarian populism, a demagogic leader arising not "because of his parliamentary accomplishments," not because he has "proved himself in a circle of *honoratiores*," but by "means of mass demagogy"? (p. 1451). If Weber is right, then a "bureaucrat" at the head of state would probably be replaced by a demagogue as head of state.

The Armistice and "Democratization"

Weber's voice was heard; but he had no say in what happened next. The war was not going well; nor were things going well on the home front. In January 1918, the USPD called for a massive nationwide strike directed at a just peace. Remarkably, perhaps a million workers, about half of them in the Greater Berlin area, responded. The High Command saw that Germany's lack of quick success could be made the responsibility of an indecisive government, bowing to the "pacifist" tendencies of democrats. According to the High Command, it was only through military pressure that Germany "could make her enemies ripe for peace; not a Peace Resolution, which must arouse the impression that the German Reich was near collapse."[35]

The desperate, sixty-two-division German offensive in the West, on 21 March 1918, was at first successful. The Kaiser could literally shout, "If a British parliamentarian comes to sue for peace, he must first kneel before the imperial standard, for this is a victory of monarchy over democracy."[36] His joy did not last the summer. Of the July retreats, General Ludendorff wrote: "The attempt to make the Entente peoples ready for peace by defeating them before the arrival of the American reinforcements had failed. The impetus of the army had been insufficient to deal the enemy a decisive blow .... I realized clearly that this made our general situation very serious."[37] By September, Ludendorff decided that there was little choice but to try to save the Army and its honor. That meant a quick armistice, and an armistice requested by the Government, not the High Command.

Ludendorff's superior was *Generalfeldmarschall* von Hindenburg, chief of the High Command. The chief warlord, of course, was the Kaiser, Wilhelm II. The "government" was led by Count Hertling, Bethmann Hollweg's replacement as chancellor. It included Admiral Paul von Hintze as Foreign Minister and a number of other key ministers of the inner circle: Karl Helfferich, von Berg, von Stein, von Waldow, von Breitenbach, and others of the Prussian aristocracy. Although not formally part of the "government," a number of prominent "citizens" also had easy access to the Kaiser. These included Albert Ballin, director of the Hamburg-America Steamship Company, Carl Duisberg, president of I. G. Farben, Hugo Stinnes, the coal and shipping magnate, and the industrialist and arms producer Gustav Krupp, among others.

Ballin has left us notes of a 5 September meeting with the Emperor and Admiral von Müller, head of the Naval Cabinet. As Fischer says, it gives us "a singularly clear picture of the principles governing Germany's policy in the autumn of 1918." Three propositions are at the center of this:

1 Peace in the West through Wilson, using the areas occupied in France and Belgium as pledges
2 Democratization of the Reich before the negotiations begin, under the characteristic name of "modernization"
3 Formation of a front against Bolshevism.[38]

The success of these proposals was stunning.

On 29 September, Generals Hindenburg and Ludendorff informed the

Kaiser that "at once, as early as at all possible," a request for an armistice must go to President Wilson. The Kaiser responded that "the war has ended — quite differently, indeed from how we expected." He had no reproach for his generals. He offered, instead, that "our politicians have failed us miserably."[39] The idea would be put to use and would have significant consequences.

The Reichstag had already agreed, on 27 September, to constitutional changes; so, just prior to issuing the request for an armistice, the men responsible for Germany's fate decided that a new group of "politicians" would make the peace. It is not clear whether it was Hintze or Ludendorff who first used the phrase "revolution from above" to describe the policy of "channeling democratization," but there was no doubt as to the motivation.[40] On 30 September 1918, liberal Prince Max of Baden was appointed to succeed Hertling, and two days later he was joined by Scheidemann of the SPD, Erzberger of the Zentrum, and Stresemann of the National Liberals. The Cabinet had "a parliamentary character for the first time in German history" — or, as Liebknecht had it, the *Kaisereich* was fitted with "a fig-leaf of absolutism." On 28 October, under pressure from Wilson, Parliament had become "the repository of sovereignty," and on 11 November the new "democracy" signed the armistice. It was, as Fischer notes, "too late . . . to avert the revolution which broke out."[41]

The Revolution that never Happened

"A German Revolution after the first world war?" Robert Wheeler tells us that "a West German undergraduate in [his] German history survey indicated that she had never heard of such a thing." He continues, "And until the early 1960s the same was probably true of most Western academics."[42] There are both good and bad reasons for this intriguing omission. The good reasons include the fact that, for us, revolution has come to mean violent structural transformation, change in the fundamental relations of power in society. There is no doubt, of course, that the Kaiser was forced to abdicate and that the monarchy was replaced by a liberal constitutional regime. In 1650 or 1776, such an occurrence would have been called a "revolution," regardless of whether there was violence or whether state power was seized. In the German case, as in the Russian February Revolution, power was not seized; nor at that time was there any violence. So, if revolution means change in the relations of power in society, then, after all is said and done, there was no revolution in Germany in 1918–19. It is striking, of course, that the SPD "leadership" was not revolutionary in this sense, even if the same cannot be said of either the Communists (KPD), the USPD, or, more significantly, the German people.

This suggests the bad reason for the historical omission of the "revolution." Presumably, Germans, including German socialists, were wiser than their counterparts in Russia. Except for a fanatical fringe of Communists whose eyes were riveted on Bolshevism in the East, Germany escaped the *madness* of revolution — indeed, even the serious threat of revolution. But all this is palpably false — as the remainder of this chapter tries to show. We can begin by noticing that even though there is disagreement as to its nature, everyone by now agrees that, beginning in November 1918, Germany experienced a remarkable revolutionary situation which for a brief period, at least, might have ended differently from how it did. We need some detail.

There had been mutinies in the German Navy as early as August 1917, although none in the Army. By October 1918, things had changed. On 30 October, sailors of the *Thüringen* and the *Helgoland* refused to sail, protesting that their mutiny was against mutineers, officers who refused to acknowledge the new government. One thousand were arrested, and the naval engagement planned against the British was abandoned. In a sense, both sides had won. The crews of the Third Squadron returned to Kiel, where, three days later, they joined thousands of workers in a great protest march. It ended with bloodshed, the first of the revolution. Soldiers' and sailors' councils were formed, as in Russia; and by November, Kiel was in control of 40,000 revolutionaries. On the next day, the revolution had spread to Lübeck and Brunsbüttelkoog; on 6 November to Hamburg, Bremen, and Wilhelmshaven; on 7 October to Hanover, Oldenburg, and Cologne. By 8 October, all the major cities of the west, as well as Leipzig and Magdeburg, were experiencing rebellion.

These were rebellions, spontaneous and anti-militarist. They expressed a desire to break with the old order and to constitute forms of democracy and self-rule. They were not Bolshevik or Spartacist; nor were they necessarily Social Democratic. On this almost all commentators agree.[43] An eye-witness report by the poet Rainer Maria Rilke perhaps captures the mood of 7 November:

> Although you sat round the beer-tables and between the tables in such a way that the waitresses could only eat through the dense human structure like weevils — it was not in the least oppressive, not even for the breadth; the fog of beer and smoke and people did not strike you as uncomfortable, you barely noticed it, so important was it and so clear above everything else that things could be said whose turn had at last come, and that the simplest and truest of these things, in so far as they were presented more or less intelligibly, were seized upon by the immense crowd with heavy and massive applause. Suddenly a pale young worker rose up, spoke quite simply: "Have

you or you or you, have any of you," he said, "made the offer of an
armistice? And yet *we* are the people who ought to have done it, not
these gentlemen at the top; if we could get hold of a radio station and
speak as common people to the common people over there, Peace
would come at once.[44]

It was hardly surprising that the German High Command could not suffer
such sentiment; but, as it turned out, the spirit of democracy was something
that neither the liberals nor the Social Democrats could suffer either.

On Wednesday, 6 November co-chair Friedrich Ebert of the SPD had
come to the Imperial chancellery to seek the Kaiser's abdication. It had
become necessary "if the masses were to be prevented from going over to
the camp of the revolutionaries." General Groener, Ludendorff's replacement, argued that it was "completely out of the question."[45] The next day
Ebert returned, this time with Prince Max. Max asked Ebert: "If I succeed
in convincing the Kaiser, can I count on your support in fighting the social
revolution?" Prince Max's record continues: "Ebert's answer was un-
hesitating and unequivocal: 'Unless the Kaiser abdicates, the social revolution is inevitable. But I will have none of it. I hate it like sin.' "[46]

Nothing is inevitable, perhaps; but Ebert was almost certainly correct in
this particular prediction. On 9 November, the Kaiser discovered that units
called from the front could not be used for action in a civil war, since they
would refuse to fire on Germans.[47] The Kaiser's abdication was announced –
prematurely, as it turned out. When a huge crowd reached the Reichstag,
Scheidemann proclaimed the Republic. The crowd which had expected
machine-gun fire was joined by "brothers" who helped them hoist Red
flags. They entered the prisons and set free political prisoners; they occupied the railroad stations and the Royal Palace. Released just two weeks
before from his two and half years in prison, Karl Liebknecht appeared on
the balcony and for the second time proclaimed the Republic – this time
"the Free Socialist Republic of Germany."

Ebert had been infuriated by Scheidemann's gesture, anticipating perhaps
that the mass, once unleashed, could not be constrained. To be sure, a
revolutionary situation existed. In Berlin alone, the revolutionary shop
stewards had organized some 120,000 armed workers with military experience. An executive committee had already worked out plans for the
takeover of the city. As Prince Max realized, "We can no longer suppress
the Revolution by force, we can only stifle it."[48]

It must surely have seemed to many that the revolution was in good
hands. At the head of the government which replaced the coalition headed
by Prince Max were three leaders of the SPD. However, they knew from
early reports emanating from the factories that if order was to be salvaged,
USPD participation would be essential. Evidently, the USPD had not even

considered the possibility of a coalition. Instead, as Morgan writes, "their attention had been turned to mass action."[49] The first offer to the USPD to participate was scorned by Ledebour. Haase was not in Berlin. Finally, enough of the leadership had gathered for the lengthy debate that followed. Most of the left wing of the USPD, Ledebour, Däumig, Richard Müller, and others, were adamantly against a coalition. They argued that the SPD leadership was untrustworthy. Many argued that the old state machinery had to be destroyed. There was also the problem of the viability of workers' councils, especially if they were taken to be "a permanent alternative to a revolutionary cabinet that would reform the existing state apparatus."[50]

The conditions for partnership further complicated matters. Moreover, this was exacerbated by the fact that the words could have such different meanings for the opposing groups. Thus, the USPD demand that "Germany should be a socialist republic" was accepted as a common goal; but the SPD offered the proviso that "the people must decide on this through the constituent assembly."[51] It was hard to reject this. Similarly, the 10 November response by the USPD insisted that "political power lies in the hands of the workers' and soldiers' councils," and that "a general congress of councils in all of Germany shall be called immediately." This was accepted, but the critical question of the constituent assembly was left vague. The USPD had said, "The constituent assembly question shall be posed only after the gains of the revolution shall have been consolidated; it is therefore reserved for further discussion."[52] But what counted as consolidation of "gains of the revolution"?

That afternoon, 10 November, leaders of the two parties reached an agreement. Ledebour, Liebknecht, and Müller refused to represent the USPD; but Haase was joined by Wilhelm Dittmann and Emil Barth, the only revolutionary shop-steward leader who would consent. According to plan, representatives from workers' and soldiers' councils gathered the same day at the Circus Busch to elect a provisional government. Richard Müller, a shop steward and member of the USPD, seems to have diagnosed the situation exactly. He wrote:

> After the result of the voting it was clear that the right-wing Socialists together with the right-wing Independents ... had a majority. A government without the right-wing Socialists was out of the question. They had to be taken into account. It was also clear to everyone that the right-wing Socialists would try to break the power of the workers' and soldiers' councils in order to bring about a National Assembly and as a result a bourgeois-democratic government. If they succeeded, the Revolution was lost.[53]

The SPD leadership had not been idle. The message given out in thousands of leaflets which had been printed during the night, as well as the headline of *Vorwärts,* the party newspaper, was "No Fratricidal War." No doubt, this had enormous appeal to workers, who, rightly, had little concern with theoretical problems regarding the nature and role of the councils (soviets), problems which are still lost on people who should know better. At this meeting in the Circus Busch, the assembly of some 3,000 ratified the "Council of People's Representatives" (*Rat der Volksbeauftragten*), the council of six, and elected an executive committee of the councils (*Vollzugsrat*) consisting of their representatives. Although resisted, the SPD was able to win parity on these. Ebert had taken the firt step in acquiring legitimacy as the leader of the revolution.

Events moved quickly. When Ebert returned from the Circus Busch assembly, he received what is by now a very famous phone call from General Groener. If Ebert could agree with him on what the real danger was, Groener would put the High Command at the new government's disposal. When Groener testified in the so-called stab-in-the-back trial of 1925, he acknowledged that the "alliance" was aimed "against the danger of Bolshevism and against the system of councils."[54]

Further steps had then to be taken. On 8 December, Hindenburg requested of Ebert the *immediate* summoning of the Constituent Assembly, so as to squash the influence of the workers' and soldiers' councils. Shortly thereafter, the first *Freikorps* were formed — "volunteer units from professional officers and soldiers of the old army, to protect the government against the revolutionary left."[55]

Ebert hated revolution "like sin." This "alliance" was surely a tab in the back for socialism. But it was not, contrary to what some have said, a stab in the back for liberal democracy. The left lost the argument that the Assembly had to be comprised of representatives from the soldiers' and workers' councils; and, pressed by their military allies, on 9 January 1919, the regime held an open national election for deputies to an American-style "constitutional convention" to be held at Weimar — where it would be difficult for the "radicals" to upset plans. On 9 February the Assembly convened and elected Ebert as president.

The Weimar Assembly agreed on a novel parliamentary system with features which resembled the American presidential system, a hybrid which people hoped would have the advantages of both systems. Weber's hopes had not been realized; but, under the circumstances, one had to do what one could do. With no monarch, there would be a strong president, elected directly. His term would be seven years. He would be "a symbol at home and a representative abroad." Recognizing Weber's points regarding the problems of coalition governments, like the Kaiser, he would choose and dismiss the chancellor, and if "public security and order [were] seriously disrupted or endangered," he could, according to the famous Article 48, take control. But instead of a hybrid with the advatanges of a parliamentary and a presidential system, the Germans got, tragically, a system which had the *dis*advantages of both.

In the meantime, Ebert did not mind the cooperation of the High Command to secure law and order. Yet, as Count Kessler put the matter, "The paradox of a republican-social-democratic government allowing itself and the capitalists' safes to be defended by hired employed [the *Freikorps*] and by royalist officers, is simply too insane."[56] To add to the difficulties, in June the new government was forced to accept the unexpectedly harsh terms of the Versailles Treaty, including the demand that the Germans turn over for trial their "war criminals," including the Kaiser. Wilson's ideological politics had issued in a disastrous peace. Such was the basis on which Germany arrived at representative democracy.

Of course, things did not settle down exactly. By the end of December, the three USPD members of the Government had already resigned, refusing to be further involved in a regime which on Christmas Eve had sent Groener's troops against Red sailors. On Sunday, 5 January, the revolution again erupted. While some histories still refer to this week as "Spartacus Week," the label is far off the mark. The Prussian "state" government which was responsible for the largest unit in the "federation" had not been "smashed". When it dismissed Emil Eichhorn, the popular USPD Berlin police chief, USPD leadership and shop stewards called for a mass protest demonstration for the weekend. The response far outran expectations. That Sunday evening, "the whole [Berlin] leadership of the USPD" came together for an emergency meeting. They were joined by Liebknecht and Pieck. Their presence had been authorized by the newly formed KPD, since the communists, significantly, had decided not to participate. Luxemburg is said to have shouted at Liebknecht, "Karl, what has happened to our programme?"[57] Their program, like Lenin's in April 1917, was to build a mass base *before* an attempt at insurrection. At the meeting, the USPD leadership proposed a general strike, and if the response was as hoped, a coup would be attempted.[58] Only six of the eighty or more present dissented. The dissenters included the "radicals" Däumig and Müller. They argued that a coup could not succeed, that the promised support of the Berlin garrisons would not materialize. They were correct. There was a stalemate, broken on 8 January, when the USPD mediators gave up. The *Freikorps* occupied Berlin.

This was the beginning of an intermittently violent *stasis* which lasted until March 1920. On the government's side were *Freikorps*, battalions of hired guns created by Groener and the Ebert regime; Prussian security police; and finally, troops of the "republican" *Reichswehr*.[59] The revolt in the Ruhr, in reaction to the failed right-wing Kapp putsch of March 1920, powerfully stimulated the improvised Red Guard which had come into existence the previous year. As Moore notes, at the height of the struggle, bordering on civil war, the Red Army of the Ruhr had between 80,000 and 120,000 men in arms. Before it capitulated, this army captured Dortmund and Essen and a number of less critical heartland cities.

The war was waged against Communists and against Rosa Luxemburg and Karl Liebknecht, murdered on 15 January. It was waged against the Bavarian Republic and its murdered leader, Kurt Eisner of the USPD. It was waged against independents who headed councils throughout Germany and against many who had voted SPD in the elections for the Constituent National Assembly on 19 January. But it is important to see that it was waged also against what surely looked like democracy. General Maercker, commander of the *Landesjägerkorps* which brought the Leipzig Independents to heel, is as clear as could be on this:

> The fight of the Reich government against the left-wing radicals was exclusively concerned with the maintenance of political power. The soldiers were sent into action with this purely political aim: as an element of force in the strengthening of internal politics. But the Government's weakness did not permit it to say so openly. It was afraid to show its hand and to announce that the volunteer force was being used to abolish Council rule wherever this was still to be found. For in the last resort, this was what it was about. They got round this by using military matters as an excuse for intervention.[60]

It may be argued here that the war was fought to save democracy from Bolshevism. But before considering this question directly, we need to consider another critical contemporaneous text: Rosa Luxemburg's "Speech to the Founding Convention of the German Communist Party," given on the second day of its first convention, on 1 January 1919.[61] This is in many ways an extraordinary address, comparable to Lenin's *State and Revolution*, resembling it in being written in the heat of a revolutionary situation, with the aim of articulating a plan of revolutionary action, and taking its point of departure from the *Communist Manifesto* and the texts rejected by Marx and Engels in 1872.

Since Luxemburg was a founding Communist, and since, as everyone knows, Communists were the radicals of the radicals, reconsidering her tract in its concrete setting may help throw light on "communism" in Germany in 1919. This may help as well in coming to grips with the historically significant question of a "third way."

The Program of Rosa Luxemburg and the Communists

As Lenin had done, Luxemburg begins her speech with an account of the "out of date" passages in the *Communist Manifesto*. But in a striking turnabout she holds that "the historical evolutionary process has brought us back to the standpoint which Marx and Engels had in 1872 abandoned as erroneous." (p. 407). It is easy, however, to miss completely her problem and intention.

First, she agrees fully with the position which Lenin took in *State and Revolution* regarding the "smashing of the state." The Paris Commune *did* prove that "the working class cannot simply lay hold of the ready-made state machinery and wield it for its own purposes." Indeed, more than Lenin, she insists that "for us the conquest of power will not be effected at one blow. It will be a progressive act, for we shall progressively occupy all the positions of the capitalist state, defending tooth and nail each one that we seize" (p. 426).

Second, on her view, the error which, presumably, was corrected concerned the role and aims of the party. She writes:

When, after the disillusionments of 1848, Marx and Engels had given up the idea that the proletariat could immediately realize socialism, there came into existence in all countries socialist parties inspired with very different aims. The immediate objective of these parties was declared to be detail work, the petty daily struggles in the political and industrial fields. Thus, by degrees, would proletarian armies be formed, and these armies would be ready to realize socialism when capitalist development had matured. The socialist program was thereby established upon an utterly different foundation. (p. 407).

Plainly, Luxemburg's paradigm was the SPD. Historians, having the advantage of distance, give us the picture: "Its unity, discipline, and organizational strength were the envy of the other socialist parties of Europe." Still, as Morgan writes:

Party work was an elevating aspect of life for many simple members and functionaries; for the editors and officials it was an all-absorbing task, a "substitute for [the] political action" that seemed precluded by the circumstances of Imperial Germany. The party turned upon itself and its own affairs, its perspective constricted by concern for its own operations. The "party," meaning the established forms and procedures of the political labor movement, became nearly the highest value of all.[62]

Indeed, this fits Weber's analysis exactly. Here was a party functioning in a "weak parliament." It could barely engage in "negative politics," still less conceive of forming a government. Here were party members who had found a life-world in the activities of the party. That its "leadership" should eventually have been what it was follows absolutely.

For Luxemburg, of course the SPD had become the paradigm of the parliamentary party, and had lost touch with both the masses and its own revolutionary ideals. She argues that Ebert, David, Scheidemann, and the so-called moderates were no longer revolutionaries, that their "shirking of the revolutionary class struggle" was the product of party development in the recent past. Indeed, "the fourth of August [of 1914, the date that the party voted for war credits] did not come like thunder out of a clear sky . . . but was the logical outcome of all that the German socialists had been doing day after day for many years" (p. 411).[63]

In her view, Engels must share some of the blame for this. In what turned out to be the *locus classicus* of Social Democracy's views on insurrection, his 1895 Introduction to *The Class Struggles in France*, Engels had held that "rebellion in the old style, the street fight with barricades, which up to 1848 gave everywhere the final decision, was to a considerable extent obsolete." This was because the state had available "the whole military machine," and military technology had improved. Luxemburg points out that Engels here assumed, wrongly, that the "proletarians in uniform" were "absolutely inaccessible to socialist influences," that "anyone who becomes a soldier, becomes thereby once and for all one of the props of the ruling class" (p. 410).

Luxemburg evidently did not know that Engels had changed his mind on this absolutely critical issue; nor did she know that pertinent passages in Engels's account had been excised by *Vorwärts* editors so as to lead readers to conclusions *not* held by Engels. In any case, the damage had been done. It was surely true, as Luxemburg argued, that many in the party had come to two important conclusions: first, that "parliamentary struggle was counterposed to direct revolutionary action by the proletariat," and second, that the former was "the only practical way of carrying on the class struggle." For these Marxists, "parliamentarianism and nothing but parliamentarianism, was the logical sequel of this criticism" (p. 409). Yet, it is important to see that the *critical* conclusion was the first, that one must choose either parliamentary struggle or direct revolutionary action. Luxemburg and many others in the USPD were "radicals" not because they had abandoned parliamentary struggle, but because they insisted that even a parliamentary conquest must be revolutionary. Further, for them, "direct revolutionary action" was an essential aspect of this. Indeed, the council idea was not its linchpin.

Luxemburg's account of "the first act" of the German Revolution is incisive. "The revolution of November 9 was characterized by inadequacy and weakness," she writes. The events were a sequel to the collapse of imperialism, a "more or less chaotic movement, one practically devoid of plan." The "only source of union, the only persistent and saving principle, was the watchword: 'Form workers' and soldiers' councils'" (p. 414). But those who made this their watchword came quickly to be disappointed. They came to see that the union between Haase and Ebert "serves merely as a fig leaf for the decent veiling of a counterrevolutionary policy" (p. 415). Indeed, as we have seen, Ebert had agreed with Groener and Hindenburg that if the councils were the linchpin of transformation, counterrevolutionary policy had to be aimed at their destruction. This first act was over, however.

Luxemburg judged that "more and more, the government is losing the support of the army," and she was prophetic in judging that the next stage would be more radical. This was not because radicals were in control of the masses, but because the masses were themselves "cured of their self-deceptions." On her view, counterrevolution would propel revolution. She writes, "I regard it as the very essence of this revolution that strikes will become more and more extensive until they constitute at last the focus of this revolution" (p. 419). Luxemburg, like many in the USPD and perhaps many who were rank and file members of the SPD, had not yet given up on the revolution.

What, then, should be the tactics of the party? "First, and foremost, we have to extend in all directions the system of workers' councils." "All directions" refers especially to the peasantry. "If socialist reconstruction is to be undertaken in real earnest, we must direct attention just as much to the open country as to the industrial workers, and yet as regards the former we have not even taken the first steps" (p. 425). Moreover, "what we have taken over from November 9 are mere weak beginnings, and we have not wholly taken over even these." "We have to seize power, and the seizure of power assumes this aspect; what, throughout Germany, can each workers' and soldiers' council achieve?" (p. 425). It is clear that for Luxemburg this was an entirely open question, to be decided by the councils, not by some formula.

On the other hand, she is perfectly clear that this does not mean that her position is now different from what it had been the day before, when she had argued that the Communists must participate in the constituent assembly – if comes into existence: "We refuse to stake everything upon the belief that the National Assembly will never come into existence." Indeed, while in prison, with nothing but newspaper accounts and hearsay to draw on, she had offered a contemporaneous assessment of the Bolshevik Revolution. It was a key point of her analysis that the Bolsheviks had made a serious error in dissolving the Constituent Assembly; that, given that it "reflected the Kerenskyan Russia of yesterday," the far wiser course would have been to annul it and then arrange for new elections. The situation in Russia was very different from the situation in Germany, of course. Had the SPD been the revolutionary party which many supposed it was, its mandate would have given it advantages only dreamed of by Lenin! And, as already noted, in that text she had also argued that, "without general elections, without unrestricted freedom of press and assembly, without a free struggle of opinion, life dies out in every public institution, becomes a mere semblance of life, in which only the burearucracy remains as the active element" (p. 391). Nonetheless, Luxemburg appreciated the difficulties facing the Bolsheviks.[64]

But more critically in the present context, she appreciated that very different difficulties now faced the German radicals. Ebert was in charge, not Liebknecht, not Daumig or Ledebour or Zetkin or Müller, not Haase or Levi or some other. It was now her hope "to build upwards, until the workers' and soldiers' councils gather so much strength that the overthrow of the Ebert–Scheidemann or any similar government will be merely the final act in the drama." She was clear that "for us the conquest of power will not be effected by one blow," that before the councils have all the power in the state,

> the members of our own party and the proletarians in general must be schooled and disciplined .... We must make the masses realize that the workers' and soldiers' council has to be the central feature of the machinery of the state, that it must concentrate all power within itself, and must utilize all powers for the one great purpose of bringing about the socialist revolution (p. 426).

This would not be easy. Those now organized in councils "are still very far from having adopted such an outlook .... But there is no reason to complain of this, for it is a normal state of affairs." Indeed, "there is no other way."

Luxemburg may have been a founding Communist, but these views do not differ fundamentally from the views (and practices) of a very large number of the members and leaders of the USPD. Two weeks after this address, of course, Rosa Luxemburg was murdered by members of the *Freikorps*.

Communists and Independents

The entire chronology is important here. Luxemburg's speech is a founding speech of the Communist Party; but we need to be reminded that in 1914, there was already a left wing of the SPD and that in 1915, Lebedour, Haase, Katusky, and Bernstein, the nucleus of the USPD, had joined Liebknecht's "radical circle." But because they feared the consequences of a split, because for them the unity of the party was critical, they had remained in the party until April 1917. We should also remember that less than a week had elapsed between the resignation of Haase and the other two USPD members from the Ebert Cabinet and the founding of the Communist Party. A revolution was in the process. It was being thwarted by a regime which claimed to be socialist. No doubt, the USPD had been utterly unprepared for this and was floundering. Something had to be done.[65]

If recent scholarship is to be believed, we can say that many leaders of the USPD never lost sight of the revolutionary vision which made them socialists, and that in practice the majority of them were hardly to be distinguished from the Communists. Of course, there were those who could be distinguished quite easily. They continued to believe that government action was essential, and that a purposeful alliance of the two party leaderships could still be constructed.[66] It may have been wrong to believe that a coalition could still be constructed, but it was not idiotic. As already noted, the working class had opposed "fratricidal war;" and many who voted for SPD delegates were far more radical than the men they voted for. It was not easy to judge what effects this might have. There were many key places in which leaders of the SPD were forced into radical coalitions: for example, "the socialization movement in the Ruhr was a genuinely multiparty, even supraparty movement."[67] This last suggests the second alternative.

Independents "set their socialist hopes on grass-roots organization, specifically on the characteristic institution of the revolution, the workers' and soldiers' councils."[68] This must not be underestimated, even if the Independents were unclear about the "theory" – whether, for example, councils were temporary, "the bearers and guarantors of the revolution whose activity had to be sustained under the consolidation of [new] conditions," or whether they would be more or less permanent features of the socialist landscape. Thus, in terms reminiscent of the radicals in colonial America, Haase argued that "the source of all power is in the workers' and soldiers' councils; the government, too, derives its power from this source." Yet he was *not* reluctant to call this "a dictatorship of the proletariat."[69] Similarly, Däumig wrote:

> Give the proletariat genuine, tangible, and honest guarantees that it is no longer to be the object, but rather the subject of the state and the economic order, and you will see that order and confidence, desire to work and joy in work will take root again in the German people. The most significant guarantee consists in allowing the institution which the proletariat has created for itself out of its revolutionary impulse, the workers' councils, to come to full development, and not trying to strangle it by trickery and force.[70]

Nevertheless, "the leaders of the USPD never turned their backs on the parliamentary system, and still less on majority rule."[71] Nor were USPD members absent in revolutionary practice. As already noted, they were critical in January 1918 and again in January 1919. In the Ruhr, they were active; in the Halle district, the socialization movement was politically united under Independent leadership.[72] Independents played a central role in Bavaria, especially after the murder of Eisner, on 7 April. They were crucial to the "disciplined radicalism" of Leipzig, where, on 11 May, General Maercker ended, for all practical purposes, the first stage of the "civil war."

A Historiographical Problem

Some commentators have argued that the Ebert government had no choice, that "the Spartacist tactics of revolt was a policy of catastrophe which drove the Majority Socialists into the arms of reactionary militarists."[73] This view is not patent nonsense, even if it is nearly so. It is certainly false that it was the Spartacists who "began a policy of strikes, riots, street fighting, insurrections"; although it is true that "the danger from the left [was] the severest and most critical problem for the new revolutionary regime."[74]

The strikes and insurrections *were* a probelm for the new regime, but that was because the new regime was not revolutionary, and because once that was seen — indeed, once the regime began counterrevolutionary activity, people responded with demonstrations, strikes, and street fighting.[75]

Others have argued, more plausibly, that "the radical wing of the SPD" — presumably the Spartacists and the USPD — did not acknowledge "the strength of Germany's anti-socialist forces, conservative, liberal, and Catholic — and the probable reaction of the other European powers."[76] Of course, this last remains an unknown; and much depends on just how some possible "third way" might have been perceived by the other European powers and, as in Russia, on the price of intervention by them. Still, most historians would agree that the anti-socialist forces in Germany were in bad disarray.[77] At the critical moment, even the Army had balked. Moore comments, "By their policies Ebert and his colleagues created in the *Freikorps* and parts of the old army the necessary instrument for counterrevolution of the old prefascist model (i.e., without massive popular support) and handed it to the right on a steel platter."[78] The question is whether these forces could have been broken, something not even tried by Ebert and his colleagues.[79]

Among recent commentators, Moore comes closest to the real issue. Yet he too misstates the problem. Getting a handle on this has importance beyond understanding the situation in Germany. A critical discussion of Moore's views of the alternatives that define the two poles which set the terms for a possible "third way" will demonstrate, and perhaps help to demystify, assumptions which nearly everyone takes for granted today.

Moore writes, "The problem before us is ... whether in fact a 'third way' was possible somewhere between a de facto alliance with the old order and revolutionary dictatorship."[80] Moore assumes, oddly, that the *de facto* alliance was not "liberal" in the vague sense that stresses "the importance of rights of free expression and protection against the abuses of authority."[81] This is surely a red herring, not because the Weimar Republic did not abuse these rights — what republic seeking to establish itself has not? — but because Moore seems to assume that, since the new regime rested on a *de facto* alliance with the old order, Weimar was not a liberal democracy. The point is important.

It is true that the Weimar Republic was not revolutionary insofar as power was not redistributed. But the state did change from being something between a monarchy and a despotism in Montesquieu's sense to being almost a paradigm parliamentary democracy! Sovereignty was vested in an elected parliament, and the chief of state was elected. There was equal, general suffrage, a multiparty system, secret elections, and a free Press. Moore would not deny this; but if so, then surely something more is at issue.

Of course, the old order, although a monarchy with elements of an aristocratic culture, was for all that essentially a capitalist state. *Nor* was this changed. That in the new republic the ruling class was badly fractioned and, more critically, that it had immense difficulties securing a mass base are all too true. But this makes it an unstable liberal order, not a nonliberal order.

Indeed, that is just the problem of the "third way:" a way which was revolutionary in the sense that it would alter the fundamental relations of power in society. If this could have been accomplished, then the problems of a fractioned capitalist ruling class and a *missing* mass base might have been foreclosed. To transpose this into Weber's perspective, in the absence of a revolution that would break power, there was no hope for a strong parliament. Moreover, in the absence of a monarch, it was precisely because Weimar was a liberal republic with a missing mass base and a fractioned capitalist class that authoritarian populism was a possibility that was realized.[82]

But the other side of Moore's polarization is also misformulated. What is meant by "a revolutionary dictatorship"? A right-wing version was not impossible, although it was unlikely. Since the Army would not fight a civil war for the monarch in November 1918, it was hardly surprising that it would not stand behind Wolfgang Kapp and General von Lüttwitz in their putsch of 1920.[83] It is important to remember that the *Reichswehr* was a *royal* army, "inconceivable without the King." "The Prussian officer was tied by bonds of special loyalty to the monarchy and to the bearer of the Crown, to whom alone he was responsible."[84] The idea of his abdication was, accordingly, unthinkable: "It removed the basis of the existence of the officers, their guiding principle."[85] Still, when General Count von der Schulenburg announced that "the army will march home in peace and order under its leaders and commanding generals, but not under the command of Your Majesty, for it stands no longer behind Your Majesty," there had already been a revolution of sorts!

What then of a left-wing revolutionary dictatorship, almost certainly what Moore had in mind? Whether this was possible also depended on the Army. Surely, the Army would not have led such a dictatorship. But it is just as unlikely that there would have been sufficient numbers in the Army to follow such a lead had a revolutionary party made the effort. By the summer of 1919, there were between 200,000 and 400,000 *Freikorps*, fighting for an SPD-led regime *against* USPD and Communist councils, the groups which, presumably, would have constituted the nucleus of a putative revolutionary dictatorship. But this misses the point. Nobody on the left of any significance even considered that he might be struggling to establish what we think of as Leninism! That anyone should have supposed that this was the opposite pole of the two possibilities is plausible only by seeing the Spartacists as a real revolutionary threat, then making them into Bolsheviks, and then ignoring the fact that at exactly this time the Bolsheviks were in the midst of a civil war which was critical only because it had the support of the "democracies" of the West and the Empire of Japan![86]

We need to explain this pervasive historiographical confusion, beautifully expressed in the view that it was the Spartacists who "drove the Majority Socialists into the arms of the reactionary militarists." Getting at the source of this confusion takes us back into history, back, indeed, into a great deal of the argument of this book. It will be well here to identify explicitly the key assumptions.

It is quite clear that many writers assume an identity between the party of "revolutionary dictatorship" and Bolshevism, and that is easily explained. But we need to see that this assumption leads to the desired conclusion only on the basis of background assumptions which have nothing to do with the situtation in Germany. They involve, in the first place, the persistent assumption that Lenin and the Bolsheviks had no democratic aspirations, and that the disastrous outcome in Russia was entirely due to their bankrupt philosophy. In chapter 11 I tried to show that this view cannot be sustained. This assumption, in turn, depends upon the belief that *parliamentary* democracy is the only viable, sound form of democracy. Much of this book has tried to provide some of the reasons for this belief.

Bearing on the understanding of Bolshevism as a "revolutionary dictatorship" is a third assumption: namely, that a revolutionary state can be "democratic" while it is fighting a counterrevolutionary war! In highly favored circumstances, with *no* interests in social transformation, the American Revolution did not altogether escape this, as noted in chapter 5; but the

French Revolution should have put modern historians on guard on this point. This, of course, was a feature of the account of chapter 9. Certainly war, interventionist and counterrevolutionary, has been a heavy burden of all twentieth-century socialist revolutions. Accordingly, it has been easy to assume that antidemocracy flowed from the socialist intentions of the leadership of these movements, instead of from the imperatives of war. In some cases it might well have done so, of course; in others — Nicaragua in recent years, for example — this was clearly not so.

Finally, then, we need to explain the identification of the party of revolutionary dictatorship with Bolshevism. Essentially, this grew out of the belief that German radicals were simply imitators of their Russian counterparts who, for the reasons just noted, were construed as antidemocrats. This, in turn, depended on the fact — and fact it was — that the Russians had provided an example and some vocabulary for both the German people and the radical leadership. The revolution occurred first in Russia, and everyone in Germany knew that in Russia a revolution against the old order was in process. Moreover, the language was indeed the same, the "dictatorship of the proletariat," "workers' and soldiers' councils," and "red guards." The question, then, is, did the Russians provide *only* an example and some vocabulary, or was the Bolshevik *experience* being repeated, including presumably, its terrible outcome?

Remarkably, German socialists joined German generals in promoting the idea that unless dramatic steps were taken, the Bolshevik experience would be repeated. This was not just because Ebert hated revolution "like sin"; it was due , in part at least, to reasons which go back to 1848 and then to the summer of 1918, in the critical first year of the Bolshevik Revolution.

The term "dictatorship of the proletariat" had been a problem since the *Communist Manifesto* (as we saw in chapter 10). In the summer of 1918, German socialists had a debate over Bolshevism. As is well known, Kautsky was the main representative of the by then orthodox Marxist view which forbade any socialist seizure of power until capitalism had generated the appropriate conditions. The Bolshevik Revolution had repudiated this doctrine. Kautsky began his attack on the Bolsheviks from this perspective within weeks of the Bolshevik coup, on 15 November 1917. He gave it full "theoretical" treatment in his *Dictatorship of the Proletariat*, published, significantly, in Vienna — despite a plea from Haase to let the matter rest.[87]

German socialists knew, of course, that conditions in Russia were radically different from what they were in Germany — a fact of considerable importance. Moreover, even those who shared the doubts of Kautsky and the "moderates" had sympathy for the Bolshevik effort which, of course, was only just beginning. Thus, Hilferding could write, "One's heart is on their side, ... but one's mind just will not go along."[88]

All we need do now is read history backwards! As it turned out, the "moderates" were not altogether right in their perception of the Russian outcome. But – and this is the point – they were half right. Contrary to everyone's expectations, the Bolsheviks succeeded in holding power; but they did not and could not realize the Marxist vision of socialism. From the Bolshevik point of view, however, this was precisely because their German comrades failed to bring revolution to Germany! Regardless, there are many Marxist revolutionaries, democratic socialists, and historians of all stripes who have taken that summer 1918 debate, sometimes explicitly, though usually not, to mark the great divide between "responsible" social democracy and "dictatorial" Leninism. But this ignores utterly the fact that Kautsky's 1918 posture did not represent the views or program of the USPD, nad it ignores, as argued, the effort by the Bolsheviks to establish council democracy in Russia.

The identification of Bolshevism with Red Guards and workers' and soldiers' councils is striking, and even more easily explained. Significantly, it was the generals of the High Command who first identified workers' and soldiers' councils with Bolshevism. As noted, Groener could not wait to secure an "alliance" with the new regime of Ebert, precisely because he had instantly made this identification. His reasons could not have been clearer. The High Command was getting information from the eastern front and was aware of what had so recently happened to the Russian army, "the greatest mutiny in history." Indeed, on 9 November 1918, Hindenburg himself sent this urgent telegram to all army units:

> Since the movement to form soldiers' councils has already penetrated into the field army and in my opinion can no longer be stopped by resistance, it is necessary to get the movement into the officers' hands. For this purpose councils of trusted men (*Vertrauensräte*) are to be formed in all companies, batteries, squadrons, etc,.... It may be announced that the High Command intends to cooperate with the Chancellor Ebert, hitherto the leader of the moderate Social Democrats, to prevent the expansion of terrorist Bolshevism into Germany.[89]

After all that had happened, was this to happen to their army? One needed no fancy theory to see that one could not run an army, especially an army with the Prussian military tradition, on democratic principles! Indeed, one suspects that soldiers' councils with absolutely no "socialist" interests would have been equally anathema to them. Red Guards, similarly, were militia units in the classic sense, formed by civilians to fight the standing army of a monarch.

Finally, the creation of these images was profoundly assisted by difficulties in getting any sort of clear picture of what was happening in Russia from February 1918 on. Writing in 1922, Walter Lippmann, who knew about the imperatives of both the modern state and journalism, observed that not only did the difficulties of the Russian language restrict information, but Russia was "closed to effective news reporting by the fact that the hardest thing to report is chaos, even though it is evolving chaos." This put Russian news "into the hands of censors and propagandists .... Until they made themselves ridiculous they created, let us admit, out of some genuine aspects of the huge Russian maelstrom, a set of stereotypes so evocative of hate and fear, that the very best instinct of journalism, its desire to go and see and tell was for a long time crushed."[90]

We now return to the question of whether the Russian experience was being repeated, including, presumably, its outcome in a one-party, anti-democratic state. First, as recent scholarship has shown, "In fact, for all the talk of learning from the Russians, there was very little thought of copying their methods; the only Russian practices followed in Germany in November 1918 were the workers' and soldiers' councils and, to a lesser extent, the Red Guards."[91] But these were, as Daumig said, a "natural" outcome of the "revolutionary impulse," or in Luxemburg's apt metaphor, "as instinctive as the cry of a newborn child."[92] Indeed, the idea of democracy was at least as old as the democratic counterrevolution of 404 BC Athens![93]

But, far more important, everyone understood that Russia in 1917 was not Germany in 1918. In Germany a very large working class had already been radicalized, and there is considerable evidence that "a broad unified socialist middle current existed in the working class that transcended party lines."[94] As Oertzen says, "when the bloody so-called 'Spartacist disturbances' were taking place all over Germany, Social Democrats, Independents, and Communists collaborated for four weeks on the basis of common program .... This unity was forced upon the leaders by the workers."[95] Of course, the Ruhr miners, even "the workers of Germany," are not Germany. Nevertheless, there was in Germany a very large working class, perhaps some 30 percent of the population; and no doubt, this considerable number could easily have been the basis for a far more radical restructuring of German society. Moore comments that "there can be no doubt that they [the workers] would have welcomed policies to the left of those actually pursued."[96]

Second, in Germany, the peasantry represented a very different kind of problem from that which it had presented in Russia. Not only was it far smaller relatively, but it did not have the land hunger and *muzhik* sensibilities which had so complicated Bolshevik plans for feeding the population, not to mention for socialist transformation. Third, a moderate program, no more radical than Lenin's program for Russia, might well have won at least the passive consent of the small bourgeois, including the "new" middle class. Even more important, Ebert's regime did not face counterrevolution abetted by foreigners. Quite the opposite: it faced revolution by the ordinary people of Germany. In Germany, as in the United States in 1787, a far more radical form of democracy was possible.

This is the main point. The people who feared Bolshevism and workers' and soldiers' councils — Ebert, Groener, Hindenburg, Erzberger, Stresemann, and many more — feared them because they feared *democracy*, not because they feared a dictatorship. To be sure, they were endorsing the views of Plato, Aristotle, Madison, and Kant in this. Democracy is rule of the poor, enslaved by the necessities of dull labor. The poor are not able to govern themselves, still less others. They will bungle everything, not least the system which has made "civilization" possible, not least any system which rewards the wise and industrious!

The Third Way

Moore's misformulation of the two poles has been discussed in an effort to clarify some pervasive distortions about a critical period in recent history. But if, on the present view, Moore's formulation of the two poles is a misformulation, he certainly offers a plausible "third way." He distinguishes two aspects to this. On the one hand, the government in Berlin would have had to "intervene decisively in the affairs of the army and the bureaucracy by putting its own men in key positions to control policy. In the army that would have meant using and influencing the soldiers' councils as well as sending representatives with broad plenary powers to the High Command."[97] On the other hand, "in social and economic policy it would have been necessary for the government to take control of some key sectors of the economy ... and give the workers additional influence over conditions in the pit and on the shop floor."[98] Gerald Feldman goes somewhat further:

> Without wanting to define all the elements of a third way, I nevertheless would place myself in basic agreement with those who argue that a good deal more could have been done by way of curbing the military, of creating a democratic army, of taming the bureaucracy and eliminating some of its more objectionable elements. Socialization of the coal mining industry was quite possible. I think as a matter of fact that some of the industrialists expected it.[99]

But these steps are "not very different from what the moderate wing of the USPD wanted."[100] This seems unexceptionable. Indeed, for *all* the radicals, including here the Communists, the problem was to establish conditions for the flowering of the councils and for encouraging that "education" which would give the people the capacity to rule themselves.

As Luxemburg had it, "The masses must learn how to use power by using it."[101]

Why was a More Radical Policy not Attempted?

This is Moore's question, and his answer is this:

> With the leaders of the industrial working class justifiably suspicious of each other on the basis of wartime experience, and with no obviously powerful enemies to contend with on their right, the quarrelling and polarization could gather momentum until they fatally damaged the whole left and rendered powerless those between Ebert and the Spartacists. Hence the old order in this largely abortive revolution was able to rely upon the "responsible" moderates to do *its* dirty work, that of suppressing radicalism."[102]

Moore argues, rightly, that "relatively slight changes in timing and tactics in this fluid situation could . . . have brought about quite different consequences." Indeed, "slightly different changes in leadership and tactics" might well have made a monumental difference so that "not only Germany but the rest of the world might have been spared enormous tragedies."[103]

Surely, this last is true – and must be emphasized. On the other hand, Moore's explanation too quickly distributes the blame between Ebert and the Spartacists. To repeat, the Spartacists were not some antidemocratic lunatic fringe. Ebert was a "responsible" moderate, not a socialist. But for Germany in 1918–19, it was too late to be a bourgeois moderate: the masses wanted democracy.[104] To be sure, Ebert, a bourgeois moderate dressed up in the suit of "democratic socialism," found it useful to say that anything left of his posture was antidemocratic, especially since the profoundly democratic idea of workers' and soldiers' councils could be described as antidemocratic. Still, given that there were no powerful enemies on the right, one can only conclude that Ebert and his colleagues, like so many, did not attempt a more radical policy because, when push came to shove, they feared the enlarged democracy which the workers and the "radicals" were calling for.

Finally, there is the question of Ebert and his group. There were remarkable contingent facts that thrust him into leadership on 10 November. That he was so thrust into leadership is absolutely critical to everything that followed. But he was so thrust into leadership because he was a chairman of the SPD and not one of those who had been part of its left wing but had left the party in 1917 to form the USPD. That the SPD was what it was is also critical. But at this point, one must advert to Weber's analysis.

The historical experience of the German parties explains the SPD and explains Ebert. He was also part of the tragic legacy of Bismarck. His party was a bureaucratic organization functioning in a "weak parliament." It could not even successfully engage in "negative politics" – hence the USPD. Ebert was the chairman of the SPD because he was a competent bureaucrat.[105] A competent bureaucrat was first made chancellor, then elected president; and hence the tragedy of Germany and all the world.

13

American Democracy: A New Spirit in the World

John Dewey believed that Americans "were not an over-agile people morally," (X. 261).[1] Like many, then and since, he was struck by the stunning turn in their attitudes toward the Great War in Europe.

Our remoteness from the immediate scene of international hatreds, the bad after-taste of the Spanish American war, the contentment generated by successful industrialization, the general humanitarianism of which political progressivism was as much a symptom as social settlements, the gradual substituion of calculating rationalism for the older romantic patriotism, all these and more had created an American sense that war was "the supreme stupidity." (X. 260)

When the Great War came, some managed the shift in attitude easily. It was, in fact, depressing that so many "who when war was actually declared merely clumsily rolled their conscience out from under the imperative of 'Thou shalt not kill' till it settled under the imperative of 'Obey thy law,'" – and this despite the fact that "they still saw the situation exactly as they had before" (X. 263). For others, seeing the situation exactly as they had before, "the pacific moral impulse" remained steady. Now a troublesome minority, Dewey worried that they were being treated badly. Not yet clear that this was but a tip of the iceberg, he wrote that they deserve "something better that accusations, varying from pro-Germanism and the crime of Socialism to traitorous disloyalty" (X. 261).

For others, a "moral wrench" had been necessary, a "moral adjustment which if not involving a tragedy of the inner life has been effected only with some awkward trampling of what has been cherished as the finer flowers of the soul." Indeed, Dewey could "hardly believe [that] the turnover could have been accomplished under a leadership less skillful than that of President Wilson, so far as he succeeded in creating the belief that just because the moral impulse retained its full validity Germany must be defeated in order to find full fruition" — the war to end all war.

Dewey's view that it took the "skillful leadership" of Wilson must not be taken lightly. It may be that few others could have so successfully fostered the belief among Americans that by entering the war they could fulfill a unique historical task. Moreover, in these passages, Dewey was not suggesting that Wilson had created a *false* belief. On the contrary, right along Dewey had been insisting that "this is not merely a war of armies, this is a war of peoples." Accordingly, "there is no aspect of our lives to which this war does not come home or which it does not touch." In his judgment, "we ought not to be neutral when the war comes home in one form or another and to talk of being neutral is to talk foolishness" (X. 158). "There is," he insisted, "such a thing as interests being vitally affected without a vital interest being affected" (X. 258).

Unlike most Americans, Dewey had convinced himself early on that the United States had to be in the war. He was also confident that the Allies would win the war. But he was not thoroughly convinced that the aims of American entry would be realized. The United States could not enter the war "with full heart and soul though we join with unreserved energy." "Not until the almost impossible happens," he continued, "not until the Allies are fighting on *our* terms for *our* democracy and civilization, will that happen" (X. 259; my emphasis).

That Dewey should himself have believed, with Wilson, that this war was a great opportunity to further "our democracy and civilization" is stunning, given what we now know. The texts quoted above are from Dewey's "In Time of National Hesitation," written with relief that "at last we were in it ourselves." Dewey concluded this remarkable text by offering that "the war has shown that we are no longer a colony of any European nation nor of them all collectively." "We are," he continued, "a new body and a new spirit in the world" (X. 259).

This was surely true. But as he later came to see, he had misread that "new spirit." Dewey did not then know that "*our* democracy" and "*our* civilization" were not what he had thought them to be. He did not then appreciate that this Great War would prove that the chauvinists, pacifists, internationalists, and cynics were correct. The "new body" would be a globally powerful America which would occupy its "rightful" place in what Dewey was to call "the war system."

In this chapter, the focus is on the role and thought of two of America's most important political philosophers and analysts, John Dewey and Walter Lippmann. The idea is to use them to recover a critical moment and argument in American history over democracy in the epoch of modern war. Dewey and Lippmann played important roles as regards American entry into the war and, in different ways, as regards the terms of the peace. Although little has been made of this, for Dewey the war was a transforming experience. It forced him to articulate a philosophy of democracy which was profoundly radical. Lippmann was not transformed; but the war forced him to become clear on some critical themes which he had previously left unclear. In the process, the two of them came to share a diagnosis of the problems of American society, even if their prescriptions were leagues apart. Their positions on science, government, mass society, democracy, and war say much about America, before and after the Great War.

The New Republic

The first *Republic*, of course, had been written by Plato. Reflecting on the problem of war in his world, Plato had envisioned a radically reformed *polis*. The second republic was that of Cicero, who, while approving of empire, nonetheless wanted Rome to return to its more virtuous republican days. The "New Republic" referred to in this part of the book, however, is neither Athens nor Rome, but, with appropriate equivocation, the magazine which was created in 1914 by Herbert Croly and funded by Willard Straight and his wife, Dorothy. Straight was a Morgan banker and an "arch-exponent of American imperialism"; Dorothy Straight was a Whitney with the benefits of ample Standard Oil royalties. The young Walter Lippmann – he was but four years out of Harvard College, the first president and founder of its Socialist Club – was a key member of the magazine's original staff. The much older John Dewey, born in 1859, was an enthusiastic contributor. There were a host of other notables who were close to the new magazine, including as an editor, Walter Weyl, author of *The New Democracy* (1912) and Felix Frankfurter, who was then teaching at Harvard Law School. Among the first contributors were Van Wyck Brooks, the youthful author of *America's Coming of Age* (1915). Indeed, the list of early contributors reads like a who's who of English-speaking intellectuals. More interesting, perhaps, Theodore Roosevelt looked on the magazine – with the encouragement of its editors – "as his own personal stepping-stone back to the White House."[2]

On the face of it, this array of personalities seems like a disparate group; but they shared in thinking that the United States was to be a new republic. Croly had been a Harvard philosophy student and had become instantly famous with his *The Promise of American Life* (1909), the perfect title for a new vision of American liberalism, a "nationalist liberalism" which would give "a democratic meaning and purpose to the Hamiltonian tradition and method."[3] Croly had savaged the Jeffersonians as individualists, isolationists, and defenders of a bankrupt laissez-faire economic philosophy. He had argued that Big Business was here to stay, but that with Big Government and Big Labor, there were totally new possibilities. He had insisted that this would call for strong leadership — the answer to the "devil-take-the-hindmost" individualism of the Jeffersonians.[4] As Forcey notes, although "clouded by a certain horror of the former Rough Rider's lusty militancy," Croly had a "deep and abiding admiration of Theodore Roosevelt."[5] But then there are always trade-offs in politics.

Lippmann's first book was *A Preface to Politics* of 1913. It was an iconoclastic book, influenced by Croly and by his old teachers at Harvard, William James and especially Graham Wallas, the famous British Fabian and political theorist. But the then fashionable Freud, along with Nietzsche and Sorel, were even more in evidence. In the background, usually unnoticed, is Woodrow Wilson's new theory of democracy.

Lippmann distinguished between "routineers" and "inventors" and argued that government, dominated by "routineers," had failed.[6] "The trusts had appeared, labor was restless, vice seemed to be corrupting the vitality of the nation. Statesmen had to do something" (p. 35). Their training was legal and therefore "utterly inadequate." But it was all they had. As "routineers," they panicked and "reverted to ancient superstition. They forbade the existence of evil by law." Lippmann insisted that what was needed was an entirely different approach. It was necessary to put this restless, untamed energy to work. The impulses were "like dynamite, capable of all sorts of uses." "Instead of tabooing our impulses, we must redirect them" (pp. 49–50). Accordingly, the United States needed a "real government that has power and serves a want, and not a frame imposed upon men from on top" (p. 45).

But the United States was no Greek *polis*:

Plato and Aristotle thought in terms of ten thousand homogeneous villagers; we have to think in terms of a hundred million people of all races and all traditions, crossbred and inbred, subject to climates they have never lived in before, plumped down on a continent in the midst of a strange civilization .... Nor can we keep the problems within our borders. Whether we wish it or not we are involved in the world's problems, and all the winds of heaven blow through our land. (p. 105)

In the face of this, "improvements in knowledge seem meager indeed." What is demanded is a different conception of government and different kind of statesmen.

Princeton political scientist Woodrow Wilson had been concerned since the 1890s with "leaderless government."[7] He was correct in arguing that the American Founding Fathers, "with genuine scientific enthusiasm," had followed Montesquieu in yearning for "equipoise and balance in a machine-like system" *(Constitutional Government,* p. 56). But on his view, if what had been wrought by them had been good enough for their sons, it was not good enough for the sons of their sons or, presumably, for their daughters either. Sharply critical of a disjointed, hence incapacitated government, Wilson responded to the same currents that had moved Max Weber; but he seemed to endorse what Weber had feared. Modern societies were mass societies, complex and inchoate. Wilson offered that "policy – where there is no absolute and arbitrary ruler to do the choosing for the whole people – means massed opinion, and the forming of massed opinion is the whole art and mastery of politics" ("Leaderless Government" p. 339).

This was truly a remarkable idea, pregnant with implications which Lippmann was shortly to pursue – with a vengeance. Wilson argued that since the president was the only official with a national mandate, he had this special role. The air of German philosophy still present in America surely influenced his next move. In a text that Hegel could have endorsed, he argued that leadership is "interpretation:" "The nation lay as it were unconscious of its unity and purpose, and [the leader] called it to full consciousness. It could never again be anything less than what he had said it was. It is at such moments and in the mouths of such interpreters that nations spring from age to age in their development" *(Constitutional Government,* p. 21).[8]

In *A Preface to Politics,* Lippmann fully shared in rejecting "the machine conception of government" (p. 13). He insisted that "the object of democracy is not to imitate the rhythm of stars but to harness political power to the nation's need" (p. 21). "Our choice," he maintained, "lies between a blind push and a deliberate leadership, between thwarting movements until they master us, and domesticating them until they are answered" (p. 286). But if Wilson had grasped what was needed, Lippmann was unsure about whether Wilson could fill the bill. "Woodrow Wilson has a talent which is [William Jennings] Bryan's chief defect – the scientific habit of holding facts in solution" (p. 102–3). On the other hand, "Wilson understands easily, but he does not incarnate: he has never been part of the protest he speaks. You think of him as a good counselor, as an excellent presiding officer." "Roosevelt has seemed to me the most effective, the most nearly complete .... He is a foretaste of a more advanced statesmanship" (p. 103). Indeed, "Roosevelt in his term did much to center government truly. For a time natural leadership and nominal position coincided, and the administration became in a measure a real sovereignty" (p. 23).

A Preface to Politics is surely a criticism of "tradition" – the "record and machine-like imitation of the habits that our ancestors created" – and of the traditional view of politics in a republic. Lippmann criticized the "mystical democrats" who believe that "an election expresses the will of the people, and that that will is wise" (p. 115). Like Wilson, he was struggling to rearticulate democracy for a complex mass society. But he stepped back from the Nietzschean implications of the new language of masses and urged instead a "break-up of herd politics." What was needed, on his view, was a more robust pluralism. Accordingly, he saw the reformation of party politics somewhat differently from either Wilson or Max Weber. He condemned "the rigidity of the two-party system." For him, it "ignores issues without settling them, dulls and wastes the energies of active groups, and chokes off the protests which should find a civilized expression in public life" (p. 262). And he appealed to just those mechanisms which Weber had rejected, saying that "the initiative and referendum will help" (p. 263).

Like Wilson, Lippmann wanted leadership and saw the leader as an "interpreter;" although for him the relation of leader to mass was more dialectical than it had been for Wilson. "Social movements" had tendencies and energy, but they needed an "inventor" if they were to be "imbued with life" (p. 63). At the same time, "to govern a democracy you have to educate it: . . . contact with great masses of men reciprocates by educating the leader." He was optimistic, indeed enthusiastic. "In a rough way and with many exceptions, democracy compels law to approximate human need" (p. 116). Given all that he himself said, it is not clear what could possibly be the mechanism for this.

Lippmann's second book, *Drift and Mastery*, published in 1914, represents a decided shift.[9] It carries forward some of the earlier themes, but in many ways it is a more democratic book; and, with its enormous emphasis on the application of science to politics, it is much closer to the vision which we now associate with Dewey. Indeed, one is tempted to say that if James had ever written a political book, it would have been *Drift and Mastery*! Both the title and the main argument are Jamesian: "A nation of uncritical drifters can change only the form of tyranny, for like the Christian's sword, democracy is a weapon in the hands of those who have the courage and skill to wield it; in all others it is a piece of junk" (p. 16). The book "begins with the obvious drift of our time and gropes for the conditions of mastery" (p. 19).

What is this "obvious drift"? "We have lost authority. We are 'emancipated' from an ordered world" (p. 111).

> We are all of us immigrants in the industrial world, and we have no authority to lean upon. We are an uprooted people, newly arrived, and *nouveau riche*. As a nation we have all the vulgarity that goes with that, all the scattering of soul. The modern man is not yet settled in this world. It is strange to him, terrifying, alluring, and incomprehensibly big . . . . We make love to ragtime and die for it. We are blown hither and thither like litter before the wind. Our days are lumps of undigested experience. (p. 118)

Worth emphasizing is the fact that for Lippmann, America *is* "the modern world," the land of immigrants and the land where "all of us are immigrants spiritually." Surely industrialization and urbanization are part of this; but of themselves, they do not make a people "modern." Americans, we are asked to believe, are modern because they are the first people to acknowledge the failure of all absolutes. The theme runs throughout the book: "Our ancestors thought they knew their way from birth through all eternity: we are puzzled about the day after tomorrow." "The guardianship of the master and the comfort of the priest" have evaporated. "The iconoclasts didn't free us. They threw us into the water, and now we have to swim" (p. 112).

But this remarkable diagnosis, along with its "existential" tone, is Jamesian, in that it allows for the most characteristic of Jamesian themes: the purposive effort to shape the environment, to make relations, to create and recreate an unfinished world. "Mastery," an ill-chosen word, is possible; but we must be clear about what it means:

> When we cultivate reflection by watching ourselves and the world outside us, the thing we call science begins. We draw the hidden into the light of consciousness, record it, compare phases of it, note its history, experiment, reflect on error, and we find that our conscious life is no longer a trivial irridescence, but a progressively powerful way of domesticating the brute.
>
> This is what mastery means: the substitution of conscious intention for unconscious striving . . . . You cannot throw yourself blindly against unknown facts and trust to luck that the result will be satisfactory. (p. 148)

This is a distinctly Jamesian view in which there is nothing "inhuman about the scientific attitude" (p. 158). By now the idea has all but been lost, a victim of the distance of esoteric language, unintelligble to all but specialists, the image of anonymous men in white coats "experimenting," the modern magic of technology and the Bomb. For James, as for Lippmann, there was nothing about science properly understood which "need make it inevitably hostile to the variety of life" (p. 161), nothing putting the scientific attitude at odds with impulse, intuition, imagination, creativity, or indeed, religious belief:

> There have been hasty people who announced boldly that any interest in the immorality of the soul was "unscientific." William James, in fact, was accused of treason because he listened to mystics and indulged in physical research. Wasn't he opening gates to superstition and obscurantism? It was an ignorant attack. For the attitude of William James toward "ghosts" was the very opposite of blind belief.

He listened to evidence. No apostle of authority can find the least comfort in that. (p. 161)

This was no scientism or positivism. Science was controlled inquiry; but, as with Dewey, it was "creative intelligence," purposive, and in the service of human impulses. Neither was it a technologism.[10]

Accordingly, it did not call for a technocracy. "The method of a self-governing people is to meet every issue with an affirmative proposal which draws its strength from some latent promise" (p. 174). For Lippmann, "mastery, whether we like it or not, is an immense collaboration, in which all the promises of today will have their vote" (p. 175). Indeed, "there is nothing accidental ... in the fact that democracy in politics is the twin-brother of scientific thinking. They had to come together. As absolutism falls, science arises. It *is* self-government .... The scientific spirit is the discipline of democracy, the escape from drift, the outlook of the free man" (p. 151). To be sure, Lippmann is usefully unclear here as to exactly how the leadership which was so important in *Preface* functions in this scheme of things; and as before, he is unclear about the mechanisms which might join the scientific spirit with the machinery of a democracy. Moreover, as he became clear, after the war, he also changed his mind.

This vagueness, as well as certain other strands in the book, make it easy to see a continuity which has thrown off more than one commentator. It also makes it easy to see why the book could receive adulation from almost all sides. Lippmann had not given up on Croly's notion that organized labor could be a "countervailing power," to adopt Galbraith's term. To this he added the idea that consumers would be a power to be reckoned with; but, more than that, in anticipation of Adolf Berle, he argued that "the real news about business ... is that it is being administered by men who are not profiteers" (p. 42). The "established" magazines and newspapers, ready to accept Lippmann's deflation of socialism and his celebration of America's uniqueness could easily be enthusiastic.

So too could the women of America. In a chapter devoted exclusively to the topic of "the Women's Movement," Lippmann saw that there had to be confusion and conflict within the movement, precisely because "every step in the woman's movement is creative" (p. 123). Randolph Bourne, who was shortly to lay blame for America's entry into the war on "the war intel-letuals," said that he would have given his soul to have written *Drift and Mastery*. And with much less good reason, even the revolutionary magazine, *The Masses*, concerned perhaps with the good relations between Reed and Lippmann, received it with warmth.[11]

Drift and Mastery was a "pragmatist's" political book and important; but it was anything but Lippmann's last word on the topic under discussion. We need first to see what, during this same period, the active, influential pragmatist, John Dewey, was up to. For some time prior to the publication of *Drift and Mastery*, Dewey had been insisting on the application of "experimental methods" to social change, arguing that in crucial ways the problem of a better society was a problem of knowledge. Yet the most striking thing about Dewey's thought up to World War I was the absence of a political philosophy. Until that time, as an intellectual and a theorist, Dewey was a psychologist, a moral philosopher, an educationist, a defender of his new "instrumentalist" version of pragmatism, a "philosopher" engaged in philosophical problems which, if they would touch "the problems of men," had not yet issued a clear vision of the good society.[12]

One here suspects a kind of characteristic American innocence. Dewey, reared in the town-meeting atmosphere of Vermont, had no reason to doubt that if there were problems in America, "the American way," erected on solid foundations, was essentially sound. Of course, he had always been more than a theorist. He had always been involved practically, in Chicago with the work of Jane Addams and the experimental lab school at the University of Chicago, and in New York, especially with the schools.

The Great War prompted Dewey's first systematic political work, *German Philosophy and Politics*.[13] But if the book was motivated by the war, it was guided by Dewey's conviction that there is a "mutual relationship of philosophy and practical social affairs" (p. 13). As the title suggests, the book is an effort to grasp the German politics of "World Policy" by a study of German philosophy, from the esoteric inquiries of Kant's *Critique of Pure Reason* to the philosophy of history, the state, and of war in the philosophy of Hegel.[14] Both German philosophy and politics come off badly. Like Marx, Dewey had been nurtured on Hegel, but had long since broken with that tradition. So far as politics is concerned, *German Philosophy and Politics* is Dewey's *German Ideology*.

At the root of German politics, Dewey finds the "two worlds" of Kantian philosophy and its subsequent "correction" by Hegel. Thus:

> The division established between the outer realm, in which of course acts fall, and the inner realm of consciousness explains what is otherwise so paradoxical to a foreigner in German writings: The constant assertion that Germany brought to the world the conscious recognition of freedom coupled with the assertion of the relative incompetency of the German folk en masse for political self-direction. To one saturated with the English tradition which identifies freedom with power to act upon one's ideas, to make one's purposes effective in regulation of public affairs, the combination seems self-contradictory. To the German it is natural. (p. 34)

General Friedrich von Bernhardi's frank and immodest *Germany and the Next War* of 1912 is extensively quoted. Drawing on the Reformation and

Kant, Bernhardi had concluded: "To no nation except the German has it been given to enjoy in its inner self 'that which is given to mankind as a whole.' ... It is this quality which especially fits us for leadership in the intellectual domain and *imposes upon us the obligation to maintain that position*" (quoted by Dewey, p. 35; emphasis original). This was no metaphor, of course. In this book, Bernhardi had called for "the elimination of France" (*die Ausschaltung Frankreichs*), the foundation of a Central European federation under German control, and the acquisition of new colonies.

In a masterful understatement, Dewey comments: "Outside of Germany, cavalry generals who employ philosophy to bring home practical lessons are, I think, rare. Outside of Germany, it would be hard to find an audience where an appeal for military preparedness would be reinforced by allusions to the Critique of Pure Reason" (p. 35). Dewey does not stop at bashing German philosophy, however. He draws more general conclusions. There is a real difference between "a theory which is pinned down to belief in an Absolute beyond history and behind experience, and one which is frankly experimental. For any philosophy which is not consistently experimental will always traffic in absolutes no matter in how disguised a form. In German political philosophy, the traffic is without mask" (p. 89). America, unsurprisingly, is said to be experimental: "America is too new to afford a foundation for an a priori philosophy .... For our history is too obviously future" (p. 129). On the other hand, "our country is too big and too unformed ... to enable us to trust to an empirical philosophy of muddling along .... We must have system, constructive method .... I cannot help but think that the present European situtation forces home the need for constructive planning" (pp. 129–30).[15]

Indeed, there is a pressing need "to clarify and guide our future endeavor;" but to do this, we need to "articulate and consolidate the ideas to which our social practice commits us" (p. 130). Current American social practices were sound. They needed to be discerned so as to provide leverage on the future. He allows himself one "illustration:" "The present situation presents the spectacle of the breakdown of the whole philosophy of Nationalism, political, racial and cultural" (ibid.). The philosophy of "isolated national sovereignty" will no longer suffice. But just for that reason, neither will those remedies which were then in the air. "Arbitration treaties, international judicial councils, schemes of international disarmament, peace funds and peace movements are all well in their way. But the situation calls for more radical thinking" (p. 130–1). There is an unacknowledged "depth and width of human intercourse," and this needs to be applied "without and within our national life." As to the remedies just mentioned, "an international judicial tribunal will break in the end upon the principle of national sovereignty" (p. 131).

For Dewey, political, racial, and cultural nationalism will take on an increasing prominence and urgency during the next three years. We find the theme in *Democracy and Education*, published in 1916.[16] Because it is rich in the philosophy and practice of education, readers usually fail to notice the underlying tension created by Dewey's insight into the problem of nationalist and statist politics. He asks, "Is it possible for an educational system to be conducted by a national state and yet the full social ends of the educative process not be restricted, constrained, and corrupted?" (p. 97). The problem is plain enough. As Plato knew, no polity can escape from the demands of creating citizens, and no educational system can escape from the fact that to be a citizen is to value and honor the distinct features of the polity. In *German Philosophy and Politics*, Dewey had both applauded and condemned the German system of education: "Germany is the modern state which provides the greatest facilities for general ideas to take effect through social inculcation. Its system of education is adapted to that end" (pp. 14–15). Surely, American schools had to make Americans. But what was an American? The solution presented itself. If we are talking about education "in and for a democratic society," then it is possible for an educational system to be conducted by a national state without a corruption or restriction of "the full social ends of the educative process." While the "if" was a big one, Dewey did not yet have any doubts that education in America was *in* and *for* a democratic society, and that in this regard America was leading the way.

Democracy and Education introduced a critical Deweyan distinction, that between democracy as "a mode of associated living" and democracy as "a form of government." He had little to say about the latter except to notice that the two ideas went hand in hand. Education in a political democracy has as its aim "sustaining and extending" democracy as a mode of associated living, of "conjoint communicated experience." As a way of life, democracy was "the extension in space of the number of individuals who participate in an interest so that each has to refer his own action to that of others, and to consider the action of others to give point and direction to his own" (p. 87).

There was an unnoticed difficulty. Given the increasing "depth and width of human intercourse," it would seem that democracy as a way of living would present an increasingly difficult – perhaps even intractable – problem. This surely was the conclusion Lippmann had already come to. It would, indeed, be the basis of Lippmann's incisive analysis of the postwar American polity. But in 1916, at least, Dewey seems not to have been in the least disturbed. He noted that there was definitely a "widening of the area of shared concerns." He concluded, optimistically, that these would break down "the barriers of class, race and national territory." Moreover, such widening was not "the product of deliberation and conscious effort." On the contrary, it was the result of "the development of modes of manufacture and commerce, travel, migration and intercommunication which flowed from the command of science over natural energy" (p. 87). Like Lippmann, he saw that "all the winds of heaven blow through our land"; or, to adopt Graham Wallas's influential term, that there was now a "Great Society" which was international and interdependent. For Dewey, as for Marx and Engels in the *Communist Manifesto*, if for different reasons, the implications of this were entirely hopeful.

We can, no doubt, instantly agree with Dewey that these forces were giving rise to problems whose solutions were increasingly intractable to local instrumentalities; but it was far from clear that these forces were in fact generating the appropriate instrumentalities for their own solution. As he came to appreciate, the problem of democracy was to provide ways whereby problems could be recognized as shared concerns and to provide the means and the instruments for dealing with them as shared. In 1916 he seems still to have been a victim of an element of that same German philosophy which had victimized Marx. Just as Marx had supposed that capitalist modes of production would destroy national boundaries, make for international proletarian solidarity, and politicize workers, so Dewey seems to have thought that "the machine age," once hooked to genuine American experimentalism, would propel democracy as a way of life![17]

The United States, forced to invent, had invented well. The idea that the Old World was just that − old − had always been a feature of American thought, to be sure. But the new psychology, new experimental philosophy, new nationalism, new democracy, new freedom, and new internationalism offered a new promise. When America entered the war, Wilson and the "war intellectuals" were ready to commit Americans to a fight for "*our* democracy and *our* civilization."[18]

"Armed Neutrality," "Preparedness," and War

The editors of *The New Republic* were democratic nationalists, not democratic socialists. But, as Forcey comments, "to be a nationalist amidst the carnage that followed Serajevo [sic], . . . was no longer so easy as it had been in the innocent days that gave birth to the new liberalism."[19] This was especially difficult, since it was hard for anyone to imagine why America should have entered the war.

We cannot here review the difficulties on this score faced by the *New Republic* nationalists, except to notice that, to begin with, they probably did better than most of the violently partisan press.[20] They ridiculed the pacifists, to be sure, and on this they got ample assistance from Dewey. In the January 1916 *New Republic*, Dewey offered the classic pragmatist response to pacifism: "Until pacifism puts its faith in constructive, inventive intelligence instead of its appeal to emotions and in exhortation, the disparate unorganized forces of the world will continue to develop outbreaks of violence" (*Middle Works*, X. 214). In any case – and more fundamentally – the issue of whether force was justified depended on the consequences. If war cannot be shown "to be the most economical method of securing the results which are desirable with a minimum of undesirable results, it marks waste and loss" (X. 214–15). But plainly, it might be so shown.[21]

The editors also resisted Roosevelt's shrill calls for "preparedness," asking, reasonably, "Preparedness for What?" In this they also got considerable support from Dewey, who wrote a series of essays against the idea that compulsory military service would overcome the admitted "defects" in our educational system. Indeed,

> when Mr. Roosevelt writes with as much vehemence about national aid to vocational education, national aid to wipe out illiteracy, and national aid for evening and continuing schools for our immigrants, as he now writes in behalf of military service, I for one shall take him more seriously as an authority on the educational advantages of setting-up exercises, firing guns and living in camp. (X. 186)

But most striking, perhaps, are the Orwellian terms which the men of the *New Republic* helped to create and promote as they moved closer and closer to militancy. They called for "differential neutrality." Their "constructive radicalism" became "constructive patriotism." With the sinking of the *Lusitania*, they called for a "new kind of war," "armed neutrality," forgetting that they had only recently been telling Americans who sailed on British ships that they did so "at their own risk."[22] It was now perfectly justifiable for the United States to use defensive convoys, confiscate German assets, and intern its shipping. Wilson's actions showed that he appreciated that the option was not to do nothing. Similarly, the *New Republic* men had been ecstatic when Wilson called for "Peace without Victory," believing, with good cause, that Wilson had got the idea from them.[23] The only question was whether Wilson really understood "Aggressive Pacifism." It turned out that he did.

Historians remain in disagreement over the explanation of America's entry into the Great War: whether, as American schoolbooks have it, the United States (by which they *must*(?) mean the President and the Congress) was *forced* into war,[24] whether there were "deep causes" having to do with securing imperial interests, or whether, as Randolph Bourne had suggested, it was the result of failure of some distinct aspects of the American *Weltanschauung*.

However, there are some facts upon which everyone can agree. For one, as Morison writes, "No citizen of a neutral state lost his life as a result of the British blockage, and all neutral cargoes seized were paid at war prices." On the other hand, "U-boat warfare took a toll of some 200 [actually 118] American lives on the high seas while America was still neutral."[25] And it is surely the case that the infamous Zimmerman telegram[26] was critical as regards Wilson's final decision — whether as the last straw or the perfect excuse. Still, it is hardly self-evident that the German proposal of a German-Mexican alliance was good reason to send troops 3,000 miles across the Atlantic to France.

Nor could there be any doubt that *some* Wall Street interests were served by war, and that many of their spokesmen, such as Teddy Roosevelt and Willard Straight, wanted war. Still, unless we assume that Wilson was a dupe for these interests, more needs to be said.[27]

But however this may be, although it is often supposed that in the 1916 campaign Wilson was "the peace candidate," this is very far from being the truth. The slogan "He kept us out of war" was part of the campaign, to be sure; but not only was no promise ever made that Wilson would continue to keep the United States out of the war, but the importance of the slogan has been magnified by Republicans who, retrospectively, like to believe that they were right all along and that Wilson had played a game of duplicity.[28] After all, nearly everyone was for peace, motherhood, and apple pie. Even those who, like the editors of the Chicago *Tribune,* were vigorous in their support of Teddy Roosvelt were saying that "preparedness" was the only hope for peace.

Domestic Politics and America's Entry into the Great War

We need here to look, if only briefly, at American domestic politics. By the time of the 1912 presidential campaign, the Republican party, whose right to rule had scarcely been questioned since the Civil War, had collapsed into open schism. The result had been the election of Wilson as a minority president over William Howard Taft and Teddy Roosevelt's splinter Progressive Party candidacy. Wilson's presidency had not satisfied the Progressives, and the war had not made things any easier for Wilson. For one thing, ethnic politics had taken on entirely new dimensions.

The census of 1910 showed some 91,972,266 Americans of whom 9,827,763 were Afro-Americans. Politicians could safely ignore them. Of the remaining 82,144,503, 32,413,723 were foreign-born or had a foreign-born parent, and 10,984,614 had either been born in Germany or Austro-Hungary or had a parent who had — that is, around one in eight. But there were also 4,505,360 who were Irish-born or of Irish parentage. Displeased with Wilson's policy of "differential neutrality," they joined a chorus of anti-British sentiment which grew louder after the unsuccessful Irish Rebellion at Eastertime of 1916. Wilson had never been happy with the "hyphenated movement," and he probably did as much as anyone to give currency to the term. In his widely quoted May 1914 remarks at the unveiling of a statue in memory of a revolutionary hero, he said impatiently: "Some Americans need hyphens in their names because only part of them has come over. But when the whole man has come over, heart and thought and all, the hyphen drops of its own weight out of his name."[29] In his "Leaderless Government" address to the Virginia Bar Association, an address which, with appropriate changes, he evidently repeated many times, he was distressingly frank: "We have the immemorial practice of the English race itself, to which we belong. Nowhere else has the pure strain of the nation which planted the colonies and made the independent government under which we live been kept so without taint or mixture as it has been in Virginia, and hitherto in all the South" (*Public Papers*, p. 337). Of course, Americans of less "pure strain" could find little to attract them in Roosevelt either, an attitude then shared by the big shots in the Republican party who were not about to forgive Roosevelt's recent, disastrous bolt of the party. Nonetheless, Roosevelt's hopes were decidedly boosted by the vocal – if minority – "preparedness" sentiment.

When the Republicans met for their convention, there were those who counted on a stampede for Roosevelt. This group almost certainly wanted war and knew that Roosevelt would not disappoint them. When the movement to Roosevelt did not materialize, efforts to seal the schism led, on the fourth day, to the nomination of Charles Evans Hughes, who at least seemed electable. Roosevelt's well-publicized dislike of him, along with his ancestry, made him a plausible friend of the Germans. Moreover, since he had said nothing to indicate that he leaned toward the cause of the Allies, the Irish might go along as well. So might Catholics and others who were angry with Wilson's confused interventions in the Mexican civil war and pacifists *and* militarists unhappy with "armed neutrality." More than that, he might appeal to the Progressives, the "hyphens," and the non-hyphens. After all, Hughes had been "one of the craftsmen of the movement."[30] But Dewey, writing in the *New Republic*, seems to have got it right: "Were one to judge from the style of campaign undertaken by the Republican managers, one would conclude that there are no issues in the present campaign – unless the business of ousting Mr. Wilson from the Presidency be called an issue" (*Middle Works*, X. 252). As Dewey saw, Hughes's "undiluted Americanism" was but "the mask" for a "contradictory medley."[31] Nevertheless, this perfectly clear perception of the nature of American party politics seems not to have disturbed Dewey. Or at least, it did not disturb him enough to deter him from saying, "I find myself, along with many others who have not been especially enthusiastic in the past about Mr. Wilson, warming up to him more and more every day" (X. 253).

Worth noting, the Socialists did not even have a convention. For them a mail primary was sufficient. Senator Bob La Follette optimistically prophesied, in April 1916, that "the day is coming when the people, who always pay the full price, are going to have the *final say* over their own destinies .... They who do the fighting will do their own deciding."[32]

Wilson's campaign was a combination of exploiting "undiluted Americanism" and a belated, energetic shift to progressivism. Jeremy A. O'Leary's "American Truth Society" had been saying, reasonably, that Wilson's neutrality was fraudulent. Knowing that the group had been cultivated by Count von Bernstorff, the German ambassador, Wilson's response to O'Leary was brief: "I would feel deeply mortified to have you or anybody like you vote for me. Since you have access to many disloyal Americans and I have not, I will ask you to convey this message to them."[33] But that was still not the end of the matter. The Democratic National Committee discovered that Hughes "had been in conference" with O'Leary's group. With good effect on the campaign, they accused Hughes of being in secret alliance with disloyal "hyphens."

On the other side, Wilson nominated the notoriously pro-labor Louis Brandeis to the Supreme Court; and in the few closing weeks of the congressional session, a raft of Progressive measures, stemming from presidential initiative, got passed: the Federal Farm Loan Act, the creation of the United States Tariff Commission, an important new labor bill restricting child labor, and the Adamson Act, a novel piece of legislation which had been the favorite of railroad labor.

Still, Wilson won only barely. In the electoral college, the victor needed 266 out of 531 votes. With California still out, Hughes had 254 and Wilson 264. The thirteen California electoral votes made the difference. Paxson comments: "Indeed, with a well-placed smile Hughes might have won the needed four votes in a thousand from the opposition, nearly half of them Republican at heart, but they had been snubbed."[34] The fact that Governor Johnson of California had combined the non Democratic vote to win in that state makes this a convincing argument.[35]

Nevertheless, it had been clear enough to Lippmann that Wilson would be a war president. Steel reports a summer 1916 interview granted to him by Wilson, then strenuously cultivating Progressive support. After almost two hours on domestic questions and "benevolent neutrality," the discussion turned to war. Steel writes:

Wilson knew what Lippmann wanted to hear. Neutrality, "benevolent" or otherwise, Wilson said, was becoming more difficult. "Let me show you what I mean," he added, and dramatically pulled out a cable from the embassy in Berlin predicting that the Germans would resume unrestricted submarine warfare after the American elections in November. "It's a terrible thing to carry around with me." The implication was clear. When the Germans sank the *Sussex* five months earlier Wilson had said that he would break relations if they resumed unrestricted submarine warfare. Now he had to either back down or go to war . . . .

Lippmann hurried back to New York to meet Croly and Straight. "Now we'll have to face it," Lippmann told them. "What we're electing is a war President, – not for the man who kept us out of war. And we've got to make up our minds whether we want to go through the war with Hughes or with Wilson.[36]

We shall never know, of course, whether Hughes, too, would have been "forced" into the war – any more than we can be sure about Wilson's true motivations and beliefs either prior to the election or up to his call for war. Historically, these are of little consequence. Far more important is the fact that up to the day on which Wilson delivered his stirring war message to Congress, 2 April 1917, few Americans could have found *any* reason to enter the war in Europe. Wilson himself offered but one reason, and that one reason, ironically, had been a gift of the Russian Provisional Government just one month before: "We desire," he declared, "no conquest, no dominion." "We are but one of the champions of the rights of mankind. . . . America is privileged to spend her blood and her might for the principles that gave her birth." "The world must be made safe for democracy."

As important, surely, is the fact that *he* decided that America should go to war, and that he could have decided otherwise. But this is not a statement that Wilson had "free will." Rather, unlike the similar judgment by Thucydides in reference to the Spartans, it is to say that he could have decided otherwise without in any obvious way compromising the "interests" of the United States. Of course, this claim may be contested. One might argue, for example, that a victorious Germany would have been a threat to the United States and to its interests. It is hard to know what sense to make of this sort of defense, especially in light of the fact that Germany was defeated and Hitler had even greater aspirations than the Kaiser!

The German High Command had blundered disastrously in believing that America was not disposed to enter the war and that therefore it could renew the submarine campaign with impunity.[37] This gave Wilson all the justification – or excuse? – he needed. To be sure, America could have adopted a consistently neutral stance, could have abided by the principles of a neutral country under international law, marked her ships appropriately, and engaged only in shipping that was pacific. Wilson knew that he was within his authority in protecting American rights at sea, even if that meant abandoning a consistently neutral posture and, thus, encouraging war. But he preferred "not to act upon general implication."[38] Nonetheless, his request for an immediate bill arming merchant ships was blocked in committee by La Follette. On Wilson's view, "a little group of willful men, representing no opinion but their own, have rendered the great Government of the United States helpless and contemptible."[39] Indeed, this same "little group of willful men" had been doggedly demanding a national referendum on war before any further step toward war be taken. We can only guess what its outcome might have been. But there is no doubt that the Congress supported Wilson: the declaration passed 82 to 6 in the Senate and 373 to 50 in the House. With less good reason than the German Social Democrats, these men were not going to be parties to a posture of cowardice which would make the United States look "helpless and contemptible."

Finally, and not to be overlooked, it is by no means clear that they did the right thing in endorsing Wilson's war policy. They could not know, of course, the consequences of the American entry; nor can *we* make any sort of sensible judgment about the consequences of that war had they acted otherwise. But surely it was as clear then as now, that the proferred reason for war was, at best, highly dubious.

The New Republic?

Dewey was instantly distressed by official and unofficial responses to the exigencies of war. In December 1917 he addressed a group at DeWitt Clinton High School in New York City. Three teachers had been charged with disloyalty and suspended. Dewey saw that it was no coincidence that the three had been active in promoting the new Teachers' Union. There had been no trial, no opportunity to present evidence or weigh testimony. It was, said Dewey, an inquisition. He offered that he was pro-Ally; but to be so, it was not necessary "to be in favor of establishing Prussianism in New York City" (X. 159).

Repression justified by war was not a novelty in the liberal democracies and had not been so in America. What was new was a new capacity to use repression, now coupled with a fantastic new ability to obiterate the distinction between "information" and "propaganda." It is not clear whether at this time Croly, Lippmann, Dewey, or indeed anyone, – appreciated this or its implications or how far it would go. But as the repression increased, so did the protests which issued from these men, especially from Dewey. The Espionage Acts (1917) and the Sedition Act (1918), aided by Justice Holmes's famous articulation of a "clear and present danger," provided the "legal" ground for slapping a ten-year jail sentence on Eugene Debs for an anti-war speech and for the mass indictment of the leaders of the IWW and others equally proteced by "due process." The editors of the *Masses* went on trial; an issue of Oswald Garrison's *Nation* was suppressed; the *Jewish Daily Forward* was threatened; and Simon Patten and Charles Beard joined the list of academics who lost their posts. The atmosphere of suspicion resulted in the withdrawal of the subsidy which had kept Bourne's *The Seven Arts* in print. Even the *New Republic* came under government surveillance until George Creel, the chief of President Wilson's new propaganda bureau, the Committee of Public Information, pointed out to federal agents that the magazine was a supporter of the Administration![40]

In order to satisfy the need for "an authoritative agency" for the dissemination of "facts about the war," the Committee of Public Information (CPI) had been created seven days after the declaration of war. It had no congressional authority and was primarily supported out of the President's fund. Its efforts were monumental. Not only did Creel's office "release the news," which meant that it had control over what Americans learned about the war; but, as Creel said, there was "no medium of appeal that we did not employ": films, posters, cartoons, prepared speeches, and widely distributed pamphlets. A sample of their titles gives the flavor: *How the War Came [sic] to America, The War Message,* [Wilson's speech before Congress] *and the Facts [sic] Behind It, Why Working Men [sic] Support the War,* and the *Official Bulletin,* a novel experiment in "government journalism." In his summary Paxson concludes that "the Wilson doctrine was the doctrine of his C. P. I. It was elaborated in the war of pamphlets and was explained out of the history of the United States and of the world. It was rationalized as a reasonable outgrowth of United States experience. It was grounded in the ideas implicit in the phrase, 'a world safe for democracy.'"[41] Plenty of people saw the films, read these tracts, and passed on what they had read. Still more were influenced by the CPI effort at disseminating "information." The pieces of printed matter and presentations number in the millions.

Moreover, with the Government providing the example, private organizations, especially hate mills like the National Security League, could go to work. Seeing traitors everywhere, their strident, irresponsible publications attacked "liberals" as traitors, especially those with Teutonic names, at the same time giving the CPI a benign, centrist, responsible look.

The February Revolution in Russia had made Wilson's war for democracy plausible, but the Bolshevik Revolution now gave the defenders of reaction wonderful new fuel. Because it was quite impossible to get any clear picture of what was happening in Russia; because, since at least the Haymarket bombing, American WASPs had associated socialism with "foreigners," especially Slavs and Jews; because, in turn, these were "terrorists;" because the German High Command and German "Social Democrats" had chimed in with the threat of "Bolshevism," it was easy for Americans to believe whatever they were told about the Russian Revolution. Lippmann, who surely knew this, could observe that "the people are shivering in their boots over Bolshevism, and they are more afraid of Lenin than they ever were of the Kaiser." He concluded by noticing what may be a characteristic trait of American culture in this century: "We seem to be the most frightened lot of victors that the world ever saw."⁴² Nor have those "truths" about Russian history been erased.

The Red scare had by then begun. The Palmer raids and the mass deportations of "dangerous" Americans – without trial – made previous efforts at repression seem sweet. Lippmann had confessed to Colonel House that he had "no doctrinaire belief in free speech," but that he could not be sanguine over the hysteria. Dewey, who had been on platforms with many of the "radicals," including the deported anarchists Emma Goldman and Alexander Berkman, responded, in 1920, along with Roger Baldwin, Norman Thomas, and Clarence Darrow, by forming the American Civil Liberties Union (ACLU). Dewey had insisted that Goldman's "reputation as a dangerous woman was built up by a conjunction of yellow-journalism and ill-advised police raids." The "trial" of Sacco and Vanzetti, in 1921, propelled Dewey to the conviction that the ACLU was anything but sufficient, a discovery that would motivate his thought from then on.

But there were other unintended consequences of the war. One was the realization of at least the main features of the *New Republic* image of a nationalist liberalism. Perhaps Dewey was in the best position to see this clearly. In a remarkable essay entitled "What are we Fighting For?" of June 1918, he spelled it out. The war had brought forward "the more conscious and extensive use of science for communal purposes." It had "made it customary to utilize collective knowledge and skill of scientific experts of all kinds, organizing them for community ends." This was, he concluded prophetically, "the one phase of Prussianism . . . which is likely permanently to remain" (XI. 98–9). The warfare state had laid the foundations for the new liberalism! Still, "Prussianism" was hardly a democratic image.

Further consequences of the war were "the formation of large political groupings" (XI. 99) and "domestic integration within each unit" (XI. 101). But this too seemed to propel democracy. "Production for profit" had been "subordinated to production for use." On Dewey's view, "the war has . . . afforded an immense object lesson as to the absence of democracy in most important phases of our national life, while it has also brought into existence arrangements for facilitating democratic integrated control" (XI. 102). It did not matter what you called this, "state socialism," "state capitalism," "socialization," or something else. The fact of "deeper import" was "the creation of instrumentalities for enforcing the public interest in all the agencies of modern production and exchange" (XI. 102). This was the key. At this time, Dewey surely believed that the instrumentalities of representative government were being extended and that they could do the job. But he was incredibly vague on the possible dangers.⁴³

He did not deny that the "absorption of the means of production and distribution by government" and "the replacement of the present corporate employing and directive forces by a bureaucracy of officials" led to centralized government. Moreover, "so far as the consquences of war assume this form, it supplies another illustration of the main thesis of Herbert Spencer that a centralized government has been built up by war necessities and that such a state is necessarily militaristic" (XI. 104). Dewey did not even comment on the idea that "such a state is necessarily militaristic." He seemed satisfied to point out merely that "in Great Britain and this country, and apparently to a considerable degree even in centralized Germany, the measures taken for enforcing the subordination of private activity to public need and service has been successful only because they have enlisted the voluntary cooperation of associations which have been formed on a non-political, non-governmental basis." The workplace too was being democratized: "The wage-earner is more likely to be interested in using his newly discovered power to increase his own share of control in an industry than he is in transferring that control over to government officials" (XI. 104–5). Still, these words, published just as the workers' and soldiers' councils in Russia had begun to solidify and just before a workers' revolution had come to Germany seemed hardly true of America.

Indeed, Randolph Bourne's appraisal of the situation was very much closer to the truth. In a series of articles published between June and October 1917, Bourne had offered an extraordinary criticism of "the war intellectuals," and especially of Dewey's *New Republic* articles.[44] Bourne had noted that for "war intellectuals," "democracy remains an unanalysed term, useful as a call to battle, not as an intellectual tool, turning up fresh sod for the changing future" (p. 123). He asked, rhetorically, "Is it the political democracy of a plutocratic America that we are fighting for, or is it the social democracy of the new Russia? Which do our rulers really fear more, the menace of Imperial Germany, or the liberating influence of a socialist Russia?" (pp. 123–4).

"To those of us who have taken Dewey's philosophy almost as our American religion," he noted that "it never occurred that values could be subordinated to technique." He agreed that "the young men in Belgium, the officers' training corps, the young men being sucked into the councils of Washington and into war organization everywhere have among them a definite element, upon whom Dewey, as veteran philosopher, might well bestow a papal blessing" (p. 128). Liberal and enlightened, they had "absorbed the secret of scientific method as applied to political organization." "Creative intelligence" was indeed "lined up in the service of war technique."

"We were instrumentalities," he admitted; "but we had our private utopias so clearly before our minds that the means fell always into its place as contributory .... You must have your vision and you must have your technique. The practical effect of Dewey's philosophy has evidently been to develop the sense of the latter at the expense of the former" (pp. 130–1).

Bourne was a pragmatist. He began his essay "Twilight of Idols" by evoking James and concluded by again evoking him:

> A more skeptical, malicious, desperate, ironical mood may actually be the sign of more stirring life fermenting in America today. It may be a sign of hope. That thirst for more of the intellectual "war and laughter" that we find Nietzsche call us to may bring us satisfactions that optimism-haunted philosophies could never bring. Malcontentedness may be the beginning of promise. That is why I evoked the spirit of William James, with its gay passion for ideas, and its freedom of speculation, when I felt the slightly pedestrian gait into which the war had brought pragmatism. It is the creative desire more than the creative intelligence that we shall need if we are ever to fly. (pp. 138–9)

Bourne's remarks are, perhaps, a confession of his rude awakening, not so much to the traps and ambiguities of instrumentalism, but to the nature of those "nebulous ideals" which so many had presumed to be instantiated in American democracy. It would take Dewey a bit longer before he would get clear on the critical issues. But, contrary to many of his later critics and epigones, get clear he eventually did.

Two Inquiries

As the war labored to an end, Lippmann and then Dewey had the chance to be engaged in projects which put their pragmatic philosophies to work. Lippmann's project was an enormous success; Dewey's was not.

Colonel House, Wilson's powerful man for all seasons, initiated Lippmann's project in September 1917. So secret that it had no name, the group which formed its directorate decided on "the Inquiry."[45] The name, a member noted, would be "blind to the general public, but would serve to identify it among the initiated."[46] The directorate included Sidney Meses, House's brother-in-law and a philosopher who was then president of City College, David Hunter Miller, a law partner of House's son-in-law Gordon Auchincloss, Columbia historian James T. Shotwell, and geographer Isaiah Bowman. Eventually it came to number some 150 academic experts, including Samuel Eliot Morison; but Lippmann was its general secretary and, as it turned out, its motivating spirit. Evidently, Dewey was tempted by Lippmann to head a Moscow branch, but in the end decided against the plan. It is interesting to speculate on how that experience might have affected his political philosophy.

The mandate of the inquiry was broad. It was to consist "not only of a study of the facts but of quiet negotiation, especially among the neutrals, so that America could enter the peace conference as the leader of the great coalition of forces."[47] It was just at this time that the Bolsheviks published the secret treaties. Because Wilson feared, rightly, that these would adversely affect American public opinion — how would Wilson maintain the fiction that the war was not "an unholy alliance of bribes and rewards"? — he tried, but failed, to prevent their publication in America. In consequence, there was an urgency in House's early December invitation to Lippmann to come to his home. Wilson had to disconnect himself from the manifest imperialism of his Allied partners and to set out a peace of his own. The terms had to "purge and pacify" the Allied cause and, at the same time, be so tempting to the German people that they would reject their own leadership.

This rather incredible mandate was brilliantly managed by Lippmann. On 22 December 1917, Lippmann presented House with a document entitled "The War Aims and Peace Terms It Suggests." The President got it on Christmas Day. On 2 January, Lippmann responded to requests for clarification with a revised memorandum. Wilson accepted the recommendations, adding six points of his own, and on 8 January he assembled Congress to offer them his historic Fourteen Points. Lippmann was rightly exultant.

Dewey's inquiry, by contrast, bore absolutely no fruit. It had been initiated in the summer of 1918 by Albert Barnes, a self-made millionaire who had been a student in Dewey's social philosophy course at Columbia. Barnes had asked Dewey "whether he would like to come down to Philadelphia and attempt to put his social theory into practice," to address a large group of Polish immigrants on questions of national identity and democratic pluralism. It turned out that Philadelphia was just the starting place for a wide-ranging inquiry with direct pertinence to the terms of the peace.

Dewey and his graduate students quickly discovered that Poles in America — like other groups, presumably — were caught in a set of intractable dilemmas. By virtue of their understandable affection for their own language and traditions, they quickly became isolated, reinforcing their otherness versus the mainstream. This prevented them, as the Handlins remark, "from getting their fair share of [America's] rewards."[48] At the same time, it made them vulnerable to exploitation and manipulation. As Dewey said, "We discovered much fear and intimidation in a certain part of the Polish population, much manipulation and exploitation in another part, together with much criticism of leaders who they were nominally following with much enthusiasm" (XI. 260–1). To get at this complex web of fear, manipulation and exploitation, and contradictory responses to leadership, however, Dewey saw that it would be necessary to extend the study "to European and international relations."

The problem was focused by a forthcoming convention in Detroit, which aimed to unite the Poles in America behind the faction of Ignace Paderewski, the famous pianist and prospective first president of the new Polish Republic. The United States had already set in motion its plans to make Paderewski's group, exiled in Paris, "the official representatives of the Polish people." But Dewey quickly came to believe that this faction was not terribly interested in democracy, that Paderewski represented a tiny minority in his homeland, and that the leaders of the KON – the acronym (from the Polish) of the Congress (or Committee) of National Defense which opposed Paderewski – had a far broader democratic base. The Poles in America were being manipulated with the full, if unintended, cooperation of American media and officialdom.

As to the European aspect, Dewey saw that the struggle went way back into history. It was between a party "whose chief policies were monarchial, reactionary and clerical and a party which was radical, often revolutionary and socialistic, anticlerical and republican" (XI. 262). This, of course, was the characteristic form of struggle going on in all those "nations" which, through no fault of their populations, had achieved neither modern, industrial civilization nor, in consequence, republican institutions.

Neither side was "especially favorable to the cause of the Jews but the record of the conservative party is much the more aggressively anti-Semitic." Similarly, "both parties share the tendency among all Poles to exaggerate territorial claims based upon events of past history, some of them as old as the twelfth century." Still, Dewey continued, "the conservative party is the more imperialist and extreme, being 'Pan-Polish.' Since the Russian revolution particulary, the radical party has moderated its claims" (XI. 262).

As to the American aspect, there existed an alliance between Polish clergy, "opposed to and admittedly afraid of Americanization," and the conservative European faction. The radical group, on the other hand, had suffered continuous accusations of pro-Germanism, anarchism, Bolshevism, and antidemocracy, all this despite the fact that one of their leaders, General Pilsudski, was then in a German prison, and that "the adherents of K.O.N. in this country have been officially expelled from the socialist party" (XI. 293)! Indeed, based upon his personal knowledge of the leadership, Dewey asserted that he could not "speak too strongly of the malicious campaign of insinuation, misrepresentation and personal attack carried on against the leaders of the K.O.N." (XI. 294).

The problem, or better, the set of problems which Dewey had diagnosed were anything but unique in domestic *and* international American politics. They have re-occurred steadily, from World War I to the present. (Compare, most recently, immigrant Salvadoreans and Vietnamese.) The official response to Dewey's efforts is perhaps typical. Dewey tried desperately to get his detailed seventy-five-page report into the hands of pertinent officials, and eventually to House himself. Yet, although he finally managed this, he did not have Lippmann's success. This is hardly surprising, for Dewey said nothing that House wanted to hear. Indeed, House was later to write: "He [Paderewski] came as the spokesman of an ancient people whose wrongs and sorrows had stirred the sympathies of the entire world. This artist, patriot, and statesman awakened the Congress to do justice to his native land, and sought to help make a great dream come true" (quoted in XI. 406).

The "great dream come true" is summarized by the conservative historian Paul Johnson: "Of the beneficiaries of Versailles, Poland [the Paderewski faction?] was the greediest and the most bellicose, emerging in 1921, after three years of fighting, twice as big as had been expected at the Peace Conference." The Polish government had, of course, exploited Western fears of Bolshevism and interests in a *cordon sanitaire* around Russia. But now, with the largest minorities problem in Europe, "with a third of her population treated as virtual aliens," it would not be long before "she maintained an enormous police force, plus a numerous but ill-equipped standing army to defend her vast frontiers."[49]

There is no doubt that Dewey's inquiry was, for him, a profoundly educative experience, perhaps, indeed, the decisive turning point as regards his hopes for a more democratic world. Lippmann's direct experience in Europe as a propagandist for the Military Intelligence Bureau had already given him all the education he needed when, in *Public Opinion*, he returned to the topic of democracy. But before turning to this Lippmann–Dewey argument, we should look at another Lippmann–Dewey argument, this one regarding the League of Nations and the campaign to outlaw war.

The League and the Outlawry of War

As Lippmann quickly saw, the Versailles Peace was a sham, whatever he might at one time have hoped. With Allied troops on their way to intervene in Russia, the Fourteen Points was a vehicle for constructing a *cordon sanitaire* around Bolshevik Russia. "We've got no business taking part in unauthorized civil war in Russia. We've got no business either in law or morals or humanity trying to starve European Russia in the interests of Kolchak, Denikin and the White Finns."[50]

Central Europe was "balkanized;" but millions of people, including Germans, were forcibly put under alien rule. The reparations imposd on Germany were contrary to anything Lippmann had expected, and the League of Nations, although it was not a defense pact, incredibly excluded an unarmed Germany. "For the life of me I can't see peace in this document," he wrote.[51] Lippmann got it exactly right: "Unless the bridges to moderate radicalism are maintained, anarchy will follow." It was not just that American policy was illegal and immoral; it was also counterproductive.

Now Lippmann found himself saying things that no one wanted to hear.

But surely he had to share the blame. Like Dewey, he had contributed to ·. Wilson's ideological war politics, now so successful that those who were still *able* to distinguish between reality and ideology were suspect — if not accused of downright disloyalty. Nor has it become easier since then to distinguish reality from ideology.

After a hostile Senate committee caught the administration in a host of highly dubious claims and outright lies, the Treaty, with its provision for the League, might still have passed had Wilson, its creator, been willing to compromise. In any case, it is clear that Europe got a League which it did not want, and that Wilson, who seemed to believe throughout that the League was as he said it was, was thoroughly discredited.[52]

In Dewey's first comments on the League, he was enthusiastic about the idea of "permanent international government whose powers shall be even more executive and international than judicial" (XI. 138). In another essay, of November 1918, he had argued that the League was not, as he understood it, merely to "enforce peace." This betrayed the same logic of the "old military-political system." What distinguishes Wilson from the "other statesmen of the epoch," he said, was "his prompt recognition that, given the conditions of modern life, no adequate defense and protection of the interests of peace can be found except in a policy based upon positive cooperation for interests which are so universal as to be mutual" (XI. 128). This was not merely a shared interest in peace, of course. Rather, it involved interests which "grew out of common everyday necessities, and which operated to meet the commonplace needs of everyday life with respect to food, labor, securing raw materials ... and so on." He continued, "An organization which grew out of wants and met them would, once formed, become so indispensable that speedily no one could imagine. the world getting on without it" (XI. 129). The idea had been important to Dewey since at least his *German Philosophy and Politics*.

Dewey was surely correct about the limits to the idea that peace could be enforced. But, as with his remarks regarding shared concerns in *Democracy and Education*, because global interdependence had accelerated and mechanisms were needed to respond to the new problems generated by interdependence, were we to suppose that the League proposed by Wilson would be such an instrument? Might we not suppose that "sovereignty" would stand equally in the way of what Dewey had hoped for?

In another essay of the same month, he linked the League to "the New Diplomacy" and argued that the question was whether the end of the war will reverse the "relative eclipse" of democracy, whether "the efforts of a nation that entered the war to make the world safe for democracy will effect a transformation of sentimental valuations." In particular, the question was whether we continue with "an unconscious adoption of the older morale of honor and defense of status," or whether the democratic movement has "the intellectual courage to assert the moral meaning of industry, exchange and reciprocal service" (XI. 132).

For some time, Dewey was relatively silent in judging which of the two roads had been taken. But by March 1920, he had decided. "There is no use in blinking the non-democratic foreign policy of the democratic nations, of France and Great Britain." Did Dewey forget to include the United States here, or was this simply taken granted? He continued, "The Versailles Conference was not an untoward exceptional incident. It was a revelation of standing realities" (XII. 5). "Diplomacy is still the home of the exclusiveness, the privacy, the unchecked love of power and prestige, and one may say the stupidity, characteristic of every oligarchy. Democracy has not touched it" (XII. 7). The distinction between peoples and governments was important, but by 1923, he could write that "the League of Nations is not a League of Nations but of governments, and of the governments whose policies played a part in bringing on the war and that have no wish to change their policies" (XV. 79–80). Like Lippmann, he seems not to have remembered that he was once an important soldier in the army of writers whose words had served to obscure these important facts.

His whole posture had indeed changed. One shift regarded the little understood – and now forgotten – campaign to outlaw war.[53] The idea derived from Salmon O. Levinson, and by 1923, in addition to Dewey, it had picked up the support of Senator William Borah, Republican leader of the assault on the League and sponsor of Senate Resolution 411 (introduced 14 February 1923). Borah's Resolution had three parts: a universal treaty making war "a public crime," the creation of a "code of international law of peace," and the creation of a "judicial substitute for war . . . in the form of an international court" (XV: xvi). At first blush, the idea seems incredibly naive and utopian. To most of its critics, it also seemed impossible that its supporters could at the same time be such adamant opponents of the League and the Hague World Court. Yet the idea was neither naive nor utopian; nor were its supporters inconsistent. Indeed, the main idea is startlingly reasonable.

"There is no such thing as an illegal war, except the kind of war that appears to most persons the most justifiable from the moral standpoint – internal wars of liberation" (XV. 62). In denying the sovereignty of an imperial power or the authority of a regime, a group or a people must make themselves "outlaws." But for a sovereign state in its relation to other states, "war is the most authorized method of settling disputes between nations which are intense," the "*ultima ratio* of states" (ibid. 54).

Yet we insist that individuals in conflict face some sort of mechanism for nonviolent resolution, that they engage in some kind of negotiation or adjudication. The point has nothing to do with the justice or injustice of a particular war. The point is that by not making war illegal, we utterly abandon the idea of nonviolent resolution of conflict. Nor is Dewey saying that a law making war illegal, signed by all, will end war. Even given the heavy sanctions available to lawmakers *within* states, crime does not cease. Nor is Dewey saying that the international mechanisms to be created should include coercive sanctions. "The measure is logical − not merely formally logical but substantially logical in its adherence to the idea that war is a crime" (XV. 94). The use of police power against an individual is not at all like its use against a nation. "The latter is war, no matter what name you give it . . . . You cannot coerce an entire nation save by war. To outlaw war and in the same measure to provide for war is to guarantee the perpetuation of the war system" (ibid.). This, of course, is one of the implications of Dewey's old objection to the League, one which also applies to the court at The Hague. Both lack coercive sanctions. Yet, incredibly, if one thinks about it, "they operate under an international law which sanctions recourse to war" (XV. 96).

Nor is this a form of pacifism. It is not claimed that force is never to be used or that nations should disarm. On the contrary, they may well have to fight a war. It is to say, by contrast, that unless and until war is outlawed and there are alternative mechanisms for settling disputes, we will not have taken one single stride toward lasting peace. Indeed, all "steps" taken within "the war system" are useless; for "it is not a step we need, it is a right-about-face" (XV. 98).

The choice, then, is between "political methods based upon a system which legalizes war, and political methods which have as their basic principle that war is a crime, so that when diplomacy and conferences cannot reach agreement the dispute shall be submitted to a court" (XV. 119−20). But isn't this naive?

Consider the possibilities. Suppose that we choose the second alternative and outlaw war and create an international tribunal. Then there are three alternatives: first, issues are settled by the open inquiry of the court; second, one party (or both) refuses to assent to the court's decision; or third, one party (or both) refuses to even submit the dispute to the court. In the latter case, then, assuming that there are mechanisms for publicity, it should be clear to the people of the world, including the people of the nations involved, that the party has no case, that the regime's rationale for war cannot stand up to the public scrutiny. The refusal to submit to publicity indicts them. In the second case, the world, including the people of the recalcitrant regime, can judge who, if anybody, has right on their side. Dewey argues that the proposition to outlaw war has never been put to the people of the world. If they do not want war, they will respond. Similarly, if such a mechanism existed, the people could decide whether they wanted the particular war which they were being asked to fight.

At the risk of pedantry, I have tried to make the foregoing absolutely clear. But Walter Lippmann, surely one of the most perceptive men around, never seemed to quite grasp what Dewey and the others had in mind. This is striking. Dewey's position is open to criticism, of course; but Lippmann's criticisms are utterly off the mark. He argued, for example, that Dewey's proposal was a plan to "enforce peace" (XV. 405), that it committed people "to a code so radical that it destroys the patriotic code which they are accustomed to associate with their security and their national destiny," that nations could never agree on the code to which they would be bound (XV. 409–10), that any test would require an abrogation of sovereignty (XV. 411), that the advocates "propose to continue to legalize all kinds of wars" (XV. 412), that the idea calls for the elimination of diplomacy and other voluntary mechanisms of adjudication (XV. 414), and more.

Dewey fielded these objections in two essays in response to Lippmann's polemic, and in each instance it was easy to show that Lippmann had been mistaken, that he had distorted the text or missed the point.[55] The main objection to Dewey's plan, of course, was that no government, not even in the democracies, was willing to submit its foreign policy aims to anybody's scrutiny, still less the scrutiny of its own people. It seems fair to say that Lippmann simply took this for granted.

There was nothing wrong with Dewey's *logic*, even if his position made him a holdout for the "new diplomacy." Perhaps he did not see that in this world, vested interests were, if anything, more powerful than they ever had been; that, if anything, people would have less say with regard to war than ever in the past. By 1923 there was an urgency in his posture. In his 1927 response to Lippmann's mature views on democracy, he converted urgency into radical analysis.

Public Opinion and Democracy

It is no exaggeration to say that Lippmann's *Public Opinion* is one of the most important books in modern democratic theory. Published in 1922, it is a masterful account of the epistemology, conditions, and mechanisms of mass-opinion formation in a modern mass society. It also includes a brilliant chapter which annihilates the individualist's image of democracy, of "the self-centered man" and the "self-contained community." As Dewey saw, the only disappointing aspect of the book was Lippmann's constructive suggestions.[56] In *Public Opinion* Lippmann did not draw the deep implications of his analysis for democracy, although they were clear enough. He did this in his *The Phantom Public* of 1925. And this is the book which prompted Dewey to his full-dress response, in *The Public and Its Problems* of 1927.

Part I of *Public Opinion* sets the parameters: "The World outside and Pictures in our Heads." Lippmann does not doubt that there is "a World outside," and that in some sense it is knowable. People in modern mass societies have "direct acquaintance" with their milieus; but even the latter involve "the selection, the rearrangement, the tracing of patterns upon, the stylizing of, what William James called 'the random irradiations and resettlements of our ideas'" (p. 16).[57] Knowing is through "the medium of fictions." But fictions are not lies. A fiction is "a representation of the environment which is in lesser or greater degree made by man himself." It may have "almost any degree of fidelity," depending on its construction. The "persistent difficulty," he concludes, "is to secure maps on which their own need, or someone else's need, has not sketched in the coast of Bohemia" (p. 16). The problem is that most people believe that they have a good map without having any way to know this.[58] The materials of "public opinion" are the "pictures inside the heads ... of themselves, of others, of their needs, purposes, and relations." "Those pictures which are acted on by groups of people, or by an individual acting in the name of groups, are Public Opinion with capital letters" (p. 19).

In successive chapters, Lippmann develops the mechanisms for the formation of public opinion. Part II, "Approaches to the World Outside," has chapters on "censorship and privacy," "contact and opportunity," "time and attention," and "speed, words and clearness." Members of modern mass societies are not *polis*-dwellers directly engaged in a world where the causes and consequences of acting can be used to check one's maps. Nor have they the time or the opportunity to range across the spaces of indirect involvement. Always subject to mediation by others, from the childhood books put into their hands to the representations of the *Official Bulletin*, they have no way to discriminate among the representations set before them or to judge whether someone's need has not "sketched in the coast of Bohemia" on their map. Moreover, it has now become possible, when necessary, to create something "that might almost be called one public opinion all over America" (p. 47).

Lippmann gives a devastating account of the Committee on Public Information and its unwitting conspirators in manipulation. He argues that the Committee drew in a host of willing helpers, from the Boy Scouts who delivered the President's annotated addresses to doorsteps to the 600,000 teachers who received the fortnightly periodicals and passed on the "information" contained therein to their pupils to "Mr. Hoover's far reaching propaganda about food" to the Red Cross, the YMCA, the Salvation Army, and other groups who carried out the campaigns. Largely voluntary, the Committee's effort was insidious, an achievement which far outran the hopes of the small group who sat at its center.

In Part III, Lippmann illuminates the overwhelming role of stereotypes in forming thought. "We see a bad man. We see a dewy morn, a blushing maiden, a sainted priest, a humorless Englishman, a dangerous Red, a carefree bohemian, a lazy hindu, a wily Oriental, a dreaming Slav, a volatile Irishman, a greedy Jew, a 100% American" (pp. 119—20). Taken as an ordered ensemble, they provide "a picture of a possible world to which we are adapted." "No wonder," Lippmann concludes, that "any disturbance of the stereotypes seems like an attack upon the foundation of the universe" (p. 95). Indeed, when these are reproduced *ad nauseam*, in authoritative histories, magazines, stories, cartoons, movies, radio shows, television productions and more, — their grip is irresistible.

Part VII is an insider's account of the role and limits of newspapers. They deal with news, not truth. "The news does not tell you how the seed is germinating in the ground, but it may tell you when the first sprout breaks through the surface" (p. 341). Moreover, where there is a good machinery of public record, statistics on crime, stock prices, election returns, and the like, the modern news service is excellent. But where information is "spasmodically recorded," unclear, explanatory, contestable, or "hidden because of censorship or a tradition of privacy," the service fails.

Worse, "news and truth are not the same." "The function of news is to signalize an event, the function of truth is to light the hidden facts, to set them in relation with each other, and make a picture of reality on which men can act" (p. 358). The Press is "like the beam of a searchlight that moves restlessly about . . . . Men cannot do the work of the world by this light alone." And, critically, the press cannot do otherwise. The newspaper is neither a church nor a school. It is a business. Indeed, "the citizen will pay for his telephone, his railroad rides, his motor car, his entertainment. But he does not pay openly for his news" (p. 322). Unreported scandals by dry-goods merchants who advertise are not the problem. "The real problem is that the readers of a newspaper, unaccustomed to paying the costs of newsgathering, can be capitalized only by turning them into circulation that can be sold to manufacturers and merchants" (p. 324). Dewey, who thought that Lippmann had given up too quickly, neatly summarized the point. He wrote: "To get advertisers [a paper] must get readers. To get readers it must defer to their own experiences and prejudices as setting the standard; it must adapt itself to sell newspapers" (XIII. 341). The problem is not the immorality of editors or publishers. It is structural, a self-reproducing, closed, causal loop. Indeed, it may be a loop which is well-nigh impossible to break!

Part V illustrates the mechanisms of the "making of a common will" with a case study of the building of the Wilsonian picture of the Great War. It joins all the previous themes and deserves a full airing here. We must settle, however, for only its flavor. Well before the Committee of Public Information geared up and well before Wilson's dramatic congressional speech, the Republican candidate Hughes unwittingly contributed. At the critical moment of the campaign of 1916 he did what was expected of him. He played politics. His first speech set the tone. Lippmann summarizes it thus: "On the non-contentious record, the detail is overwhelming; on the issue everything is cloudy" (*Public Opinion*, p. 210). "What cannot be compromised must be obliterated, when there is a question on which we cannot all hope to get together, let us pretend that it does not exist" (p. 201). With regard to Wilson, the "experiment" of the Fourteen Points, "addressed to all the governments, allied, enemy, neutral, and to all the peoples," would have been impossible "without cable, radio, telegraph and daily press" (p. 207). And there was the opportunity. By the end of 1917, "the earlier symbols of the war had become hackneyed, and had lost their power to unify. Beneath the surface a wide schism was opening in each Allied country" (p. 209). Moreover, "the whole Allied cause had been put on the defensive by the refusal to participate in Brest-Litovsk" (p. 210). Wilson filled the gap. But, of course, the Fourteen Points served precisely because "no one risked a discussion." Indeed, on pain of exposing their roles, they could not. "The phrases, so pregnant with the underlying conflicts of the civilized world, were accepted. They stood for opposing ideas, but they evoked a common emotion" (p. 215). The two previous chapters of the present study have sketched some of the consequences of this.

Lippmann then turns to democracy. The never true, fanciful, democratic image of "the self-centered individual" autonomously and directly confronting the world as it is makes no sense. Nor does the idea that the community is "self-contained," and that, accordingly, there is no "unseen environment" which escapes everyone's "direct and certain knowledge." We are not *polis*-dwellers. We are a mass.

Yet Lippmannn does not for a second pretend that the Founding Fathers were democrats, mystical or otherwise. On the contrary, "when they went to Philadelphia in May 1787, ostensibly to revise the Articles of Confederation, they were really in full reaction against the fundamental premise of Eighteenth Century democracy" (p. 277). They were "determined to offset as far as they could the ideal of self-governing communities in self-contained environments .... The problem, as they saw it, was to restore government as against democracy" (p. 278). To be sure, "the American people came to believe that their Constitution was a democratic instrument, and treated it as such." Moreover, "they owe that fiction to the victory of Thomas Jefferson, and a great conservative fiction if has been .... It is a fair guess that if everyone had always regarded the Constitution as did the authors of it, the Constitution would have been violently overthrown, because loyalty to the Constitution and loyalty to democracy would have seemed incompatible" (p. 284).[59]

What then is the upshot? What is the solution? One might guess here that Lippmann believes that all is well, on the grounds that, mythology notwithstanding, the people do not rule anyway. Representatives rule, and surely *they* have good maps. But Lippmann thinks otherwise. Everywhere in the world, he says, representative bodies are discredited. And there is a good reason: "A congress of representatives is essentially a group of blind men in a vast unknown world" (p. 288). Indeed, for Lippmann, one of the preconditions of a "strong parliament" can never by satisfied: "There is no systematic, adequate, and authorized way for Congress to know what is going on in the world." The president "tells Congress what he chooses to tell it" (p. 289).

Recurring now to his earlier views, he concludes that this is why the prestige of presidents has grown in modern democracies. He seems to throw a bouquet to the Congress, but it ends up being more like a crumb. He writes, "There is no need to question the value of expressing local opinions and exchanging them." Accordingly, "Congress has a great value as the market-place of a continental nation" (p. 288). But since the president, "presiding over a vast collection of bureaus and their agents, which report as well as act," frames and directs policy, the congressional "market-place" is effectively the congressional talking shop!

Although it would appear that Lippmann did not know what Max Weber had recently said on the subject, he has further limited the capacities of a representative body and, without any apparent fear of the consequences, has celebrated the singular importance of leadership in the modern mass state. As an Amercian, he could still have special faith in experts. Predictably, this was the "entering wedge" which allowed him to join "knowledge" and power.

As Dewey and the pragmatists had been saying all along, the problem of the modern state was the problem of "organized intelligence." Lippmann, having forgotten his William James, it seems, now gives an unabashed elitist, technocratic version of this. "Gradually ... the more enlightened directing minds have called in experts who were trained, or had trained themselves, to make parts of this Great Society intelligible to those who manage it" (p. 370). Though these "enlightened directing minds" knew that they needed help, they were "slow to call in the social scientiest" (p. 371). Lippmann hopes that the lesson has been learned. What is needed is presidential leadership responsive to the best of "social scientific knowledge"![60]

Lippmann ended *Public Opinion* by referring to Plato's parable of the ship at sea. "In the first great encounter between reason and politics, the strategy of reason was to retire in anger," "leaving the world to Machiavelli" (p. 412). Whenever one makes an appeal to reason in politics, the parable recurs. But Lippmann's answer is not the one just given. His answer is to combine Plato and Machiavelli: "Even if you assume with Plato that the true pilot knows what is best for the ship, you have to recall that he is not so easy to recognize, and that uncertainty leaves a large part of the crew unconvinced,' (p. 413). Worse, during a crisis at sea there is no time "to make each sailor an expert judge of experts."

> It would be altogether academic, then, to tell the pilot that the true remedy is, for example, an education that will endow sailors with a better sense of evidence . . . . In the crisis, the only advice is to use a gun, or make a speech, utter a stirring slogan, offer a compromise, employ any quick means available to quell the mutiny, the sense of evidence being what it is.[61]

Indeed.

By the time of *The Phantom Public*, Lippmann had groped his way to a clearly articulated, novel conception of democracy. He could now insist that the democratic ideal is a false ideal because it is unattainable, "bad only in the sense that it is bad for a fat man to try to be a ballet dancer" (p. 39). Things are too complicated, too changing, too obscure, and too difficult; and ordinary people simply have no time to get the information they need in order to make intelligent judgments. Even if each person is equipped for 1925, this "will not equip him to master American problems ten years later." "That is why the usual appeal to education as the remedy for the incompetence of democracy is so barren" (p. 26).

> The individual man does not have opinions on all public affairs. He does not know how to direct public affairs. He does not know what is happening, why it is happening, what ought to happen. I cannot imagine how he could know, and there is not the least reason for thinking, as mystical democrats have thought, that the compounding of individual ignorances in masses of people can produce a continuing directing voice in public affairs. (p. 39)

What, then, is democracy?

> To support the Ins when things are going well; to support the Outs when they seem to be going badly, this, in spite of all that has been said about tweedledum and tweedledee, is the essence of popular government. Even the most intelligent large public of which we have any experience must determine finally who shall wield the organized power of the state, its army and its police, by a choice between Ins and Outs. (p. 126)[62]

But is there, then, any important difference between democracy and dictatorship? "A community where there is no choice [between Ins and Outs] does not have popular government. It is subject to some form of dictator-ship or it is ruled by the intrigues of the politicians in the lobbies" (ibid.).

The Public and Its Problems

Tweedledum and Tweedledee did not satisfy Dewey. Eleven incredible years had separated *Democracy and Education* from *The Public and Its Problems*, Dewey's direct response to Lippmann and almost certainly the best twentieth-century defense of the idea of democracy. The distinction between democracy as a way of living and democracy as a form of government remained. However, not only had Dewey developed a critique of democracy as a form of government, but, aided and abetted by Lippmann, he had come to see that democracy as a way of life was *not* being fostered by the new interdependencies and the new capacities of technogoical society. On the contrary, democracy as a mode of associated living was being profoundly undermined by these forces. Since the problem was deep, Dewey was driven to a radical solution.

In the first part of the book, Dewey attempts a generic empirical approach to the question What is the State?[63] Viewed from a long term historical perspective, most people have not lived in states. We can see two extremes. At one extreme are associations "which are too narrow and restricted in size to give rise to a public" (p. 39). "Immediate contiguity, face to face relationships, have consequences which generate a community of interests, a sharing of values, too direct and vital to occasion need for political organization." Indeed, within a community, "the state is an impertinence" (p. 41). Dewey here seems to be thinking not merely of some pre-modern forms of association − for example, the democratic *polis* of the ancient world − but of pre-political forms as well. At the other extreme are "empires due to conquest where political rule exists only in forced levies of taxes and soldiers, and in which though the word state may be used, the characteristic signs of a public are notable by their absence" (pp. 43−4). Indeed, "for long periods of human history ... the state is hardly more than a shadow thrown upon the family and neighborhood by remote personages .... It rules but it does not regulate" (p. 41).

In Dewey's view, when those who are "indirectly and seriously affected ... form a group," we can speak of "The Public" (p. 35). and when this public "is organized and made effective by means of representatives" who "care for" its special concerns, "then and in so far, association adds to itself political organization, and something which may be government comes into being: the public is a political state" (p. 35). Dewey sees *all* modern states as "representative" in the sense that there are governments which presume to act for the nation. One of the forms of the modern, national state − but surely not the only one − is the democratic state.

Mythology surrounds the idea of the democratic state, not merely the mythology of "individuals who in the privacy of their consciousness make choices which are carried into effect by personal volition" (p. 119), but that of the democratic movement having "originated in a single clearcut idea," and then "proceeded by a single unbroken impetus to unfold itself to a predestined end" (p. 83). However, in fact, the democratic state, skewed by "individualist philosophy," emerged for reasons largely unrelated to the goal of realizing democracy, understood as a form of association in which people collectively govern themselves. At best, political democracy — the idea of a republic — "represents an effort ... to counteract forces that so largely determined the possession of rule by accidental and irrelevant factors, and ... an effort to counteract the tendency to employ political power to serve private instead of public ends" (ibid.).

But political democracy — now in the form of a republic — has failed to realize even these limited goals. "'The individual,' about which the new philosophy centered itself, was in process of complete submergence in fact at the very time in which he was being elevated on high in theory." It was thus that "the new governmental agencies." created especially to minister to the new problems, "were grasped and used to suit the desires of the new class of business men" (p. 96). "In a word the new forms of combined action due to the modern economic regime controls present policies, much as dynastic interests controlled those of two centuries ago" (p. 108).[64]

There were unintended consequences. The new property relations, the new forms of commerce and industry, and the emancipation of persons from "a mass of old habits, regulations," have indeed brought about the forms of democratic government — general suffrage and executives and legislators chosen by majority vote — but these same forces have thrown huge barriers in the way of the realization of publics.[65] Woodrow Wilson's "'new age of human relationships' has no political agencies worthy of it" (p. 109).

Lippmann's analysis of the mechanisms of the formation of public opinion was surely not wrong; but in describing the public as "a phantom," he drew the wrong conclusions. As Dewey had it, "The democratic public is inchoate and unorganized"; it is "lost," "eclipsed," "confused," and "bewildered." There is a Great Society, but organized into a war system of states, individuals, who are impersonally dependent, commodified, alienated, and disempowered, are prevented from identifying themselves as members of publics.

"Where extensive, enduring, intricate and serious indirect consequences of the conjoint activity of comparatively few persons traverse the globe," the absence of publics is a catastrophe. Surely the Great War is "a convincing reminder of the meaning of the Great Society" (*Public and Its Problems*, p. 128). Indeed, in another essay published in 1927 , Dewey suggested that a state without a public is a monstrosity. He writes: "Patriotism, National

Honor, National Interests and National Sovereignty are the four foundation stones upon which the structure of the National State is erected. It is no wonder that the windows of such a building are closed to the light of heaven; that its inmates are fear, jealousy, suspicion, and that War issues regularly from its portals."[66] The problem admitted no easy solutions; for surely it did not involve perfecting the institutions of political democracy. "The old saying that the cure for the ills of democracry is more democracy is not apt if it means that the evils may be remedied by introducing more machinery of the same kind as that which already exists, or by refining or perfecting that machinery" (p. 144). The problem was much deeper and concerned the disintegration of the conditions for democracy *as a way of life:* the incapacity of interdependent people even to perceive the consequences of "combined action," still less to perceive shared goods and to act on them.

The problem of the public was the problem of democracy as a way of life; it was the problem of community.

> Where there is conjoint activity whose consequences are appreciated as good by all singular persons who take part in it, and where the realization of the good is such as to effect an energetic desire and effort to sustain it in being just because it is a good shared by all, there is in so far a community. The clear consciousness of communal life, in all its implications, constitutes the idea of democracy. (p. 149).

Dewey is at pains to emphasize the role of knowledge and participation in the constitution of democratic community. Although as individuals we are interdependent, there is at present no way for the countless "I's" to become "we." Moreover, as Rousseau and then Marx had discerned, "interdependence provides just the situation which makes it possible and worthwhile for the stronger and abler to exploit others for their own ends, to keep others in a state of subjection where they can be utilized as animated tools" (p. 115).

Community requires both communication and knowledge; but Lippmann and the technocrats failed to realize that the kind of knowledge which is "the prime condition of a democratically organized public *is a kind of knowledge and insight which does not yet exist*" (p. 166; my emphasis). For Dewey, such knowledge is knowledge of the causes and consequences of activity; but it is knowledge which funds experience by transforming needs and wants into mutually understood ends, knowledge which can be used in the conscious direction of conjoint activity.

Dewey believes, with Lippmann, that there is a need for experts and for expert knowledge, but also that Plato's parable of the ship at sea profoundly misleads. Plato assumes that the pilot not only has a knowledge of navigation, but that he has a *privileged* knowledge regarding the choice of destination. Because Plato believed that the *demos* were incompetent to decide on the destination, they were to be forbidden the knowledge necessary to decide. If, on the other hand, one denies the plausibility of this theory of knowledge — and the theory of politics which it entails — and says, instead, that *only* those affected can determine their good, then Lippmann's "solution," while easy, is immoral. For Dewey, outcomes requiring conjoint action require participation precisely because only the participants can decide whether a particular outcome is a good for them.[67]

War is surely the clearest case. It takes the combined energies of many, and the sufferings of many, many more; but unless there is someone — the philosopher-king — who knows what all the rest *cannot* know, they have a rightful claim to the requisite information and to being parties to the decision. It is one thing to argue that the people lack the knowledge they need to make a decision, quite another to argue that they cannot have it. In rejecting the democratic ideal as a *false* ideal, Lippmann, like so many before and after him, takes everything as it is and offers us, dangerously and naively, a wise technocracy. By contrast, Dewey refuses things as they are. He is a democrat, and his vision is immense. Assuming that

> The Great Society is to become a Great Community; a society in which the ever-expanding and intricately ramifying consequences of associated activities shall be known in the full sense of the word .... The highest and most difficult kind of inquiry and subtle, delicate, vivid, and responsive art of communication must take possession of the physical machinery of transmission and circulation and breathe life into it. When the machine age has thus perfected its machinery it will be a means of life and not its despotic master. Democracy will come into its own, for democracy is the name for a life of free and enriching communion. It had its seer in Walt Whitman. It will have its consummation when free social inquiry is dissolubly wedded to the art of full and moving communication. (p. 184)

It is easy to become impatient here. What are the institutional conditions for realizing "free social inquiry" and joining it to "full and moving communication"? If, as Dewey says, the national state, the Constitution, the Supreme Court, private property, and free contract are falsely deemed "sacred," "not to be approached or touched, save with ceremonial precautions and by specially anointed officials" (p. 170), then what are the new forms needed for transforming the Great Society into a Great Community?

Dewey tells us precious little. He clearly believes that national sovereignty is an enormous obstacle, and that governments and the ideologists of the modern state are fully to blame for reproducing the conditions for antidemocracy.[68] Further, he surely believes that the neighborly community must be the primary locus of the Great Community; although, as his experience with the Poles in Philadelphia had taught him, local communities cannot be barricaded and provincially defined. Thus:

> In its deepest and richest sense a community must always remain a matter of face-to-face intercourse .... The Great Community in the sense of free and full communication is conceivable. But it can never possess all the qualities which mark a local community. It will do its final work in ordering the relations and enriching the experience of local associations. (p. 211)

This vision is Jeffersonian and cosmopolitan. If today it seems utopian in a vicious sense, it is worth remembering that not long ago, it seemed not only possible, but imminent! On the other hand, Dewey remained hopeful that people could find one another and act for themselves.

The Soviet Union: Dewey and Lippmann

The year after the publication of *The Public and Its Problems*, Dewey visited the Soviet Union. In a series of six articles published in the *New Republic*, he offered his impressions. In the first, "Leningrad Gives the Clue," in terms reminiscent of deTocqueville, he wrote that he was "inclined to think that not only the present state of Communism (that of non-existence in any literal sense), but even its future is of less account than is the fact of this achieved revolution of heart and mind, this liberation of a people to consciousness of themselves as a determining power in the shaping of their ultimate fate."[69] The spirit of democracy remained irresistible. Here, as throughout these essays, Dewey notes right away that, given conventional beliefs about Bolshevism and Bolshevik Russia, what he says may "seem absurd."

In the second essay, "A Country in a State of Flux," he insists that anything said about Russia must be dated, since Russia was, again, rapidly undergoing change. "From the World War, the blockade and the civil war," the government did "practically take over the management of co-operatives," even while, as he remarks parenthetically, the legal forms of the cooperatives were "jealousy guarded." But, he reports, "this state of affairs no longer exists: on the contrary, the free and democratically conducted cooperative movement has assumed a new vitality – subject, of course, to control of prices by the State" (pp. 209–10).

In the third, "A New World in the Making," he writes of "the sense of energy and vigor released by the Revolution ... a sense of the planned

constructive endeavor which the new regime is giving this liberated energy";
and he says, "I certainly was not prepared for what I saw; it came as a
shock" (p. 217). And in his concluding essay, "The Great Experiment and
the Future," he sees an "experiment" with two purposes:

> The first and more immediate aim is to see whether human beings
> can have such guarantees of security *against* want, illness, old age,
> and *for* health, recreation, reasonable degree of material ease and
> comfort that they will not have to struggle for purely personal acquisition
> and accumulation, without, in short, being forced to undergo the
> strain of competitive struggle for personal profit. In its ulterior reaches,
> it is an experiment to discover whether the familiar democratic ideals
> — familiar in words, at least — of liberty, equality and brotherhood
> will not be most completely realized in a social regime based on
> voluntary cooperation, on conjoint workers' control and management
> of industry, with an accompanying abolition of private property as a
> fixed institution — a somewhat different matter, of course, than the
> abolition of private possessions as such. (p. 244)

Dewey should have known that the Western democracies had played no
small role at a critical moment in 1918 in derailing the "experiment,"
although he knew that until then, the United States was still steadfastly
refusing the Soviet Union even diplomatic recognition. He had gone to
Russia almost indifferent to this. It would not, he wrote, "go far in bringing
about the kind of relations that are in the interest of both countries and of
the world." Now in language as strong as he can find, he expressed his
altered perception: "I came away with the feeling that the maintenance of
barriers that prevent intercourse, knowledge and understanding is close to
a crime against humanity" (p. 249). Nor did he then realized that too much
damage had been done, that with the failure of Lenin's last struggles, the
October grain crisis would be all the excuse that Stalin would need for the
"great leap" of 1929–30.

In 1933, Lippmann also commented on the future of the Soviet Union.
Even without the advantage of the five more years that had passed, one
would expect him to be less confident than Dewey regarding the possibilitites
of democracy in the Soviet state. Indeed, his account of the critical determining factors of the Soviet state is very nearly a summary of the argument
of chapter 11 above. A lengthy quotation can serve both as a summary of
this account and as a transition to some thoughts on the last war to be
considered in this book.

> Lenin's slogan before the seizure of power was: "Under a Soviet
> government, state capitalism constitutes three-quarters of socialism"

– the idea being that the proletarian dictators could control the organization which capitalism had already created. He thought this could be done by nationalizing the banks on the theory that capitalist industry is itself controlled by the banks . . . .

But within a year, by the summer of 1918, Lenin knew that this method of realizing communism had failed, that the Marxian theory of the old order, pregnant with the new, did not hold in Russia . . . .

This is, I believe, a crucial point in any and every effort to understand the inwardness of the communist regime. The circumstance which compelled Lenin to depart from the Marxian idea of controlling the economy organized by capitalists, and to adopt the idea of organizing a new economy, was the civil and international war which broke out in July 1918 and lasted until November 1920 . . . .

At the critical period of this war the Russian Soviet state was practically surrounded by enemies. There were German and Austrian troops in the Ukraine, a White army in the Caucasus, a Czech army in Siberia and the Urals, an Allied army, Japanese and American, at Vladivostok, a British, French and American army at Archangel, French naval forces in the Black Sea ports, and then, within this ring the counterrevolutionary armies of Kornilov, Denikin, Yudenich, Wrangel, and Kolchak. Red Russia was cut off not only from the outer world but from the Russian regions which produced wheat, meat, coal, and oil. In this desperate struggle the communists had to create an army and supply it . . . . This brings us to the question of whether in its subsequent development Russian collectivism has continued to be predominantly military in its aims and methods . . . .

The proof is to be found in the fact that the two Five-Year Plans have had as their primary objective the creation of heavy industries in the strategically invulnerable part of Russia, and that to finance this industrial development the Russian people have been subjected to years of forced privation . . . .

I do not mean to suggest that they have not done many incidental things which are not military in origin. But I think it is evident that the fundamental decision as to the form of the political state, the plan of the economy, the determining policies of the regime, are what they are because Russia has been preparing for war on her European and Asiatic frontiers.[70]

Epilogue

In 1933 it was already "evident" to Walter Lippmann that "the world was moving towards a gigantic war."[1]

> From 1914 to 1918 all the belligerents were driven step by step into a planned and politically directed economy. The Bolsheviks... were driven into it by the civil and international war they were forced to fight. They have continued with it under the Five-Year Plans, which, in their strategy and in the order of their priorities, are fundamentally military. The fascists have adopted collectivism, more or less frankly proclaiming their intent to solve all their social problems by developing their military power. In all the nations which are still democratic and capitalist, plans are drawn for their rapid transformation into totalitarian states. The only difference is that these plans are not described as schemes of social reconstruction. They are called more candidly plans of rearmament and mobilization and they are drawn up in War Colleges, Committees of Imperial Defense, in General Staffs and Naval Boards. (p. 89)

Lippmann was essentially correct. "The class war" had been "diverted toward international war." This was the critical fact. "The people, habituated in the class struggle to appeals calling them to fight for their rights and for better opportunities, to strike at privilege and oppression, are told by the fascists that they must continue to fight, not as traitorous members of a class, but as patriots in a national cause" (p. 144). Mistakenly thinking that the New Deal was revolutionary, but rightly fearful of the enthusiasm for fascism in America,[2] Lippmann exaggerated regarding the incipient totalitarianism of nations which were still "democratic and capitalist;" but while his book was still in press, he watched first a republic, then a struggle for radical democracy crushed by Franco's Falangists, aided and abetted by

Nazi dive-bombers, Mussolini's tanks, and the "malevolent neutrality" of nations which were "democratic and capitalist."[3] The suspicion he had voiced in 1919 that the Allies feared Bolshevism more than fascism was confirmed.

The Spanish Civil War was but the first stage of the unfolding Second World War. Nazi Germany and fascist Italy did not restrict themselves to supporting fascism in Spain; nor did Hitler stop at the Sudetenland. Still trying to complete the project of World War I, the Nazis sought "to annihilate all rival powers in Europe" (p. 149), including the states which were democratic and capitalist. Meanwhile, Imperial Japan, at the expense of China, Russia, Korea, and what could be gained in the Pacific, would secure Eastern hegemony.

And the "Peace"

Nor were matters made easier for democracy when World War II ended. After six years of horror, two giants, one crippled but nevertheless both awesome and antidemocratic, the other in its full power, the classic modern democracy, came face to face in the middle of Germany. Rooted in the incomplete struggles of World War I, the decisive fact in the greatly exacerbated woes of the struggle for democracy is what we call "cold war." The historian E. P. Thompson is surely correct in arguing that assigning responsibility for the cold war is far less important than ending it. Nor is it the present intention to settle the many questions.[4] Still, something must be said in this regard.

There was a striking analogy to both Athens and Sparta, with similarities and, as with any analogy, critical differences. Truman and Stalin were not in the situation of Athenians and Spartans, of the Greek "superpowers," "compelled" to make the moves they did. On the contrary, Truman had wide latitude in constructing a postwar policy which would have guaranteed the security and the interests of the United States. Stalin's options were more limited; but they existed, nevertheless. Still, it is easy enough to explain, at least in outline, how it was that, led by these two men, the United States and the Soviet Union established conditions which made democracy of any sort an increasingly precarious alternative in the contemporary world, not only for new nations struggling to overcome centuries of stunted development, but for the more fortunate early "republics" as well.

We can begin by noting that the United States, like Athens, was a powerful "democracy," fully ready to impose its ideas of freedom and democracy on a world which was reasonably suspicious of its motivations and of what, concretely, this American version of "democracy" might mean. It is also true that the Soviet Union, like Sparta, was a dictatorship, paranoid, and desperate to secure itself against interference from the capitalist colossus. The pictures of the world held by the Americans, the Soviets, and those caught in between were clearly products of propaganda and their respective experiences at the end of World War I.

Containment and the Cold War

The United States had always been fortunate, a new nation on a rich, nearly empty continent, free of the constraining legacy of the old order, and isolated from the dynastic struggles of Old World politics. Invented as a special experiment in democracy and a model to the world, it was also free to reject militarism. Assertions of its unwillingness to allow Old World politics to infect "its" hemisphere were not tested.[5] World War I armed America and brought her out of her hemispheric domain, but the change seemed merely temporary. America subsequently disarmed and returned to her earlier ways. But the regime of the Japanese put an end to this. The air attack on Pearl Harbor showed Americans that the oceans were no longer a barrier, that the United States too was vulnerable. But more than that, the United States was now irreversibly implicated in the affairs of the world. As General George Marshall observed, "It no longer appears practical to continue what we once conceived a hemisphere defense as a satisfactory basis for our security. We are now concerned with the peace of the entire world."[6]

This involvement in the affairs of the world was not a neutral one. As far as the West was concerned, the Soviet Union had never been merely a state among states, "a country like any other that operates in a complex international environment, often very hostile to it, and has its problems with it."[7] The Great Communicator's movieland term "evil empire" is a recent invention; but the idea surely is not. By 1945, with Stalin cast in the role of a modern Tartar emperor, there was little reason to alter the perception. The *cordon sanitaire* which had motivated Allied behavior in World War I was the model for the "containment" policy which has directed American foreign policy ever since.

George F. Kennan, writing as Mr X, articulated and defended the idea of "containment" in July 1947. The vehicle was the prestigious journal *Foreign Affairs*. This led to a series of articles by Walter Lippmann, by now acknowledged as America's foremost analyst of foreign affairs. When these were hastily reprinted as a book entitled *The Cold War: A Study in U.S. Foreign Policy*, "cold war" entered the world's vocabulary.[8] Here were two movers and shakers of America's role in the world, now posed on opposite sides of the issue which would be the most critical determining factor of the second half of the twentieth century.

Lippmann's incisive critique is immensely instructive. The policy of containment, he wrote, was "fundamentally unsound." "It cannot be made to work," and "the attempt to make it work will cause us to squander our substance and our prestige" (p. 869). Lippmann systematically attacked the assumptions. First, Mr X assumes that "Soviet power ... bears within itself the seeds of its own decay and the sprouting of these seeds is well advanced." Accordingly, the United States can enter "with reasonable confidence upon a policy of firm containment, designed to confront the Russians with unalterable counterforce at every point where they show signs of encroaching upon the interests of a peaceful and stable world." But Lippmann could not find much ground for "a reasonable confidence in a policy which can be successful only if the most optimistic prediction should prove to be true" (p. 870). Indeed, history suggested that preparation for war is the best excuse that any regime could have to *maintain* power. Why would this be less true of the Communists?

Second, "if history has indeed intended us to bear the responsibility of leadership, then it is not leadership to adapt ourselves to the shifts and maneuvers of Soviet policy at a series of constantly shifting geographical and political points" (p. 871). This allows Moscow, not Washington, to define the agenda.

Third, "Mr X is surely mistaken ... if he thinks that a free and undirected economy like our own can be used by diplomatic planners to wage a diplomatic war against a planned economy at a series of constantly shifting geographical and political points" (p. 873). Here again, the Soviet Union has the advantage. Unlike American policy planners, its planners have full control over its economy. Unencumbered by the foibles of electoral politics and the independence of capitalists, it can far more easily make the choice of guns over butter, just as it has in fact done, ever since its inception as a modern state.

Fourth, "American military power is peculiarly unsuited to a policy of containment which has to be enforced persistently and patiently for an indefinite period of time." "The Eurasian continent is a big place, and the military power of the United States, though it is very great, has certain limitations which must be borne in mind if it is to be used effectively" (p. 874). Lippmann was being generous here, for just a few months earlier, in the famous speech which articulated the Truman Doctrine, Truman had made a vague promise to aid "free peoples" *everywhere*. Lippmann had written that "a vague global policy, which sounds like the tocsin of an ideological crusade, has no limits. It cannot be controlled."[9]

Fifth, because the policy offers "intolerable alternatives" to our old allies – "either Europe falls under the domination of Russia, or Europe becomes the battlefield of Russian-American war" – the real aim of every European nation is "to extricate itself from the Russian-American war" (p. 877). On Lippmann's view, instead of "devoting our energies to lining up and bolstering up the Chinese Nationalists, the Iranians, the Turks, the Greek monarchists and conservatives, the anti-Soviet Hungarians, . Romanians [and] Poles," the United States ought to be strengthening "the natural alignment of the British, French, Belgians, Dutch, Swiss and Scandinavians" (p. 877).[10]

Sixth, "there is still greater disadvantage in a policy which seeks to 'contain' the Soviet Union by attempting to make 'unassailable barriers' out of the surrounding border states." The problem is that the latter are "admittedly weak," and "a weak ally is not an asset." Indeed, Lippmann continued, "it is a liability. It requires the diversion of power, money and prestige to support it and maintain it" (p. 875). As a consequence of its unfortunate history, not only was this borderland underdeveloped, but it was "a seething stew of civil strife" (p. 876). What was curious, he noted, was that the supporters of the Truman Doctrine say that this strife is due to the "machinations of the Soviet Union." But this argument, if true, "destroys the last reason for thinking that the policy of containment can be made to work successfully" (ibid.).

The point may be missed. If this "strife" − *stasis*, revolution, domestic conflict − lacked an independent ground, then it could be ended simply by ending Russian involvement. But what would this take? Presumably, it would mean eliminating those partisans who, as Truman had said vis-à-vis the situation in Greece, "were actually agents of Soviet expansionism in Greece."

This is quite remarkable. But, apart from the technically bizarre, immoral character of such an undertaking, one would have thought that, having fought Germans and Italians to establish their freedom, the partisans in the mountains would be reluctant to enslave themselves to Russians. From at least 1920, Lippmann had been insisting that revolutionary movements in the not yet fully modern parts of the world had ample *independent* motivation to overthrow the existing order, and that American policy ought to be aimed at building bridges to "moderate radicals." Moreover, good sense seems challenged by the further assumption that the Russians had the capacity to "control" these movements. Despite the fact that the United States had been profligate in sending help in support of various generals in Latin America, going back at least to the coup of General Chamorro in 1926, it has been surprisingly unable to "control" them, including most recently Panama's General Manuel Antonio Noriega.

Seventh, "at the root of Mr X's philosophy about the Russian-American relations and underlying all the ideas of the Truman Doctrine there is a disbelief in the possibility of a settlement of the issues raised by this war" (p. 882). The policy is tantamount to an abandonment of diplomacy. It is to treat the Soviet Union not as a rival, unfriendly power, but, to use Ronald Reagan's terms, as an "evil empire." Lippmann had no illusions about the unfriendliness or rivalry of the Soviet Union; but he argued that "the method by which diplomacy deals with a world in which there are rival powers is to organize a balance of power which deprives the rivals ... of a good prospect of successful aggression." Lippmann pointed out that it had not been ideology or the desire for conquest which had brought the Russians into Eastern Europe; it had been Hitler. So too with American troops in Europe. Soviet troops had remained because history had taught them that their internal security depended heavily on the character of the states on their western borders. Lippmann did not note here an analogy with Sparta; but he might have.

As he saw it, the presence of invading armies in "the heart of Europe" had upset the balance of power in Europe. Accordingly,

a genuine policy would ... have as its paramount objective a settlement which brought about the evacuation of Europe .... The communists will continue to be communists. The Russians will continue to be Russians. But if the Red Army is in Russia, and not on the Elbe, the power of the Russian Communists and the power of the Russian imperialists to realize their ambitions will have been reduced decisively. (p. 883)

There was one final point, which I have placed last. In arguing that the United States was "peculiarly unsuited" to pursue a policy of containment, Lippmann asked rhetorically: "How, for example, under the Constitution of the United States is Mr X going to work out an arrangement by which the Department of State has the money and the military power always available in sufficient amounts to apply 'counterforce' at constantly shifting points all over the world?" (p. 872).

What Lippmann did not then appreciate was that the policy committed the United States to a new kind of war in which, alongside armies of aggression and "balance of power" diplomacy, there would be atomic diplomacy and "covert activities." Moreover, he did not appreciate that ways would be found to fight this new kind of war, and that there would be a price. The wars of the twentieth century had already established the conditions for an imperial presidency. The new kind of war and the new way to fight it would realize the national-security state with a commander-in-chief whose capacities would have made Napoleon envious.

The National-Security State

Volumes have already been written on the development of the "national-security state," and it is not my intention to review and assess this important literature.[11] Still, it is legitimate to wonder about the indignation over Irangate in the light of this development, the main features of which seem already to have passed from memory.

For most of its history, in no meaningful sense could it be said that the American state was a warfare state. It lacked a standing army and had no mechanisms for organizing and coordinating its economy or its military or foreign policy. These were created, as emergency measures, during the war. But the war also created the "ideology of national preparedness." In May 1943, Navy Secretary James Forrestal put the matter in a distinctly Orwellian mode: "There is no such thing as security, and the word should be stricken from our dictionary. We should put in every school book the maxim that power like wealth must be either used or lost."[12] As it turned out, no official had to issue an order to carry out the idea. Today no one can escape that belief.

That same year, Chief-of-Staff General George Marshall organized the Project Planning Division to plan America's postwar military structure. The result of this was the National Security Act of 1947. It established changes in the executive branch which included an independent Air Force, a Joint Chiefs of Staff, and the creation of a Secretary of Defense, a National Security Council, and an independent intelligence department, the Central Intelligence Agency.

Prior to 1946, the military chiefs did not fear Soviet aggression.[13] They wanted military bases in Japan, Okinawa, the Philippines, Guam, and Hawaii so as to preserve newly acquired Pacific hegemony; they wanted bases in Canada, Greenland, Iceland, the Caribbean, and the west coast of Africa to counter attack from the north and the east; and they identified for "protection" six areas of Latin America — the "traditional" locus of American military and economy hegemony.

For some time, George Kennan had been a leader of the State Department view that Russia was the only real danger. This was because "the endless pursuit of power is a habit of Russian statesmanship, ingrained not only in the traditions of Russian State but also in the ideology of the Communist party."[14] By 1946, the military chiefs had come around to the views of the State Department. But by now new assumptions had entered the picture.

A New Kind of War

The old kind of war was to be joined by covert activities and the Bomb. The Bomb irreversibly altered the problem of national security, needless to say. It would be an effective deterrent only if, in the event of war, the United States was fully prepared to use it. It is unnecessary to review here this critical history, except to emphasize that at no time did military planners preclude a first-strike use.[15] The Commander-in-Chief and his men acknowledged that "the atomic bomb would be a major element of Allied military strength in any war with the U.S.S.R. and would constitute the only means of rapidly inflicting shock and serious damage to vital elements of the Soviet war-making capacity."[16] The myth of "defense" and deterrence persists, of course, in Star Wars.[17]

The other aspect was "covert operations," "something more than diplomacy but still short of war," according to the official CIA history.[18] It continues: "As such, it held the promise of frustrating Soviet ambitions without provoking open conflict." It is important to emphasize that this aspect of the new kind of war assumed a new kind of enemy, an enemy which might *not* send invading armies into territories. If deterrence fails and invading armies cross frontiers, then the Bomb must be used. If deterrence succeeds – then the enemy constitutes a different kind of threat.[19]

Kennan, the theorist of containment, put this at the heart of his analysis. In a recent reappraisal of the containment policy, he explained that "there was no way that Russia could appear to me to be a military threat." But then, in a magnificent turn of phrase, he continued, "What I *did* think I saw ... was what I might call an ideological-political threat."[20] This ideological-political threat could be fought, presumably, on the economic front – for example, with the Marshall Plan. It could also be fought on the ideological front – for example, with Radio Free Europe. But Kennan was correct in thinking that this would not be sufficient, that, as Lippmann had pointed out to him, the forces which he wanted to constrain were not under the "control" of the Comintern, however hard these foolish men tried to carry out their missions; nor was it to be bought by reconstituting the prewar order. The peoples of the world wanted democracy, but they did not necessarily define it the way Kennan and most Americans had done.

The CIA history maintains that the idea of "covert operations" dates from 1946. "Sometime in late 1946, Secretary of War Robert Patterson suggested to Forrestal that military and civilian personnel study this new form of war for future use."[21] In an early use of the term, in a State-War-Navy-Coordinating Committee (SWNCC) guideline, "covert operations" seems to be restricted to "psychological warfare," though it was by no means clear what that might include. SWNCC noted that "covert operations" were properly the responsibility of the State Department. Within three weeks of Truman's 4 November 1946 approval, the decision was reversed. General Marshall objected that, since the United States aimed at bringing democracy to the world, "such activities, if exposed as State Department actions, would embarrass the Department and discredit American foreign policy both short-term and long-term" (p. 40). Yet, if "psychological warfare" meant nothing more than propaganda, it is hard to see the problem. One suspects that "covert operations" meant a great deal more than that — indeed, that it meant practices which were contrary to democracy, practices which, if known, would indeed discredit American policy. In any case, Marshall's argument was accepted, and the task went to the CIA.

In May 1948, the director of the State Department's Policy Planning Staff, George Kennan, suggested that in addition to attempts to influence public opinion, the CIA should develop a covert political action capability which would include "direct intervention in the electoral processes of foreign governments" (p. 41). The cards were now fully on the table — at least the card tables of the executive branch of the American government.

Kennan seems also to have believed that in the implementation of National Security Council memorandum 10A, "political warfare activity [would] be conducted as an instrument of U.S. Foreign Policy and subject in peacetime to direct guidance by the State Department," a branch of the Executive, but presumably a thoroughly responsible, republican branch (p. 42). He did not think that this activity needed to be subject to congressional scrutiny, presumably, still less to the scrutiny of the public.

However this may be, the history of the CIA is a tragic record of congressional irresponsibility. Today it is not at all clear whether there is *anyone* — still less anyone in Congress — who can say exactly how much the CIA has spent and exactly what it has done. Indeed, consider but the briefest sample of facts that are widely known: the overthrow of Premier Mohammed Mossadegh in Iran (1953) and the coup against President Jacobo Arbenz Guzman of Guatemala (1954) — regarded as early operational "successes" — and the "Family Jewels" revealed during Watergate, which showed that the CIA had engaged in acts of repression which defied law and that the United States was well on the way to becoming a police state. Then there is the CIA debasement of the democracy in the Philippines with the stage-managed election of Ramon Magsaysay (1953) and the destruction of democracy in Ecuador (1961), the Dominican Republic (1963), Brazil (1964), and Chile (1973), and, more recently, the scandal of Irangate.[22]

If we cannot say, with confidence, how these nations would have evolved in the absence of CIA intervention, it is hard to believe that they would have come out worse. Surely the victims of the Shah's American-trained Savak, the death squads in Latin America, and more generally, the decades of one-party repression by governments supported by the United States are among the products of the cold war. Surely the United States did not even need Lippmann's 1920 advice that it maintain connections with "moderate radicals." It had only to take the risk *for* democracy, just once even. Indeed, had it put its economic might to use to help the nations listed above end their exploitation of the poor, it is clear that it would not have "squandered its substance and its prestige."[23]

The Cold War Consensus and US Domestic Politics

The cold war consensus was the condition for CIA license. Further, as part of the sky-rocketing dialectic of presidential aggrandizement and congressional irresponsibility, there were other clearly identifiable actions contributing to the erosion of republican institutions in the American state. These include the repeated willingness of Congress to give "blank checks" to presidents, as regards Formosa in 1955 and the Gulf of Tonkin in 1964, the sanctioning of executive classification and executive privilege, the use of executive agreements to bypass congresssional authority, and, most dramatically in Irangate, the utter nonaccountability of executive branch personnel who establish little "governments" with more resources at their disposal than some genuine states have.[24]

Along with this came the full development of the "rhetorical presidency," to use Jeffrey Tulis's apt expression. Through promotion as a response to an immediate "national security" crisis, every important foreign policy decision thereby secures a legitimacy; but surely what Weber would have called a "caesarist" legitimacy. Yet, this is not because people come to hold new beliefs. Rather, it turns on the fact that by virtue of the cold war consensus, the president fashions the terms of elite debate and, accordingly, of media coverage.[25]

The beginnings of this date from World War I and the administration of Wilson.[26] Franklin D. Roosevelt was surely a master, and Truman's speech in "justification" of the doctrine that bears his name was a decisive turning point. But no president since then has failed to follow the pattern. The Formosa Resolution is typical. Following the practice of Truman, Eisenhower created a crisis over the Quemoy and Matsu Islands in the Straits of Formosa. Reichart comments, significantly, that "a small number of democrats opposed the resolution as a dangerous 'blank check,' but most ... believed it was innocuous because unnecessary" – the very conclusion Eisenhower and Dulles hoped to inspire. As one congressman put it, Eisenhower had shown "his deep adherence to the principles of constitutional government."[27] Remarkably, Eisenhower had secured "consent" for whatever he chose to do from a Congress which was not going to be blamed for losing Taiwan as it had been for "losing" China. Only three dissenting votes in each house were recorded.

In fact, it is fair to say that because the cold war consensus is so taken for granted, Congress never chooses to confront a president over the *substance* of his policies. Rather, the major debates have been couched in *constitutional* terms: from the Bricker Amendment, aimed originally at limiting Truman's foreign policy, which failed under Eisenhower, in 1954, to the Mansfield Resolution for a CIA oversight committee, which was defeated in April 1956, right through to and including Irangate. Here we have a Weberian "weak parliament" with a vengeance!

Ronald Reagan has perhaps consummated the development of the rhetorical presidency. His startling ability to mine the harbors of Nicaragua, invade Grenada, shrug off the needless loss of life in Lebanon, bomb Libya, promote Star Wars, and so forth perhaps gives him credit; but it can only be explained by acknowledging the complete absence not merely of parliamentary politics, but of any sort of serious public debate in the American polity. Indeed, not only can a president cow members of Congress, who, like the Social Democrats of pre-World War I Germany, are not going to be accused of disloyalty and Communist sympathizing, but in the paranoid atmosphere which has come to be taken for granted, "competition for the vote" becomes competition for a profoundly distorted "center."[28]

Still, the claim is not that American presidents are caesars or that the United States has been solely responsible for the failures of the new nations to achieve democracies. The world is far more complicated than that. Indeed, it is my contention that *everyone* contributes to the making of history, and that they do so in circumstances not of their own choosing. Leaders need followers; bureau chiefs need bureaucrats; people need employment and find it in work which often contributes to outcomes they would not have chosen. Of course, because of their position in society, the decisions and actions of *some* people have consequences which affect many, many people. Accordingly, some people have much greater capacity than others to "make history." In the modern mass state, commanders-in-chief have capabilities which would have stunned Alexander, Caesar, the Kublai Khan, or Napoleon. This is well known, and in this book, I have tried, however incompletely and inadequately, to offer an explanation of how this has come to be. That is one main point. But there is another.

Truman and Stalin, like all agents, acted out of a legacy which had been inherited from previous makers of history who had passed on ideas, institutions, and structures which had been transformed by still others, and so on. But, like all people, they had real choices. They could have made different and better decisions, and — what is more to the point — different and better possibilities are currently available to their successors. As Arthur M. Schlesinger Jr. puts it vis-à-vis Americans and their presidents:

When the American presidency conceives itself as the appointed savior of a world in which mortal danger requires the rapid and incessant deployment of men, weapons and decisions behind a wall of secrecy, power rushes from Capitol Hill to the White House. . . .
If America's mission is to redeem a fallen world, then the United

States must have a new constitution. And if a messianic foreign policy bursts the limits of our present Constitution, then the wisdom of the Framers is even greater than one could have imagined, for such a policy is hopeless on its merits and can only bring disaster to the American republic.[29]

But this is only part of the point: for one needs to add here — and add emphatically — that such a policy can only bring disaster to those peoples who continue to struggle to realize forms of self-rule. Indeed, we are now in the midst of a race between democracy and, because of the possibility of nuclear war, the destruction of human civilization. Hence we are all obliged to make choices which will foster and encourage democracy.

Notes

Introduction

1 Oxford: Basil Blackwell, 1987.
2 Barrington, Moore, *Injustice, The Social Basis of Obedience and Revolt* (White Plains, N.Y.: Sharpe, 1978), p. 500.

Part I War and Democracy in Ancient Greece Introduction

1 All references to Greek authors will be to the Loeb Classical Library editions (London: Heinemann). All citations of Herodotus are of his *History*, of Thucydides, his *History of the Peloponnesian War*, by book and chapter numbers; and of Plato and Aristotle, by title, book and chapter or page.

   With respect to *stasis*, consider also Herodotus: "*Stasis* is a thing as much worse than war ... as war itself is worse than peace" (VIII. 3). Thucydides concluded that "*stasis* gave birth to every form of wickedness in Greece" (III. 83); and an unknown pamphleteer of Larissa, writing just before Athens capitulated in that struggle, affirmed this, asserting that "war is conceded to be the greatest of all evils by as much as peace is the greatest of all blessings. Yet *stasis* as far exceeds war in the magnitude of its evil as war exceeds peace" (quoted from W. S. *Ferguson, Greek Imperialism* (Boston: Houghton Mifflin, 1913)).

   Greek terms and phrases, translations of which are often contestable, are given in this book in italics, without accents.

   A number of modern authors have considered various aspects of Greek *stasis*. See M. I. Finley, esp. his *Politics in the Ancient World* (Cambridge: Cambridge University Press, 1983) and "The Ancient Greeks and Their Nation," in *The Use and Abuse of History* (New York: Viking, 1971). He writes in the former that "the aim of *stasis* was to bring about a change in some law or arrangement, and any change meant a loss of rights, privileges, wealth to some group, faction, class, for whom the *stasis* was accordingly seditious. But from that standpoint all politics are seditious in any society in which there is a measure of popular participation, of freedom for political manoeuvring" (p. 106).

G. E. M. de Ste Croix's massive *The Class Struggle in the Ancient World* (Ithaca: Cornell University Press, 1981) is rich in scholarly detail and offers always sound judgments, but is burdened, I believe, by his effort to force matters into a somewhat reductionist class theory. I find quite the opposite weakness in Andrew Lintott, *Violence, Civil Strife and Revolution in the Classical City* (Baltimore: Johns Hopkins University Press, 1982), which identifies many instances of *stasis* and is thus a most useful compendium. However, Lintott's treatment suffers, in my view, from the absence of any sort of explanatory theory or comprehensive framework. He does shed some light on the etymology of *stasis*, though. While its primary meaning is "standing" or "place of standing," a posture or position, Lintott speculates that it may have come to mean civil strife "after being used to refer to a political faction, a position taken in politics" (p. 34).

Chapter 1   The Invention of Politics

1 I have found most useful in this regard Anthony Snodgrass, *Archaic Greece* (Berkeley: University of California Press, 1980). See also M. M. Austin and P. Vidal-Naquet, *Economic and Social History of Ancient Greece: An Introduction* (Berkeley: University of California Press, 1977), who write: "As a matter of fact the process of the emergence of the *polis* eludes us entirely and it could hardly be otherwise" (p. 51).

2 See M. I. Finley, *The World of Odysseus*, rev. edn. (New York: Viking, 1978).

3 As regards the critical question of the hoplite reform, I have essentially followed Paul Cartledge, "Hoplites and Heroes; Sparta's Contribution to the Technique of Ancient Warfare," *Journal of Hellenic Studies*, 97 (1977), a careful review and discussion of existing literature. For further discussion and references, see Snodgrass, "The Hoplite Reform and History," *Journal of Hellenic Studies*, 85 (1965), and *idem, Archaic Greece*.

4 Cartledge, "Hoplites and Heroes," pp. 15–16.

5 F. E. Adcock, *The Greek and Macedonian Art of War* (Berkeley: University of California Press, 1957), p. 7.

6 Cartledge, "Hoplites and Heroes," p. 18.

7 Ibid., p. 23.

8 Various elements of the Spartan configuration are found elsewhere – e.g., helotage in Crete and Thessaly – but the particular ensemble is substantially unique. The most detailed study of Sparta is that of Paul Cartledge, *Sparta and Lakonia: A Regional History 1300–362 BC* (London: Routledge and Kegan Paul, 1979), which replaces A. H. M. Jones, Sparta (Cambridge, Mass.: Harvard University Press, 1967), and W. G. Forrest, *A History of Sparta, 950–192 BC* (London: 1968). See also J. F. Lazenby, *The Spartan Army* (London: Aris and Phillips, 1985), and M. I. Finley's perceptive essay "Sparta," in *Use and Abuse*. Considerable debate remains about both the genesis of the Spartan *polis* and its constitution. See e.g. A. Andrewes, "The

Government of Classical Sparta," in E. Bawan (ed.) *Ancient Society and its Institutions* (Oxford: Basil Blackwell, 1966), and G. E. M. de Ste Croix's careful critique of Andrewe's's views in *The Origins of the Peloponnesian War* (Ithaca: Cornell University Press, 1972), pp. 124—51. The main problem, as noted earlier, is the lack of sources. They are scarcest prior to ca. 460, increasing dramatically thereafter. J. K. Davies has remarked that the choice is between "the risky creation of an interpretation and the stultifying regurgitation of what the surviving sources happen to say" (*Democracy and Classical Greece* (Hassocks: Harvester, 1978), pp. 95—6). Perhaps Finley has been the severest critique of the effort to write history under such conditions. See his "Myth, Memory and History," in *Use and Abuse.*

On helotage and slavery, see, in addition to the foregoing, Austin and Vidal-Naquet, *Economic and Social History*, Ancient pp. 86—91, 239—41, 251—4; Ste Croix, *Origins* pp. 89—93; Finley, *The Ancient Economy* (Berkeley: University of California Press, 1973), pp. 63—4; *idem*, "Was Greek Civilization Based on Slave Labor?" in *Economy and Society in Ancient Greece* (New York: Viking, 1981).

9   Cartledge, *Sparta and Lakonia*, pp. 178—80.
10   Ibid., p. 222.
11   Finley, "Sparta", p. 170.
12   The best overview of the early period is perhaps W. G. Forrest, *The Emergence of Greek Democracy* (New York: McGraw-Hill, 1966). See also Martin Ostwald, *Nomos and the Beginnings of Athenian Democracy* (Oxford: Clarendon Press, 1969). R. W. Connor, *The New Politicians of Fifth-Century Athens* (Princeton: Princeton University Press, 1971), is excellent for fifth-century Athenian domestic politics. A. H. M. Jones, *Athenian Democracy* (Oxford: Basil Blackwell, 1977) is excellent on the fourth century and on the social and economic structure of Athens. A more recent book is Mogens Herman Hansen, *The Athenian Assembly* (Oxford: Basil Blackwell, 1987).
13   Finley, *World of Odysseus*, p. 57. The point is that not only was a *thes* dependent, but worse, he was unattached, not part of any *oikos*. See also E. S. Stavely, *Greek and Roman Voting and Elections* (Ithaca: Cornell University Press, 1972). Stavely remarks, "Solon is unlikely to have taken the step of so radically altering the composition of a body which until his own time had been little more than the equivalent of the Homeric assembly of warriors" (p. 26). de Ste Croix suggests that *thetes* was used in Athens in a specialized sense to refer to "those who were too poor to be hoplites" (*Class Struggle*, p. 281).
14   Ostwald, *Nomos*, p. 159.
15   Snodgrass, *Archaic Greece*, p. 96.
16   Ibid. The point bears emphasis. We think of a tyranny as a regime which violates rights; but Aristotle saw it as a regime which ruled in its own interests rather the interests of those ruled (*Politics* III. 5). But originally the word seems to have referred to the mode of acquiring power, by usurpation. This sense remains in Marx's use of the term "dictatorship". See also de Ste Croix, *Class Struggle*, pp. 279—83. He quotes Glotz: "The people regarded tyranny only as an expedient. They used it as a battering-ram with which to demolish the citadel of the oligarchs, and when their end had been achieved

they hastily abandoned the weapon which wounded their hands" (*La Cité grècque* (Paris: 1928)).

17 Snodgrass, *Archaic Greece*, pp. 199–200.

18 Ivon Garlan, *War in the Ancient World: A Social History*, tr. Janet Lloyd (New York: Norton, 1975), is a very useful study, even though Garlan, like so many others, implies that war was the main feature of life in the *polis*. Sir Frank E. Adcock provides a corrective when he writes, "It is rash to assert, as has been done by some, that war was the permanent characteristic of all Greek communities" (F. E. Adcock and D. J. Mosely, *Diplomacy in Ancient Greece* (New York: St Martin's, 1975)). See also Adcock's brief, but extremely lucid, *The Greek and Macedonian Art of War* (Berkeley: University of California Press, 1957). Perhaps the most complete account of war in the ancient Greek world is W. K. Pritchard, The Greek State at War, 2 vols (Berkeley: University of California Press, 1971), which replaces Hans Delbruck, *History of the Art of War*, vol. 1, tr. Walter Renfroe (Westport, Conn.: Greenwood Press, 1975). A masterful history of the Greek trireme is given by J. S. Morrison and J. F. Coates, *The Athenian Trireme: The History and Reconstruction of an Ancient Greek Warship* (Cambridge: Cambridge University Press, 1986). A fine collection of maps and drawings may be found in Peter Connolly, *Greece and Rome at War* (Englewood Cliffs, N. J.: Prentice-Hall, 1981).

19 Athens, it should be noted, had long since lost its autarchy; Sparta never did. Aristotle agreed with Plato that Athens was an "over-swollen multitude." The idea that the *polis* was "territorarily inelastic" derives from Perry Anderson, *Passages From Antiquity to Feudalism* (London: NLB, 1974).

Chapter 2 War, *Stasis*, and Empire

1 J. B. Bury, *A History of Greece*, 3rd edn, rev. Russell Meiggs (London: Macmillan, 1951), ch. 6.

2 One gets some idea of this from a list of the "nations" which Xerxes assembled for his march on Greece. According to Herodotus, it included, in addition to Persians – "the Ten Thousand" – and Medes, Cissians, Hyrcanians, Assyrians, Bactrians, Sacae, Indians, Arians, Parthians, Chorasmians, Sogdians, Gandarians, Dadicae, Caspians, Sarangians, Pactyans, Utians, Mycians, Paricanians, Arabians, Ethiopians, Libyans, Paphlogonians, Phrygians, Armenians, Lydians, Mysians, Thracians, Cabalians, Milyans, Moschians, Tibarenians, Macronians, Mossynoecians, Mares, Colchians, Aloradians, Saspirians, and "islanders from the Red Sea" (VII. 61–80).

3 F. E. Adcock, *The Greek and Macedonian Art of War*, p. 12.

4 Ibid., p. 30.

5 See J. S. Morrison and J. F. Coates, *The Athenian Trireme*.

6 Jones, *Athenian Democracy*, pp. 8–9.

7 See esp. Russell Meiggs, *The Athenian Empire* (Oxford: Clarendon Press, 1972). See also Donald Kagan, *The Outbreak of the Peloponnesian War* (Ithaca: Cornell University Press, 1969), ch. 2.

8 Here I follow Ste Croix, *The Origins of the Peloponnesian War*, and Meiggs, *Athenian Empire*. Sealey offers a minority view in arguing that the purpose of

the alliance was "piratical" and neither emancipatory nor defensive. See his "The Origin of the Delian League," in E. Badian (ed.), *Ancient Society and its Institutions.*

9   My discussion draws on Ste Croix, *Origins*, pp. 298–307 and, regarding the Peloponnesian League, pp. 101–24. I know of no more detailed account of Greek symmachies.

10 Ste Croix, *Origins*, p. 36.

11 The famous Melian Dialogue (Thucydides, V. 84–113) raises many interesting problems and difficulties, which cannot be developed here; but Ste Croix's account (*Origins*, pp. 13–16) is an excellent place to begin. In general, I believe that it is an error to read the dialogue as proclaiming an Athenian defense of "might is right" or to hold that the dialogue establishes that Thucydides is an early Machiavellian. See also Jones, *Athenian Democracy*, pp. 65–7.

12 I follow in its essentials Ste Croix, *Origins*, which offers a penetrating critique of the views of those who hold that Athens wilfully provoked the war, that she was at least "morally the aggressor," or that Thucydides did not understand the "real forces" at work. The book has come in for considerable criticism as regards Ste Croix's most innovative interpretation, that of the Megarian Decree; but his main theses need not fall if this particular interpretation falls. For some references and discussion, see Ronald P. Legon, *Megara: The Political History of a Greek City-State to 336 B.C.* (Ithaca: Cornell University Press, 1981), esp. pp. 213–17.

For a different orientation, see Kagan, *Outbreak.* Kagan criticizes the view that the "bipolar" nature of the Greek world at that time made war inevitable. First, he argues that the Greek world was not bipolar, since Thebes and Corinth at least might have opted for an independent foreign policy. Second, he argues that both sides "allowed war to come" because each supposed that something could be gained "at a reasonable cost." In part, this is true – and important. Neither side could have predicted the costs. One must agree with his philosophical conclusion, that "the Peloponnesian War was not caused by impersonal forces, unless anger, fear, undue optimism, stubbornness, jealousy, bad judgment, and lack of foresight are impersonal forces. It was caused by men who made bad decisions in difficult circumstances. Neither the circumstances nor the decisions were inevitable" (p. 356).

13 See Ste Croix, *Origins*, esp. pp. 97–8 and 292. In speaking of the Peloponnesian League, Kagan remarks: "Fear of Argos, the other great Peloponnesian power, and fear of popular unrest which might result in the expulsion of oligarchies and the establishment of tyrannies provided these cities with a strong motive for accepting Spartan leadership" (*Outbreak* p. 11). Kagan, who agrees that Sparta's helot problem constrained its foreign policy, also says that "another problem continually affected the conduct of Spartan policy," its "mixed constitution," of which it was a "fine example." Thus, it produced "the rarest of flowers, political stability," a stability "which might appear to be the best guarantee of a consistent and well-conducted foreign policy" (ibid., p. 27). Political stability is indeed a "rare flower," but surely Kagan deludes himself if he supposes that it is always a virtue!

14 Ste Croix, *Origins*, p. 208.

15   Finley, *Politics in the Ancient World*, p. 74.
16   Ibid., p. 76.
17   Ferguson, *Greek Imperialism*, p. 61.
18   Finley, *Politics*, p. 54.
19   Hannah Arendt, *The Human Condition* (New York: Doubleday, 1959), p. 35.
20   Douglas M. MacDowell, *The Law in Classical Athens* (Ithaca: Cornell University Press, 1978), p. 40. As Jones points out, Athenian democrats would say that Aristotle and the conservatives got it backwards: "'Tyrannies and oligarchies', according to Aeschines, 'are governed by the ways of their governments, democratic cities by the established laws.' 'No one, I think, would assert', says Demosthenes, 'that there is any more important cause for the blessings which the city enjoys and for its being democratic and free, than the laws'" (*Athenian Democracy*, p. 53).
      In addition to MacDowell, *Law in Classical Athenes*, see M. Mion, "Athenian Democracy: Politicization and Constitutional Restraints," and B. Campbell, "Constitutionalism, Rights and Religion: The Athenian Example," both in *History of Political Thought*, 7 (1986).
21   Ostwald, *Nomos*, p. 87.
22   Jonés, *Athenian Democracy*, p. 17.
23   Finley asserts: "I hold the empire to have been a necessary condition for the Athenian type of democracy. Then, when the empire was forcibly dissolved at the end of the fifth century B.C., the system was so deeply entrenched that no one attempted to replace it, difficult as it was in the fourth century to provide the necessary financial underpinning" (*Democracy Ancient and Modern* (New Brunswick, N. J.: Rutgers University Press, 1972), pp. 49−50). See also *idem*, "The Athenian Empire: A Balance Sheet," in Finley, *Economy and Society in Ancient Greece*, where he writes that "the empire provided both the necessary cash and the political motivation" (p. 58). He there rejects Jones's claim, holding, as above, that "it is easily demonstrated that institutions often survive long after the conditions necessary for their introduction disappeared" (ibid., p. 258).
      The problem is clear enough. Finley may be right that the full flowering of democracy — "extreme democracy" — would not have happened in the absence of empire, so that in this sense, empire was "necessary." As I have been arguing, extreme democracy and empire were no doubt connected. But even if it was only social inertia that kept the system going after 404, it did keep going, which if nothing else shows that it could!
24   Finley, *Politics*, p. 36.
25   See Jones, *Athenian Democracy*, pp. 78−9. Finley, *Economy and Society*, p. 102, maintains that Jones's figures are too low. He estimates that for the peak periods in the fifth and fourth centuries, there were 60,000−80,000 slaves in Athens. It seems that most chattel slaves were non-Greeks, and that they were either victims of war, often between non-Greeks, or had been purchased. We should note too that some of the free adults were "metics," free aliens who were forbidden by a law of 451 from becoming citizens. There seems to be no reliable information on their numbers in the fifth century or in most of the fourth either. Jones reports that a census taken at the end of the fourth

century shows 21,000 citizens and 10,000 metics. We should also note that metics enjoyed full civil rights, except that they could not own land in Attica.

26 Finley, *The Ancient Economy*, p. 69.

27 Finley, *Economy and Society*, p. 114.

28 Jones, *Athenian Democracy*, p. 11.

29 Ste Croix, *The Class Struggle in the Ancient World*, pp. 116–17, rightly insists that the freedom of the propertied class was what Aristotle had in mind, that "free" meant literally free from all constraining toil, as opposed to "unfree," meaning "working for another's benefit." But that does no violence to the foregoing. To be sure, the ideal was no menial work at all (*scholia*); but the critical distinction was between self-directed work for oneself and other-directed work for others. Ste Croix later writes: "The essential fact which, in Aristotle's eyes, makes the hired man a less worthy figure than the ordinary artisan is not so much his comparative poverty (for many independent artisans are likely to be poor too) but his 'slavish' dependence upon his employer" (ibid., p. 184).

30 The problem of Socrates and of Plato and the Sophists is far too large to treat here. On the Sophists, see G. B. Kerferd, *The Sophist Movement* (Cambridge: Cambridge University Press, 1981), and Eric A. Havelock, *The Liberal Temper in Greek Politics* (New Haven: Yale University Press, 1957). George Grote's treatment remains valuable; see his *History of Greece* (London: Murray, 1888), vol. 7. A more conventional treatment is W. K. C. Guthrie, *The Sophists* (Cambridge: Cambridge University Press, 1971). For Socrates, see I. F. Stone, *The Trial of Socrates* (Boston: Little, Brown, 1988).

It is often said that the Greeks left no democratic theory. The Sophists may well have begun such; but, given that no writings survive from any of the Sophists and that we are so thoroughly dependent on Plato's hostile treatment of them, we can only guess. Nevertheless, Plato's *Protagoras* surely contains an incipient democratic theory, albeit turned inside out. While I have sympathy for the task that Ellen Meiksins Wood and Neal Wood have set themselves in their *Class Ideology and Ancient Political Theory* (Oxford: Basil Blackwell, 1978), I find their treatment both anti-historical and shrill. For a balanced review of Stone's book, see Jasper Griffin, "Stone's Philosopher," *Times Literary Supplement*, 7–13 Oct. 1988, p. 1104.

31 Aristotle reminds us of the lack of originality of Plato's conclusion when he writes: "That it is proper for the polis to be divided into castes and for the military class to be distinct from that of the tillers of the soil does not seem to be a discovery of political philosophers of today or one made recently" (*Politics*, VII. 9).

32 What, indeed, is wrong with a city "chock-full of liberty and freedom of speech" or a condition in which "everyone would arrange a plan for leading his own life that pleases him" or a form of constitution which "assigned a kind of equality indiscriminately to equals and unequals alike"? Aristotle concurs with this characterization of democracy and likewise disdains it. "For justice is supposed to be equality, and equality the rule of multitude, and liberty doing just what one likes. ... But this is bad" (*Politics*, V. 7).

33 M. I. Finley, "Plato and Practical Politics," in *Aspects of Antiquity*

(Harmondsworth: Penguin, 1972), p. 75. Finley would have agreed, I think, that our beliefs about "democracy" are mostly ideological. See his *Democracy Ancient and Modern.*

Part II   Early Modern War and State Formation   Introduction

1   See Michael Oakeshott, "On the Character of the Modern European State," in *On Human Conduct* (Oxford: Clarendon Press, 1975). For a discussion of the features of the "longue durée" and for specific detail, see Fernand Braudel, *The Mediterranean and the Mediterranean World in the Age of Phillip II*, 2 vols (New York: Harper Colophon, 1976). For an excellent overview, see Anthony Giddens, *The Nation-State and Violence* (Berkeley: University of California Press, 1985), ch. 1−4. Also very useful are the essays in Charles Tilly (ed.), *The Formation of National States in Europe* (Princeton: Princeton University Press, 1975), especially Tilly's "Reflections on the History of European State-Making" and Samuel E. Finer's "State- and Nation-Building in Europe, the Role of the Military."

2   Perry Anderson, *Lineages of the Absolutist State* (London: NLB, 1974), p. 48.

3   Braudel, *Mediterranean*, vol. 2, pp. 657−8.

Chapter 3   Machiavelli and the Imperative of Modern Politics

1   Quotations from *The Discourses* are from the Modern Library Edition, Christian E. Detmold tr. (New York: Random House, 1950), cited in the text by book and chapter.

2   This sketch of the early history of Rome appeals to a number of standard sources. A convenient overview is that of Michael H. Crawford, *The Roman Republic* (Cambridge, Mass.: Harvard University Press, 1982). See too, the much older treatment by M. Rostovtzeff, *Rome* (New York: Oxford University Press, 1960). More detail be found in R. Syme, *The Roman Revolution* (Oxford: Clarendon Press, 1939); P. A. Brunt, *Italian Manpower 225 B.C. − A.D. 14* (New York: Oxford University Press, 1971); Zwi Yavetz, *Plebs and Princeps* (Oxford: Clarendon Press, 1969); and Claude Nicolet, *The World of the Citizen in Republican Rome* (Berkeley: University of California Press, 1980), which provides a wealth of detail on the Roman "militia."

3   Crawford, *Roman Republic.*

4   Rostovtzeff, *Rome*, pp. 29−30.

5   Brunt (*Italian Manpower*) argues that in 225 BC, citizens and their families may have numbered 923,000 of the total population of 2,752,000. The census of the year 14 registered a civic population of 4,937,000, and Brunt estimates that this might be too low by as much as 20−25 percent. Regardless of the actual figures, "citizens" constituted somewhere between a fifth and a tenth of the total population of the empire.

6   Crawford, *Roman Republic*, p. 22. It is amazing how easy it has been to read Cicero as a defender of "democracy". This is mainly because it has been easy

to assume that Cicero's approval of Roman institutions which protect against "invasion of the rights of the people" — e.g. the tribunes of the plebs or the Lex Hortensa of 287 — amounted to an approval of democracy. But Cicero, whose *De Re Publica* was intended to be the Roman equivalent of Plato's *Politeia*, thought otherwise. Likewise, while Cicero could not be clearer on the motivation underlying the tribunate, a writer as sophisticated as G. H. Sabine can guilelessly remark, "Strangely enough, the tribunate is intended to play a repressive role, curbing the otherwise uncontrollable impulses of the commons" (Introduction to Cicero's *On the Commonwealth* (Library of Liberal Arts, Indianapolis: Bobbs-Merrill, 1929), p. 83). As Finley remarks, both *De Re Publica* and *De Legibus* are "filled with valuable explanations of the working and the 'spirit' of the Roman political system, notably of the ways in which the plebs were held so completely in check." But they also contain, if you will, a great deal of hot air; and it is this last, unfortunately, which still draws praise. For a brief assessment, see Finley, *Politics in the Ancient World*, pp. 127—9.

7 Quoted in William J. Bouwsma, *Venice and the Defense of Republican Liberty* (Berkeley: University of California Press, 1984), p. 52.

8 Ibid., p. 63. Bouwsma slips, revealingly, in remarking that "the spirit of the Venetian government was quite as important as the machinery of this admirable constitution" (p. 64). His own account suggests that what he should have said was "admired constitution."

9 Bouwsma, *Venice*, p. 95. See also Braudel, *The Mediterranean and the Mediterranean World in the Age of Phillip II*, vol. 2, ch. 4.

10 Machiavelli, *The Prince*, tr. Luigi Ricci, rev. E. R. P. Vincent (New York: Modern Library, 1940), ch. 26. See too, J. H. Hexter, *The Vision of Politics on the Eve of the Reformation: More, Machiavelli and Seyssel* (New York: Basic Books, 1973).

11 Quentin Skinner, *The Foundations of Modern Political Thought* 2 vols (Cambridge: Cambridge University Press, 1978), notes that Francesco Giucciardini (1483—1540) may have been the first to use the term. A Counter-Reformation Jesuit, Giovanni Botero, offered a clear statement of this doctrine in his *Della Ragion de Stato*, of 1589. Carl Friedrich, *Age of Baroque* (Ithaca: Cornell University Press, 1957) reports that it was defined somewhat later by Pietro A. Canonheiro as follows: "The reason of state is a necessary violation [*eccesso*] of the common law for the end of public utility (*per fine di publica utilita*)."

12 Neal Wood, Introduction to Machiavelli, *Art of War*, rev. edn. of the Farnsworth translation (Library of Liberal Arts, Indianapolis: Bobbs-Merrill, 1965), p. lix.

13 Isaiah Berlin, "The Problem of Machiavelli," *New York Review of Books*, 4 Nov. 1971, p. 26.

14 Carl J. Friedrich, *The Pathology of Politics* (New York: Harper and Row, 1972), p. 232. It should be noted that this book was published a year before Watergate.

15 Wood, pp. liv—v.

16 Felix Gilbert, "Machiavelli: The Renaissance of the Art of War," in Peter

Paret (ed.), *Makers of Modern Strategy: From Machiavelli to the Nuclear Age* (Princeton: Princeton University Press, 1986), p. 13.

17 Ibid., p. 14. See also Geoffrey Parker, *The Military Revolution* (Cambridge: Cambridge University Press, 1988), p. 17.

18 Machiavelli, *The Art of War*, p. 15.

19 Whether Roman legions were either "voluntary" or "temporary" is highly arguable. After 106 BC, the troops were probably all volunteers *and* full-time professionals; but this is *after* the period which Machiavelli idealizes. A Roman male was always liable, it seems, for military duty, up to the "retirement" age of sixty. The *dilectus* was not a mass levy, and in theory no one was obliged to serve in more than between sixteen and twenty "campaigns." But it is not clear what this meant in practice. While the army was basically a conscript force, comparable to a contemporary "selective service," the republic came to maintain a regular force, a standing army, as well (Nicolet, *Republican Rome*, p. 97).

20 Polybius reports that cavalrymen were the best paid, and that centurions (hoplite-type soldiers) received twice as much pay as light-armed infantry. I am not claiming of course, that these sums were in any way exorbitant; only that, as in the Hellenistic world when mercenaries came to dominate armies, paid service did constitute a livelihood. Caesar doubled the pay of his troops. But pay was perhaps the least of it; for certainly after the Second Punic War (218–01 BC), the troops received increasingly large amounts of distributed booty and, following victories, grants of double pay. Nicolet reproduces a table from Brunt which gives some approximations. Further, a "retired" soldier could hope for security, ideally on conquered land. Finally, from the Second Punic War onward, "some Roman soldiers were able to make a fortune out of trading." Indeed, "pillage and commerce were two complementary and interconnected methods of exchange and transfer of wealth" (Nicolet, *Republican Rome*, p. 121).

Yavetz shows that Caesar "did not discover any new means of dealing with Roman masses – he only changed the scale." See his excellent *Julius Caesar and his Public Image* (London: Thames and Hudson, 1983).

Machiavelli did not ignore these facts, as his account in Book V of *The Art of War* makes clear. But he painted a rosy picture, arguing, e.g., that *quaestors* ensured that booty was returned to the public treasury.

21 J. R. Hale, *War and Society in Renaissance Europe, 1450–1620* (Baltimore: Johns Hopkins University Press, 1986), p. 78. This is a very valuable book as regards the period and the problems treated.

Chapter 4 Monarchies, Despotisms, and Peaceful Republics

1 Most of these statistics come from William H. McNeill, *The Pursuit of Power* (Chicago: University of Chicago Press, 1982), pp. 110–11, and Finer, "State- and Nation-Building in Europe: The Role of the Military," in Tilly (ed.), *The Formation of National States in Europe*, p. 122. See too Hale, *War and Society in Renaissance Europe, 1450–1620*, ch. 9. My account is indebted to all three of

these excellent summaries of what are extremely complicated matters.

2 See Henry Guerlac, "Vauban: The Impact of Science on War," in Paret (ed.), *Makers of Modern Strategy*, and McNeill, *Pursuit of Power*, pp. 90—3.

3 McNeill, *Pursuit of Power*, p. 102.

4 Hale, *War and Society*, p. 70.

5 The preceding depends on Peter Blickle, *The Revolution of 1525*, introduction and translation by T. A. Brady Jr. and H. C. E. Midelfort (Baltimore: Johns Hopkins University Press, 1981). Perhaps the most remarkable of the mercenary entrepreneurs was Albrecht von Wallenstein, who during the Thirty Years' War raised an army of 50,000. Starting out as a petty nobleman, he acquired enormous properties and was "almost a sovereign in his own right" (McNeill, *Pursuit of Power*, p. 120).

6 This paragraph draws on Hale, *War and Society*. I make no effort here to try to identify the causes, whether, e.g., the war created the modern state or the other way round. This way of putting the question seems to me to be misconceived. Not only were the structural linkages between economy and polity not reducible, but developments in technology — e.g., in artillery and in ocean-going vessels — and organization — e.g., administrative competence — and the possibilities opened up by successful maritime exploration were complex and always subject to particular circumstances. For an excellent discussion, see Giddens, *The Nation-State and Violence*, ch. 4—7; Finer, "State-and Nation-Building in Europe," and Hale, *War and Society*, ch. 9. This is not to say, of course, that the foregoing agree on all the salient issues. Questions of causal primacy at critical junctures become important.

7 McNeill, *Pursuit of Power*, p. 130. See also Gunther E. Rothenberg, "Maurice of Nassau, Gustavus Adolphus, Raimondo Montecuccoli, and the 'Military Revolution' of the Seventeenth Century," in Paret (ed.), *Makers of Modern Strategy*.

8 McNeill, *Pursuit of Power*, p. 133.

9 Rothenberg, "'Military Revolution' of the Seventeenth Century," p. 47.

10 Lawrence Stone, *The Causes of the English Revolution, 1529—1652* (New York: Harper, 1972), p. 141.

11 Richard H. Kohn, *The Eagle and the Sword: The Federalists and the Creation of the Military Establishment in America, 1783—1802* (New York: Free Press, 1975), p. 4.

12 R. R. Palmer, "Frederick the Great, Guibert, Bulow: From Dynastic to National War," in Paret (ed.), *Makers of Modern Strategy*, p. 97. There were, of course, deep structural differences between the Prussian and English cases. For further detail and discussion of these, see Anderson, *Lineages of the Absolutist State*, pp. 113—41 and 236—78.

13 Finer, "State- and Nation-Building in Europe," p. 138. The foregoing paragraph draws on Finer.

14 Montesquieu, *The Spirit of the Laws*, tr. Thomas Nugent (New York: Hafner, 1966) Bk XVIII, ch. 11. Hereafter, citations from Montesquieu are abbreviated and are from *The Spirit* unless otherwise indicated. I have discussed Montesquieu's conception of a social science in my *A History and Philosophy of the Social Sciences* (New York and Oxford: Basil Blackwell, 1987).

15   John Dewey, *The Public and Its Problem's* (Chicago: Swallow Press, 1927), p. 41.

16   Anderson notes that Montesquieu's very sophisticated theorization of this prejudice was further influential, carrying through to Marx and Engels, whence it became part of the belief system of German Social Democracy. In 1914 the prejudice bore fruit. Anderson's account of "Oriental despotism" is not only stimulating from a historical point of view, but analytically important as well. See *Lineages*, pp. 463–73.

17   Montesquieu solved his problem and saved his classification easily; he merely rejected the testimony of the Jesuit missionaries! For some discussion, see Walter Watson, "Montesquieu and Voltaire on China," *Comparative Civilizations Review*, 2 (Spring 1979).

18   J. H. Plumb, *The Origins of Political Stability: England, 1675–1725* (Boston: Houghton Mifflin, 1967), p. 69.

19   J. R. Pole, *Political Representation in England and the Origins of the American Republic* (London: Macmillan, 1966), p. 408.

20   Ibid., p. 402.

21   John Plamenatz, *Man and Society*, vol. 1 (London: Longmans, 1963), argues that Montesquieu "understood how England was governed much better than those who accuse him of making a gross mistake about the English system imagine" (p. 283).

22   This is not the place to develop the problems associated with "mixed constitutions." There are a number of different issues, which are usually, and confusingly, conflated. It is necessary to distinguish between theories which look at abstraet functions of government, the fusion and separation of powers (e.g., Montesquieu and the American Federalists), theories whose primary concern is the mix of status and class groupings in society (e.g., in the writings of Harrington and sometimes Aristotle), and finally, theories like Aristotle's and Polybius's which assume a *polis* form of constitution and mix institutions from the three "pure" forms of rule by one, a few, and many. Failure to see the difference between a mixed constitution in a *polis* and a mixed constitution in a modern state has led to enormous confusion. Montesquieu's theory is well analyzed by Louis Althusser, *Politics and History* (London: NLB, 1972).

23   See John Locke, *Two Treatises of Government: A Critical Edition with an Introduction and Apparatus Criticus* (New York: Mentor, 1965). Laslett's introduction to this edition is valuable. See also John Dunn, *The Political Thought of John Locke: An Historical Account of the Argument of the 'Two Treatises of Government'* (Cambridge: Cambridge University Press, 1969). See below n. 25.

24   The question of whether there is a useful sense in which it can be said that ancient polities experimented with "representative government" has been disputed. There are many examples of "representative machinery," such as the *boule* or council in Athens. However, it is misleading to use the term "representative government" so broadly as to include ancient polities. Although J. A. O. Larsen entitles his book *Representative Government in Greek and Roman History* (Berkeley: University of California Press, 1955), he emphasizes that "the

antithesis of representative government is direct government," and that "this is something that the modern state at times tries to secure through the use of initiative and referendum." "The Greek and Roman city-state, on the contrary, secured direct government by the use of primary assemblies in which all adult, active, male citizens had a right to take part" (p. 2). This is absolutely critical.

25 Since what made a government "rightful" (legitimate) was a function of the *source* of its authority, "oligarchy," as well as hereditary and elective monarchy, could be rightful. Thus "the Community" may place the power of making and executing laws "into the hands of a few select Men, and their Heirs and Successors ... or else into the hands of one Man ...; if to him and his heir, it is an Hereditary Monarchy; if to him only for life, but upon his Death the Power of nominating a Successor to return to them; an Elective Monarchy" (*Second Treatise*, X. para. 132). See also XIX. para. 213, where Locke considers the government of England.

26 Edmund Burke, *Thoughts on the Cause of the Present Discontents* (1770); quoted in Pole, *Political Representation*, p. 442.

27 Pole, *Political Representation*, p. 412.

28 Plumb, *Origins*, p. 29.

29 David Hume, *Essays, Moral, Political and Literary* (London: Oxford University Press, 1963), pp. 259–74.

30 Montesquieu *Considerations of the Causes of the Greatness of the Romans and Their Decline*, tr. David Lowenthal (Ithaca: Cornell University Press, 1968) ch. 9. See also Lowenthal, "Montesquieu and the Classics: Republican Government in The Spirit of the Laws," in Joseph Cropsey (ed.), *Ancients and Moderns* (Chicago: Rand McNally, 1964). Lowenthal's discussion has influenced the present account.

31 See J. H. Parry, *The Establishment of European Hegemony, 1415–1715* (New York: Harper, 1965).

Part III Modern War and Modern Democracy Introduction

1 See Robert R. Palmer's valuable *The Age of Democratic Revolution*, 2 vol (Princeton: Princeton University Press, 1969). Palmer is not entirely comfortable with this label, and rightly so. He acknowledges that the revolutionaries were not "democrats," a coinage unknown before the 1780s. Indeed, even when it was used, this term was almost always a term of abuse. "Democracy" is used by Palmer, misleadingly in my view, as a term that contracts with "aristocracy." Overall, however, I would see the revolutions of the period as *liberal* revolutions even though they included radical elements which were democratic but had been co-opted and submerged.

2 Joyce Appleby has written that it was "one of the great ironies" of American history that "those gentlemen who supported the [United States] Constitution because they wanted to remove power from the local level where it was exposed to manipulation by popular majorities actually created the national forum that made possible the democratization of American politics" (*Capitalism*

and a New Social Order: The Republican Vision of the 1790s (New York and London: New York University Press, 1984), p. 76). The unintended consequences of decisions made by anti-democrats created democracy!

3 See Charles Beard, *An Economic Interpretation of The Constitution of the United States* (New York: Macmillan 1913); Jackson Turner Main, *The Anti-Federalists (Chapel Hill, N.C.: 1961); Merrill Jensen, The New Nation: A History of the United States during the Confederation 1781–1789* (New York: Knopf, 1950); Gordon Wood, *The Creation of the American Republic, 1776–1787* (New York: Norton, 1969); William Appleman Williams, *The Contours of American History* (New York: Wm Morrow, 1971).

Chapter 5   The American War of Independence

1 The following relies heavily on Don Higginbotham, *The War of American Independence: Military Attitudes, Policies and Practice, 1763–1789* (Bloomington: Indiana University Press, 1971).

2 The view, still popular in the United States, that all the virtue was on the American side derives from the authoritative work of George Bancroft, *History of the Formation of the Constitution of the United States of America* (1882). This view rests on the notion that George III was a tyrant, as the Declaration so dramatically attempted to detail. While brilliant polemically, most of the particular charges of the Declaration were either false or distorted. The pro-American interpretation has been corrected by Lawrence Gipson, *The Coming of the Revolution, 1763–1776* (New York: Harper and Row, 1954). Gipson argues that the King and Parliament were not guilty of tyranny, that they were pursuing a justified imperial policy, which, by virtue of altered expectations on the part of the colonists, led inevitably to conflict. Thus Britain had to reorganize its administration so that the colonists would contribute to the unprecedented war debt and to maintaining imperial security in North America. However, precisely because the redcoats had succeeded in North America, the colonists were relieved of the pressures on their borders and thus "felt impelled to demand greater autonomy than ever" (ibid., xi). Further complicating matters is the pertinence of domestic politics, in both Britain and the Colonies. A provocative review is Edmund S. Morgan's "Revisions in Need of Revising," repr. in his *The Challenge of the American Revolution* (New York: Norton, 1976).

3 Morgan "Conflict and Consensus," in his *Challenge*, p. 182. These facts were also critical as regards the possibility of a more democratic political order than the one which was in fact realized after the Constitution had been ratified. See next chapter.

Higginbotham points out that the fact that the revolutionaries were "haves" and not "have-nots" affected military policy – e.g., the decision not to burn New York when Washington was forced to evacuate. Moreover, "the opinion of many pessimistic colonists that the fabric of American life would be ripped apart explains their espousal of loyalism. Congress determined this should not happen, and Washington shared its resolution" (*War of American Independence*, pp. 160–1). Again, compare twentieth-century wars of liberation.

4   See Walter Millis, *Arms and Men: A Study in Military History* (New York: Capricorn, 1956), who comments: "The citizen who, as a citizen rather than a mercenary, bore arms in the state's service was establishing new claims upon the state and new power over its institutions" (p. 27).
5   Higginbotham, *War of American Independence*, p. 7.
6   Ibid.
7   Ibid., p. 159.
8   Ibid., p. 169.
9   Ibid., p. 197.
10 Quoted from ibid., p. 392.
11 On the other hand, as Millis has remarked, "it was the militia which presented the greatest single impediment to Britain's only practical weapon, that of counter-revolution" (*Arms and Men*, p. 34).
12 Higginbotham, *War of American Independence*, p. 181.
13 Ibid., p. 184. Why this "mirage" persisted in British minds may be explained relatively easily; but it is less easy to explain why leaders of modern states, who send foreign troops off to "liberate" peoples who have succeeded in bringing about a revolution or who have been prevented from doing so have been taken in by similar mirages.

    Worth noting here is the number of refugees, loyalists who chose to leave the Colonies. Estimates run as high as 100,000, but Palmer more conservatively judges 60,000. There were about 2,500,000 people in America at this time, perhaps one-fifth of whom were slaves. If we exclude these, the ratio is 30 emigrés per 1,000. In France, by contrast, the population numbered some 25,000,000, and the refugees numbered 129,000, including 25,000 clergy who were deportees rather than emigrés. With these excluded, the ratio was 4 emigrés per 1,000. And this with the Terror!

    Palmer uses similar numbers to argue that since dislocation is a reasonable measure of revolution, the American Revolution was a genuine one. On the other hand, it has been observed that the American ratios are the highest ever, even including twentieth-century wars of national liberation! This should chasten one's judgments about the latter. The distribution of wealth (and the nature and distribution of the relevant classes) would have a bearing on these comparative numbers. But of course, so do other factors, including ideology and the amount of assistance provided to potential emigrés.
14 Higginbotham, *War of American Independence*, p. 119.
15 Ibid., p. 262.
16 Ibid., pp. 330–1. For the Indians, the critical fact was the uncontrolled western expansion (west of the Allegheny divide to western Pennsylvania, Ohio, and western New York), formally prohibited by Britain after 1763. The British had both commercial interests in the frontier and responsible people concerned with Indian affairs, including Indian Superintendent Sir William Johnson. As Francis Jennings puts the matter,

> Johnson's appointment [in 1756] signified more than an effort to manage Indian affairs with greater competence; it was the beginning of substantial change in the constitution of empire. Previously the colonies had been under the Crown's protection and the Indians under the

colonies' protection – or at their mercy. Johnson represented not only the Crown's assumption of administration over Indian affairs, but also the extension of the Crown's protection directly to the tribes. ("The Indians' Revolution," in Alfred F. Young (ed.), *The American Revolution* (DeKalb: Northern Illinois University Press, 1976), p. 332)

But of course, as Jennings argues, if "the colony-states fought for independence from the Crown, the tribes had to fight for independence from the states" (ibid., p. 322). See Jennings' book *The Invasion of America: Indians, Colonialism, and the Cant of Conquest* (Chapel Hill: University of North Carolina Press, 1975). I return to this problem in the next chapter.

17   Higginbotham, *War of American Independence*, p. 52.

18   Ibid., p. 198.

19   Palmer, *Age of Democratic Revolution*, p. 197. One does not need to deny the revolutionary character of this process in order to affirm that there was no *social* revolution in America. For some discussion of this see, ibid., pp. 185–206.

20   Quoted in Jack N. Rakove, *The Beginning of National Politics: An Interpretative History of the Continental Congress* (New York: Knopf, 1979), p. 69. Although I reject Rakove's overarching effort to provide a convincing "nationalist" interpretation, I have learned much from him.

21   Ibid., p. 288.

22   Ibid., p. 208.

23   Ibid. See also Higginbotham, *War of American Independence*, ch. 12. He remarks, "A backward glance enables us to see that if Congressional authority was weak, the same was true of state authority." Geography, hamstrings on the governors – the outcome of legislative supremacy – and the absence of an effective civil service all contributed to this.

24   Rakove, *Beginnings*, p. 145.

25   Ibid., p. 160.

26   Quoted in ibid., p. 166.

27   Quoted in ibid., p. 267.

28   The best account of the history of the idea of sovereignty is to be found in Skinner, *The Foundations of Modern Political Thought*, vol. 2, ch. 8. Transforming the ancient concept of *imperium*, as developed by Chasseneuz and Moulin, Bodin was probably the first to treat "the doctrine of non-resistance as an analytical implication of sovereignty" and to hold that "sovereignty must be fundamentally legislative in character" (pp. 287–8). An exceptional analytical account of the by now much confused concept of sovereignty may be found in W. J. Rees, "The Theory of Sovereignty Restated," in Peter Laslett (ed.), *Philosophy, Politics and Society*, 1st ser. (Oxford: Basil Blackwell, 1967). Rees's account influences what follows.

29   Rakove, *Beginnings*, p. 167.

30   Ibid., p. 185.

31   The obscurity of the current discussion is nowhere better indicated than in Richard B. Morris's suggestion that

> The adoption of Burke's amendment does not necessarily mean that the Articles endorsed a "compact" view of the formation of the Union, in which the states agreed to confederate and delegate limited aspects

of their sovereignty to a central government. Rather, since the Articles recognized in Congress exclusive authority over peace and war ... [it] may be read as simply retaining in the states all aspects of internal sovereignty not expressly delegated to the United States. "The Forging of the Union Reconsidered: A Historical Refutation of State Sovereignty Over Seabeds." (*Columbia Law Review*, 74 (1974), p. 1057).

If the reader has lost the force of the difference between a "compact" view and the creation of a national government, he may be further discouraged to notice that Rakove writes that his rejection of a "states'-rightest interpretation," the main theme of his valuable book, is "essentially consistent" with the view just quoted from Morris, a view endorsed, he remarks, by Samuel Beer, "Federalism, Nationalism and Democracy in America," *American Political Science Review*, 72 (1978).

Rakove asserts that "in addition to congressional prerogatives over war and diplomacy, the procedures used to authorize the creation of new governments in 1775–6 clearly demonstrate that sovereign powers were vested in Congress from the beginning, and that emerging provincial regimes were regarded as subordinate bodies" (p. 174n). The fact that Congress had prerogatives over war and diplomacy and so was "sovereign" in this sense does not prove what Rakove supposes. The states were "subordinate" as regards war, as would be expected in *any* confederation. It seems unlikely that he intends by the remainder of his remark that the Congress created the states and that their authority derived from its authority. Yet this is exactly the view recently developed by Morris in his book *The Forging of the Union, 1781–1789* (New York: Harper and Row, 1987). See next chapter.

Eighteenth-century political thinkers could not, of course, read into their understanding future developments, especially the total absence of a viable confederation in the modern world. While they had a deeper knowledge of ancient political institutions and contemporaneous political theory than we do we may find it difficult to believe that they believed what they said they believed!

32 Rakove, *Beginnings*, p. 279.
33 Ibid., p. 281.
34 E. James Ferguson, *The Power of the Purse: A History of American Public Finance, 1776–1790* (Chapel Hill: University of North Carolina Press, 1961), p. 244. This portion draws considerably on Ferguson's outstanding account. On the other hand, my conclusions regarding the Morris program seem closer to those of Rakove. Rakove writes: "Neither in 1777 nor in 1781 did congressional leaders presume that the Articles were meant to reduce Congress to a choice between solvency and a precarious balance on the voluntary gifts of states ... In seeking independent sources of revenue, the delegates were asking the states to enable Congress to discharge its acknowledged responsibilities" (*Beginnings*, p. 306). But, to repeat, this is no argument that from the beginning, Congress constituted a national government. Indeed, it suggests quite the opposite, that the thirteen states formed a confederation for purposes of fighting a common enemy. Both Rakove and Ferguson read the period in terms of the Constitution. Ferguson is correct in

holding that "the power of the purse was [to eighteenth-century Americans] the determinant of sovereignty and upon its location and extent depended the power of government" (*Power of the Purse*, pp. xiv−xv). This perception was critical and explains much of the controversy. But one cannot assume that the "nationalists," (*alias* Federalists), had all the clarity on their side. See next chapter.

35 Elbridge Gerry summarized the "republican" view thus: "If we have no standing army, the Militia, which has ever been the dernier Resort to Liberty, may become respectable, and adequate to our Defense ... but if a regular army is admitted, will not the Militia be neglected, and gradually dwindle into Contempt? and where are we to look for Defence of our Rights and Liberties?" (quoted by Higginbotham, *War of American Independence*, p. 444). As it happened, the United States got neither what Washington wanted nor what Gerry wanted: instead, it got the worst of all possible worlds! The best treatment of the pertinent issues, to which the foregoing owes a considerable debt, is in Richard H. Kohn, *Eagle and Sword*, esp. ch. 3 and 7.

36 Bernard Bailyn, *The Ideological Origins of the American Revolution* (Cambridge, Mass.: Harvard University Press, 1967), p. 164.

37 J. R. Pole, *Political Representation in England and the Origins of the American Republic*, ch. 3; Jack P. Greene, "The Role of the Lower Houses of Assembly in Eighteenth Century Politics," *Journal of Southern History*, 27 (1961).

38 Letter to James Sullivan, 26 May 1776; in *The Works of John Adams*, 10 vol (Boston: Charles C. Little and James Brown, 1856) vol. 9.

39 Gordon Wood, *The Creation of the American Republic, 1776−1787*, pp. 173−96; Morgan, "Colonial Ideas of Parliamentary Power," in Morgan, *Challenge*. The American idea of proportional representation begins to make sense when one assumes that individuals are to be represented. Similarly, the idea, also new to the period, that, as James Wilson put it, "the legislature ought to be the most exact transcript of the whole society," a miniature of the society writ large, makes sense where actual participation is considered desirable but has given way to "representatives."

40 Extensive documentation that Montesquieu was the point of departure for almost every figure writing in the United States between 1748 and 1789 is provided by Paul Merrill Spurling, *Montesquieu in America, 1760−1801* (Baton Rouge: Louisiana State University Press, 1940). John Adams read *Spirit* in 1760 and pledged "to write, in the margins, a sort of index to every paragraph" (ibid., p. 88). Samuel Adams and James Madison had memorized Montesquieu. Madison wrote in a letter to Jefferson of 1793, "I use Montesquieu also, from memory, tho' I believe, without inaccuracy" (ibid., p. 90). Jefferson read *Spirit* between 1774 and 1776 and copied extensive amounts of it into his common-place book. Significantly, he omitted altogether text and references to Bk XI, ch. 6, Montesquieu's famous discussion − and approbation − of the Constitution of England. This section, repeatedly cited in debates of the period, was copied verbatim in Adams' *Defense of the Constitutions of the United States* (1787). These facts provide important evidence for a major thesis of the next chapter. For the eighteenth-century "republican," Bk XI, ch. 6, was the best in Montesquieu; for the democrat who hankered

after a version of the ancient republic extended over a large territory, it was the worst in Montesquieu.

41 Wood, *Creation*, ch. 8. See also Main, *The Anti-Federalists*, pp. 104ff. Charles Carroll offered the opinion, by this time a commonplace among literate eighteenth-century men, that the Americans "will be ruined, not so much by the calamities of the war, as by the intestine divisions and bad govern[men]ts wh[ich] I foresee will take place in most of the United States: they will be simple Democracies, of all govern[men]ts the worst, and will end as all other Democracies have, in despotism" (cited by Rakove, *Beginnings*, p. 121).

42 See Hannah Fenichel Pitkin, *The Concept of Representation* (Berkeley: University of California Press, 1967).

43 The text is by an anonymous contributor to the *Maryland Journal* of February 1787, quoted from Melvin Yazawa (ed.), *Representative Government and the Revolution: The Maryland Constitutional Crisis of 1787* (Baltimore: Johns Hopkins University Press, 1975), p. 20. Most of the pertinent documents are collected in this volume, which is the source of the quotations which follow.

A stunning feature of this particular debate is the fact that Chase and Paca were land speculators in heavy debt. Their very special interests, accordingly, led them to make "democratic" arguments probably despite themselves, judging by their later behavior. As Morris points out, "contrary to tradition as Populist-Progressive historians would depict it, [the creditors-debtors] division was neither geographical nor a clear-cut alignment of the rich against the poor" (Morris, *Forging of the Nation*, p. 155).

44 Quoted from Wood, *Creation*, pp. 373ff. The text perfectly illustrates the transitional nature of the key ideas. How many Americans would say today that the president *rules* them, even if in concert with Congress? Compare also, of course, Rousseau: "The people of England regards itself as free: but it is grossly mistaken: it is free only during the election of members of parliament. As soon as they are elected, slavery overtakes it, and it is nothing" (*Social Contact* (New York: Dutton, 1950) Bk III, ch. 15).

45 "Class interests" arguments are as unnecessary as they are unhelpful. In the first place, as Morris notes, the division of interests was not as clear-cut as one might like to suppose. Second, it is true – and important – that there accrued an enormous concentration of paper money; but, as Ferguson shows, it cannot be argued that, in order to profit, these individuals conspired to end the Confederation. Perhaps 100 individuals held $5,000,000 in securities, and another $2,600,000 was subscribed by another 170. Perhaps no more than 15,000–20,000 held public securities of some $40,000,000. But this happened during the 1780s as the outcome of capitalist tendencies. Speculators did not buy securities in anticipation of federal funding at profitable rates. There was far too much uncertainty for that.

Similarly, the movement toward democracy was diffuse, even if it was real enough. Elites surely perceived it, and clearly it caused them enormous anxiety. When this is coupled with the plain economic advantages which the new order gave the rich, it is easy to see why the class perspective has the appeal it has. From the present point of view, "class interest" views depend on the assumption that there is always some simple correspondence between a class relation, "objective interests," and perceived interests. But outside some simple model, Beard's or the model of Marx's *Capital*, reality is rarely so neat. See my *A History and Philosophy of the Social Sciences*.

It is idle to replace this with some sort of "dialectic of virtue and commerce." See Isaac Kramnick's valuable bibliographical essay "English Middle Class Radicalism in the Eighteenth Century" in *Literature of Liberty*, 3 (1980), pp. 5–48, and Jeffrey Isaac, "Republicanism and Liberalism: A Reexamination," *History of Political Thought*, 9 (Summer 1988), pp. 349–77.

Chapter 6   The Invention of Modern Democracy

1   For discussion of the overall economic situation, see E. James Ferguson, *The Power of the Purse*; Merrill Jensen, *The New Nation*; and the balanced account in Richard B. Morris, *The Forging of the Union, 1781–1798*, ch. 6.

2   Rakove comments: "Despite occasional gloomy outbursts, few American leaders believed that the new nation was actually poised on the brink of crisis. After eight years of war and the turbulence of the pre-revolutionary years, it was scarcely surprising that most Americans showed little interest in public affairs" (*The Beginnings of National Politics*, p. 365). Although this is a most welcome corrective, Rakove may have gone too far here. Certainly the level of political activity fell sharply after the cessation of hostilities; but it is not easy to make comparative judgments. Compare here Gordon Wood's otherwise fine discussion of political activity prior to and during the war, which is easy to misread. See *The Creation of the American Republic, 1776–1787*, ch. 3, "Conventions of the People." First, Wood's "state of nature" motif is dangerous; the discovery by people of their own agency is not identical with "anarchy." Second, and more important, it is easy to blur the first years of this period, the seventies, with the years following the end of hostilities.

3   Rakove, *Beginnings*, p. 381.

4   Ibid., p. 390.

5   Ferguson, *Power of the Purse*, p. 245.

6   Morris, *Forging of the Union*, p. 264. In writing that "the ratification of the federal Constitution seems to have laid a basis of economic recovery," Morris implies that the recovery would not have occurred had the existing arrangements prevailed. But we shall never know, of course. Still, if any inference is possible – and perhaps Morris would not disagree with this – the new arrangements as such seem to have had little to do with the recovery.

7   The first of these was George R. Minot, clerk of the Massachusetts lower house, who wrote a *History of the Insurrection in Massachusetts in 1786*. James Wilson, Nathaniel Chipman, Nathan Dance, Joseph Story, and George Ticknor also offered versions of the rebellion. Curtis wrote, "The Constitution of the United States was the means by which republican liberty was saved from the consequences of impending anarchy" (cited from Robert B. Morris, "The Confederation Period and the American Historian," *William and Mary Quarterly*, 13 (1956), repr. in S. Fine and G. S. Brown (eds), *The American Past*, vol. 1 (New York: Macmillan, 1961).

Morris notes that it was probably, William Henry Trescot who, in 1857, coined the term "critical period" ("Confederation Period," p. 163). Richard Frothingham (1872) and H. von Holst (translated 1899–92) affirmed the idea, as did Bancroft in his 1882 history. It is the philosopher John Fiske, however, who seems to have fixed the idea indelibly with his 1888 *The Critical Period of American History, 1783–1789*. Morris, on whom I rely here, points out that while academic historians have gone in for abusing Fiske as "showing almost no evidence of first-hand acquaintance with the sources," the issue concerns the validity of his synthesis which, undeniably, "had enormous impact both upon the public and upon fellow historians" (p. 165), including, to be sure, Fiske's "professional" critics.

There have been dissenters from the conventional view regarding the impending "anarchy," including in the nineteenth century, the military historian Henry B. Dawson (1871), the "political scientists" J. Allen Smith (1907) and Arthur Bentley (1908), and a number of writers inspired by Charles Beard's *An Economic Interpretation of the Constitution*, including Merrill Jensen, whose work is most valuable.

Morris summarizes one aspect of the issue in concluding that "in truth, the real difference between the nationalist and Antifederalist schools of historiography turns neither on the extent of the depression nor on the amount of anarchy in the 'critical period,' but springs from a deep divergence in interpreting the American Revolution and the issues for which it was fought" ("Confederation Period," p. 171). Morris argues that because the radicals were not engaged in an "internal revolution" and because democratic forces did not seize control originally, there could be no "counter-revolution" in 1787 by antidemocrats. This seems true enough; but what is missing here is an acknowledgment that the idea of a "crisis" was largely the invention of contemporary "nationalists" and then of conservative historians, who understandably wished to celebrate the Constitution. What would have been the meaning of the period had the convention at Philadelphia failed to take place or to acquire legitimacy? What if the Virginia Plan had not been ratified, or if the New Jersey Plan (discussed below) had been adopted? The period between 1781 and 1787 would have had an entirely different meaning. Yet any of these was possible.

8   Pole, *Political Representation in England and the Origins of the American Republic*, p. 228.

9   Ibid., p. 229.

10   Cited from Paul A. Varg, *Foreign Policies of the Founding Fathers* (East Lansing: Michigan State University Press, 1963), p. 49. Varg asserts: "The most conspicuous failure of the Confederation was in meeting challenges from abroad. In the realm of domestic affairs Congress and the state governments performed reasonably well" (ibid., p. 46). We can agree that in the realm of domestic affairs, Congress performed well enough. Was the "crisis" then a crisis in foreign policy? Surely not. To be sure, Varg does not hold that it was, although he argues that "foreign affairs played a major rule in undermining the Articles of Confederation and contributed in an important way to the movement that led to the Constitution of 1787" (ibid.). Most probably the Confederation as constituted could not solve all these problems. But it does not follow, as almost everyone assumes, that the only or the best alternative

was the new Constitution. A *strengthened* Confederation might have succeeded – and have been more democratic.

11   One does not need to be cynical to appreciate the wheeling and dealing of some notables over the possibility of exploiting these vast acres. For some discussion, see Samuel Eliot Morison, *The Oxford History of the American People* (New York: Oxford University Press, 1965), pp. 196–7. Benjamin Franklin was party to the Vandalia Company, which, just before the Revolution, set as its goal the acquisition of some 10 million acres "for which they proposed to pay the Crown £10,000." See also Peter S. Onuf, *The Origins of the Federal Republic: Jurisdictional Controversies in the United States, 1775–1787* (Philadelphia: University of Pennsylvania Press, 1983).

12   Onuf, *Origins*, p. 5. Onuf's useful book is seriously burdened by his assumption that because the states did not act like "true states," the Constitution was "truly an unremarkable achievement." Onuf, like almost everyone else, fails to see the enormous differences in possible consequences of alternative "articulations" and "embodiments" of the widely shared view that America was a "community of states" (ibid., p. 172). He sees that Jefferson had in mind an equally "complicated" alternative for a new union, but chides Jefferson for being "trapped by an outmoded and highly abstract theory of the union" (ibid., p. 168). Such is the power of Federalist ideology.

13   *Notes of Debates, in the Federal Convention of 1787 Reported by James Madison* with an introduction by Adrienne Koch (New York: Norton, 1966), p. 165.

14   Rakove, *Beginnings*, ch. 15 treats these themes beautifully.

15   Ibid., p. 377.

16   Morris, *Forging of the Union*, p. 269.

17   Rakove, *Beginnings*, pp. 398–9.

18   Madison, *Notes of Debates*, p. 35. Subsequent page references are given in the text in parentheses.

19   The matter of "dual jurisdiction" is irrelevant. James Wilson was "tenacious" with regard to preserving the state governments and argued that "they were absolutely necessary for certain purposes" (ibid., pp. 151–2). K. C. Wheare has said that "what the authors of *The Federalist* claimed for the Constitution of 1787 was not that it substituted a federation for a league but that it substituted an efficient federation for an inefficient federation" (*Federal Government*, 4th edn (New York: Oxford University Press, 1964), p. 11). Of course, this is what was claimed, but Wheare's endorsement of this claim cannot be excused.

20   In these first remarks, a rambling disquisition of some six hours, Hamilton felt obliged "to declare himself unfriendly to both plans." Critical for him was the absence of sufficient coercive power in *either* plan: "A certain portion of military force is absolutely necessary in large communities." With reference to Shay's Rebellion, an event to which he and others returned again and again, he noted that "Mass[achusetts] is now feeling this necessity and making provision for it. But how can this force be exerted on the States collectively? It is impossible" (ibid., p. 131).

This was a genuine argument, which may have been persuasive to many. If the states were to have their own military in order to maintain "domestic tranquility," then the arrangement woyld seem to "amount to a war between the parties." But we should take note of the assumptions underlying it. Here was an eighteenth-century American assuming that enforcing the laws of society required not merely civilian authority but an army! Shades of "banana republics"! See the account of *Federalist* No. 8 below. Moreover, "the extent of the Country to be governed discouraged him." While "he did not mean to shock the public opinion," the general government would be expensive, and a "great oeconomy [sic] might be obtained" by eliminating altogether the state governments (ibid., p. 134). The striking point, usually missed, is not that Hamilton had designs for a strong central government, which was fully realized in any case, but his view that there was no need for lower-level jurisdictions. This discussion took place before the modern state was fully realized, of course.

It was irrelevant that "piracy" was under the aegis of the Congress. Ships at sea were not within the jurisdiction of particular states, and the policing power was, thus, sensibly assigned to the Congress. The piracy point was picked up by Madison on the next day of the Convention (see ibid., p. 140).

By far the best account of Hamilton is that of Gerald Stourzh, *Alexander Hamilton and the Idea of Republican Government* (Stanford: Stanford University Press, 1970), a wonderful, yet little appreciated, book.

21 It is important to notice that, at least in Philadelphia, Madison's view was different from either Hamilton's or Wilson's. After the New Jersey Plan had been rejected, considerable attention was paid to the way in which the Virginia Plan proposed to treat the states. Many present believed that the latter required that incompatible principles be joined: legislation over states as political societies with legislation over individuals. At first, Madison argued that "too much stress was laid on the rank of the States as political societies. There is a gradation ... from the smallest corporation, with the most limited powers, to the largest empire with the most perfect sovereignty .... [T]he limitations on sovereignty of the States, as now confederated[,] their laws in relation to the paramount law of the Confederacy were analogous to that of bye laws to the supreme power within a State" (*Notes of Debates*, p. 213). Madison was correct in holding, in effect, that sovereignty *could* be divided; but this particular view of the Confederation was manifestly false. "The supreme law" was not in the Congress. Indeed, if it had been, one would wonder what the Convention was all about!

In any case, Madison seems to have concluded subsequently that legislation over states was no longer in question: "The practicality of making laws, with coercive sanctions, for the States as Political bodies, had been exploded by all hands" (ibid., p. 294). In other words, once the New Jersey Plan had been rejected, the idea that "the General Government" should attempt to legislate against states was rejected. Indeed, Madison "called for a single instance in which the General Government was not to operate on individuals." Put another way, Madison saw, correctly, that they were no longer really talking about a federation at all! See, by comparison, the accounts of the Kentucky and Virginia resolutions in ch. 7 below.

22 Cited from J. R. Pole (ed.), *The Revolution in America, 1754–1788, Documents*

on the *Internal Development of America* (Stanford: Stanford University Press, 1970), p. 203.

23   Wood, *Creation*, pp. 529ff. The same argument also meant that a Bill of Rights was unnecessary, since "the people" did not need to be protected against themselves. I return to this in the next chapter.

24   Ibid., p. 532.

25   Quoted from Wood, *Creation*, p. 535. Wood's work on this issue was, as far as I know, ground-breaking. But the full implications of what happened have not yet been appreciated. It helps to explain how Locke came to be read as a philosopher of democracy. His contract had allowed a hereditary king to be sovereign, since it was not concerned with the location of sovereignty but with the question of "rightful" (legitimate) government. A second implication is that we can see more clearly why, after the American invention, it was easy for *any* government to claim that it was democratic simply because it rested on "consent," active or tacit!

26   This point is made by Stourzh, *Alexander Hamilton*, p. 49.

27   See Cecelia Kenyon, "Republicanism and Radicalism in the American Revolution: An Old Fashioned Interpretation," *William and Mary Quarterly*, 3rd ser., 19 (Apr. 1962); repr. in Fine and Brown (eds.), *The American Past*, 3rd ed, vol. 1 (New York: Macmillan, 1970). Kenyon notes that "if we accept the reasoning and conclusions of the Anti-Federalists ... then we must conclude that the House of Representatives is not and never has been democratic," from which it follows that "the United States is not a democracy, has never been one since 1789 and can never be one" (ibid., pp. 146–7). This, she admits, is "plausible," but is not a "useful" conclusion. But useful to whom?

In an important essay published the same year, Pole pinned down the problem:

It is possible to concentrate all our attention on those aspects of the systems which we would now call democratic, to assert that these elements exerted a controlling influence and that all the rest was a sort of obsolescent window dressing. Such a view may not be particularly subtle, but on the other hand it is not absolute nonsense ... [I]t leaves unfulfilled the rather more complex task of perceiving the democratic elements in their proper place within a system conceived in another age, under a different inspiration. ("Historians and the Problem of Early American Democracy," *American Historical Review*, 68 (Apr. 1962), repr. in Fine and Brown (eds) *American Past*, 3rd edn, vol. 1, p. 55).

28   The "mutation" in political culture among the French notables, including Lafayette, Condorcet, Morellet, and Dupont de Nemours, men who often dined with Jefferson, had not made them "radicals," even though by this time their thinking had moved well to the left of Montesquieu's. Striking proof was the response to John Adams's *Defense of the Constitutions of the United States* (discussed in the next chapter). Jefferson had promised to arrange for its publication in France but soon discovered that his French friends saw the

Defense as no more than an American version of Montesquieu. Accordingly he got no cooperation from them. Interesting in this regard is the little noticed tract of Destutt de Tracy, *Le commentaire sur Montesquieu*, composed in 1807 but first published in English translation with the significant help of Jefferson. De Tracy attacked head on Montesquieu's trichotomy of republics, monarchies, and despotisms as "essentially erroneous" (*A Commentary and Review of Montesquieu's Spirit of the Laws* (Philadelphia: William Duane, 1811), p. 9). For de Tracy, there were but *two* types of polity: "national," with "social rights common to all," and "special." Adopting the brand new Federalist formula, de Tracy wrote that in national governments, "all rights and power originate in, reside in, and belong to, the entire body of the people or nation" (ibid.), and not, as in the "special government" of pre-revolutionary France, to the king. "National governments" – the designation is itself significant – can take several forms, depending on who actually exercises power; but "representative democracy" is his preference. De Tracy notes further that "representative government" was "unknown in Montesquieu's time" (ibid., p. 19). In the marginalia of his copy, Jefferson wrote: "This is almost certainly an error, for Montesquieu gives us a clear exposition of the theory of representative government." This is striking. In terms of the new theories, grasped by de Tracy but not by Jefferson (as I argue below), Montesquieu admitted "representation," just as Polybius had; but for a representative *government*, one needed the concept of *a sovereign people*. This was an entirely new idea.

29 In addition to the differences in prevailing institutional forms, a critical difference between the United States in the 1780s and *all* subsequent movements for democracy, including the French situation of the next decade, is the class base. As Marx well understood, advancing capitalism put the problem of democracy to proletarians posed against a decaying aristocracy and a well-established bourgeoisie. And in industrial civilizations, peasant movements have faced even greater obstacles. America, lacking an aristocracy, a peasantry, and a significant proletariat, had all the advantages.

30 Quoted from Wood, *Creation*, pp. 227–8.

31 See also the letter to Major John Cartwright of 5 June 1824: "As Cato concluded every speech with the words, *Carthago delenda est*, so do I every opinion, with the injunction, 'divide the counties into wards.'" In this letter he expressed the hope that the Virginia Constitution might be changed so that "each ward would be ... a small republic in itself, and every man in the State would thus become an acting member of the common government, transacting in person a great portion of its rights and duties within itself, subordinate indeed, yet important, and entirely within his competence." See also Hannah Arendt, *On Revolution* (New York: Viking, 1965), pp. 252ff.

32 All citations from the *Federalist Papers* are from the Wesleyan University Press edition, edited by Jacob E. Cooke (Middletown, Conn., 1961); page references are given in the text in parentheses hereafter.

33 David Hume, "Idea of a Perfect Commonwealth," in *Essays, Moral, Political and Literary* (Oxford: Oxford University Press, 1963), p. 514. Remarkably, Hume's influence was not noticed until Douglas Adair's excellent analysis,

"'That Politics may be Reduced to a Science': David Hume, James Madison and the Tenth 'Federalist,'" *Huntington Library Quarterly*, 20 (Aug. 1957), repr. in Brown and Fine (eds.) *The American Past*, 3rd edn, vol. 1. I believe that the connections between Hume and Montesquieu and between them and Madison and Hamilton are more complicated than is generally supposed. See the next chapter.

34   See Robert A. Dahl, *Preface to Democratic Theory* (New Haven: Yale University Press, 1956), esp. ch. 1.

35   It is one of the aims of this book to try to explain this. It is fascinating to note that Marx, like both Madison and Plato, believed that the majority who lacked property would attack property rights. That this is a reasonable enough motive, is clear. But while popular majorities have often sought debt relief, they have never, in fact, sought to overturn systems of private property! For an account of Marx and democracy, see ch. 10 below. This is not to say, of course, that popular majorities have always done the right thing!

36   Dahl, *Preface*, p. 9.

37   For some discussion, see Morris, *Forging of the Union*, ch. 1.

38   This view, hinted at by Rakove, *Beginnings*, has recently been developed by Morris, *Forging of the Union*. Morris, an eminent Jay scholar, argues that Congress was the creation of "the people," not the states, not only because there were then only colonies, but because the first Congress was the product of "conventions," not the colonial legislatures. This argument is surely inspired by Madison and by Federalist arguments during and after the Philadelphia Convention; but it is an anachronism to transpose Federalist notions of "the sovereign people" into the war period. Indeed, the consequence is peculiar; for it leads Morris to conclude that "in essence, it was Congress which declared the colonies to be 'states'" (ibid., p. 59)! Because "the people" created Congress, and because Congress, in managing the war, assumed "the role of national sovereignty," the United States was *always* one nation united, or so the argument goes.

Morris has a difficult time producing any evidence that this was what anybody thought he was doing. Admittedly, most people assumed that Congress was acting legitimately in carrying out the war; but it was not simply "a few intractable states' righters, such as Thomas Burke," who believed that its authority to do this derived from the states. Indeed, as Morris's own account in the chapter entitled "Congress and the States" suggests, *everyone* did.

Morris cites a 1779 text of Jay, who was president of the Congress at that time, in support of his view: "For every purpose essential to the defense of these states in the progress of the present war, and necessary to the attainment of the objects of it, ... the States now are fully, legally, and absolutely confederated as it is possible for them to be" (ibid., p. 61). How this confirms his interpretation is unclear. It shows that Jay knew that Congress did not need the legitimacy which ratification by twelve states had already given it. But does it show more than this? Indeed, if it meant what it would have to mean if it were to support Morris's interpretation, it is hard to see what all the difficulties were about, and why Jay and the nationalists worked so hard for the new Constitution!

Of course, by the time the *Federalist Papers* were written, it was already possible to begin to rewrite the history of the confused recent past. Jay may have wanted "one nation" from sometime earlier, but now hoping to get one, he happily put to use whatever he could find to support the idea.

Chapter 7 Politics and War in the New United States

1 Quoted from Kohn, *The Eagle and the Sword*, p. 94. On the critical military questions of the period, here and later, I follow Kohn.

2 On Hamilton's program, see Ferguson, *The Power of the Purse*, ch. 13. Remarkably, Madison attacked Hamilton's plan for not discriminating between original and present holders of public securities. While it may be pleasant to believe that he did this on moral grounds, the fact is that this question had never bothered him before. Ferguson guesses that "Madison's sudden turn is better explained as the opening move in a resumption of state-oriented politics" (ibid., p. 298). While this seems true as far as it goes, Ferguson's very sketchy explanation of the motivation and meaning of it is not satisfying. See below for further evidence of a Madisonian change of mind.

The assumption issue was a horse of a different color. While complicated, it seems that Madison's obstructionism was designed to guarantee Virginia's interests even at the high cost of making individuals and states "pensioners of the Union" (ibid., p. 316). It is of some interest to note that Jefferson played a critical role in the passage of assumption. He seems to have consummated a deal with Virginia congressmen Alexander White and Richard Bland Lee for their votes on the assumption of the debts in return for location of the capital on the Potomac! See Noble E. Cunningham Jr., *The Jeffersonian Republicans: The Formation of Party Organization, 1789–1801* (Chapel Hill: University of North Carolina Press, 1957), p. 5.

Hamilton's program, including assumption, was surely a boon to a number of insiders who, knowing Hamilton's plans, were in a position to generate huge profits. And, worthy of emphasis, this fact certainly aided subsequent "republican" ideological attacks on the eastern big-monied men. See below.

3 At its deepest level, it concerns the question of democracy in its classical sense. In the period under examination, the "riotous democracy" of the First Republic was posed against both the British and the Federalist image of a "republic." Socialism, of course, was to enormously compound and confuse all the pertinent issues. See below.

4 See, among other treatments, George Lefebvre, *The Coming of the French Revolution*, tr. R. R. Palmer (Princeton: Princeton University Press, 1967), esp. pp. 187–97; R. R. Palmer, *The Age of Democratic Revolution*, vol. 1, pp. 493–502. Palmer comments that, as regards the "Monarchicals or Anglomaniacs," as their opponents dubbed them, "it was at least as much to American as to British examples that they pointed." The significance of this must not be underestimated. As noted (ch. 6, n. 28), French liberals, including, e.g. Lafayette, Condorcet, and Destutt de Tracy, had already accepted American teaching on the irrelevance of Montesquieu and had accepted the

ideas of the "sovereign people" and "representative government" as defined in America. Americans were not wrong in their perception that the French Revolution owed a great deal to American ideas, even if the French use of these outran many Americans perceptions of what had been created in America or of what a proper republic should be.

5 Edmund Burke, *Reflections on the Revolution in France* (New York: Doubleday, 1960), p. 38, repr. in a double volume with Paine's *Rights of Man*.

6 Quoted from Cunningham, *Jeffersonian Republicans*, p. 10. I follow Cunningham here and in the paragraph which follows.

7 The foregoing draws on Richard Hofstadter, *The Idea of a Party System: The Rise of Legitimate Opposition in the United States, 1780–1840* (Berkeley: University of California Press, 1969). Hofstadter notes that, as late as 1826, "when Sir John Cam Hobhouse first referred in a spirit of levity to 'His Majesty's Opposition,' the notion was greeted with the amusement he had anticipated, and was not yet taken as an important constitutional conception" (ibid., p. x). Hofstadter provides an excellent account of the particular difficulties of Madison. *Federalist Paper* no. 10 is discussed on pp. 64–73, and the several papers on parties which Madison wrote for the *National Gazette* are discussed on pp. 80–6.

8 Quoted from Lance Banning, *The Jeffersonian Persuasion, Evolution of Party Ideology* (Ithaca: Cornell University Press, 1978), p. 168. Madison's language is striking: the government created by his Constitution was "partisan" and was acting against "the liberty of the many."

9 Ibid., p. 212.

10 Joyce Appleby, *Capitalism and a New Social Order*, pp. 55 and 58. We should note here that it was the intrusion of the sans-culottes which so profoundly radicalized the revolution in France. Unlike the Jacobins, they were not bourgeois, even petit bourgeois, and they rejected "representative democracy" for a form of "direct democracy." See Albert Soboul, *The Sans-Culottes: The Popular Movement and the Revolutionary Government, 1793–94*, tr. Alan Forrest and Remy Inglis Hall (New York: Doubleday, 1972), and ch. 9 below.

11 Cunningham, *Jeffersonian Republicans*, p. 13. For additional detail, see Frank Luther Mott, *Jefferson and the Press* (Baton Rouge: Louisiana State University Press, 1943).

12 Cunningham, *Jeffersonian Republicans*, p. 168.

13 Banning quotes Uriah Tracy: "The House, he protested, was not seriously deliberating upon 'the welfare of our citizens but upon the relative circumstances of two European nations.' Members were not debating 'the relative benefits of markets to us,' but 'which government is best and most like our own'" (*Jeffersonian Persuasion*, p. 221).

14 Quoted from Paul A. Varg, *Foreign Policies of the Founding Fathers*, p. 73; see also p. 98. The disagreement with Hamilton could be simply put: Hamilton believed that the United States then lacked the power so confidently assumed by Madison. Varg's treatment is flawed by his view that, as regards foreign policy, the Federalists were advocates of "*realpolitik*" and the Republicans were "idealists." If "idealist" means that they "defended 'republican' visions of the world," then, by definition, the Republicans were "idealists." As I

argue below, both parties were quite capable of allowing ideology to influence policy. Perhaps Varg means that they were idealists in making secondary the national interests of the United States. Yet this seems not to be the case. There could be real differences regarding the genuine interests of the young nation. Madison and Jefferson had a poorer grasp of the "reality" than did the Hamiltonians; perhaps this is principally what Varg had in mind. But this does not make them "idealists." The issue of supposed "idealism" continues to haunt interpretations of American foreign policy.

15 Quoted from Kohn, *Eagle and Sword*, p. 179. The foregoing and the paragraph which follows derive largely from Kohn.

16 Hofstadter, *Party System*, p. 94.

17 Cunningham, *Jeffersonian Republicans*, p. 93.

18 There is no consensus on this point. Some interpreters, including Varg, have argued that "the troubled situation in Europe would have restrained the British from provoking a war." He continues: "The Hamiltonians did not fear that the British would deliberately make war, but they did fear that the American government would be pushed into more and more extreme measures until the British would feel that they had no alternative" (*Foreign Policies*, p. 109). This seems correct. Hamilton would appear to have been correct also in charging that the opposition "seems to consider the United States as among the first-rate powers in the world in point of strength and resources" (quoted in ibid., p. 108).

19 Banning, *Jeffersonian Persuasion*, p. 247.

20 Ibid., p. 252.

21 Ibid., p. 254.

22 With regard to the flurry of repressive legislation, Kohn asserts, arguably, that historians have tended to support the Republican view of the matter, implying that while the Republicans retained a balanced view of the situation, the Federalists were paranoid. He tries to argue that Federalist fears, of both imminent war and treason at home, were justified. So, accordingly, were their efforts to guard American interests (see *Eagle and Sword*, ch. 10).

It seems, however, that Kohn would have been better advised to argue that *both* sides were somewhat paranoid, the result of deep confusion, propelled by ideology, over what was going on in both America and the world. Kohn is correct in saying that the Federalist attempt "to silence dissent with the Sedition law, and to arm the country, was not an attempt to destroy liberty." *Both* sides believed that the other side was out to destroy "liberty;" but they had very different views regarding what should be done to prevent this. Kohn lapses into errors concomitant with the "liberal" interpretation in holding that the objective of the Sedition Act was "to prove to France that the nation was united, and should war come, to keep ranks closed for what all agreed would be a monumental struggle" (ibid., p. 195). The problem was that "closing ranks" required, on Federalist views of the matter, eliminating the opposition. See Hofstadter, *Party System*, pp. 102–11.

23 Strictly speaking, there were three alien acts: the Naturalization Act spelled out the conditions of citizenship; the Alien Enemies Act was a permanent wartime statute which had bipartisan support in Congress; and the Alien

Friends Act was temporary and pertained in times of both peace and war. It had little "Republican" support.

Two indispensable books here are James Morton Smith, *Freedom's Fetters: The Alien and Sedition Laws and American Civil Liberties* (Ithaca: Cornell University Press, 1956), and Leonard Levy, *Jefferson and Civil Liberties* (New York: Quadrangle, 1973), ch. 3. Samuel Eliot Morison represents the mainstream, perhaps, in holding that "for the Sedition Act of 1798 there was a legitimate need" (*Oxford History*, p. 353). David Brion Davis has collected some key texts and commentaries in *The Fear of Conspiracy: Images of Un-American Subversion from the Revolution to the Present.* (Ithaca: Cornell University Press, 1971). There is also a vast literature on the constitutional questions, which will be discussed in ch. 8.

24   Levy, *Civil Liberties*, p. 51.

25   Quoted in ibid., p. 52.

26   Ibid., p. 53.

27   Quoted in ibid., p. 59.

28   Robert M. Johnstone Jr., *Jefferson and the Presidency: Leadership in the Young Republic* (Ithaca: Cornell University Press, 1978), p. 247; my emphasis.

29   Quoted from Smith, *Freedom's Fetters*, p. 170. This paragraph derives from Smith. Smith gives a host of further evidence of the capricious, oppressive character of enforcement of these Acts.

30   Cited by Kohn, *Eagle and Sword*, p. 327.

31   Ibid., p. 244.

32   Ibid., p. 248.

33   Cited by Banning, *Jeffersonian Persuasion*, p. 166n.

34   See Kohn, *Eagle and Sword*, pp. 259–73; Banning, *Jeffersonian Persuasion*, pp. 266–70; and Cunningham, *Jeffersonian Republicans*, pp. 185–7, 229–30.

35   John Adams, *Defense of the Constitutions of the Government of the United States of America*, in Charles Francis Adams (ed.), *The Works of John Adams* (Boston: Little and Brown, 1851), vol. 4, p. 358.

36   The text is quoted from John Howe, Jr., *The Changing Political Thought of John Adams* (Princeton: Princeton University Press, 1966), p. 183. Howe, whom I largely follow here, argues that Adams's earlier confidence in American "virtue" was undermined. In explaining this, he attempts to show how incidents in Adams's personal life and the dramatic events of the period influenced the way in which Adams employed the legacy of ideas which were the materials of his thought.

37   Adams, *Defense*, in *Works*, vol. 6, p. 57. This view, worth mentioning, is the outcome of a detailed critique of Marchamont Needham's 1656 "The Excellency of a Free State, or The Right Constitution of a Commonwealth." The argument is played out against the examples of ancient history. It is truly unfortunate that for most contemporary readers, not only is Needham's name unknown, but the history which both he and Adams studied so thoroughly is utterly alien.

38   Cited by Howe, *Changing Political Thought*, p. 153.

39   Ibid., p. 151.

40   Ibid., p. 154.

41 Adams, Letters to Roger Sherman on the constitution of the United States, 17 July 1789, in *Works*, vol. 6, p. 428.
42 Quoted by Gordon Wood, *The Creation of the American Republic*, p. 585.
43 Adams, *Works*, vol. 4, p. 430.
44 Ibid., p. 380.
45 It is misleading to say, as Banning does, that "wholly elective, neither national nor federal, [the American system of government] could not be fully understood or justified in Adams' older terms" (*Jeffersonian Persuasion*, p. 98). It was simply understood and justified *differently*. According to the present view, Adams's understanding is greatly to be preferred; but given both the unleashing of democratic sentiments and the commitment of so many to the "sovereignty" of the states, his justification would no longer suffice.
46 Quoted from Palmer, *Age of Democratic Revolution*, vol. 1, pp. 26–7. Condorcet, Mirabeau, and Turgot had all argued that a republic presupposed one nation, one interest, and hence that a senate was incompatible with a republican equality. Later Leninist doctrines found inspiration in this.
47 Adams, *Defense*, p. 270.

Chapter 8 Jefferson and the Revolution of 1800

1 See Merrill Peterson, *The Jeffersonian Image in the American Mind* (New York: Oxford University Press, 1960).
2 Unless otherwise noted, quotations from Jefferson are from Andrew A. Lipscomb (ed.) *The Writings of Thomas Jefferson* (Washington, D.C.: The Thomas Jefferson Memorial Association, 1903), 20 vols.
3 It is because the modern state is acknowledged that "anarchism" – easily defined as an anti-statist political philosophy – emerges. Auguste Comte rightly referred to Rousseau as the founder of "the anarchical school," precisely because for Rousseau, sovereignty could not be alienated to government. See J. B. Noone Jr., *Rousseau's Social Contract* (Athens, Ga.: University of Georgia Press, 1980). Jefferson seems to have seen this. It is part of the reason why his definition of a "republic" differs from that of Madison. One might add that with the modern state and with appropriation of "democracy" in the first decades of the nineteenth century by theorists of government, both French and American "democrats" in the Greek sense become "anarchists." See my *A History and Philosophy of the Social Sciences*, ch. 2.
   "Individualism" coupled with anti-statism is "libertarian anarchism." It is the anarchism of Robert Nozick. Libertarians would have found Indian society profoundly oppressive. So-called left-wing anarchism is democracy coupled with anti-statism. It is the anarchism of the Paris Commune and of Kropotkin. See below, ch. 10.
4 In a *tour de force*, Gary Wills has argued that Jefferson was a long way from the atomism of "state of nature" theory, and that he had a version of an "affectionate community" derived from the "moral-sense" theory of the Scottish Enlightenment. See his *Inventing America: Jefferson's Declaration of Independence* (New York: Doubleday, 1978). For criticism of this, see R. Hameway,

"Jefferson and the Scottish Enlightenment, A Critique of Gary Wills," *William and Mary Quarterly*, 36 (1979).

5 John Dewey grasped it, however, See his brief *The Living Thought of Thomas Jefferson* (New York: Fawcett, n.d.). This aspect has been given a persuasive treatment more recently by Richard K. Matthews, *The Radical Politics of Thomas Jefferson: A Revisionist View* (Lawrence Ka.: University of Kansas, Press, 1984). I would see Matthews as developing only half of Jefferson's "radical" politics in that he fails to see that Jefferson's views of democracy were profoundly connected with his views on federalism.

6 With regard to Jefferson, the level of civilization relates to the question of the "agrarian" versus the "commercial" impulses in his thought, and thus too to his perception of foreign policy, sketched below. In addition to Matthews, *Radical Politics*, see Joseph Dorfman, "Thomas Jefferson: Commercial Agrarian Democrat," in Fine and Brown (eds), *The American Past*, vol. 1, 1st edn (1961). In the same volume, A. Whitney Griswold rejects the idea that there was a fusion of agrarian and commercial elements in Jefferson's thought. See his "The Agrarian Democracy of Thomas Jefferson." While I favor Dorfman's view, how this issue is settled does not affect the foregoing.

7 See Pole, "Historians and the Early American Democracy," and Cunningham, *Jeffersonian Republicans*, pp. 105–6.

8 Quoted from Gilbert Chinard, *Jefferson et les ideologues* (Paris and Baltimore: Johns Hopkins University Press, 1925), pp. 77–8; my emphasis. See also *Writings*, XIII.

9 The authorship of the Kentucky Resolution did not generally become known until 1821. The Kentucky and Virginia resolutions were motivated, of course, by the Alien and Sedition Acts. The irony should not go unnoticed. Jefferson gave a "state's rights" argument in defense of the central government's attack on civil liberties. It is true, of course, that, as a result of slavery, "state's righters" have usually been reactionaries, who have used Jeffersonian arguments to *deny* civil liberties, a fact of some importance in American historiography and ideology. One of the results of this has been to collapse liberalism and democracy. Neither Democrats nor liberals have ever dominated state houses in the South; but liberals have dominated the White House and the Supreme Court. But even a *classic* democracy for white males *only* would not be preferable to a *liberal* nondemocracy! We should choose the United States over Athens; but we should keep straight why.

10 I here follow Harry Jaffa, "The Political Theory of the Civil War," in R. A. Goldwin (ed.), *A Nation of States*, 2nd edn (Chicago: Rand McNally, 1974), pp. 109–37. It is obviously not possible here to review even a sample of the literature. The following citations from the pertinent texts are from Jaffa's essay.

11 How the Constitution itself became the source of authority is beautifully treated by Wood, *The Creation of the American Republic*, ch. 7. We can see this in two conceptual stages: the idea of a (Lockean) community which then forms a government; then, in the United States, the drawing up by the community of a Constitution, the fundamental expression of the people. The best statement of the new understanding as regards the Supreme Court is in

Hamilton's *Federalist Paper* no. 18. The new understanding of the Constitution did not mean that fundamental law was no longer rooted in God or Nature, as nineteenth-century positivist conceptions had it. In the American context, Blackstone was critical, as Stourzh's *Alexander Hamilton* emphasizes. Similarly, this paper of Hamilton's built on Blackstone and the Madisonian notions expressed in *Federalist Paper* no. 39.

12 An analogous problem arises as regards civil disobedience. Do individuals have the right to "nullify," failing redress, to act outside the constituted law? Jefferson affirmed that they did; but recent "federalists" have not agreed. Similarly, the stability of the community depends not on the capacity to coerce, but on the voluntary acceptance by the great mass of the people of the law and its ends. See my *The Death of the State* (New York: Putnams, 1974).

13 See Merrill D. Peterson, *Thomas Jefferson and the New Nation* (New York: Oxford University Press, 1970), p. 359.

14 *Idem, Adams and Jefferson, A Revolutionary Dialogue* (Athens, Ga.: University of Georgia Press, 1976), p. 94.

15 To clarify the question of the nature of "the Revolution of 1800," we need to distinguish changes in policy from changes in institutions. As everyone agrees, there were no changes of the last kind, although, as I argue in what follows, people comprehended very differently what it was that they had. There were changes in some of the policies, but with the deep irony that Republicans did just what they had restrained Federalists from doing! This is the force of the classic charge by Henry Adams that the Republicans "out-Federalized the Federalists."

16 The foregoing categories overlap, of course. Many ordinary people were also "Anglophiles," defenders of American autarchy, etc. For expressions of views "from the bottom," see all the essays in Alfred F. Young (ed.), *The American Revolution*; also Jesse Lemisch, "Jack Tar in the Streets: Merchant Seamen in the Politics of Revolutionary America," in Irwin Unger (ed.), *Beyond Liberalism: The New Left Views American History* (Waltham, Mass.: Xerox, 1971); and Lemisch, "The American Revolution Seen from the Bottom Up," in Barton J. Bernstein (ed.), *Toward a New Past: Dissenting Essays in American History* (New York: Pantheon, 1967).

All this complexity is overlooked or de-emphasized by "nationalist" views which underplay the *structural* revolution which the Constitution had wrought. Since for them, no essential structural changes resulted from the Constitution, it could not represent an antidemocratic "counter-revolution." Similarly, Jefferson's administration could not embody "apostasy" because, from the beginning, Republicans and Federalists were in agreement over essentials: the great and enduring "consensus" in American history.

There is always agreement at some level of abstraction. Thus, most Americans (not merely the leading elites) were "liberals" in their assumptions regarding "liberty" and "property." As Hofstadter put it, this was a "democracy of cupidity" rather than fraternity, and this is vitally important. But we lose too much history if we submerge the genuine differences and real struggles.

Appleby is absolutely correct in concluding that the election of 1800 represented "the defeat of aristocratic values in American politics," and that "it was the people – ordinary men, political parvenues, outsiders, interlopers, mere voters without office – who created the turmoil, defined the issues, formed the clubs, manned the demonstrations, arranged the July 4th celebrations, and filled the newspaper columns with the rhetoric of Republicanism" (*Capitalism and a New Social Order*, p. 104). Moreover, she is correct, versus progressive historians, that the Republicans were not "agrarian democrats." But in my view she fails to see that this was a victory *only* in ideology. She writes as if Jeffersonian democracy, not merely the ideology of democracy, was the victor.

17 Dumas Malone writes: "Nothing was more characteristic of the Patriots at the birth of the Republic than the conviction that the American people were unique and that their experiment in self-government was destined to set an example for the world. To that faith and vision Jefferson proposed that the country should return" (*Jefferson the President: First Term, 1801–1805* (Boston: Little, Brown, 1970), p. xvii). Indeed, they did see themselves as unique and it did become an example to the world. What is obscured is the reference to "Patriots at the birth of the Republic." Was this 1776? Or was it 1789? Or doesn't it make any difference? If it makes a difference, then between 1776 and 1812 or somewhat later, the "glittering generality," the "experiment in self-government," came to mean something very different from what many in 1776 had thought it meant, what Republican rhetoric in the 1790s would have led one to believe it meant, and surely what Jefferson took it to mean.

18 Hofstadter, *The Idea of a Party System*, pp. 150–1.

19 I here follow Gerald Stourzh, *Alexander Hamilton and the Idea of Republican Government*, pp. 189–201. Stourzh observes that "for a century and a half, the study of political theory and the study of international relations have been divorced from one another," and that "this divorce has left its imprint on our approach to the study of the Founders' intent and procedure while framing new forms of government" (p. 128). As I hope is clear, this book in many ways pursues this insight across history. That is why I take it that Thucydides and Machiavelli are absolutely fundamental to political theory.

20 Hamilton gave his views under the pseudonym "Pericles" in the *New York Evening Post* in February and July 1803; collected in Richard B. Morris (ed.), *Alexander Hamilton and the Founding of the Nation* (New York: Dial Press, 1957), pp. 118–21.

21 Michael H. Hunt develops the difference between Hamilton and Jefferson and shows that it has been a recurring debate in American policy. Hunt also sees that the Hamiltonians have always prevailed. Indeed, it is a key theme of his account that the Hamiltonians not only won, but succeeded in incorporating Jeffersonian themes as justification for Hamiltonian empire! I believe that the argument of this chapter shows why this was so easy. The upshot, familiar enough, was American self-righteousness, making the world "safe for democracy." See Michael H. Hunt, *Ideology and U.S. Foreign Policy* (New Haven: Yale University Press, 1987).

By contrast, Lawrence S. Kaplan has very recently suggested that the ideological difference between Jefferson and Hamilton was of small importance, that both believed that the goal of American foreign policy should be to secure American national independence. But, even if this is true, their very different choice of means was a straightforward result of deep ideological differences in their goals. See Lawrence S. Kaplan, *Entangling Alliances with None: American Foreign Policy in the Age of Jefferson* (Kent, Ohio: Kent State University Press, 1987).

22 Cited in Robert M. Johnstone, *Jefferson and the Presidency*, p. 72. I have found much of value in Johnstone's treatment.

23 See Thomas F. Abernethy, *The Burr Conspiracy* (New York: Oxford University Press, 1954); Levi, *Jefferson and Civil Liberties*, ch. 4; and Johnstone, *Jefferson and the Presidency*, pp. 109–207.

24 The "Quids" were followers of John Randolph. They were strong defenders of legislative supremacy who had broken with the Republicans over the sorry Yazoo scandal. Briefly, just when states were ceding lands to the Confederation, in 1789, some 25 million acres were sold to a group of seasoned speculators, including Patrick Henry, George Rogers Clark, and others. They paid only $207,580 and, in consequence, reaped handsome profits. In 1795 the exercise was repeated, but even more outrageously. The new companies, securing most of Alabama and Mississippi for about one cent per acre, were all members of the Georgia state legislature! The scam was cut short, however, when Georgians found out. An "anti-Yazoo ticket" swept the next election, and the sale was rescinded. By this time, however, some of the property had been bought by third parties. When the Yazoo land was ceded to the United States in 1802, Jefferson plainly had a problem. How could he settle this without spurring party division? A commission was appointed, and 5 million acres were set aside to settle claims. Although none of the original claims were held to be valid, innocent third parties would presumably be protected; but the compromise did not satisfy the rabidly anti-Yazoo Randolph.

25 Cited from Levy, *Jefferson and Civil Liberties*, p. 98.

26 Perhaps 30,000 seamen were put out of work, as well as all those engaged in enterprises which depended on seaborne trade. Johnstone notes that while the loudest protests came from the merchants, the working classes suffered most. New Yorkers suffered more than Bostonians, and, worthy of emphasis, as the prices of domestic produce fell and the prices of imports soared, southern agrarians suffered most of all. It is also important to notice, as Johnstone says, that while the fiercest resistance came from the New England states, it was, as Jefferson surmised, politically motivated, rather than the outcome of economic hardship. There were many who believed that the embargo was "a direct assault upon one section of the economy – the commercial interests – and one section of the country – New England – by a party dominated by southern agrarians" (Johnstone, *Jefferson and the Presidency*, p. 269).

27 This is now the consensus among historians of the period. See esp. Levy, *Jefferson and Civil Liberties*; Peterson, *Thomas Jefferson*; and Malone, *Jefferson the President*.

28 Levy, *Jefferson and Civil Liberties*, p. 139.

29 This is Johnstone's judgment (*Jefferson and the Presidency*, p. 299), confirming Louis Sears, *Jefferson and the Embargo* (Durham, N. C.: Duke University Press, 1927).

30 Quoted from Johnstone, *Jefferson and the Presidency*, p. 294. The mystique of

Jefferson, no doubt, was sufficient to keep him from "censure" at the time. Until recently, historians have chosen to be uncritical of those actions which he rightly feared might bring him censure. This has also contributed, obviously, to the tendency to accept Jefferson's own view of the "Revolution of 1800."

31 The whole business is profoundly ironical. Here was Jefferson riding a crest as a "true" Republican against "Anglophiles" at just the time when Robespierre was redefining "democracy" on the Federalist model of the sovereign people, a model never quite internalized by Jefferson. The Republican "Revolution of 1800" maintained that it had restored the "principles" to the "form" of the American Revolution at just the time when the republic created by the French Revolution gave way to the crowning of Napoleon! No wonder the American system of government is the very model of modern democracy!

Part IV Absolute War and Social Democracy Introduction

1 Jacques Godechot, "The French Revolution," in *Chapters in Western Civilization*, 3rd edn, vol. 2 (New York: Columbia University Press, 1962) p. 27. I have relied heavily on the work of George Lefebvre, *The French Revolution, From its Origins to 1793*, 2 vols (New York: Columbia University Press, 1962); *idem*, *Napoleon*, 2 vols (New York: Columbia University Press, 1969).

2 General Carl von Clausewitz, *On War*, Bk VIII, ch. 6B. I have used two translations of this. What is quoted in the text here is from the newer translation by Michael Howard and Peter Paret (Princeton: Princeton University Press, 1984). The more widely available translation is that of J. J. Graham, with Introduction and Notes by F. F. Maude, 3 vols, 8th impression (London: Routledge and Kegan Paul, 1966).

Chapter 9 The Revolution in France and the Revolution in War

1 W. Walker Stephens, *The Life and Writings of Turgot* (New York: Burt Franklin; repr. 1971), p. 303.

2 Ibid., p. 301.

3 Ibid., p. 302.

4 Ibid.

5 Immanuel Kant, "Idea for a Universal History with a Cosmopolitan Purpose," in Hans Reiss (ed.), *Kant's Political Writings*, tr. H. B. Nisbet (Cambridge: Cambridge University Press, 1971), p. 47; original italics omitted.

6 I have found W. B. Gallie's *Philosophers of Peace and War: Kant, Clausewitz, Engels and Tolstoy* (Cambridge: Cambridge University Press, 1978) extremely useful, not only as regards Kant, but as regards all the writers he discusses.

7 Kant, "Perpetual Peace: A Philosophical Sketch," in Reiss (ed.), *Kant's Political Writings*, p. 99. It is a background theme of this book, although I do not pursue it, that liberalism and democracy are conceptually independent, even if in the modern "democratic state" they came together. While the literature on liberalism is vast, the following are recommended: Michael Oakeshott, *On*

Human Conduct, Roberto Mangabeira Unger, *Knowledge and Politics* (New York: Free Press, 1975); C. B. Macpherson, *The Real World of Democracy* (Oxford: Clarendon Press, 1965); *idem*, *Democratic Theory* (Oxford: Clarendon Press, 1973); John Dunn, *Western Political Theory in the Face of the Future* (Cambridge: Cambridge University Press, 1979); and Ian Shapiro, *The Evolution of Rights in Liberal Theory* (Cambridge: Cambridge University Press, 1986).

Recent liberal theory has shown a remarkable inattention to democracy. Consider here the two influential recent books on liberal political philosophy, John Rawls's *A Liberal Theory of Justice* (Cambridge, Mass.: Harvard University Press, 1971) and Robert Nozick's *Anarchy, State and Utopia* (New York: Basic Books, 1974). In the extensive index to Rawls's impressive book, neither "democracy" nor "political democracy" appears. Following Mill, Rawls allows that since "government is assumed to aim at the common good" and "some men can be identified as having superior wisdom and judgment ... plural voting may be perfectly just" (p. 233). Notably, in this context he drags out Plato's metaphor of the captain and his passengers!

Nozick outdoes this. On his view, "after we exclude from consideration the decisions which others have a right to make, and the actions which would aggress against me ... and hence violate *my* (Lockean) rights, it is not clear that there are *any* decisions remaining about which even to raise the question of whether I have a right to a say in those that importantly affect me" (p. 270)! How about war?

8   Reiss (ed.), *Kant's Political Writings*, p. 100. Subsequent quotations from Kant are from this volume, with page references in the text in parentheses unless otherwise stated.

9   There are two points here, not to be confused. I believe that Kant's argument for perpetual peace is plausible *if*, as in the ancient *polis*, the citizens *are* the army and *are* the government. But Kant is twice removed from this. As I will argue more systematically below, the second remove, passive citizens, is far less critical than the first, citizens whose only *power* is eligibility to vote for officials of government.

10 See Lefebvre, *The French Revolution*; Vivian Gruder, "A Mutation in Elite Political Culture: The French Notables and the Defense of Property and Participation, 1787," *Journal of Modern History*, 56 (1984).

11 Stephens, *Turgot*, p. 367.

12 It is striking that Kantian liberals give authority to representative governments which they disallow the people themselves! See J. L. Talmon, *The Origins of Totalitarian Democracy* (New York: Praeger, 1960), ch. 3.

13 Gallie, *Philosophers*, p. 29.

14 An extremely useful account of Clausewitz's life and times is Peter Paret's *Clausewitz and the State* (New York: Oxford University Press, 1976). The title is misleading since, as Paret himself argues, Clausewitz was a philosopher of war, not of the state.

15 The quotations which follow are from the Graham translation, pp. 90–101.

16 Clausewitz reported that his intention in *On War* was to proceed in somewhat "the manner in which Montesquieu dealt with his subject" (quoted by Paret,

Clausewitz and the State, p. 361). This was more than a stylistic fancy. More interesting perhaps is Paret's report that Marie von Bruhl's older friend, the Countess Caroline von Berg was a friend and patron of Herder and Fichte, as well as Goethe and others. It seems hard to believe that Clausewitz was unaffected by these contacts. Commentators tend to emphasize a Kantian influence. Perhaps so. Yet his implicit philosophy of history is Herder's, not Kant's, and his historical method, especially his treatment of the relation of the abstract to the concrete, is pure Herder. I have sketched my views of Herder vis-à-vis Montesquieu and Kant in my *A History and Philosophy of the Social Sciences*, pp. 33–6 and 73–86.

17   Anatol Rapoport's *Strategy and Conscience* (New York: Harper, 1964), a detailed polemic against neo-Clausewitzeans, remains valuable. As Rapoport later noted, his attack was aimed not just at game theory, but at the Clausewitzean assumptions shared by all foreign-policy planners. These assumptions are summarized in a text quoted from Robert Osgood: "The problem is this: How can the United States utilize its military power as a rational and effective instrument of national policy.'" It was, he says, against "this framework of thought that I directed my polemic" (Editor's Introduction to Clausewitz, *On War* (Harmondsworth: Penguin, 1968), p. 73). See below.

18   See Geoffrey Best, *War and Society in Revolutionary Europe, 1770–1870* (New York: St Martin's, 1982), pp. 71–2.

19   It is worth remembering, perhaps, that in America, militia responded to the call to overcome Shay's little rebellion, and that although Washington was reluctant to use force against whiskey tax delinquents in 1794, for fear of civil war, he himself led a force of some 15,000 to restore "law and order." Similarly, Jefferson, remembered for the remark that "a little rebellion now and again" is good for "the tree of liberty," used the regular army and navy to enforce the embargo.

20   Quoted by Paret, *Clausewitz and the State*, p. 22.

21   For discussion, see Lefebvre, *The French Revolution, 1793*, pp. 210–26.

22   Quoted by Paret, *Clausewitz and the State*, p. 289. France was not then a "democracy," of course, even if it was sometimes thought to be one. But until 1795, when the election of officers was discontinued, the army continued to be remarkably "democratic." With the *amalgame* of "regulars" and "volunteers" in 1793 the elective principle was compromised, so that only holders of the particular rank to be filled voted.

23   Quoted from ibid., p. 293. This text is from Clausewitz's memorandum of 1819, in which he states the objections to a *Landwehr* and attempts to refute them. His experience had taught him that reform of the army and the government were sorely needed if Prussia was to prevail. On his view, the Prussian regime was caught on the horns of a dilemma: Was it to suffer threat of rebellion or threat of invasion? In his judgment, "We know nothing of any revolution, of any genuine rebellion. Do we know nothing of invasion?" (pp. 294–5).

24   Godechot, "The French Revolution," p. 27.

25   The text from the Committee of Public Safety is quoted from Best, *Revolutionary Europe*, p. 87. The leave order of Felicité Duquet is quoted from George

Pernoud and Sabine Flaissier (eds), *The French Revolution* (New York: Capricorn, 1961), p. 283. McNeill remarks that "in retrospect the revolutionary success in creating vast armies seems relatively simple and straightforward, given the dynamic of exploding population and economic dislocation from which France both profited and suffered" (*The Pursuit of Power*, p. 194). If these were necessary conditions, they were not sufficient, as I am sure McNeill would acknowledge. One must add, at the very least, the dynamic of a *new kind* of war fought by "citizens." This is surely *not* to be taken for granted. As McNeill says, the task of arming these huge numbers was even more remarkable. That this was accomplished attests to the involvement of almost everyone in the nation.

26 It is sometimes implied that it was Napoleon who produced the revolution in war which so impressed Clausewitz. Clausewitz is clear, however, that Napoleon only "perfected" it. For example, he writes of a "technical incompleteness with which the French [at the time of the Directory] had to contend" and says, "After all this was perfected by the hand of Buonaparte, this military power, based on the strength of the whole nation, marched over Europe, smashing everything to pieces so surely and certainly, that where it only encountered the old-fashioned Armies the result was not doubtful for a moment" (Bk VIII, ch. 3).

As Rothenberg notes, "from the Revolution, Napoleon inherited huge conscript armies, led by young and ambitious commanders, accustomed to a mobile, offensive and ruthless way of war" (Gunther E. Rothenberg, *The Art of Warfare in the Age of Napoleon* (London: Batsford, 1977), p. 126).

Still, Napoleon's coup was of great historical significance. Paret offers the fascinating counterfactual that "had Napoleon been killed before Toulon [December 1793] or captured off the coast of Crete on his way to Egypt, France would have ceased or at least slowed its efforts to destroy the European balance of power .... The Revolution and transformation of war would have still left France the most powerful country in Europe, but a country integrated in the political community, rather than dominating and indeed, almost abolishing it" (Peter Paret, "Napoleon and the Revolution in War," in Paret (ed.), *Makers of Modern Strategy*, p. 126). Would there have been another Napoleon? Paret suggests that the answer is no.

27 Prussia, a "comprehensively regulated machine for producing revenue and soldiers," was perhaps the extreme case. In response to the trauma produced by Napoleon, Clausewitz took an active role in trying to reform both the state machinery and the army. In the eighteenth century both had been well adapted for the state's purposes. Clausewitz saw that they no longer were. The reformers got some of the reforms they wanted, but most of these did not last. The *Freikorps* was adapted to the times, and was followed, at the time of the crisis of 1812–13 by the enlistment of 12,000 *Jager*, strictly middleclass volunteers who could afford their own uniforms and equipment. *Landwehr*, militia, were then created. All men between seventeen and forty who were not in the regular army or the *Jager* were asked to volunteer. The Army Law of 1814 mandated universal military service, providing a variety of options for Prussian males, including signing on as "one year volunteers." By 1819,

however, with "peace" restored, conservative *Junkers* managed to emasculate the *Landwehr*, leaving the *Landsturm* as training units for men who were then available for regular army service. For discussion, see Best, *Revolutionary Europe*, ch. 11 and 16. For Clausewitz's role in the reform movement, see Paret, *Clausewitz and the State*, esp. pp. 137–46, 255–85. The Prussian army, never "liberalized," remained the province of the right. The implications of this as regards the history of modern Germany, and thence the world, are tremendous. See ch. 12 below.

28   See Benedict Anderson, *The Imagined Community* (London: Verso, 1983), whom I follow here. A useful historical account of modern nationalism, including the emergence of the modern nation-state, is Boyd C. Shafer, *Faces of Nationalism* (New York: Harcourt, Brace, Jovanovich, 1972). See also Anthony D. Smith, *Theories of Nationalism* (New York: Harper and Row, 1971). I have sketched the concept of the nation-state against the backdrop of the philosophies of Herder and Hegel in my *A History and Philosophy*, ch. 5 and draw on this in what follows.

29   Anderson, *Imagined Community*, p. 78.

30   We know that Clausewitz had enormous admiration for the *Discourses* – as well he might. Thus he wrote:

> No book on earth . . . is more necessary for a politician than Machiavelli. . . . What he says about the princes' policies toward their subjects is certainly largely outdated because political forms have considerably changed since his day. Nevertheless, he gives some remarkable rules, which will remain valid forever. . . . But this author is especially instructive in regard to foreign affairs, and all the scorn cast on him (to be sure, often out of confusion, ignorance, affectation) belongs to his teaching on the treatment of the citizenry, insofar as it is justified at all. (Quoted by Paret, *Clausewitz and the State*, p. 171)

31   The relevant work had a double title, *Naturrecht und Staatswissenschaft im Grundrisse* and *Grundlinien der Philosophie des Rechts* ("Natural Law and Political Science in Outline" and "Elements of the Philosophy of Right"). The quotations which follow are from the translation by T. M. Knox, *Hegel's Philosophy of Right* (New York: Oxford University Press, 1967), and citations (in parentheses in the text) are to the numbered paragraphs therein. Additional material is cited from Hegel's *The Philosophy of History*, tr. J. Sibree (New York: Dover, 1956).

32   The clearest, if arguably the best, treatment is Charles Taylor, *Hegel* (Cambridge: Cambridge University Press, 1975). The problem is that because Hegel was the systematic philosopher *par excellence*, the arguments for the distinct view of *Philosophy of Right* cannot be isolated from the encompassing arguments of his whole systematic philosophy. My description of his "conclusions" is unavoidably selective and omits, in terms of his inclusive philosophy, much that is of enduring value. Further pertinent to the present volume, Hegel believed that radical participation cannot create common purposes – indeed, quite the opposite, that radical participation presupposes such purposes. He saw this as the error of the Terror. On this, see Taylor, *Hegel* esp. pp. 403–27. In this regard, Hegel contrasts sharply with both Marx and Dewey; see below.

33 Hegel, *Philosophy of History*, tr. Sibree, p. 450.
34 Ibid.
35 Ibid.
36 The root of the tension, responded to by Hegel, is between political individualism and nationalism. A consistent political individualist like Kant is a cosmopolitan. Compare here, perhaps, Robert Nozick, *Anarchy, State and Utopia*. Marxists are up against the same tension of course, except that they are faced with the dilemma of being members of a class as well as members of a nation. The American War of Independence and the French Revolution, as I have been suggesting, allowed for an easy accommodation of liberalism and nationalism. Marxists have found this considerably more difficult.
37 Some American presidents have better "represented" the United States than others. Is Ronald Reagan's success, for example, in part, at least, due to his capacity to "represent" the nation? See Gary Wills, *Ronald Reagan's America* (New York: Penguin, 1988).
38 Hegel, *Philosophy of History*, tr. Sibree, p. 19.
39 Charles R. Beitz argues that the required analogy between "nations" and "persons" breaks down altogether, empirically, theoretically, *and* morally. See his most useful *Political Theory and International Relations* (Princeton: Princeton University Press, 1979).

Chapter 10   War and Revolution: Marx and Engels

1 The biographical facts given here and taken from Franz Mehring, *Karl Marx* (Ann Arbor: University of Michigan Press, 1969).
2 The following has profited from James Schmidt, "A *Paideia* for the '*Burger als Bourgeois*': The Concept of 'Civil Society' in Hegel's Political Thought." *History of Political Thought*, 2, no. 3 (Winter 1981).
3 Hegel, *The Philosophy of Right*, tr. T. M. Knox, para. 289. See also ch. 9 above.
4 Marx, "On the Jewish Question," in L. Easton and K. Guddat (eds). *Writings of the Young Marx on Philosophy and Society* (New York: Doubleday, 1967), p. 236. Quotations from this volume in this and the next section are given in the text in parentheses. Later in the chapter it is cited in the text as *Writings*.
5 Hegel, *The Philosophy of History*, tr. J. Sibree, p. 452.
6 Paul Thomas, *Karl Marx and the Anarchists* (London: Routledge and Kegan Paul, 1980), p. 196. Thomas provides an invaluable account of Marx's relations, ideological and political, to nineteenth-century anarchism. See also his "Alienated Politics," in Terence Ball et al. (eds), *After Marx* (Cambridge: Cambridge University Press, 1984).
7 I have developed the implications for the social sciences of the idea that the social world is the unintended product of deliberative action in my *A History and Philosophy of the Social Sciences*, ch. 13.
8 A deep and troublesome problem in Marxian theory is the question of whether there is a *telos* to history; whether, as Hegel had it, history has a goal and that what happens as part of realizing this is therefore "inevitable." This is the *bête noire* of most unsympathetic critiques of Marx. I have argued that

while it is easy to read Marx and Engels as holding some such view – "historical materialism" or, more perversely, "economic determinism," – this reading cannot be sustained. But this is not the only troublesome theoretical issue. As important is the problem of the meaning of "scientific socialism." I develop these issues in my *History and Philosophy*, ch. 6. But it can hardly be denied that Marx and Engels believed in progress, and in particular that socialism was *somehow* inevitable. This optimism has left a tragic legacy and has both promoted revolutionary messianism and discredited their genuine insights.

Thus, by the time we get to Plekhanov's *In Defense of Materialism: The Development of the Monistic Theory of History* (1894), "dialectical materialism," a monistic hypernaturalism comparable in many ways to the "old materialism" which Marx and Engels set out to refute, had been joined to an eschatological history in which human agency had disappeared altogether! This perverse reading subsequently became the dominant one within Marxist circles. These "theoretical" issues were important in Russia and Germany in 1917–18 and contributed to the confusion. But their worst effects were felt later, with their codification in the Soviet Union. Still, one needs to try to avoid reading history backwards.

9 Marx, "Communist Manifesto," in *Collected Works* (Moscow: Progress, 1976), vol. 6, p. 513.

10 Eric J. Hobsbawm, "Marx, Engels and Politics," in *The History of Marxism*, vol. 1: *Marxism in Marx's Day* (Bloomington: Indiana University Press, 1982), p. 238. Compare also this letter of 1871:

> The ultimate object of the political movement of the working class is . . . the conquest of political power for this class; and this naturally requires that the organization of the working class, an organization which arises from its economic struggles, should previously reach a certain level of development. On the other hand, however, every movement in which the working class as a *class* confronts the ruling classes and tries to constrain them by pressure from without is a political movement. For instance, the attempt by strikes, etc. in a particular factory or even in a particular trade to compel individual capitalists to reduce the working day, is a purely economic movement. On the other hand, the movement to force through an eight-hour day, etc., law is a political movement. And in this way, out of the separate economic movements of the workers grows up everywhere a *political* movement, that is to say, a *class* movement, with the object of enforcing its interests in a general form, in a form possessing general, socially coercive force. While these movements presuppose a certain degree of previous organization, they are in turn equally a means of developing this organization. (Marx to Sorge, 23 Nov. 1871)

11 Compare Ralph Miliband, *Marxism and Politics* (New York: Oxford University Press, 1977), ch. 6.

12 Frederic L. Bender (ed.), *Karl Marx: The Essential Writings*, 2nd edn. (Boulder, Co.: Westview Press, 1986), p. 499.
An excellent contextual reading of Marx's politics is Alan Gilbert's *Marxs*

Politics: Communists and Citizens (New Brunswick, N.J.: Rutgers University Press, 1981). Gilbert, following a path marked out by Michael Harrington (in his *Socialism* (New York: Bantam, 1973)), shows that Marx persistently altered his political strategies in the light of experience, and that he was no economic determinist inflexibly committed to pat formulas – unlike most of his later epigones.

13 See Thomas, *Marx and the Anarchists*, ch. 5.

14 Minutes of the Central Committee of the Communist League, 15 Sept. 1850, in *Collected Works*, vol. 10, p. 626. Already, against Stirner, he had argued that "it is only in the mind of the ideologist that [the 'will' to abolish competition and with it the state and law] arises before conditions have developed far enough to make its production possible" (*The German Ideology*, cited by Thomas, *Marx and the Anarchists*, p. 343). To emphasize, the conditions referred to are political; they concern the political capacities of the people whose activities had sustained "competition" and "law and the state."

15 F. L. Bender, whose account of the *Manifesto* very much influences mine, points out that Marx's argument *requires* workers' control, since only then "could the state ever become subordinate to the proletariat rather than its master." Still, as he says, "nowhere to my knowledge does Marx make this point explicitly." In this, of course, Marx did not discourage confusion over what *we* know to be a critical point. But the explanation of actual existing socialisms has less to do with misreadings of texts than with other factors – e.g. the conditions of their genesis. On the other hand, Bender seems to me to go too far in saying that the *Manifesto* contains grounds for holding that Marx is ambiguous regarding a centralized *economy*. In my view, Bender does not carry his own historically concrete reading of the ten points far enough. See his very useful "The Ambiguities of 'Proletarian Dictatorship' and 'Transition to Communism,'" *History of Political Thought*, 2, no. 3 (Winter 1981).

16 In addition to Thomas, *Marx and the Anarchists*, see Martin Buber's *Paths in Utopia* (Boston: Beacon, 1949), which remains valuable.

17 In *Selected Works* (Moscow: Foreign Languages Publishing House, 1962), vol. 2, pp. 29–31. This text was intended for circulation within the party. Perhaps understandably, commentators have concentrated on Marx's theory of distribution in a fully developed socialist society; but they have tended to miss the point of Marx's criticism. Lassalle may have lacked an understanding of political economy, but Marx offered his detailed account "in order to show what a crime it is to attempt, on the one hand, to force on our party again, as dogmas, ideas which in a certain period had some meaning, but have now become obsolete verbal rubbish, while again perverting, on the other, the realistic outlook." The "realist outlook" regarded the problem of being realistic *without* betraying one's revolutionary aspirations. It was for this reason that it was "in general a mistake to make a fuss about so-called distribution and put the principal stress on it." As he insisted again and again, the problem was the proletarian conquest of political power, so poorly articulated in the Gotha program. After it had achieved this, the proletariat could move to distributional questions. Accordingly, "if the material conditions of production are the co-operative property of the workers themselves, then there likewise results a

distribution of the means of consumption different from the present one."

18 This had been a theme of Marx's from early on. "In politics," Marx wrote in 1843, "the Germans have thought what other nations have done" (Easton and Guddat (eds), *Writings*, p. 257). This also influenced his view that only insurrection would bring Germany to socialism. The peculiarly uneven political development of Germany was obviously an enormous problem for the German Social Democrats of the prewar period. See ch. 12 below.

19 See Bender, "Ambiguities." See also Harrington, *Socialism*, ch. 3; Gilbert, *Marx's Politics*, ch. 8. As Harrington remarks, Sidney Hook's interpretation of "dictatorship" is probably correct. In *Towards the Understanding of Karl Marx (New York: John Day 1933)*, Hook wrote, "Wherever we find a state we find a dictatorship."

20 Quoted by Hobsbawm, "Marx, Engels and Politics," p. 253, from an 1889 letter to Lafargue. Hobsbawm's very brief account of the question of nationalism is a good summary. A more extensive treatment is that of Solomon F. Bloom, *The World of Nations: A Study of the National Implications in the Work of Karl Marx* (New York: Columbia University Press, 1941). It is striking that it has been nearly fifty years since these questions have been addressed systematically.

21 The following depends upon the very useful book by Martin Berger, *Engels, Armies and Revolution: The Revolutionary Tactics of Classical Marxism* (Hamden, Conn.: Archon, 1977).

22 Ibid., p. 36.

23 Quoted in ibid., p. 37.

24 Quoted in ibid., p. 78.

25 Quoted in ibid., p. 79.

26 Quoted in ibid., p. 80.

27 Quoted in ibid., pp. 81–2.

28 Quoted in ibid., p. 84.

29 Quoted in ibid.

30 Marx, *The Eighteenth Brumaire of Louis Napoleon* (New York: International Publishers, n.d.), p. 16.

31 See Michael Howard, *The Franco-Prussian War* (St Albans: Granada, 1961), ch. 2.

32 What follows derives from Stewart Edwards, *The Paris Commune, 1871* (New York: Quadrangle, 1971).

33 The designation "Government of National Defection" was, of course, Marx's. See *The Civil War in France*, Marx's nearly contemporaneous account of the Commune. Citations from this and other pertinent writings on the Commune by Marx and Engels are quoted from *On the Paris Commune* (Moscow: Progress, 1971), and are hereafter given in the text in parentheses.

34 Quoted from Edwards, *Paris Commune*, p. 60.

35 Quoted by Thomas, *Marx and the Anarchists*, p. 184.

36 As Bender points out, Engels confirmed that as a new type of polity, the Commune was not a state. In an 1875 letter to Bebel, Engels wrote:

> The whole talk about the state should be dropped [from our party's statements], especially since the Commune ... was no longer a state

in the proper sense of the word [because it was a state in-the-process-of-dissolving] .... We would therefore propose to replace *state* everywhere by *Gemeinwesen*, a good old German word which can very well convey the meaning of the French word "commune." (Cited by Bender, *"Ambiguities,"* p. 549)

37 It should be emphasized here that Marx's furious battle with Bakunin and the anarchists in the First International reached its peak at the time of the Commune. To my knowledge, all the nineteenth-century literature on federalism belongs to the anarchist tradition. Important here is Proudhon's very interesting tract *Du Principe federatif et de la necessité de reconstituer le parti de la révolution* (Paris, 1863). There is an English translation by Richard Vernon, *The Principle of Federation* (Toronto: University of Toronto Press, 1979). If Marx knew it (which seems likely), he ignored it – understandably. He would have taken it to be another utopian exercise in "mutualism." Bakunin's *Federalism, Socialism, and Anti-Theologism*, an unfinished tract, had been written for the predominantly liberal and pacifist League of Peace and Freedom. It is excerpted in G. P. Maximoff (ed.), *The Political Philosophy of Bakunin* (Glencoe: III. Free Press, 1953). See E. H. Carr, *Michael Bakunin* (New York: Octagon, 1975), ch. 25–31.

38 Bloom, *World of Nations*, p. 17. Hobsbawm, "Marx, Engels and Politics," notes that Marx used "society" and "nation" interchangeably.

39 See Bloom, *World of Nations*, ch. 3. Marx's conception of a nation as an integrated, cultural, economic unity is distinctly "sociological"; but it is fair to say that he failed to appreciate fully the more irrational aspects of "nationalism." In this, he was probably closer to Goethe, who believed that while people would continue to identify with the "fatherland" as the place where they were most comfortable, "above the nations is humanity." Engels was, it seems, far more sensitive to the worst aspects of the sentiment of nationalism.

40 With regard to what we would call the problem of "national liberation," in the Balkans or the colonized areas of the world, they hardly took it seriously. This has bothered modern writers, since it seems to imply a condescending attitude toward "less developed" societies. Perhaps so. But regardless it is one of the great tragedies of the modern world that capitalist imperialism did not promote development, as Adam Smith, Kant, and Marx and Engels believed that it would. In consequence, wars of national liberation have been fought by peoples who, faced with superpower fears and aspirations, have had no chance to realize socialist democracy.

41 Marx to Domela-Nieuwenhuis, 1881, *Paris Commune*, p. 293. The judgment that the Commune was not socialist was inconsistent with Marx's earlier quite exaggerated comments, of course. The composition of the Council showed that of eighty-one members, about eighteen came from middle-class back-grounds and about thirty from the professions, *"la bohème,"* journalists, three doctors, a veterinarian, three lawyers, an architect, and three teachers. Thirty-five were manual workers, but were mainly craftsmen in small workshops. Although there were some newer, heavy industries in the suburbs of Paris, only a small number of members came from these. In this remarkable

group, there was no obvious leader. See Edwards, *Paris Commune*, pp. 204–7.

42 Quoted in Berger, *Engels, Armies, and Revolution*, p. 85.

43 Edwards, *Paris Commune*, p. 339.

44 See James Joll, *The Second International, 1889–1914* (New York: Praeger, 1956).

45 See Berger, *Engels, Armies, and Revolution*, ch. 7.

46 Engels, *New York Daily Tribune*, 18 Sept. 1852; Repr. in L. Krieger (ed.), *Germany: Revolution and Counter-revolution* (Chicago: University of Chicago Press, 1967), pp. 227–8.

47 Engels's Introduction to Karl Marx, *The Class Struggles in France*, (New York: International, 1964), p. 21. The publication history of this becomes pertinent in ch. 12 below. Written for a new edition in 1895, this introduction was "edited" by *Vörwarts*, the party newspaper of the German Social Democrats and was never published in full by them. Engels was extremely displeased by this, even though the deleted portions of his text do not make a convincing case for an insurrectionary Marxist politics. See n. 48. Still, there is little doubt that the more "opportunistic" members of the SPD did all they could to make it seem that Engels had abandoned his revolutionary posture; and, as we shall see, Rosa Luxemburg was led to lay some blame on Engels for misdirecting German revolutionary politics.

48 A deleted passage here reads:

> Does this mean that in the future the street fight will play no further role? Certainly not. It only means that the conditions since 1848 have become far more unfavourable for civil fights, far more favourable for the military. A future street fight can therefore be victorious when this unfavourable situation is compensated by other factors. Accordingly, it will occur more seldom in the beginning of a great revolution than in its further progress, and will have to be undertaken with greater forces. These, however, may then well prefer, as in the whole Great French Revolution on September 4 and October 31, 1870 in Paris [prior to the events of the Commune], the open attack to the passive barricade tactics. (ibid., p. 24)

This seems hardly arguable, but what is described sounds far more like a military response to counterrevolution than an insurrection. This would square with Engels's views on the changing character of the army. See below.

49 There are precious few discussions in English of Engels's theories on war and revolution. Berger's *Engels, Armies, and Revolution* is the most extensive. But I depart somewhat from his account of Engels's later theories. Gallie's *Philosophers of Peace and War*, ch. 3, is subtle, especially as regards the later theory, even if, as Mark von Hagen says, it suffers from a typical tendency: "Gallie describes Marx and Engels as rigorously dogmatic theorists, only to devote most of his essay to faulting them for failing to live up to his claims on their behalf." The comment is in his annotated bibliography, which includes German sources, in Paret (ed.), *Masters of Modern Strategy*, pp. 890–2. Von Hagen substantially revised the older essay by Sigmund Neumann. The essay is too brief but is nonetheless valuable.

50 Quoted in Berger, *Engels, Armies, and Revolution*, p. 162. This is as good a
place as any to raise the question of how, in terms, of "historical materialism,"
Engels saw war. There is first of all the more general question of whether
Marx and Engels were committed to a version of fatalist, eschatological history.
As in the remark in the foregoing, that "this is coming, as inexorably as a
decree of fate," Marx and Engels often wrote as if their "predictions," rooted
in their new "science," were guaranteed. But as already noted, it can easily be
shown that this was not meant seriously. In both their concrete historical
writings and in their most systematic theoretical accounts, they acknowledge
all sorts of contingency in history.

The second question, discussed by Gallie, is whether Marxism claims to
explain wars "as calculable and gradable effects of deeper-lying changes in
the ways in which societies organize their productive power" (*Philosophers of
Peace and War*, p. 75). Engels's *Herr Eugen Dühring's Revolution in Science*,
Pt II, ch. 2 (1878), may be taken as a typical text. Engels argues explicitly
against Dühring's claim that "force," "the formation of political relationships
is, historically, the fundamental fact, and the economic facts dependent on
this are only an effect, ... and consequently always facts of the second
order" (ibid., p. 176). It is easy to suppose that Engels reverses this, making
political relations, including war and wars, "effects" of economic facts. Even a
cursory reading shows, however, that this way of talking misrepresents the
issue. You cannot have modern war without modern industry. The former
"depends" on the latter but is not "caused" by it. That is the burden of
Engels's account. On the other hand, nowhere does Engels say that all wars
have economic *causes*. Indeed, in his many concrete analyses of wars, the
Austro-Prussian War, the Italian War, the American Civil War, the Franco-
Prussia War, and so forth, he finds all sorts of causes. Moreover, he explicitly
holds, with Clausewitz, that wars, once begun, can have unpredictable tra-
jectories; for, "once the first shot is fired, control is at an end, the horse can
bolt" (cited in Berger, *Engels, Armies, and Revolution*, p. 129). Gallie's review
concludes that Marx and Engels pay "lip service" to the idea that wars are
explained as epiphenomona of deeper causes, but then go on to "show us war
as a relatively independent variable in the every-changing human scene"
(*Philosophers of Peace and War*, p. 79). Of course.

It is of considerable importance to note that Engels was speaking as an
acknowledged military authority. His specifically military writings encompass
hundreds of pages. Unfortunately, they are nowhere conveniently collected.
One collection of his published essays which emphasizes specifically technical
military questions is W. H. Chaloner and W. O. Henderson (eds), *Engels as a
Military Critic: Articles Reprinted from the Volunteer Journal and the Manchester
Guardian of the 1860's* (Westport Conn.: Greenwood Press, 1976).

Berger writes that Engels's *Pall Mall Gazette* series on the Franco-Prussian
War "was a major triumph, and 'The General,' as Marx's daughter Jenny
named him, achieved considerable acceptance in military circles. On the eve
of his first visit to England in 1894, Hellmut von Gerlach discussed travel
plans with his circle of reactionary notables, and was astonished to hear
Major Otto Wach of the German Great General Staff, 'the strategic authority

of the whole right-wing press,' declare that Gerlach must 'look up my friend Frederich Engels.' ... As a military writer, Engels had made it" (*Engels, Armies, and Revolution*, p. 53).

51   Quoted in Berger, *Engels, Armies, and Revolution*, p. 167.

52   Berger's point that the army will *begin* the revolution leads him to an important conclusion: "Unless a socialist accepted the full Theory of the Vanishing Army – and no socialist did – he was presented by the Marxist founders with a tactical vacuum" (ibid., p. 170). Some, like Bebel, accepted the contradictions and "could do no better than combine revolutionary goals with moderate, legal activity." Others followed Bernstein, who maintained that the revolutionary goal was impossible, since revolution would always be crushed by the army. For him, of course, "revolution" was also unnecessary. Others, including Lenin and Sorel, proposed new schemes for effectuating revolution.

This is quite a powerful argument, but it seems to me that there was no tactical vacuum. The question was, as Gallie suggests, would the Socialist parties have time? Could sufficient numbers of men who were at least sympathetic to socialism be recruited? Would they at least be unwilling to squash a revolution? These become terribly pertinent in the Russian and German contexts of 1917–18. Workers' and soldiers' councils became the core of the revolutionary hopes of both the Bolsheviks and the USPD and the Communists in Germany. See Part V below.

53   Marx to Liebknecht, 4 Feb. 1878; quoted by Gallie, *Philosophers of Peace and War.*

54   Quoted in Berger, *Engels, Armies and Revolution.*

Worth noting is the fact that Engels does not see war between nations as the inevitable outcome of capitalist expansionism. Neither is this view found in Marx, who in *Capital* has precious little to say about the economics of colonialism. By the last decades of the century, however, the idea was in the air and found expression in J. A. Hobson's influential 1902 *Imperialism – A Study* (Ann Arbor: University of Michigan, 1965). Hobson argued that Britain acquired colonies as a dumping ground for surplus capital, but insisted that there was nothing *necessary* about this, that "whatever is produced in England can be consumed in England, provided that the 'income' or power to demand commodities, is properly distributed." The theory that this was *not* possible makes its first clear appearance in Lenin's 1917 *Imperialism, The Highest Stage of Capitalism* in *Collected Works*, 4th edn, vol. 22 (Moscow: Foreign Languages Publishing House, 1961–5).

Part V   War and Mass Democracy   Introduction

1   Quoted from Ronald Steel, *Walter Lippmann and the American Century* (Boston: Little, Brown, 1980), p. 113.

2   Fritz Fischer, *War of Illusions, German Policies from 1911 to 1914* (London: Chatto and Windus, 1975), p. viii. Plainly, the question of the causes of World War I is complex. Nevertheless, it seems safe to say that if the

"immediate motives" were neither "directly imperialist" nor wholly domestic, there can be no understanding which ignores these. Thus, all the governments were "sharks," as Hobsbawm has recently put it (*Age of Empire 1875–1914* (New York: Pantheon, 1988)). Or, as James Joll writes: "Imperialist thinking has always accepted the risk of war and regarded armed struggle as an essential part of imperial expansion . . . . By 1914 this intensified the crisis in which German ambitions, French grievances, Russian expansionism, British anxieties and Austrian fears led to the decision that war was inevitable if vital national interests were to be preserved" (James Joll, *The Origins of the First World War* (London and New York: Longmans, 1984), p. 167).

The view that domestic crisis was a critical component has been put forward by many historians. In addition to Fischer, see Eli Halévy, "The World Crisis by 1914–1918" (1929), in Halévy, *The Era of Tyrannies* (New York: Doubleday, 1965), and G. Baraclough, *The Origins of Modern Germany* (Oxford: Basil Blackwell, 1962), p. 435. More recently Arno Mayer has put it at the very center of his account. On his view, "domestic crises were the precondition and cause rather than the consequence of foreign wars [from 1870 to World War I], and that the end-purpose of external conflicts was to affect the outcome of the internal crisis in which they originated" ("Internal Crisis and War Since 1870," in Charles L. Bertrand (ed.), *Revolutionary Situations in Europe 1917–1922: Germany, Italy, Austria-Hungary* (Montreal: Centre for European Studies, 1977). If Mayer overstates his case, he nevertheless provides an extremely useful framework. He emphasizes "the politics of over-reaction" and the success of the "ultras" in preventing the reaccommodation of what had become, with socioeconomic development, a backward political structure. This was a theme of Max Weber's analysis in 1917. See also Arno Mayer, "The Domestic Causes of the First World War," in L. Krieger and F. Stern (eds), *The Responsibility of Power* (Garden City, N.Y.: Doubleday, 1967), and *idem, The Persistence of the Old Regime: Europe to the Great War* (New York: Pantheon, 1981).

3 Briefly, on 28 June Archduke Francis Ferdinand, heir to the throne of Austro-Hungary was shot at Sarajevo. Fearing nationalist stirrings in Serbia and the distintegration of the Empire and urged on by the German government which pledged full support in any war, the Emperor delivered a predictably provocative ultimatum, to be answered within forty-eight hours. The Serbian government, itself in the midst of a domestic crisis, responded in a conciliatory tone; but, probably because it could expect Russian assistance and perhaps because of some complicity in the inner circle in the assassination plot, it objected to the clause which demanded the participation of Austro-Hungarian officials in the Serbian inquiry into the assassination. In the event, the Russians responded to the "Slavic compatriots" and began a partial mobilization. From the point of view of Germany, the key was France. The Kaiser assumed and hoped that France would join Russia. Thus, Germany could, through war, satisfy its imperial aims. The key then became England. Bethmann Hollweg had carefully secured agreement from Lord Grey that "[England] will neither make nor join in any unprovoked attack on Germany." It was critical, accordingly, that Germany's entry be "provoked." The so-

called Schliefflen Plan, drawn up in 1891 and elaborated in 1905 by General Moltke, called first for a quick defeat of Russia's ally, France, England remaining neutral, and then an attack on Russia. One serious complication was that Germany could not attack France with sufficient forces without trespassing on Belgian neutrality. Bethmann Hollweg hoped that this would not bring England into the war. The foregoing follows Joll, *Origins*.

For analysis of the "fateful alliance" between France and Russia, see George F. Kennan, *The Fateful Alliance: France, Russia and the Coming of the First World War* (New York: Pantheon, 1984). For Germany, in addition to Fischer's *War of Illusions*, see *idem, Germany's Aims in the First World War* (New York: Norton, 1967). It was by no means a foregone conclusion that England would enter the war. See John Viscount Morley, *Memorandum on Resignation, August 1914* (London: Macmillan, 1928), and discussion in Mayer, "Domestic Causes." For an account of the domestic crisis of liberal England, see George Dangerfield, *The Strange Death of Liberal England, 1910–1914* (New York: Putnams, 1980).

4   To be sure, Lord Grey did have a majority of the House of Commons with him, but the die had been cast. Indeed, in his speech in the House on 3 August 1914, he observed that there was but one way "in which the Government could make certain at the present moment of keeping out-side this war, and that would be that it should immediately issue a proclamation of unconditional neutrality." He continued, "We cannot do that. We [that is, Lord Grey!] have made the commitment to France that I have read to the House which prevents us [Great Britain?] from doing that." Foreign policy, including the giving of "assurances," was in the hands of the executive.

5   Quoted by Joll, *Origins*, p. 116.

6   Gordon Craig, "The Revolution in War and Diplomacy," in Jack R. Roth (ed.), *World War One: A Turning Point in Modern History* (New York: Knopf, 1967), p. 122.

Chapter 11   Bolshevism and the Question of Democracy

1   In what follows, dates prior to 14 Feb. 1918 are according to the Julian calendar, thereafter according to the Gregorian calendar in standard use in the West and from that date in Bolshevik Russia.

2   Moshe Lewin, *The Making of the Soviet System* (London: Methuen, 1985), p. 210. The following derives primarily from Lewin.

3   Ibid., p. 211.

4   Quoted from Paul Avrich, *Kronstadt 1921* (Princeton: Princeton University Press, 1970), p. 9. This paragraph derives from Avrich.

5   Lewin, *Making of the Soviet System*, p. 51.

6   Ibid.

7   Avrich, *Kronstadt 1921*, p. 9.

8   Stephen F. Cohen observes that "the civil war years ... remain largely un-studied" (*Rethinking the Soviet Experience: Politics and History Since 1917* (New York: Oxford University Press, 1985), p. 33. I have found William Henry

Chamberlin's study, *The Russian Revolution*, 2 vols (New York: Macmillan, 1935), most valuable. More recent non-Soviet studies offer differences in interpretation but depend largely on the sources available to Chamberlin. See Peter Kenez, *Civil War in South Russia, 1918* (Berkeley: University of California Press, 1971); *idem, Civil War in South Russia, 1919–1920* (Berkeley: University of California Press, 1977); Richard Luckett, *The White Generals* (New York: Viking, 1971); George Brinkley, *The Volunteer Army and Allied Intervention in South Russia, 1917–1921* (Notre Dame: University of Notre Dame Press, 1966); and Richard H. Ullman, *Britain and the Russian Civil War, November 1918–February 1920* (Princeton: Princeton University Press, 1968). But in addition to the limits on sources, most specialist writing makes little effort to grasp the many, confused connections which constitute the civil war.

9   Chamberlin, *Russian Revolution*, vol. 2, p. 171.
10 In 1929, Churchill wrote:

> The Bolsheviks were absorbed during the whole of 1919 in the conflicts with Kolchak and Denikin. Their energy was turned upon the internal struggle. A breathing-space of inestimable importance was afforded to the whole line of newly liberated countries which stood along the western borders of Russia ... Finland, Esthonia, [sic], Latvia, Lithuania and, above all, Poland were able during 1919 to establish the structure of civilized states and to organize the strength of patriotic armies. (Winston Churchill, *The World Crisis: The Aftermath* (London Butterworth, 1929), p. 250; cited by Chamberlin, vol. 2, p. 171)

11 Alexander Rabinowitch, *The Bolsheviks Come to Power: The Revolution of 1917 in Petrograd* (New York: Norton, 1976), p. 95.
12 Quoted by Chamberlin, *Russian Revolution*, vol. 1, p. 197.
13 Rabinowitch, *Bolsheviks Come to Power*, p. 102.
14 Ibid., p. 139.
15 Quoted, in. ibid., p. 191.
16 See Chamberlin, *Russian Revolution*, vol. 1, ch. 10–14, and Stephen F. Cohen, *Bukharin and the Russian Revolution* (New York: Knopf, 1971), p. 46. Rabinowitch writes:

> Historians of the Soviet Union have stressed historical inevitability and the role of a tightly knit revolutionary party led by Lenin in accounting for the outcome of the October revolution, while many Western scholars have viewed this event either as a historical accident or, more frequently, as the result of a well-executed coup d'etat without significant mass support ....
> Studying the aspirations of factory workers, soldiers, and sailors as expressed in contemporary documents, I find that these concerns corresponded closely to the program of political, economic and social reform put forth by the Bolsheviks at a time when all other major political parties were widely discredited .... As a result, in October the goals of the Bolsheviks, as the masses understood them, had strong popular support. (*Bolsheviks Come to Power*, p. xvii)

Theodore von Laue (*Why Lenin? Why Stalin?* (New York: Lippincott, 1971), p. 118) concludes that "one can hardly deny that theirs [the Bolsheviks'] was a democratic revolution." Still, his book is spoiled by cold war rhetoric. He says, e.g., that "mercilessly they exploited the ignorance of the masses," both fantastically exaggerating the capacities of the Bolsheviks (who, e.g., surely did not control the press) and, worse, denigrating the capacities of "the masses" to decide for themselves what they wanted. Similarly, in his chapter on the first months of the regime, he asserts, remarkably, that the Bolsheviks "aimed at nothing less than overthrowing the entire world order" (ibid., p. 123).

17 Richard Pipes, *The Formation of the Soviet Union: Communism and Nationalism 1917–1923*, rev. edn (Cambridge, Mass.: Harvard University Press, 1974), pp. 107–8.

18 For discussion of the Brest–Litovsk Peace, see E. H. Carr, *The Bolshevik Revolution 1917–1923*, vol. 3 (New York: Macmillan, 1961); Rex Wade, *The Russian Search for Peace, February–October, 1917* (Stanford: Stanford University Press, 1969; Richard H. Ullman, *Intervention and the War* (Princeton: Princeton University Press, 1961), ch. 3, and 4; Fritz Fischer, *Germany's War Aims in the First World War*, Pt III.

19 Pipes, *Formation*, p. 108.

20 Ibid.

21 Quoted by Chamberlin, *Russian Revolution*, vol. 1, p. 374.

22 Pipes, *Formation*, p. 92.

23 Ibid., p. 100.

24 Quoted in ibid., p. 107.

25 Ibid., p. 108.

26 Kenez, *Civil War*, p. 37.

27 Ibid., p. 3.

28 Chamberlin, *Russian Revolution*, vol. 1, p. 380. The Terek Cossacks had more than twice the acreage of the natives. In addition to the *inogorodnye* (literally "people from other towns"), who were largely Russians, rented land from Cossacks, and comprised an urban class of workers, merchants, etc., were the native peoples: Kabardians, Ossetins, Chechens, Ingush, etc. These elements were critical to the ultimate Bolshevik victory in the region.

29 Ibid., vol. 1, p. 375.

30 Avrich, *Kronstadt*, pp. 14–15.

31 Carr, *Bolshevik Revolution*, vol. 3, p. 65.

32 Brinkley, *Volunteer Army*, pp. 44–5.

33 Ibid., p. 48.

34 Quoted by Chamberlin, *Russian Revolution*, vol. 2, p. 3.

35 This remarkable episode is treated by George F. Kennan in his *Soviet–American Relations, 1917–1920*, 2 vols (Princeton: Princeton University Press, 1956, 1958), vol. 2, ch. 6. Kennan argues that "in view of the importance of this uprising for subsequent Allied, and particularly American policy with regard to intervention," the question of who instigated the confrontation is important. He notes that according to Soviet histories the blame is fully on the Allies. He rejects this view and decides that

all in all ... one is reduced to the conclusion that external instigation or encouragement, either from the Allies or from central headquarters of the underground Whites, played no significant part in the decision of the Czechs to take arms against Soviet power. The outbreak of these hostilities was a spontaneous occurrence, resulting from decisions and actions promulgated, respectively and almost simultaneously, by the Soviet authorities in Moscow and in Siberia and by the Czech commanders on the spot. (Ibid., p. 164)

On the other hand, he acknowledges that there is a sense in which "the Czechs began the uprising" (ibid., p. 152). More important perhaps, when the situation became known, it was enthusiastically greeted by the Allies – as Churchill said, "as if by magic" – and especially by the Americans. See ibid., esp. vol. 2, ch. 17.

36 Ibid., vol. 2, p. 416.
37 Quoted in ibid., vol. 2, p. 101.
38 Ibid., vol. 2, p. 145.
39 Chamberlin, *Russian Revolution*, vol. 2, p. 163.
40 Kennan, *Soviet–American Relations*, vol. 2, p. 417.
41 Quoted in ibid., vol. 2, p. 247.
42 Chamberlin, *Russian Revolution*, vol. 2, p. 165.
43 Kenez, *Civil War ... 1919–1920*, p. 188.
44 Ibid., pp. 193–202.
45 Chamberlin, *Russian Revolution*, vol. 2, p. 168.
46 Ibid.
47 Churchill, *The World Crisis*; quoted in ibid., vol. 2, p. 152.
48 Kenez, *Civil War ... 1919–1920*, p. 179.
49 Quoted in Kennan, *Soviet–American Relations*, vol. 2, pp. 460–1.
50 Quoted in ibid.
51 Chamberlin, *Russian Revolution*, vol. 1, p. 371.
52 The Marxist celebration of the "proletariat" and concomitant prejudices against the "idiocy" of peasant life surely worked against them. Lenin had appreciated this from at least his "What is to be Done?" (see below). But it was not until Russian Marxists, locked into the historical monism of Plekhanov, were forced to acknowledge the need for the peasantry, that the latter became part of Marxist plans for revolution. This was due in part to the fundamental failure of a simple-minded class analysis, illustrated most poignantly – and in the Stalin era most tragically – by the continued vitality of the terms "kulak" and "village bourgeois" in the vocabulary of the Marxist parties. In addition, there was a failure to grasp the nature and role of religion and of customary law in the countryside, facets better appreciated by SRs and anarchists. These important themes are analyzed by Moshe Lewin, *Making of the Soviet System*, Pt I. See also Nicholas Berdyaev, *The Origin of Russian Communism* (Ann Arbor: University of Michigan Press, 1960), ch. 2.
53 See Paul Avrich, *The Russian Anarchists* (New York: Norton, 1978).
54 Carmen Sirianni, *Workers' Control and Socialist Democracy: The Soviet Experience* (London: Verso, 1982), pp. 82–3. See also the most useful history by Helène

Carrère D'Encausse, *Lenin, Revolution and Power*, vol. 1, tr. Valence Ionescu (London and New York: Longmans, 1982).

55   Quoted in Rabinowitch, *Bolsheviks Come to Power*, p. 294.

56   Quotations from Lenin are from *Collected Works*. Subsequent citations are given in the text in parentheses and include volume and page numbers. Bernstein, of course, is Eduard Bernstein, the German Marxist, whose 1899 *Die Voraussetzungen des Sozialismus und die Aufgaben der Sozialdemocratie* (literally "The Premises of Socialism and the Tasks of Social Democracy" – misleadingly entitled in English *Evolutionary Socialism*) codified a debate over the theory which grounded the tactics of a Marxist politics. Bernstein's views were formally condemned in 1899 and then again at the Dresden Congress of 1903. Millerand is Alexander Millerand, an ex-socialist who became France's Minister of War. Worth mention, student editions of Lenin's "What Is to be Done?" invariably excise the last sections, which deal with the object and aim of the essay, Lenin's plan for an all-Russian newspaper.

57   The best account is by Lucio Colletti, "Bernstein and the Marxism of the Second International," in Colletti, *From Rousseau to Lenin* (New York: Monthly Review, 1972).

58   Quoted in Colletti, *From Rousseau to Lenin*, p. 57; my emphasis.

59   Lenin berated those revolutionaries who "insult the workers by [their] desire *to talk down* to them when discussing working class politics and organization .... We must educate workers (and university and gymnasium students) so that we *may be able to discuss* these questions with them" (V. 471).
      The Greek roots and subsequent connotations of "pedagogic" and "demagogic" bear noting. Since the fifth century, their connotations had been propelled by the power of Plato's philosophy. "Teachers of children" (*paide*) are noble in providing them with knowledge (*episteme*). "Teachers of the people" are sophists! Did the only choice lie between treating the people as children, as in the *Republic*, or swaying irrationally grounded opinion (*doxa*) in the public forums of the Assembly?

60   There is much evidence in support of this. For example, while still in Zurich, just after the overthrow of the Tsar, Lenin wrote: "We are not Blanquists, not advocates of the seizure of power by a minority." And later, "We are now in a minority – the masses [N.B. *not* the workers] do not trust us yet. We know how to wait." This was then expanded: "We are not charlatans .... We must base ourselves only upon the consciousness of the masses. Even if it is necessary to remain in a minority, be it so .... We must not be afraid to be a minority .... We will carry on the work of criticism in order to free the masses from deceit. ... Our line will prove right. All the oppressed will come to us" (quoted by Trotsky, *The History of the Russian Revolution* (New York: Monad, 1980), vol. 3, p. 127, vol. 2, p. 306).

61   See her "Organizational Questions of the Russian Social Democracy," in Mary Alice Waters (ed.), *Rosa Luxemburg Speaks* (New York: Pathfinder, 1970).
      As Norman Geras points out, Bertram Wolfe's retitling of this essay as "Leninism or Marxism?" is symptomatic of the widespread misreadings of both Lenin and Luxemburg. Not only do the views they shared, *versus* the

quite different views of, say, Bernstein and Kautsky, far outweigh their differences; but the failure to be historical in analyzing these, coupled with a willingness to employ their differences in the service of Stalin's version of "Leninism" or, at the opposite extreme, of bourgeois liberalism, does enormous injustice to the facts. For example, not only did Luxemburg understand the crucial role of a revolutionary party, but in "Blanquisme et socialdemocratie" (1906), she wrote: "We do not accept Comrade Plekhanov's reproach that [the Bolsheviks] have been the victims of Blanquist mistakes during the course of the [1905] revolution. It is possible that there were traces of this in the organizational project drafted by Lenin in 1902, but that is something which belongs to the past ...." This is cited by Geras in his excellent *The Legacy of Rosa Luxemburg* (London: NLB, 1976), p. 102n.

He also points out that it is remarkable, but also symptomatic, that Peter Nettl and all three editors of English-language editions say, wrongly, that Luxemburg's essay was aimed at "What Is to be Done?" Even a cursory reading shows that its object is Lenin's "One Step Forward, Two Steps Back."

62   Cohen remarks that "even in the 1920's, after the bureaucratization and militarization fostered by the civil war, the high party elite was not (nor had it ever been) the disciplined vanguard fantasized in 'What Is to be Done?' It remained oligarchical, in the words of one its leaders [Bukharin], 'a negotiated federation between groups, groupings, factions, and "tendencies"'" (*Rethinking the Soviet Experience*, p. 53; original emphasis omitted). Cohen may read too much into "What Is to be Done?" and take Bukharin too much at his word. See also Robert Service, *The Bolshevik Party in Revolution: A Study in Organizational Change, 1917–1923* (London: Macmillan, 1979).

63   A third interpretation is more cynical. It holds that the theses of *State and Revolution* were put forward only to win support from the masses. That Lenin and the Bolsheviks acted on these theses suggests, however, that this view cannot be sustained. Some defenders of the Bolshevik seizure of power share in holding that Lenin justified anti-democracy in terms of a future democracy, except that by redefining "democracy," as rule by the revolutionary party, the unity of means and ends is preserved. More subtle is the claim that "facts were to show that Lenin's analysis was correct, that it was possible to establish Soviet power through armed insurrection, and that this power, the establishment of which opened a new stage in world history, would be remarkably firmly grounded" (Charles Bettelheim, *Class Struggles in the USSR, First Period 1917–1923* (Hassocks: Harvester, 1976), p. 83. Unless this is an equivocation on "soviet," the problem is exactly that soviet power was not and could not be established.

64   See Oskar Anweiler, *The Soviets: The Russian Workers, Peasants and Soldiers Councils, 1905–1921* (New York: Pantheon, 1974); Chamberlin, *Russian Revolution*, vol. 1, pp. 52, 112; and Sirianni, *Workers Control*, ch. 3. By the time of the October Revolution, there were perhaps 900 Soviets.

Anweiler's treatment is indispensable, even if he sometimes falls victim to reading history backwards. Thus, in passing, he offers that "Lenin's centralization of both state and economy, which robbed the soviet system of its inherent strength, was Marx's belated answer to Proudhon" (*The Soviets*, p. 9). But he fully appreciates that the program announced in the April theses had evolved during the Great War (ibid., p. 149), that "the system of 'dyarchy' could not endure" (ibid., p. 139), and, remarkably perhaps, that "the Bolsheviks were absolutely correct in demanding a radical solution to the problem: 'All power to the soviets' (ibid.).

At the same time, Anweiler is profoundly sensitive to the problems which this "solution" created, and his summary of these is excellent. First, the soviets were class organizations and thus, "Should soviet rule be established, other strata – especially the bourgeoisie, but also sections of the peasantry – would reject the revolution, and the proletariat, the nucleus of soviet power, would be isolated" (ibid., p. 140). This was a view shared by most Bolsheviks, of course. But his next two observations are striking, because they are both obvious, yet ignored in criticism of the outcome. Thus, "a soviet government could solve Russia's enormous problems no better than could a broadly based coalition government. Waging war, especially, required union of all national forces," and finally, "establishment of soviet power would reinforce centrifugal tendencies inherent in local soviets, and thereby defeat unity" (ibid.).

65 Bukharin is quoted in Cohen, *Bukharin*, p. 49; Trotsky from his *History*, p. 300. Avrich (*Russian Anarchists*, p. 128) reports the words of I.P. Goldenberg, "a Veteran Russian Marxist" as follows: "Lenin has made himself a candidate for one European throne that had been vacant for thirty years – the throne of Bukunin!"

66 Cohen recounts a dispute between Lenin and Bukharin regarding the theory of the state. Lenin had charged Bukharin with "semi-anarchism," a charge that had surprised Bukharin. Cohen judges that there was a "volte-face" in Lenin's thinking and concludes that "the arguments and conclusions" of *State and Revolution* were Bukharin's. See Cohen, *Bukharin*, pp. 40–2.

67 It is not denied by anyone, I believe, that as far as *socialist* transformation was concerned, the Bolsheviks were extremely cautious. They insisted on nationalization of the banks and "most important cartels;" but Lenin was careful to make clear that nationalization and confiscation of private property are totally different measures. "Whoever owned fifteen million rubles would continue to be the owner of fifteen million rubles after the nationalisation of the banks" (Works, vol. 25, p. 360). It was only with war communism that, on 28 June 1918, the decree expropriating heavy industry appeared. As to workers' control, the policy of limiting their power to control of management fell short of the workers' expectations. As regards the peasantry, the policies which the Bolsheviks adopted were straightforwardly petty bourgeois.

It is striking that Marxists writers have devoted countless pages to the question of whether socialist states, beginning with the state that emerged from the Bolshevik Revolution, are really socialisms and have devoted so few pages to the question of why they are not democracies. Of course, I have put war at the center of this; but subsequent revolutionary leaders, misled by poor theory, a poor understanding of the Bolshevik revolutionary experience, and antidemocratic sentiments must share some of the blame. One would need, of course, to consider each case as the particular case it is!

68 Trotsky, *History*, vol. 1, p. 214.
69 Quoted in Chamberlin, *Russian Revolution*, vol. 1, p. 101.
70 Quoted by Carsten, "Revolutionary Situations in Europe," in Charles L. Bertrand (ed.), *Revolutionary Situations ... Germany, Italy, Austria-Hungary*, p. 21.

On "dual power," Bettelheim asserts: "'Dual power' meant that in April 1917 the democratic dictatorship of the proletariat and the peasantry was both realized (for 'actually, in Petrograd, the power is in the hands of the workers and soldiers') and not realized, for through the SRs, the majority of the people supported a line of class collaboration, so that 'the bourgeoisie is in power'" (*Class Struggles in the USSR*, p. 84). Of course, Bolshevik control of the Petrograd soviet was not in any sense a realization of "the democratic dictatorship of the proletariat and the peasantry." Nor, as noted, were the bourgeoisie "in power."

71 Quoted in Cohen, *Bukharin*, pp. 55—6.
72 Martin Buber, *Paths in Utopia*, pp. 99—100.
73 Rabinowitch, *Bolsheviks Come to Power*, p. 311.
74 Anweiler, *Soviets*, pp. 212—13.
75 Quoted in ibid., p. 219.
76 See A. J. Polan, *Lenin and the End of Politics* (Berkeley: University of California Press, 1984), for a bizarre version of this view. Adopting a remarkable ahistorical methodology in which "texts" have lives of their own, he first accuses Lenin of being an "ill-read ignoramus" and then argues that *State and Revolution* "is guilty of subsequent developments: that is, the features of the authoritarian Soviet regime are present within every line and concept of the text" (p. 128). For Polan, "the issue is not what the author intended, but what the text dictated." Thus "the 'crime' of the text is not that it did not work; it is that it did" (ibid., p. 130). This stunning conclusion is reached by arguing that by collapsing all political functions into one kind of institution, the soviets, the "text" allows for "no distances, no spaces, no appeals, no checks, no balances, no processes, no delays, no interrogations and above all, no distribution of power" (ibid., p. 129).

This is a fairly conventional criticism of democracy, of course; and it does not appear to make any difference to Polan that civil war, economic chaos, and the demand to preserve the revolution quickly deepened the gulf between Bolshevik ideology and practice. One can only wonder what Polan might have said had the explicit hopes of *State and Revolution* been achieved, hopes as intelligible to Polan as to any moderately literate reader.

One might offer a sympathetic "reading" of Polan and say that his position, following Weber, is that only via a parliament can one control a bureaucracy, and that, accordingly, in the best of circumstances, Soviet democracy was a hopeless delusion. Perhaps. Weber's views on this are discussed in the next chapter. But clearly, once the choice was made for Soviet democracy, the parliamentary route was foreclosed. It is hard to say whether an alternative was possible. Would the outcome have been similar if the Bolsheviks had adopted a compromise position, Kamenev's or Luxemburg's?

77 Lewin, *Lenin's Last Struggle* (New York: Vintage, 1970), p. 31.

78   Cohen, *Bukharin*, p. 87.

79   Ibid., p. 98.

80   On Kronstadt and the suppression of factions, see Avrich, *Kronstadt 1921*. Avrich writes: "Kronstadt presents a situation in which the historian can sympathize with the rebels and still concede that the Bolsheviks were justified in subduing them. To recognize this, indeed, is to grasp the full tragedy of Kronstadt" (p. 6). To say that the Bolsheviks were "compelled" to subdue them, of course, rests on the assumption that any regime will make the effort to maintain itself. It is not clear however, whether Avrich thinks that they were right in doing so.

81   Cohen, *Bukharin*, p. 106.

82   Lewin, *Lenin's Last Struggle*, p. 31.

83   The following draws on Lewin, *Lenin's Last Struggle*, and Pipes, *Formation*, pp. 291–3.

84   Lewin, *Lenin's Last Struggle*, p. 103.

85   Quoted in ibid., p. 51.

86   Quoted in Pipes, *Formation*, p. 286.

87   Ibid., p. 41.

88   Ibid., p. 42.

89   Quoted in ibid., p. 43.

90   Luxemburg, "The Russian Revolution," in *Rosa Lexemburg Speaks*, ed. Mary-Alice Waters (New York: Pathfinder, 1970). p. 378.

91   Bettelheim provides a useful summary in his *Class Struggles in the USSR*, pp. 106–10.

92   Mensheviks and SRs were sometimes permitted to hold conferences; but after Lenin's analysis in *What Is to be Done?* this was liable to result in Cheka arrests of the leaders. Until the middle of 1919 there were periods in which Menshevik and SR newspapers could be printed; but this ceased thereafter. While it is not a justification for Red Terror, unless one accepts the Machiavellian imperative, we need to remind ourselves that Russia was engaged in a bloody civil war.

93   See Jerry A. Hough, *The Soviet Union and Social Science Theory* (Cambridge, Mass.: Harvard University Press, 1977).

94   Luxemburg, "Russian Revolution," p. 391.

95   Lewin, *Making of the Soviet System*, p. 195. From 24,000 at the beginning of 1917, there were 300,000 party members by the end of the year. But the war cost the party some 150,000. These were replaced by new members, so that by 1921 there were some 500,000. By 1927, there were 1,000,000 and in 1933 about 3,000,000. A survey prepared for Lenin concluded that for every 1,500 officials, some 900 were from the former "working intelligentsia," 250 were former workers, and about 300 were former landowners, priests, officers, top managers, and high Tsarist officials. See ibid., p. 212.

96   Lewin argues that "this was becoming a key factor in shaping the whole system." He continues: "It was becoming important to study not only the social potential of the proletariat, or the peasantry, but the potential, interests and aspirations of the growing and changing Soviet State machinery. It is doubtful, however, whether such an analysis is available in the Soviet Union even today" (ibid., p. 261).

97 Luxemburg, "Russian Revolution," p. 391.
98 Lewin, *Lenin's Last Struggle*, p. 122.
99 Ibid., p. 279.
100 The best effort to comprehend Stalinism is Lewin's *Making of the Soviet System*. His judgment that it is an enormous error to believe that Stalinism followed inevitably from the situation at the time of Lenin's death is shared by a number of other writers, including Cohen, *Rethinking the Soviet Experience*; Avrich, *Kronstadt 1921*, pp. 228–9; R. C. Tucker, *The Soviet Political Mind* (New York: Praeger, 1963), and the essays collected by Tucker, *Stalinism: Essays in Historical Interpretation* (New York: Norton, 1977.) Though at the opposite pole of the political spectrum, the inevitability argument is shared by writers sympathetic to the revolution, including Carr, *History of Soviet Russia*.

Chapter 12 War and the Weimar Republic

1 Max Weber, "Parliament and Government in a Reconstructed Germany (A Contribution to the Political Critique of Officialdom and Party Politics)," in Max Weber, *Economy and Society*, vol. 3, ed. Guenther Roth (New York: Bedminster Press, 1968), p. 1385.
2 I draw here on the useful sketch in Fritz Fischer, *Germany's Aims in the First World War*, ch. 1, and from Weber's almost forgotten essay cited above.
3 Compare Arthur Rosenberg, *The Birth of the German Republic, 1871–1918* (London: Humphrey Milford and Oxford University Press, 1931), ch. 1, 2; and Fritz Fischer, *War of Illusions, German Policies from 1911 to 1914*, ch. 2.
4 Weber, "Parliament," pp. 1387–8.
5 Ibid., p. 1397.
6 Fischer, *War of Illusions*, p. 15.
7 Ibid., p. 272.
8 Quoted in ibid., p. 17.
9 Quoted in ibid., pp. 511–12.
10 Barrington Moore Jr., *Injustice, The Social Bases of Obedience and Revolt* (White Plains, N.Y.: Sharpe, 1978), pp. 225–6.
11 Quoted in Fischer, *Germany's Aims*, p. 97.
12 Fischer judges that "without the Social Democrats and the workers controlled by [the party] the war could not be carried on" (ibid., p. 97). Fischer seems to attribute more authority to the SPD than it had. Not only did the shop stewards play a critical, independent role, but the workers were capable of acting independently of both. In fairness to the SPD, it should be noted that the unions declared on 2 Aug. 1914, *before* the SPD actions, that strike activity would be suspended indefinitely. Within two years, factory-based, worker-inspired opposition to the war began. Perhaps the first incidents to gain widespread attention were partial strikes in Berlin, Braunschweig, and Bremen in June 1916. Notably, these were in response to the jailing of Karl Liebknecht. See below.
13 Ibid., p. 327.
14 Fischer, *Germany's Aims*, p. 97.
15 Quoted in Fischer, *War of Illusions*, p. 463.

16 See David W. Morgan, *The Socialist Left and The German Revolution: A History of the German Independent Social Democratic Party, 1917—1922* (Ithaca: Cornell University Press, 1975), ch. 1, 2.
17 Sebastian Haffner, *Failure of a Revolution, Germany 1918—1919* (Chicago: Banner, 1986), p. 12.
18 Fischer, *Germany's Aims*, p. 336.
19 Quoted by Ronald Steel, *Walter Lippmann and the American Century*, p. 127.
20 Ibid., p. 113.
21 See E. H. Carr, *The Bolshevik Revolution*, vol. 3 (New York: Macmillan, 1961).
22 Fischer, *War of Illusions*, pp. 613—18.
23 My brief account has been influenced by Arno Mayer, *Political Origins of the New Diplomacy, 1917—1918* (New Haven: Yale University Press, 1959).
24 Ibid., p. 55.
25 Quoted in Carr, *Bolshevik Revolution* vol. 3, p. 16.
26 Weber, "Parliament," p. 1383. Subsequent page references are given in parentheses in the text.
27 Quoted in Fischer, *War of Illusions*, p. 32.
28 Ibid.
29 Weber asks rhetorically, "Does anybody believe that the present director of Krupp, formerly a civil servant and active in East-German colonization politics, was destined to manage Germany's largest industrial enterprises rather than to run a key ministry or a powerful parliamentary party?" (p. 1413). "Why does he do the one," he continues, while he would refuse the other? It is not the money. Rather, "in face of the powerlessness of parliament and the resulting bureaucratic character of the ministerial positions a man with a strong power drive and the qualities to do with it would be a fool to venture into this miserable web of mutual resentment and on this slippery floor of court intrigue" (ibid.).
30 It is difficult to overstate the centrality of the role of parties for the "strong" versus "weak" parliament distinction or its importance. Weber held that England was superior in this regard, and that the United States did not have a strong parliament even though it had managed to escape difficulty for historical reasons. Thus, rather than ideological combat between parties, there was a patronage system at work in the United States. "Despite the resulting corruption this system was popular since it prevented the rise of a bureaucratic caste. It was technically feasible, as long as even the worst management by dilettanti could be tolerated in view of the limitless abundance of economic opportunities" (p. 1398). The practice of direct election encouraged "caesarism," but this too had not yet created a problem. See below. By now, of course, the conditions favoring the United States are surely past. See next chapter.
31 E. O. Wright offers an excellent comparison and critique of Weber and Lenin vis-à-vis the problem of the state bureaucracy. He finds complementary flaws in their respective accounts. See his *Class, Crisis and the State* (London: Verso, 1979), ch. 4. We should notice here that "weak parliaments" are everywhere the order of the day.

32   Irangate is the most dramatic recent instance, perhaps, but other examples are easy to find. In the debate over reform of the British Official Secrets Act, the former Prime Minister, Edward Heath, was led to assert: "I am beginning to realize that there is a period of history through which I lived about which I shall never know the truth" (*The Guardian*, 16 Jan. 1988).

33   "Teutonic" Germany is "naturally" aligned against "Slavic" Russia. "Backward" Russia is not "naturally aligned" with Britain, France, and the United States. In his view, the ideological politics of Wilson, lately promoted by the Russians, was made possible by blunders beginning with the Boer War and continuing to the Moroccan crisis. For some discussion, see Fischer, *War of Illusions*. Weber believes that intelligent elites in powerful nations can conduct a mutually satisfactory foreign policy which is free from the irrationality of ideology. He should be alive today!

34   Weber looked at the United States. At the time he was writing, he could say, "It is true that, by and large, the popular election of a head of state has not worked out badly. The number of really unsuitable presidents has at least not been larger during the last decades than that of unfit monarchs in the hereditary monarchies" (p. 1455). Putting aside the fact that leadership was not in the hands of the monarch in some of these, one might or might not quarrel with this judgment. In any case – and this is important – for reasons hinted at (n. 30) and others besides. There was as yet no demand for effective centralized leadership in the United States. It was only with World War I that the United States became a world power. See Lippmann's account in the next chapter. The question is, would Weber have altered his appraisal in the light of this development?

35   Fischer, *Germany's Aims*, p. 397. General Ludendorff was easily the match of the radicals as a propagandist. He had distributed to every unit in the army a brochure entitled "The Future of Germany under a Good Peace, or a Bad One." I quote Fischer's summary:

> Grotesquely distorting the data, this screed says that "a German peace" would leave Germany "a free people with only 5,000 millions of debt" (!) while "a Scheidemann peace" would leave her "a wage-slave of England's with 170,000 million of debt." Coloured maps of the Central Powers and the ethnically non-Russian parts of Russia show Germany's new European order, the possibilities of colonisation for the German people, the coal, iron and oilfields which were to make Germany self-sufficient in raw materials, and the continuous Central Africa which was to supplement her European basis. (ibid., p. 340)

36   Quoted in ibid., p. 618.
37   Quoted in ibid., p. 625.
38   Quoted in ibid., p. 632.
39   Quoted in ibid., p. 634.
40   Said General Groener, "The High Command deliberately adopted the position of refuting the responsibility for the armistice and all later steps. Strictly legally seen, it did so without justification, but to me and my associates it was vital to keep the armour shining (*die Waffe blank*) and the general staff free of

burdens for the future" (quoted by Francis Carsten, *The Reichswehr and Politics, 1918−1933* (Oxford: Clarendon Press, 1966), p. 6).

Arthur Rosenberg remarks, "The parliamentarization of Germany was not fought for the Reichstag; it was arranged by Ludendorff" (*Birth of the German Republic, 1871−1918*, p. 242).

41 Fischer, *Germany's Aims*, p. 636.
42 Robert F. Wheeler, "'Ex orient lux?' The Soviet Example and the German Revolution, 1917−1923," in C. L. Bertrand (ed.), *Revolutionary Situations in Europe, 1917−1922*. On the historiographical situation regarding this period, see Reinhard Rurup, "Problems of the German Revolution 1918−1919," *Journal of Contemporary History*, 3, no. 4 (1968).
43 Wheeler, "'Ex orient lux?'," p. 45.
44 Quoted in Haffner, *Failure*, p. 61.
45 Quoted in ibid., p. 65.
46 Quoted in ibid., p. 66.
47 On this critical point, see Carsten, *Reichswehr*, pp. 12−18. He writes: "It became more and more obvious that the units which returned from the western front soon disintegrated when they reached their garrisons, that they came there under the influence of the political left and could no longer be used against political disorder emananating from it" (p. 15).
48 Quoted in ibid., p. 72.
49 Morgan, *Socialist Left*, p. 124.
50 Ibid.
51 Many of the critical documents are conveniently translated in John Riddell (ed.), *The German Revolution and the Debate on Soviet Power: Documents 1918−1919, Preparing the Founding Congress* (New York: Pathfinder, 1986). Although Riddell's head-notes are sometimes seriously misleading, the collection is most useful.

Especially significant is the newspaper debate initiated on 13 Nov. by Friedrich Stampfer of the SPD on the question of workers' and soldiers' councils and their relation to the Reich government to be constituted. Liebknecht and Luxemburg responded. Luxemburg's 20 Nov. *Rote Fahne* essay produced, in *Die Freiheit* of 5 and 6 Dec., a lengthy rejoinder by Kautsky, now on the right of the USPD. Kautsky had made a powerful argument which did not get an answer. Riddell says that there was no time; but this is hardly the case. This debate must not be confused with the debate stimulated by Kautsky's *The Dictatorship of the Proletariat*. The latter concerned Russia and had occurred the previous summer, *before* German socialists were actually faced with responding to a revolution in Germany. See below.

52 Riddell (ed.), *German Revolution*, p. 47.
53 Quoted in Haffner, *Failure*, p. 96.
54 Quoted by Francis Carsten, "Revolutionary Situations in Europe, 1917−1920," in Bertrand (ed.), *Revolutionary Situations*, p. 26.
55 Carsten, *Reichswehr*, pp. 15−16.
56 Quoted by Peter Gay, *Weimar Culture* (New York: Harper and Row, 1968), p. 19. If we put aside the fact that the parties were not Tweedledee, Tweedledum parties, we can agree with Gay when he says, "The Weimar coalition

had received a strong mandate" (p. 149). In the 19 Jan. elections for deputies, the SPD polled 11,500,000 votes for 163 seats; the Catholic Center got less than 6,000,000 votes and 89 seats; the Democratic Party, the newly founded party of liberal intellectuals and progressive industrialists, polled 5,500,000 votes and got 75 seats; the new National People's Party, "the Conservatives of the Empire, unchanged in all but name," received 3,000,000 votes and got 42 seats; the USPD managed 2,500,000 votes and got 22 seats; and Stresemann's new party of big business did the worst, receiving only 1,500,000 votes and 21 seats. What is most striking, perhaps, is how by June 1920 this had changed. While, the SPD "declined spectacularly, dropping to almost a third of its earlier voting strength," both the conservatives and the USPD became forces, to be reckoned with. The Weimar coalition had already collapsed, and Germany was well on the way to disaster.

57 Quoted in Haffner, *Failure*, p. 137.
58 Morgan, *Socialist Left*, p. 214.
59 It is not easy to keep straight the fighting forces of the right. In general, *Reichswehr* refers to the regular army, before 1918 comprised of units from the federal states and under the High Command. *Freikorps* refers to "voluntary" units, formed under Groener's leadership when *Reichswehr* officers lost confidence in their ability to use troops in a civil war. First among the *Freikorps* units were the *Freiwillige Landesjägerkorps* and the *Gardekavallieriechutzendivision*, recruits from guards regiments. Under the terms of the Versailles Treaty, the army of the Weimar Republic was to be limited to 100,000 and to be responsible to the civilian government. The *Freikorps* then became a way around this mandate. There were conflicts within the military, between, e.g., the "Black Reichswehr," the future leaders of Hitler's stormtroopers, and those who tried to "stay free of politics," between those *Freikorps* officers who were adventurers and those whose main concern was the preservation of the German army and its traditions. For discussion, see Carsten, *Reichswehr*.
60 Quoted in Haffner, *Failure*, p. 158.
61 In *Rosa Luxemburg Speaks*, pp. 405–27. Subsequent page references are given in parentheses in the text.
62 Morgan, *Socialist Left*, p. 20.
63 Compare Carl E. Schorske, *German Social Democracy, 1915–1917* (Cambridge, Mass.: Harvard University Press, 1955).
64 She wrote:

> Everything that happens in Russia is comprehensible and represents an inevitable chain of causes and effects, the starting point and end term of which are: the failure of the German proletariat and the occupation of Russia by German imperialism. It would be demanding something super-human from Lenin and his comrades if we should expect of them that under such circumstances they would conjure forth the finest demopracy, the most exemplary dictatorship of the proletariat and a flourishing economy. (p. 394)

And her text concludes prophetically: "The danger begins only when they make a virtue of necessity and want to freeze into a complete theoretical system all the tactics forced upon them by these fatal circumstances, and want to recommend them to the international proletariat as a model of socialist tactic" (ibid.). These words were both prophetic and unheeded. Not only did they anticipate the disastrous decisions of the Third International of October 1920; but, had they been heeded, they might have prevented eager revolutionaries from the error of taking the Bolshevik Revolution as *the* pertinent model for twentieth-century revolution. For discussion of the decision of the October convention of the Third International, see Morgan, *Socialist Left*, pp. 355–80.

65   There is in general a powerful tendency to reify categories – SPD, USPD, Communist, Bolshevik, "moderate," "radical," and so on – and to fail to see that the individuals who fell into these categories were responding to a fluid situation, that their application of abstractions to concrete situations was not predetermined, and that they may often have failed to get past abstractions whose meanings had shifted.

66   Morgan, *Socialist Left*, p. 119.

67   Ibid., p. 225.

68   Ibid., p. 119.

69   Quoted in ibid., pp. 141, 135.

70   Quoted in ibid., p. 249.

71   Ibid., p. 135.

72   Ibid., p. 230.

73   Koppel S. Pinson, *Modern Germany, Its History and Civilization* (New York: Macmillan, 1954), p. 380. Although the premises of this conclusion have been undermined by more recent scholarship, the view continues to inform a large body of conventional opinion. See n. 75.

74   Ibid.

75   The point is treated by a number of recent German scholars. Wheeler writes:

> As Volker Rittberger has observed [,] the SPD leadership attempted to give its participation in the "coalition of order" a certain credibility by playing up the so-called and non-existent "Spartacist threat." But it was the Social Democrats' foot-dragging which gradually led to radical reaction by those who believed they saw their Revolution being betrayed and not the other way round .... The result was regional civil war or what Rurup and Eberhard Kolb refer to as the second phase of the Revolution. ("'Ex oriente lux?'" p. 46)

76   Klaus Epstein, "Three American Studies of German Socialism," *World Politics*, II (1959), repr. (with abridgment) in Richard H. Hunt (ed.), *The Creation of the Weimar Republic: Stillborn Democracy?* (Lexington, Mass.: Heath, 1969), p. 67.

77   Carsten concludes, "In central Europe the conservative forces were completely dead for a short time. In 1918–19, they showed no strength whatsoever and they only came back into power with the failure of the Communist uprisings and their suppression by the Free Corps or the white terror in Hungary" ("Revolutionary Situations," p. 35).

Carsten considers the possibilities of British intervention in his *Britain and the Weimar Republic* (New York: Schocken, 1984). He reports that in March

1919, due to "alarming reports of British officers and the fear of Bolshevism spreading westwards," large shipments of food were sent despite the formal existence of the blockade. General Malcolm was saying that "it is ... most important that the present government, or something like it, be kept in power, and I would urge that the Allied governments should do whatever they can do support it" (p. 22). But what they could do at that time was very limited. It is also striking that Lord Curzon, the British Foreign Secretary, questioned the claim that the regime was "a constitutional regime." "According to his information, the German government was accepting 'an extreme Socialist programme' to maintain itself in power" (ibid., p. 37). This distortion of events in Russia and Germany was widespread. Was it the result of paranoia? See below.

78 Moore, *Injustice*, p. 388.
79 Again, Carsten writes:

> In my opinion, there was ... a very good chance that [the Ebert regime] need not have relied on the General Staff and its generals. Such a regime could have created it own military force .... As German "Social Democracy" was considerably stronger than the Austrian Social Democrats, they also could have created a "Volkswehr"; and indeed the Germans passed a law that created the "Volkswehr" and local "Volkswehr" units came into being in many parts of Germany. The elements were there, but the chance was not used. ("Revolutionary Situations," p. 33)

For some discussion, see Richard N. Hunt, "Friedrich Ebert and the German Revolution of 1918," in Krieger and Stern (eds), *The Responsibility of Power*. Of course, after the first phase of the civil war was over, one could hardly encourage a *Volkswehr*, when the *Volk* were in the process of creating a Red Army in response to counterrevolution!

80 Moore, *Injustice*, p. 386.
81 Ibid., p. 385.
82 See David Abraham, *The Collapse of the Weimar Republic*, 2nd edn (New York: Holmes and Meier, 1986). It is fair to say, I believe, that Abraham provides the materials for a powerful explanation of an "authoritarian populist" solution to the unsolved problems of Weimar but does not at all explain National Socialism, the particularly virulent form which it took.
83 Carsten, *Reichswehr*, pp. 78–89.
84 Ibid., p. 8.
85 Ibid.
86 Carsten said, "In my opinion, there was no possibility whatever to establish a Leninist or Communist regime in Germany in 1918–1919 for the simple reason that the Spartacists, or later, Communists were extremely weak; the left-wing workers at that time, if they supported any party, did not support the Communists, but supported the Independent Social-Democratics, the U.S.P.D., which was a large left-wing party, but not ... a revolutionary party" ("Revolutionary Situations," p. 33). No one would argue with his judgment regarding the strength of the Communists; but it is hard to know what to make of his assertion that the USPD was not a "revolutionary party."

It seems that Carsten has accepted, perhaps despite himself, the dichotomy: between what actually occurred or something like it and "revolutionary dictatorship." It is striking that there are contemporary "Leninists" who would agree with this! See below.

87   Morgan, *Socialist Left*, p. 103.
88   Quoted in ibid., p. 101.
89   Quoted in Carsten, *Reichswehr*, p. 10.
90   Walter Lippmann, *Public Opinion* (New York: Macmillan, 1954), p. 354. See below for a discussion of Lippmann's insights regarding the problem of "pictures in their heads."
91   Morgan, *Socialist Left*, p. 99.
92   Luxemburg, *Rosa Luxemburg Speaks*, p. 414.
93   See Hannah Arendt, *On Revolution* (New York: Viking, 1965).
94   See Peter von Oertzen, "The Ruhr Miners and the Third Way," abridged trans. in Hunt, *Creation of the Weimar Republic*, p. 77. Oertzen's 1963 monograph *Betriebsräte in der Novemberrevolution* (Dusseldorf, 1963) is put to use by Morgan, who, supplementing it with other research, is led to conclude: "The ideal of workers' councils in some form was held by a broad section of the socialist movement, not only by Communists and radical Independents but also by most moderate Independents, much of the Majority Socialist rank and file, and even a few leading members of the SPD" (*Socialist Left*, p. 251).
95   Oertzen, "Ruhr Miners," p. 000.
96   Moore, *Injustice*, p. 389.
97   Ibid., p. 386.
98   Ibid., p. 387.
99   Gerald D. Feldman, "Socio-economic Structures in the Industrial Sector and Revolutionary Potentialities, 1917–22," in Bertrand (ed.), *Revolutionary Situations*, p. 175.
100 Moore, *Injustice*, p. 392.
101 Luxemburg, *Rosa Luxemburg Speaks*, p. 426.
102 Moore, *Injustice*, p. 396.
103 Ibid.
104 Wheeler, "'Ex orient lux?'", pp. 39–40.
105 Schorske, Hunt, and others have suggested, perhaps extravagantly, that, as Hunt puts it, "in a large sense Ebert was the creator of the famous SPD bureaucracy" (*Creation of the Weimar Republic*, pp. 317–18). But however this may be, it may be worth pointing out that Ebert was considered for a post on the party executive in 1904, a suggestion which was vetoed by Bebel, who described him as "standing too far to the right." The next year he was elected as one of four party secretaries, "because of strong support given by the reformist-minded trade unions" (ibid., p. 317). He "soon found himself busy developing and rationalizing the party apparatus in accordance with a newly adopted organizational statute. He introduced modern office methods ... appointed paid functionaries to staff new regional organizations, and required regular reports from both regional and local units" (ibid.). The USPD schism left Ebert in command. After Haase and the anti-war "radicals" left, at the Würzburg Congress of 1917, he became, along with Scheidemann, the SPD senior co-chairman.

Chapter 13   American Democracy: A New Spirit in the World

1   Unless otherwise indicated, citations from Dewey are from *John Dewey, The Middle Works, 1899–1925*, ed. Jo Ann Boydston (Carbondale and Edwardsville: Southern Illinois University Press, 1976–83), cited by volume and page numbers in parentheses in the text.

2   The foregoing draws on Ronald Steel, *Walter Lippmann and the American Century*, ch. 6, 7, and Charles Forcey, *The Crossroads of Liberalism: Croly, Weyl, Lippmann and the Progressive Era, 1900–1925* (New York: Oxford University Press, 1961). ch. 5. The *New Republic* was to be "radical without being socialistic." How radical is arguable, of course. The magazine ran a deficit, except toward the end of the war, when it was selling more than 40,000 copies. For four years, the Straight subsidy ran to $100,000 per year.

3   Forcey, *Crossroads*, p. 129.

4   Ibid., p. 38.

5   Ibid., p. 40.

6   Walter Lippmann, *A Preface to Politics* (New York: Mitchell Kennerly, 1913). Page references are given in the text in parenthesis hereafter.

7   This is the title of an oft-given speech and essay. A version may be found in Ray Stannard Baker and William E. Dodd (eds), *The Public Papers of Woodrow Wilson* (New York: Harper and Row, 1925). See also Wilson's very influential *Congressional Government: A Study in American Politics* (Boston: Houghton Mifflin, 1885), which, by 1900, was in its fifteenth edition; and his later *Constitutional Government in the United States* (New York: Columbia University Press, 1908). These are cited in the text respectively as "Leaderless Government," *Congressional Government*, and *Constitutional Government*.

   Congressional Government shows striking similarities to the analysis of Weber; See ch.12 above. Wilson finds that "the Senate can have in it no better men than the best men of the House of Representatives; and if the House of Representatives attract to itself only inferior talent, the Senate must put up with the same sort" (p. 195). Moreover, "in governments like our own, in which legislative and executive services are altogether dissociated," there is no adequate way "to train men for practical statesmanship . . . and secondly, to exhibit them to the country, so that when men of ability are wanted, they can be found without anxious search and perilous trial" (ibid., p. 251). Moreover, for men in Congress, "independence and ability are repressed under the tyranny of the rules" (ibid., p. 110). In America, "public opinion cannot be instructed or elevated by the debates of Congress, not only because there are few debates seriously undertaken by Congress, but principally because no one not professionally interested in the daily course of legislation cares to read what is said by the debaters when Congress does stop to talk, inasmuch as nothing depends upon the issue of the discussion" (ibid., p. 101).

   Wilson, like Weber, is impressed by the British parliamentary system, for most of the same reasons. "The British system is perfected party government" (ibid., p. 117). By contrast with the American system, in which power is divided and hence not responsible (ibid., p. 93), in the British system "of closely organized party government, . . . legislation is saddled upon the majority." This locates responsibility and "gives to the debates and action of parliament an interest altogether denied the proceedings of Congress" (ibid., p. 117).

Finally, "we have in this country . . . no real leadership; because no man is allowed to direct the course of Congress, and there is no way of governing the country save through Congress which is supreme" (ibid., p. 205).

Jeffrey K. Tulis has given an excellent account of Wilson's transformation of the presidency. See his *The Rhetorical Presidency* (Princeton: Princeton University Press, 1987). The Great War gave Wilson the chance to bring to realization his idea that the systemic difficulties of "mechanical government" could be overcome by a president who had the capacity to form mass opinion. See below.

8   The idea of the leader as "interpreter" has a distinguished German history. It runs from Wilhelm von Humboldt to Hegel, Ranke, Droysen, Treitschke, Dilthey, and Meinecke. The fundamental premise is well expressed by Ranke: "No state ever existed without a spiritual basis and spiritual content. In power itself a spiritual essence manifests itself. An original genius, which has a life of its own, fulfills conditions more or less peculiar to itself." By means of "interpretation" (*Verstehen*), the historian discerns this "genius" and thereby makes history intelligible; and the leader (*Der Führer*) who "expresses" it becomes, as for Hegel, a "World-Historical Individual." I have discussed these remarkable notions in my *A History and Philosophy of the Social Sciences*, pp. 86–96, 117–24.

On General von Bernhardi's use of these ideas, see below. Do we need to be reminded here that these ideas also had a remarkable future in fascist and Nazi ideology. See e.g., Benito Mussolini, *Fascism: Doctrine and Institutions* (Rome: "Ardita," 1935).

9   Walter Lippmann, *Drift and Mastery: An Attempt to Diagnose the Current Unrest* (1914; repr. Englewood Cliffs, N.J.: Prentice-Hall, 1961). Page references to the 1961 edition are given in the text in parentheses hereafter.

10 David Hollinger properly insists that James had an importantly distinct notion of science and its relation to culture, a notion thoroughly grasped by Lippmann. See Hollinger's "Science and Anarchy: Walter Lippmann's *Drift and Mastery*," *American Quarterly* (1977), and *idem* "William James and the Culture of Inquiry," *Michigan Quarterly Review* (1981), both repr. in Hollinger, *In the American Province* (Bloomington: Indiana University Press, 1985).

11 Reed and Lippmann, friends since Harvard, had been part of a group which had recently put on a Madison Square pageant dramatizing the situation of striking IWW silk-workers in Paterson, New Jersey. But in *Drift and Mastery*, Lippmann had applauded "conservative unions" and condemned the IWW as preferring "revolt to solidarity" and, in practice, being "ready to destroy a union for the sake of militancy" (p. 62).

12 The 1908 *Ethics*, a collaboration with James H. Tufts, contains much social philosophy and sensible social philosophy at that. Still, these parts were Tufts's contribution. See my discussion, "John Dewey and the Problem of Justice," *Journal of Value Inquiry*, 15 (1981).

13 John Dewey, *German Philosophy and Politics* (New York: Henry Holt, 1915).

Subsequent page references are given in the text in parentheses.

14   Dewey seems to have liked Marx's little joke which he cites in a note attached to Hegel's famous reference to "the bird of Minerva which takes its flight only at the close of day": "Marx said of the historic schools of politics, law and economics that to them, as Jehovah to Moses at Mt. Sinai, the divine showed but its posterior side" (ibid., 110)!

15   The text is worth calling to the attention of critics of Dewey who say that Dewey's experimentalism kept him from insisting on the need for an inclusive plan. The idea stayed with him throughout. But, like his associates at the *New Republic*, he was no socialist – at least until later. Accordingly, he waffled regarding the key features of a "constructive plan".

16   John Dewey, *Democracy and Education* (New York: The Free Press, 1966). Subsequent page references are given in the text in parentheses.

17   Dewey was reluctant to refer to the capitalist epoch by this name, preferring instead "machine age," "industrial order," "new forms of commerce and industry," and so forth. This had some severe consequences, especially after his "radical turn." See my essay "Marx or Dewey?" in M. Murphey (ed.), *Values and Value Theory in Twentieth Century America* (Philadelphia: Temple University Press, 1988).

18   For the early period in American culture, see Sacvan Berkovitch, *The American Jeremiad* (Madison, Wis.: University of Wisconsin Press, 1978).

19   Forcey, *Crossroads*, p. 221.

20   Ibid., p. 231.

21   See also Dewey's April 1916 essay for *The International Journal of Ethics*, "Force and Coercion" (*Middle Works*, X. 244–51). In terms of Dewey's altogether sensible moral posture, the pacifist case against World War I, of course, was much stronger than it was against World War II.

22   In June 1915, the issue had brought about the resignation from Wilson's Cabinet of Secretary of State William Jennings Bryan. Bryan had wanted the United States to bring all disputes between it and the thirty countries with which it had treaties before an international commission. He wondered, moreover: "Why should an American citizen be permitted to involve the country in war by travelling upon a belligerent ship when he knows that the ship will pass through a danger zone?" Finally, he could not understand how American passenger ships were permitted to carry cargoes of ammunition, a policy which plainly and provocatively threatened the ships and encouraged war. Wilson would not submit the issue to impartial inquiry; nor would he disclaim responsibility for the precipitous actions of private citizens. See "Bryan's Letter of Resignation," in S. Cohen (ed.), *Reform, War and Reaction: 1912–1932* (Columbia, S.C.: University of South Carolina Press, 1972), p. 58.

23   Forcey, *Crossroads*, pp. 265–8.

24   The conventional opinion regarding the American entry is ably represented by Samuel Eliot Morison, *The Oxford History of the American People*, pp. 851–6. See also Frederic L. Paxson, *American Democracy and the World War*, 3 vols (repr. New York: Cooper Square, 1966).

25   Ibid., p. 851.

26 In January 1917 Arthur Zimmermann, the German Foreign Minister, had
    sent a telegram to Mexican President Carranza which had been intercepted
    by British intelligence. It read (in part):

> We intend to begin unrestricted submarine warfare on the first of
> February. We shall endeavor in spite of this to keep the United States
> neutral. In the event of this not succeeding, we make Mexico a proposal
> of an alliance on the following basis: make war together, make peace
> together, generous financial support, and an understanding on our part
> that Mexico is to reconquer the lost territory of Texas, New Mexico
> and Arizona.

Given the circumstances, the idea was hardly shocking. Not only was the
United States arming ships which carried munitions to Britain; but *if* the
United States was to be in a full-scale war with Germany, then Germany
would obviously hope for all the help she could get. For anyone wanting war,
of course, the note was a gift from heaven. Wilson released it on 28 Feb and
in April received a vote in favor of war. See below.

27 It is certainly true that American foreign policy was imperialist. It had been so
    from the beginning. But its imperialist designs had been confined to the
    western hemisphere and, more recently, to the Pacific. It was also true that at
    the time of the Russo-Japanese War, President Roosevelt had notified Germany
    and France that if they took Russia's side, he would "promptly side with
    Japan and proceed to whatever length necessary on her behalf." In 1911 he
    further asserted that, "owing to our strength and geographical location," the
    United States had become "more and more the balance of power of the
    whole globe." Nevertheless, Wilson seems not to have shared these views.
    See below.

28 Paxson, *American Democracy*, I. 347.

29 Ibid., I. 205.

30 Ibid., I. 341.

31 Ronald Steel quotes a "spleen-filled passage" from Lippmann's report of the
    Republican convention. A piece of this gives the flavor:

> I think that there were fifteen nominations plus the secondary orations.
> It was a nightmare, a witchs' dance of idiocy and adult hypocrisy . . . .
> The incredible sordidness of the convention passes all description. It
> was a gathering of insanitary callous men who blasphemed patriotism,
> made a mockery of Republican government and filled the air with
> sodden and scheming stupidity. (*Walter Lippmann*, p. 103)

Lippmann gives a brilliant analysis of Hughes's speech in his *Public Opinion*.
See below.

32 Quoted in Paxson, *American Democracy*, I. 274.

33 Quoted in ibid., I. 350.

34 Ibid., I. 363.

35 The foregoing is influenced by Walter Karp, even though it departs from his
    account. See Walter Karp, *The Politics of War: The Story of Two Wars Which
    Altered Forever the Political Life of the American Republic (1890–1920)* (New
    York: Harper Colophon, 1980). Karp argues: "If the interests of the country

or even the desire to win the elections had shaped the policy of the Republican Party leaders, Wilson's diplomacy would have provided a political target impossible to miss" (p. 216). No doubt it is true that for the Republicans, "straightforward warmongering was out of the question. It would have brought not war, but political disaster to the agitators" (ibid., p. 220). "Wilson's diplomacy," he writes, had "opened up the prospect for war, and war was what the Republican oligarchy wanted and needed" (ibid., pp. 216–17). But they wanted war "to undo the deep damage of the preceding ten years." As Bourne saw, "they wanted war . . . because they saw in war the opportunity to become the great captains of an industrial war machine and partners, once again, in the governance of the country" (p. 219).

This explanation would plainly suit a theme of this part of the book. No doubt America's elites shared the perception that, as in Europe, growing democratic sentiment was undermining the privilege of the business-dominated Republican oligarchy. Nevertheless, by contrast with Germany and England, it is much less clear that this perception motivated the key American actors, especially Wilson. Karp recognizes the problem and shifts gears to argue that Wilson was motivated "to play 'the noblest part that ever came to a son of man'" (ibid., p. 175). Presumably, then, Wilson's high-sounding idealism played perfectly into the hands of the Republicans, who, though they lost the election, got what they wanted. Even so, it remains true that Wilson took America into the war for reasons not in the least related to oligarchic interests.

36 Steel, *Walter Lippmann*, pp. 106–7.
37 Commentators agree that the German High Command had a tremendously confident assessment that the United States government would not confound its plans, and that even if it choose to do so, America would be unable to raise, train, and send much of a force. See Paxson, *American Democracy*, I. 394, and Fritz Fischer, *Germany's War Aims in the First World War*, p. 307. These views were very much the product of German thinking about the war-making capacity of democracies!
38 Quoted in Paxson, *American Democracy*, I. 399.
39 Quoted in ibid., I. 401.
40 Since "exclusion from the mails was near-equivalent for silencing," the Espionage and Trading-with-the-Enemy Acts permitted Postmaster-General Burleson to repress by administrative fiat (Paxson, *American Democracy*, II. 286). Not only did second-class mail come under his autonomous purview, but he had the power to examine private correspondence as well. Even before the war had begun, the Attorney-General had developed a vast network of agents, law-enforcement officers, and voluntary coadjutors, who persistently prosecuted complaints, sometimes malicious, sometimes hysterical, against accused "saboteurs". and "traitors." The Sedition Act prescribed language which was "disloyal, profane, scurrilous, or abusive." It did not take many successful prosecutions before Americans got the idea.

It is still very much worth reading George Creel's enthusiastic *How We Advertised America* (New York: Harper and Row, 1920).
41 Paxson, *American Democracy*, II. 48.
42 Quoted by Steel, *Walter Lippmann*, p. 156.

43 The comparison with Weber's contemporaneous writings is stunning.

44 Randolph Bourne, *Untimely Papers* (New York: Huebsch, 1919). These beautiful essays, so Jamesian – and Sartrean! – in style and thrust, have been too soon forgotten. Page references are given in the text in parentheses.

45 See Lawrence E. Gelfand, *The Inquiry: American Preparations for Peace, 1917–1919* (New Haven: Yale University Press, 1963).

46 Steel, *Walter Lippmann*, p. 128.

47 Ibid., p. 129.

48 Dewey, *Middle Works*, vol. XI, contains the full materials on Dewey's study of Polish conditions, including a valuable note, presumably by Lilian and Oscar Handlin, who introduce the volume.

49 Paul Johnson, *Modern Times: The World from the Twenties to the Eighties* (New York: Harper and Row, 1985), p. 39.

50 Quoted in Steel, *Walter Lippmann*, p. 164.

51 Quoted in ibid., p. 158.

52 See Johnson, *Modern Times*, pp. 23–34, and Steel, *Walter Lippmann*, pp. 159–66.

53 *Middle Works*, vol. XV, contains all Dewey's essays on the campaign to outlaw war, along with Walter Lippmann's polemical rebuttal to Levinson and Dewey. Carl Cohen's introduction to the volume is also most useful.

54 After World War II, the United Nations made both war and imperialism illegal. On this code, wars of national liberation were the only legal wars. The upshot, not foreseen by Dewey and Levinson, was that thereafter there would be no declared wars, only "police actions," or "advisors" sent to suppress national liberation movements!

55 See Lippmann's "The Outlawry of War" (XV. 404–17) and Dewey's rejoinders: "What Outlawry of War Is Not" (XV. 115–21) and "War and a Code of Law" (XV. 122–7). Sovereignty is not denied, since the state will decide whether to submit its claims and whether to abide by the judgment of the court. No third party exists to enforce decisions. No complicated code is required beyond the ordinary, vague conventions governing international law. The plan hardly denies that diplomacy is necessary for maintaining peace.

56 Walter Lippmann, *Public Opinion* (New York: Macmillan, 1954). Subsequent page references are given in the text in parentheses. Dewey's review is contained in *Middle Works*, XV. 337–44.

57 "The facts we see depend on where we are placed, and the habits of our eyes" (Lippmann, *Public Opinion*, p. 80). Lippmann went on to enlist Dewey on the same point.

58 Dewey was later to make the point vividly:

> Schooling in literacy is no substitute for the dispositions which were formerly provided by direct experience of an educative quality. The void created by lack of relevant personal experiences combines with the confusion produced by impact of multitudes of unrelated incidents to create attitudes which are responsive to organized propaganda, hammering in day after day the same few and relatively simple beliefs asseverated to be the "truths" essential to national welfare. (*Freedom and Culture* (New York: Capricorn, 1963), p. 46)

59   Compare ch. 6–8 above. How far we have traveled since 1922!

60   It is not irrelevant here that the social sciences as we now know them had just then completed their institutionalization in the universities of America. See my *A History and Philosophy of the Social Sciences*, Pt II. Perhaps thinking here of Veblen's critique of the social sciences, Lippmann writes that if so much social science is "apologetic rather than constructive, the explanation lies in the opportunities of social science, not in 'capitalism'" (*Public Opinion*, p. 373). Lippmann, who usually sees the pertinence of the fact that practices are influenced by conditions external to them, clearly forgets this here.

61   Lippmann's unabashed Machiavellianism is also clear in *The Phantom Public* (New York: Harcourt, Brace and World, 1925). There he writes:

> We do know, as a matter of experience, that all the cards are not laid face up upon the table. For however deep the personal prejudice of the statesmen in favor of truth as a method, he is most certainly forced to treat truth as an element of policy .... In so far as he has power to control the publication of truth, he manipulates it to what he considers the necessities of action, of bargaining, morale and prestige. (p. 158)

62   Compare Robert A. Dahl's important *Preface to Democratic Theory* (Chicago; University of Chicago Press, 1956). Dahl agreed with Lippmann that there is no way for populations in democratic mass states to influence policy; yet he supposed that he had shown that "elections are a crucial device for controlling leaders," and thus that "the distinction between democracy and dictatorship still makes sense" (pp. 131–2). But what, apart from what Lippmann says, can "control leaders" mean? It is true, I believe, that two-party representative systems are important in preserving hard-won civil liberties, and that these are fundamental and not to be scorned. Nevertheless, we should not confuse civil freedom with democracy. Compare Dewey, below.

63   Dewey, *The Public and Its Problems* (Chicago: Swallow Press, 1954). Subsequent page references are given in the text in parentheses. See my essay, "John Dewey: Anarchism and the Political State," *Transactions of the Charles Peirce Society*, 18 (Spring 1982).

64   This judgment and the analysis which leads to it is very much in keeping with Marx's analysis. See also Dewey's "Philosophies of Freedom" (1928), in *Later Works, 1925–1953*, vol. 4 (Carbondale and Edwardsville: Southern Illinois University Press, 1981).

65   Dewey was to repeat this theme often and emphatically in books and essays of the next few years. For example, in *Individualism Old and New* of 1929, he spoke of "the lost individual," lost because, while "persons are now caught up in a vast complex of associations, there is no harmonious and coherent reflection of the import of these connections into the imaginative and emotional outlook of life." "Rapacious nationalism" is seen to result from the fact that, detached from "their old local ties and allegiances," individuals lack "a new center and order of life." Where "armies and navies exist to protect commerce, to make secure the control of raw materials, and to command markets," and peace cannot establish "a common life," "the emotions are mobilized in the service of a war that will supply its temporary simulation" (*Individualism*

Old and New (repr. New York: Capricorn, 1962), pp. 85–6, 61–2).

By this time, Dewey had taken his socialist turn. In a text that could have been written by Engels, he said, "There is a difference and a choice between a blind, chaotic and unplanned determinism, issuing from business conducted for pecuniary profit – the anarchy of capitalist production – and the determination of socially planned and ordered development. It is the difference and the choice between a socialism that is public and one that is capitalistic" (pp. 119–20)

66   Dewey, "The Fruits of Nationalism," *Later Works*, vol. 3, p. 157.

67   See my essay "Philosophy and Politics: A Historical Approach to Marx and Dewey," in W. J. Gavin (ed.), *Context Over Foundation* (Dordrecht: Reidel, 1988).

68   In *Reconstruction in Philosophy* of 1920, he had argued that, despite wide differences, political philosophies were "agreed upon the final consummating position of the state,"; and he concluded that assumptions regarding the "unique and supreme position of the State in the social hierarchy" had solidified into "unquestionable dogma" (*Reconstruction in Philosophy* (repr. Boston: Beacon, 1957), p. 201).

69   *Later Works*, vol. 3, p. 204. Subsequent page references are given in the text in parentheses.

70   Walter Lippmann, *The Good Society* (Boston: Little, Brown, 1936), p. ix.

Epilogue

1   Walter Lippmann, *The Good Society*, p. ix. Subsequent page references are given in the text in parentheses.

2   See John Diggins, *Mussolini and Fascism: The View from America* (Princeton: Princeton University Press, 1972). I would quarrel, however, with Diggins's analysis of the response of Lippmann, Dewey, and Niebuhr.

3   See Douglas Little, *Malevolent Neutrality: The United States, Great Britain and the Origins of the Spanish Civil War* (Ithaca: Cornell University Press, 1985).

4   See D. F. Fleming, *The Cold War and its Origins, 1917–1960* (Garden City, N. Y.: Doubleday, 1961); John Gaddis, *The Origins of the Cold War, 1941–1947* (New York: Columbia University Press, 1972); and Walter LaFeber, *America, Russia and the Cold War, 1945–1980*, 5th edn (New York: Knopf 1985). There will always remain the unresolvable counterfactual, however; what if Roosevelt had lived?

5   In saying that the United States was free to reject militarism, this should not be taken to mean that it had been free from imperialist adventure. As noted, American imperialism spread initially westward across the vast lands made use of by the many Indian nations. Early on – after the war of 1812 – it accepted the boundaries of Canada, then turned southward and to the Pacific. For this history, see, interalia, Francis Jennings, *The Invasion of America: Indians, Colonialism, and the Act of Conquest* (Chapel Hill: University of North Carolina Press, 1975); Walter LaFeber, *Inevitable Revolutions: The United State in Central America* (New York: Norton, 1984); Noel Kent,

Hawaii: Islands Under the Influence (New York: Monthly Review, 1983), Pt I;
Renato and Leticia Constantino, *The Philippines: The Continuing Past* (Quezon
City, Philippines: The Foundation for Nationalist Studies, 1978).

6 Quoted from Norman Graebner, Introduction to *The National Security: Its
   Theory and Practice, 1945–1960* (New York: Oxford University Press, 1986),
   p. 8.

7 Moshe Lewin, *The Making of the Soviet System*, p. 5.

8 Kennan's essay "The Sources of Soviet Conduct" is reprinted in *Foreign
   Affairs* (Spring 1987), along with substantial excerpts from the series of
   articles originally published in the *New York Herald Tribune* which constitute
   Lippmann's reply. The full series is available under the title *The Cold War: A
   Study in U.S. Foreign Policy* (New York: Harper and Row, 1947). I am quoting
   from the *Foreign Affairs* abridgment, giving page numbers in the text in
   parentheses.

9 See Ronald Steel, *Walter Lippmann and the American Century*, ch. 33, 34.

10 On Iran and its subsequent history, see James A. Brill, *The Eagle and the Lion*
   (New Haven: Yale University Press, 1988). Brill argues that the United
   States chose the monarchy of Mohammed Reza Pahlevi when Mossadegh
   offered a reasonable democratic option, afraid that the latter was a "stalking
   horse" for Iran's Communists. The CIA intervention was "a momentous
   event in the history of Iranian-American relations." By aborting the nationalism
   of secularist, Western-educated Mossadegh, the Americans alienated Iranian
   patriots of all classes and broke with middle-class nationalism. The outcome,
   of course, was the Ayatollah Khomeini.

   With regard to Greece, see Lawrence S. Wittner, *American Intervention in
   Greece, 1943–1949* (New York: Columbia University Press, 1982). The
   "success" made possible by Marshal Tito as acceptance of Stalin's suggestion
   to close the border led, of course, to General Papadopoulos setting back any
   sort of democracy in Greece for a decade.

11 See Daniel Yergin, *Shattered Peace: The Origins of the Cold War and the
   National Security State* (Boston: Houghton Mifflin, 1977) and more recently,
   Norman A. Graebner (ed.), *National Security*.

12 Quoted in Graebner (ed.), *National Security*, p. 8.

13 Ibid., p. 9.

14 This is a 23 Oct. 1945 text drafted by Kennan. It is quoted from Graebner
   "The Source of Postwar Insecurity," *National Security*, pp. 7–8. It is hard to
   judge the impact of Kennan's famous Feb. 1946 "long telegram," an 8,000-
   word message from the Moscow Embassy. There is considerable evidence to
   suggest that Truman and Forrestal had already redefined American posture
   vis-à-vis the Soviet Union, and that Kennan's message merely confirmed
   this.

15 See, e.g., Thomas Powers, *Thinking About Nuclear War* (New York: Knopf,
   1982); Gerard H. Clarfield and William M. Wiercek, *Nuclear America: Civilian
   and Nuclear Power in the United States, 1940–1980* (New York: Harper and
   Row, 1984); Gregg Herken, *The Winning Weapon* (New York: Knopf, 1980);
   Michael Mandelbaum, *The Nuclear Question: The United States and Nuclear
   Weapons, 1946–1976* (New York: Cambridge University Press, 1979);
   Martin Sherwin, *A World Destroyed: The Atomic Bomb and the Grand Alliance*

(New York: Knopf, 1977); and George Kennan, *The Nuclear Delusion* (New York: Pantheon, 1982).

16   General H. R. Harmon, quoted in Graebner (ed.), *National Security*, p. 25.

17   See Phillip M. Boffey, William J. Broad, Leslie H. Gelb, Charles Mohr, and Holcomb B. Noble, *Claiming the Heavens: The New York Times Complete Guide to the Star Wars Debate* (New York: New York Times Books, 1988); Kurt Gottfried et al., "Reagan's Star Wars," *New York Review of Books* 31 (16 Apr. 1984); Ashton B. Carter, *Directed Energy Missile Defense in Space* (Washington, D.C.: Government Printing Office, 1986); "Reverberations of the Space Crisis: A Troubled Future for 'Star Wars,'" *New York Times*, 15 June 1986.

18   *The Central Intelligence Agency, History and Documents*, ed. William M. Leary (Birmingham: University of Alabama Press, 1984), p. 38.

19   One can argue that nuclear bombs have deterred nuclear war – to date, since there is no way to determine that they have not! We can admit this, however, and still attack the assumptions underlying the nuclear arms race. On the one hand, deterrence means having sufficient numbers of weapons which are invulnerable and available to *respond* to an attack. The logic is perfectly clear: neither side will make a first strike because there is no way of guaranteeing against losses which would make the strike irrational. Because there is no scientifically plausible way of making *all* nuclear weapons invulnerable, the conditions of deterrence have long since been satisfied. The evidence is overwhelming that they will remain so. See the references already cited on Star Wars. For an unsuccessful effort to refute this, see Robert Jastrow, "Reagan vs. the Scientists: Why the President is Right about Missile Defense," *Commentary* (Jan. 1984).

If the Russians have conventional superiority, an assumption which is plainly contestable, and if emptying Europe of nuclear weapons would encourage Russian aggression in Europe, then obviously Europe needs conventional armies. Still, this argument depends upon assumptions which seem, at least, to have been vitiated by the two world wars. Imagine armies marching across Poland into Germany. Is it likely that the Russians would test American intercontinental missile capacities in order to conquer Europe? For what purpose? See Edward Thompson et al., *Exterminism and Cold War* (London: Verso, 1982). On deterrence, see Leon Wieseltier, *Nuclear War, Nuclear Peace* (New York: Holt, 1983).

20   Of course, it is not clear whether we are supposed to believe that he has now changed his mind on "the political ideological threat." He has surely changed his mind on the nature of the Russians. While his language in 1946 included phrases such as "the Kremlin's neurotic view of world affairs," "Oriental secretiveness and conspiracy," "particular brand of fanaticism, unmodified by any of the Anglo-Saxon traditions of compromise," he found himself subsequently complaining about the news media's "endless series of distortions and oversimplifications," its "systematic dehumanization of a leadership of another great country," and the "monotonous representation of the nature and attitudes of another great people." For Kennan, "the view of the Soviet Union that prevails today [1982] in large portions of our government and journalistic establishments [is] so extreme, so subjective, so far removed from what any sober scrutiny of external reality would reveal, that it is not only

ineffective but dangerous as a guide to political action" (quoted by William A. Dorman, "Playing the Government's Game: The Mass Media and American Foreign Policy," in Charles W. Kegley Jr. and Eugene R. Wittkopf (eds). *The Domestic Sources of American Foreign Policy* (New York: St Martin's, 1988).

The quotations are drawn from Kennan's "On Nuclear War," *New York Review of Books*, 21 Jan. 1982, pp. 21–2. Of course, Kennan is now rightly frightened by the trajectory of the ideological mind-set which he played such a large role in promoting.

21 *Central Intelligence Agency*, p. 38. Subsequent page references are given in the text in parentheses.

22 A fuller account may be found in William Blum, *The CIA: A Forgotten History* (London: Zed, 1986).

23 American policy in Latin America is overdetermined by imperialism and cold war ideology. During the cold war period, anti-communism, considered a sufficient ground for policy, simply reinforced the older imperialist motivations, for obvious reasons. Long before the cold war, American governments happily used state power against the peoples of Latin America in the interests of American corporations. This fact has led many Marxist-oriented analysts to argue that cold war policy throughout the world, including Vietnam, has imperialist or neo-colonial motivation. This has been reinforced by the manifest failures of United States policies. Thus, if one assumes that United States policy-makers have an adequate grasp of the world and can rationally connect means to ends, then since its policy is so manifestly counterproductive vis-à-vis its explicitly stated goals, it must be that these goals are merely a cover for unstated imperialist goals! For a vigorous defense of the United States as a post-World War II imperial power, see Harry Magdoff, *The Age of Imperialism* (New York: Monthly Review, 1966). For a critique, see Alexander Erlich, "A Hamlet Without a Prince of Denmark," *Politics and Society*, Fall 1973.

24 On these topics up to 1973, see Thomas M. Franck and Edward Weisband (eds), *Secrecy and Foreign Policy* (New York: Oxford University Press, 1973). For some more recent discussion, see Kegley and Wittkopf (eds), *Domestic Sources*.

25 Dorman adopts Lippmann's phrase in characterizing "a journalism of deference to the national-security state." He writes, "the pictures about foreign affairs in the heads of most Americans are largely put there by the news media, and these pictures throughout the Cold War have been neither reassuring nor substantively at odds with official Washington's dark vision of the world" ("Playing the Government's Game," p. 79).

26 See Jeffrey K. Tulis, *The Rhetorical Presidency*, Tulis compares the "Old Rhetoric" and the "New Rhetoric" and shows two extraordinary shifts between the nineteenth and twentieth centuries. First, since Wilson, speeches have been aimed at "the people," and second, they have contained no arguments whatever! Tulis remarks, "In Ronald Reagan, America found the rhetorical president."

27 Gary Reichard, "The Domestic Politics of National Security," in Graebner, ed., *National Security*, p. 260. Reichard offers, thereby misleading his reader: "Nor, except in the most general sense, did a 'cold war consensus' prevail." Plainly, the "most general sense" is the critical sense. He acknowledges this

in saying that "leaders of both parties, with few exceptions, were reluctant in the 1950's to break from the cold war assumptions and adopt the prescriptions that flowed from the critical writers of the decade" (ibid., p. 267). The same holds true today.

Perhaps Reichard was caught in the puzzling argument over the idea of a cold war consensus in the United States. Usually this takes the form of a debate over the existence or nonexistence of "partisanship" with regard to foreign policy matters. A particularly interesting implication is drawn by I. M. Destler, Leslie G. Gelb, and Anthony Lake. They write:

> For two decades, the making of American foreign policy has been growing far more political — or more precisely, far more partisan and ideological. The White House has succumbed, as former Secretary of State Alexander Haig recently put it, to the "impulse to view the presidency as a public relations opportunity and to regard Government as a campaign for reelection (*Domestic Sources*, p. 18)

They suggest that up to 1960, this was not true, and that, for all the failures of the 1945–60 period, these were years of bipartisan, responsible government, even of "considerable political creativity."

It is hard to know what to make of this. These writers suggest that mass opinion has been exploited by "ideologues of both the right and left of our political system" and that in the recent past, presidents have succumbed to this mass opinion — that is, American foreign policy has been irresponsible because the United States is a democracy! One emendation would make this plausible: it is irresponsible because it is a *republic* and, as Dewey saw, there is no public.

If consensus means that everyone agrees on particular cold war policies, of course there is no consensus. It is precisely because there is disagreement that foreign policy can be exploited in American domestic politics. But, of course, the disagreements within the ruling elite are not over cold war assumptions or ends, but over means. In the struggle of aspiring politicians to find the center, there have been shifts in means, but, as could hardly be denied, every administration since Truman has been led by a "cold warrior."

Haig is still correct, however. But what is tragic is that this is happening within a cold war consensus so taken for granted by these writers that they do not even notice it. See I. M. Destler, Leslie H. Gelb, and Anthony Lake, "Breakdown: The Impact of Domestic Politics on American Foreign Policy," in Kegley and Wittkopf (eds), *Domestic Sources*, pp. 17–29, and *idem Our Own Worst Enemy: The Unmaking of American Foreign Policy* (New York: Simon and Schuster, 1964).

28   C. W. Mills argued this in his *Power Elite* (New York: Oxford University Press, 1956). His final chapter, entitled "The Conservative Mood," employs the Deweyan conception of a public, and, like Dewey, he laments its disappearance. The United States, he says, was never an ensemble of publics, just as it is not now a full-fledged mass; but the direction in which it is going is clear.

29   Arthur M. Schlesinger Jr., "The Presidency and the Imperial Temptation," in Kegley and Wittkopf (eds), *Domestic Sources*, p. 30.

Index